Dimensions of
Multicultural Counseling

*To Kip, with gratitude, for the courage to choose
me as a friend and partner for the journey. To Nic, Melissa,
and Jessica, who each in their own way continue to feed my pride and admiration.*

SS

*This version is dedicated to Benjamin and Bethany, who are beginning
their exciting cultural journey.*

AJT

Dimensions of
Multicultural Counseling

A Life Story Approach

Sara E. Schwarzbaum
Northeastern Illinois University

Anita Jones Thomas
Loyola University Chicago

SAGE Publications
Los Angeles • London • New Delhi • Singapore

For information:

Sage Publications, Inc.
2455 Teller Road
Thousand Oaks, California 91320
E-mail: order@sagepub.com

Sage Publications India Pvt. Ltd.
B 1/I 1 Mohan Cooperative Industrial Area
Mathura Road, New Delhi 110 044
India

Sage Publications Ltd.
1 Oliver's Yard
55 City Road
London EC1Y 1SP
United Kingdom

Sage Publications Asia-Pacific Pte. Ltd.
33 Pekin Street #02-01
Far East Square
Singapore 048763

Printed in the United States of America

Library of Congress Cataloging-in-Publication Data

Schwarzbaum, Sara.
Dimensions of multicultural counseling : a life story approach/Sara E. Schwarzbaum, Anita Jones Thomas.
    p. cm.
Includes bibliographical references and index.
ISBN 978-1-4129-5136-4 (pbk.)
    1. Cross-cultural counseling. 2. Minorities—Counseling of—Case studies. I. Thomas, Anita Jones. II. Title.

BF636.7.C76S33 2008
158′.3—dc22   2007036394

This book is printed on acid-free paper.

08 09 10 11 12 10 9 8 7 6 5 4 3 2 1

Acquisitions Editor:	Kassie Graves
Editorial Assistant:	Veronica Novak
Production Editor:	Kristen Gibson
Copy Editor:	Bill Bowers
Typesetter:	C&M Digitals (P) Ltd.
Proofreader:	Eleni-Maria Georgiou
Indexer:	Kirsten Kite
Cover Designer:	Janet Foulger
Marketing Manager:	Carmel Schrire

Contents

Preface   **xiii**
     Organization of the Book   xv

Acknowledgments   **xix**

SECTION I: Conceptual Frameworks   **1**

1. Multiculturalism, Theory, and Competence   **3**
     History of Psychotherapy   4
     Multicultural Theory as a Fourth Force   5
     Multicultural Theory   8
     Multicultural Competency   9
     Oppression and Social Justice   11
     Conclusion   12

2. Oppression and Resilience   **13**
     Definition of Oppression   14
     Relationship Between Oppression and Privilege   15
     Models of Oppression   16
         Exploitation   17
         Marginalization   17
         Powerlessness   17
         Cultural Imperialism   18
         Violence   18
     Personal, Interpersonal, Institutional, and
         Internalized Oppression   19
         Personal and Interpersonal Oppression   19
         Institutional or Cultural Oppression   20
         Internalized Oppression   21
     Types of Oppression   22
         Ableism   22
         Anti-Semitism   23
         Classism   24
         Ethnocentrism   26
         Homophobia   26
         Racism   28

Sexism   29
Xenophobia   30
Resilience   32
What Is Resilience?   33
Factors Associated With Resilience   34
   Personal Protective Factors   35
   Gender Differences   37
   Religion and Spirituality   37
   Family Connectedness   38
Why Use a Resilience Approach?   38
Assessment of Oppression and Resilience   39
   Assessing Oppression   39
   Assessing Resilience   40
Implications for Professionals   40
   The Power of the Service Provider   40
   Reactions to Oppression Training   41
   Who Serves Oppressed Clients?   43

3. **Self in Context**   **45**
   Human Development   45
   Development of the Self   47
   Contextual Dimensions of the Self   48
      Shifting Selves   49

SECTION II: Dimensions of Race and Ethnicity   **51**

   Limitation of the Concept of Ethnicity   53
   Intragroup Differences: A Framework for
      Understanding Ethnicity   54
   Racial Identity Models   56
   Intergroup Differences   57
      White Europeans   63
      African Americans   64
      Native Americans   66
      Latin Americans   67
      Asians   69
   Implications for Professionals   70
   Stories in This Section   70
      Discussion Questions   71

4. **Julie's Story: So What if I'm a Black Woman?** **73**
   Julie's Story   74
   Content Themes   80
      Race and Stereotypes   80
      Interpersonal Relationships   80

Racism 81
Self-Definition/Authentic Self 82
Clinical Applications 83
Assessment 83
Techniques and Interventions 84
Countertransference 86
Toolbox Activity—Julie 89

5. Butch's Story: Who Am I? **91**
Butch's Story 92
Content Themes 101
Contextual Dimensions 102
Family Socialization Patterns 103
Intragroup Differences 104
Self-Image 105
Clinical Applications 105
Assessment 106
Techniques and Interventions 106
Countertransference 107
Toolbox Activity—Butch 109

6. Betsie's Story: I Am 100 Percent Jewish **111**
Betsie's Story 111
Content Themes 121
Pride About Ethnic Background 121
The Connection Between Ethnicity and
Family Values 122
Pressure to Conform to Ethnic Values 123
Relationship Between Ethnicity and Religion 124
Relationship Between Sociohistorical Contexts
and Identity 124
Clinical Applications 125
Assessment 125
Techniques and Interventions 126
Countertransference 127
Toolbox Activity—Betsie 131

7. Maribel's Story: When Are You Going to Have Kids? **133**
Maribel's Story 134
Content Themes 139
Ethnicity, Immigration, Social Class, and Racism 139
Ethnicity and Language 140
The Double Life of a Hybrid Identity 140
Gender Role Shifts 141
Clinical Applications 142

	Assessment	142
	Techniques and Interventions	143
	Countertransference	146
	Toolbox Activity—Maribel	148
SECTION III: Dimensions of Immigration and Acculturation		**149**
	Historical Dimensions	149
	The Beginnings	149
	African American Migration	151
	Anti-Immigrant Sentiment	152
	Legislative Restrictions to Immigration	152
	Current Controversies	154
	Reasons for Immigration	157
	Dimensions of Acculturation	157
	Implications for Professionals	160
	Stories in This Section	161
	Discussion Questions	162
8.	**Vu's Story: I Am an American**	**163**
	Vu's Story	163
	Content Themes	173
	Forced Migration and Refugee Status	174
	Second Language Acquisition	175
	Acculturation and Assimilation Processes	176
	Survivor Guilt	176
	Clinical Applications	177
	Assessment	177
	Techniques and Interventions	179
	Countertransference	180
	Toolbox Activity—Vu	182
9.	**Esteban's Story: Still Uprooted**	**183**
	Esteban's Story	183
	Content Themes	190
	Tragic Loss	190
	Language Loss	191
	Language, Acculturation, and Ethnicity	192
	Immigration and Social Class	193
	Clinical Applications	194
	Assessment	195
	Techniques and Interventions	195
	Countertransference	196
	Toolbox Activity—Esteban	198
10.	**Maria Luz's Story: Here We Are Not Free**	**199**
	Maria Luz's Story	199
	Content Themes	203

Ambivalence	203
Voluntary Versus Involuntary Migration	204
Documented Versus Undocumented Status	204
Language Issues of the First-Generation Immigrant	205
Immigration and Geographic Origin	206
Clinical Applications	206
Assessment	206
Techniques and Interventions	210
Countertransference	212
Toolbox Activity—Maria Luz	214

11. Teresa's Story: I Didn't Want to Go to Church on Sunday 215

Teresa's Story	215
Content Themes	220
First- Versus Second-Generation Immigrants	221
Language Issues of the Second Generation: Loss or Rejection	221
Intergenerational Conflicts and Gender	223
Clinical Applications	224
Assessment	224
Techniques and Interventions	225
Countertransference	226
Toolbox Activity—Teresa	228

SECTION IV: Dimensions of Religion and Spirituality 229

Spirituality	230
Religion	230
Christianity	231
Islam	232
Judaism	233
Buddhism	234
Hinduism	235
Native American Spiritual Traditions	236
Summary	237
Religion and Identity Development	239
Religion and Culture	240
Religion and Wellness	240
Reactions to Religious Socialization	241
Implications for Professionals	241
Stories in This Section	242
Discussion Questions	242

12. Frank's Story: Hearing God's Voice 245

Frank's Story	245
Content Themes	256

Relationship With God 256
Submission in Religion 257
Religion as a Strength or Resource 258
Clinical Applications 259
Assessment 259
Techniques and Interventions 260
Countertransference 261
Toolbox Activity—Frank 263

13. **Bob's Story: The Good Christian Son** **265**
Bob's Story 265
Content Themes 269
Religious Socialization 269
Shift in Religious Identity 270
Internal Migration and Religious Identity 271
Clinical Applications 271
Assessment 272
Techniques and Interventions 273
Countertransference 274
Toolbox Activity—Bob 275

14. **Katie's Story: Catholic and Jewish? How Can It Be?** **277**
Katie's Story 278
Was This a "Crisis" of Faith? 281
The Wedding Plans 282
And the Rest of the Story . . . ? 283
Practice, Practice, Practice: A Practicing Catholic 285
Content Themes 287
Religious Identity Development 287
Decision Making 289
Family Socialization 290
Influence of Current Events 290
Clinical Applications 291
Assessment 291
Techniques and Interventions 292
Countertransference 293
Toolbox Activity—Katie 294

SECTION V: Dimensions of Social Class **295**

Social Class and Social Justice 299
Implications for Professionals 301
Stories in This Section 301
Discussion Questions 302

15. **Carla's Story: One More Mile** **303**
Carla's Story 304
Content Themes 310

The Impact of Poverty   310
Lack of Access to Resources   312
Importance of Education   313
Link to Race/Dominant Values   313
Clinical Applications   314
Assessment   314
Techniques and Interventions   315
Countertransference   318
Toolbox Activity—Carla   320

16. Anthony's Story: From Radical to Bohemian to Suit Me   321
Anthony's Story   322
Content Themes   328
Changes in Socioeconomic
    Status and Social Class   328
Dominant Class Standards   329
Clinical Applications   330
Assessment   330
Techniques and Interventions   331
Countertransference   333
Toolbox Activity—Anthony   335

SECTION VI: Dimensions of Sexual Orientation   337

Heterosexuality, Homosexuality, and Bisexual
    Gender Orientations   338
Historical Data   338
Current Views on Gender Socialization
    and Sexual Orientation   340
Clinical Considerations   342
Homophobia   343
Ethnicity and Sexual Orientation   343
Suicide and Substance Abuse   344
HIV   345
Gay and Lesbian Youth   346
Human Rights Issues   347
GLB Client/Clinician Match   347
Gay and Lesbian Couples and Families   348
Social Support   349
Resiliency Factors   349
Implications for Professionals   350
Discussion Questions   350

17. Karen's Story: Midlife Growing Pains   351
Karen's Story   351
Content Themes   356
Coming Out   356

	Bisexuality	359
	Shame and Internal Judgment	361
	Clinical Applications	361
	Assessment	362
	Techniques and Interventions	362
	Countertransference	364
	Toolbox Activity—Karen	366
18.	**Transgender and Intersex Sexuality**	**367**
	Implications for Professionals	369
	Discussion Questions	370
19.	**Rachel's Story: Nurturing the Spirit**	**371**
	Rachel's Story	371
	Content Themes	376
	Trapped in Wrong Body/Gender Identity	376
	Transition	377
	Harassment	377
	Clinical Applications	378
	Assessment	378
	Techniques and Interventions	379
	Countertransference	380
	Toolbox Activity—Rachel	382
Appendix		**383**
	Author Guidelines	383
	Multicultural Genogram	384
	Ethnicity	384
	Immigration/Acculturation	384
	Gender	385
	Socioeconomic Status (SES)	385
	Spirituality	385
	Other Areas of Concern	385
References		**387**
Index		**413**
About the Authors		**419**

Preface

Nothing is more fascinating than looking at old photographs. We love viewing people captured in time by a photograph as much because of what we see as because of what we do not see and do not understand. The same can be said about the stories that people tell about their lives—to themselves, to others, and to therapists. Stories only capture one moment, one perspective, one snapshot of individuals' lives. This includes not only the individuals' recollections of activities, thoughts, and feelings but also their current understanding of their circumstances and their past. Like the elusive nature of memory, truth, and reality, some recollections stay the same, but others change with each telling of the story. As the future alters the past, some details become lost or forgotten, while others become exaggerated and provide more intrigue, eliciting sympathy or enhancing the humor in the story. Our clients afford us the opportunity to look at them in the same way we look at old photographs, both seeing what is there and also wondering what is missing. Working as clinicians provides us with the joy and the privilege of participating in the reconstruction of clients' stories and in the co-creation of brighter futures. This book is about the dimensions we need to know in order to work with diverse clients and about people's life journeys, the stories they tell about themselves, and a few of the possible clinical applications derived from them. The stories provide us with a glimpse into the subjects' pasts and an opportunity to imagine their futures.

As a young child, I, Anita, was raised and encouraged by my parents to embrace my cultural heritage. I vividly remember messages that were given both implicitly and explicitly about being an African American female. Because I was raised in a predominantly White environment, my parents were worried about whether I was developing a positive self-concept in the face of often racist and oppressive experiences. Due to their positive encouragement and diligent efforts to protect me and to help me process oppressive experiences, I grew to love, appreciate, and embrace my cultural heritage. Most would say that I have a passion or obsession for cultural issues, and I have dedicated my personal and professional life to helping people understand the importance of culture.

When Anita came up with the idea of coauthoring a book based on autobiographical stories to help emerging clinicians, I, Sara, was eager to get started. I was raised in a multilingual and multiethnic household, and long before I became interested in psychology and psychotherapy, I was curious about people's cultural backgrounds, ethnic affiliations, and language abilities. Close friends and relatives tell me that I am insatiably curious about people's lives, but what I am most interested in are people's cultural lives.

One of our favorite courses to teach is the multicultural counseling course. Our experience of training professional clinicians, therapists, and social service providers has been rewarding because we like to help students figure out how best to understand, and then influence, the lives of their clients. The Multicultural Theory course stands out because it increases students' level of self-awareness and encourages them to explore the full influence of culture, with its multiplicity of meanings and clinical implications.

We have been confronted with four difficulties in the course that we are sure other instructors, students, and clinicians experience as well. First, many textbooks that cover multicultural theory focus solely on the racial and ethnic aspects of clinical work with minorities, and exclude other cultural factors. This approach helps to build understanding of values, beliefs, lifestyle, and perspectives for each group, but it is fairly limited in promoting an understanding of intragroup differences and may promote stereotyping of groups. The second difficulty is helping students understand the full influence of culture on individuals' functioning and identity. Most instructors incorporate the use of popular movies, case vignettes, and media resources to help portray the concepts covered. Though case vignettes and movies can be helpful, they are limited because they do not tell a full story and lack the characteristics of a counseling situation. Third, although such courses promote awareness of the importance of cultural factors, self-awareness of the clinician, and knowledge of cultural factors, the courses often do not promote culturally sensitive skills, which include the ability to assess and understand the interactional effects of the cultural dimensions in the shaping of a person's identity and the interventions that may be necessary at certain moments in time. Fourth, new clinicians are generally exposed to "cookbook" approaches for understanding culture (Speight, Myers, Cox, & Highlen, 1991), in part because it may be difficult for clinicians to consider the multiplicity and complexity that understanding cultural dimensions of identity demands.

This book attempts to fill these gaps in the multicultural training literature by providing cultural autobiographies from individuals who have contributed their life stories. We have highlighted and summarized multicultural theory, research, and literature on oppression and resilience. We have provided a brief overview of racial identity models for the ethnic minority groups. The special focus of this text, however, is the cultural autobiographies that highlight themes from multicultural theory. We selected these contributions to emphasize the effects of cultural factors on values, beliefs, and the development of identity and self-concept. These stories also present the interaction of multiple cultural factors including intragroup differences and sociohistorical developments that affect individual identity. We collected the stories from students in a graduate program, from professionals, and from ordinary people who agreed to share their personal histories. To prepare their contributions for this book, the storytellers used a questionnaire (see Appendix) as a guide, answering some of its questions and ignoring others, creating personal narratives that give the reader an intimate glimpse of each individual storyteller's life. Each is written to give the reader an understanding of the personal significance and meaning that cultural factors play in the authors' lives, as they perceive them. The identifying characteristics of the storytellers and their families—such as names, locations, and certain characteristics—have been changed to preserve their anonymity. The language, punctuation, and style of the stories have not been altered much, however, to preserve the authenticity of the stories and to honor the storytellers.

Organization of the Book

This book is an expanded version of *Culture and Identity: Life Stories for Counselors and Therapists* by A. J. Thomas and S. Schwarzbaum. This book can be used in upper undergraduate courses that cover multicultural and diversity topics in psychology and social work, and in graduate courses in counseling, psychology, social work, human services, or marriage and family therapy and in practicum or internship courses. This book would also be of interest to new professionals eager to sharpen their clinical skills, their level of empathy, and their self-awareness. The book has six sections. Section I contains the conceptual frameworks chapters that precede the cultural life stories. Chapter 1 covers multicultural theory, Chapter 2 examines oppression and resilience, and Chapter 3 covers topics related to understanding the self in context. Sections II through VI contain the life stories. Each section starts with an opener that covers the theoretical dimensions associated with the main topic of the section, providing an overview of the predominant cultural factor, and is followed by the chapters containing the life stories of that section. Sections and chapters can be read independently from the others. Although stories have been grouped together according to the predominant themes of race and ethnicity (Section II), immigration and acculturation (Section III), religion and spirituality (Section IV), social class (Section V), and sexual orientation (Section VI), other themes, including gender, regional concerns, and educational background are present within the stories. Two subsections follow each story: "Content Themes" and "Clinical Applications." The content themes are the issues that appear to be most predominant for the individual in the story. They are extracted from the story and describe cultural concepts and cultural variables and how those variables interact in the individual's life. Some of the content themes are applications of known conceptual ideas pulled from the literature of multicultural theoretical frameworks. Others are less well known conceptually, stemming from the authors' experience as teachers, counselors, and consultants. They are intended to help the reader find applications of the multicultural theory concepts in a real-life story and to understand the complexities of identity formation. The content themes described are not the only ones that can be extracted from these stories.

Not all themes that are obvious in a story have been described because, in some cases, those themes have been explored in a different chapter. Readers might be able to extract additional content themes, and we wholeheartedly encourage that exploration with the help of the Toolbox Activity at the end of each chapter. The "Clinical Applications" section contains assessment questions, clinical interventions, and cross-cultural countertransference issues. The assessment questions are generally related to the content themes and are intended as guidelines, not as an exhaustive list of the possible topics to be assessed in a clinical situation. They serve as a way to remind clinicians about topics or issues that might be salient or relevant to a certain client at a certain time, and counselors need to be sensitive to the relevance and timing of the questions. The clinical interventions generally flow from the content themes and the assessment questions, but not always. The clinical interventions are intended to be used in all types of therapeutic encounters, including individual, family, couple, and group therapy. We have tried to present culturally sensitive interventions existing in the literature that are related to the individual experiences of each storyteller but can be extrapolated and used in other, similar cases. A complete explanation of the intervention is not possible, but the reader is invited to consult with the original sources for the ideas presented in the section.

The final portion of the "Clinical Applications" section includes a discussion of reactions clinicians may experience when working with diverse clients—countertransference reactions. Therapists carry into their interactions with their clients their character, values, and ideals about a good life, a good marriage, and good parenting; their perspectives on "normal" behaviors drive the treatment goals and the therapeutic process. This experience is even more critical to examine when working with culturally diverse clients because clinicians deal with their own cultural socialization, cultural norms, and standards (Comas-Diaz & Jacobsen, 1991) that affect the clinical situation. As we received feedback from reviewers, student readers, and others, it became clear to us that the readers' reactions to the stories were influenced by the readers' own life stories, their own cultural factors, and their own experiences. These included a variety of emotions: annoyance, rage, sorrow, frustration, sympathy. Readers also reacted strongly to the authors' choice of content themes, choice of placement of the stories, choice of clinical interventions, and descriptions of counter-transference reactions. This indicated to us that the readers were having their own countertransference reactions to the cultural issues that we decided to cover or not cover in our book, content themes and clinical interventions we decided to include or exclude, and so on. The reactions of our readers reinforced our conviction that each story needed a section on countertransference because they are proof of the powerful influences strong personal reactions exert on clinical work with individuals, couples, and families. Countertransference reactions can be understood as useful data that can guide clinicians in their quest to provide culturally sensitive clinical services. Social service providers who do not take the time to wrestle with, and become aware of, personal reactions to issues presented in a clinical encounter engage in unethical professional behavior (Gorkin, 1996; Perez-Foster, 1998). We encourage readers to embark on an exploration of their reactions to the stories and the clinical applications in this book. We invite our readers to ask themselves questions that could elucidate the meaning and origin of those reactions.

We use the words "therapists," "clinicians," "providers," and "counselors" interchangeably because the helping professions are populated by individuals of varied theoretical orientations, degrees, and interests.

It is clear from the stories that each individual storyteller has embarked on a journey of growth, which has included both joy and pain. It is our hope that readers feel enriched by the stories presented and that they gain a better understanding of the importance that comes from exploring the rich cultural heritage of their clients in their varied dimensions.

Acknowledgments

We could not have written this book without the contributions from our storytellers. Thank you for being so open with us and sharing your personal tragedies and triumphs! Your stories inspire and move us. Thank you also for not complaining about the changes in identity that we had to make to fit our needs and protect your privacy. We hope that we have been able nonetheless to honor your voice and spirit.

We would like to express gratitude to the original reviewers for their comments and feedback: Randall L. Astramovich, University of Nevada, Las Vegas; Suzanne E. Degges-White, Purdue University Calumet; Sandra A. Lopez, University of Houston, Graduate School of Social Work; Lillian Huang Cummins, California School of Professional Psychology at Alliant International University; and Christopher Weiss, Syracuse University. Thanks also to the reviewers of the current textbook: James Bartee, West Virginia University; Donna Davenport, Texas A&M University; Pamela A. Havice, Clemson University; Sandra Lopez, University of Houston; and Steve Shuetz, University of Central Oklahoma. What results is a stronger product. Also, thanks to Art Pomponio for thinking this was worth doing, to Kassie Graves for her encouragement and support of the expanded version, and Veronica Novak for her invaluable assistance. Thanks to Kathleen Franzwa for her meticulous editorial assistance. We also thank Cheryl Duksta for her assistance and feedback during copy editing of the original *Culture & Identity*. A very special thank you to Jessica Harlow, without whom this book would not have seen the light of day. Another special acknowledgment to Kristen Gibson for her wonderful work as the production editor and for having the brilliant idea of hiring the best copy editor in the world, Bill Bowers. Finally, we want to thank PFLAG Philadelphia, who allowed us to use a version of the story "Nurturing the Spirit," which originally appeared in a booklet *The Agony of Nurturing the Spirit*.

SS & AJT

Section I

Conceptual Frameworks

This section contains three chapters. Chapter 1 is titled Multiculturalism, Theory, and Competence. Chapter 2 covers Oppression and Resilience, and Chapter 3 is titled Self in Context. These chapters explore the theoretical frameworks usually encountered in the syllabi of multicultural theory, multicultural counseling, and diversity theory courses. They can be read independently. They can also be assigned concurrently with the chapters in Sections II through VI that contain the life stories.

Multiculturalism, Theory, and Competence

1

Individuals are like all persons, like some persons, and like no persons (Sue & Sue, 2003). That is, individuals share universal human traits, such as the ability to love, express, and understand emotions, the ability to communicate, and develop intimate relationships. Individuals also have unique personality traits, characteristics, and features based on temperament, life experiences, socialization experiences, and family structure. In addition, individuals share values, beliefs, behaviors, traditions, and customs based on membership, affiliation, and attachment to particular groups. These groups are usually based upon cultural factors, such as race, ethnicity, nationality, immigration status, gender, social class, sexual orientation, and spirituality. To understand any individual, it is necessary to understand the expression of universal traits, the unique traits of the individual, and the cultural affiliations, as these factors operate in a recursive fashion (Speight, Myers, Cox, & Highlen, 1991; Sue & Sue, 2003). To focus on one particular aspect limits full understanding of the individual, including choice of behaviors, worldview, beliefs, and decision-making abilities, as it fails to consider the complexity of human lives.

Psychologists, counselors, and social workers are increasingly working with diverse clients, clients who differ in background from the therapist on a number of factors, including race/ethnicity, gender, social class, immigration, spirituality, and sexual orientation. The demographics in the United States are changing, such that ethnic minorities or persons of color will become the numerical majority by the year 2035 (U.S. Bureau of the Census, 2000). In order to provide effective services, psychologists, counselors, and social workers should be culturally competent (Arredondo, Toporek, Brown, Jones, Locke, Sanchez, & Stadler, 1996). The training that most future providers receive, however, does not adequately prepare them to be culturally competent, for two reasons. First, a Western perspective of mental health and counseling is emphasized in most training programs that focus on traditional approaches to work with clients. Second, the training that incorporates multicultural concerns primarily focuses on race, racial identity, or ethnicity, to the exclusion of other important cultural factors. The programs also tend to focus on helping students to develop multicultural awareness and knowledge, but often do not incorporate training in multicultural skills or culturally sensitive techniques and interventions. The training also does not help trainees to understand the vast intragroup differences, and to understand the interactional effects of multiple cultural factors.

History of Psychotherapy

Psychology and counseling have focused as fields on the complexities of human behavior. This focus has included an examination of individual functioning, especially intrapsychic and interpersonal influences in human behavior. Traditionally, psychology and counseling have focused on understanding human universals and individual characteristics and traits, but have neglected understanding the role of shared customs, traditions, values, and beliefs from cultural influences. The traditional psychotherapy orientations—psychodynamic, behavioral, and humanistic approaches—also have focused on universal traits and unique characteristics without considering the influences of culture (Katz, 1985). Although the emphasis on the traditional approaches is supposed to focus on universal traits and be applicable to all individuals, the theories are embedded within a specific cultural context. The theoretical approaches were developed with White, middle-class clients and are suited for individuals with dominant or Western values, beliefs, and behaviors. The science of multicultural theory has attempted to correct this imbalance by encouraging social service professionals to reconsider the importance of culture on human functioning. Multicultural theory has highlighted the two shortcomings of traditional approaches: the sociopolitical context of traditional counseling and psychotherapy approaches, and the conceptualization of culturally diverse clients.

Traditional psychotherapy approaches are value laden with a Western perspective and tend to favor clients who have dominant values, beliefs, and attitudes. For example, when clients do not present with a strong self-agency or self-improvement orientation, they might be labeled resistant or dependent, and when clients' nonverbal expressions are more predominant that their verbal ones, they may be pathologized. These conclusions can be understood as deriving from the traditional approaches. Examining the worldview embedded in each theoretical orientation will help to understand their inherent cultural values. Worldview is a holistic concept that ties together the belief systems, values, lifestyles, and modes of problem solving for a particular cultural group (Sue & Sue, 2003). There are five dimensions to worldview: view of human nature (good, bad, neutral); perspective on time (past, present, future); human activity (being, being-in-becoming, doing); social relationships (lineal, collateral, individualistic); and relationships with nature (harmony with, mastery over, subjugated by). Psychodynamic approaches espouse a worldview in which there is a negative view of human nature (drives and instincts, annihilation fantasies), an emphasis on the past (early childhood experiences), a doing orientation, an individualistic focus, and mastery over nature (the importance of intrapsychic functioning). Behavioral approaches have a neutral view of human nature (blank slate); a present time focus (observable behaviors); a doing orientation (behavior modification and token systems); an individualistic focus, and a belief in mastery over nature (internal controls over behaviors). Humanistic approaches have a positive view of human behavior (capacity for growth and self-actualization); present time orientation (emphasis on the here and now), being-in-becoming orientation, an individualistic focus, and a belief in mastery over nature. Katz (1985) has stated that essentially, the three major orientations focus on the individual, promote a Protestant work ethic, and hold that individuals can master and control their own environment. They also tend to be goal-oriented, rely heavily on verbal communication, follow linear causality models, highlight the importance of insight, and value the scientific method, observable and concrete behaviors, and a literal time perspective (50-minute sessions).

Multicultural Theory as a Fourth Force

Clients with a worldview that is different than the one postulated by traditional psychotherapy models are often not helped in treatment. In fact, the biased perspective of the traditional approaches has historically labeled ethnic minority clients as deviant and deficient, and has tended to blame them for "dysfunctional" behaviors or the failure to be responsive in treatment. Historically, there are two phases of the pathological view of ethnic minority clients: the genetic deficiency model and the culturally deficient model. According to the genetic deficiency model, ethnic minorities are viewed as pathological due to their physiological makeup and genes. This model was most widely used to explore differences in intelligence across racial groups (Katz, 1985; Trickett, Watts, & Birman, 1994), which was measured with diverse methods, from cranial size and the size and shape of the brain, to intelligence tests. Ethnic minorities were viewed as inferior because they did not have the gene structure to function appropriately and successfully within society and were seen as helpless. During the Civil Rights movement, ethnic minority psychologists highlighted the role of oppression and racism on the functioning of ethnic minorities. The mental health field began to view diverse clients from the culturally deficient model. Although the standard of comparison was still the Eurocentric mainstream perspective, psychologists began to view differences as due not to genetic factors, but to environmental factors, particularly those related to poverty, gender socialization patterns, and racism.

Influenced by developments of the Civil Rights and feminist movements, and the disciplines of anthropology and sociology, the science of multicultural theory has attempted to correct this imbalance of emphasizing human universals and the Western perspective by encouraging social service professionals to consider the effect of culture on human functioning without considering diverse clients as deviant or deficient. Multicultural theory is supposed to counteract the extremes of universalism and relativism by focusing on unique socialization experiences of members in various cultural groups (Speight, Myers, Cox, & Highlen, 1991).

Another factor that led to the development of multicultural theory was the examination of premature termination of clients in treatment (Sue & Sue, 2003). Process and outcome research suggested that many clients of color were leaving treatment after the first and second session, and it was assumed that for many, the reason was that they did not feel understood by their counselors. While results were mixed regarding whether client-therapist match makes a difference to maintaining a therapeutic relationship, it was clear that therapists needed to become more aware of and attend to cultural values and that providers needed to understand how culture influences values, beliefs, and behaviors in order to understand the functioning of the clients. There was also a realization that cultural values are related to the development of the helping relationship, to the nature of presenting problems, and to expectations of the therapeutic process. For example, people of color often attribute credibility to clinicians in ways that differ from the way White clients attribute credibility. Due to the mistreatment and discrimination individuals have faced from medical professionals (i.e., the Tuskegee syphilis studies), from social service professionals (i.e., involvement in an often oppressive social service system), and from the legal system (i.e., minorities of color with less money have fewer access to legal resources) people of color may approach the relationship cautiously. They may mistrust White therapists or assume that the counselor does not understand issues of oppression. Asian clients may immediately treat the clinician with respect due to the therapist's role as an authority figure (Sue & Sue, 2003). Latino and Latina clients may expect a "treatment" after the talking, following a medical model, and may find it difficult to relate matters of intimate content to strangers to whom they are not related (Falicov, 1998a).

Once the need to understand culture was established within the field of multicultural psychology and diversity, several notable historical trends occurred. First, the focus of the theoretical formulations in multicultural theory as a discipline as well as the ideas for training multicultural competent clinicians have changed since its introduction into the mental health field as a fourth force in the 1980s. Initially, the multicultural competency literature focused on the importance of knowledge, awareness, and skills in working with diverse populations. These competencies are still central to the training of clinicians (Arredondo, et al., 1996). The inclusion of the perspectives of social justice (Vera & Speight, 2003), community psychology (Nelson & Prilleltensky, 2005), and critical psychology (Prilleltensky & Prilleltensky, 2003) in the multicultural literature has accrued salience in a field that initially focused on the individual and group interventions as a way to deal with oppression. The importance of training for social justice is being increasingly recognized as a need inherent in the multicultural competency of any clinician (Fouad, Gerstein, & Toporek, 2006).

Second, the multicultural literature tended to focus in the early 1980s primarily on oppression related to ethnicity and race and their relative importance for identity formation. Later scholarship included other dimensions of diversity, such as social class, religious background, geographic origin, sexual orientation, and others (Hays, 2001). Discussions in the field ensued as to the relative importance of these dimensions. Which is more important? Which affects people more? Recent literature points in the direction of multiple intersecting identities and their concomitant multiple oppressions, recognizing the constrictions inherent in focusing on one single factor (Hays, 2001). Similarly, the dimensions of identity formation were initially conceptualized as discrete, describing individuals fitting into one or another category. People were viewed as primarily White or primarily African American or Latino, for example. More recently, however, individuals are being described using a multiplicity of dimensions, their relationship to each other, and the differing weight these dimensions may have in the construction of an individual's cultural identity. Individuals are now understood as having a complex identity that includes their ethnicity, social class, geographic origin, religious background, or sexual orientation without assuming that one (ethnicity or sexual orientation) is necessarily more important than the others (Fuertes & Gretchen, 2001). Individuals may give more salience to one dimension than to another according to their personal experiences, but that is not to be assumed.

Third, there has been a language shift from the use of the terms "minority" and "majority" to the use of the terms "dominant" or "subordinate," which coincided with the examination of privilege, power, and oppression in the multicultural literature (Adams, 2000c). It is now considered that individuals have ". . . social identities, some are dominant or agent such as male, White, heterosexual, able bodied or upper class and others are subordinate or target (female, black or Latino/a, gay or lesbian, disabled or working poor). These distinctions help to understand social privilege and power" (Adams, 2000c, p. 6).

Fourth, there has been a refining of the term "diversity" as having two meanings: One refers to the different worldviews and experiences that we learn as we are socialized within our social groupings. "The nuances of these differences are infinite in their complexity, given our socialization within specific, intersecting social communities and cultures" (Adams, 2000c, p. 7). The other meaning of the term "diversity" refers to social groups that not only are different but also unequal, which are not equally valued and occupy different places in a social hierarchy. Diversity is often equated with deficiency and with the poor in our society (Parham, 2001).

Multicultural theory has benefited the practices of psychology, counseling, and social work as it has developed and evolved. First, understanding diversity and cultural factors helps therapists to shift beyond the focus of universal traits and factors (Breunlin, Schwartz, & Mac Kune-Karrer, 1997). Multicultural theory allows counselors to understand both intercultural issues—concerns between cultural beliefs and behaviors based on commonalities and similarities of experience—as well as intracultural issues, including concerns within recognizable cultural groups. Second, multicultural theory has placed an emphasis on oppression and the difficulties that often occur in identity development and the development of positive self-concept in an oppressive society (Fukuyama, 1990). Multicultural theory has also highlighted issues of language and communication (Ibrahim, 1991). The approach has been so influential that it has been labeled as the fourth force behind psychodynamic, behavioral, and humanistic approaches (Pedersen, 1991). There are three areas that are the focus of multiculturalism: multicultural theory, multicultural competency, and social justice.

Multicultural Theory

Multicultural theory developed in response to the need to provide more culturally sensitive treatment. Because the traditional psychotherapy approaches have a Western perspective, they are sometimes limited in their effectiveness in work with nondominant clients. Sue, Ivey, and Pedersen (1996) developed multicultural theory, which is a metaframework or approach for working with culturally diverse clients. The theory holds six propositions, with supporting corollaries.

Proposition 1 states that Multicultural Theory (MCT) is a metatheory of psychotherapy. The corollaries hold that theories are grounded in particular cultural contexts, which makes them biased and therefore suitable for the particular population for which they were designed. While MCT is a metatheory, it combines and utilizes materials from other theoretical approaches. It is important for therapists to be "coconstructionists" with their clients and to help them find new ways of adaptive living.

Proposition 2 holds that both clients and counselors develop identities within multiple contexts and layers, and that the totality of these experiences and layers needs to be considered in a clinical encounter. Corollaries state that individuals develop identities in individual and group contexts, and that as contexts shift and change, identities are also fluid and adjust to contextual factors. Counselors and clients share cultural similarities despite overt dissimilarities. It is important to consider the culture of both client and counselor, as counselor identity and values affect the relationship. Because culture and identity change and are fluid, the cultural influence and factors that are important will also vary within the counseling process.

Proposition 3 holds that for clients and counselors, the development of cultural identity influences attitudes for both the self and for other groups, including the dominant group. Corollaries include the notion that identity represents cognitive, behavioral, and emotional progression, and that the rates of progression may differ. It is important for therapists to understand identity development, to work with clients within social contexts, and to recognize intragroup differences. Behavior needs to be interpreted within contexts, and counselors need to be cognizant of the dangers of assumptions and racist beliefs.

Proposition 4 states that counselors are more effective when using MCT when they are using multiple modalities in their work with clients. Corollaries note the importance of recognizing universal and culturally specific frameworks for treatment, and generating new theories based on cultural context. The counseling process can be blocked or enhanced by recognition and acknowledgment of culture, and interventions need to be selected according to the cultural context.

Proposition 5 stresses the importance of using multiple forms of interventions, including group, community interventions, or work with larger systems. The importance of nontraditional therapeutic settings, accurate and appropriate diagnosis and treatment, and two-directional counseling, which includes dialectical issues, is stressed in the corollaries.

Finally, Proposition 6 stresses the liberation of consciousness as the basic goal of MCT. Corollaries stress critical consciousness, helping clients to become aware of their cultural identity, and the importance of using both Western and Eastern approaches.

Multicultural Competency

In order to treat clients effectively, counselors must have a level of multicultural competency (Arredondo, et al., 1996). Cultural competence is the ability to use skills, behaviors, or interventions to respectfully provide services to individuals through the appropriate systems, agencies, and organizations. "'Cultural competence' demands that clinicians develop flexibility in thinking and behavior, because they must learn to adapt professional tasks and work styles to the values, expectations, and preferences of specific clients. This means that practitioners must choose from a variety of strategies that are useful for the range of cultural groups and social classes, levels of education, and levels of acculturation that exist among clients" (Pinderhughes, 1989, p. 163). The content of competencies has changed and expanded as the field of multicultural theory has grown, from suggestions by leaders of the field to endorsement of policy statements by the major social service professional organizations. Basic multicultural competence requires awareness of the importance of culture, self-awareness, knowledge of cultural groups, and skills for working with diverse clients. Pedersen (1991) indicated that therapists must have an awareness of cultural differences and similarities of behaviors, attitudes, and values. In addition, counselors must have knowledge of cultural groups, including facts and information on values, beliefs, behaviors, communication styles, and social preferences. Finally, counselors should develop culturally sensitive skills, including methods for efficient and effective action with diverse clients. Counselors need to have the ability to present a solution that matches the client's language and cultural framework.

The professional organizations developed competencies for practice, research, and training. The first major position paper was published in 1982 by the American Psychological Association (APA), and required that clinicians have awareness, knowledge, and skills for working with culturally diverse clients (Casas, Ponterotto, & Gutierrez, 1986). While the competencies were drafted specifically by counseling psychologists, they were applied and adopted by psychologists of all specializations. These competencies were expanded in 1992 to include research and training by counseling psychologists and presented to and adopted by the American Counseling Association and the APA. In 1992, Sue, Arredondo, and McDavis (1992) developed a conceptual framework that outlined cultural competence. The model, which was represented by concentric circles, included dimensions of identity, worldview, and culturally sensitive interventions and strategies. It was a comprehensive model that included not only the importance of counselor self-awareness, but the notion of multiple components within identity, the importance of assessment of cultural variables, and the need for culturally sensitive interventions. This model was widely followed by counseling psychologists, counselor educators, and counselors. In 1998, a group of counseling psychologists expanded competencies to be used across an ecosystem at micro, meso, and macro levels, and these were expanded and adopted by APA. In 2003, *Guidelines on Multicultural Education, Training, Research, Practice, and Organizational Change for Psychologists* was adopted as a policy statement. The policy includes six guidelines for psychologists.

Guideline 1 states that psychologists are aware of themselves as cultural beings with attitudes and beliefs that influence functioning, beliefs, and their work. These attitudes may detrimentally affect work with clients.

Guideline 2 states that psychologists understand the importance of multicultural sensitivity, and knowledge and understanding of ethnically and culturally diverse clients. Guideline 3 encourages educators to include multiculturalism in education.

Guideline 4 provides suggestions for the inclusion of cultural issues in research. Guideline 5 encourages the use of culturally relevant skills and applied work, and Guideline 6 promotes the use of organizational change processes to influence and change policies and organizational development. (The complete guidelines may be found at http://www.apa.org/pi/multiculturalguidelines/homepage.html.)

Social workers also developed competencies for their work. Lum (2006) developed a cultural competence framework for social workers. In 1996, the Council on Social Work Education Board of Directors, Cultural Diversity Subcommittee presented a proposal for a conference examining cultural issues and developing guidelines. Two conferences were held, one on social work education in 1998, and the second on child welfare practice in 2001 (Lum, 2006). In 2005, the National Association of Social Workers (NASW) published the *Standards for Cultural Competence in Social Work Practice,* which provided 10 standards. Standard 1 states that social workers who follow ethical guidelines of the profession recognize that personal and professional values may conflict with the needs of diverse clients. Standard 2 states that social workers have self-awareness, Standard 3 promotes cross-cultural knowledge, and Standard 4 encourages cross-cultural skills. Standard 5 suggests that social workers are knowledgeable of services provided within the community and society and make appropriate referrals. Standard 6 refers to the importance of understanding the influence of policy on clients and engaging in advocacy and empowerment as necessary. Standard 7 recommends the promotion of a diverse workforce in social service agencies. Standard 8 upholds the importance of education and training in cultural competence. Standard 9 advocates for providing services in the language of the clients. Standard 10 promotes social workers as leaders in cultural competence with other professional groups. (The complete guidelines may be found at http://www.socialworkers.org/sections/credentials/cultural_comp.asp.)

Oppression and Social Justice

A discussion regarding the redefinition of what it means to be a multiculturally competent clinician is taking place in the scholarly literature and among practitioners (Arredondo & Perez, 2003; Vera & Speight, 2003).

Multicultural competency is not always defined solely in terms of the ability of the provider of services to engage in a relationship with an individual or a family, and often includes the ability to function as a change agent in agencies, organizations, and institutions (Vera & Speight, 2003). In many cases, multicultural competency is viewed not only as including the ability to recognize oppression, but also as the ability to enact alternatives that attempt to eliminate it (Prilleltensky & Prilleltensky, 2003). Although this discussion is not new (Arredondo & Perez, 2003), it has taken a renewed emphasis in the field of psychology and counseling.

Counseling and psychotherapy are two possible ways to provide services for the oppressed but certainly not the only ways (Vera & Speight, 2003). The restoration of social justice is the real aspiration of those who are committed to the elimination of oppression, inequality, and injustice, both for individuals and for the society at large. But despite good intentions, many clinicians often reinforce oppression when they seek to categorize, pacify, or otherwise adjust the people to whom they provide services (Fox, 2003). A professional who is interested in developing the skills to engage in social justice work would be interested in the elimination of oppression, and attempt to dismantle oppressive environments, systems, and structures.

Social justice work can include the practice of advocacy, prevention, and social activism to combat poverty, racism, homophobia, domestic or community violence, and other oppressive practices. It can also include an examination of the ethics of managed care, the ethics of social control of poor families, inequalities in education or access to health care, and others (Fouad, Gerstein, & Toporek, 2006). In this context, the main goals of social justice advocacy are to help disadvantaged or marginalized groups gain access to self-determination and to help them become participants in the decisions that affect their lives (Toporek & Williams, 2006).

Conclusion

Multicultural theory has highlighted the importance of understanding diversity in work with clients. Today's culturally competent clinician has awareness of the importance of culture on psychological functioning, and has an awareness of his or her own cultural identity, socialization experiences, and the influence of culture on functioning and the therapeutic relationship. Culturally competent professionals have a good knowledge base of various cultural factors and skills to translate this to the therapeutic relationship. Competencies developed by the American Counseling Association (ACA), APA, and NASW also promote cultural competence in training and education, as well as in standards for research, testing, and assessment. Finally, a social justice perspective is important to consider in the interest of working toward eliminating oppression, inequality, and injustice.

Oppression and Resilience 2

People of color, women, immigrants, and the poor have been overlooked, dismissed, ignored, or mistreated in a number of ways. When individuals experience discrimination in a way that makes them feel marginalized or powerless, they have experienced oppression. Multicultural theory has helped clinicians to understand the role that oppression and discrimination has played on individuals who are oppressed and on those who serve as oppressors. Oppression is linked to psychological functioning, and is often related to presenting problems. Oppression affects the therapeutic relationship through majority/minority status and trust and credibility issues for the provider of services.

Marginalized and oppressed clients make up a disproportionate number of those who seek counseling or who are involved in the mental health or the social service system (Hanna, Talley, & Guindon, 2000). Many clinicians are, or were, oppressed themselves (Anderson & Middleton, 2004; Ponterotto, Casas, Suzuki, & Alexander, 2001). Understanding the nature of oppression is fundamental for any professional who intends to work competently with other human beings within a social justice perspective, particularly as psychology and psychotherapy are often inadvertently used as tools to continue the oppressive status of clients. This occurs when counselors ignore or deny the sociopolitical conditions that create suffering and psychopathology (Prilleltensky, 1994; Sue & Sue, 2003; Vera & Speight, 2003). The underlying Western perspective of individual counseling that strong-willed individuals—with a large sense of personal responsibility and a strong self-improvement program—can change their lives, no matter how adverse and oppressive their conditions, is often at the base of many practitioners' ideology (Prilleltensky, 1994). That is why it is so important for providers of services to develop an understanding not only of oppression, but also of social justice, social action, and advocacy (Falicov, 1998a; Fouad, Gerstein, & Toporek, 2006). Understanding the

nature of oppression, resilience, and social justice will help emerging clinicians and change agents put their clients—and their clients' stories—in a
broader context from which to derive their meaning by connecting their
clients' mental health with their experiences of oppression (Atkinson,
1998; Falicov, 1998a; Ponterotto, Jackson, & Nutini, 2001; Prilleltensky &
Prilleltensky, 2006).

Oppression has been identified as the basis of a considerable range of
psychopathology (Hanna, Talley, & Guindon, 2000), but also as the source
of strength and resilience (Luthar & Cicchetti, 2000; Luthar, 2006; Walsh,
1999a). Understanding the nature of resilience and the relationship
between oppression and resilience is important for any competent practitioner. This chapter will explore the subject of oppression from a variety
of perspectives, the subject of resilience, and the issue of training emerging clinicians in the assessment of both.

Definition of Oppression

Webster's dictionary defines oppression as "unjust or cruel exercise of
authority or power" (Merriam-Webster, 1998, p. 1282). Oppression needs
to be understood conceptually as a relational term that involves "asymmet-
ric power relationships between individuals, groups, communities and
societies" (Nelson & Prilleltensky, 2005, p. 25). It can lead to discrimination, exclusions, exploitation, or violence directed at the oppressed by
those who dominate. The core of oppression is, then, the inequality in
power. To be oppressed is to be unjustly denied the opportunity of "resilient
autonomy" (Zutlevics, 2002, p. 84) or "self-determination" (Prilleltensky
1994, p. 204). All just societies are nonoppressive, but oppression cannot
be analyzed solely in terms of injustice, because not all instances of injustice are oppressive (Zutlevics, 2002).

The concept of oppression has changed over time and currently reflects
the influence of contemporary social movements that have entered the
political discourse in the United States during the last several decades. In
the traditional understanding, oppression implied the activities conducted
by Conquistadors, colonizers, tyrants, or slave owners against their conquered people (Young, 1990; Todorov, 1984). Individuals used to the traditional understanding of oppression will deny that what occurs in the
United States today can be labeled as oppression (Young, 1990). But in its
contemporary conceptualization, oppression is based on systemic and
structural constraints that do not stem from the actions of an individual
tyrannical ruler, but rather are the result of rules and practices related to the
power afforded by the privilege and domination of some groups with
severe consequences for the subordinate groups with less power (Young,

1990). Additionally, the concept of oppression is always tied to the concepts of race, class, gender inequalities, or sexual orientation (Macedo, 2001).

To understand the nature of contemporary oppression and why it is unjust, it is also important to view its relationship to the concepts of autonomy and self-determination. Society's failure to provide basic resources such as health care, education, security, and food and shelter to individuals in need constitutes oppression because it is an injustice that impedes the expression of resilient autonomy and self-determination (Prilleltensky, 1994; Zutlevics, 2002). To have resilient autonomy and self-determination means that people can live their lives not only according to their own choosing, but also that they can project their lives into the future with the ability to continually decide what they are to become.

In a system that privileges some groups and disenfranchises others, differences and diversity are often equated with inequality. However, freedom and diversity are frequently at odds with each other too, and the tensions between them are not always easily resolved (Appiah, 2006). Human variety and diversity matter because people are entitled to options. Different people require different conditions for their development and autonomy. Just as not all plants can exist and grow in the same atmosphere and climate, similarly, what helps one person to grow and self-determine may be a problem for another. A wide range of human conditions are needed in order to allow free people to make choices about their own lives. As much as diversity should not be made to reflect inequalities and oppressive practices, by the same token, diversity cannot be enforced by force, as this also constitutes a form of oppression. A sustainable global ethics, and by extension an ethical psychology, has to strike a balance between a respect for difference with a respect for the freedom of actual human beings to make their own choices (Appiah, 2006).

Relationship Between Oppression and Privilege

A complex system of domination and subordination exists in the world that stigmatizes some groups and privileges others (Adams, 2000c). Influenced by the disciplines of anthropology, sociology, political economy, and feminist theory, among others, authors in the field of multicultural theory have recognized that there are groups that are systematically advantaged and others that are systematically disadvantaged because of their memberships in certain social groups. Male privilege has been described in the feminist literature for at least three decades (Dolan-Del Vecchio, 1998). Inspired by the ideas related to male privilege, McIntosh wrote the seminal article on the invisibility of White privilege (McIntosh, 1998). Since White and male privilege have been identified as having oppressive effects towards those who do not possess these characteristics, other societal privileges have been identified, including Christian privilege (Blumenfeld, 2006), and privileges afforded by the physically and psychologically able (Castaneda & Peters, 2000), and those who are heterosexual (Miller, 1995), and have more wealth (Liu, 2002), among others. Though descriptions of each type of privilege's roots and consequences may differ, there are some ideas that are common to all. First, there is a positive relationship between privilege and power. The more privileges a person or a group holds, the higher its power. Second, because the privileged characteristics tend to be considered the norm against which all others are compared, they are invisible, that is, they are not recognized as privileges. Finally, people or groups who hold privileges tend to resist accepting their power in society. That resistance, in turn, makes change difficult, since any change involves loss of power, never easily abdicated.

People can be both oppressed and privileged at the same time (Anderson & Middleton, 2004; Hays, Chang, & Dean, 2004). For example, a person can be both gay (subordinate) and upper-class (dominant), a White student (dominant) can belong to a working-class background, (subordinate), a Latina (subordinate) teacher can be middle-class (dominant), and so on. Additionally, a person can be simultaneously oppressed and oppressive, as in the example of the sex offenders who were sexually abused and are sexually abusive (Hanna, Talley, & Guindon, 2000) or as in the case of individuals who currently express other kinds of abusive behaviors who have a history of abuse in their own lives. These connections between multiple social identities and the interaction between multiple forms of oppression affect each other in the lives of people and groups in complex ways.

Models of Oppression

Several authors have attempted to conceptualize a general theory of oppression. Allport (as cited in Ponterotto, Utsey, & Pedersen, 2006) presented a five-phase model of prejudicial acts as a continuum from least to most extreme, namely antilocution (prejudicial talk); avoidance (efforts to avoid contact with individuals of certain groups); discrimination (official segregation in education, employment, political life, or social privilege); physical attack (destruction of property, harassment, vandalism); and finally, extermination (systematic destruction of a group of people based solely on their membership in that group as in lynching, pogroms, and genocide).

Young's model provides a classification of oppressive practices and involves the exploration of exploitation, marginalization, powerlessness, cultural imperialism, and violence. Following is a description of the five faces of oppression as conceptualized by Young (1990).

EXPLOITATION

Exploitation describes the work of people who are involved in menial work that is servile, unskilled, low-paying, and lacks autonomy. The exploited maintains a position of subordination in a system in which the energies of the exploited are expended to maintain and augment the power, status, or wealth of a group that has the resources. Power differentials, subordinations, and inequality are the defining features of exploitation. A woman can be said to be exploited by a man when his freedom or status are possible because a woman works so he can have them. Hotel maids or restaurant busboys, earning minimum wage, tend to perform servile work that enhances the status of those served without recognition for the job done.

MARGINALIZATION

Marginalization is defined as affecting people whom the system of labor will not or cannot use. An entire category of people is excluded from useful participation in social life and therefore, severely deprived materially. These are the people dependent on bureaucratic institutions who are generally involved with social services agencies (i.e., the old, the poor, and the physically or mentally disabled). The public administrators of these organizations end up making decisions with an invasive authority, enforcing rules with which marginalized individuals have to comply. This is the group most affected by oppressive practices in psychotherapy whose basic rights to privacy and individual choice seem to have ceased to exist.

POWERLESSNESS

Powerlessness describes what generally happens to mostly nonprofessional, working-class men and women. They exercise little creativity or judgment in their work and have no technical expertise or autonomy. They lack the opportunity and the possibility of making decisions that affect their lives or to make progress or advance in their status. They lack both direct and mediated power. They take orders but never give them. People are powerless if they are not free to leave their jobs for fear of losing their health insurance, for example. This group is often treated with less respect than other groups. To the extent that a woman of color can establish respectability by revealing that she is a college professor, and is consequently treated differently than before the disclosure of her professional status, or to the extent that a man loses respectability by revealing that he is of the working class, they are powerless.

CULTURAL IMPERIALISM

Cultural imperialism is defined as the universalization of the values of a dominant group, established as the norm, together with the repression of the values of the nondominant group. It is oppressive to the extent that people who are under it are not able to exert influence on the dominant culture. Groups who do not comport to the dominant one are viewed as "other" and inferior. The other reason this could be oppressive is because these values are, in some societies, imposed against the will of the non-dominant minority.

VIOLENCE

Violence involves overt cases of physical violence and also harassment, intimidation, ridicule, or stigmatization of members of a particular group just because they are members of that group. It could be legitimized if the perpetrators are never punished or if nobody is surprised by its occurrence. Violence becomes oppressive when embedded within a system that makes it both possible and acceptable. Solely on account of their group identity, people who are the target of violence live under threat of attack. Typical examples are gays in homophobic environments or adolescents with disabilities in a large public high school, unable to defend themselves from the attacks of bullies. When the properties that would make an individual a target of violence are difficult to hide, such as color, gender, or age, freedom of movement is seriously limited. For example, young women have to limit where they go or when because of the possible consequences of walking alone late at night in certain areas.

Young's model of oppression represents the different factors that constitute the oppression of different groups, and is an example of the difficulties of reducing the concept of oppression to one single factor. Zutlevics (2002) argues against Young's idea that it is not possible to reduce oppression to a single factor and states that to be oppressed is to be unjustly denied the opportunity for what he calls "resilient autonomy" (Zutlevics, 2002, p. 85). He contends that each of Young's different faces of oppression falls within this analysis, and that the lack of resilient autonomy is the ultimate consequence of all forms of oppression, regardless of their nature. "To be non-oppressed one must be able to reasonably project one's plans into the future" (Zutlevics, 2002, p. 92).

Prilleltensky (1994) suggests that three factors, i.e., economic inequality, male dominance, and racism, all of which lead to inequalities in power, form the basis for oppression in society that creates obstacles to self-determination, distributive justice, and collaboration and democratic participation. To be helpful, psychology and psychotherapy need to reformulate their traditional roles as "scientific" and "apolitical" in order to be successful at combating oppression and its consequences for individual well-being (Nelson and Prilleltensky, 2005; Prilleltensky, 1994). Otherwise, psychology and psychotherapy end up supporting the oppressive status quo, by blaming the victims for their fate and utilizing a supposed expertise to define the realities of the oppressed and marginalized (Kagan & Burton, 2005).

Personal, Interpersonal, Institutional, and Internalized Oppression

It is unquestionable that significant progress has been made in the United States regarding numerous forms of oppression (D'Andrea & Daniels, 2001). White racism is no longer blatant; the correlation between race and poverty, or between race, ethnicity, and educational achievement, though still positive, is not as pronounced as it once was. Large numbers of African Americans have benefited from the upward mobility formerly associated only with Whites and are now part of the middle and upper middle classes. Women's occupational choices are wider than they once were. The gay rights movement has resulted in some advances. In spite of the courageous efforts of social justice and civil rights advocates over the last 30 years, there has been a resurgence of conservative leadership since the 1980s in the United States. This resurgence should bar the complacency of those involved in the quest for well-being and remind us that oppression continues to exist in its many forms (D'Andrea & Daniels, 2001; Nelson & Prilleltensky, 2005).

The oppressed include victims of oppressive governments; racial and ethnic minorities; gays, lesbians, and bisexuals; women; persons with disabilities; victims of physical, verbal, and sexual abuse; children and adolescents; aboriginal or indigenous peoples; the poor; and the colonized (Hanna, Talley, & Guindon, 2000; Prilleltensky, 1994; Steinem, 2000).

PERSONAL AND INTERPERSONAL OPPRESSION

Personal oppression can be observed when acts of prejudice, discrimination, or violence interfere with individuals' ability to evolve as complete human beings. Individuals who are burdened spiritually or mentally, or suppressed or crushed by an abuse of power, can be considered oppressed.

Individual oppression can be conscious or unconscious, that is, individuals may or may not be aware that some of the issues in their lives can be attributed to past or current oppressive experiences. Often the oppressed do not know that they are oppressed and are immersed in a "culture of silence" (Freire, 1970/2001, p. 32) or have a fatalistic worldview (Kagan & Burton, 2005), which assumes that their destiny is out of their control.

Some groups have acquired critical consciousness about their situation, but many have not. Paulo Freire (1970/2001; 1999) has written that in order to acquire critical consciousness it is important for the oppressed to stop their adherence to their oppressors, step back, and gradually begin to perceive both the personal and the social realities in order to deal critically with them. Becoming critically conscious (that is, aware) and altering that reality is necessary to acquire a sense of dignity and renew hope.

Interpersonal oppression is an often-overlooked category in the writings about oppression and can be defined as oppressive attitudes and behaviors that are the result of imbalances in power within intimate or close relationships, such as those that exist between parents and children or between intimate pairs or spouses. Interpersonal oppression also takes place between employers and their subordinate employees, in which one of the members of the pair, the one with more power, oppresses the less powerful member. Interpersonal oppression is frequent, often lethal, and though generally relegated to the privacy of the home, has profound political and social costs. The relationship between cruelty toward children, violence, and democracy is rarely examined (Steinem, 2000), nor are the effects on the economic and judicial system of violence toward women. Another form of interpersonal oppression takes place in factories and restaurants, for example, where abusive and oppressive bosses mistreat their powerless (frequently non-unionized or undocumented) employees caught in the double bind of losing their livelihoods or their integrity, with profound implications on public health costs related to exposure to chronic stress.

INSTITUTIONAL OR CULTURAL OPPRESSION

Cultural oppression can be found in those practices, laws, and customs that produce—or result in—social inequalities, whether they are intentional or unintentional. Racial and ethnic groups, gays and lesbians, and women are often the targets of cultural oppression, but are not the only ones. Examples are differential earnings for equal jobs based on gender, property tax laws that effectively set up a two-tier educational system, banking practices that prevent low-income people and minorities from receiving loans with competitive interest rates, discrimination in housing by realtors—who are not necessarily personally racist—who steer minorities of color away from White neighborhoods, and countless others. Cultural oppression is often expressed in collective stereotypes, cognitive schemas, and political and ideological narratives reflected in the ways nondominant groups are portrayed, considered, and treated (Sonn & Fisher, 2005; Young, 1990), and denies them equal access and equal rights. It is important to keep in mind that individuals do not act independent of their social determinants, and therefore, historical and political events that take place create the conditions that produce unequal social relations and oppressive systems (Gimenez, 2005). From this viewpoint, it would be a mistake to place the fault solely in the hands of individuals, for they are embedded in a system that maintains conditions of inequality. It would be equally unhelpful to feel personally guilty for the systemic oppressions affecting groups and individuals on a daily basis. However, there are social justice practices that can be implemented, described later in this chapter.

INTERNALIZED OPPRESSION

Oppression can also become internalized, creating negative psychological and physical effects (Ponterotto, Jackson, & Nutini, 2001; Sue & Sue, 2003). Internalized oppression can exert a powerful influence on people's behavior and feelings. Religious, racial, or ethnic minorities, as well as sexual orientation minorities, may develop self-hatred and engage in self-deprecating behavior, believing the cultural stereotypes assigned to them, identifying with those beliefs, and acting accordingly. The fatalistic outlook of many oppressed groups can also be understood as a form of internalized oppression (Kagan & Burton, 2005). With the internalization of social dominance, the oppressed are rendered helpless and "their impotence becomes proof of their worthlessness" (Kagan & Burton, 2005, p. 298).

Internalized oppression can be expressed in many ways. One way of expressing internalized oppression is the denial of a certain category or dimension of identity. For example, because it is common for darker-skinned Latino, Latina, or African American children to be less preferred than lighter-skinned children by their relatives within a family, it is not surprising that nearly half of all Latinos and Latinas consider themselves White (Gimenez, 2005). Another type of internalized oppression occurs when oppressed individuals begin to believe in the perception that the oppressor has of them. Women in abusive relationships may believe that they are inferior, or that they cannot survive without a man. Abused or oppressed children may exhibit signs of low self-esteem and low self-worth. The poor, marginalized, or disabled may begin to believe in the dominant or experts' definition of what is wrong with them. Internalized oppression can also result in identification with the oppressor. In this case, the internalization of negative stereotypes can be turned outward, making individuals react against others of similar background, mistreating or oppressing them in surprisingly harsh ways. It is not uncommon for Latinos or Latinas, for example, to question the qualifications of other successful Latinos or Latinas. African Americans or Latinos or Latinas in dominant or supervisory positions sometimes mistreat their subordinate counterparts with an exaggerated virulence not warranted by the subordinates' behavior. It is not unusual for women in positions of power to adopt overly competitive or aggressive attitudes toward other women.

Internalized homophobia can occur when gays, lesbians, or bisexual (GLB) people internalize the negative messages perpetuated by society relative to their sexual orientation (Morrow, 2006c). GLB individuals who receive negative messages from society regarding their sexual orientation may internalize those messages, and perpetuate them toward themselves and other GLB persons.

Types of Oppression

The following paragraphs present descriptions of different types of oppression. The list is organized in alphabetical order and, obviously, these are not the only types of oppression that exist.

ABLEISM

Ableism is a negative judgment about the characteristics and capabilities of an individual with a disability (White, 2005). It is considered to be one of the biggest barriers to the full integration of an individual with disabilities into the world of employment and education. Many people with disabilities or chronic conditions are marginalized, ostracized, or disenfranchised, preventing them from participation in their communities and society. Unlike the other "isms" that have a large body of literature, the scholarly field of disability and of ableism as an oppression theory (Castaneda & Peters, 2000) has only recently begun to develop. Until recently, persons with disabilities were the often-neglected category when considering marginalized or oppressed groups. One of the main reasons for the oppression of people with disabilities has to do with cultural prescriptions of what is considered normal, and with definitions of disability based on a deficit medical model (White, 2005). Like other forms of oppression, ableism operates at individual, interpersonal, and institutional levels (Castaneda & Peters, 2000). At the personal level, people with disabilities report being either invisible or viewed with pity. People with disabilities are more vulnerable to interpersonal violence, they experience varied difficulties in their relationships with the health care establishment, and they have difficulties with access to power within institutional structures.

The disability rights movement spearheaded changes in how people with disabilities view themselves and also impacted federal laws. People with disabilities started to understand themselves as a minority and to view their oppressed status as a civil rights issue. The Rehabilitation Act of 1973 and the Americans with Disabilities Act of 1990 are efforts to eliminate discrimination and to protect the civil rights of individuals with disabilities at the federal level (Castaneda & Peters, 2000). To prevent ableism in social services, providers need to train in the areas of diversity of disabilities, covering subjects that include rehabilitation, resilience, assumptions, accommodations, and clinical work with individuals and families affected by a disability. Providers also need to be aware of current laws regarding disabilities in their state, the rights of individuals with disabilities, and the community resources available.

ANTI-SEMITISM

Anti-Semitism is discrimination against Jews and is considered to be the "longest hatred" (Wistrich as cited by Adams, 2000a, p. 133) and the most persistent form of racism in the Western and Muslim worlds. Throughout history, it has taken all the forms in the Young (1990) model. Jewish communities have been established mostly in Diaspora all over the world, experiencing cycles of relative acceptance and assimilation alternating with cycles of enslavement, expulsion, pogroms, and genocide (Adams, 2000a). Jewish communities were regularly subject to massacres in Christian Europe (Dinnerstein, 2000), for example during the Crusades, and preceding their expulsion from Spain in 1492. Jewish communities were also subject to expulsion from England in 1290, from France and Germany in the 14th century, and from Portugal in 1496 (Doniger, 2006). Pogroms destroyed Jewish communities in Russia, Poland, and the Ukraine during the late 19th century and early 20th century, and the government of Nazi Germany perpetrated the genocide of six million Jews during World War II (Gilbert, 2000). Anti-Semitic sentiment and actions also exist in various countries in the Middle East, with continued calls for the destruction of Israel by countries in the Arab world that had previously tolerated their Jewish communities (Doniger, 2006).

In the United States, both organized and community-based anti-Semitism reached its peak during the 1930s, 1940s, and 1950s, with immigration restrictions, restrictions in university and country club admissions, vandalism of Jewish cemeteries and synagogues, beatings of Jewish children by youth gangs, Jewish hate propaganda pamphlets, and other acts (Wyman, 2000). Direct or overt anti-Semitism in the United States has diminished in the last few decades (Anti-Defamation League, n.d.), but by no means can it be said to be nonexistent. It has been replaced by "modern" or "new" anti-Semitism, in which actual anti-Semitism is denied by perpetrators who nonetheless engage in anti-Jewish acts. There are many groups of neo-Nazis, Holocaust deniers, and conspiracy theorists (who claim that the terrorist attacks of September 11, 2001 were part of a Jewish conspiracy) who actively engage in anti-Jewish harassment and intimidation in the schools, and anti-Semitic activity on college campuses, among others. The Anti-Defamation League's annual tracking of anti-Semitic hate incidents reported that there were a total of 1,757 anti-Semitic incidents in 2005 (Annual ADL Audit, 2006) including threats, harassment, and vandalism. The American Psychological Association has recently adopted a resolution calling for the end of anti-Semitic and anti-Jewish prejudice (American Psychological Association, 2005).

Providers working with Jewish clients need to know the basic history of the Jewish people. They also need to be cognizant of the diversity within the Jewish community, have a basic understanding of the fundamental Jewish traditions, and avoid biases and stereotypes commonly related to Jewish people.

CLASSISM

Classism cannot be formulated without the construct of social class (Liu, 2002; Liu, Soleck, Hopps, Dunston, & Pickett, 2004) and can be explained as prejudice and discrimination based on socioeconomic level or social class. The traditional Marxist view of classism is that it is discrimination, stereotyping, or prejudice from the upper class directed toward the lower classes (Liu, et al., 2004). Classism can also be understood as the process of denying the existence of class differences created by political and social structures while blaming the poor for being poor. Classism disproportionately affects minorities of color and is the result of a capitalist economy in which wealth and power are concentrated in a small elite class, leaving those at the bottom with minimal resources and power (Nelson & Prilleltensky, 2005). In the United States, the idea of equating political equality with economic equality leads many individuals to believe in the myth of meritocracy and social mobility as a way out of poverty (Adams, 2000b; Prilleltensky, 1994). If the individual characteristics of intelligence, hard work, and ambition are responsible for success, those who do not exhibit these qualities are solely responsible for their failures. These beliefs create social policies that, in turn, have the effect of influencing people's beliefs about themselves. For example, the lack of affordable child care for working mothers who earn minimum wage may eventually force a single mother to quit her job, which, in turn, may lead her to believe that if she is poor or unemployed, she is to blame for her condition. This makes it difficult for people who do not belong to the middle or upper classes to have class consciousness. If oppressed people believe that there exists equality of opportunity, they may internalize blame for their position (Langston, 2000).

There is documented evidence suggesting that poverty is inversely correlated with well-being (Prilleltensky & Prilleltensky, 2006). Individuals who live in deprived communities have disadvantages including lack of affordable housing, clean air, accessible transportation, health care, education, and job opportunities. These conditions, in turn, affect psychological and physical well-being because economic deprivation affects self-determination, sense of control, and self-efficacy. A groundbreaking study found that workers who experienced little control over their jobs were up to four times "more likely to die than those who experienced a lot of control over their lives" (Marmot as cited in Prilleltensky & Prilleltensky, 2006, p. 16). This is because the stress involved in so-called high-demand, low-control jobs further down the occupational scale is more harmful than the stress of professional jobs that come with greater autonomy and control (Scott, 2005).

Social capital, consisting of a community's collective resources, is also affected by poverty. Economically deprived communities are less cohesive and feature less volunteer participation in organizations, which in turn, affects the health, education, crime rates, and general welfare of the community. In communities where people do not volunteer and participate in social affairs and social networks, there are lower educational achievements, more crime, more child abuse, and more health problems than in communities with high rates of volunteerism (Putnam, as cited in Prilleltensky & Prilleltensky, 2006, p. 20).

Internalized classism is another consequence of classism. It is the result of the perceived "violation of the values, norms, and expectations of an individual's economic, culture, and social class worldview" (Liu, et al., 2004, p. 109). People can become angry or develop feelings of failure because of their inability to meet the perceived demands of their social class culture (Liu, et al., 2004).

In the field of mental health, classism is revealed in the fact that most empirical research tends to be based on middle-class, educated individuals. For example, the majority of empirical studies published in peer-reviewed journals are based on the recruitment of research participants on college campuses by academics (Liu, 2002). In addition, there is an upward mobility classist bias (Liu, et al., 2004) that can have harmful effects on the relationship between providers and their clients. Providers often operate under the assumption that everyone strives for a better social class, and wants to move "upward, and become wealthier than they are in the current situation" (Liu, et al., 2004, p. 98), which implies that every individual is industrious, ambitious, wants to delay gratification, and strives for material success. People who do not adhere to this Protestant work ethic (Liu, et al., 2004) are viewed as deviant. Providers who assume that their clients share similar worldviews, expectations, and goals in life may be engaging in classist attitudes that can hurt the clients rather than be helpful (Liu, et al., 2004; Sue & Sue, 2003). Moreover, training programs in counseling and psychology (social work programs are often an exception) rarely devote content material related to working with the poor, even though the poor constitute a majority of the clientele of recent graduates in the field of mental health (Schwarzbaum, Consoli, & Zalaquett, 2006). In fact, the training of counselors and psychologists tends to focus on individual clinical work with middle-class, highly verbal, voluntary clients who are interested in personal change (Sue & Sue, 2003).

ETHNOCENTRISM

Ethnocentrism is the belief that one ethnic or religious group is superior to others and implies a concomitant belief in the inferiority of other religious or ethnic groups (Sue & Sue, 2003). It can lead to ethnic or religious prejudice and oppression (Blumenfeld & Raymond, 2000; Ponterotto, Utsey, & Pedersen, 2006). Ethnocentrism can be manifested in mild ways or in extreme ways, and in overt or covert ways. Historical events involving one ethnic group tend to increase violence toward that ethnic group. Since September 11, 2001, for example, there has been a surge of ethnocentric manifestations of violence and hatred toward Muslims in the United States (Elliott, 2005).

It appears that ethnocentrism is a universal characteristic of human beings. People seem to like their own food, music, political systems, and languages more than they like those of others. It is common for people to prefer their own "in group" and people of their "own kind" than the "out group" (Ponterotto, Utsey, & Pedersen, 2006, p. 12). It is also common for people to exaggerate the positive characteristics of their own group and to vilify those of other groups, less known or different. Though all groups appear to be ethnocentric, not all groups have the same power in a society to impose their values on others. When ethnocentrism is practiced by dominant groups that have more power, the characteristics of the dominant group tend to prevail and be seen as the normative group to which to aspire. Sue & Sue (2003) argue that ethnocentrism as a concept can be used only to characterize the dominant White majority. Since ethnic and religious minorities do not generally have power in a society, "the damage of oppression is likely to be one sided" (Sue & Sue, 2003, p. 71). The question is not whether or not African American or Latinos and Latinas or Muslims are ethnocentric (they can be), rather the question is: Do they have the power to oppress another group?

In the mental health field, ethnocentrism can be manifested when clinicians fail to understand that variations in verbal and nonverbal behavior, in motivation for personal self-improvement and change, in levels of disclosure, and in other clinical behaviors need not be judged as deviant (Sue & Sue, 2003).

HOMOPHOBIA

Homophobia is a term used to describe individuals who have an intense fear or dread of homosexuals and/or homosexuality, and it can be experienced by persons who are not gay as well as those who are gay (Moses, 1982). Homophobia can also be conceived as a toxic action that is comprised of shame, disgust, and contempt for those who are homosexual (Kaufman & Raphael, 1996). Homophobia is a part of our cultural landscape, and from discrimination in the workplace to the "don't ask, don't tell" policy of the U.S. military, the message is clear that homosexuality is not acceptable.

Perhaps the most extreme example of homophobia was the Nazi persecution of homosexuals during World War II. A more recent example of extreme homophobia was the 1996 verbal and physical assault of Jamie Nabozny, a student in Ashland, Wisconsin, by several students, during which they held him down and urinated on him due to his sexual orientation (Rossman, 1997). Other examples of recent "gay murders" are those of Scotty Joe Weaver, in Alabama in 2004; Raymund Catolico, in New York in 2006; Schlomy Rejwan, in New York in 2006; Matthew Shepard, in Wyoming in 1998; and Paul Broussard, in Texas in 1991 (Bartee, 2007). Although homophobia is still pervasive in society, the gains made by gays and lesbians since the Stonewall Rebellion of 1969 have lessened the overall acceptance of homophobic behavior (Miller, 1995). It is no longer legal in many states to discriminate against gays or lesbians in employment or housing (Swan, 1997). Some employers now choose to offer domestic partner benefits such as insurance coverage for those who are in permanent same-gender partnerships (Swan, 1997). Because it is so ingrained in contemporary society, homophobia is often expressed in subtle ways. Even when they are not making a directly homophobic remark, the tone and wording individuals use can express the contempt and loathing they feel (Moses, 1982).

As mentioned, homophobia can lead to direct attacks on GLB individuals. D'Augelli & Dark and Dean, Wu, & Martin (as cited in Rivers & D'Augelli, 2001) suggest that GLB youth are often victims of direct attacks or assaults because of their identified or perceived homosexual orientation. The social stress experienced by GLB persons due to this victimization can be understood in terms of the minority stress model, which suggests that social conditions such as stigmatization, prejudice, and discrimination can lead to mental health problems (Meyer, 2003). Meyer (2003) found that gay men and lesbians suffer from more mental health problems than their heterosexual counterparts, including substance abuse disorders, affective disorders, and suicide.

In a clinical situation, homophobia can be expressed when clinicians agree to counseling a gay or lesbian, provided that no relationship issues are discussed, or when clinicians agree to parents' requests to institutionalize a gay, lesbian, or bisexual youth because of the child's sexual orientation. Social service agencies can be viewed as homophobic when they do not provide clear indications that they are open to serving the GLB community, when they fail to use inclusive language in their printed materials or conversations, or when they fail to train the staff about the needs of gay youth and the community resources available (Bass & Kaufman, 1996).

RACISM

Due to the history of colonialism and slavery, white skin is still believed to be normative and better, and darker skin is thought to be inferior (Ponterotto, Utsey, & Pedersen, 2006). Aside from poverty, racism and discrimination are powerful challenges in the daily lives of minorities of color. Though racism is not as overt as it once was, it continues to exist, both overtly and covertly. For example, the result of a recent study revealed that lighter-skinned immigrants earn more on average than those with darker skin, even when controlling for race and nationality (Study of immigrants, 2007). A nationwide survey found that 44.4 percent of non-Hispanic Whites reported that they had "never" experienced day-to-day discrimination, in contrast to only 8.8 percent of African Americans; 3.4 percent of Whites experienced discrimination "often," while 24.8 percent of African Americans reported experiences of discrimination (Szalacha, et al., 2003 as cited in Luthar, 2006). In a sample of African American adults, 98 percent reported personally having experienced a racist event in the last year, and 100 percent had experienced such in their lifetimes (Landrine & Klonoff, 1996). Research with Latinos showed that 94 percent reported that they experienced some form of racist event the year before and over 70 percent reported being treated unfairly by people in service jobs (Szalacha et al., 2003 as cited in Luthar, 2006).

The relationship between prejudice, oppression, and psychological well-being is a complex one (Cassidy, O'Connor, Howe, & Warden, 2004). Research suggests that most, if not all, African Americans experience some type of racist oppression, and that this oppression can lead to negative consequences (Landrine & Klonoff, 1996; Luthar, 2006; Thompson, 1996). Reactions to racist experiences differ according to the level of threat involved, perceptions of the intent of behavior, and the presence of internalized oppression (Clark, Anderson, Clark, & Williams, 1999; Cokely, 2002; Harrell, 2000; Krieger, 1996; Utsey, Ponterotto, Reynolds, & Cancelli, 2000). Research has linked experiences with racism to physical and psychiatric symptoms including high blood pressure, somatic symptoms, anger, paranoia, anxiety, frustration, resentment, helplessness and hopelessness, low self-esteem, and subjective distress (Clark, Anderson, Clark, & Williams, 1999; Harrell, 2000; Jackson, Brown, Williams, Torres, Sellers, & Brown, 1996; Klonoff, Landrine, & Ullman, 1999; Krieger, 1996; Landrine & Klonoff, 1996; Thompson, 1996).

In the mental health field, racism is unlikely to be expressed directly, but indirect expressions are frequent. Blaming minorities of color for their own social and economic fate, denying the existence of racism, and denying White privilege are all examples of indirect forms of racism (Neville, Worthington, & Spanierman, 2001). In a clinical situation, racism exists in the form of racial microaggressions revealed in patronizing messages or stereotypic assumptions, often uttered in subtle ways by White therapists who treat minorities of color (Constantine, 2007). From the organizational perspective, it is worth noting that the great majority of presidents of organizations representing counselors and psychologists are White, so are most of the chairs of graduate programs in counseling and psychology and the majority of the editors-in-chief of the scholarly journals (D'Andrea, Daniels, Arredondo, Ivey, Ivey, Locke, O'Bryant, Parham, & Sue, 2001).

SEXISM

Sexism is defined as discrimination on the basis of gender, most often by men toward women. It stems from a belief in male dominance and control, which keeps women subordinate to men and is evident both at the institutional and at the personal levels. Gender is a major component of the inequalities that it produces. Poor women of color have less power, prestige, or economic rewards than other women. Acts of violence (rape, incest, sexual harassment in the workplace) against women, low-paid and gender-segregated employment, denigrating jokes, media portrayals of women as objects, and curtailment of reproductive rights are some examples of sexism. In spite of gains made by several waves of the women's movement spearheaded primarily in the United States and other Western societies to combat sexism, each wave of feminism has been followed by cultural, social, and political backlashes that aim at eroding the gains obtained (Hackman, 2000; Faludi, 1992). It is important to understand that while it is true that the gains women have accomplished in the Western world within the past 30 years are equivalent to a revolution, it is also true that the systems of power—government, business, judiciary, law enforcement, the media, and organized religion (Hackman, 2000; Lorber, 2000)—are still dominated primarily by men, who hold the positions of authority and leadership.

To varying degrees, all women experience multiple oppressions (Gimenez, 2005). Some men in patriarchal societies in the world murder their wives if they do not bear sons, or if they were raped by another man. In the United States, women still do most of the housework and child rearing, even if they work full time; women are paid less than men for the same occupation; occupations typically filled by women (i.e., teaching, caregiving, nursing) receive lower salary rewards than occupations typically filled by men; young women are afraid to go out alone at night and/or to be alone in certain places; and violence is a major daily threat to women of all ages. In spite of decades of feminist activism, men are still sexually abusing, battering, raping, and murdering girls and women at an alarming rate, and sexual harassment is pervasive in the workplace, at school, and in the streets (Katz, 2000). After 35 years of antidiscrimination laws, women's earnings as a percentage of men's, currently at 91 percent, are still lower for the same positions in the United States (Leonhardt, 2006). Some earning differences are the result of differences in occupations. In New York City, women earned 79.4 percent of what men did in 2005 (Roberts, 2006), which is above the national average. In Wyoming, that percentage is only 63 percent, and in Wisconsin it is 70 percent (U.S. Bureau of Labor Statistics, 2006). The only groups of women who are better off economically than they were in 1960 are the subgroups of young, white, unmarried, and well-educated women (Lipsitz Bem, 2000).

It is a mistake to fault individual men for the continued institutional oppression of women. It is important to remember that men (as well as women) do not act independent of their social determinants, and therefore, the historical conditions that produce the current unequal social relations need to be analyzed (Gimenez, 2005). Until men as a group begin to ask themselves continually the question: "How can I combine career and family?" as women do, and be as equal in the home as some women have become in the workplace (Steinem, 2000), sexism will not be eradicated.

In the mental health field, sexism can be examined by its consequences. Women experience sexism, including being called names, institutional discrimination, and sexual harassment (Klonoff, Landrine, & Ullman, 1999). Experiences with sexism have been linked to premenstrual symptoms, somatization, obsessive-compulsive behaviors, interpersonal sensitivity, depression, and anxiety (Landrine & Klonoff, 1996). Depending on the age of the victim and the severity of the oppressive acts (sexual abuse, rape), lifelong consequences, including physical illness, personality disorders, and post-traumatic stress disorder can occur (van der Kolk, MacFarlane, & Weisaeth, 1995).

Because sexism in mental health is a subject that encompasses a broad spectrum of issues, readers are encouraged to consult Morrow, Hawxhurst, Montes de Vegas, Abousleman, & Castaneda (2006); Morrow & Hawxhurst (1998) for a social justice perspective of sexism; the writings of the feminist family therapists, particularly the Women's Project (Walters, Carter, Papp, & Silverstein, 1991); and the work of Judith Lorber (2005), on contemporary inequalities related to sexism.

XENOPHOBIA

Xenophobia can be defined as "fear or hatred of strangers or foreigners or anything that is strange or foreign" (Merriam-Webster, 1998). The fear and hatred of immigrants implied in xenophobic attitudes exist in all societies, and the pervasiveness of xenophobia fluctuates according to several cultural, economic, and political factors. It is conceptually related to ethnocentrism, anti-Semitism, and racism, but it is not the same. Xenophobia implies a belief—accurate or not—that the target is in some way foreign. The target of xenophobia is often a recent immigrant group within a society, which is not considered part of that society. But xenophobia may be also directed against a group that has been present for centuries. Xenophobia can elicit or facilitate hostile and violent reactions, such as mass expulsion of immigrants, or in the worst case, genocide. Most expressions of xenophobic attitudes in the United States are rejections of immigrants reflected in exclusionary policies. While intercultural contact has been a feature of most societies throughout history, international migrations are now at historic highs, and so is xenophobia. In the United States, there is a growing exclusionary response toward immigrants that is reflected in language used (i.e., "illegal aliens"), federal legislation (i.e., the proposed 700-mile fence along the U.S.-Mexico border), and numerous policies proposed or adopted by individual states.

Prejudice and racist attitudes do not seem sufficient to understand xenophobia. Social researchers theorize that the model of group conflict is important to understand xenophobia, positing that perceived competition over scarce resources may have an impact on intercultural group relationships by increasing hostility, which, in turn, is reflected in ethnic prejudice and discrimination (Ponterotto, Utsey, & Pedersen, 2006; Sonn & Fisher, 2005).

Other explanations include the idea that lack of intercultural contact (i.e., ignorance of the "other") is at the heart of xenophobic attitudes because there is a natural tendency in people to fear or distrust those who are not like themselves (Todorov, 1984). Insofar as people are ignorant of each other, xenophobic reactions prevail. There is some support for the theory that people in large urban areas exposed to a variety of cultural manifestations may be less xenophobic than people in isolated or homogeneous communities, where immigrants' differences stand out (Sonn & Fisher, 2005). However, other theorists contend that in larger cities, when contact is brief and impersonal, it can lead to "urban insecurity" of one group toward another (Blumenfeld & Raymond, 2000, p. 29). As in racism, ethnocentrism, and religious fundamentalism, at the heart of xenophobia is a belief that differences are threatening.

In social services, xenophobic attitudes are expressed when policies and procedures are not tailored to the needs of the immigrant groups the organization serves (including hiring qualified and trained translators to interpret or to translate printed materials), or when organizations do not make a commitment to hiring and training qualified staff in the target languages. This lack of commitment can be seen, for example, when there are no differential salary adjustments to attract qualified professionals who speak a foreign language, when relatives or janitorial staff without professional training are used as translators and interpreters, and in countless other situations where adjustments are not made, reflecting the idea that immigrants, because they are in the U.S., are expected to act more like Americans.

Resilience

In spite of the well-documented relationship between oppression and psychopathology, the link is often not apparent. Oppression does not always lead to psychopathology. About half the people exposed to multiple or severe oppressive stressors do not develop serious disabilities or persistent mental health problems (Werner & Smith, 2001; Walsh, 1998). The combination of constitutional factors, lived experiences, resources, and personality formation is so complex that predictions about outcomes are quite difficult to make. Why do some people exposed to severe trauma or oppressive experiences develop mental health problems while others do not? What accounts for the fact that some women who are victims of sexual abuse develop post-traumatic stress disorder and others do not? Why do some adolescents exposed to homophobia develop suicidal ideation while others thrive? How is it possible that so many African American and Latino and Latina students educated in school districts located in economically depressed neighborhoods and exposed to crime, gang life, drugs, or severe parental psychopathology, abuse, or neglect overcome low achievement expectations and attain academic success instead of failing?

In the last two decades, researchers in the behavioral sciences have begun to shift their focus, spearheading a new body of literature that deals with the phenomenon of resilience (Werner & Smith, 2001; Luthar, 2006). In the mental health field, whose practitioners and academic scholars have historically been more comfortable thinking in terms of deficits, diagnostic labels, and psychopathology, there is a growing body of scholarship devoted to the study of resilience and resilience factors. Researchers interested in investigating the relationship between oppression and resilience seek to understand the protective factors and mediating mechanisms that account for normal development, high competence, sustained mental health, and successful recovery from oppression. Researchers are focusing on the mechanisms that buffer, ameliorate, or mediate an individual's or a community's reaction to oppression and lead to well-being (Luthar, 2006; Prilleltensky & Prilleltensky, 2006; Walsh, 1998).

Whether to focus on negative consequences of oppression or not—in other words, whether to concentrate on psychopathology and community breakdown, or on resilience and community survival—is not devoid of political implications. According to one conservative scholar (Steele, 2006), the Civil Rights movement had the unintended effect of creating a culture of victimhood of those affected by racism, from whom responsibility is not expected, "lest the larger nation seem to be oppressing them all over again" (Steele, 2006, p. 56). For Steele, White supremacy was replaced during the 1960s by the view of White as evil that, in turn, led eventually to the development of White guilt. Politically conservative thinkers, then, do not support the continuing focus on the consequences of oppression, but propose that the culture of victimization, with its focus on oppression and its consequences, needs to be replaced by the culture of responsibility, with its focus on resilience. This focus on resilience, on the other hand, can be opposed by social activists on the left of the political spectrum, who contend that resilience is not a personality trait but a privileged outcome of a few, which not every oppressed individual has the luxury of possessing (Luthar & Cicchetti, 2000). Because resilience can be misrepresented as a "personal attribute of the individual" (Luthar & Cicchetti, 2000, p. 862), it can lead to perspectives or policies that, intentionally or unwittingly, blame individuals for not having the characteristics needed to function well.

In spite of political considerations that may color the understanding of resilience, it is important for practitioners in any setting to have clear knowledge of the concept and its implications, for several reasons. First, understanding resilience, and the characteristics of resilient people and communities, helps practitioners to develop preventive tools for helping the clients and the communities their clients live in (Prilleltensky & Prilleltensky, 2006). Second, it moves practitioners from a deficit focus to the focus on strengths, competence, survivorship mechanisms, and positive outcomes, not just negative ones (Duncan, Miller, & Sparks, 2004; Seligman, 2006). Third, making a commitment to understand the links between protective factors and resilience provides a means for practitioners to advocate for their clients by empowering them to overcome oppression (Luthar & Cicchetti, 2000). Finally, by studying the mechanisms and characteristics of resilient people and families, we learn about the processes that underlie them and can utilize them to promote growth in less resilient individuals and families (Walsh, 1998).

What Is Resilience?

The concept of resilience needs to be understood contextually, culturally, and relationally. It is difficult to define resilience because it is not a fixed characteristic that can be measured, and it is not a personality trait or an individual attribute (Luthar & Cicchetti, 2000). Resilience has been defined as "requiring exposure to significant risk, overcoming risk or adversity and success that is beyond predicted expectations" (Richman & Fraser, as cited in Ungar, 2004, p. 18). Another definition states that resilience is a dynamic process involving displays of positive adaptation despite experiences of significant adversity that evolves over the course of the life cycle (Everall, Altrows, & Paulson, 2006; Luthar & Cicchetti, 2000; Werner & Smith, 2001). These definitions do not take into account that resilience needs to be understood contextually and culturally, and as a process rather than as a fixed and invariant trait (Ungar, 2004). In addition, there exists not just one type of resilience but multiple types, i.e., emotional resilience, social resilience, and academic resilience (Everall, Altrows, & Paulson, 2006).

It seems more useful, then, to discuss resilience from a multidimensional and multicultural perspective, remembering that what constitutes a "significant risk" in one community or for one person may not be so for another, or that what constitutes a "success" may not be the same for everyone in every context (Ungar, 2004). For example, women's anger in response to certain sexist oppressive situations can be viewed as resilient by a feminist practitioner, or as the reaction of a borderline personality disorder by a male psychiatrist. If a disenfranchised youth joins a gang, is that showing resilient or criminal traits? Because there are social and cultural factors that determine what are good or bad outcomes, resilience needs to be understood contextually.

Additional cultural perspectives in the understanding of resilience include its relationship to class, race, and ethnicity factors. For example, strict parental monitoring and discipline have been linked to positive adjustment outcomes among poor Latino adolescents (resilience), but not for middle-class adolescents (Luthar & Cicchetti, 2000; Kilpatrick & Holland, 2002). Therefore, forces that appear as sources of vulnerability in some contexts can be protective in others.

Finally, resilience needs to be understood relationally because there is a reciprocal interaction between the environmental factors and the behavior, cognitions, and feelings of the person exposed to risk factors or oppressive environments (Everall, Altrows, & Paulson, 2006; Luthar & Cicchetti, 2000). This means that oppressive events alone are generally not sufficient to understand the development of mental health–related problems or other negative outcomes, because the oppressive events are mediated by cognition, perception, language, and the environment in which the oppression takes place. A mother's depression may affect a poor child much less than it affects a middle-class child, because a poor adolescent may be much more affected by community violence (Luthar & Cicchetti, 2000). Understanding resilience relationally also means that resilience is "forged through adversity, not despite it" (Walsh, 1998, p. 6). Studies of resilient people found that they became stronger as a result of suffering, which made them more resilient. Resilience that comes from overcoming oppression results in the establishment of competence and confidence, which may result in the restoration of dignity and hope and overall positive functioning (Freire, 1970/2001).

Factors Associated With Resilience

It is not true that "early or severe trauma can't be undone; that adversity always damages people" (Walsh, 1998, p. 4), because even a "bad start" does not necessarily imply a "bad outcome" (Walsh, 1998, p. 13). In fact, often the very fact of being abused or oppressed, or having fundamental rights denied, may elicit attempts to rectify the situation, develop resilience, push in positive directions, or develop collective actions (Kagan & Burton, 2005). The existence of protective resilient factors needs to be taken into consideration (Luthar, 2006; van der Kolk, MacFarlane, & Weisaeth, 1995). What are some of the protective factors related to resilience in the midst of oppression? What do Nelson Mandela, Martin Luther King, Jr., Mahatma Gandhi, Betty Friedan, Rosa Parks, and countless others have in common? Their biographical information reveals that they were each exposed to severe forms of oppression. How did they overcome it? First, they have a strong sense of self-efficacy and personal identity, essential ingredients of mental health. Second, they did not accept culture's assessment of themselves as lazy, stupid, or inferior. Third, they developed a strong sense of purpose or mission. Fourth, they learned to advocate for a whole class of people and experienced transcendence, which allowed them to dispute the reality in which they lived and became powerful social activists (Hanna, Talley, & Guindon, 2000). Some researchers contend that the protective factors that foster resilience may have more buffering effects on a person than the specific risk, adverse, or oppressive factors (Morales & Trotman, 2004; van der Kolk, MacFarlane, & Weisaeth 1996; Werner & Smith, 2001).

PERSONAL PROTECTIVE FACTORS

The following protective factors found in the literature on resilience appear to protect minorities of color and other oppressed minorities from developing psychopathology. Protective factors can each derive from multiple levels of influence (Luthar & Cicchetti, 2000) and can be related to each other and influence each other, creating a chain of reciprocally influencing factors.

Attachment, Nurturance, and Support

People who grow up in nurturing and supportive environments may forestall the effect of oppression later in life, no matter how intense or severe (Luthar, 2006). Early attachment seems to be of particular importance. However, it also appears that those who do not have that early secure attachment, but have access to at least one caregiver or a supportive adult who believes in them or cares about them later in life unconditionally, can develop resilience (Walsh, 1998).

Self-Efficacy and Self-Esteem

Resilient people seem to have a strong sense of self, self-identity, and self-efficacy, which increases a sense of mastery and control in spite of adversity, stress, or oppressive environmental circumstances (Everall, Altrows, & Paulson, 2006). One theory regarding the lack of a link between prejudice and psychological distress is that self-esteem moderates the impact of prejudice on depression, i.e., lower levels of self-esteem place the individual at higher risk for depression. Higher levels of self-esteem may protect individuals from distress because there is less vulnerability and more resilience for stressful events (Cassidy, O'Connor, Howe, & Warden, 2004).

Capacity for Emotional Self-Modulation and Self-Regulation

This has to do with the ability to tolerate the fear, anger, and frustration that oppressive environments present to an individual, which in turn has an effect on the ability to cope (van der Kolk, MacFarlane, & Weisaeth, 1996).

Availability of Emotional and Cognitive Processing

Resilient individuals can express their feelings more openly, and are open to making cognitive shifts in perspective (Everall, Altrows, & Paulson, 2006). If discrimination and prejudice are cognitively appraised events, psychological distress depends on whether or not the individual who is the target determines that the event is indeed stressful. In other words, individuals experience higher or lower levels of distress according to whether or not they cognitively determine the event to be stressful (Luthar, 2006).

Problem-Solving Focus

People who are resilient seem to face their problems head on, instead of avoiding them (Everall, Altrows, & Paulson, 2006) and seem to have a variety of coping strategies, not just one (Walsh, 1998).

Social Competence

Resilient people tend to have strong social skills. For example, resilient youth reach out to adults other than their parents, and engage in activities that provide affiliations with other people and have peer support systems (Everall, Altrows, & Paulson, 2006).

Help-Seeking Behavior

Related to a problem-solving focus and the social competence of resilient people, seeking help—whether from professionals or social, religious, or family networks—appears to be a sign of strength. Highly resilient people do not hesitate to reach out for help when they need it (Walsh, 1998), mobilizing the resources available to them, or creating resources when none exist. Resilient individuals have the strength to admit that they have difficulties and need help, and they are more likely to turn to extended family, friends, neighbors, community services, and counseling or psychotherapy (Walsh, 1998).

In addition, the following factors need to be taken into consideration when examining resilience.

GENDER DIFFERENCES

Men and women may react differently to oppression and oppressive environments. Male gender can be a vulnerability marker, and female gender can be a protective one in some situations because boys are typically more reactive than girls to negative influences (Luthar & Cicchettti, 2000). Men and women may respond to ethnic discrimination and other forms of oppression in different ways. In one study that measured depression, anxiety, personal and ethnic self-esteem, and perceived discrimination among young Chinese, Pakistani, and Indian men and women, men who experienced a high level of perceived discrimination were found to have lower levels of personal and ethnic self-esteem, which predicted increased depression, but women did not (Cassidy, et al., 2004). One possible explanation is that compared with ethnic minority women, ethnic minority men are less likely to experience gender discrimination, have more access to open spaces during leisure time, and may therefore be more likely to attribute negative experiences to ethnic discrimination than to gender discrimination.

Another possible explanation is that men's ethnic identity is more relevant for men's well-being than for women, who appear to have other means to obtain well-being, such as interpersonal relationships. Ethnic self-esteem may be a possible target for clinical interventions, particularly for male victims of ethnic discrimination (Cassidy, et al., 2004).

RELIGION AND SPIRITUALITY

The concept that everyone has a personal purpose in living is present in the minds of many oppressed people. The search for meaning and life's purpose engages the minds of many people affected by oppressive environments. For some individuals, the most vital ingredient of resilience is faith. For some, it is faith that exists in the context of a formal religion; for others, it is the contact with a deep level of the eternal or expressing spirituality in everyday life (Walsh, 1998). Many people burdened with the oppression and disadvantages brought about by poverty, or who have any other undervalued status in society, find in religion a resource that helps transcend their personal discouragement, that enhances their identity, increases their self-worth, and can give meaning to their personal struggles (Aponte, 1999). When people lack autonomy or self-determination, the strength of the person's religious convictions often provides connections to God and the sense of empowerment that goes with it. This gives people the strength and resilience they need to go on with their lives, even when they are oppressed.

FAMILY CONNECTEDNESS

The family connectedness that some families espouse can be a great source of power, strength, and resilience. Asian and Latin American adolescents, for example, may have stronger values about their duty to respect, support, and help their families than their peers of European backgrounds (Luthar, 2006; Falicov, 1998a). It seems that the emphasis on family obligations tends to be associated with more positive relationships with family and peers, as well as higher academic motivation in adolescence. In African American families, it has been shown that extended kin support helps promote positive outcomes among both parents and children in poverty (Luthar, 2006).

Why Use a Resilience Approach?

The mental health field has traditionally focused on deficits, pathology, and on what is not working for the person exposed to trauma and oppression. One aspect of the complexity of human beings resides in their ability to survive and thrive heroically in spite of oppressive suffering. One paradoxical aspect of the human condition is that the worst calamities impinged on individuals can also bring out the best in them (Duncan, Miller, & Sparks, 2004). Though trauma, oppression, and their aftereffects can linger on for a lifetime, people often do reorganize their lives, find meaning, and do not succumb to psychopathology (Bettelheim, 1980). Additionally, while it is true that some people can exhibit more resilience in the face of adversity and oppression than others, it is also true that even in the worst adverse circumstances, all people carry around some alternative version of their "bad story" narrative (Ziegler & Hiller, 2001, p. 12) that involves survivorship mechanisms stemming from their strengths, their talents, their successful coping, and the discovery of their resources. Part of the job of a multiculturally competent clinician involves helping clients become aware of the resources they have utilized to survive. When clinicians use a resilience approach, assess for resilient factors, and focus on what is working in the individual in addition to what is not working,

clients are encouraged to develop their competent side, their heroic side, and their survival skills.

Assessment of Oppression and Resilience

When counseling individuals or families in any setting, it is important to assess the experiences of oppression. At the same time, it is important to assess for resilience factors that may be present and to look for expressions of resilience.

ASSESSING OPPRESSION

As we have seen, exposure to discrimination, stigma, and prejudice creates hostile and stressful environments that are linked to mental health problems (Meyer, 2003). Many of the clients who request, or are mandated for, services at social service agencies may have been exposed to multiple oppressive experiences that need to be assessed. It is important to pay attention to how clients perceive their experiences and whether or not they attribute their symptoms, distress, or overall psychological state to the oppressive experiences. For example, it is common for women who are depressed or anxious not to connect their depression or anxiety with their exposure to sexism in the workplace or in their relationships. It is also not unusual for men to fail to connect anger and addiction to experiences of racism or abuse.

Following are areas to consider that may facilitate the assessment of oppressive experiences.

Did the client hasve experiences growing up that could be labeled oppressive, alienating, marginalizing, exploitive, or discriminatory?

Is the client currently having experiences that could be labeled discriminatory, alienating, or oppressive?

Are the experiences taking place at home, in the workplace, among peers?

What are the psychological and interpersonal consequences of these experiences for the client?

Does the client present signs of internalized oppression?

Does the client present with a fatalistic outlook?

Is the client aware that the experiences are or were oppressive in nature?

Is he or she connecting the oppressive experiences with their presenting problem, symptoms, or reactions?

ASSESSING RESILIENCE

People exposed to discriminatory, stigmatizing, and prejudicial experiences often survive and sometimes thrive; it is important to call attention to those characteristics, strengths, and resources that help protect oppressed people from developing psychopathology (Kilpatrick & Holland, 2002). Calling attention to strengths and resources, rather than psychopathology and deficits, may result in increases of hope, and has the potential for eliciting well-being (Prilleltensky & Prilleltensky, 2006). It is also important to assess the heroic aspects of the clients' lives (Duncan, Miller, & Sparks, 2004). Assessing resilience factors and the heroic aspects of a client's life is as important as assessing oppressive experiences. Following are some questions for assessing resilience.

What resources do clients have at their disposal that they use?

What resources do they have that they have not used but could use in the future?

What personal strengths can clients identify that have been helpful to them to overcome and survive adversities?

How are clients making meaning of their personal experiences?

How do they keep from being depressed? Anxious?

If clients were to give advice to others in their same situation, what would they say?

What people or places do the clients seek that give them hope, comfort, or trust?

What persons, places, or things do clients seek that help them to feel safe?

How do they find dignity in the midst of oppressive and/or denigrating experiences?

What keeps them going and helps them to not give up?

Implications for Professionals

THE POWER OF THE SERVICE PROVIDER

After years of multicultural competency training experience, it is still not clear what is a multiculturally competent provider, nor whether there is a difference between a multiculturally competent provider and

a merely competent one (Ponterotto, et al., 2001). In addition, we have very little information from clients about whom they consider to be multiculturally competent clinicians (Pope-Davis, Liu, Toporek, & Brittan-Powell, 2001).

What we do know is that psychologists, counselors, and social workers have the power to influence the opinions and behavior of the people with whom they work. Considering how many children and adults consume the services of providers of mental health services, voluntarily or involuntarily, it is imperative to understand the ideological, political, and social implications of what they do. Many providers of psychological practices perpetuate the oppression of the clients they serve, in part by blaming its victims and "silently endorsing unjust social practices" (Prilleltensky, 1994, p. 12). In cross-racial supervisory relationships, supervisors can sometimes ignore important issues of the work of their supervisees, or engage in microaggressions (Constantine & Sue, 2007). It is important to recognize how power differentials between the provider and the clients, or between the supervisor and his or her supervisees (Constantine & Sue, 2007), can potentially victimize the clients the therapists are trying to help (Sue & Sue, 2003). Social service providers have a witting or an unwitting role as either social reproducers or social reformers. They can have a role as promoters of change or as proponents of the conservation of the status quo (Prilleltensky, 1994), which occurs particularly if they do not connect the experiences of oppression with mental health issues their clients present.

REACTIONS TO OPPRESSION TRAINING

The importance of training future providers of social services regarding issues of oppression and resilience cannot be emphasized enough. Clinicians who are exposed to formal coursework and practicum experiences seem to be more culturally competent (Mio, 2003), even though, as noted earlier, it is difficult to assess multicultural competency outcomes (Pope-Davis, et al., 2001).

There is a relationship between reactions to oppression training and attention to the issue of oppression in the delivery of services. There are several reasons why it is important to understand the reactions that future providers of services have to their training regarding the issue of oppression. First, lack of awareness of privilege and oppression or pronounced defensiveness about those subjects can lead to resistance to learning about oppression (Hays, Chang, & Dean, 2004; Mio, 2003). Second, it is important to increase awareness of the cognitive dissonance that sometimes exists between the egalitarian ideology of counselors and their racist, homophobic, ethnocentric, xenophobic, and other feelings, thoughts, and behaviors (Washburn, Manley, & Holiwski, 2003). Finally, it is imperative for future providers to develop awareness of their own privilege and their own oppression (Ponterotto, et al., 2001) because power differential in the client–provider dyad is often maintained in mandatory reporting, expert witness duties, and other instances in which the provider can wittingly or unwittingly become an oppressor.

Much of the understanding and subsequent quality of services depends on providers' reaction to the training on oppression they receive as students. In the last two decades, researchers have collected some data related to the reactions of undergraduate and graduate students to the information presented in this chapter.

When issues or racism, classism, ethnocentrism, sexism, or homophobia are presented, student reactions vary. Students' reactions to the material include discomfort and resistance and vary according to whether the students are White or members of the majority or belong to ethnic or other minority groups (Mio, 2003). The most dramatic variations occur according to whether students have been subjected to oppressive experiences themselves or not. For example, men may feel personally attacked when discussing sexism, and White students may feel accused of being racist in the discussion of racism, ethnocentrism, or xenophobia.

It is not unusual for White students' reactions to fall into several categories including hostility ("I am not a racist." "I didn't have anything to do with it."); apathy ("This is not happening now, why are we spending so much time devoted to racism?"); or guilt ("When I graduate, I will make everything right with my clients."). White individuals (or males, or heterosexuals) may feel unusually burdened with guilt as if they were personally responsible (D'Andrea & Daniels, 2001).

Negative responses to discussions regarding White privilege are not unusual among White students, who may lack awareness of their privilege and be resistant to learning about racism (Hays, Chang, & Dean, 2004). When male privilege is explained or discussed, it is common for male students to feel defensive, as if this discussion implied that all males are villains, and that all women are good-hearted victims. Students of color who have experienced oppression of any kind may feel grateful for having an opportunity to discuss issues of oppression in the classroom, sometimes for the first time in their academic lives. But Latino, Latina, or African American students may also feel as if they are being used as representatives of their race or ethnicity in classrooms where those students' experiences are thought of as representing their group and may feel tired of always being put in the position of the ethnic minority "educator" (Mio, 2003, p. 133). Similar reactions may develop in gay or lesbian students or in Jewish students, but only if they reveal themselves. The reactions of other minorities of color to the issues of oppression may include "I already know about this," or "I don't need to study this material."

WHO SERVES OPPRESSED CLIENTS?

Clients who are marginalized or belong to oppressed groups are often served by recent graduates with little or no clinical experience. The most marginalized and oppressed of clients end up being served by students in their internship years, or who have recently graduated and may be supervised by clinicians who are overworked and underpaid. Many clinicians who are committed to work with this population can also be burned out. Because staff turnaround rates are high in agencies that serve marginalized, oppressed, and poor clients, the clients end up having to start over numerous times, repeating the stories of their lives to different and strange providers, reliving—in the agencies that are supposed to help them—the oppressive stories with which they are trying to come to terms. It is important for interns and recent graduates to delve into issues of oppression and social justice to help the clients they serve.

Self in Context 3

P ersonal identity *is* cultural identity. Culture is a powerful organizer of people's lives. How we view ourselves and who we are as individuals cannot be separated from when, where, and how we grew up. How adults behave, love, work, and make decisions is related not only to their individual psychological development but also to how their individual development intersects with the political, geographical, sociological, and historical factors that precede and surround their lives. Culture is one of the most influential determinants of identity (Waldegrave, 1998), and therapists who do not address cultural meanings in their clients may be engaging in oppressive practices rather than therapeutic ones. The stories in this book provide a window into individuals' lives as they reflect on important aspects of their cultural identity. It is important to view the stories as snapshots along a continuum in the storytellers' lives, one possible view of their journey toward identity development. It is also important to view the stories in the authenticity of the moment for the storyteller. How people decide to tell their story at one moment in life may vary according to their self-concept, their developmental stage, and the contextual dimensions of their lives. Our framework includes a description of human developmental models, together with other areas that must be explored to understand self-concept and cultural identity, such as descriptions of life cycle stages and other contextual dimensions of development.

Human Development

The models of human development teach us about human nature and the formation of identity. When working with clients across the lifespan, it is important to consider developmental tasks and activities, particularly as they relate to behaviors and functioning. Human development is plastic, fluid, and holistic; occurs within multiple contexts; and is often bidirectional because skills gained during one time period may be lost in another (Berger, 2004). For example, cognitive development is important to consider when understanding cultural identity and individuals' perceptions of themselves as cultural beings. In Piaget's model, for example, when school-age children move from concrete to formal operations, they are engaging in a cognitive shift that allows them to understand the world in logical terms and from multiple perspectives (Berger, 2004). In terms of cultural identity development, it is generally at this stage that children begin to move from a conceptual understanding of race and gender from a physical standpoint to a social perspective, with the beginning notions of the sociopolitical context from which culture is derived (Quintana, 1998; Wright, 1999). In Piaget's final formal operations stage, abstract and rhetorical thinking skills are mastered, allowing individuals who reach it to understand multiple perspectives simultaneously. When examining clients' stories, it is important to consider how cognitive development influences their understanding of the events in their lives and their ability to develop effective coping and problem-solving strategies. The stories in this book reflect the storytellers' shifts in their cognitive appraisal of their cultural identity as they tell us about their cognitive understanding.

Erickson's stages of psychosocial development help us to understand development and its relationship to culture (Berger, 2004). As children move through their developmental tasks, the role of cultural factors cannot be ignored. As they move through the stages, they begin to understand the social connotations of their identities. For example, preteens begin to base their friendships solely on gender and develop strict rules for behaviors that signify group membership. Children who may not strictly follow the norms for gendered behavior are often teased and ostracized. The same can be true for other cultural factors. As adolescents try to answer the crucial "Who am I?" question, they begin to assess their roles within society, including an understanding of stereotypes and the importance of values. For ethnic minority children, issues around career aspiration and expectation, for example, are colored by their perceptions of reactions and acceptance by others, the presence of role models, and financial concerns. In reading the stories in this book, the reader should be able to comprehend complex relationships between personality development and cultural identity.

The final area of development that serves as part of the framework for the stories is moral development. The three major moral development models (Piaget, Kohlberg, and Gilligan) include the significance of social norms and interpersonal relationships in resolving moral dilemmas (Berger, 2004). Piaget postulates that children develop a sense of right and wrong based on cooperative relationships with each other and conforming to what works best for the group. Kohlberg suggests that children move from avoiding punishment to receiving rewards and social praise for their decisions. Individuals move to an understanding of democratic principles and social norms before developing a set of universal moral principles. Gilligan argues that moral development of women differs from that of men because women are socialized to consider connection and intimacy in decision making (Berger, 2004). No matter which model is considered, it is important to remember that the issues of justice and equity need to be taken into account, particularly for people in oppressed groups. The incongruence that individuals often feel between the sense of these principles and their lived experiences needs to be reconciled in the process of cultural identity development.

Development of the Self

These traditional developmental models are not enough to understand cultural identity because they do not address the richness, complexities, and shifting of an individual's identity (Almeida, Woods, Messineo, & Font, 1998). In addition to understanding the role of human development in personality development and behavioral functioning, it is important to understand the development of the self and the intersection of cultural factors with self-concept. There are generally three components that influence the development of the self: the notion of the self, the ideal self, and the self reflected in the perceptions of others. The first layer of the self includes individual components, including unique personality traits, characteristics, and abilities, along with innate dimensions of temperament. The second layer of the self includes the self-ideal, traits and characteristics that are aspired to, along with goals and aspirations. Additionally, identity is not made up of a self that develops in isolation and holds still, but is constructed by the social context a person has been in, is in, and will be in. The view of oneself is not constant but is complex, multifaceted, and reflected by others in the person's life (Tomm, 1989). Identities are shaped through social interactions with others (Rockquemore & Laszloffy, 2003). By the time they reach school age and develop the ability to classify on multiple dimensions, children begin to understand that others have perceptions of them (Quintana, Castaneda-English, & Ybarra, 1999; Selman, 1971), and they begin to incorporate others' perceptions into their perception of themselves. They become hypersensitive to others' perceptions and will often elicit feedback from others on their personality traits, abilities, and characteristics. The knowledge that others have perceptions that may differ from one's own underscores the need for acceptance by peers and the desire to fit in, to be "normal," and to feel validated (Rockquemore & Laszloffy, 2003). School-age children begin to have a solid understanding of group membership, and they become aware that group membership includes social status (Kerwin & Ponterotto, 1995). This is carried into the adult years.

Cultural identity models outline development that includes a sense of reference group orientation along with self-group orientation (Atkinson, 2003). During preadolescence and the awareness of the sociopolitical connotations of cultural group affiliations, the pressure for conformity and acceptance increases. Preteens develop rigid definitions of criteria for group membership based on behaviors, dress, speech, and relationships. As you read the stories, it becomes clear that the storytellers' sense of identity includes not only how they view themselves, but also how others view them or have viewed them in the past, and their future aspirations for themselves.

Contextual Dimensions of the Self

Cultural identity and self-concept are developed not only within the context of the consciousness of others' perceptions but also within historical images and stereotypes of culture. Dominant cultural patterns are embedded in our cultural discourses and social institutions, perpetuating certain ideas and ignoring others. Cultural identity is constructed historically and socially within groups and is influenced by contact with differences within those groups or differences between different groups; it also evolves as ideas and historical times change (Falicov, 1998a). Individuals need to integrate their individual traits, their ideal selves, and their perceptions of others, including current perceptions and historical stereotypical roles, as they form their self-perceptions across the lifespan.

Therefore, the sense of self is not developed in a vacuum but within multiple contexts. In the field of psychotherapy, explanations for human behavior have traditionally been individual and psychological in nature and have tended to contain the narrow idea that an individual's or a family's behavioral patterns are regulated by personal decision, with an implicit notion of existential freedom devoid from the shaping of contextual dimensions. Although it is true that individual psychological explanations are important and that people do have the freedom to choose their fate to some extent, these individual dimensions are not enough to understand human behavior, motivation, and change. People do not wake up one day and decide to act in a certain way. Historical, sociological, anthropological, political, and geographical explanations are needed to make sense of a person's life choices, life cycle events, and patterns of individual or relational behavior. If therapists lack the curiosity of an anthropologist to seek out information or do not become interested in the statistics that a good sociologist provides, much harm can be done. Counselors, social workers, and psychologists may feel discomfort facing the daunting task of becoming acquainted with so many other disciplines to understand human behavior. But the discomfort of feeling ignorant may be a preferable reaction than indifference and the illusion that only psychological and individual explanations account for human behavior. As Monica McGoldrick (McGoldrick, Giordano, & Pierce, 1996) pointed out in *Ethnicity and Family Therapy,* the typical middle-class White American, often unaware of his or her own ethnic background, believes that ethnicity is something that other groups have, while the Americans are regular, as if the Western, middle-class, individualistic societies were the norm and not just one possible cultural norm. Our storytellers will not let us forget that.

SHIFTING SELVES

Given that personality development, self-concept, and cultural identity are developed with multiple components and within multiple contexts, it is important to remember that the development of cultural identity is not static but dynamic and fluid as individuals continuously relate to institutions, communities, and other individuals. In this "relational reality" (Gergen, 1991, p. 242), individuals discover new talents or traits, have a better understanding of the perceptions of others, and become aware of historical images and stereotypes while the self continues to evolve. Although we often think of optimal functioning for development, or compare others against norms and standards, what is clear is that self and identity are perpetual processes. "Psychologists have proposed that a sense of one's own past, present and future life and identity is created through the telling of life narratives. The properties of the narrative form create a sense of temporality and coherence in an uncertain chaotic world, enabling us to learn from our past and predict aspects of the future" (Ellis-Hill & Horn, 2000, p. 280). As we mature, grow, and add experiences, our view of self shifts and changes, existing in a state of continuous construction and reconstruction (Gergen, 1991). The storytellers in this book demonstrate this idea in their own narratives. Some of them write about how their sense of self changes across developmental age periods, within particular time periods, and across contexts. It is also certain that engaging in a period of self-reflection, in a way that resembles the self-reflection of a person engaged in a therapeutic relationship, also caused them to shift their views. That leads to a unique reflection and representation of the development of their cultural identity. Others do not write about their shifts, but as they go through the stages of their life cycle, predictions of future shifts are possible.

Section II

Dimensions of Race and Ethnicity

In America, race has long been a primary distinguishing cultural factor and a basis for oppression. Indeed, racial bias has underpinned many oppressive acts, including slavery, the removal of Native Americans from their lands to reservations, and the internment of Japanese Americans during World War II. Both subtle and institutional forms of oppression occur due to race. Race is associated with many emotionally laden issues, including racism, affirmative action, race-based quotas, acts of personal prejudice, political correctness, and sentiments against ethnic minorities (Ponterotto, Utsey, & Pedersen, 2006; Sue & Sue, 2003). The experiences of most racial and ethnic minorities are colored by their status as minorities, and while it is true that conditions have changed dramatically since the days when "Blacks were not permitted to drink from the same water fountains as Whites. . . . we still live in an essentially segregated society" (McGoldrick & Giordano, 1996, p. 15).

The significance of race as a term and concept has been debated. Race has been based on phenotypical differences in skin color, facial features, and hair and has been extended to include judgments on intelligence and other psychological characteristics. These physical differences, however, were determined to be inappropriate measures of separateness, so much so that the American Anthropological Association (1998) issued a statement suggesting that race no longer be used as a biological classification but instead be viewed as a product of sociopolitical issues and economics. Skin color, for example, is a historical adaptation to climate and environmental conditions rather than a representation of genetic differences. Contrary to people's beliefs, purity of the races is a myth (American Anthropological Association, 1998). Race has sociopolitical connotations in the United States and has historically been a way to justify political oppression (McGoldrick & Giordano, 1996; Sue & Sue, 2003). Race was used for determining citizenship and land ownership and served as a justification for oppressive acts. Ethnicity is a broader concept in the field of multicultural theory that affords more depth of analysis than race. Focusing on ethnicity allows for inclusion of various groups categorized within racial groups, such as differences between Japanese and Chinese or Mexicans and Puerto Ricans. The emphasis on ethnicity also allows for the exploration of cultural norms for Whites.

Although often associated with nationality and national origin, ethnicity influences functioning, the nature of relationships, and life cycle transitions (Breunlin, Schwartz, & Mac Kune-Karrer, 1997). Phinney (1996) defines ethnicity as an aspect of a person's social identity that is a part of an individual's self-concept that derives from his or her knowledge of membership in a social group, together with the value and emotional significance attached to that membership. Ethnicity includes three components: cultural values, attitudes, and behaviors; a subjective sense of group membership; and experiences with minority/majority status (Phinney, 1996). Ethnicity directs actions; thoughts; affective experiences, including work and career, interpersonal relationships, rituals, and traditions; and eating habits and patterns (McGoldrick & Giordano, 1996). Members of ethnic groups differ in the nature of their interpersonal relationships, rules, family and personal dilemmas, and strategies for resolving conflict (Hines, Garcia-Preto, McGoldrick, Almeida, & Weltman, 1992). Individuals differ in terms of ethnic identity, which includes the sense of membership in the ethnic group, and attitudes and feelings about group membership (Phinney, 1996). Racial identity, a similar concept, is derived from socialization experiences and the psychological and sociopolitical attitudes individuals hold toward their racial group and other groups (Helms, 1995). Racial and ethnic identity models postulate that individuals progress through stages of low salience and awareness of race to integration of values and beliefs prescribed by race (Sue & Sue, 2003). It is important to explore racial and ethnic identity because it explains behaviors and attitudes. Ethnic identity varies in family members (Gushue, 1993), and there are often conflicts in families resulting from differences in ethnic identity and values (McGoldrick & Giordano, 1996).

There are a variety of racial and ethnic identity models (Atkinson, 2003; Cross, 1995; Helms, 1995; Sue & Sue, 2003). Individuals can progress from having neutral or negative and deprecating attitudes toward their own racial group and positive attitudes toward the dominant group to immersion in their own culture, sometimes with accompanying anger toward the dominant group. This is often, but not always, followed by a more sophisticated psychological and cognitive exploration of the meaning of their culture and an integration of cultural values and racial and ethnic identity into self-concept. Racial identity is self-determined and is inclusive of values from both cultural groups. It is important for therapists to determine the identity levels of their clients. It should be noted that the racial and ethnic identity process is dynamic and recursive and that individuals may move fluidly back and forth through various stages as a result of experiences, personal growth, and self-awareness.

Limitation of the Concept of Ethnicity

In multicultural theory, it is important to examine the concept of differences *between* ethnic groups (intergroup differences) as well as the differences *within* groups (intragroup differences). Examining the differences between groups allows readers to clarify some of the cultural differences that exist between people, and helps to legitimize the idea that the sense of belonging to an ethnic group is necessary to some people's identity. In addition to the diversity and heterogeneity of ethnic groups, there are important similarities for certain groups that share a legacy of oppression, genocide, slavery, colonization, or conquest and that makes it necessary to examine them separately (Bernal, Trimble, Burlew, & Leong, 2003). This is why it is sometimes helpful to differentiate between White Europeans, African Americans, Latinos and Latinas, Asians, and other different ethnic groups. The concept of ethnicity, however, has several limitations.

Although understanding an individual's ethnic group membership may be a good framework for examining behaviors, values, and beliefs, generalizations could also lead to inappropriate stereotypes and misunderstandings of intragroup differences. First, most ethnic groups are a combination of multiple cultural groups, and the labels that name ethnic groups generally do not reflect the diversity that exists within the groups (Hays, 2001; McGoldrick & Giordano, 1996). Second, it is nearly impossible to find pure ethnic groups that have not been "contaminated" by others (Appiah, 2006, p. 1). This contamination makes it difficult to describe a typical Latino or Latina or African American. Third, conceptualizing ethnicity as a categorical variable (you are either Asian or Latino or Latina, or you are not), simplifies the complexities of identities (Phinney, 1996). Finally, the descriptive characterization of ethnic group differences does not take into consideration the origins of those characteristics, always rooted in economic, social, historical, and political reasons. For example, the Latino or Latina elderly is often described as a person who did not plan for retirement and depends on his or her adult offspring during their later years. This description fails to acknowledge the fact that in many economically depressed areas of Latin America, planning for retirement is not possible. It is also a Western, middle-class concept derived from the economic structures that make planning for retirement a feasible goal. The different characteristics of ethnic groups are often wrongly understood as different from the middle-class, Western "norm," from which they "deviate" (McGoldrick & Giordano, 1996). From this point of view, there is a risk of understanding "not planning for retirement"—or any other different characteristic—in a pejorative way.

Intragroup Differences: A Framework for Understanding Ethnicity

Since people cannot be understood apart from the sociohistorical, political, and geographical backgrounds into which they were born, a useful approach might be to understand where people can be placed along a continuum of certain cultural characteristics. Table II.1 provides a way of thinking about personal characteristics, values, and worldview as stemming from individuals' contact with, and exposure to, different cultural milieus. For example, societies—and the individuals and families who live within them—are exposed to more or less autocratic governments, live in more or less urban environments, and that are more or less patriarchal. They can be more or less individualistic, have more or less education, more or less access to material goods, and so on. A male individual raised in a patriarchal society, holding traditional gender roles, who has attained a high educational level, in an urban setting will differ from another person of the same patriarchal society, belonging to a lower socioeconomic class, raised in a rural area, even if that person belongs to the same ethnicity. Additionally, individuals can be at different points in the continuum regarding different personal characteristics. For example, an individual can be at a certain point in the continuum Individualism-Collectivism and at another point in the continuum Egalitarian-Patriarchal. Finally, individuals can change along some continuums more than along others, depending on numerous factors, including exposure to other cultures, immigration, and societal changes.

Because gender socialization differs so greatly across cultural groups, comparing two women who are at opposites ends of the continuum might be helpful. First, let's examine the hypothetical life of a woman raised within the cultural characteristics at the right end of the continuum (see Table II.1), in a patriarchal, non-Western, autocratic society, who lives in a poor, rural area or the world, with little access to material goods, health care, or education. This composite of a woman is likely to be one of many siblings. Her parents will likely have differing expectations of her as compared to her male siblings in terms of her education. The parental expectations of her are that she will grow up to marry and have children, like her mother. Some of her siblings might not have survived beyond the first five years of their lives. She is likely to live in a household composed of more

Table II.1   Continuum of Ethnicity and Culture (Sociopolitical Characteristics of Society or Origin)

Sociopolitical Characteristics of Society or Origin

Democratic --Autocratic
Secular---Religious
Economic stability----------------------------Economic instability
Western-------------------------------------Non-Western
Urban/suburban-----------------------------Rural

Characteristics of Culture

Individualism----------------------------------Collectivism
Independence/Self-reliance----------------Rely on other
Non-hierarchical-----------------------------Hierarchical
Egalitarian----------------------------------Patriarchal
Material comforts-----------------------------Lack of material comforts
Mobility--Lack of mobility
Change--Stability
Compartment by age-------------------------No compartment by age
Scientific-------------------------------------Folklore, superstition

Access to Resources

More Access to education	Limited access to education
More Access to health care	Limited access to health care
More access to mental health care	Limited access to mental health care

Other Cultural Dimensions to Consider

- Socioeconomic level
- Level of religious commitment
- Historical facts
- Geographical characteristics
- Gender socialization patterns
- Levels of exposure to oppression
- Sexual orientation

than two generations; she might marry before age 18 to someone who comes with the approval of, or has been selected by, her parents and who shares her religious orientation and her social class standing. Upon getting married, she might move in with the family of her husband, where single aunts and uncles also live. If she works, her income might be considered the property of her husband. She might never divorce, even if the marriage is unhappy, she might have several children raised, in some cases, by her mother-in-law. Her status in the family hierarchy might rise as she gets older and begins to have her own grandchildren, whom she would raise, the way her mother-in-law raised hers. Each one of the families' life cycle events (births, marriages) would be punctuated by specific, ritualized ceremonies involving several generations of the family. This composite woman will almost never be alone in the course of her lifetime, surrounded by her siblings, her children, or her in-laws. In her old age, she will expect to be taken care of financially by her children and will be not be expected to provide for her own care.

Now let's examine a composite woman who was raised within the cultural characteristics of the left side of the continuum in a democratic, Western, secular, middle-class, egalitarian, White American household, and has never been exposed to oppressive experiences. She is likely to have only one sibling and have been raised in a single-parent home. She is expected to go to college, and have an occupation that will allow her to support herself. She may obtain a higher level of education that her male siblings or the males with whom she went to school. She might move out of the house at age 18 to go to a college several hundred miles away from where she grew up and live by herself or with other women her age, without supervision. She might choose a mate whom her parents do not know, or do not approve, who is of a different religious background or a different social class. It would be possible for her to enter into a relationship with another woman. If she were to engage in a same-sex relationship, she might disclose that to her friends and family. She might decide either to have children after age 35 or not to have children at all. She might choose to concentrate on her career and never marry. If she does get married, and has children, both she and her husband might work after the children are born. It would be possible for her to work and for her husband to stay home and raise the children. They would likely live in a home by themselves, without other relatives, and they are likely not to live in the town where they grew up. She is likely to have her own bank account. She and her partner or husband are likely to consult a therapist if their have any concerns regarding their relationship, and they have a high probability to get divorced after less than 10 years of marriage. If they do get divorced, the children are likely to spend some time with each of their separate parents in different households. She is likely to get remarried. She is likely to plan for her retirement during her work years, and after she retires, she might move to a place where there are other people her age. She is not likely to share a household with any of her children in her old age.

The advantage of examining people as falling along continuums across several dimensions is that it allows for the understanding of people's worldviews, beliefs, behaviors, and values as being subject to, and influenced by, the cultural milieu in which they grew up.

Racial Identity Models

While it is important to understand values and characteristics associated with each racial or major ethnic group, it is also important to understand intragroup differences, as noted. Differences may occur due to acculturation rates, experiences with oppression, educational and social class differences, or socialization experiences. Racial identity models have been postulated as another way to help understand intragroup differences. Racial or ethnic identity has been defined as the part of an individual's self-concept or sense of self that is related to group membership status and perceptions of membership. Most racial/ethnic identity models hold that individuals begin with low salience or awareness of race, or strong pro-dominant-group values, until some type of significant encounter occurs, usually with a member of a different racial group. The encounter phase is typically accompanied by confusion, anxiety, depression, and guilt over previously held beliefs. The third stage includes an immersion into cultural activities, including social and political activities, and may include a change of dress, hairstyles, speech, and friendships. The fourth stage includes an integration of racial identity into larger self-concept, and awareness and acceptance of all cultural groups. Table II.2 summarizes major racial and ethnic identity models.

Intergroup Differences

Though it seems unfair to group all White Europeans, Asians, Latinos and Latinas, and African Americans in one big category, some very general characteristics do exist, as noted earlier, that define them as a group, distinct from others. Concepts such as discrimination, marginalization, and segregation, which characterize oppressed groups, or hegemony, which characterizes dominant groups, are salient features in different groups that warrant separate descriptions (Potts & Watts, 2003). The idea, though controversial, that membership in a devalued racial or ethnic group is the most defining experience for an individual living (Utsey, Gernat, & Bolden, 2003) justifies the continued descriptions based on ethnic and racial characteristics. Additionally, some groups share many characteristics, i.e., ways of relating to ancestors, nature, or kin; notions of time; ways of speaking; and so on, that are distinctively different from the way other groups behave, think, or believe (Potts & Watts, 2003). It is important to realize that it is not a question of choosing *either* to emphasize between group descriptions *or* within group variations, but to find a way to integrate *both* between and within group differences in order to make sense of the cultural identity of an individual (Saba, Karrer, & Hardy, 1989).

Additionally, it is important to consider the following aspects that affect ethnic identity. First, some individuals and families maintain their ethnic identity longer than others, depending on their migration history and acculturation processes, i.e., whether they live in heterogeneous or homogenous neighborhoods, whether they socialize with members of their own group, and whether they feel threatened by the lack of loyalty

Table II.2   Racial/Ethnic Identity Models

General racial/ethnic models	Models for specific groups	Models for White Americans
Marcia (1966)	African Americans Cross (1995)	Helms's White Racial Identity Model (1995)
Identity diffusion—has not experienced an identity crisis.	Preencounter—Assimilation (pro-American values and low salience to race).	Contact—Unawareness or denial of White privilege, does not see racism in society as a reality
Foreclosed identity—has committed to an identity that was externally imposed, but has not undergone self-exploration or crisis.	Miseducation (negative stereotypes and African Americans). Self-hatred (negative attitudes about the self due to race).	Disintegration—Begins to see the realities of racism, conflicted over new knowledge and what to do with it.
Moratorium—identity crisis, active identity exploration.	Encounter—occurs after an experience happens that changes awareness of race and is characterized by confusion, depression, or alarm.	Reintegration—Rejection of minority groups and a desire to protect privilege, conflict from disintegration stage is transformed into negative feelings toward minority groups.
Achieved identity—commitment to identity, based on self-exploration and experimentation.	Immersion/emersion—Individuals have an overromanticized immersion into Black culture (intense Black involvement) or strong feelings against White culture and values (anti-White)	Pseudo-independence—Begins to reject racism, but rejection is superficial and directs feelings toward society's racism rather than own actions, more intellectual than personal.
	Internalization—Working to empower the Black community (Black nationalist) or by Black self-acceptance with other cultural variables emphasized (bicultural and multiculturalist)	Immersion—Immerse in search for deeper understanding of racism as it relates to their own experience as a member of the White culture.
	Sellers's (1998) Salience—The extent to which a person defines him- or	Emersion—With a new sense of identity and a deeper sense of what it means to be White, seeks other Whites who have

General racial/ethnic models	Models for specific groups	Models for White Americans
	herself with regard to race. Regard—Private regard (individual evaluation of self and other Blacks) Public regard (others' views of African Americans). Ideologies—Nationalist (emphasizes the uniqueness of being Black, and the belief in the importance of Blacks controlling the destiny of Blacks without the input of other groups. Oppressed minority—Recognizes the oppression experienced by all minority groups. Assimilation—Emphasizes similarities in African Americans and other American (dominant) groups Humanist—Emphasizes the similarities of all humans.	undergone similar transformation. Autonomy—Avoidance of activities that require participation in racism, activism for oppressed groups, active rejection of unearned privilege.
Phinney Ethnic Identity Development Model (1996) Diffusion and foreclosure—feelings about ethnicity are unexplored. While adolescents at this stage may have internalized negative stereotypes,	Asian Americans Kim's Model of Asian American Identity Development (1981) Ethnic awareness—Prior to entering school, ethnicity is understood through interactions with family members, own ethnic	Hardiman's White Identity Development Model (1982) Lack of social consciousness—Birth to five years, passive indoctrination into majority norms and expectations. White children may feel uncomfortable in situations

(Continued)

Table II.2 (Continued)

General racial/ethnic models	Models for specific groups	Models for White Americans
the majority have not. Identity search or moratorium—Awareness of ethnic identity, may be precipitated by any number of events, large or small, often resulting in feelings of anger or embarrassment over previous lack of awareness. Achievement—Confident and comfortable with one's own ethnic identity, open to experiencing other cultures without feeling threat to own group and identity.	identification usually positive or neutral. White identification—Entering school precipitates this change, children develop a sense of being different and the begin to internalize racism toward own identity. Awakening to sociopolitical consciousness—This is usually precipitated by a major life event, and individuals begin to develop a more realistic idea of their place in society, self-concept becomes more positive as they identify more with being a part of an oppressed group. Redirection to Asian American consciousness—They reject the White culture while turning to their own with a new appreciation for their heritage, often feel angry at White culture. Incorporation—Healthy overall appreciate of own culture, see self as more pluralistic and not simply Asian, stop measuring everything against White culture.	with individuals of other racial groups, but have not developed negative associations. Acceptance—Through socialization, children develop an internalized understanding of what race means in society, stay in this stage until an event triggers transition to the next stage. Resistance—Challenging transition, causes embarrassment to Whites as they learn that they passively accepted and propagated racism. Unsure how to change, but actively seeks information to facilitate change. Redefinition—Search for a new White identity that allows pride in group, receptions of aspects that are racist, and awareness of White culture's limitations. Internalization—White identity is positive, works to help other Whites move through the stages.

General racial/ethnic models	Models for specific groups	Models for White Americans
Atkinson, Morten, & Sue (1998) Minority Identity Development Model Conformity—Prefer dominant culture, feel negatively toward self and group, see others as the dominant culture sees them. Dissonance—Enter this stage because of race-related experience. Stage represents a time of transition and mixed feelings towards self and others. Resistance and Immersion—Complete acceptance of ethnic group, complete rejection of White culture, mixed feelings toward other ethnic groups. Introspection—Increased comfort with ethnic identity allows a more flexible view of other groups, starts to differentiate between self identity and group identity. Whites not seen as monolithic. Synergetic articulation and awareness—Racial identity is secure and positive, seen as one aspect of identity, not	Ruiz (1990) Casual—Lack of identification with Latino culture, lack of affirmation of one's ethnic identity. Cognitive—Distorted images of Latinos is incorporated into mental sets: (A) ethnicity is associated with poverty and prejudice; (B) assimilation with Whites is beneficial; (C) assimilation is necessary for success. Consequence—Shame and embarrassment at ethnic identity and markers. Rejection of Latino/Latina heritage. Working-through stage—Distress over negative feelings and not being identified with heritage. Increased ethnic consciousness. Successful resolution stage—Acceptance of culture and ethnicity.	Rowe, Bennett, & Atkinson's White Racial Consciousness Model (1994) Achieved Types—Characterized by some level of exploration around racial attitudes. Dominative—Believes in the superiority of Whites. Conflictive—Does not actively support racism, but does not want to change the current balance of White privilege. Reactive—Speech is very pro-minority, but may be unaware of own unexplored racism. Integrative—Has understanding of a variety of issues related to the dynamic between minority and majority groups and holds positive racial attitudes. Unachieved types—Characterized by disinterest or unawareness around racial attitudes. Avoidant—Consciously ignores or minimizes race-related issues. Dependent—View of race issues depends on what they are told by others.

(Continued)

Table II.2 (Continued)

General racial/ethnic models	Models for specific groups	Models for White Americans
completely defining, selective respect and appreciation for other cultural groups.		Dissonant—Have experienced conflict between their racial beliefs and their experiences, but are unsure what to do with the information.
Helms (1995) People of color Conformity—Unaware of internalized racism, or groups' sociopolitical history Dissonance—Begins to realize that they are not White, and that they know little about their actual group membership Immersion—Seeks positive information about racial group to replace previous negative beliefs, idealizes own group while rejecting White culture Emersion—Prefers same-group experiences, pride in group. Internalization—Able to balance positive membership in own group, while responding objectively to White culture. Integrated awareness—Identifies more on a continuum than an either/or. Comfortable identifying with aspects of more than one group, including White.		

of their offspring (McGoldrick & Giordano, 1996; Sue & Sue, 2003). Second, the attachment to one's ethnic identity is greatly influenced by exposure to racism and discrimination (Ponterotto, Utsey, & Pedersen, 2006). Third, individuals and families without a strong sense of ethnic affiliation may resort to their "ideological ethnicity" (Harwood, cited by Falicov, 1998a, p. 132) when faced with crisis, struggles, or illnesses. Fourth, social class affects ethnic identity greatly because it determines what people value, and the options and resources that people have or don't have (Kliman, 1998). Social class also determines differences in family life cycle sequences (i.e., age of marriage and procreation), and attitudes toward illness, death, and help-seeking behavior (McGoldrick & Giordano, 1996). Fifth, ethnic affiliation also differs, as noted, according to levels of identity development, gender socialization patterns, and sociohistorical developments. Finally, it is important to not idealize or denigrate any culture, because there are adaptive and nonadaptive features in each cultural value.

Let us turn our attention to the differences between groups, with a particular emphasis on ethnic characteristics that may affect help-seeking behavior. The following descriptions come from the work of Bernal, Trimble, Burlew, & Leong (2003); Falicov (1998a); McGoldrick, Giordano, & Pierce (1996); Sue & Sue (2003); and from our own clinical observations. The reader is encouraged to consult these and other references for more comprehensive descriptions of ethnic groups.

WHITE EUROPEANS

White Americans of European ancestry are the largest ethnic group in the United States, comprising two thirds of the population (Page: 1 http://www.census.gov/prod/2001pubs/c2kbr01-4.pdf). In some geographical areas, Whites are no longer a majority (Roberts, 2007). As a group, they tend not to be included in articles that describe ethnic populations. As is the case with all ethnic groups, White European Americans are not a homogeneous group. The majority have German, British (including English, Welsh, Scottish, and Irish) origin, followed by Italians, Scandinavians, Greeks, and people of Slavic origin. Most White Americans have been in the United States for more than two or three generations and have increasingly married outside of their own ethnic groups, which generally means that they are of mixed European origin. It is not uncommon for White Americans of European origin not to identify with a specific ethnic group, and many do not attach significance to their ethnic affiliation after a couple of generations. But that is more true of the groups that have been in the United States the longest (i.e., German and English) than of the Eastern European (Russian and Polish), Southern European (Greek and Italian), or the Irish, in part because these subsequent groups were subject to ridicule, prejudice, or discrimination. Though there are poor and lower-class Whites, the majority are not poor.

By the second or third generation, most European Americans' history is characterized by upward mobility and a weak affiliation with their ethnic identity—they prefer to be identified as Americans. The early Anglo-Americans and German Americans were greatly influenced by Protestantism, valuing independence, hard work (Protestant work ethic), loyalty and fidelity in relationships, generosity to those less fortunate, civic responsibility, good deeds, and tolerance for religious diversity. Additionally, the spirit of entrepreneurship, organization, problem solving, risk taking, resourcefulness, and autonomy demonstrated by the early pioneers influenced the possibilities for social mobility and economic growth. There are, however, traits that characterize some White ethnic groups more than others. For example, people originally from England or Germany may prefer restraint and stoicism in dealing with adversity. Emotionally, they would rather not complain and not express anger, affection, and emotion, contrasting with the Irish or Italians, who may appear to be more boisterous or animated in the same situation. Help is sought with difficulty, as it is acknowledgment that they cannot solve a problem themselves, because, as noted, independence and autonomy are greatly valued. Anglo-Americans may feel that saying too much about themselves may burden other people.

This contrasts with Irish and Italians. The Irish are more prone to use humor, wit, and sarcasm to express pain indirectly. The Catholic Church may be the primary cultural force that unifies the Irish, and provides strict guidance for suffering as well as codes of sexual behavior. The legacy of English occupation influences the Irish character to this day. In therapy, the Irish may act as if in confession, seeking forgiveness by revealing the sins. For Italians, separation from the family is not desirable, and they have tended to turn to the family first for help in solving problems. The intense involvement with family members may make it difficult to set boundaries and negotiate their individuality.

People of Slavic origin (Czech, Slovak, Hungarian, Russian, and Polish) are as diverse as their countries of origin, but share a history of living under oppressive political regimes. The White European female client often self-refers to therapy and may be the most assiduous consumer of clinical services.

AFRICAN AMERICANS

African Americans comprise the second largest ethnic minority group within the United States, approximately 13 percent of the population (U.S. Bureau of the Census, 2005), and are the only group whose heritage in this country includes slavery. While Irish immigrants and Native Americans often worked as indentured servants or slaves, when laws in this country established slavery as a legal institution, Africans were the primary target. Census data suggest that more than two centuries of enslavement still has negative consequences for many African Americans. A disproportionate number of African Americans live in poverty (33.1 percent), are unemployed (11 percent), or undereducated (U.S. Bureau of the Census, 2000).

History books often treat the African American legacy as beginning in this country. Africans, however, thrived for many generations, and have a distinct culture that includes values, beliefs, lifestyles, and traditions that influence African Americans today. Boykin and Toms (1985) outlined nine Afrocentric cultural values that influence functioning: harmony, spirituality, communalism, movement, verve, expressive individualism, affect, oral tradition, and the social time perspective. Harmony refers to a sense of connection and attachment of all living beings, and is an essential component of the sense of spirituality for many Africans and African Americans. African spirituality holds that all beings have worth and dignity, and honors the connections between all things, animate and inanimate. The sense of harmony and spirituality extends to a respect for nature. Communalism includes the importance of connections between people, families, and groups. In communalistic societies, group functioning is viewed as more important than individual functioning, and behaviors and choices are seen as a reflection of the group. Movement and verve reflect the level of spontaneity, and the importance of rhythm. Expressive individualism and affect refer to the importance of self-expression. The oral tradition refers to the importance of storytelling, and oral histories. Social time perspective focuses on the importance of connections and relationships within dimensions of time and space.

Boyd-Franklin (2003) outlines five strengths of African Americans that are a reflection of the Afrocentric values. The first strength is the importance of extended family relationships, which include family, friends, community members, and important religious leaders. Family therapy is often recommended for African Americans due to the importance of social connections and communalism. The second strength is the importance of flexible gender roles. While many African Americans live in single-parent families or mother-headed households, there are not rigid stereotypes or expectations based on gender. Children are expected to contribute in multiple ways to the household, and are able to engage in a variety of roles. The third strength is spirituality. Clinicians should include religious leaders— such as pastors or ministers—in treatment, and assess the importance of prayer as a coping mechanism, and the role of the church in providing resources for the client or family. The fourth and fifth strengths are the importance of education and hard work. Educational achievement is stressed in African American families, and is often reinforced through religious institutions, and civic and community organizations. The communal nature of Africans requires that individuals contribute to the functioning and well-being of the group or tribe. This is reflected in valuing education and achievement as an adult competency for African Americans.

African Americans are often seen as underachieving, are often disproportionately placed in special education classrooms, and have a higher high
school dropout rate than other groups. Social services providers need to
work with clients around achievement, but also promote culturally relevant curriculums, work with teachers around expectations, and engage in
programs that promote career development. Helping children and adolescents find mentors may also be effective for helping with achievement and
career development.

NATIVE AMERICANS

Native Americans comprise a small percentage of the total U.S. population, about 1.5 percent (U.S. Bureau of the Census, 2005). Native
Americans experienced oppression and discrimination, which led to the
almost total annihilation of the population that existed prior to European
settlement. Today, there are more than 500 federally recognized tribes,
many of whom have treaties with the United States. These treaties often
allow the tribes to establish their own set of laws and policies, which clinicians may need to know. For example, the Indian Child Welfare Act holds
that children who need placement should be placed with family members
or members of the tribe, and sometimes outside placements need to be
approved by a tribal council.

Native Americans hold values that often differ from those of the dominant culture, and need to be understood by therapists (Garrett & Garrett,
1994). The first value is the importance of the tribe, family, and extended
family. Tribes are seen as interdependent systems, and individuals within
the tribes are seen as a part of the tribe. Decisions, behaviors, and values
are derived from tribal and group membership. Elders within tribes are
treasured and seen as wise. Second, Native Americans value sharing and
cooperation. Third, resources are to be shared and used as needed, without the notion of ownership or proprietorship. Native Americans try to
live in harmony with nature, and believe in the importance of giving to
nature in the same manner as taking from nature. Fourth, Native
Americans have a worldview that includes the importance of being, choosing behaviors to meet current needs for individuals or the groups. The
fifth value is noninterference, the importance of respecting others and
observing rather than acting impulsively. This translates into a parenting
style that is seen as more permissive or allowing freedom for the child, and
promoting self-awareness. Spirituality is another important value, which
includes the connection with all beings. Many believe that we are spiritual
beings living within a particular time, and that noninterference helps individuals to grow and actualize. It also includes an awareness of supernatural
phenomena (Garrett & Garrett, 1994; Herring, 1999).

There are several common psychological issues or presenting problems for Native Americans. First, Native Americans have a high rate of substance use. Substance use may occur as a coping method for dealing with oppression, discrimination, high rates of poverty on reservations, lack of employment, or cultural identity concerns. The rate of substance use is growing among adolescents and may be related to elevated school dropout rates (Beauvais, Chavez, Oetting, Deffenbacher, & Cornell, 1996). The second issue is education. Native Americans have the highest high school dropout rates in the country. Although the experience of boarding schools is seen as a historical phenomenon, many children currently leave reservations to attend public school programs. Because there is not typically employment or business on reservations, many are hypothesized to drop out because they do not see education as useful. Violence, particularly domestic violence and sexual assault, is an issue on reservations. Young girls are used as sexual objects in exchange for alcohol. There is also a high suicide rate on reservations.

Finally, clinicians need to use a holistic approach when working with Native American clients. Providing culturally sensitive treatment to Native Americans could include the use of the medicine wheel (Garrett & Garrett, 1994). The wheel incorporates spiritual, natural, physical, and mental components. Many clients may have seen a medicine man for treatment, or expect the use of supernatural methods.

LATIN AMERICANS

Latinos and Latinas in the United States, also known as Latin Americans or Hispanics, are the largest and fastest-growing ethnic group and also the largest language minority group, comprising almost 13 percent of the American population (U.S. Bureau of the Census, 2005). Hispanics are not a race, and there are both light-skinned and dark-skinned Latinos and Latinas, depending on ancestral mixing among Europeans, the indigenous peoples, and Africans. Many are foreign born, but most are not. A lot of Latinos and Latinas are poor, and in the United States, they tend to have lower levels of educational achievement when compared with non-Hispanics. Part of the reason for the high level of poverty has to do with conditions in their countries of origin and the relative closeness of the countries to the United States. They are a heterogeneous group composed of Mexicans, the largest by far (about 65 percent), followed by Puerto Ricans (about 10 percent), Cubans (about 6 percent), and Central and South Americans (about 14 percent). Each group has a different history and different migration patterns into the United States. In many cases, they share a language. Even Latinos and Latinas who do not speak Spanish most often have a parent or a grandparent who does. Most Latinos and Latinas also share a religion, Catholicism, even though Protestantism has grown in the last several decades. There are also Latinos and Latinas who are Muslim or Jewish, depending on migration patterns to Latin American countries.

For Latinos and Latinas, the family is a source of identity, cohesiveness, and support and includes the nuclear and extended family. The extensive attachment possibilities afforded by extended families are generally viewed as increasing relational resources, and therefore better for psychological well-being. As in other collectivistic societies, the family stresses dependency over independence, and demands loyalty. As in other patriarchal societies, there is firm hierarchical organization in the Latino family, and men and women are often taught two different codes of sexual behavior. These double standards are decreasing in urban areas, but may persist even among Latinos and Latinas of higher education and higher socioeconomic status. Divorce rates tend to be lower, and families tend to have more children than Anglo-American families. Religion may provide a framework and meaning for life that includes meaning assigned to family life cycle events and that may affect marital life.

The Roman Catholicism of Latinos and Latinas is often blended with native religious beliefs and practices, and varies from region to region. Beliefs in folk healing and practices, such as *curanderismo* and *espiritismo*, may coexist with belief in scientific Western practices. Colonized or oppressed people and those who live under poor economic conditions, with little or no self-determination, often have a fatalistic outlook, which includes beliefs that events are determined by fate, rather than personal will. Within this fatalistic worldview, death and suffering are part of life. Suffering may be more accepted, which may serve an adaptive purpose, but at the same time constitutes an expression of powerlessness. There is certain dignity attached to suffering stoically, and without complaints, about events, illnesses, death, and other tragedies. Even though only a small percentage of Latinos and Latinas are undocumented immigrants, many suffer discrimination and other forms of social oppression. For many Latinos and Latinas in the United States, immigration, and the uprooting and losses associated with it, are common denominating factors in their lives. Depression, family violence, school failures, and delinquency are some of the consequences of migration and social change. Latinos and Latinas are often referred to services by schools and the legal system in relation to concerns regarding their children, but they are not likely to seek help voluntarily. Many Latinos and Latinas are not aware of the function or roles of mental health professionals, and might relate to clinicians with the respect and deference afforded to the authority of a professional. Many Latinos and Latinas will express emotional problems through somatic concerns.

Some of the most important issues to consider in a clinical situation with Latino and Latinas are their migration experience, their acculturation and acculturative stress, their experiences with racism and discrimination, language issues, and gender roles and expectations. Many individual, couple, and family conflicts arise when there are differing and changing levels of acculturation within the same family.

ASIANS

Asians are generally grouped together in texts that define ethnic groups, even though they are an extremely diverse group of people, coming from many countries, with different languages, and a variety of religious orientations. Census figures estimate the total Asian population of the United States at around 5 percent (U.S. Bureau of the Census, 2005). The countries of origin may include India, China, Japan, Korea, Vietnam, Cambodia, Indonesia, and the Philippines. Sometimes people from Middle Eastern countries (Iran, Lebanon) are included with the Asian groups. Asians can be Hindus, Christians, Muslims, or Buddhists. The majority of Asians in the United States are foreign born, with the exception of the Japanese. Compared to other ethnic groups, nonrefugee Asians, such as the Indians or the Chinese, tend to have higher income levels and higher educational levels. This does not mean that poverty does not exist in the countries of origins, or that Asians work harder or are smarter than people from other ethnic groups, but simply that voluntary migration from countries that are geographically more distant is only possible for those who can afford it. On the other hand, groups such as the Cambodians or the Vietnamese have lower levels of education and income than other groups, and may have arrived as refugees of war. Culturally, the Asian ethnic groups are the most "other" in relation to Western cultures. Collectivism, with its emphasis on mutual family obligations and interdependence, may be one of the issues that cuts across all Asian groups. Authoritative, hierarchical, and patriarchal family structures are common. Duties and clearly defined roles based on gender, age, and social class are valued and expected. The expectation of self-disclosure and verbal expression of feelings may go against the culturally sanctioned practices of expected self-restraint and repression of emotions. Somatic complaints (headaches, dizziness, fatigue; gastrointestinal, sleep, and appetite disturbances; or chest pains) may be the way through which emotional, relational, or mood problems are expressed; indirect communication patterns are not uncommon. Many Asian individuals would not accept dealing with their personal problems by seeking the help of a mental health professional. Public disclosure of family problems can be a source of shame and embarrassment. As in other patriarchal and authoritative families, traditional husbands may be reluctant to attend sessions for fear of losing face. University students and more acculturated Asians of the second or third generation might seek professional help from a mental health practitioner. More traditional Asians are unlikely to seek help voluntarily and may be referred for help by medical doctors or the school system. The clinician needs to gain the trust of the individual or the family, which may be difficult to engage initially. Clinical work with Asian individuals or families requires the assessment of migration history, acculturative processes, differences in levels of acculturation, and expectations of the therapy process. It can also involve taking into consideration the particular group's explanatory theories of mental health–related problems and the availability and use of traditional healing practices. Explanatory theories can include energy imbalances and supernatural interventions due to transgressions of family expectations or rituals. Healing practices can include nutrition therapy or traditional medicines.

Implications for Professionals

Although race has little biological basis, clinicians would be wise to consider how the constructs of race and ethnicity influence a client's functioning. Race and ethnicity may exert subtle or overt influence on behaviors, functioning, values, and beliefs. Ethnic beliefs, in fact, influence beliefs about normal and adaptive functioning and perspectives on mental health and emotional and psychological well-being. It is imperative that therapists initiate discussions on race and/or ethnicity, because even clients whose experience of oppression is the presenting problem may be reluctant to discuss it. Therapists should assess the influence of race and ethnicity and experiences of racism or ethnocentrism. The intersection of race and ethnicity with other cultural variables including gender, social class, and immigration status should be examined. Finally, the racial and ethnic identity of clients should be included as a component of assessment and throughout the therapeutic process.

Stories in This Section

This section includes four chapters. In each story, the themes of race and ethnicity play a prominent role. The first story chronicles Julie's experiences of racism, internalized oppression, and racial identity development. The second chapter follows the identity development and functioning of Butch, a multiracial individual. The reader will discover the challenges that he faces in integrating each of the cultural groups that comprise his racial heritage. The third chapter focuses on ethnicity and ethnic identity development, as Betsie chronicles the values from her Jewish family traditions. The fourth story of Maribel reflects her struggles with being both Puerto Rican and American.

Discussion Questions

What are the benefits and drawbacks of depicting people according to their ethnic group affiliation?

What is your opinion of the inclusion of Whites as a distinct ethnic group category, along with the others?

How do the conceptualizations of race, ethnicity, and culture affect the quality and nature of the services the provider offers?

Which ethnic groups are you most and least familiar with?

How would familiarity or lack of familiarity with a certain ethnic group affect the provision of services?

What kinds of questions could you ask to assess the stage of identity development of a White young adult? An African American adolescent? An older Latina woman? A middle-aged Asian male?

Julie's Story 4

So What if I'm a Black Woman?

Race remains one of the most contentious issues in our country. When we are at cocktail parties, race, along with politics and sex, is often a forbidden subject. We are often socialized to pretend that race does not exist, encouraged and rewarded to see people as individuals without color. Yet, for many, particularly ethnic minorities, race is a primary identifier. It provides a sense of pride, a sense of connection and belonging; it becomes an all-encompassing source of identity. One's racial affiliation can determine lifestyle choices and values, and it influences relationships and behaviors. But race can also lead to a sense of shame, discomfort, embarrassment, and fear as individuals encounter experiences of oppression and racism. Race can lead individuals to engage in stereotypical behaviors or behaviors that serve as attempts to fight against stereotypes. Although our relationship to race is a lifelong fling, our connection to it changes with new experiences and with changes in development.

In her story, Julie explores the development of her racial identity. Although she has always had an awareness of her status as an African American woman, race had little salience or meaning until she was confronted with racial concerns and episodes of racism in high school and college, which, according to Erikson (1968), is the time when identity development begins. As you read her story, you should think about the influence that racism can have in shaping identity, an individual's sense of self, and self-esteem. Also, begin to think about how Julie's level of social class interacts and intersects with race, along with the role of gender in her life.

Julie's Story

As a 30-year-old African American female, it feels like I have had to deal with my race and its impact on me and how I view the world since the day I was born. I was raised in a single-parent African American household. My maternal grandfather lived with me most of my life and acted as a surrogate father. I saw my father pretty frequently, and he did give me an allowance and took me shopping; however, I always got the feeling he only did it to please my mother. I viewed my father as being very distant and never looked forward to his constant put-downs and negative comments. When I mentioned this behavior to my mother, she usually defended him and made excuses for his behavior: "He just feels if he says that about you, you'll work harder to prove him wrong," or "He's just having some problems right now. Just ignore him." I soon stopped telling her because the excuses were worse than the comments.

As a young girl, I searched for affirmations of my beauty and intellect. On television, I did not see many African Americans, and my earliest dreams of being a career woman were colored by how I thought the "White" people did things. You see, my community was poor and Black. Some of the schoolteachers were White, but for the most part, I didn't interact with Whites until I went to the store with my family outside of our community. I often dreamed of traveling and seeing all the places White people came from. It's funny—visiting Africa never entered my mind until high school.

During my search for an identity as a young girl, I remember hating to go get my hair done. We would go to a friend of the family who had a beauty shop in her basement. She was an older woman, and my weekly press and comb was done by her. Here my mother talked and got cooking lessons and life lessons. I always felt I was being tortured and talked about. I have very thick, coily hair, and it was the topic of many discussions. My "bad" hair was difficult and hard to manage, and I was often teased about cutting it off. Although I never said anything, this early experience made me feel I should have been born White. I remember getting mad at my mother on a few occasions and asked her why my daddy couldn't have been White so my hair could be "good." My mother, probably unable to understand the full magnitude of what I meant, would tell me my father was chosen because he was the person she loved. As I began to develop and get noticed by men in a sexual way, I went through a very uncomfortable and difficult time, which still plagues me to some degree to this day. At home, my father constantly told me I was fat and would have to be pushed through the door by the time I was 18. My grandfather would yell at me to take off the shorts or whatever else I happened to be wearing, and my mother would just say, "Your father used to tell me I was fat when I was your size, and I look back now and see I wasn't." The only people who seemed to think I was beautiful with coily hair and large hips, thighs, and buttocks were the boys who lived in the area. Because I did not have a great relationship with my father, it's safe to say I didn't trust men, so, thankfully, I did not fall prey to any male sexual advances during this time of turmoil. Also, because I was heavily involved in church activities, I believed that sexual activity before marriage was forbidden, and I was determined not to fall prey to it. Lastly, because my father wasn't around much and my mother was raising me alone, I never wanted a child out of wedlock. I had been called a bastard too many times and never wanted my child to endure such a thing, nor did I want to be the subject of the Supremes song "Love Child."

All of this physical development and turmoil began when I was 12 years old. During this same time, I got the greatest shock of my young world. One day as I sat in the kitchen eating my dinner alone, my father was in the den (located the next room over) watching television. The doorbell rang. Suddenly my mother appeared to tell my father someone wanted him at the door. Well, this was most unusual because my father did not live with us and most definitely did not receive any visitors. As I peeked out of the window, I saw my father's van double-parked and a woman standing near it with her hands on her hips and her head moving from side to side. It was apparent she was yelling from the way her hands would occasionally wave in the air. My mother stood in the darkness on our enclosed porch, listening. I ran back to my seat in the kitchen as my father came past me to get his shoes and prepared to leave. I asked who was at the door, and his only response was, "Who do you think?" After I told him who I thought it was, he said, "Yep," and walked out the door. We were never to speak of her again, and, in fact, my mother and I never spoke of her until a few days before my wedding, when I told her I had reservations because I was not confident a man could be faithful. Her only response was, "I knew you would have problems with this eventually. I just didn't know when."

As a Black woman, this early event had dramatic effects on me. Did only White families have faithful husbands who took care of their families and loving and devoted wives? Was it a Black woman's fate to raise her children alone and to bear them outside of marriage? (There sure were a lot of single female parents at church.) Why was I not considered beautiful, and because of my appearance, would I ever meet someone who would love me and think I was beautiful? It's funny, but as I continued to struggle with these issues and entered high school, I remember my father telling me he would not walk me down the aisle on my wedding day. Like the glutton for punishment I was, I asked why. He told me that when I got divorced because the man was no good and could not take care of his responsibilities, I couldn't blame my father for giving me away.

In high school, I attended a magnet school with a very mixed ethnic population. I discovered that there were intelligent Blacks and Hispanics as well as intelligent people from other ethnic groups. To me, we got along great. I do not recall having any racial discussions or hearing people put down because of their race. You were considered elite because you were able to get into the school, and if you were able to stay, well, you were destined for greatness, regardless of your race. I never really thought about race during this time. Granted, my time at school was very different from my time at home. At home, I was surrounded by African Americans who engaged in the use and distribution of drugs, there were gang fights and shootings, and many of the young girls my age were pregnant or soon to be, but somehow I wanted to believe I was better than they were. I was going to make it, and in my mind I would be a credit to my race. How awful to admit such a thought, but nonetheless it is what I thought. I began to imitate my White classmates. I spoke proper English and worked very hard at sounding White. I even worked on my accents: British, California Valley girl, and so on. I see now that I wanted to be anything but Black. As I left my neighborhood for school each day, I dreamed of being a doctor or anything else that would take me around the world and make me important. In some of my daydreams, my hair was a bouncy, wavy texture, and my skin was much lighter. I was considered beautiful, and all the men—White and Black and everything else—thought I was the most beautiful woman they had ever met. See, I knew I was Black, but I hated everything about being Black. I hated the way Black people spoke, and I hated the way they laughed and drank and looked. I hated that they all didn't want to do better, wouldn't go to school, didn't find jobs, had unprotected sex, and so on. I didn't realize it, but I hated me. I didn't like my full figure, and I definitely found nothing beautiful about my skin or my hair. I wanted to be White, and I identified with the White culture. I felt that Blacks were in the shape they were in because of the decisions they made. I was unable to see anything differently. My grandfather would also make comments about the neighborhood gang-bangers or other members of the community, which helped to reinforce my beliefs.

In high school, we were all required to take an African American history class, which I thought was an awful requirement. After all, I was Black, so therefore I didn't need the class. Right? Wrong! I remember feeling overwhelmed at the material and somewhat confused. All of my grammar school history books never even mentioned Blacks. We simply were the slaves. Now here was this new information that said we contributed greatly to the world and to the United States. How could this be? The instructor assigned a research paper for us to write, and I still remember part of it and the changes it began to make in me. We were assigned an African country, and we had to write about the land and its people. Additionally, we needed to first start our research at home, in the family encyclopedia. Well, this was great because, for a poor family, we did own a set of encyclopedias, and I thought I would finish this assignment on Egypt in a hurry. Well, I looked up Egypt and found all the pictures of the people to be drawings of White people. I remember feeling hurt and furious. Were Egyptians White or Black? Then I discovered that they never really said Egypt is in Africa (which I found out later during my research). I was floored. How much did I not know about being Black and why were they (I wasn't sure who "they" were) trying to hide this information?

As I entered college, I still had these grand dreams of being accepted into the White world as one of them. I knew I would have to work hard and felt that every word I spoke or wrote was a reflection on how much like them I could become. I did join the African American student union, but this was only because a Black girl I met during orientation introduced me, and I just began hanging out. I also began to discover that making friends with other people (those who were not Black) was much harder than it had been in high school. In fact, most people wouldn't even talk to me, let alone be my friend, but I attributed it to my unattractiveness and not my race.

While walking through the community area one day, I noticed that many clubs were attempting to bring in new members. I was looking to move on campus and began to talk to a resident of an off-campus dorm. The dorm had a chef and many other benefits, and they seemed very eager to have me apply. Cool, I thought. I can move in here, and this would be great. I didn't realize that they wanted me because they didn't have any Blacks living there and thought it would be a good idea to integrate. I also did not know I was in for some trauma that I was not prepared to deal with on an emotional level. I was accepted and moved in right away. It was the beginning of my sophomore year, and I already had a 3.8 average and wanted to keep up the good work. During the first week of classes, I went to the study area in the dorm and prepared to study. Suddenly, these two humongous White males entered the room and began talking to each other. I didn't know them, and they never introduced themselves to me. I continued to try to study, but they just got louder and louder. Eventually, I asked them if they would quiet down so I could continue studying, and this is when I began to understand who I was to the outside world. The two men came over to my table and began to taunt me. One said, "Oh, it looks like we've made the little nigger mad." The other said, "Yes, I wonder what the nigger thinks she can do about it." Well, I was taken off guard, and I definitely didn't know what to say. I had never been called the "N" word, and I had only heard it used from one Black person to another as a word of affection and familiarity. As these two men continued to call me names, something inside of me began to fall into the pit of my stomach. I wanted to fight, to hit, to scream, to kill them for calling me that horrible name. But instead I said nothing. I picked up my books and left the area, telling myself I couldn't take them both; they were too big. I hid. I hid in my room and began to look at each person in my classes. I soon discovered that in all my classes I was the only Black person. I became paranoid. I was depressed and petrified. My mother was not speaking to me because I had moved into the dorm, and everyone else in my family seemed so busy. I didn't know where to turn. Meanwhile, life at the dorm just got harder.

My roommate was a white Hispanic. This meant she was Hispanic but looked White. She dated a White male and was very confused about who she was. She acted and thought White and began to make racial comments. Her boyfriend was my most incessant source of grief because on some occasions I would wake up with him looking in my face, making a racial comment about me. At a party, he told me he asked everyone to turn the lights on so he could find me. The other women on my floor were just as awful. When I woke up in the morning, they made comments about my hair. When I exited the shower after washing my hair, they made comments about that. The time I blow-dried my hair and it stood out in a huge Afro, they all screamed when I entered my room, where they were waiting to see my hairdo. And let's not forget the time they kept harassing me because they wanted to touch Black hair. I won't even mention the times they made comments about how fat I was, although looking back I know I was considered small by all standards; I just had a fuller, rounder figure than they did. I won't even go into detail about my English composition teacher who, during this same time, wrote on my final paper/presentation that I should consider going into a profession where I could do public speaking, like the entertainment field, because I couldn't write, and my people were not known for their writing ability anyway. But with all of this, my breaking point came when an African American male was allowed entry to the dorm, and he proceeded to rob many of the rooms. I was not home at the time, but later that evening the dorm leaders called a family meeting where the robbery was discussed. Many felt I was in on it because I was Black, and others thought he was my friend and wanted me to go get their items back. I sat there in disbelief, fighting back the tears and horror. I found the courage to ask how I could possibly be involved if I was in class at the time. Someone said the man rang the doorbell and was let in. I asked why.

"He wanted to see you."

"Did he ask for me?"

"No, but he was Black, so I just assumed he wanted you, and I let him enter."

"Oh, that makes sense. I know all the Black people in the world."

"Well, why didn't he take any of your stuff?"

"Because I don't have anything to take except my underwear."

It was after these experiences that I began to change my racial identity.

I began hanging out with the other Blacks on campus. I joined and attended Black club meetings. I began to take African American studies courses and became friends with some of the instructors. I ran for office in the clubs and soon began running workshops and bringing prominent Blacks to the campus to speak to the student body. Suddenly, I hated those White people, and I wanted them to know it. I started fighting back at the dorm. When they made comments, I became sarcastic. When it was my turn to cook dinner, I made African dishes and made them eat with their fingers. For dessert, I made a chocolate pudding pie with the words "Black is beautiful" written on top. I even invited some of my Black friends over, and, dressed in black, red, and green, we stood in front of the dinner table with our fists held high while the various artists' versions of "Lift Every Voice and Sing" played in the background. I hated the Whites, and I picked any opportunity to make comments, to scare them, and to do whatever I could to regain my sense of dignity and self-worth. I played on their stereotypes of me, and I loved it. Soon I saw the dorm as a great place because of the benefits of the chef, unlimited kitchen privileges, the guest rooms, and so on, and decided I would take it over and make it a Black dorm. I began a huge crusade to get more Blacks into the dorm, and I was successful. The next year, six Blacks moved into the dorm, and with them came their friends. It was great, and many of the Whites began to move out.

One day, one of the senator's nephews who lived there had to be hospitalized for a mental breakdown. The rumor was that the Blacks had driven him crazy. The truth? He made all kinds of racial comments and was constantly confronted. This particular day, he was caught writing "Millie and Vanilli" on the room door of a Black girl who was dating an Iranian man. She caught him and physically attacked him, knocking him to the ground and pouncing on him. I thought it was great. He called his uncle, and some important-looking men came to get him and took him away, while he cried and blubbered like a little baby.

Life began to take a turn when one of my instructors pulled me and several other students to the side for a group discussion one day after class. During class time, we had become upset with a White student's presentation. In it, he showed a home movie where all the people in authority were White, and all the villains and down-and-outs were Black. We ate him alive, and he was quite insulted. The instructor wanted us to process what happened and told me and the other Black girl in the group that we would have to apologize to him. I laughed and refused. This began the first of many talks with me on racial identity and how to succeed in a multicultural world.

I would like to say that I left college a changed woman. I would even like to say that I got through all the stages, and when I entered the work world I was totally open to a multicultural world and confident in who I was as a Black woman. I can't say that. I did not leave totally aware, but hurt and angry and determined not to allow Whites to get close. I had been discriminated against by my peers and quite a few instructors, and I was not going to stand for it. If I thought I was being put down because of my race, I was going to scream and shout. I was accepted into the minority internship within the psychology and sociology departments, and I began to assist with research projects on racism and multicultural issues during my last year of school. It was during this time that I began to see the racial tension in the world not just toward Blacks but toward other ethnic groups. I also began to hear positive overcoming stories from Blacks who were able to navigate life despite being discriminated against.

My first job in my field after college was at a women's treatment facility. One of my coworkers was a young White woman, who was a little older than me. She constantly wanted to talk to me and offered me rides home from work, and it became apparent she wanted to be my friend. One day, I sat her down and told her quite bluntly that I did not want her friendship and that I didn't like White people, so she should leave me alone. She replied, "Some White people must have really hurt you bad. I'm going to show you we're not all that way." She and I are still friends today, and that incident occurred more than 10 years ago. Her friendship and my work with clients and on myself helped me to continue to grow and develop a positive racial identity. This actually sounds crazy, but my White coworker affirmed my Blackness every day. She loved and kissed the children of our Black clients, she spoke of adopting Black children, she was always braiding her hair and even wearing beads, and she ignored all the comments and stares by other Whites. She thought I was smart and never seemed to mind that I was Black. She came to my home, met my boyfriend, and was just a cool person. I even went to her all-White suburb, met her biased mom, and sat in her outdoor hot tub with my coily hair frizzing into an Afro. (By the way, her mother is like an aunt to my kids today, and our extended families get along great.)

Currently, I work in an affluent, predominantly White town where I am now one of only two Black police officers. In this capacity, I have felt a lot of strain and stress from my coworkers, and although they won't say anything to my face, it is apparent that a lot of them operate on some unspoken racial beliefs about my character, and no matter how hard I work, it just isn't good enough for them. I became increasingly conscious of my figure and body image, my hair became an issue, and I started to watch every word I spoke. Recently, I cut my hair into a really short style as a sort of liberation. I wanted to swim and engage in other activities in which my hair requires too much effort and time (which I don't have), and I cut it. I have never felt so free. I also began to allow my coworkers to see me in my street clothes, with my stomach or legs showing, as a way of showing I am proud of my figure and who I am.

As I get older and experience life, I am beginning to love myself for who and what I am. I used to cry and wonder why God would make me Black and then make Black the thing people despised and mistreated. Why make me Black and then make my hair so thick and tangly that I can't comb it or so coily that it sticks straight out? Why make my nose so large along with my buttocks, hips, and thighs? Wasn't one of these enough, without having all of them? And then why make the other people like me confused and full of self-hatred, self-destruction, and color consciousness? I may not have all the answers, but I am confident that I will find them and am learning to embrace myself more.

Content Themes

Julie's story, though it is unique in many ways, helps us to understand the process and journey that many undergo in the development of a positive racial identity. Her story suggests that the identity development process can be difficult, not only because of stereotypes and experiences of oppression from the mainstream or dominant culture, but also because of internalized racism and socialization experiences from family and friends. Her story teaches the difficulties individuals face when oppression and racism are internalized, the impact of stereotypes and racism, the effect of socialization experiences with family and peers, and the importance of self-definition.

RACE AND STEREOTYPES

The first issue in Julie's story is the influence that perceptions of race and stereotypes have on identity development and psychological functioning. Julie was raised in a poor, predominantly African American neighborhood. She had few positive role models of African Americans and developed a sense of shame about being Black. Negative stereotypes played a role in her self-concept. Julie indicates that she was concerned about the speech and levels of intelligence of African Americans. The negative image of African Americans was reinforced through her education; it was not until high school that she was exposed to African American history and heritage and more positive role models. This is a typical experience for many racial and ethnic minorities, who are frequently portrayed in the media as criminals, on drugs, less intelligent than Whites, unemployed or underemployed, and on public welfare. The media also often portray challenges experienced in families of racial minorities, including single-parent families and absent fathers. Asian Americans are often presented differently as the model minority, high-achieving and successful, but this portrayal can be limiting as well and can cause many Asian Americans to be ignored if they are underachievers (Sue & Sue, 2003). All of Julie's behaviors, values, and decisions were influenced by her perceptions of race. She imitated Whites in speech to be perceived as more intelligent and to be accepted by Whites. After she experienced racism on campus, she began to associate more with Blacks and to participate in Black activities on campus.

INTERPERSONAL RELATIONSHIPS

Race also influenced Julie's gender role expectations and views on interpersonal relationships. First, her family experiences caused her to question the roles of African American women and men in relationships. This, combined with negative stereotypes of African Americans, led Julie to believe that African American men were unfaithful and that African American women were destined to be single or single parents. It is important to note that her gender role expectations were colored not only by her racial identity but also by her family relationships. If both parents had raised Julie, her perceptions might have differed.

Second, Julie's perception of physical attractiveness was influenced by her race. Julie was faced with images of White women as attractive and was self-conscious about her weight, her hair texture and length, and other features. Her level of concern about her appearance was so great that she dreamed of being more White in appearance. Although Julie's family dynamics might exacerbate her self-consciousness, her experience is not unique. Many racial minorities struggle with standards of beauty set by the dominant culture and may internalize a negative self-perception (Greene, White, & Whitten, 2000). Some dye, perm, or relax their hair or use hair extensions to make it straighter, lighter, or longer. At an extreme, some individuals pursue plastic surgery to gain Eurocentric facial features. Julie's concern with her physical attractiveness certainly influenced her interpersonal relationships and may have placed her in a vulnerable position where men may have taken advantage of her.

Third, racial identity influenced the nature of her friendships and social relationships. During her teenage years, Julie was more interested in being accepted by White people and limited her association with other Blacks. She tried to adopt various speech accents to sound White. The mixed ethnic magnet school allowed her to transcend race, or adopt a raceless persona (Fordham, 1988), an option that is often taken by racial minorities. Her efforts to change her speech, however, suggest that the raceless stance was not always a successful strategy to use. After significant experiences of racism, she changed her relationships to associate only with other African Americans. Julie's racial identity influenced her relationships with authority figures, particularly teachers. She describes an incident in which a professor attempted to lead her to critically examine her behaviors. However, Julie was too hurt and angry at Whites to benefit fully from this experience. Her relationships with coworkers were equally affected because she was initially mistrustful and distant.

RACISM

The most striking component of Julie's story is the experiences with racism that she encountered on her college campus. Although college is often a time of intellectual enlightenment, Julie's story reminds us that individuals often become more aware of their cultural identity and even more aware of the oppressive and prejudicial opinions of others. The pain from the experiences was intense, and led Julie to change her perceptions of herself. What is striking in the story is the level of threat she faced, both in terms of concerns for her physical safety and, more important, the threats to her sense of self. Although it is not clear whether Julie ever felt completely accepted by Whites, the sense of security that she did have was completely shaken by her peers' reactions to her in the dorm. Her concerns about physical differences were constantly stirred, even through small experiences such as exiting the shower. Her problem-solving resources were challenged because she had to overcome negative stereotypes of African Americans and reach out to her peers for support and comfort. It was the accumulation of the experiences, or microaggressions (Feagin & Sikes, 1995), that influenced the intensity of Julie's response. Single episodes of racism may not have a devastating influence on individuals, but repeated experiences and assaults of the self can be damaging.

Julie's college experiences caused her to begin the process of racial identity (Atkinson, 2003; Cross, 1995; Sue & Sue, 2003). This process generally occurs with individuals having neutral attitudes about race, low salience to race, or negative internalized attitudes about their own race. Often, this continues until the individual has racial encounters, which lead to a shift in attitudes and immersion into his or her racial group. Finally, the individual integrates race and racial identity into self-concept. Julie clearly followed this path as she began to develop her sense of positive racial identity. Julie began her racial identity development as a child with negative attitudes about Blacks and being African American. Entering a magnet school allowed Julie to continue to see herself as different from other Blacks and close to equal with Whites. Julie had two periods in which significant encounter experiences occurred, seeming to propel her into further stages. The first period was when she took an African American history class and was exposed for the first time to positive historical images of Blacks. The second encounter period occurred during her study time in the college dorm, when students called her a racial slur. Julie experienced the typical psychological distress that occurs after significant racial encounters, including paranoia, depression, and fear. These experiences shifted Julie into an immersion phase, in which she participated in Afrocentric activities and joined Afrocentric organizations and changed interpersonal relationships. Julie seems to be continuing to develop her identity and completing tasks in the final stage of integrating her racial identity into her self-concept. She admits that her journey was not complete when she left college, but self-acceptance and pride are increasing as she continues in her adult development.

SELF-DEFINITION/AUTHENTIC SELF

The final theme from Julie's story is the importance of self-definition. Julie spent most of her childhood and adolescence reacting to negative reactions and stereotypes of African Americans. She defined herself in opposition to her negative perceptions of African Americans. Julie changed her speech to sound like and be accepted by Whites. She worried about her physical attractiveness and body size. After experiences of racism, she changed her self-definition and immersed herself in African American activities. Although this seems positive in many ways, her behaviors and attitudes were defined to combat others' perceptions. It was not until she was confronted by a professor and a White colleague that Julie began to examine her behaviors more critically. She changed her hair to a style that is more suitable for her lifestyle without being worried about others and is more comfortable with her body image. She has relationships with people from various racial groups and interacts comfortably with them. And she continues to have pride in her race. It is clear that Julie is in the process of defining herself more authentically and that, although she may continue to experience oppression and racism, she is secure in her identity and will continue to thrive.

Clinical Applications

This section explores the clinical implications from Julie's story for counselors, including assessment of race and racial identity, techniques and interventions to use in treatment, and countertransference concerns.

ASSESSMENT

Influence of Race

Race influences the identity, behaviors, values, and psychological functioning of individuals. It is important to understand how clients conceptualize group membership and their understanding of the stereotypes and others' perceptions of their race. Values from racial groups should be explored. Clients often internalize racial stereotypes and prejudices and engage in self-fulfilling behaviors or attempt to act in opposition to them. Clinicians should assess the level of internalized oppression of their clients and the relationship between the client's presenting problem and his or her experiences with racism. Therapists should also explore how race intersects with other cultural factors. For example, Julie was raised in a poor neighborhood. What would her experiences have been like if she had been raised in a middle- or upper-middle-class neighborhood? Social class intersects with race and influences expectations on education and careers, exposure to role models, and access to resources. Julie's family did not need public aid, but how would her life be different if she had been raised in poverty? Finally, therapists need to examine the level of racial identity of their clients. Treatment with Julie over therapeutic issues would have been different if Julie had been in the immersion stage for longer periods of time, or if her immersion experience had occurred during high school instead of college.

The following questions may be used to assess race and racial identity. Clinicians should feel comfortable directly asking questions on race because clients will generally not initiate these discussions, even if the issues are related to the presenting problems.

How important is your racial background to you?

Have you experienced any incidents of racism or oppression?

What messages about race did you receive from your family? From peers? From your school? From your community?

Have you felt negatively about your race? Has your race served as a source of strength or resource?

How is your racial background related to your presenting problem?

TECHNIQUES AND INTERVENTIONS

Critical Consciousness and the Authentic Self

One technique for clients dealing with racism is to help them to develop critical consciousness, the ability to assess their experiences in light of the context, and to separate their personal response from societal expectations (Watts & Abdul-Adil, 1997). Once individuals have the ability to critically examine their experiences, they can begin to develop their authentic self—self-concept that is self-defined. The development of an authentic sense of self involves the following process: see it, name it, question it, resist it, and transform it (Isom, 2002).

The first step is the development of awareness of the pervasiveness of oppression—seeing racism for what it is. For Julie, this beginning awareness came in high school when she was exposed to African American history. Therapists should help clients to understand the reality of racism, understand the history of stereotypes and sociopolitical context, and recognize individual acts of oppression as well as the institutional structures that support and maintain oppression. For example, in Julie's story, one wonders if the residence hall staff were aware of the oppression she experienced and whether any attempts to intervene were made. Julie may not have seen the staff or university administrators as allies in the process, suggesting that the racism she experienced was a part of the institutional climate.

The second step in the development of authentic self is to name it, to define the true nature of oppression as it occurs. It is the process of separating societal influences, thereby allowing correct labeling of the experiences. It was important for Julie to recognize the racism for what it was and to not make personal attributes for her experiences. The third step includes questioning one's experiences, to allow for the externalization of the problem to occur. Questions to be asked include the following: Am I responsible for this image? Did I cause the person to respond to me in a particular way? Julie began to question why information on African Americans was excluded from her textbooks in high school and why Egyptians were portrayed as Whites. She also began to question who was responsible for the misinformation. The fourth step is to resist, which includes being assertive and defending the self. Resistance may also mean confronting oppressors, letting people know that their comments or behaviors are hurtful. Once oppression is resisted, individuals are freed from the restrictive context of oppression and are not ruled by the stereotypes and biases of others. The process of self-definition can begin, and people are free to behave and react in a way that is authentic.

Racial Heritage

The second recommended technique is to encourage clients to explore their racial history and heritage. Another way to overcome negative stereotypes and perceptions is to replace them with more positive information and images. Julie began to build a more positive self-concept when she began to explore her African heritage. Clients can be encouraged to attend cultural events, to read historical pieces or cultural literature, and to join social activities and organizations that promote racial heritage. Clients also can be encouraged to speak to or interview senior citizens in their racial group about their experiences. The interviews and conversations should focus on problem-solving techniques and available resources. Clinicians should be aware of cultural organizations within their communities, as well as cultural leaders. Caution must be used in the timing of this intervention, and clinicians may want to consider the client's level of readiness to explore his or her cultural heritage. The more oppressed the client, the higher the risk of self-hatred. Assessing the client's level of racial identity may be helpful in determining the appropriateness of this intervention (Atkinson, 2003; Cross, 1995). Clients who feel negatively about their own racial group may benefit from exploring racial heritage but may not be psychologically ready to begin such exploration.

Racial Socialization

Racial socialization is the process of helping racial minority children develop positive self-images within an oppressive community. Research shows that parents give messages in a variety of categories, including the presence and reality of racism, preparation for and overcoming of bias and racism, cultural heritage, racial pride, self-pride, racial equality and humanistic values, mainstream Eurocentric values, and spirituality and coping (Stevenson, Cameron, Herrero-Taylor, & Davis, 2002; Thomas & Speight, 1999). It is important for clinicians to assess the racial socialization messages their clients receive. For example, Julie's grandfather often made disparaging comments regarding the poor African Americans in their community. This affected Julie's perspectives on race and gender roles by perpetuating and reinforcing her internalized negative attitudes. Parents should be especially encouraged to discuss racial issues and the possibility of racism with their children (Hopson & Hopson, 1992). Greene (1992) outlines a model for including racial socialization as part of the therapeutic process. The first step includes helping children to correctly label racism and handle accompanying feelings. The second phase includes the parents serving as role models for dealing with racism. The third step is providing emotional support for the emotional reactions to racism, including anger and powerlessness. The final phase includes helping families to adjust by developing coping mechanisms.

COUNTERTRANSFERENCE

Clinicians may experience a variety of reactions to hearing about racial issues in clients. Race is one issue—along with politics and religion—that individuals are often socialized not to discuss, so many therapists may find it awkward to initiate a discussion about racial identity or experiences of oppression. However, because race is so important, it is critical for counselors to explore these factors in their clients' lives and functioning. Clinicians may experience feelings of sadness, anger, frustration, anxiety, and guilt (Comas-Diaz & Jacobsen, 1991).

Reactions to Racism

Julie's story reflects the racism and oppression that occur from membership in a particular racial or ethnic group. Because Julie's experience occurred in the 1990s, it can be easily dismissed as a historical artifact. One reaction that counselors have is to experience sadness over the mistreatment that clients have experienced. Acts of racism and discrimination can have a negative effect on self-esteem, and counselors may become overwhelmed with feelings over these acts. For example, Julie reports mistreatment by other students in her college dormitory. A clinician who feels sadness for her may express sympathy for her pain in an effort to relieve some of the discomfort of the client and the therapist. However, it is critical to remember the difference between empathy and sympathy. Although comforting comments may be helpful for the client, if the comment is based more on the therapist's sadness, it may come across as patronizing, which may alienate the client. Sympathy from a counselor in this situation may be experienced by the client as the counselor feeling sorry for the client, leading the client to feel disconnected from the therapist or needing to "help" the counselor by minimizing the pain from the incident. Empathy is the ability to place oneself in the experience of another and to understand it from their perspective. Although counselors may not have experience with racism, they can empathize with the feelings of anxiety, depression, or discomfort that may arise.

A second common reaction to racism and acts of oppression may be a rationalization of the event, in which the clinician suggests to clients that perpetrators may have other motives for their behavior. Providing a rationale for perpetrators, however valid an alternative explanation may seem, minimizes the issue for the client and may lead the client to feel invalidated. The end result of an explanation is that it often trivializes the problem and may prevent the client from feeling comfortable in disclosing painful experiences. Underlying this response may be some anger at the client for assuming the victim role or for personalizing the experiences of oppression. The therapist may feel that the client is paranoid or too sensitive to issues. This reaction also may hamper the therapeutic relationship.

Therapists may experience a sense of frustration or hopelessness about the likelihood of racism or oppression ending. One common response is a sense of incredulity about the prevalence of oppression in today's society. When racism is brought up, some White people typically respond that racism is a part of history and that ethnic minorities should move on and not be so sensitive to racial issues. Public and violent acts of oppression, such as the killings of James Byrd, Jr. and Matthew Shepard, remind us all of the continued presence of bigotry and prejudice. While ethnic minorities may be reminded of the importance of being prepared for racism, some Whites may perceive the experiences as isolated events that do not represent the majority's feelings. In many instances, the stories presented by clients stir up feelings of frustration that racism will never end. Some clinicians feel some level of powerlessness and helplessness while listening to the clients' experiences. Powerlessness often serves as a parallel process for the clients, who may also be experiencing depression, anxiety, and feelings of hopelessness. Clinicians who experience these feelings may help clients in reflecting on their feelings of helplessness, which validates the experience of the clients and possibly opens the door for further dialogue on personal responsibility and the development of coping mechanisms for oppression.

Race of the Therapist

Some reactions may occur based on the racial background of the client–counselor dyad. White counselors may feel some guilt about being members of an oppressive group. This sense of guilt may lead to feelings of sadness for the client and attempts to overcompensate for the actions of others. The therapists may feel that clients will blame them for oppression and that the clients may harbor feelings of anger and resentment toward them. This may be a reality for nonvoluntary clients, who view the therapist as part of the court and social services systems. This may lead therapists to treat clients gingerly, and therapists may avoid confronting clients over tough issues that need to be addressed in treatment. At an extreme, clinicians may engage in unethical treatment of clients by allowing problematic behaviors to go unreported to maintain rapport with clients.

Counselors who are the same race as the client but at a different stage of identity development may experience anger over the client's stories and may suggest problem-solving skills that promote assertiveness or sometimes aggression as a reaction to acts of oppression. Although endorsing active problem solving may be helpful to some clients, if the client is experiencing depression, he or she may need to resolve those feelings before moving to problem solving. Same-race therapists may also feel powerlessness and helplessness and may be unable to provide solutions as they experience memories of their own experiences of oppression. Same-race clinicians may also experience overidentification with their clients and project their feelings onto the clients' experiences. When therapists begin to overidentify with their clients, they lose the ability to feel and express empathy as they work to attempt to take care of their own emotions. At this point, clinicians often become frustrated when clients deny the emotional reactions that the clients are experiencing. Clinicians of the same race or ethnicity may have difficulty distinguishing between behaviors within the cultural norms and those that are pathological.

Finally, same-race counselors may ignore pathological behaviors in an attempt to foster solidarity within the race. The example of the reactions to the Anita Hill trials exemplified this notion: Some African Americans were angry that Anita Hill decided to come forward with her accusations against Clarence Thomas, believing that it should have been kept private to protect an African American man. Many counselors, for example, may ignore signs of abuse to prevent another member of their race from entering the social services system.

TOOLBOX ACTIVITY—JULIE			
Resources and Suggested Readings	*Videos*	*Activities*	*Discussion Questions*
Feagin, J. R., & Feagin, C. (2002). *Racial and ethnic relations.* Englewood Cliffs, NJ: Prentice Hall. Rodriguez, R. (2002). *Brown: The last discovery of America.* New York: Viking. Tatum, B. (2002). *Why are all the Black kids sitting together in the cafeteria?* New York: Basic Books.	*Boyz n the Hood* *The Joy Luck Club* *Smoke Signals*	Visit a cultural center or museum that focuses on Native American, African American, Asian, or Latino heritage. Write in your journal about the feelings that are elicited as you visit. How will the experience influence your work with clients?	Content Themes What other themes do you see emerging in the story that the author did not identify? Assessment Are there any questions you would like to ask Julie? Interventions What other interventions could you propose with Julie? Countertransference What countertransference reactions were emerging in yourself as you read this story? Other Scenarios What would have occurred if Julie's father had played a more prominent role in her life and lived with the family? What would Julie have been like if she had been raised in a middle- or upper-class family? What roles did strengths such as spirituality and extended family play in Julie's life?

Butch's Story 5

Who Am I?

Developing racial identity can be complicated for individuals because they must balance self-perceptions, stereotypes and biases, and socialization processes. Racial identity development is more difficult for people with multiple or mixed racial backgrounds. Biracial individuals are the offspring of parents with differing racial heritage. *Interracial* is the term given to describe the marital process, and *multiracial,* a newer term, describes individuals from two or more heritages (Kerwin & Ponterotto, 1995). The idea of the existence of mixed racial heritage has been troublesome. The prevailing notion was—and still is today—that individuals from mixed racial heritages, particularly Whites and Blacks, would have difficulty functioning. It was also believed that mixing the races would "dilute" Whiteness, leading to an inferior race or group of people. In the early 1800s, interracial marriages began to be outlawed, and it was not until 1967 that the Supreme Court ruled these laws were unconstitutional (Kerwin & Ponterotto, 1995).

Complicating the identity process were laws that defined the notion of race, which varied from state to state, including the "one-drop rule" for individuals with African heritage, which stated that a person with any African ancestry was categorized as African or African American (Rockquemore & Laszloffy, 2003). The consequences of the negative reactions to racial mixing included the development of a social status classification system, leading to intragroup differences and judgmental attitudes. Biracial individuals were often forced to choose a racial group, but some biracial people attempted to "pass" and be accepted as Whites. The tragic mulatto syndrome, personified in the movie *Imitation of Life,* was a by-product of the attitudes toward biracial individuals; it includes the dilemma of having to choose a racial identity, often as a result of denying a part of one's racial heritage (Kerwin & Ponterotto, 1995). It should be noted that this process included not only the denial of part of one's own heritage but also a denial of family members or associates.

The 2000 U.S. Census data show that 6.8 million individuals, or 2.4 percent of the population, reported a multiracial heritage, the majority of whom reported two races in their background (Grieco & Cassidy, 2001). The majority of individuals indicating more than one race included White as one race (about 80 percent), followed by "some other race," Black, Native American, or Asian. (For more information, visit www.census.gov). Hispanics are counted as an ethnic group and can have a variety of racial designations, according to the U.S. Census Bureau. Although historically more attention has been given to White–Black intermarriages, it is clear that the multiracial category is expanding, and clinicians may be confronted with more biracial and multiracial clients. It is more acceptable today to claim multiracial heritage; however, individuals still need to engage in the complex task of identity development. Butch's story describes this complex process, which occurs with people of mixed racial heritage. The reader should pay close attention to the negotiation process that must occur with each component of Butch's racial background, including acceptance from various racial groups, pressures to accommodate to particular racial groups, and intragroup oppression from racial groups.

Butch's Story

Who am I? What race am I? What nationality am I? Where do I fit into American society? Where can I find total acceptance? For most of my 47 years, I have struggled to find answers to these questions. I am an American of multiracial descent and culture. In this aspect, I am not very different from many Americans. The difference for me is that I have always felt an urge to feel and live the intermingling of blood that runs through my veins. American society has a way of forcing multiracial and biracial people to choose one race over the other. I personally feel this pressure every time I have to complete an application form with instructions to check just one box for race category.

My own racial and cultural background consists of American Indian from two nations, Lahkota and Creek; African American; Italian American; and Puerto Rican. I am Spanish-speaking, with some knowledge of the Lahkota language. Possessing such a diverse background has often placed me in a position to hear many insensitive and racist remarks from one group or another—obviously, I have often been the target. In the eyes of White Italian people, I am viewed as a Black person. Blacks often view me as a weak and tainted half-breed. American Indians have either cautiously accepted or rejected me. The Puerto Rican community has offered the most acceptance.

A family tree would be next to impossible in our family, largely due to secrets (skeletons in the closet), question marks, and taboo subjects. The matriarch of our family was my maternal grandmother, Anna, who was half Black and half Creek Indian. My paternal grandfather was Oglala Lahkota from the Pine Ridge Indian Reservation in South Dakota. He was called Jimbo, which was short for Jim Bull. I am told that my mother's father was an Italian immigrant who lived in a "little Italy" neighborhood. My father's mother was Black. Her husband, Jimbo, called her Pipe because she always smoked a pipe. So when all of this was finally sorted out, it looked liked this: My mother, Laura, is one fourth Black, one fourth Creek, and half Italian. My father is half Black and half Oglala Lahkota.

The Italian side of our family was—and to a large extent remains—a mystery seldom discussed in our family. My mother and her siblings were born and raised in a "little Italy" neighborhood. At about the age of 12 or 13 years, I learned of our Italian ancestry. I received this information through one of our family historians, or storytellers, our Aunt June. Aunt June was one of my mother's younger sisters. Aunt June was very fair-skinned, with dark eyes and hair. She never had children of her own, and she also had a drinking problem, which I realized after I was grown. While I don't believe she told us everything about the family, she did let us in on many family secrets. Probably because she never had children of her own, it seemed like she really enjoyed spending time with my siblings and me.

We have fond memories of Aunt June babysitting for us on the weekends. She loved to watch horror flicks with us, which we thought was very cool, since no other adult we knew did. We would all lie down on the floor together, eating popcorn and enjoying all the old, original *Frankenstein, The Wolf Man, Dracula,* and *The Mummy* flicks. After the movie, Aunt June would tell us old family stories of when she and her brothers and sisters were young children. Sometimes after drinking a few beers, Aunt June would cross the forbidden line and tell us things that my mother and her other sisters had secretly kept hidden in the closet. I can remember my mother and her other two sisters pulling Aunt June in the bedroom, closing the door, and scolding her about talking too much. (Of course, as many children do, we eavesdropped.)

Well, one day, Aunt June pulled out this old wallet-size photo of a dark-haired White man with a Hitler-style moustache. She said to me, "This is your grandfather, my father. You can keep this picture, but don't let my sisters know." Aunt June later went on to tell me that my grandfather was an Italian immigrant from Calabria, Italy. Aunt June didn't seem to know much more about him. With a very sad face and with tears welling in her eyes, she told me that she never knew her father. Even though I never asked her, I always wondered why she chose me to keep the picture instead of my brothers and sisters. In some ways, learning about my grandfather helped me to make sense of some things. Between the ages of five and seven years, I began to perceive and question the differences in skin colors, which were quite evident in our family. My mother and Aunt June were very fair-skinned, while Candace, my mother's oldest sister, and Lily were brown and olive. Their brother, Tony, had black skin. So learning about my Italian grandfather took me back to a question I had asked my mother at about the age of seven years. I was gazing at a picture of my mother's brother, Tony, when I thought to myself, "If Tony is my mother's brother, then why are they virtually opposite colors?"

So, as a child, I popped this question to my mother: "If Uncle Tony is your brother, then why is he so dark, and you are so White?" My mother responded with a quick, sharp slap to my face and told me, "It's not your business, and Tony is my brother, and that's that." As I was to learn later in life, this was just the beginning of hard questions to come with no easy answers.

When I was about 11 years old, our family moved to an extension of the "little Italy" neighborhood. While the Italian community didn't exactly throw a welcoming party for us when we first moved there, all in all we were not harassed. We had some Italian childhood friends, although I don't remember being invited into many homes. Our family would go on living here for the next six years—years that would challenge our multiracial status like never before.

Ironically, the very neighborhood my mother had been raised in, "little Italy," claimed me as a beating victim. One day, possessing an urge to visit my mother's old neighborhood, I was approached by two grown Italian men who had been standing on their front porch stairs. One of the men appeared to be in his 50s, the other in his mid-20s, probably father and son. The younger man had a metal pipe in his hand. They asked me what the hell I was doing around here. At the time, I was 18 years old and had this feeling of invincibility. So, as they approached me, I stood my ground in defiance and proceeded to ultimately receive a beating that cost me 10 stitches on my head, along with numerous bumps and bruises, mostly on my arms, which I had used to ward off some of the blows aimed at my head. I was to learn later from the "Gents," a Puerto Rican street gang, that they had been warring with some of the Italians. This, of course, explained why they had called me a dirty Puerto Rico Gent as I was being beaten. Somehow, after what seemed like an eternity, I was able to escape, and later was picked up, bleeding and dazed, by two plainclothes detectives. After showing the detectives the house where my assailants entered after the beating, I was driven to the emergency room. Shortly before leaving the hospital, I was told by the returning detectives that they couldn't locate the perpetrators. It was apparent that I was the wrong person in the wrong place at the wrong time. It was this incident that created a deep hatred on my part toward Italians. In a sense, it was also the beginning of self-hatred for the Italian side of myself. Afterward, whenever anyone asked what my ethnicity was, I would not mention the Italian blood that ran through my veins.

I also had trouble with my African American heritage. As the neighborhoods in which we lived continued to become more Black, it became increasingly difficult to cope. My oldest brother, Landon, was forever getting beaten up. The Black girls thought he was gorgeous, which didn't help to ease the hatred that the Black males had toward my brother. Landon was a star athlete in track, basketball, and baseball. Since Landon didn't hang out in the neighborhood in which we lived, I was put in the uneasy position of trying to protect my younger brother, Paul. We were always getting socked on because we weren't quite the same as our friends, according to them. I was, quite frankly, afraid to fight Blacks. The blacker they were, the more afraid I was to fight. I remember being told on numerous occasions that my family was physically weak because we were mixed.

There was one kid in our neighborhood who happened to be our friend, sometimes. But whenever he felt like beating up on two little light-skinned, curly-haired boys, there my younger brother and I were, ready to be someone's doormat. One day, like so many others, he felt like taking his rage out on us, so he began beating me up. Paul ran home to get our mother. During the beating, I saw my mother coming, so I knew I had to find some courage to fight back, even though at the same time I was glad that my rescue was on the way. When my mother arrived, she shouted out to me, "Don't you stand there and let him beat you up. Fight back!" Well, I suddenly got this renewed energy and courage and began to try to turn the tide. Unfortunately, it was not to be. I was afraid. I was totally lacking in confidence. I was a victim, buying into the belief that, because of my mixed blood, I was not Black enough; I could not and would not overcome my adversary. It would be years before I would grow to understand and confront my fears.

Another incident that occurred when I was about 12 or 13 years old would leave another deep wound in my already shaken and mixed-up mind. My siblings and I had made friends with the new Black kids who had moved into the neighborhood. At first it seemed that they were very eager to make friends with us. We all seemed to get along well, and we hung out and played together often. One day I got into a fight, for reasons I don't recall, with this kid whom everyone else called a nerd. Franky, as he was called, certainly wasn't very popular; he wasn't even part of our little group that regularly hung out together. As I was pinning him down to the ground in a straddle position, I couldn't actually believe it, but it appeared I was winning the fight. Franky meanwhile was swearing at me, telling me that as soon as he got up he was going to kill me. Suddenly, my friends (or so I thought), who had been standing in a circle around us watching, began shouting, "Get up, Franky! You can beat this little light-skinned nigger's ass any day!" At that point, the little confidence and courage I had gained was quickly destroyed. As they continued urging Franky on, I began to panic, and Franky started to sense my panic. He began struggling even harder, even though my growing fear was the only thing that gave me strength to keep Franky subdued.

When I looked up at what had turned into a mob, all I could see was hateful faces, salivating for my ridicule and defeat. In desperation, I scanned the crowd for a sympathetic, helping face. And then, bingo! There it was—the face that seemed to say, "Pity you! What can I do?" Speaking low, hoping that the mob wouldn't hear, I asked this person if he could go and bring my mother back. The person nodded slightly, indicating that he would. At the same time, some of the other kids had heard my request and began to tease me and laugh at me. Unfortunately, my would-be messenger was physically threatened and ordered to stay put. About that time, my mother stepped out on the terrace and saw the incident. She rushed down to get me. My ordeal was over, though the fear, pain, and humiliation were for me very real. I was in shock—I really thought they were my friends. After the incident, I stayed inside for about two weeks. I was very hurt and embarrassed. But eventually I would go back out and try to be part of the group. I knew I needed to try to fit in some way. It would be difficult because I certainly couldn't change my looks. Why did I go back to these kids, who I knew hated me for who I was? Simply put, I had no choice. It was either adapt or stay locked up at home. I wanted and needed to be accepted. It was at this point in my life that I really wondered why I couldn't have been born Black—Black meaning black in skin color, hair texture, facial features, everything.

From this point, it was pretty much open season on my family and me. At times, things seemed to go well with my friends. Friends? We would play basketball, softball, and follow-the-leader, and sometimes we would just hang out on each other's front porches. But when things got boring or the right situation presented itself, my family would become a target again. I remember one day we were all sitting out on the front porch, and my mother was walking down the street. As she was going up the stairs to our apartment, one of the guys asked, "Hey Butchie! Ain't your mother White?" Knowing that I needed to fit in, I answered back, "No!" They all laughed in response to my answer and said I was lying. Being very sensitive, I lowered my head and went home.

In the fall of 1963, I began my freshman year at a high school that had a Black student population of about 95 percent. There were six or seven White students, about five Asian students, and approximately 15 to 20 Puerto Rican students. Academics aside, the school was primarily known for its top athletics teams. It was also known for its violence. With my shy, sensitive, introverted personality, I felt even less than a number. During my entire four years of high school, I was never able to fit in. My freshman year, I decided to take Spanish. I was already partly fluent due to our family's early experience with the Puerto Rican culture. I began learning Spanish at the age of six from my mother's fiancé, who had moved to the States from Puerto Rico. I did so well the first year that I was immediately placed in honors Spanish for my remaining three years of high school. I struck up a friendship with another student in Spanish class, Sue. Sue was racially mixed, part Dominican, part Santee Sioux, and part Black. We were the most fluent speakers in honors Spanish and often shared our experiences of trying to fit in. Needless to say, our experiences mirrored each other.

By my junior year, I was able to make friends with a Puerto Rican student, Rosa. Rosa in turn introduced me to the Puerto Rican connection, or body of students. I was received very graciously, with open arms. Like myself, the other Puerto Ricans had been beaten up and harassed on the way to and from school. They told me to walk with them to school and invited me to sit at the two lunch tables they had assigned themselves to. Sometimes, I would go out for lunch. There was a small family-owned restaurant that served Puerto Rican food, Mexican food, and the traditional student's fare: hot dogs and hamburgers. The owner's stepdaughter, Cristina, a student from my school, also helped out part-time. I began eating there frequently. Cristina and I seemed to be attracted to each other, began dating, and moved in together. We would later become common-law husband and wife, living together for 16 years. By the time I began dating Cristina, I was totally immersed in the Puerto Rican culture but still tried to relate to the African American side of me.

In my second year of living with Cristina, I began looking for something to connect to. This was a time of soul searching for me. Politically, there was a lot going on. The late 1960s and early 1970s was an era of civil strife and unrest. There was the Black Power movement, the Students for a Democratic Society (SDS), the Weathermen, the second battle of Wounded Knee in South Dakota, and the assassinations of Martin Luther King, Jr. and Robert F. Kennedy. The list goes on and on. The drug culture was also in full bloom. I had started to affiliate myself with the Black Panther Party and the Young Lords, a Puerto Rican revolutionary group. I would sometimes go to their meetings and help pass out revolutionary literature. It was also a time of the Back to Africa movement. Afros and Dashikis were commonplace. We were all sporting huge Afros. In the 1970s, the African movement struck me as very exciting. I actually felt more of a closeness or kinship with Africans than I did with American Blacks. To me, African Americans were a lost and deculturalized people, segregated from everyone else for so long that anyone different was deserving of being set upon.

At any rate, the African thing was very exciting to me. Cristina and I began wearing African clothes and sporting big Afros. I went out and bought a bunch of African records. Later on, I purchased two congas and would go out and beat them with a group of drummers who would congregate in the summer at various beaches. I even wound up giving some of my children African names.

Sometimes, we would visit some of my cousin Roy's closest friends to smoke weed and listen to African music. At first, everything would seem fine. But after a while we would get little side cracks thrown our way, things like "You guys aren't Black enough! If you moved to Africa you wouldn't be accepted." One of Roy's friends, Tim, had a girlfriend named Kenya who saw herself as the African spokesperson (whatever that's supposed to mean). Kenya was very black, with a very short natural hairdo, and she actually looked like she was Nigerian. She would always make some negative comments about Cristina. Kenya would ask Cristina why she was wearing an Afro since Cristina was Puerto Rican. Cristina's shyness exceeded my own, so I usually had to talk up for her. I explained that Cristina's father was dark-skinned Puerto Rican. I also told how African slaves had been taken to Puerto Rico and other Caribbean islands. Afterward, Kenya, along with other members of the group, would tell us not to speak Spanish. (Cristina and I would speak Spanish to each other at times.) Eventually, the negative comments escalated. One day, Kenya told Roy to tell me not to bring Cristina to the group since she wasn't Black. When I angrily called Kenya up to question her about the comment, she added, "You and your cousin Roy are lucky we let you half-breeds in." When I told Roy what Kenya said, he passed it off by saying I was too sensitive, saying Kenya was just joking. Well, that was the last time Cristina and I set foot in their house. But apparently I hadn't learned my lesson.

There was a new revolutionary group of Blacks who were conducting educational and revolutionary seminars. My cousin Roy had attended a few of these meetings and was very excited. One day he asked me to go with him. It sounded very appealing, so I brought a friend of mine named Ricardo. Ricardo was from Puerto Rico and had been in the United States about a year. Ricardo spoke very little English, although he understood more than he could speak. As we entered the building and were waiting in line to be searched, I was explaining to Ricardo in Spanish what the meeting was about. Just then, one of the security guys pointed to Ricardo and said to me, "This guy can't come in!" When I asked why, he told me "This is only for Blacks." I then tried to explain that Ricardo was Puerto Rican with some African heritage. The security guard responded by saying, "You have to be all Black to come in here!" I responded by saying that I wasn't all Black, so I wouldn't go in either. Roy and a couple of his friends went inside, while Ricardo and I waited in the front lobby. Since we all had all ridden in the same car, we had no choice. Not long after, Roy's older brother, Randy, showed up. Randy was concerned about our interest in these revolutionary groups and had decided to follow us. When we explained why we were sitting outside, Randy immediately went into the meeting, interrupting the speaker, by calling them Black racists who were no better than White racists for refusing Ricardo admittance. Roy, of course, disagreed with his older brother and told Randy that he was off base. Randy thought Roy was completely wrong to have entered the place when Ricardo, our friend, was not allowed in. Randy then told his brother that he was a sucker for punishment, that he was nothing but a mixed-breed, high-yellow chump who would never be accepted by Blacks. I agreed in heart.

It was about this time that I began to minimize my social contact with Blacks. I was bewildered, rejected, and abused. On top of all of this, I was quite simply tired of the mistreatment. I began to take a close look in the mirror. Here I was telling Blacks that I was the same as they were, with no takers. They saw me as different. I thought to myself, "If they see me as different, then maybe I am different." It hit me right in the face. The coffee was there for me to smell. From that point on, I was never to refer to myself as a Black person. If someone were to ask if I was Black, I would answer by saying, "No. I'm brown. I'm a person of color," or "I'm multiracial." I was comfortable with this. I knew at that point that I would no longer allow someone else to tell me who I was. As a human being, I felt it was my God-given right to say who I was. Unfortunately, what I knew right then was that I certainly didn't feel Black anymore. The negative experiences I suffered had pushed the Black side of me to the farthest recesses of my mind, body, and soul, and at the time I wasn't sorry for it.

My very first Indian contact began with my maternal grandmother. We always referred to her as simply "Mama." On the other hand, we called our mother, Laura, by her name. Because our grandmother lived with us from a very young age, we more or less copied our mother and her sisters when referring to our grandmother. Grandmother Jenna was half Black and half Muscogee Creek. Mama's physical appearance pretty much typified a Black woman, although her demeanor was very Indian. Mama often talked of her father, who was of the Eastern Band of the Creek Nation. The Creeks were originally from the southeastern portion of the United States, particularly Georgia. Somehow my grandmother's father settled for a time in Kentucky, although he later went to live with his disconnected relatives in Oklahoma.

I can vividly remember the various American Indian foods my grandmother would make, food that today is commonly referred to as soul food. Corn pones, hominy soup, succotash, grits, okra, sassafras tea, Indian sumac lemonade, and wild mustard greens are just a few of the dishes my grandmother made that originally came from the Indian nations of the South. I am often surprised that many African Americans who to this day still eat many of these foods are unaware that they are gifts borrowed from Indian America.

While my grandmother viewed herself as Indian and Black, neither my mother nor her three sisters did. I think to this very day they have more or less seen themselves as Black, which in my opinion complicated their lives in regard to the racial prejudice and harassment they endured. In contrast, my mother's lone brother, Tony, also viewed himself as Indian and Black. Uncle Tony was the first male figure in my life who inspired me to dance. Because Tony was always traveling across the country, we rarely got to see him. But when he visited, he always performed powwow Indian dances for us. There was one dance he would perform called the stomp dance, which, according to him, originated from the intermarriage of Creeks and Black runaway slaves. This was my first inspiration to dance. Uncle Tony was my second inspiration and influence in regard to the Indian side of our family.

The other person who was very influential in instilling Indian culture in my life was my paternal grandfather, Jim Bull, otherwise known as Jimbo. Jimbo was a member of the Oglala band of Teton Lahkota, otherwise known as Sioux.

Jimbo was born on the Pine Ridge Oglala Reservation around the turn of the 20th century. I was told by a cousin that his tribal name was Short Bull, although the name *Short* was taken out somewhere along the way. My grandfather's agency name was Johnson. An "agency" name for Indians is like a plantation name for African American slaves. My grandfather actually lived between three homes: Pine Ridge, South Dakota; Wisconsin; and Chicago. Jimbo in stature was a short man, with olive skin and black wavy hair, which, on the few occasions I saw him, he usually wore in a single ponytail. Because of family infighting, I can count my visits with him on two hands. Even still, the impression he left on me was obviously very strong.

Once when my mother was in the hospital, I remember my grandfather taking me up by Oshkosh, Wisconsin. I can remember us going to a lake, where he baited some fishing lines, and after throwing them in, began to walk through the fields gathering plants, which I was to later learn were for medicinal purposes. Before gathering, he always prayed in his language and left some tobacco. Many tribes use tobacco as an offering to God. I didn't know what I was gathering (I was only eight or nine years old at the time). I simply gathered the plants he pointed out. What was amazing was what occurred years later when I was a young adult. I had always enjoyed the outdoors. When I was about 19 years old, I got this incredible interest and urge to gather and use medicinal plants. Once my own children were old enough, whenever we would go to the woods, I would have them help me gather as well. I continued through the years to follow my urge for medicinal knowledge by studying tribal medicinal lore. To this very day, at the age of 47, I continue to forage for wild plants. For each of the four seasons, there are different plants to gather. And just like my grandfather and grandmother, I carry on the tradition of always leaving an offering of tobacco. Foraging for wild plants is cathartic; for me it is equal to worshipping at a church. There is an inner feeling of peace connecting me to a closer understanding of the creator of life. The physical act of gathering brings on a sense of spiritual and physical healing.

When I was about 35 years old, it suddenly occurred to me that I was continuing this tradition of gathering left from my grandparents because I had received a calling. Of all my brothers, sisters, and cousins, why me? In fact, neither of my grandfathers told me that I was the one to carry the torch, and yet now when I gather, it's as if I can sense their approving presence. I would soon learn that this was just the beginning of reconnecting with the disconnected Indian side of our family.

Because my cousin Randy was about three years older, he got an opportunity to spend more time with our grandfather. In this way, Randy was able to pass a lot of the wisdom and knowledge from our grandparents to me. Randy was very aware of his position as an older grandson. Strangely enough, Randy and I, of the grandchildren, were the only ones who tried to stay connected to our Indian family. We saw ourselves as Indian. The rest of our brothers, sisters, and cousins were very aware that we were part Indian, but they simply thought of themselves as Black. Randy, in a sense, inspired me to stay connected. During our teen years at summer camp in Indiana, Randy and I performed dances for the campers at night around a fire. We put on our homemade dance regalia and even painted our horses, which we rode into camp bareback. After our camp days, I started to drift away from things Indian; of course there were lots of distractions. I graduated from high school, started working, and was busy raising a family.

I was also experimenting with drugs while at the same time involving myself with the antigovernment, civil unrest scene, which occupied me into the late 1970s. I'll never forget the date: November 1979. That was the year I reconnected with my Indian self.

It was a Friday afternoon. I was at home with my children when my cousin Randy stopped by. My children were five, seven, and eight years of age. Randy said, "Come with me and bring the kids. I want to show you something." We got in the car and drove to the National Armory. When we entered the armory, I was completely awestruck. I had never seen so many Indians in one place in my life.

Randy had taken me to the American Indian Center Powwow. My children and I stood for a long time and watched the various dancers dance around the arena. As I watched, it seemed as if I were dreaming. I immediately thought of my grandparents. I suddenly felt their presence. It felt as though I had been lost for many years and had finally found home. I had arrived at the circle. Randy and I looked at each other. He had brought me here because it was his duty to do so. We didn't need to say anything to each other. We knew that our grandparents had entrusted in us the responsibility of not allowing our Indian family to wither away and die. By the enthusiasm I saw in the faces of my children, I sensed that they, too, felt a strong relationship to the dancers, the sacred drummer, and the circle.

When we left the armory that night, I knew right then that the cultural and spiritual aspects of my life would be greatly affected. Through my cousin Randy, I found out about the American Indian Center (AIC). The AIC was created to address the needs of American Indians who were relocating from reservations. At the monthly fundraiser powwows held at the AIC, there was also a potluck dinner where various participants brought dishes from home. For about two years, I brought food for the potlucks. The meals were usually eaten before the dancing. Afterward, someone from the powwow committee publicly thanked all the people who brought food or helped to serve. It wasn't long before I noticed my name was never mentioned. At first, I thought maybe I was accidentally overlooked. But after about six or seven months of attending the fundraiser, it became apparent that the snub was intentional. At that point, I began to feel a familiar sense of rejection very similar to the rejection Blacks had tossed my way—except there was one difference in the style of the rejection. The Blacks had rejected and harassed me openly and directly. They were vocal in their feelings toward me and right to the point. In contrast, many of the Indian people at AIC rejected me silently. Usually nothing was ever said directly to my children or me. This in itself was not surprising or new to me. It was the type of stony silence and penetrating looks I can remember from my grandparents. They didn't need to physically discipline us when we stepped out of line. We knew what the look and silence symbolized. But I quickly realized how naive I had been to enter into the Indian community as a mixed-blood, thinking that they would be waiting to accept me with open arms. It was indeed another painful eye-opener for me.

As in the past, instead of confronting the resistance, I slowly began to retreat. There were some people who never spoke to us—some of the elders included— although I remember other elders who didn't have too much to say but would occasionally give me an approving nod when my children would dance. One of the AIC employees, Ron, a Vietnam veteran and a member of the Mesqualic (Sac & Fox) tribe of Tama, Iowa, turned out to be one of my biggest supporters.

Ron began telling me more about the tribal conflicts that had been going on for years at the center. The vast majority of the people who frequent the center are from the Midwest—generally Ojibwa, Winnebagos, Menominees, Potawatomies, and Ottawas. At any given time, other tribes come from more distant locations, such as Lahkotas, Mesquakie, Choctaw, Iroquois, and Navajos. But according to Ron, it had always been the Ho-Chunks, or Winnebagos, who controlled the center, to the disdain of the other tribes. In fact, he said that the Ho-Chunks, as far as he could remember, always had this aura that they were better than other Indians. According to Ron, the Ho-Chunks' way of thinking was "We're more Indian than you, and we have a monopoly on everything that's Indian. Our ways and customs are more sacred than yours." After receiving this information, I began to notice that many of the people from the center who had given my family a cold shoulder indeed were Ho-Chunks. Ron told me as he ended our conversation, "Don't think the Ho-Chunks dislike you and your family because you're of mixed blood. Those people are prejudiced against anyone who isn't Ho-Chunk." Like Whites who romanticize Indian people, in a sense I too learned that I was also guilty of romanticizing the Indian side of our family, wondering why I couldn't have been born a full-blood, naively thinking that maybe Indian people were perfect, without blemish or flavors. My yearning for Indianness was not one of nostalgia, but very much like a homeless person searching for a niche in society. It was what I felt the strongest. Likewise, when the door was slammed in my face, the hurt and pain ran deep. Reality, however, boldly revealed that Indians, like all people, are indeed not perfect. Nor were Indian people perfect before the coming of the White man to these shores. That Whites conquered, and Indians became conquered, is proof enough of imperfections on both sides. On the other hand, it would be safe to say that Indian peoples had fewer imperfections before the White man's arrival. The broken treaties (lies), theft of ancestral lands, the rape and plunder of villages, the implementation of the reservation system, genocide, and the deculturalization process of Indian peoples certainly adds up to just one word—colonialism. The results of colonialism produced things that had never before been recorded, seen, or heard: alcoholism, tuberculosis, fetal alcohol syndrome, unemployment, incest, domestic abuse, child abuse, tribal infighting, fatherless children, reservation and street gangs, and the list goes on. So, with all this in mind, the AIC—indeed, the Indian community—is heir to the results of colonialism from its inception. As I began to learn more about the history of my Indian and African American ancestors, I became less bitter but not less hurt.

Content Themes

Butch's journey demonstrates several important components of racial identity development. There are moments that are quite painful in his story, suggesting that identity development is difficult for biracial individuals. The first component is the importance of examining the multiple contexts in which identity development occurs. The second component is the role of the family, particularly the role of socialization and the family's role in confronting and dealing with oppression. The most important component of Butch's story is the nature of intragroup differences. This includes the importance of the sense of acceptance from individuals and cultural groups on identity development and psychological functioning.

CONTEXTUAL DIMENSIONS

Butch's story illustrates the importance of examining the context of development. The ecosystem framework developed by Bronfenbrenner (1977) is a useful model for understanding the multiple influences. The first level, the individual level, represents the intrapsychic component of identity and includes temperament, personality traits and characteristics, and cognitive processes. The second level, the microsystem, includes all the immediate influences on individual development, including the nuclear family, peers, and the school system or work community. The mesosystem includes the interactions between the individual and the microsystems. The macrosystem includes more distal systemic influences on development, including immediate and extended family relationships, the neighborhood, legal systems, social services, the community, and community organizations. The exosystem, the next level, includes broader societal influences, including cultural and sociopolitical ideology. Finally, individual development needs to be examined within the particular time perspective, or the chronosystem. Butch's development is reflective of the process outlined in the model. Throughout his childhood and adolescence, experiences with the microsystem were prominent. He and his siblings were consistently teased by neighborhood children and were the victims of physical violence, allegedly due to race. Butch was accused of not being "Black enough" by both neighborhood children as a child and then by members of an organization as a young adult. These experiences contributed to feelings of shame and doubt about his racial identity. His family seemed to have a more tacit influence on his racial identity. Although his mother was aware of the teasing and violence against him, her response seems to have been more related to his self-defense and protection rather than to messages about his race. The family, according to Butch, did not have overt discussions about race and culture. In fact, the discovery of his Italian heritage was cloaked in secrecy. It is also not clear whether his mother helped to intervene with his sense of isolation in high school. The active components within the microsystem seemed to contribute to Butch's difficulties in identity development.

The school system, particularly the high school, reinforced mainstream values, and Butch continued to struggle with experiences of oppression within the school, along with feelings of isolation and rejection from his peers. Community organizations, AIC, had more influence on Butch's adult identity though, again, in a negative fashion. It is also important to understand Butch's development in light of the current events of his time and the cultural ideology within society, the exosystem and the chronosystem. Butch experienced adolescence and young adult development during the era of the civil rights movement. Butch was able to experience the sense of liberation and racial pride and made attempts to take pride in his Black heritage. Ironically, during the time that he was attempting to be empowered, he experienced intragroup oppression and was accused of not being truly Black and therefore not worthy of participating in the movement or empowerment. His story reminds us of how important it is to consider the context in identity development and psychological functioning of individuals.

FAMILY SOCIALIZATION PATTERNS

The role of the family is an important consideration in examining the role of race in people's lives and is often critical in understanding the identity functioning of biracial individuals. Butch's story provides an example of the complications that can occur when families have not only different racial backgrounds but also differing values. Butch has made attempts to be reconciled with and integrate each of the components of his background into his identity. His family did not have overt discussions about racial heritage. Butch learned about his Italian side from an aunt who secretly told him about his grandfather. For Butch, this answered several questions, particularly the variation in skin colors. When he tried to follow up with questions, however, his mother slapped him, ending his questioning. Butch felt that he could not continue to pursue further questions on this topic. It also seems as if the family did not have overt conversations on his Native American heritage. His cousin introduced him to the Native American culture and encouraged him with his dancing. Yet it seems as if he and his cousin are the only ones interested in learning about the heritage and the culture.

What is interesting about Butch's story is that acts of physical violence occurred due to racial differences. Yet although his mother was aware of the fights, there was no indication that overt discussions about racial issues took place. Butch experienced some very real threats and a sense of social isolation. Neither the nuclear nor the extended family engaged in a socialization process that may have served as a buffer against some of the discrimination. One wonders if Butch would have been so vulnerable if he had been shielded from some of the oppression or given coping mechanisms or resources to deal with them.

INTRAGROUP DIFFERENCES

Due to historical factors around multiracial heritage, a caste system has developed involving race and racial group membership. Biracial or multiracial individuals often have to choose a racial identity or affiliation, sometimes at the expense of neglecting or denying another. Because outward appearances are often our first connection to racial group membership, this choice is often reinforced in families through favoritism based on skin color; hair color, texture, and length; or facial features. When Butch began to recognize and understand his multiracial heritage as a child, it seemed linked to the physical differences within the family. It is not clear whether siblings were more favored in Butch's family because of physical appearance, but Butch's skin color led to some of the neighborhood fights. Because of the physical differences between Butch and other family members, he became an easy target for intragroup oppression. African American children teased him because his mother appeared White and because he was not "Black enough." The caste system and forced racial group affiliation led to intragroup differences. For example, during the period of slavery in America, mulatto children, the offspring of slave owners and slaves, experienced preferential treatment and did not have to labor as hard in the fields (Rockquemore & Laszloffy, 2003). Issues of superiority were established as people who were closer to White in terms of racial mixing and skin color and features were given more status and clout. The intragroup difference affected identity for people because both physical and psychological characteristics were used to determine group membership. One example of this consequence is the brown paper bag test that African American civic organizations used to determine membership. Even today, notions still exist of what constitutes membership within certain groups and the concept that people have to meet various criteria to belong to a race. Butch was certainly caught up in this phenomenon. As a child, his and his mother's skin color became the benchmark for group membership as African Americans. Because his mother appeared to be White, and Butch was biracial, this precluded his true membership. Butch could have theoretically compensated for the skin color issues through his behaviors, but he was also judged as not behaving Black enough. He did not receive socialization and encouragement from his family to learn to connect to his African American heritage and connect with his peers. Butch continued to be judged harshly when joining Black groups as an adult. When Butch joined the AIC and attempted to reconnect with his American Indian heritage, he experienced similar rejection based on his multiracial heritage. Only the Puerto Ricans in his high school accepted him openly, which may have led to his marriage to a Puerto Rican woman.

SELF-IMAGE

The development of identity is complex for everyone, but more so for multiracial individuals. Kerwin and Ponterotto (1995) developed a model of identity development for multiracial individuals based on research. The first stage, preschool, includes low salience to racial heritage as a component of the self. Although Butch was confused about skin color as a child, he did not base his sense of self solely on racial group membership. Children in this stage are aware of physical differences in their parents. The second stage, school-age, occurs as individuals feel compelled to select a racial group for membership. Children in the school-age stage are often asked to identify their heritage and select a response usually based on parental messages. Butch's journey through identity development reflects this stage as he, one by one, almost in a sequential fashion, attempts to explore his heritage and integrate it into his self-concept. Preadolescence and adolescence, the third stage, are characterized by growing awareness of the social connotations of race and are usually triggered by specific environmental circumstances. Butch experienced rejection from Italians, African Americans, and American Indians. This rejection led him at some points in his life to deny his Italian and Black heritage and to feel angry with members of these groups. What complicated this process for Butch was his exposure to the negative stereotypes and biases against certain groups. Butch appears to have internalized the stereotypes, sometimes leading him to be more vulnerable to assault. For example, regarding fights with neighborhood children, he reports that he did not have the confidence to fight them because he thought Blacks were stronger. This of course denies a part of his own heritage. The internalized oppression may have made it easier to reject parts of himself.

The fourth stage in the model occurs in college and young adulthood, as individuals continue with immersion in one culture due to rejection from another. Butch continued the exploration of his identity after high school and into early adulthood. Adulthood, the final stage, is characterized by the continuing integration of identity and an appreciation of a variety of cultural groups. Butch seems to have moved in this direction as he proudly proclaims his multiracial status and acknowledges all of his parts.

Clinical Applications

This section explores the clinical applications from Butch's story for counselors, including assessment, techniques and interventions to use in treatment, and countertransference concerns.

ASSESSMENT

The assessment of racial issues for multiracial individuals is similar to the concerns for individuals with a single racial heritage. Therapists should examine racial identity stages and understand how race intersects with other cultural variables, including social class and gender. More specific information should be assessed to determine how each racial group heritage influences identity development. The following questions are suggested:

What messages did you receive on each of your racial heritages?

Did you experience pressure to accept or deny any of your racial heritages from family members or peers?

Did you feel more accepted by one or more particular groups?

What historical information did you receive on your racial heritage?

What were the societal messages you received about your racial heritage?

TECHNIQUES AND INTERVENTIONS

Myths About Multiracial Individuals

There are three myths associated with being multiracial that should inform treatment and therapy (Kerwin & Ponterotto, 1995). The first myth is that of the tragic mulatto, the notion that multiracial individuals live marginalized lives because they are not fully accepted by any cultural or racial group. Butch's story is a good example of this perspective because at each developmental time period in his life, he attempts to reconcile his racial identity and is denied by each racial group. He reports feeling isolated and marginalized in his childhood neighborhood, in his high school, and by community organizations. Many biracial and multiracial individuals, however, are able to find acceptance and understanding from family and friends and are able to integrate each dimension of their heritage into their identity. Therapists should facilitate the integration of identities into self-concept as a goal with clients. The goal of clinicians should be to help clients acknowledge and honor each racial heritage (Rockquemore & Laszloffy, 2003). Although therapists may not be able to foster acceptance by others, they can be instrumental in helping clients find appropriate support groups and resources. For example, when Butch felt rejected by members of the AIC, one of the leaders took him aside and explained the reactions of some of the members, thus depersonalizing the issue. Counselors may also be able to help clients find support groups for individuals of multiracial descent. The second myth is that biracial individuals must choose one racial group. Historically, many were forced to choose one racial group by denying their racial heritage or by choosing a minority race and being rejected by Whites. Dominant society encouraged individuals to associate race in a dichotomous fashion (Rockquemore & Laszloffy, 2003). Until the 2000 U.S. Census count, individuals were asked to check one, and only one, race. Today, the option exists of identifying with and associating with various groups. Clinicians can help clients to research and understand the cultural heritage of both groups, working as cultural brokers (McGoldrick & Giordano, 1996). Clients can be encouraged to participate in and share rituals from one heritage with family members of the differing racial groups. The third myth is the notion that multiracial individuals do not want to discuss their cultural heritage. Butch's story highlights why the opposite view is so important. Many multiracial children have questions about their heritage, particularly because the values, beliefs, and lifestyles of each racial group differ. This was not evident in Butch's story, but often child-rearing difficulties arise based on different cultural values. While courting, a couple may agree to certain principles, child-rearing techniques, and values, but the actual birth of the children may change the priorities and focus. Families often experience more pressure from extended family members to maintain traditional cultural and racial activities (McGoldrick & Preto, 1984). Children often find themselves caught up in the cultural struggles, which may influence identity development. Many multiracial children look for opportunities to discuss their racial heritage in an attempt to solidify their development. Rockquemore and Laszloffy (2003) recommend a relational-narrative approach to therapy to allow clients to be able to process and tell their stories.

Family and Racial Socialization Processes

Racial socialization is the process of helping racial minority children to develop positive self-images within an oppressive community. The racial socialization process is even more critical for people of multiracial descent. Therapists should be encouraged to discuss and dialogue with their clients about their racial heritage. The process is more complicated with multiple racial backgrounds because individuals need to be socialized to each of the cultural groups to which they belong. Individuals also need to understand the historical influences on and societal messages about interracial marriages. Finally, clients need to be socialized on intragroup oppression.

COUNTERTRANSFERENCE

There are two areas in which countertransference may occur when working with multiracial clients, myths of multiracial persons, and client self-hatred. As in any other area, it is important for clinicians to monitor the personal reactions that arise when working with clients. Therapists should consider their own perspectives on interracial relationships before working with multiracial clients.

Myths and Misperceptions

One area of countertransference for clinicians working with multiracial clients is to become caught up by the complexity of identity development. It is important for therapists not to make the assumptions that their clients are experiencing the tragic mulatto syndrome, that clients live marginalized lives, and that they are not accepted by any group. It is true that multiracial clients may face rejection from racial groups. One reaction of Butch's story is to be moved and feel pain from the rejection that he faces and to be anxious about the violence he experienced. One reaction that therapists may have is to alleviate the pain clients experience from the rejection. This can lead to minimizing the rejection or attempting to make excuses for the other behaviors. Therapists may also be concerned that clients are forced to choose one group over another. Therapists may inadvertently encourage clients to choose one racial group to protect clients from the pain of rejection from another racial group. Although it may be a temporary solution to encourage clients to choose a nonrejecting group and to cut themselves off from groups that are rejecting, this has the long-term effect of clients' denying a part of themselves. Clinicians must monitor the sadness they feel for their client so that they engage in empathy and not sympathy.

It is often believed that multiracial individuals do not want to discuss issues. In fact, multiracial individuals often have the experience of strangers asking, "What are you?" and having to explain their backgrounds. It is critical for multiracial clients to talk about their backgrounds because it influences their identity and functioning. Similar to individuals with single racial backgrounds, multiracial individuals may not discuss racial issues unless therapists initiate the discussion. Avoiding racial discussions may be one way that therapists protect themselves from the secondary pain and discomfort of their clients. These conversations are even more important for therapists who are part of a rejecting racial group and for therapists with multiracial or multiethnic backgrounds.

Issues of Self-Hatred

Finally, therapists may be concerned with levels of self-hatred that their clients possess. When clients enter with depressive symptoms, including low self-esteem, resolving issues of self-hatred may be easy to introduce as a treatment goal. However, there may be times when the clients are not able to acknowledge their feelings. For example, when Butch is rejected by the

African American group, he decides to reject that part of his heritage. If he were to enter treatment at that point, he may not recognize his rejection as being linked to internalized oppression or self-hatred. The therapist would then be caught in the dilemma of identifying a potential treatment goal that the client may not be willing to accept. Clinicians have to reconcile the ethical requirement of not imposing their own values and standards on clients with the need to promote optimal functioning for their clients.

TOOLBOX ACTIVITY—BUTCH		
Resources and Suggested Readings	*Activities*	*Discussion Questions*
Kandel, B., & Halebian, C. (1997). *Growing up biracial: Trevor's story.* New York: Lerner. Katz, K. (2002). *The colors of us.* New York: Henry Holt. McBride, J. (1997). *The color of water: A Black man's tribute to his white mother.* New York: Riverhead Books. Nakazawa, D. J. (2004). *Does anybody else look like me? A parent's guide to raising multiracial children.* New York: DaCapo. O'Hearn, C. C. (1998). *Half and half: Writers on growing up biracial and bicultural.* New York: Pantheon. Rockquemore, K. A., & Brunsma, D. L. (2001). *Beyond Black: Biracial identity in America.* Thousand Oaks, CA: Sage Publications.	Construct a multiracial genogram, using Butch's story or the story of a famous multiracial individual (Joan Baez, Mariah Carey, Barack Obama). Trace the racial heritage and status of each group represented. Write an essay on the influence of heritage and racial history on the person.	Content themes What other themes do you see emerging in the story that the author did not identify? Assessment Are there any questions you would like to ask? Interventions What other interventions could you propose with Butch? Countertransference What countertransference reactions were emerging in yourself as you read this story? Other scenarios What would have occurred if Butch had been female? What would Butch have been like if he were only biracial instead of multiracial?

Betsie's Story 6

I Am 100 Percent Jewish

Less visible than race, ethnicity affects lifestyle, values, and identity, regardless of the individual's awareness of its influence. People vary greatly in the way they experience their own ethnicity, from ignoring it to feeling pride or ambivalence or expressing rejection. In a clinical situation, ethnicity is often ignored as a variable (McGoldrick & Giordano, 1996) because it may be less visible or because it creates conflicts between family members or between the clinician and the client (Hays, 2001). In this chapter, Betsie tells us about her pride in her Jewish ethnic background, the pressures to conform to her ethnicity, and some of her struggles, including her job-related concerns, her experiences with substance abuse, and her romantic relationships. The reader is not to feel discouraged by the complex web of Betsie's family tree. It is important to pay attention to her descriptions of the flavors and noises during her childhood years. Following the story, a wide range of issues related to ethnicity are addressed in the content themes, clinical interventions, and countertransference sections: the perception of ethnicity of oppressed groups, the relationship between ethnicity and religion, and the reaction of clinicians of similar or different ethnicity than that of the client.

Betsie's Story

I am 100 percent Jewish, having been born to two Jewish parents, both of them born to Jewish parents. I personally remember my two paternal great-grandmothers and have heard stories about their families and those of my two maternal great-grandmothers, whom I am named after, and their families. My family was seldom dull. I have always felt this way about my family history, which includes my life and the stories of my ancestors' lives that have been passed down to me through my parents and grandparents. First, I only have three sides of family because my mother's parents were uncle and niece. My grandfather, Bert, married his oldest sister's daughter, Fran, my grandmother. This was in 1926, and they had to get married in Illinois because it was illegal in Indiana. One of the many reasons I do not consider myself a truly White person from European descent is because all of my family (the Frieds from Rumania, the Staks from Poland, and the Nobles from Russia) came to the United States because none of their home countries allowed Jews to become citizens. All three families came over between 1900 and 1905. They came both out of fear of the pogroms and for the economic opportunities, which were very limited for Jews in the aforementioned countries at that time. My maternal grandfather's (Bert's) mother died on the crossing from Rumania when my grandfather was only three months old, so he was raised by his oldest sister, Ellen, and her husband, Yeshiva, a butcher. It is a Jewish custom to name your children after dead relatives whom you were close to, and my middle name is Ethel, after Ellen, whom my mother knew as her grandmother. My maternal grandmother's (Fran's) parents were my grandfather's next oldest sister, Bluma, and her husband, Abraham, who owned a jewelry and watch repair shop. My first name, Betsie, comes from Bluma. My mother considered naming me Bluma but could not see sticking her head out a window and calling "Bluma, come in for dinner!" So she Americanized Bluma to Betsie.

Bert was always in love with Fran (they were six years apart in age), and he used to write love letters to her. The mail in Bloomington used to get delivered twice a day, and Bert would write Fran a love letter in the morning on the streetcar on his way to school, where he got his master's degree in education, and mail it from campus, and Fran would have it in the afternoon mail. She used to show my siblings and me the letters. My mother still has them, and I will eventually inherit them. One quote of my grandfather's I will always remember is: "I will always be your knight in shining armor, protecting you and our future family forever." They were very much in love with each other, happily married for 63 years until their deaths, and I think it gave my mother a much romanticized notion of love; I know it did for me. They were both in very good physical shape. Fran wore midriff tops until she died at 83—and looked good. Until the end of their lives, when they took their afternoon 3-mile walk, they did it holding hands. They were both teachers. Bert started out as a mechanical drawing teacher at a vocational school, then got his master's degree and doctorate and ended his career as a professor at Indiana Institute of Technology. He was brilliant, and I know that I got my brains from him. Fran was no slouch, either. She was also a teacher at two schools, got two master's degrees, one in reading and one in administration, and ended her career as the assistant principal in charge of discipline. It is from this side of my family that I got the most pressure to do well in school. I was always the smart one of my siblings, and as far back as I can remember my parents always took it for granted that I would get top marks in grammar school and high grades in junior high, high school, and college. Fran began working in 1928, retiring after 40 years in 1968. She always worked under her maiden name, Miss Brooks. If I ever have a daughter, I will name her Brooke (to honor both my grandmothers, Brooks and Betsie). Bert and Fran lived right behind Bluma and Abraham. Because Fran worked, Bluma cooked dinner for both families. My mother, Millie, remembers that Bluma often cooked three or four different dishes because she loved to cook what each person enjoyed.

Millie and her brother Joshua were both very picky eaters. At one time in their lives, Millie would only eat chicken, and Joshua would only eat lamb chops.

Both sides of my family followed many Jewish ideals, but closeness of family is probably the strongest one on both sides. As I mentioned, my grandparents lived right behind their parents; my father's (Jacob's) mother's (Betsie's) family was even closer. Betsie's parents came over from Kiev, Russia, before she was born in 1903. My great-grandmother's (Martha's) sister had died, leaving Isaac and six children, so Martha married him, as was tradition. I have a million stories about this side of my family, the side I have always been closer to. Martha and Isaac lived in Philadelphia and had six children together. After Isaac died, his brother Abe's wife also died, leaving him with four children, so Martha married him. Betsie always said she had 15 brothers and sisters, even though nine were actually first cousins. She was the oldest girl of the second set of six. When Isaac was alive, he was a cantor and a Torah scholar, and Martha ran a restaurant to earn enough money for their family. All the children lived around their parents. The oldest two girls, Carol and Eve, were opera singers who toured throughout Europe with an international opera company, always sending half of their money home to the family.

With 11 children, the money wasn't enough, so during the 1920s Martha added a speakeasy menu to the restaurant. Betsie was forced to quit school after eighth grade to go to work in a department store to earn money. She looked older and was able to get a job as a clerk. She always had a great love of learning and was a voracious reader until she died at 85 years of age. Meeting her, one would never guess her lack of education because she was self-taught. Betsie's older brothers, Sam and Charley, started a clothing business, which became such a success that they sent Martha and the youngest 11 children to Chicago to own an apartment building and restaurant in the late 1920s. So Martha, Abe, and the 11 youngest children, including Betsie, moved to Chicago. Leah and Hyman and their four children—Samuel, my grandfather Jack, Victor, and Silvia—were tenants in the building that Martha and Abe owned. Hyman was a tailor. Sam fell in love with Betsie, who was engaged to a man named Samson Cowen, who was going to medical school out East. Sam made a deal with Samson. Sam asked Samson to give him one year to woo Betsie while he was away at school; if Sam could not convince Betsie to leave Samson in one year, Sam would back off forever. Samson stupidly agreed and left for school, cutting off all contact with Betsie, without telling her anything. She thought he had left her, was heartbroken, and started dating Sam on the rebound.

Sam was a good-looking, smooth-talking dreamer. He was a bellboy at a prestigious hotel, with lots of connections for free tickets to concerts and shows and passes to all the fine restaurants, so he wined and dined Betsie and soothed her broken heart. By the time Samson came back from school, Sam had already asked Betsie to marry him. Samson finally told Betsie the truth. She was so angry with Samson for playing games with her emotions that she married Sam out of anger and spite. Although they did remain married for more than 50 years, until Sam's death, they fought often. I got two things from Grandfather Sam. One was his love of partying and having a good time; the other was his quick temper and big mouth. He yelled, and yelled loudly, a great deal of the time. I can get very angry, sometimes very quickly, but like him, after I let it out (I do it in a more appropriate manner than he did) it is over. I rarely hold a grudge.

Although my mother's family was close, Betsie's family took family closeness to a new art form. When Betsie married Sam, her sister, Sarah, married Sam's brother, Jack. All of Betsie's siblings who moved to Chicago lived near each other as adults, and the two brother-sister couples were no exception: They always lived next door to each other until 1948, when they bought a three-flat building with another of Betsie and Sarah's sisters and her husband. This was known as "the Building." Martha lived with Betsie and Sam for the last 15 years of her life. I get my great love of family from the many weekends spent at the Building. Betsie was the most loving, caring, giving person you could ever meet. She loved and accepted everyone, just as her mother Martha had done. Martha's youngest son, my Uncle Maurice, fell in love with a Las Vegas showgirl, an Egyptian woman, my Aunt Jessica. Martha welcomed Jessica into the family. After Maurice's death, Jessica and her new husband, Sam, came to all of our family events and continued to do so for almost 20 years. When my Uncle Jack's son, Chuck, married Sandra, an African American woman, we all welcomed her as well.

If I had to pick one person who influenced my life the most, it was my "Nonny" Betsie. I was her oldest granddaughter, and that made me the luckiest person on earth. She was my best friend and my greatest advocate. She died about five years ago, and I miss her terribly. I am crying now as I write these words. I consider myself a third-generation party animal because, with such a large, close family, there was always one event or another happening, and everyone was invited. Every other Friday (Shabbat) night we went to the Building for dinner, and then my siblings and I slept there overnight. My father's sister's family did the same on the other weeks. At 4 p.m. every afternoon, cocktail and snacktime was held. Betsie and her sisters met in one of the kitchens for one glass each of vodka, filled to the top. Each floor was filled with cousins; many were my second or third cousins, but that never mattered.

Before they bought the building, my father, Jacob, grew up very poor. Because Sam worked for tips, money was tight and did not come in on a consistent basis, which had a big impact on Jacob—and hence on me. Sam finished high school but did not go on to college. His brothers, Jack and Victor, went to college and became accountants. Jacob became a certified public accountant (CPA). As a class project, he volunteered to be the accountant for the theater department. He took the elevator to the top floor of the school, which housed all the sets and the dressing and rehearsal rooms. As Jacob got off the elevator, he saw a man carrying my mother, Millie, over his shoulder. The man said to Jacob, "Wanna pinch something nice?" Of course Jacob said yes and pinched Millie's behind, and that is how they met (Millie was a theater major). My smooth-talking father romanced my naive mother, and they were married two years later, after my father graduated. Their marriage lasted 15 years. When I look back, I see what they had in common at ages 20 and 21: They both were (are) Jewish, they both were (are) close to their families, they both have a great love of literature and the arts, and in the 1950s they both wanted to do what their parents wanted them to do—raise a family of their own to continue the Jewish traditions.

So you have now read much of my family history, and finally I am born. But just as in the movie *Avalon*, I grew up hearing all the stories I have just shared, and they have been an important influence on my life. These stories grounded me and gave me my great love and appreciation of history in general, especially my family history and traditions. In 1954, when they were 21 and 20 years old, Millie and Jacob got married. Millie quit school and went to work as a secretary, while Jacob sat for the CPA exam and started working with Victor and Jack in their accounting firm. I was born in 1958. Victor died suddenly in 1959, and Jacob became a partner in the firm. At age 26, he was giving advice to men twice his age about how they should run their businesses. My brother was born in 1960, and my sister in 1961. As I mentioned, Jacob grew up poor, which inspired him to do better for himself and his family. For example, in both the apartment we lived in until I was four years old and the house we moved to in the suburbs, we always had air conditioning. Jacob would not buy a house unless it had central air. His dream was to have an office on Market Street and to live downtown. He has accomplished both. He worked extremely hard throughout my entire childhood. Until I was seven or eight years old, he worked six and a half days a week part of the year and seven days a week from January to April, tax season. To this day I hate math, and I believe it is because I used to fall asleep to the sound of the adding machine. Whereas the Frieds are very conservative, the Staks are very liberal. When my parents looked to buy a house, my father purposely moved us to a mixed suburban community so that we would live in what today you would call a multicultural neighborhood and attend a multicultural school. My four best friends on my block were Dana (Jewish), Laurie (Japanese), Annie (Chinese), and Betty (Polish). I have always been proud to grow up there.

Education is another Jewish value I identified greatly with. Because I was the smart one of my parents' children, it was always expected of me that I would do well in school, and I did. Schoolwork always came very easy for me. My brother was the athlete, so it was okay that he did not have top grades, and although my sister did well in school, she had to work very hard to do so. I have to admit that I was actually rather lazy, but because I caught on to things quickly (I have an almost photographic memory and am able to relax when taking a test) it was very easy for me to get high grades. I was also tested for my music and dance abilities and received high marks. When I was seven years old, my parents bought a piano. The store that we bought it from had music testing. My parents were told that I had the musical ability of a 16-year-old. I took ballet classes at the Jewish Community Center (JCC) near my house. My class was taught by a prima ballerina who, after escaping from Russia, was helped by the Chicago Jewish community and was giving back to our community by teaching dance. She told my mother that I should be taking lessons at a higher level. We could not afford better ballet lessons, and I got lazy about practicing piano, so I did not go much further with either one. I am still a frustrated artist. First, I am always drawn to artists. I got involved in theater in high school and was in the National Thespian Society. Most of my friends from college were theater and music majors. I love to take pictures. I am the one on vacations and at parties who brings out the camera; it is my muse.

Another important aspect of my childhood is that I grew up in the 1960s and 1970s. I lived through and was greatly influenced by the civil rights movement, the hippies, the Vietnam War, and the women's movement. I understand that everyone has some prejudice, but I have always felt that because I am Jewish I know that there are plenty of people in this world who hate me because of my ethnicity. I hate this fact. It scares me, makes me very angry, and bothers me, so I feel that I can't do that to anyone else. This may sound corny, but I truly believe this. My family was always very politically active, and the historic events of my youth made me even more aware of how important it is to be involved in the political process.

The women's movement really messed things up for me. Even though Fran worked, she still got married at 18 and had two children. Most of the other adult women in my life were homemakers and mothers, some with part-time jobs. Millie did not work until my sister started first grade and was in school all day. Millie got a job as a secretary in the school district's central office so that she would always have the same days off as we did. All of a sudden, everything changed. Now I was expected to find a career and fight for women to have the right to be trained and work in fields dominated by men—and to earn as much as men—and to have the right to a legal abortion. All of a sudden, men and women were supposed to be equal. I remember starting junior high school in the fall of 1969. At that time, girls had to wear dresses or skirts, no slacks or shorts. One day in October, the word went around that all the girls were walking out at 10 a.m. to protest the dress code. We wanted the right to wear pants! At the appointed time, virtually every girl walked out of school. We marched around the school chanting for about two hours, and then we went home. The rule was changed, and we could wear pants. This felt so powerful, to have a voice and have it heard.

Another aspect of Jewish women is the notion of Jewish women as nurturers (to the point of worriers), always taking care of their families. Being the oldest, and a girl, I took on this role as soon as my siblings were born. One of the first messages I received as a child was "Take care of your brother and your sister!" And I did. Whenever anyone offered me candy, perhaps at a store or at the doctor's office, I would always ask, "Can I have one for my brother and sister?" My mother loved to tell people about this. Somehow I was able to understand when my sister talked baby talk. When I was 11 years old, I began babysitting my siblings when my parents went out. They would pay me a quarter per hour. Kids used to pick on my sister because she was so small. I took care of that. Being three years older, I was always bigger than her peers, at least through grammar school. Even once we were all in college, my mother would still call me and ask, "Where is your brother?" The funny thing is, often I would know. We were very close growing up and still are to this day. I talk to my sister almost every day, and I talk to my sister-in-law often also. I would talk to my brother more often, but he is a psychologist and is with clients all day.

The most traumatic event of my life was my parents' divorce. They got divorced when I was 11 years old, in 1970. They seem to have started the trend. When it happened, I only knew one other family with divorced parents. I was devastated. Sometimes I think that I still have not completely gotten over it and wonder if I ever will. I know it is part of the reason that I did not get married until I was 44 years old. My siblings were 29 and 34 years old when they got married. We all say that we will never get divorced. It was very ugly. Jacob was cheating on Millie. They told us about it in December of 1969, and the divorce was finalized in March of 1970. Jacob was married again on April 15 of that year. Fran was cruel. She would always bad-mouth Jacob. The only good thing to come out of it was that we got to spend more quality time with Jacob. Instead of him coming home late every night, tired and crabby, and doing chores around the house on his days off, he was now responsible for us every Sunday and had to spend time with us, and we still went to Betsie and Sam's every other Friday night and slept over.

Jacob's second wife, Avis, was a wonderful person. She had two daughters, Barbara (five years older than me) and Lynn (two years older than me). Lynn and I became very close. Jacob and Avis were married for five years. Avis and Lynn were major influences in my life. Lynn was thin and beautiful, and Avis was a former model, so she was beautiful, too. My mother is very good-looking, but she is short. Avis was tall and glamorous. Avis had helped her daughter Barbara with her weight problem, and she urged me to deal with mine. At age 13, I was 5 foot 3 inches tall and weighed 179 pounds. I looked eight months pregnant. My weight brings me to another aspect of what I believe is part of the Jewish culture: food. All the Jewish women in my family were avid cooks who loved to feed us and urged us all to eat, eat, eat. And I loved food, so I did. Also, after years of therapy, I have realized that this was the way that I got love from my mother: she fed me. Because Jacob worked so much, Millie was left alone to raise three little children. I was always a good girl. My brother was always mischievous. He would get lost in the grocery store or hide our toys. My sister was a big crybaby and demanded by mother's attention, so I did not get enough attention from Millie. I know that she loves me very much, but as a child what I got most from her was her excellent cooking. Avis gently talked to me about how Barbara had lost weight on diet pills (after all, it was 1971, and pills cured everything), took me to my pediatrician, and started me on amphetamines, and I have been conscious of my weight ever since. My metabolism is such that I was on the verge of needing thyroid medication, so the pills just curbed my appetite; I did not get jumpy or lose sleep.

One negative aspect of my family and the era I grew up in was substance use and abuse. As I mentioned, the three sisters always had their cocktail hour. When my father finally did come home from work, he always had a drink almost immediately after walking in the door. Alcohol was never a big deal for us as kids. We always had wine at Passover and could always try our parents' or grandparents' drinks if we asked. Although drinking was no big deal, smoking pot was much more exotic. I tried pot for the first time at age 12 after being influenced by Lynn. I only smoked once or twice a month for the five years I knew her, and though I stopped in high school, I started up again in college. I believe it was the pressure of trying to do my best and be successful at the University of Chicago. I was a lazy student in high school. If I even put my hand over a book, I would get an A. I was number 98 out of 647 in my class, I got a 29 on the ACT and an 1150 on the SAT, and I had a great interview, so I was accepted to college. Sometimes I think that maybe I was also filling their Jewish quota. Whatever the reason, there I was surrounded by class valedictorians, feeling like I did not belong. My first two years were a disaster. I loved going to class and listening to lectures and participating in discussions. I read the books, but it took me two years to really learn how to study and write papers. In the meantime, I got Cs and Ds, something I had never gotten before. In high school, I got a C in typing and one in biology and then finished my last two years with straight As, so my grades at University of Chicago were ego-shattering. I hid them from my parents and had many sleepless nights.

Another message I always got from Millie was "Don't worry, don't get upset!" Pot smoking was the perfect solution for my worry and anxiety. I began smoking every night. At least I never went to class or tried to study while high; I just smoked instead of studying. I finally developed good study habits in my junior year, after I was put on probation. I am very proud to have a diploma from the University of Chicago and that I did it in four years despite my partying, but I am humiliated about my grades. Once I was out of college, I continued to smoke pot virtually every night for 10 more years. I was still using it as a crutch, this time to ease the pressure of not being successful at a career and my lack of ability to find a husband. These relate to issues in the Jewish culture, the push for success, which for a woman from my generation means success both in a career and in a relationship.

I always loved history (my major), but in 1980, my senior year, schools were closing, and teachers were not paid nearly as well as they are now. I definitely had the desire to be successful, especially monetarily. I worked on the trading floor of the Chicago Mercantile Exchange as a summer job when I was in college. My uncle was the head of the computer department and got me the summer job. I did not have a clue what he was talking about when he offered me the job, only that it paid much more than minimum wage and that the hours were 7:30 a.m. to 2 p.m. I loved being out in the sun during the summer, so having a summer job that ended at 2 p.m. was heavenly. I carpooled with two girls from school whose fathers were commodity traders. I remember them telling me on my first day, "Forget every rule of life you know. You are about to enter the trading floor!" And they were right. It was a trip: a room full of thousands of people—mostly men, most young, and most without a college education—all excited and shouting. I thought, "Hey, I'm a University of Chicago student. I am smart, so I should do really well here!" The object of the game is very easy— buy low, sell high—but playing the game is hard: having the guts to know when to stay in as your money is ticking away or when to get out and cut your losses.

I kept moving up the ladder of jobs, and I helped many people make literally millions of dollars. Many promised me a share, but it never materialized. I had eight different jobs in 10 years. For example, my third-to-last job was as a personal clerk for an options trader. Commodity options were new, and it actually took some brains, not simply luck, to trade them successfully, so I took the job to learn how to trade options. Rick paid me almost no money (I had to work a second job at a video store to pay my bills), but he promised me he would lease me a seat to trade with him in one year if I helped him make money and learned enough about options. In one year, with my help, he went from earning $100,000 to earning $300,000. He gave me a $200 Christmas bonus and promptly went into the florist business with his brother and left the trading floor. I could go on, but needless to say, commodities and options was never a career for me: it was just a fun and exciting job. I met a lot of fun, interesting people, and to get through the nights of feeling like a failure I smoked pot. After performing well and still losing three jobs, I decided that God was trying to tell me something. Millie offered to let me live back at home while I got my master's in education to become a teacher. I did not completely stop smoking pot until four years later, but from the time I started in my career in education I only smoked occasionally on the weekends, until I finally stopped for good when I got my first teaching job.

I also felt as though I was failing in my attempts to form a marriage relationship. I have a large number of friends, a couple since high school and many since college, but I had difficulty in bonding with a man for a lifelong relationship. Part of the problem I alluded to earlier: I think I had romanticized a relationship with a man after seeing the love letters Bert wrote to Fran. Another part was my lack of confidence in my looks. I grew up with the commercials on television touting "blondes have more fun," and I was never going to be a blonde. I was a tomboy, growing up before it was popular for girls to play sports. Sometimes I think my parents fought a great deal after my birth because I subconsciously thought that a relationship with a man meant fighting, unhappiness, and divorce, and I sent out negative relationship vibes. I did not wear makeup until I was 26 years old. Until that time, I wore blue jeans and T-shirts most of the time when I was not at work. I was always busy with family and friends, so it was not like I sat home doing nothing. I think that the way I dealt with the pressure from my family was to smoke pot and avoid dealing with it. Since I was not getting an A in relationships, I was not going to even try to be in one.

Another aspect in my life that kept me away from relationships was my family experiences with my father. He has been married three times and has had two long-term relationships since his last divorce. His third wife, who was 11 years younger than he, was a jerk. After a 10-year relationship, including two years of counseling, they finally came to the same conclusion that I realized the moment I met her: that they had nothing in common. His next relationship was with a woman only three years older than me. She looked much older because she was a heavy smoker. Betsie made my father promise that he would not get married again because she got attached to his wives, and all of his divorces hurt her a great deal. She died five years ago, and I think he has finally realized that she was right. His most recent relationship has lasted 10 years and will probably last the rest of his life because she is only 51 years old and he is 70. All of the women he has had relationships with were skinny and gorgeous. Maybe part of my problem was that I felt I could never live up to my father's image of a woman.

Finally, at 26 years old I met a man, Tim, on the trading floor. He was four years younger than me. He seemed nice and very giving, and he really liked me, so we started dating. He was not Jewish, but he said that he would never ask me to convert and that even though he was raised Catholic and went to Catholic school he did not really believe in religion. I was so relieved to finally have a boyfriend that at first I did not realize that he was taking over my life. It was also nice that he came from a very wealthy family. His uncle owned a large company and was a multimillionaire. They were in the vending machine leasing business. We all went to a convention in Atlantic City, and we stayed in a luxurious hotel and were driven around in limousines. His uncle really liked me and asked us to join him in his limo for the weekend. I felt as though I had hit the jackpot: a man who loved me and who would be able to take care of me in style. So what if he had cut me off from most of my family and friends? So what if he was telling me what to wear and how to wear my hair? I had been too much of a tomboy anyway, and I was looking much better. My mother was not thrilled, but I think that she liked the physical change in me. She had always tried to get me to dress up more, and I always fought her. I used to hate shopping, which was unusual for a Jewish girl in my new neighborhood.

Maybe part of why I did not mind Tim taking over my life was because I was used to not having important things my way. So many things had already happened to me that I had no control over. We started living together after one year and lived together for four years. I was so happy that the pressure was off of me to get married. I finally felt like I fit in. Thank God that one of my college friends married a woman, Tina, who is a therapist who works with battered women. She saw what was going on and talked to me about how unhealthy my relationship was. She began to predict how Tim was going to behave. He started breaking my things, and she insisted that it was only a matter of time before he started to hit me. The turning point came when Tim's father won a trip to Cancun and gave it to us. Tina had warned me that batterers often begin battering in a place outside the United States because the woman is so distant from her family and friends. She warned me that I better have a credit card with me because Tim would start a fight, and if I tried to call the police they would just laugh at me because I was a "rich, White American girl" and do nothing, so I would have to jump on a plane myself. Sure enough, as we were having dinner one night, Tim started up with me. He had asked me to marry him a few weeks before, and I had said that I would think about it. The only thing he could not get me to change my mind about was raising my children as Jews, which I was determined to do. He agreed to this as long as they could celebrate Christmas and Easter, which I had no problem with.

So at dinner he said to me, "How can you think I would ever agree to raise my children Jewish after I went to Catholic school all of my life?" I said, "Because you said you would when we first talked about it." He started yelling at me right there in public, and all of a sudden the light bulb went off in my head. I realized that this was the fight Tina had alluded to, and I knew right there and then that I had to end the relationship. I did not want a scene. Six months before, when I had talked about ending things with him, he broke a glass table of mine. I did not want more violence to happen. I stopped the argument by agreeing to think about it and started planning how I would leave.

The trip had been in late November. I had very early work hours; Tim worked from 10 a.m. to 6 p.m. Just before Christmas, I pretended to go to work, waited at Jacob's apartment until I knew Tim was gone, and then arranged with a few of my friends to pack up all my things and move out. I went to stay with Tina. I attended her battered women's group and learned a lot about myself. I got into group and then individual therapy as soon as I got back home. I still struggle with my self-image and self-esteem, but through therapy I have gained enough insight to have a healthy career and a healthy marriage.

When I look back at my life so far, I vacillate between two feelings. On the one hand, I feel angry because I have wasted so much time being scared to live a full, adult life. I partied away 10 years of my life in commodities and have only had my real career for the past 10 years. So now I am working my behind off catching up. On the other hand, I look back at all the great experiences I have had and know that I would never have been able to have them if I had begun teaching right after college or had gotten married right away. My family's history, experiences, and lessons will continue to help me in my future.

— ▪ — ▪ — ▪ — ▪ — ▪ — ▪ — ▪ — ▪ — ▪ — ▪ — ▪ — ▪ —

Content Themes

In this story, Betsie tells us about her pride in her ethnic background, the values transmitted through her family to her, her challenges in upholding some of those values, and her struggles with employment, substance use and abuse, and romantic relationships. In looking at the themes of this story, we also learn how the implicit family norms affected and shaped her identity.

PRIDE ABOUT ETHNIC BACKGROUND

As many individuals do, Betsie speaks proudly about her ethnicity: "I am 100 percent Jewish." She also exhibits pride in her family history and in the fact that she was named after several of her ancestors. She spends a considerable amount of time writing about how her grandparents met and courted, what she considers was passed on to her from them ("He was brilliant, and I know that I got my brains from him.") and who influenced her the most ("It was my 'Nonny' Betsie . . ."). She does not introduce herself until much later in her narrative and spends the first several pages retelling the stories that grounded her and gave her an appreciation of her family history. Ethnicity is a powerful force that influences identity formation, and how an individual feels about his or her ethnicity, whether pride or contempt, has an enormous impact on the individual's views about his or her sense of belonging and sense of inclusion in a community, and that in turn influences a sense of self. Unlike the racial categories, ethnicity can be less visible. Whether people are conscious of their ethnic identity varies greatly within groups and from one ethnic group to another. Not everyone feels as Betsie does about his or her ethnic background. In general, the more pride an individual has in his or her ethnic identity, the easier the acquisition of self-identity becomes. The more people reject their ethnicity, the harder it is for them to negotiate and deal with the rejected or denied parts of themselves. This is particularly true for oppressed ethnic groups (McGoldrick & Giordano, 1996; Sue & Sue, 2003). Individual awareness of ethnic background differs according to the status of the ethnic group in a given society. The oppressed, marginalized, and less powerful individuals may shift and increase awareness of their ethnic identity as they interact with members of the mainstream, more dominant groups. Often the shifts in awareness depend on whether the minority/majority groups interact within oppressor/oppressed models or within more egalitarian models of interaction. For example, before Hitler's rise to power, the German Jews were assimilated into the German culture and considered themselves more German than Jewish, in part because, in spite of biases against Jews, they tended to be more accepted by the mainstream German society than the Polish or Russian Jews were in theirs (Elon, 2002). Similarly, in the United States, the rate of assimilation of the U.S. Jews appears to be staggering, with intermarriage the highest and rates of synagogue affiliation the lowest in the history of the Jewish people (Ashemberg Straussner, 2001). This is not surprising, considering that Jewish university quotas, employment quotas, and other discriminatory acts have begun to disappear from American mainstream society since the 1960s. Similar phenomena occurred at certain historical times with other ethnic groups. In general, the easier the group's immersion into the White cultural and ethnic values, the quicker the group seems to lose its ethnic identity in the following generations. The more the group experiences oppression, discrimination, and stereotyping, the more its members cling to and try to retain their ethnic identity (Iglehart & Becerra, 1995).

THE CONNECTION BETWEEN ETHNICITY AND FAMILY VALUES

It is difficult to separate the ethnic identity of the family from the cultural norms the family transmits. The culture of the family is in part the ethnic identity of the family and has deep ties with it (McGoldrick & Giordano, 1996). Implicit family norms tied to the ethnic identity of the family shape an individual's identity. This has an impact on how people live and the values they hold dear, or reject. The typical Jewish family is a good example of the difficulties that arise in trying to tease out the culture of the family from its ethnic background. Because Jews are not only a nationality and not only a religion, some of its general values can be observed regardless of the national origin or the religiously observant or nonobservant status of it members. That is harder to perceive in White Anglo-Saxon Protestants and has traditionally been easier to observe in other ethnic groups (Irish, Italian, Jewish). But that is because the Anglo-Saxon Protestant is the supposedly regular background against which all the other ethnicities are compared, not because the White Anglo-Saxon Protestant does not have a culture (McGoldrick & Giordano, 1996). No Jewish mother would consider herself a competent mother, for example, if she did not worry about her children and share her suffering openly with the rest of the family (Rosen, 1995). Obviously, non-Jewish mothers worry about their children, too, but they might do so differently; they might not share the worrying with the rest of the family, for example, so as to not worry the others. The offspring of these two different mothers encode worrying differently and react accordingly to their own children. Of course, neither one is right or wrong. They just become the ethnic cultural norms for the individual. In Betsie, we see the transmissions of several family values that she interprets as Jewish family values (e.g., the centrality of the family), which includes the expectation that women will marry, have children, and take care of them; the expectation of financial success and intellectual achievement; the love of food; and, of course, the notion that mothers worry and share that worry with other siblings: "Where is your brother?" Whether or not these are really exclusively Jewish family values is not as important as the fact that Betsie thinks they are.

PRESSURE TO CONFORM TO ETHNIC VALUES

We have just seen how Betsie identifies some core Jewish values and traditions that have been passed down from generation to generation. She feels influenced by them and expresses a desire to abide by and continue in the next generation: "He could not get me to change my mind about raising my children as Jews, which I was determined to do." As Betsie continues telling her story, she begins to describe the pressures those values exerted and how unsuccessful she was at keeping up with them. In the age of the feminist movement, the ancestral push for success meant that now she had to succeed both in a career as well as in a relationship. This is consistent with the findings in the literature about Jewish families who describe that, despite the impact of feminist ideas, the pressure on Jewish women to find the most appropriate mate is still high. At the same time, the expectations of intellectual achievement and professional success once exerted only on sons now seem to pertain to daughters also. Consequently, Jewish daughters are now expected to be not only good wives but also successful professionals (Rosen & Weltman, 1996).

Betsie tells us about difficulties that led to years of pot addiction as a way of dealing with the anxiety and worry of not getting the expected good grades, the unfulfilled expectations of marriage, and the unanticipated financial frustrations in the male-dominated world of commodities trading, in which she was not successful. We know little about the pressure her parents actually exerted on Betsie, but we do know from her story that she feels she has not been able to abide by what she considers to be her family expectations. She felt as though she failed in upholding the family prescriptions of success. The cost of her perceived pressure and, as she understands it, her failure to conform to her Jewish values was high.

Sometimes the fluidity of identity does necessitate breaking the family ethnic prescriptions of what constitutes a good life to figure out one's self-identity. Many family conflicts are played out in the form of stricter or less strict adherence to family ethnic rules and expectations, most often in the areas of intermarriage, mate selection, parenting, and education. Often, when the offspring do not adhere to strict ethnic family rules, violent cut-offs and hurtful rejections take place. Because this is a country that continues to absorb many immigrants, there are large numbers of second- and third-generation immigrants dealing with the issue of loyalty to, or separation from, the ethnic origin of the family. These immigrants, while struggling with whether to conform or not conform to the ethnic prescriptions of their ancestors, are making the fluidity of the shifting self-identity a hallmark of our immigrant society.

RELATIONSHIP BETWEEN ETHNICITY AND RELIGION

Ethnicity has many points of contact with religious observance, but the two are not the same. The Irish Catholics can be different from the Mexican Catholics, and the German Lutherans can be different from the Slovak Lutherans. Their ethnicity may be intersected with their religion, but not totally. The differences in levels of Jewish observance exemplify this. Families can follow secular Jewish traditions that allow for a strong ethnic identification and at the same time be religiously nonobservant. In contrast, there are many Jews who are religiously observant. Betsie thinks of herself as ethnically rather than religiously Jewish. Also, people may have ambivalent reactions to their ethnicity but tend to cling to their reservoir of ethnic traditions in times of crisis, illness, death, marriages, births, and any other markers of the life cycle. Many of these traditions tend to be grounded in religion, so that even people who in everyday life do not appear to lead lives in which religion plays a role might suddenly resort to religious customs and rituals because of a renewed need to connect with previous generations, heal losses, make a transition to the future, or repeat a familiar family rite (Imber-Black, Roberts, & Whiting, 1988).

RELATIONSHIP BETWEEN SOCIOHISTORICAL CONTEXTS AND IDENTITY

For Betsie, the historical and social contexts in which she grew up included the feminist movement, her parents' divorce, and the societal expectation of women's attractiveness. These historical and social contexts, and the values that can be derived from them, appear to be in contradiction with the values generated by her ethnic heritage (e.g., expectations of togetherness, marriage and children, emphasis on eating and food). She felt that her life was out of her control, and she understands her choice of an abusive mate and her addiction to pot in light of these contradictions. With intense regret, she attributes what she considers to be her personal failures to abide by the prescriptions of her ethnic heritage to the new social movement of her time, the Civil Rights and the feminist movements. She also talks about being negatively influenced by her father, his numerous wives, and other family members. Because of the way she ends the writing of her story, we do not have a clear sense of how she defines herself today, which aspects of her cultural and ethnic background she continues to embrace, and which ones she has decided to discard. Has her self-identity shifted or does it remain the same?

Clinical Applications

This section starts with assessment questions related to the content themes and continues with interventions useful when working with people who present with stereotypes about ethnicity, either their own or someone else's. This section ends with an extensive discussion about possible countertransference reactions when working with people of similar or different ethnic affiliations.

ASSESSMENT

Counselors can be instrumental in helping to increase their clients' awareness of their ethnic identity, including awareness of the factors that shape their current values, motivations, and actions. Also, it is important to help clients understand that their self-definition and identity may change over time or remain the same. If people receive negative images of their ethnicity, either in the societal or family context in which they develop, or if they begin to have negative views of their ethnicity as they grow and mature, self-hate and rejections of parts of their selves may result. Self-hate can be detrimental to their sense of self, their identity, and their relationships. At the other extreme, people may develop distorted, self-aggrandizing, and ethnocentric views of their own ethnicity and feel superior to people they deem inferior because these people do (or do not) possess a certain ethnic identity. Another possibility is that individuals do not recognize that how they think about themselves, their values, their motivations, and their behavior is based on their ethnicity.

It is important to assess the meanings and expectations associated with clients' ethnicity and its relation to other areas of their lives to get a sense of where they are in their identity development and help them move forward, if they so desire. Also, it is important to assess clients' constraints in relation to their own ethnic identity or the way they understand the ethnic identity of others with whom they interact (e.g., spouses, coworkers, neighbors, in-laws, employees). These therapeutic conversations are important because clients' sense of self and their relationships with others are deeply tied to issues about ethnicity.

Pride About Ethnic Background

How important is your ethnicity in your life? How do you understand your ethnic background? Has that view changed over the years or remained the same? Do other people you interact with share your positive or negative view?

Ethnicity, Family Values, and Pressures to Conform

Have any of your decisions been affected by your ethnic background, in terms of choice of spouse, child rearing, home location, your religious affiliation, and so on? How difficult were those decisions for you? For your family? Has your ethnicity constrained or made it easier for you to live your life? If you identify constraints about how you live your life, how have you dealt with those constraints?

Relationship Between Ethnicity, Religion, Sociohistorical Contexts, and Other Variables

Are you aware of any religious, historical, or social class issues that have affected the way you think about your ethnicity? Are you aware of how your ethnic background has affected the way you think about other people's ethnicity (e.g., your spouse, coworkers, in-laws)? Are there any constraints in your relationship with your spouse, coworkers, subordinates, or in-laws that you attribute to ethnic differences? Have you changed the way you deal with those constraints, or have your methods remained the same over the years?

TECHNIQUES AND INTERVENTIONS

Sometimes people attribute their problems in life to the difference between theirs and their parents', spouses', or in-laws' ethnicity: "He drinks like an Irishman," "She worries like a Jewish mother," "He cheats like a Latin lover," "She is uptight like a German." It is not unusual to hear people speak these ready-made stereotypes to justify and explain, to themselves or their significant others, their disputes, family struggles, or profound differences. When people speak this way, they are using what is known as cultural camouflage: the attribution of ethnicity to problems in a relationship (Falicov, 1995). This way of understanding people's characteristics tends to perpetuate struggles, decrease empathy, and polarize family members, coworkers, subordinates, and in-laws because they tend to present people with paralyzing, one-perspective narratives that do not include empathy for themselves or others. Counselors often do not know how to deal with clients who use explanations based on ethnicity to explain their problems with significant others in their lives.

One useful intervention is the internalized-other interviewing technique developed by Epston (1993) and Tomm (1989) to increase empathy, reduce polarizations, and help people see things from multiple perspectives. In internalized-other interviewing, the therapist asks the client to put him- or herself in the shoes of the significant other and allow the client to be interviewed as if he or she were the other person. In internalized-other interviewing, clients answer questions about the subjective experience of other members of the family being interviewed through the client. This brings awareness to the client of the feelings and needs of the other person, and, therefore, increases the client's empathy for the other person (Ziegler & Hiller, 2001). It can be helpful for clients who are struggling with their in-laws, coworkers, superiors, or subordinates, or with the mate selection of their children in terms of their or the other's ethnicity. One of us (Sara) used this technique with Jan, who attributed her difficulties with her mother-in-law, Ellen, to Ellen's ethnic background. According to Jan, Ellen's ethnicity was the reason they did not get along, why she raised her son (Jan's husband) the way she did, and why she was not a good grandmother to Jan's and her husband's baby. Sara asked Jan to answer questions as if she were Ellen and asked: "Speaking as Ellen, what do you attribute your struggles with Jan to? When was the first time you noticed a difference in the way Jan talked to you? What kind of relationship would you like to have with your grandson? What stops you from having this relationship with your grandson? What do you suppose Jan thinks of you? What would be the first thing you would notice in Jan that would give you a clue that the relationship with her will change? What do you think Jan will notice about you, Ellen, that will give Jan the clue that things are going to be different and better?" At the end of the dialogue, Jan was surprised by her increased level of empathy toward Ellen, her mother-in-law.

Similar techniques are circular questions, reflexive questions, relationship questions, outside perspective questions, and role reversal questions (Tomm, 1988; Ziegler & Hiller, 2001), which can help clients become actively reflective about a particular experience, event, or course of action from a variety of perspectives. Because one of the most valuable tools a clinician has is the art of questioning to elicit self-generating solutions, the reader is invited to explore the wide availability of experience-generating questions that can move clients toward other preferred realities and ways of relating to significant people in their lives (Freedman & Combs, 1995).

COUNTERTRANSFERENCE

When clients present with strong ethnic affiliations, countertransference reactions may depend on whether the clinician is of the same or a different ethnicity than that of the client and how much information about or exposure to the ethnicity of the client the clinician has. Therapists must be aware of their own cultural, religious, or ethnic countertransference (Crohn, 1998).

Similar Ethnicity

If the counselor's ethnicity is similar to that of the client, there is a danger that the clinician will overidentify with the client and miss intragroup differences (Comas-Diaz & Jacobsen, 1991). Sara was supervising an intern who completely missed assessing a severe alcohol abuse issue in one of her clients because she and the client were both Jewish. The stereotype of the Jewish female client is that substance abuse may be less of a problem than it would be if the client were a man or of another ethnic group (Ashemberg Straussner, 2001). Because this coincided with the circumstances of the lack of substance abuse in the intern's family, it did not occur to her that this client might be presenting with an alcohol-related problem. The attractiveness of having a client to whom the counselor can attribute similar backgrounds can mask the ability of the clinician to make accurate assessments, seduced by the idea that the clinician and the client have so much in common. The seduction of the apparent knowledge of the ethnic background of the client is no small advantage. Clients, too, feel more attracted to clinicians with whom they think they have more in common. Another possible countertransference reaction of similar background in the counselor–client dyad is annoyance, disappointment, or impatience if the client is not advancing in the way the clinician thinks the client ought to be progressing. This is quite common when the therapist is of the same ethnic background but of a different social class than the client (Comas-Diaz & Jacobsen, 1991). Having become more educated and more assertive, or having been able to overcome poverty, the therapist may have the expectation that the clients can do it too and overlook the clients' differing expectations of themselves, different contexts, or different personalities. Sara noticed that as a Latina and immigrant therapist, the clients with whom she has the strongest countertransference reactions are, paradoxically, those who have very similar backgrounds in terms of cultural context but not in terms of class. For several years, as a single mother with three children, teaching four classes a semester at a university and taking two classes a semester in a doctoral program, Sara used to write her own papers at night and grade students' papers during soccer games, at the doctor's and dentist's office, and while her kids were getting haircuts. Several years after that, Sara worked with a very depressed Latina single mother who continuously and bitterly complained about how her (only) child interfered with her ability to study for one English as a second language class she was taking. It was not until Sara was able to become aware of her annoyance, impatience, and arrogant thoughts (e.g., "If I could do it, why can't she?") and overcome them that she was able to be more helpful to her client.

Different Ethnicity

If the client–counselor dyad is culturally very different, there can be ambivalent discomfort on the clinician's part (Comas-Diaz & Jacobsen,

1991). On the one hand, the clinician is eager to help and demonstrate that he or she is not racist or discriminatory and tries hard to show this to the client by being overly friendly or accommodating. On the other hand, the clinician may be puzzled by some characteristic of the client that the clinician attributes to the client's ethnicity and tends to view these attributes negatively. Often the clinician fails to inquire about these characteristics for fear of being labeled insensitive, racist, or both by a supervisor, the clinician's peers, or the client. This is not uncommon in client–counselor dyads that correspond to traditional polarizing ethnic pairs—for example, Puerto Rican and Mexican, Irish and Polish, Arab and Israeli—but it is worse when the clinician belongs to the dominant group and the client is a member of a traditionally oppressed ethnic minority, such as between a White therapist and a Hawaiian, Native American, Latino, or Asian client (Gorkin, 1996). The ambivalent discomfort of the clinician may be more prevalent currently than it was in years past because the expectation of political correctness may push the ambivalent discomfort underground.

Another reason the discomfort may exist with dominant-group counselors is because many feel disassociated with their own ethnicity. The original European immigrant settlers shaped basic political and civic life in such a broad way that the White Protestant culture became associated with the ideal by which all subsequent ethnic groups were judged (Giordano & McGoldrick, 1996). When ethnic minorities begin to consider issues of race and ethnicity seriously, many of European descent often express surprise. Lack of acknowledgment, rejection, or denial of the ethnic background is more possible for Whites than for other ethnic groups precisely because they are seen by all groups as the norm in the United States. This is due to several historical and sociopolitical reasons. First, White Americans do not generally perceive themselves as anything other than regular Americans, perhaps in part because they fought the English for the right to be Americans and not English (McGill & Pierce, 1996). Second, to be an American has been initially equated to being White, and although the United States was very diverse from its inception, in general, acculturation meant (and often still means) acquiring White Protestant values and personal characteristics (Giordano & McGoldrick, 1996). Third, having been traditionally the ethnic group with the most dominance in the colonized world, ethnic Whites of different backgrounds have considered themselves to be superior to other peoples viewed as less civilized (Hays, 2001).

As the traditional ethnic group with the privilege and luxuries that power and dominance afford, White Americans have, therefore, been able to deny, reject, or not acknowledge their ethnic affiliation. As a concept, ethnicity is often understood by Whites as something that other ethnic minority people have. It is not often a word a White American would apply to describe him- or herself. This is obviously an illusion shared by minorities and Whites alike. When we teach a multicultural counseling course, the White students tend to be the ones who have the hardest time figuring out how to answer the questions related to their cultural identities. Interestingly, by the end of the course, they may be the ones with the biggest shift. They may realize that the denial of their ethnic affiliation is a luxury and a privilege they have been able to afford since the day they were born, a luxury that individuals in other ethnic groups may not share (McIntosh, 1998).

The lack of awareness of ethnicity is more possible for Whites who have had limited exposure to ethnic minorities during their childhood and adolescence. The invisibility of ethnic minorities for Whites is not uncommon. Contact with ethnic minorities may not have been present in the historical past and in the awareness of most Whites. In spite of continued racial hostility and residentially segregated neighborhoods, for example, racial issues are still not present in the awareness of many Whites, who can continue to be complacent about such important issues (Giordano & McGoldrick, 1996). During the multicultural counseling course, it is not unusual for White students to be the last to acknowledge that racism, bigotry, and discrimination still exist, in part because these are experiences they tend not to have, due to their privileged position in society. Their ethnic identity of Whites might remain weak or irrelevant for most of their lives. It might take a significant event to change that, such as intermarriage, a move to a less homogeneous part of the country, or exposure to workplace or classroom diversity. These events sometimes force White individuals to examine their identity as they confront the issue of difference, sometimes for the first time in their lives. Confronted with difference, they may begin to understand for the first time that the characteristics of their personalities are related to their own White cultural socialization. Clinicians need to be aware of their ambivalent discomfort, if or when it surfaces, as they work with their ethnic minority clients and are encouraged to explore the influence of their ethnicity and ethnic socialization on their own identity development and functioning.

TOOLBOX ACTIVITY—BETSIE			
Resources and Suggested Readings	*Videos*	*Activities*	*Discussion Questions*
Ben-Sasson, H. (1985). *History of the Jewish people.* Cambridge, MA: Harvard University Press. Steinberg, S. (2001). *The ethnic myth: Race, ethnicity and class in America* (3rd ed.). Boston: Beacon Press. Thernstrom, S. (1980). *Harvard encyclopedia of American ethnic groups.* Boston: Belknap Press.	*Monsoon Wedding* *The Namesake* *Bend It Like Beckham* *My Big Fat Greek Wedding* *The Way Home*	Attend a Jewish religious service or a Passover dinner. Visit Latino, Korean, Polish, Vietnamese, Indian, or Mexican neighborhoods. Find out the differences between Orthodox, Reform, Conservative, and nonobservant Jewish individuals. Interview separately individuals from India and Pakistan, Korea and Taiwan, Japan and mainland China, or Poland and Russia and write in your journal about the differences between the two closely related ethnic groups.	Content themes What other themes do you see emerging in the story that the author did not identify? Assessment Are there any questions you would like to ask Betsie? Interventions What other interventions could you propose with Betsie? Countertransference What counter-transference reactions were emerging in yourself as you read this story? Other Scenarios If Betsie were Irish, Italian, Mexican, or Polish, would your reactions to the story be the same or different? If Betsie were a Jewish man, would your reactions to the story be any different?

Maribel's Story 7

When Are You Going to Have Kids?

Ethnicity is associated with nationality and country of origin. Examining ethnicity provides clues about individuals' values, beliefs, and behaviors and often yields more information than race, particularly on intragroup differences. This is critical in working with clients of Asian or Latino descent. Generic information on racial characteristics provides a helpful starting place for clinicians, but specific information about ethnicity adds to the richness of understanding. In this chapter, Maribel, a Puerto Rican, describes growing up in a poor, Spanish-speaking household; moving around the country; and feeling like a minority everywhere she went. She talks about what she feels was her double life, her pride in her educational accomplishments, and the price she paid for her acculturation and her gender role shifts. As you read, notice how she experienced the frequent moves of her family as she was growing up, and how the exposure to racism affected not only her blended identity but also her decision to become better educated to increase her social status options. Also, notice the losses that came with her gains, and how she manages her American identity blended with her identity as a Puerto Rican. Following the story, we explore the relationship between ethnicity and racism, language, social class, gender socialization patterns, and gender role shifts that occur as the identity of the individual shifts. The clinical intervention discusses some ideas for working with ethnic minority couples who are in cultural transition from hierarchical gender roles to more egalitarian modes of relating. Finally, the countertransference section includes a discussion about possible reactions clinicians may have when working with couples who exhibit power imbalances.

Maribel's Story

I am a 30-year-old Latina woman. I was born in Puerto Rico and, beginning at the age of five years, was raised in Chicago. My parents are both Puerto Rican—born and raised in Puerto Rico. I have one brother, Osvaldo, and three sisters, Daniela, Debora, and Magdalena. Daniela and Debora are half sisters from my father's side. They have lived in Puerto Rico all their life, not once having visited the United States. Osvaldo and Magdalena both live in Chicago, but Osvaldo was born in Puerto Rico, and Magdalena was born in Connecticut.

I was raised in a Spanish-speaking household. When I was in the first grade, I was taught English and was then placed in a bilingual class. I learned English so well that I was transferred to English-only classes and afterward was exclusively in English-only classes. I was still able to retain my knowledge of Spanish because I spoke English only at school and Spanish only at home. To this day, I am very grateful that I was taught to appreciate the Spanish language, despite my need to learn English. I am proud to say I am very fluent in Spanish: I can read it, speak it, and write it well. Not many people who come to the United States are able to do so because they are faced with the challenge of learning English, abandon the Spanish language, and therefore forget it.

My current religion is Roman Catholic. Many Latinos are Catholic. Growing up, I was faced with the dilemma of being in two religions, depending on which side of the family I was hanging out with. It was very bizarre. My mother's side of the family was Pentecostal, and my father's side of the family was Catholic. I was only five years old when I learned the hard way that when I entered my grandfather's church, which was Pentecostal, I could not do the sign of the crucifix on my forehead. This was very confusing and painful for me to try to understand at such a young age. If I was visiting my father's side of the family, I was Catholic, but if I was visiting my mother's side of the family, I was Pentecostal, even if for that day only. These two religions are complete opposites of one another. As a child, I visited several churches in search of the religion that I felt comfortable with and understood. I visited Baptist, Evangelical, Pentecostal, and various Catholic churches. I even took a course in the sociology of religion at a university to further understand the different types of religions available. I must say, I thought every religion had something to offer that was of interest to me. I enjoyed reading about them and wish there was a way that I could have all of them in one, but it seems impossible. Hence, I have remained Catholic and visit church every once in a while.

My family migrated to the United States when I was five years old. We have lived in the United States ever since. We live in Chicago, Illinois, but since leaving Puerto Rico, we have also lived in several other states. When I was six years old, my family and I moved to Hartford, Connecticut. My father was doing auto body work, and my mother was a housewife at the time. When I was 10 years old, my family and I moved to Winnie, Texas. A friend of my father's lived in Texas and offered him a job in auto body work, so we all moved to Texas in search of a better life. I think we only lived there for about two years before returning to Chicago. Later, my mother decided to find employment and became a teacher's aide for a school. She has held this job for about 14 years. It was difficult moving every time my father was offered a better job. We had to adjust to a new state, a new environment, new friends, the loss of family left behind, and new beginnings at another school. My father has worked in auto body work, mechanics, and carpentry almost all his life. My mother has been a factory worker, a waitress, and a teacher's aide.

Growing up, I found that my family and I were different from other families around us. We lived in "barrios," or ghetto neighborhoods. I grew up very poor and a minority. It seemed that, even though we lived in neighborhoods where other minorities lived, we had to go to institutions, such as school, where there weren't too many minorities. I recall living in Texas and attending grammar school, where I was the only Puerto Rican girl. People used to stare at me and say things like, "Is that the Puerto Rican girl? I have never seen one before." I was made fun of in school, and riding the school bus to go to my trailer home was a nightmare. I was picked on because of my race, and I felt like a complete outsider—lonely, uncomfortable, and embarrassed—for being so different and not understanding what it meant. Living in Chicago was quite a different story. I grew up mostly in ghetto neighborhoods and still in the lower class. I did not feel as much as an outsider as I did in Texas because there were other Latinos around me, in my neighborhoods and in school. I was not made fun of because of my race or because I spoke Spanish.

As I continued going to school, I saw that there were opportunities available for my personal growth that mostly came about through education. I participated in school events in grammar school, such as the flag squad and band, so I could belong to groups in which there were people like me—Latino and poor—and feel like I belonged. Later, in high school, I also felt the need to become a part of different groups. I attended Washington High School my freshman year even though I wanted to attend Smith Tech High School. I was not allowed entrance into Smith because of my entrance exam grades. As a sophomore, I was able to transfer to Smith Tech High School after being ranked second in the entire freshman class at Washington High. At Washington, I was a member of the Reserve Officers' Training Corps (ROTC) and was the top cadet. I was very happy because I felt that I was somehow better than what I had been without this rank. All my life I had felt that I wasn't good enough because of my race, my cultural background, my being different. Having rank in ROTC made me feel that it was okay to be different, that I could still be accepted. I also joined the marching band at Washington, where I was a flute player. When I transferred to Smith, I transferred from ROTC to gym class but remained in the marching band. At that time, the Smith Tech Marching Band was quite an important group. This made me feel so good, like I was part of something special. I was very pleased to graduate from such a prestigious high school as a music major. Graduating from Smith Tech High School made me feel that I was not only intelligent but also able to succeed, regardless of my race or cultural background.

In my college years, I attended several schools, colleges, and universities. In each one of these, I found more variety of cultural groups and more people like me, Latinos, attending and making something out of their lives. I realized that there are many minorities, Latinos as well as other minorities, who have struggled throughout their lives with being different from the majority group and with what we call culture shock. We minorities spend so much time trying to acculturate that we miss our culture, and being the way our culture indicates we are when we are in that place of origin. For example, I am Puerto Rican and feel that I am Puerto Rican at all times. However, I cannot dress for work or school the way I would if I were working or going to work or school in Puerto Rico. For one thing, the climate is different, and also I would attract too much attention and would hence feel again how different I am from the majority group. Many times, I miss dressing up in "my clothes" and acting the way I would if I were in Puerto Rico. In this way, I feel like I'm living a double life.

When I graduated as a medical assistant from business school in 1993, I was so proud of myself. I remember so many great things about my graduation, but most of all I recall going on stage to give my valedictorian speech and having a crowd of people, whom I did not know, scream, "Yea! It's a Puerto Rican." I was surprised because I did not know the people in the crowd, and they did not know me, but they were proud that I was representing Puerto Ricans everywhere and that I had succeeded in having a 4.0 GPA.

Perhaps, the most I was ever involved in a cultural group was when I went back to live in Connecticut. I moved to Storrs, Connecticut, and attended the University of Connecticut for a couple of years. I became a psychology major and learned about the differences in other cultural groups and about the different people who attended the university with me. I was pleased to find that there were other Latinos becoming educated and advancing their careers by obtaining their bachelor's degrees. I joined the Puerto Rican and Latina American Cultural Center (PRLACC) and became very involved with university activities, which promoted the advancement of Latinos. As a group, we were very strong in our beliefs, in our desire to continue improving our lives, and in helping others realize that it is possible for us as minorities to have better lives through education and motivation.

In my family, I am a great role model for those who are still going to school. My mother's side of the family is just as different as my father's side of the family regarding educational background—as different as they are in religious background. Almost all the members of my mother's side of the family dropped out of high school, got married, had children, and either lived as housewives or worked in factories or performed other unskilled jobs. My father's side of the family is filled with educated individuals who almost all have careers and have continued their education to the master's and doctorate levels. I say that I have come to be like my father's side of the family.

Growing up was difficult for me, not only in terms of my cultural background but also in terms of the problems within my household. I grew up in a family where my mother was oppressed as a woman and practically a slave to my father's needs. My father has been an alcoholic most of his life, and this was difficult for me as well. I saw that part of my cultural background consisted of the woman of the house being a slave to her man, and the man of the house being the boss. I did not agree with this and saw that it was very common to the other Latino families around me, whether they were just friends of the family or my family members. I did not understand why it had to be this way and why the women put up with all the things their men would do, such as physically and emotionally abuse them and cheat on them and then come home and expect to be treated like kings of the world. I vowed to not let this become my life, and I have kept my promise to myself to become strong and better so that I do not end up like my mother and other Latina women.

I am currently divorced and have been so since January of this year. I believe that my divorce came about partly because of my cultural background and my experiences in my family as I was growing up. I do not see myself as the typical Puerto Rican woman. I am educated and intelligent, and I take advantage of opportunities to become a better person, more educated and experienced. When I was married, my husband tried to treat me the way my father treated my mother, and that was not the life I was going to live. My ex-husband was not educated in the same manner that I am. He is an intelligent young man in different fields, such as in mechanics; he was a real estate agent and is currently a mortgage loan officer at a bank. However, when we were together, my ex-husband thought that he could be my boss and that I would do as he said. He soon found out that this thinking was a mistake. Another issue that came about in my marriage was my education. I decided to continue my studies to obtain my bachelor's degree after I got married. When I notified my husband of my decision to pursue a degree, his exact words were, "When you married me, you stopped being a student." I was angry when he said this to me and hurt that the man I had chosen to accept as my husband was not supportive of my desire to continue my education. I saw that he was going to be an obstacle in my path. This made me want to continue my education even more, and I did just that. I registered for school and attended classes against his will, which created tension in our marriage for some time. With time, he tried to convince me that he was supportive of my education, but I saw that it was not true. He attended my graduation where I received my bachelor's degree, and he gave me a very hard time when I wanted to stay and take pictures with my friends before leaving campus. He thought I should graduate and leave, and that was the end of that, whether I liked it or not. I was extremely hurt and felt that it had all been an act. I ended up leaving the university without seeing any of my friends or taking any pictures with them. I lost contact with many of them, and I can't forgive him or myself for allowing him to do that to me. I recall one of his friends telling me that my ex-husband thought I was more intelligent than he was, and I honestly believe that my education was a threat to him.

In my marriage, I had several issues that brought conflict to the marriage, but I would say that family was one of them as well. I am very family-oriented, and my ex-husband, even though he is Puerto Rican also, was not family-oriented at all. He became very angry and hostile anytime I wanted to spend time with my family. I found myself in the middle, as if I had to choose between my family and my husband. This was extremely stressful, and I believe unnecessary, but it was a very big part of my life. It got to the point that my family stopped visiting because my ex-husband became very hostile when they visited me. My entire life had been about family, and there was no way I was going to let a man separate me from my family.

I believe that in the Latino culture, men believe they are the bosses and that their women and their children are to obey them. I had conflict in my marriage because I did not let my husband be my boss and because of his beliefs in raising children. In my attempt to become a mother, I lost three pregnancies, either to miscarriage or to ectopic pregnancy. These experiences were very painful for me and for my husband at that time. Later, I found out that the only way I can achieve a full-term pregnancy is through in vitro fertilization. This was difficult news for me as a woman and also as a Latina because, to me, Latinas are viewed as fertile and ready to have many kids, but I was the contrary of this stereotype. Another thing that made it difficult was my family's expectations that I would have children. I am the only woman in the family who doesn't have children, and they are very persistent that I have some, even now that I am divorced. It is almost as if I am making them look bad. It sounds crazy, but every time they see me they ask me, "When are you going to have kids?"

My ex-husband wanted children, but while married I found out that I did not like the way he treated his little nephews, and this created problems in our decision to go through the in vitro fertilization. My ex-husband thinks that children need to be raised with threats to prevent them from misbehaving, and I do not agree with this. I was raised without ever being spanked, and I think I turned out just fine. One thing I can say: I am glad I divorced my husband because we definitely kept growing apart, and my experiences as a child growing up in the type of family I have made me attentive to people being treated as people and not being oppressed because of their sex, race, or ethnicity. I later found out that he had a girlfriend, which is when I decided I wanted a divorce. Latin men have a bad reputation for being womanizers, and I definitely was not going to accept him after this. Again, my husband came to find out that I was not the typical Puerto Rican woman who was going to let her man oppress her while he hung out at bars with his friends and kept girlfriends on the side. After all is said and done, I am glad I continued my education because it is just as I said before: a man will come and go, but I will have my education with me forever, and I can do a lot with that, even if I am by myself.

I am now continuing my education to obtain my master's degree. Even though I am still a minority, I see that my education has done so much for me and always will by giving me opportunities to succeed. I may still be a minority and a woman, but I am a better minority and am very proud of my culture, no longer concerned about my differences being criticized or made fun of. I now laugh because I have found happiness within myself, in my culture, in my not being one of the majority group. Growing up poor and allowing my education to give me better opportunities in employment has allowed me to become what I consider middle class. I don't expect to ever become a member of the upper class, but if I were ever to live again in poverty, I know that I would survive, just as I did when I was a child. Changing socioeconomic status has showed me that I can survive in the worst environments if I have to become part of them again. I owe my rise to the middle class to my education and the opportunities it gave me. I am thankful to my parents, mi familia, for bringing me to the United States as a child and giving me the opportunity to live a better life than they did. If I ever find the perfect man for me, one who will respect me as a woman and an individual and who is not threatened by my education and my ability to think for myself and stand up for myself, then I will take the opportunity to have children, whether it be through in vitro fertilization or adoption, so that I can teach my children that they too can become somebody in a society where we are just another minority. I will teach them to respect others' differences and take advantage of opportunities to be as successful as those of the majority group so that they too can have a better life than the one I have.

Content Themes

The main themes in Maribel's story are how she manages the blending of her Puerto Rican identity with her American identity, her increasing awareness of the gender role shifts, and her pride in her identity as a Puerto Rican woman.

ETHNICITY, IMMIGRATION, SOCIAL CLASS, AND RACISM

Maribel's story reflects the relationships among ethnicity, immigration, social class, and racism as she describes the struggles of her family, who came to the United States to escape poverty. Once in the United States, the family had to move frequently in pursuit of better economic opportunities. According to statistical data, Puerto Ricans still hold the status of being the poorest among the Latino groups (U.S. Bureau of the Census, 2000). These statistics can be misleading because, although this fact may be true for residents of New York City—where so many Puerto Ricans live and where the concentration of urban poverty may be higher than in other parts of the country—data show that when Puerto Ricans move to other areas of the country, they fare better economically than other Latinos in those areas. In Texas, for example, Puerto Ricans' rates of high school and college graduation and income are higher than those of other Latinos (Garcia-Prieto, 1996). Other cross-national immigration studies show similar results, implying that a minority group's success or lack of success in a new cultural environment is relative to its relationship with the dominant group, rather than to intrinsic characteristics of the minority group (Green, 1998). Maribel's family moved to Texas, where her father found employment as a mechanic. In times of stress, Puerto Rican families may turn to their extended families for help (Garcia-Prieto, 1996), and this is true of many other ethnic groups whose members help each other in times of crisis. Family members who are in more stable positions usually feel obligated to help, often putting allegiance to the distressed extended family members above the needs of their own nuclear families. This may baffle some people in more individualistic or competitive family structures, whose members would never think of asking relatives for help in times of distress. Maribel's father moved to Texas because his brother had a successful business there and invited him to move. But in Texas, Maribel describes being singled out as a Puerto Rican, and she reports being made fun of in school and feeling lonely, uncomfortable, and embarrassed. This is consistent with the experiences of many Latinos in the United States. Dominant group attitudes toward Hispanics may display racist overtones, especially toward those with darker skin and less money or education. Maribel reflects that in her story.

ETHNICITY AND LANGUAGE

Immigrants of various ethnic backgrounds often encourage their children to continue speaking the language of origin, in part because there is a newly recognized need to preserve the cultural heritage, particularly the heritage of oppressed minorities. Children of immigrants whose ethnic identity is plagued by issues of discrimination, stereotyping, or other forms of oppression may resist the parental insistence on preservation of cultural and language heritage. Some may, in contrast, express a strong desire to continue their ties with their ethnic identity and their language as a way to express pride, solidarity, and loyalty to the cultural background. Clearly, Maribel not only retained her Spanish language oral proficiency, but also can read and write in Spanish. The extent to which a language is preserved or lost in the second-generation ethnic minority depends on several variables. Maribel speaks with pride about the preservation of her language abilities and is proud of her written and oral proficiency in Spanish. The racial, ethnic, and socioeconomic heterogeneity of the Latino population in the United States is well documented (Falicov, 1998a; Gonzalez, 1997; Mezzich, Ruiz, & Muñoz, 1999). However, the percentage of Latinos living below or just above the poverty line is significantly higher than the percentage of Whites living below or just above the poverty line (U.S. Bureau of the Census, 2000). For a large percentage of Latinos in the United States, loss of cultural roots, ethnic discrimination, language barriers, and difficulties with acculturation are common occurrences (Falicov, 1998a). It is not surprising that someone like Maribel, a person exposed to discrimination and poverty while growing up, and who has strived to achieve social mobility and financial independence, shows interest in continuing her ties with her Puerto Rican cultural background through the preservation and betterment of her Spanish language literacy.

THE DOUBLE LIFE OF A HYBRID IDENTITY

Even though Maribel has preserved her Spanish language, she exhibits hybridization and alternation between two cultures as she negotiates her identity as both an American and a Puerto Rican (Falicov, 1998a). Maribel says she leads a double life because she cannot dress and act in the United States as she would in Puerto Rico. To live in the United States, she feels that she has to act and dress in a certain American way, even though she feels strongly like a Puerto Rican. This can be a confusing and challenging task. As Maribel's story illustrates, her differing identities do not need to be mutually exclusive or progress in a linear or one-dimensional way. As is true with many second-generation immigrants who attempt to reconcile their various allegiances and ethnic identities, changes in Maribel's representation of self can vary over time, across settings, and within relationships. Because she identifies solidly with both the Puerto Rican and the American groups and settings, she appears to be able to simultaneously hold and merge the two worlds at times. At other times, she might experience a shift in identity from foreground to background (Hays, 2001), depending on the context. It would not be surprising if she were to experience herself as primarily American in her occupational or educational settings and primarily Puerto Rican in her family context. She may alternate or combine the uses of her language, for example, Spanish at home and English at work, or Spanish to count and sing and English to discuss schoolwork. She is also choosing what she judges to be the best from the Puerto Rican culture, what she wants to preserve, and choosing what she would like to discard. This hybridization of ethnic identity is not without its challenges (Falicov, 1998a) because, as bicultural individuals navigate life and relationships, they may be accused of being disloyal by other individuals in the same family, they may have trouble convincing others of the benefits of hybridization or biculturality, or they may be confused about the meanings of their own bicultural status. One of the challenges of alternating identities comes from the individual's simultaneous view of him or herself as an American and a Puerto Rican.

GENDER ROLE SHIFTS

Another main theme that emerges in this story is the shifting of the gender roles, from traditional or polarized gender roles to more egalitarian or balanced gender role definitions (Breunlin, Schwartz, & Mac Kune-Karrer, 1997). The struggles that result from the shift in the gender roles take place often between the men and women of a family. Usually, the movement toward gender equity comes as a result of discomforts first identified by the women in the family—the wives or the daughters—which may in turn bring discomfort to the men—the fathers or husbands—who may, as a result, resort to increased control and intimidation tactics to maintain the status quo. This is clear in Maribel's case. In authoritarian and collectivistic cultures, differing standards for men and women exist, giving men the responsibility for the welfare and honor of the family, with its concomitant privilege, and assigning women spiritual superiority, self-sacrifice, and a more passive and oppressed role (Comas-Diaz, 1987; Falicov, 1998a). Marriages can be more about the preservation of the family than about the relationship between the members of the couple, and divorce is a worse outcome than staying in an unhappy relationship. In some hierarchical societies, the status of the women may change over time, as women become older mothers, grandmothers, and mothers-in-law themselves (Ingoldsby, 1995). In Maribel's case, she does not see herself as a typical Puerto Rican woman who caters to men's needs. She struggles with the role models of other Latina women, women she sees as slaves of the men in their lives. She promised herself that she would not be like that but instead would become independent and educated. She does not describe personal intergenerational struggles with her father, as other second-generation immigrants do, but is critical of her mother's adherence to traditional gender roles. She did not agree with this role for women and vowed not to end up like her mother. Maribel feels that her view of her gender role and the shifts she elicited for herself precipitated her divorce. She describes a husband who became increasingly polarized as Maribel's gender awareness became strengthened by her exposure to education and the more egalitarian American cultural milieu. These gender role shifts generally come at a considerable cost for the family. The more freedom and equality the female member of the spousal team aspires to, the more the male may cling to his old patterns and may have more difficulty giving them up, solidifying conflicts in the couple. Maribel may shift in gender role expectations in terms of wanting a more egalitarian relationship and separating herself from what she perceives to be her mother's traditional gender roles, while at the same time expressing a wish to fulfill her own family's gender expectations of her as a mother, as she struggles with the loss of her pregnancies and her spousal relationship.

Clinical Applications

This section describes assessment questions that may be relevant for clients like Maribel. The techniques and interventions focus on gender and class differences in help-seeking behavior, couples therapy for ethnic minority couples, the engagement of the Latino male in therapy, and ideas to avoid clinical pitfalls.

ASSESSMENT

It is important to assess the identity issues of the client whose ethnicity, social class, and educational and family background differ from that of the White ethnic middle-class majority culture. Is the client resorting to rejection, to acceptance, or to a blend of both cultures? It is also important to assess the relationships among ethnicity, immigration, social class, education, and racism in the client's life, and the extent of the gender shifts and the gains or losses that come with it.

Ethnicity, Immigration, Social Class, and Racism

Were or are there any experiences with marginalization, oppression, discrimination, or racism related to the client's ethnicity, social class, or immigration status?

Have there been drastic gender or social class shifts between the client and his or her family of origin or members of his or her extended family?

Have there been shifts in educational attainments between the client and the family of origin?

If there were shifts, how have they affected the client's relationship with members of the family of origin or the extended family?

Hybrid Identity

Has the client accepted, rejected, or blended identities?

Can the client identify what she or he has accepted, rejected, or blended?
Does the client alternate behaviors in different contexts?

If the client feels or acts differently in different contexts, how easy or hard is that? What is the reaction of the significant people in the client's life to the shifts?

Gender Role Shifts

Were there any shifts in gender roles?

How and by whom were the shifts initiated?

What effect did the shift or lack of shift have on the individual or family?

How were the conflicts around gender shifts handled by the client's parents and spouse?

What were the gains or losses associated with the gender role shifts?

TECHNIQUES AND INTERVENTIONS

When traditional gender roles begin to shift, as in the case of Maribel with her former husband, conflicts in the couple may increase (Breunlin, Schwartz, & Mac Kune-Karrer, 1997). With ethnic minority couples, it is not unusual for women to be the ones requesting therapeutic help.

Because a Latina woman may see herself in the role of having to be the one to hold the family together, she may think of herself as a failure if she is not successful (Falicov, 1998a). Her willingness to seek therapeutic help may be in sync with her cultural prescriptions. Female cultural prescriptions and therapy share similar characteristics because talking to a stranger about matters of intimate concern is considered to be the cornerstone of therapy. But it can also be seen as a typical female characteristic (McCarthy & Holliday, 2004). Some men, particularly traditional men in patriarchal or hierarchical family structures, might consider talking to a stranger about intimate family matters as signs of weakness, vulnerability, potential incompetence, and lack of control (McCarthy & Holliday, 2004). It is not unusual for men to come to one therapy session and drop out or refuse to accompany the woman to therapy if the therapist reacts negatively to dropping out by mistakenly accusing him, overtly or covertly, of being resistant to change. There are gender-related issues in help-seeking behavior, particularly with respect to individuals who are embedded in traditional, patriarchal, or hierarchical family structures, and applying traditionally female expectations of therapeutic behavior to men may not be conducive to successful therapeutic outcomes. Many men view therapy as something to be avoided rather than a supportive process (McCarthy & Holliday, 2004) when they are faced with a therapist who makes them feel more embarrassed and less competent than they were before therapy started. It may be more effective to change the way therapy is offered than to criticize men for not wanting to use it as a means of getting help with their couple problems.

This is not a question of matching client–therapist dyads by gender; there are risks involved either way. Both men and women therapists can be guilty of the same therapeutic mistakes. It may help to point out men's strengths rather than deficits and to use a collaborative stance in which men are viewed as having important opinions about the issues facing the couple. The previous comments are not intended to negate or minimize in any way the power imbalances that often exist in couples' relationships or the important role that power imbalances play in those relationships. The ideas that women in traditional marriages need to be empowered (Vazquez-Nuttall, Romero-Garcia, & De Leon, 1987), or that men's position in society has given them privileges not afforded to women (Comas-Diaz, 1987), or that it is important to understand the implications of a patriarchal culture for the mental health of both women and men (Walters, Carter, Papp, & Silverstein, 1991) are not new. But to be able to have a therapeutic conversation about the effect of the distribution of power in a relationship, there needs to be a strong therapeutic alliance first. Often, couples in traditional marriages do not arrive at that point therapeutically and drop out of therapy early because the therapists may be overtly or covertly critical of the men in therapy or may understand the couple as not moving quickly enough in the direction of more equality and, therefore, may pressure their clients to move faster than they may be prepared to move at that time.

Prolonged and regular therapy may not be the staple of couples therapy with couples of ethnic and social class backgrounds other than White middle class (Falicov, 1998a). Couples may seek help as a result of a crisis, and therapists may have a small window of opportunity to prove to both members of the couple that therapy can be helpful for their problem of differing degrees of acculturation. If the couple becomes a customer (De Shazer, 1988) of therapy, it may be possible to move to other issues pertaining to the power imbalances and lack of equality in the relationship. Some couples may never reach the point of working toward gender equality. Therapists can expect ethnic minority couples to come intermittently, perhaps at the time of a crisis, rather than continuously. If the couple views the therapist as helpful for the problems they face as a family, they may be more inclined to return for more sessions when another crisis arises. The effectiveness of the therapeutic encounter is much more related to the strength of the alliance, which includes the match between client and therapist goals, than to the length of the treatment. Couples can make a lot of progress in one or two sessions (Falicov, 1998a), if they are seen by a therapist who does not judge them for not returning for more and whom the couple sees as helpful in solving their problems.

There are several interventions clinicians may implement in the beginning stages of the therapeutic process that have been successful with couples of varying ethnic and social class backgrounds.

Invite Husband to Therapy

Therapists can phone the husband and invite him to come for a session or two, appealing to his sense of duty and dedication to the family. Alternatively, therapists can appeal to a husband's "expert" knowledge about the nature and motivation of his wife's problems with him and the need to get his advice on how to best understand his wife. This is not a trick intervention; it genuinely implies that the husband may know about the problem at least as much as the wife does and may have an idea of how to solve it.

See Members of the Couple Individually

Therapists can offer to see each member of the couple individually and talk to each separately about how to understand the other member. In hierarchical societies, where direct communication between the members of the couple may be less common or not encouraged (Falicov, 1998b), talking indirectly through the therapist may offer the best option in the beginning. Also, couples seen together may be embarrassed or act as if they need to save face in front of the therapist or each other. Individual members of the couple may be more amenable to individual sessions than to couples sessions. As with family therapy, couples therapy is not about how many people are in the room. Clinicians can provide couples therapy even if only one member attends the session (Weiner-Davis, 1993).

Hypothesize Something Different

When clients present their stories and their dilemmas, therapists may have certain ideas in their minds about the meaning of those stories. Those meanings generate a hypothesis, which in turn generates the questions that follow the hypothesis (Tomm, 1989). The questions that therapists ask are more related to their own hypothesis-making process than to the presenting problems of the client. Therapists can force themselves to imagine a different or contrasting hypothesis, rather than the one they hold in the early stages of the therapeutic relationship, thus generating varied questions.

COUNTERTRANSFERENCE

Reactions to Power Imbalances

When faced with a perceived imbalance of power in a couple, therapists may feel pressured to make the relationship more balanced and less unequal. This can include wishing that women were less submissive, more direct, and more assertive, or wishing that men exerted less control. A man may contend that his wife is no longer acting in the way that she used to act in terms of her submissiveness and give examples of his wife's unwillingness to comply with socially prescribed expectations for her gender. The therapist's understanding of this complaint, his or her clinical effectiveness with this issue, and the couple's decision to stay or drop out of therapy depend largely on how the therapist views this problem. A number of possible views come to mind. First, the therapist may view the problem as one of differing cultural and gender transitions and shifts. In this case, the therapist might question the husband about when he first became aware that his wife was changing and what needs he has that are not being met because of the wife's change. Second, the therapist may react with curiosity and as a result try to find out how the husband is affected by the wife's change and what changes he foresees himself making in the future as a result of his wife's change. Third, the therapist who views the husband's complaint as an expression of his need for control and continued oppression of the wife may ask a question that implies a criticism of the male client's position with respect to his wife. Fourth, a clinician may be interested in how the wife puts up with such a difficult husband and ask a question that implies a criticism of her. Because questions imply presuppositions and are prescriptive (Tomm, 1988), what the clinician is curious about and ends up asking, based on the countertransference reactions, has profound effects on the outcome of the counseling process. A therapist may encounter a couple whose problem is presented in the way that Maribel described the difficulties with her former husband: that he did not support her educational goals and felt threatened by them and that he tried to sever her ties with her family. By using the interventions outlined previously, therapists can avoid the countertransference trap of supporting the wife against the husband, of blaming the couple's problems on the *machista* (male chauvinist) attitudes of the husband, and of prematurely expecting the wife to increase her assertiveness and reclaim her equal rights in the decision-making process. Because the clinician's countertransference reactions drive the questions asked or not asked, this may precipitate separation or divorce, put women at risk of increased violence, and require women to make drastic changes prematurely without the adequate social support needed to implement them (Falicov, 1998a). The issue is not whether clinicians are right or wrong about what they think clients ought to do or not do but, rather, whether their therapeutic conversations facilitate or block future changes (Breunlin, Schwartz, & Mac Kune-Karrer, 1997).

TOOLBOX ACTIVITY—MARIBEL			
Resources and Suggested Readings	*Videos*	*Activities*	*Discussion Questions*
Alvarez, J. (1992). *How the Garcia girls lost their accent.* New York: Plume Books. Cisneros, S. (1991). *The house on Mango Street.* New York: Vintage Books. Gutierrez, D. (1995). *Walls and mirrors: Mexican Americans, Mexican immigrants, and the politics of ethnicity.* Berkeley: University of California Press. Waters, M. (1990). *Ethnic options: Choosing ethnic identities in America.* Berkeley: University of California Press.	*Mi Familia* *Real Women Have Curves* *Double Happiness* *The Joy Luck Club*	Interview a second-generation Mexican, a Puerto Rican, and a Central American Latino and ask them the following question: What is it like to be a Mexican, a Puerto Rican, or a Central American Latino in the United States? In your journal, write how the answers might affect the way you work with Latino clients of different ethnic affiliations. Find the dictionary definition of race and ethnicity. Then, ask people of different race and ethnic backgrounds for their definitions. What conclusions can you draw?	Content Themes What other themes do you see emerging in the story that the author did not identify? Assessment Are there any questions you would like to ask Maribel? Interventions What other interventions could you propose with Maribel? Countertransference What countertransference reactions were emerging in yourself as you read this story? Other Scenarios What if Maribel hadn't divorced her husband? How would Maribel's life be different if she had not gone to graduate school?

Section III

Dimensions of Immigration and Acculturation

"Partir c'est mourir un peu, C'est mourir à ce qu'on aime; on laisse un peu de soi-même en toute heure et dans tout lieu."

To go away is to die a little, It is to die to what we love; You leave behind a part of yourself in every corner and at every hour.

—Edmond Haraucourt (n.d.)

Historical Dimensions

THE BEGINNINGS

The history of the United States is also the history of its immigration. In earlier generations, the United States was built on the basis of European immigrants. Before the September 11, 2001, attacks, more than one million mostly legal immigrants arrived annually in the United States, and since the 1960s, the majority have come from Asia and Latin America.

One way to tell the story of American immigration is to emphasize how the immigrants contributed to the success of the United States as a country

149

with one of the highest standards of living in the world. This is the traditional way of telling the story of immigration, to say that what immigrants have done for America and what America has done for its immigrants is one of the success stories of world history (Kennedy, 1964). From this point of view, each new wave helped to meet the needs of American development and made its distinctive contribution to the American character and the country as a whole. But this way of telling the story leaves out important aspects of the history of immigration, including the ethnic struggles, the challenges of nativists and other anti-immigrant expressions, controversies regarding who was and was not considered American, and who was and was not considered an immigrant, among others.

The early diversity of immigrants' religious beliefs has resulted in religious tolerance. In demanding freedom for itself, each religious group had to permit the freedom of others who came after. That each successive wave of immigrants insisted upon its right to practice its religion explains in part why freedom of worship is a central aspect of the American creed. The continued current diversity in this country results in more religious pluralism than in most areas of the world. The United States has always been a refuge from tyrannical political regimes, because for many generations it held out to the world the promise of respect for the rights of human beings. Every time a revolution failed in Europe, families gathered their belongings and set out across the sea, seeking sanctuary in the United States. Immigrants who came for economic reasons contributed to the strength of the new country. Those who came from countries with political and economic institutions brought with them faith in those institutions and experience in making them work. They also brought technical and managerial skills that contributed to economic growth, helping give America its extraordinary social mobility, which is the essence of an open society (Kennedy, 1964).

The United States has been racially, ethnically, and religiously diverse since its inception. An often forgotten fact is that the Spanish had been in what is now the United States since before the first British colonies. Spanish explorers were not only the first Europeans to cross much of America, but were also the founders of the first successful colony. St. Augustine in northern Florida was founded in 1565, 42 years before Jamestown and 55 years before Plymouth Rock (Daniels, 2002).

Before the American Revolution, the English were the majority of the first settlers, and they gave the country the basic foundations of its institutions, including the form of government, common law, language, and the tradition of freedom of religious worship. During the colonial period, people of varied backgrounds were welcome, i.e., indentured servants, profit-seeking aristocrats from England, farmers, discharged soldiers, scholars, and intellectuals, regardless of their origin or birth, so long as they could contribute to the building of the country (Kennedy, 1964). During the 17th and 18th centuries, the Irish, the Germans, Scots, French, and

Swedes followed the British. By the end of the 19th century, a significant change had taken place; people from other European countries (Italians, Russians, Poles, Czechs, Hungarians, Rumanians, Bulgarians, Austrians, and Greeks) had begun to arrive in great numbers. This was due, in part, to advances in railroad technology that allowed mass movements of people who were farther away from the coastal areas (Daniels, 1997).

One way to explain the success of the United States as a country is to invoke the entrepreneurial characteristics of those who came to the New World. In the communities they left, immigrants usually had a fixed place, carrying on a father's craft, or farming a father's land. Only with the most exceptional talent and enterprise could those early immigrants break out of the mold. There was not such mold for them in the New World. Once broken with the past except for sentimental ties and cultural inheritance, immigrants had to rely on their own abilities (Kennedy, 1964). Except for the African slaves and the Native Americans, immigrants could go any-where and do anything their talents permitted. A sprawling continent lay before them, and they had only to weld it together by canals, railroads, and roads. If the immigrants had failed to achieve the dream for themselves, they could still retain it for their children (Kennedy, 1964). It is generally accepted that this is the foundation of American inventiveness and inge-nuity, of the multiplicity of new enterprises, and of the success in achiev-ing the highest standard of living anywhere in the world. These were the major forces that triggered this massive migration.

There are at least two other aspects to this story that are seldom dis-cussed in literature regarding immigration. One is the history of the invol-untary transfer of Blacks from West Africa to American soil (Daniels, 2002) that spanned four centuries, and the other is the story of continued struggles over ethnicity and race related to immigration (Daniels, 1997; Takaki, 1993).

AFRICAN AMERICAN MIGRATION

For varied reasons, African Americans are seldom named in the history of mass migration to the United States. One reason for that omission is that it was a forced migration and not a voluntary one; other reasons also exist, including a reluctance to use the term "migration" when referring to the slave trade. The history of the struggles to uphold a White majority in power and exclude a colored minority from coming to the United States, or gaining power, contradicts the mythology of the melting pot. By the end of the 18th century, the character of what was to become the United States was well established. The United States would be English and Protestant (Blumenfeld, 2006; Daniels, 2002), regardless of the characteristics of the people who were here. History has viewed American to mean European in ancestry. Toni Morrison has explained that in the creation of the national identity, American has been defined as White (Morrison as cited in Takaki, 1993). The history of the mass migration from Africa into the United States, and the slave trade associated with it, is beyond the scope of this chapter, but it is important to remember that, except for the indigenous populations, everyone came from somewhere else. Some, like the African Americans, were forced to relocate.

ANTI-IMMIGRANT SENTIMENT

In spite of the fact that wise Americans have always understood the significance, importance, and contributions of immigrants (Kennedy, 1964), nativist or anti-immigrant movements have always existed and have risen periodically in American history. Nativism is the opposition to all or certain group of immigrants and it is not exclusively an American phenomenon. In Germany or Austria, the "others" are usually Turks or Bosnians; in France it is the North Africans; in Canada, the Chinese, and so on. Political nativists existed in the United States almost since its inception, when immigrants from Ireland or France were attacked. The early Irish were the first to be called "savages" by the British (Takaki, 1993, p. 26), and were the first to endure discrimination, later to be inflicted to some degree on each successive wave by already settled "Americans" (Kennedy, 1964). After the Irish, it was the immigrants form Germany and China, or the Catholics and Jews who were the targets of anti-immigrants. Groups who were generally racist and anti-Black tended also to be anti-immigrant. Today, even after the September 11, 2001, terrorist attacks, it is the Spanish-speaking who are usually the targets of nativist ideas (Daniels, 1997) and often, the Muslims (Elliott, 2005).

LEGISLATIVE RESTRICTIONS TO IMMIGRATION

Nativism and xenophobia (the dislike or fear of people from other countries or ethnic backgrounds) had a big impact on immigration legislation starting in the early part of the 20th century. The years between 1890 and 1924 are known in the history of the United States as the age of economic revolution because of the country's transformation from an agrarian to an industrial economy. The United States emerged as world power during this time, when more than 20 million immigrants entered this country, more than in any other period, before or since (Daniels, 1997).

With the expansion of immigration came the end of the era of free and unrestricted entry into the United States. The immigration restriction legislation had begun with the Chinese Exclusion Act of 1882. That was a minor act that was the start of the modern American immigration restriction, and even though it was repealed in 1943, it set the stage for the restrictions to follow. Many Chinese became the first voluntary illegal immigrants in American history.

The National Origins Act of 1924 was the first major restriction on immigrants, and it established a quota system to reduce the arrival of people of "undesirable" ethnic origins (Daniels, 1997, p. 138) and had the effect of increasing the immigration of the British, and reducing that of other ethnic groups, particularly from Southern and Eastern Europe. It also had the effect of reducing the immigration of non-Whites (Cole, 2006). In subsequent legislative measures, poor Mexicans and Jewish refugees, for example, were kept out of the United States by a clause that required immigrants to produce affidavits promising economic support from some person already within the United States in order to gain entry (Daniels, 1997). This made it difficult for most refugees to gain asylum. Even as late as the administration of Franklin D. Roosevelt, most people of Jewish origin encountered severe restrictions to gain admission into the United States as refugees from Nazism before World War II. The internment of 120,000 Japanese Americans during World War II in concentration camps was another example of the effect of the racially motivated quota system. The majority of them were American-born, but they were nonetheless considered "enemy aliens," and they suffered for the actions of Japan. After World War II, the long history of anti-Asian, anti-Jewish, anti-Mexican, and other anti-immigrant legislation was beginning to change. For example, in 1954, naturalization was made color-blind for the first time (Daniels, 1997). But the quota system lingered on until 1965, when Congress repealed it.

Before 1924, immigration was dominated by Europeans, but since the liberal Immigration Act of 1965, which abolished the quota system and made family reunification the keystone of immigration policy, immigrants from Asia and Latin America constitute more than 80 percent of recent immigrants. In 1980, the Refugee Act established the right for asylum for people who were already in the United States, even if illegally, if they fitted the definition of a refugee (Daniels, 2002).

During the 1990s, the number of immigrants who became naturalized American citizens skyrocketed. Several factors caused the rise, including efforts to deny public assistance to noncitizens and the large group of illegal immigrants who became eligible for citizenship through the 1986 amnesty law.

Defenders of the idea of diversity in the so-called "new immigrants" say that putting up roadblocks to citizenship of foreign-born residents is not socially just. Critics say that American identity is threatened by the government's overly accommodating immigration policies (Clark, 1997). Concerns about the number of undocumented immigrants keep the American Congress busy. In the current debate regarding immigration policies, there is a fundamental paradox that is expressed in a simultaneous desire to exclude undocumented immigrants and non-White foreigners from the United States, while continuing to need and enjoy the benefits of their underpaid labor (Cole, 2006).

Current Controversies

The immigrant population is estimated at about 12.5 percent of the total, lower than it was in the 1920s as a percentage of the total population, while the total population of undocumented immigrants is estimated at 11 million, just over 3 percent of the total population (Report: Undocumented immigrant population surges, 2005; Undocumented Immigrants: Facts and figures, 2004). The undocumented immigration surges often coincide with opportunities for employment. The current surge in undocumented immigration is considered to be related to the boom in construction, poultry processing plants, and other industries (Moreno, 2005).

Policymakers wrestle with difficult immigration policy issues, and *ambivalence* may be a good word to describe the current attitude toward immigrants in the United States (Daniels, 2002). There has been a 25-year decline in the admission of documented immigrants, in particular since September 11, 2001, which is attributed in part to new security measures and other new barriers and to a continued debate among policymakers who seek to find answers to difficult questions:

- How many immigrants should the United States admit?
- Should the United States continue the present policy of one general quota, or should future immigration be restricted to specific nations or races?
- On what criteria should these policy decisions be based?
- How should these policy decisions be enforced?

Conflicting and paradoxical attitudes from federal, state, and local governments at different historical times have been the common thread in policies that search for answers to these important questions. Some examples of recent policies follow, which describe paradoxical, ambivalent, and confusing legislative measures.

Since September 11, 2001, immigrants, whether documented or undocumented, have not been allowed state-issued driver's licenses. The need for a federally issued Social Security number has not been waived in many states, and many immigrants, regardless of their immigration status, do not have one. As a result, many immigrants either drive without licenses and without insurance, creating risks to public safety, or do not drive, which presents other, no less challenging problems (Kirkpatrick, 2005; Wald, 2004).

California's Proposition 187 made illegal immigrants ineligible for public social services, public health care, and public education. It was first passed in 1996. By the late 1990s, most of the proposition was deemed unconstitutional (Nieves, 1999).

Undocumented immigrants are not eligible to receive federal funding for tuition. However, in many communities, they are eligible to receive English lessons at local state public schools and other community agencies that do receive state funding (Mead, 2004).

Between 1960 and 1962, the U.S. government supported a clandestine program, Operación Pedro Pan, which brought about 14,000 unaccompanied Cuban children to the United States to "save" them from the evils of Communist brainwashing. These children were placed in orphanages and homes. About half of the children never saw their parents again (Daniels, 2002). But the political climate in the post–Cold War was very different in 1999, when a Cuban boy, Elián González, the most publicized refugee in the world, who had survived his family's ill-fated attempt to reach U.S. soil from Cuba by boat, was sent back on the order of United States Attorney General Janet Reno (Daniels, 2002), so that he would be not be separated from his family.

In the 1990s, the Immigration and Naturalization Service tripled the funding for border patrol programs (Daniels, 2002). Increased border security resulted, paradoxically, not in fewer border crossings but in more deaths by heat exhaustion or extreme dehydration (McKinley, 2005). At the same time, the funding for the enforcement of existing immigration laws remained the same. Once border crossers are inside the United States, immigrants can find employment easily in the fields or in the service industry (Thompson & Ochoa, 2004). Though legislation exists that bars employers from hiring undocumented immigrants, these laws are not enforced regularly, and it is often the immigrants themselves who are the targets of deportation raids in the plants where they are employed. Moreover, the House of Representatives passed legislation in 2005 that sought to criminalize the undocumented immigrant with felony charges (Section by Section Summary of the Sensenbrenner Bill, 2005).

Although official discrimination is no longer permissible, the majority of the refugees admitted into the United States in the late 1990s were from Eastern Europe and not from Africa, where most of the world's refugees are located (Daniels, 2002).

If Cubans who flee their land reach U.S. soil, they are granted asylum status and a path to apply for permanent residency within a short period of time, whereas Haitians (or any other asylum seekers for that matter) who reach U.S. soil are sent back to their countries of origin (Migration Information Source, 2006).

Thousands of Iraqis are fleeing their country every day since the start of the sectarian violence that followed the U.S.-led war in Iraq. Though a large number of Iraqis are filling out applications for asylum in the European Union, they cannot apply directly for refugee status at the United States Embassy in Iraq. The U.S. has admitted fewer than 500 Iraqi refugees since the start of the invasion (Tavernise & Worth, 2007). As of this writing, and under pressure from the new Democratic Congress, the U.S. and the United Nations are developing a plan that would bring several thousand Iraqis to the U.S. during 2007 (Swarns, 2007).

As Nacha explains to Rosa in the 1983 movie *El Norte,* "Trying to figure out the American ideas toward immigrants will give you a headache" (Nava, 1983). Government policy changes regarding immigrants (especially since September 11, 2001), shifts in the economic and budgetary outlooks, and the cultural differences of immigrants who arrive in the United States all affect public opinion about immigrants. These issues permeate the media, which translate them into bite-size chunks of information that viewers consume, often uncritically.

Periods of economic dislocation always bring unemployment and other features of economic uncertainty. It is usually during these times when the public, and sometimes the political leaders, accuse immigrants of stealing jobs from Americans. The depression of the 1890s, for example, raised fears about immigrants' unfair competition for jobs. The ethnic composition of the immigrants was changing, and although two thirds of those were from familiar regions of Western Europe, many came from Southern or Eastern Europe and seemed alien to many Americans. The U.S. is going through such a period now. Many Americans view immigrants as a drain on jobs and government social spending. The majority of Americans now want the number of immigrants reduced. For several years, states and the federal government have been planning cutbacks in welfare, health, and education benefits for both documented and undocumented immigrants. When Americans are divided and lack confidence in the future, dislike of foreigners increases (Daniels, 2002).

The United States has been racially diverse since the beginning. More than one third do not trace their origins to Europe. In some major metropolitan areas of the country, the minorities are the majority. This emerging demographic diversity raises fundamental questions about America's identity and culture. What does it mean that American society will be composed of a majority of non-Whites by the year 2053? How will the idea of what it is to be an American change? As the time approaches when Whites will become a minority, many are perplexed about national identity and the future of American society. This uncertainly provokes serious anxiety in certain social and academic groups. Author Arthur Schlesinger (1998) and others like him have throughout the 1990s reacted defensively to what they regard as a threat to assimilation and Americanization. Others are responding to the increased diversity as an opportunity to open the minds of American people (Takaki, 1993). Some of the current controversies regarding immigration have pitted two sides of the spectrum against each other, as they both wrestle with whether retention of immigrants' native languages is harmful or beneficial for the immigrants' acculturation process; whether the new immigrants threaten American racial stock; whether new immigrants take jobs from American workers; whether the United States must restrict immigration; and whether it is important for immigrants to assimilate or not.

Reasons for Immigration

Individuals migrate to this country for a variety of reasons. Scholars of immigration patterns have used special words to describe the major factors involved in immigration: push, pull, and means factors (Daniels, 2002). Push refers to the forces that exist in the place of origin that encourage or force people to emigrate, for example, poverty or the inability to use acquired professional skills. Pull refers to the attraction that draws the immigrants, or the immigrant's goals. For example, some people emigrated from tzarist Russia to the United States or South America to avoid serving 14 years in the military. That the United States and Argentina did not impose such long military service pulled immigrants out of their countries of origin. Means refers to the ability to migrate and the absence of effective barriers at the destination. Most recent immigrants undertake the journey as a result of push rather than pull factors due to economic hardship, which seems to be at the base of the decisions, even when religious or political reasons appear to be at the top. Because of the availability of affordable transportation and other advantages related to globalization and advances in technology, many recent immigrants are not forced to sever ties with the families they leave behind. Unlike immigrants of earlier generations, recent immigrants may have the opportunity to travel back and forth between countries with ease, enjoying continued contact with family and friends and keeping other cultural ties. This in turn makes it harder to acculturate or resolve the ambivalence about the immigration decision (Daniels, 2002). Obviously, not all immigrants can take advantage of the ease of travel and other means of communication, and many, particularly if they are undocumented, feel quite trapped inside the United States.

DIMENSIONS OF ACCULTURATION

A diverse group of immigrants enter the United States with their families and children as asylum seekers, refugees, through marriage to settled immigrants, or as undocumented workers. Consequently, ethnocultural diversity is the rule rather than the exception in today's cities and schools. Especially in geographical areas for which ethnocultural diversity is a new phenomenon, such as in cities or states that are not used to receiving an inflow of immigrants, the diversification of language, religion and culture is upsetting notions of national culture, identity, and values, and creating ethnic tensions (Berry, Phinney, Sam, & Vedder, 2006). The blending of the new immigrants with the American culture has not always been a smooth transition for immigrants. The White Protestant mainstream culture has historically celebrated the superiority of the native-born, and in earlier generations, many European immigrants compensated by attempting to become Americans fast and assimilate to gain acceptance. The thrust toward assimilation in language and culture that used to be common has weakened, however, in recent generations. Globalization, the end of the Cold War, and the rise of the United Nations are given by some scholars as the reasons for the weakening of the push toward Americanization of the immigrants (Clark, 1997). Others contend that new immigrants, with their changing faces, are not so quick to shed their ways and assimilate, in part, as a mechanism to preserve their identity and integrity in the face of discrimination, racism, and lack of acceptance of non-White immigrants. Resistance to assimilation may stem from the need to affirm the ethnic identity of the immigrants and make that opposition public so as to be noticed by the general public or the authorities (Turner & Simmons, 2006). Still others affirm that, by the second, or at the most the third, generation, individuals integrate into the American mainstream language and culture rather well (Kotkin, 2006) attaining social, occupational, and educational achievements comparable to those of the larger society (Berry, et al., 2006).

There is a vast literature on the psychological and social changes that take place among immigrants and their descendents in the societies that have been receiving immigrants for a long time. How the new second generation makes the transition to adult life and how they negotiate multiple cultures and identities is crucial for the success or failure of immigrant integration in a society (Chun, Balls Organista, & Marin, 2003). How do people from one culture who have a certain repertoire of behaviors, values, and attitudes adapt to living in a different culture?

Regardless of the speed and nature of cultural adaptation, the process of immigration invariably involves a redefinition of cultural identity at the individual and family levels (Beth-Shalom & Horenczyk, 2003). Immigrants always struggle with the reorganization of themselves in the context of their host society and face pressure either to acculturate or not acculturate from a variety of sources. It is important for therapists to understand the acculturation process that individuals experience (Berry, et al., 2006; Birman, 1994; Chun, et al., 2003; LaFromboise, Coleman, & Gerton, 1993). Acculturation can be defined as the process that occurs as members of one cultural group are exposed to, or come into significant contact with another (usually the dominant) cultural group. It not equivalent to assimilation, which can be thought of as the adoption or absorption of one culture by individuals of another.

Acculturation is a complex process, and the theoretical models that describe and explain them have become more refined, less rigid, and more inclusive over time (Beth-Shalom & Horenczyk, 2003; Berry, et al., 2006; Marin, Balls Organista, & Chun, 2003; Rahman & Rollock, 2004; Torres & Rollock, 2004). Older models of acculturation describe an almost forced-choice approach between two opposite poles of a continuum (Falicov, 1998a). According to these older models, immigrants could choose either to reject the culture of origin and embrace the new culture or not, navigating the either-or possibilities allowed by where they place themselves along the continuum. Such a unidimensional and unidirectional model implied that the adoption of a new identity required relinquishing the old one (Beth-Shalom & Horenczyk, 2003), and that cultural identity change eventually resulted in full assimilation (Trimble, 2003).

There are several approaches to thinking about acculturation issues, some of which do not force a choice between two necessary and useful perspectives and allow the possibilities of including hybrid, alternation, and bicultural models. (Berry, et al., 2006; Chun, et al, 2003; Falicov, 1998a; LaFromboise, et al., 1993) According to one approach (Berry, 1980, as cited in Berry, et al., 2006; Marin, et al., 2003), the acculturative process can result in four types of outcomes. Individuals who are viewed as assimilating can be defined as having given up the cultural identity of origin while at the same time wishing positive relationships with the host culture. If individuals are seen as separating, they can be viewed as keeping the original cultural ties and not relating positively to the host culture. The people who are seen as integrating retain their cultures of origin and also maintain a positive relationship with the host culture. Finally, those whose acculturative process resulted in marginalization do not retain their original culture nor desire to have positive relationships with the host culture. Which individuals fare better? What are the consequences of the acculturation outcomes? Theorists arrived at mixed conclusions (Torres & Rollock, 2004). Those who assimilate might have more problems than those who remain connected to their culture. These problems might include individual identity problems, problems with peer groups, and, in many cases, severe conflicts with family members, as is typical of immigrant youth (Berry, et al., 2006). For example, immigrant families from non-European backgrounds support the value of interdependence more strongly than do families from European backgrounds. Some families believe that adolescent children have more obligations to the family and fewer individual rights than do their counterparts in Western families. These underlying differences between the cultural values of the host society and those of the immigrant families may create intergenerational discrepancies that have the potential to create stress during the acculturation process (Berry, et al., 2006). But it is also clear that to be successful in the new cultural milieu, immigrants need to adopt the values and behavior of the majority culture, and, to avoid marginalization, immigrants need to reevaluate at least part of the original cultural identity. As biculturalism is increasingly understood as a positive outcome of acculturation processes (Falicov, 1998a; Berry, et al., 2006), it is important to remember that biculturalism is not simply a midpoint between an ethnic and an American identity (Phinney, 2003). Immigrants can acculturate in one dimension and not in another (language, peers), in one context and not another (work life, home life), and can move backward and forward according to the stage of the life cycle or experiences.

The concept of acculturative stress can also be helpful to understand the processes involved in acculturation. Adjusting to a new language, to different codes of behavior and social interactions, to new rules and laws, and to new lifestyles can be demanding and stressful and can increase the risk of mental health–related problems (Balls Organista, Organista, & Kurasaki, 2003). Severe difficulties with English language proficiency are associated with anxiety and depression among ethnic minority immigrants (Marin, Balls Organista, & Chun, 2003).

As noted, researchers have acknowledged that the process of cultural adaptation is complex and multidimensional (Marin, Balls Organista, & Chun, 2003; Berry, et al., 2006; Hays, 2001), and that the relationship between acculturation and mental distress is a complicated one (Rahman & Rollock, 2004).

There is an important relationship between social class, ethnicity, racism, and acculturation, and the extent to which and the ways in which people acculturate depend on other variables, in addition to those related to the individual decision-making process. It is important to distinguish between the acculturation attitudes of the immigrant and the acculturation attitudes of the members of the larger society and the relationship between the two. Immigrants and other ethnocultural groups may not necessarily be free to choose how they acculturate (Berry, et al., 2006). Many of the experiences of the immigrant within the larger society will determine whether they integrate, assimilate, separate, or marginalize. For some kind of integration to take place, a mutual accommodation is needed. Immigrant groups need to have the ability to live as a different cultural group and at the same time, adopt the values of the host society. But in order to be able to adopt the values of the host society, the institutions of that society need to adapt to meet the needs of the immigrant groups. How, and whether, the immigrant groups acculturate is, in part, a function of the multiculturalist, segregating, or exclusionary attitudes of the host society (Berry, et al., 2006). Not only do the oral and written ability with the English language, age at the time of arrival, and the socioeconomic status of the individual affect the ability to adapt to a new culture, but it seems clear that a significant variable is the exposure to prejudice and discrimination the immigrant experiences, which ultimately affect acculturation outcomes. The variability with which people solve their individual and interpersonal dilemmas; the existence of social, cultural, and political forces that influence individual and family decisions; and the intersection of immigration as a fact with other dimensions such as social class, racial, or ethnic discrimination are factors that influence how people live and what options they have. It is not only impossible but also naive to apply one acculturation model to all immigrants.

Implications for Professionals

Many in the United States are the children or grandchildren of immigrants. Immigration can be an issue for an individual long after the first-generation immigrant in that family took the journey. The ability to cope with the migration process in the first and subsequent generation differs according to the level of choice in migrating, gender and age of the immigrant, proximity to the country or region of origin, educational level, social support, and events that occur after migration (Falicov, 2003; McGoldrick, 2003). Regardless of the reasons for migration, immigrants of the first and second generations face a number of challenges and issues of which providers of mental health services should be aware. First, clinicians need to be aware of the reasons for migrating to this country, the method of migration, and the intent on returning to the country of origin (McGoldrick, 2003). Second, most immigrants experience a sense of loss, which may produce grief and feelings of sadness, regardless of the original intent for migration (Falicov, 2003). Third, immigrants face language issues: strains involved in learning and adapting to English, pressure to retain or eliminate the language or languages of origin, and challenges of accented speech. Fourth, life for the immigrant in the host country ranges from the reality of living at the margins of society to the possibility of mainstream acceptance, depending on whether the immigrant has documented or undocumented status, adequate language skills, and educational or work-related opportunities (Daniels, 2002), and to what extent the immigrant faces racism and discrimination.

Even though the United States is one of the largest recipients of immigrants from all over the world, the U.S. population is generally not seen as the most cognizant of other cultures, languages, and international issues. There is also a lack of information among the general public about several important issues regarding immigrants (Mills, 1994): What is the difference between a legal and an undocumented immigrant? Why do immigrants not learn English? Why do some immigrants have so many children? Is it true that they do not care about education? Are immigrants taking jobs away from Americans? Why don't immigrants act more like Americans? Clinicians do not live in cultural isolation and are exposed to these confusing aspects regarding immigrants. These ideas seep into the therapy room and plant themselves in the middle of the relationship, creating countertransference effects. Confusion, lack of knowledge, curiosity, criticism, and compassion may be common reactions to issues presented by immigrant clients in therapy and cannot be ignored by the clinician. It is important for clinicians to be informed.

Stories in This Section

This section contains four stories in which the immigration experience represents the cultural factor with the most salience for the authors. The stories constitute a sample of the complexity of identities and of the variability and heterogeneity of the immigration experience. Given the chance to interact with them and hear their stories, any counselor would be struck by their struggles with acculturation and assimilation, their resilience, their strengths, and their immense losses. These accounts chronicle how Vu, Esteban, Maria Luz, and Teresa integrate their immigration stories into the fabric of their cultural identities at the present moment. This view permeates their everyday lives, generating new stories that filter into their daily routines, furthering their fluid cultural identities, in a never-ending cycle of loss and resilience that constitutes the human experience. Chapters 8 and 9 are told by Vu and Esteban, who came to the United States as forced child refugees, without their parents. Chapter 10 contains the story of Maria Luz, a first-generation adult immigrant with undocumented status. Chapter 11 contains the story of Teresa, a second-generation immigrant who arrived in the United States as a child with her parents. Each individual constructed a sense of self quite different from the others, in spite of containing similar aspects. Each has different coping styles and strengths and various ways of looking at their gains and losses, and each has used distinct paths to reach their cultural identity. After reading these narratives, one is left with the impression, on the one hand, that it is impossible to predict the overall outcome and the effect of the immigration experience on the life of the person. At the same time, and paradoxically, one is left with the certainty that the immigrant's identity has been shaped in no small part by the experience of immigration.

Discussion Questions

What examples of nativism, xenophobia, and ambivalence toward immigrants exist in the United States today?

Do you believe that immigrants of previous generations had an acculturation experience that was different than that of the immigrants of today?

To what do you attribute that difference or lack of difference?

In your view, what are the most important factors that account for the acculturation of immigrants of the first generation? The second generation?

Why is a bicultural or integrative acculturative outcome generally considered to be more adaptive than either assimilation or marginalization?

What are some examples of how the views of a social service provider regarding immigration and acculturation issues affect the provision of services?

Vu's Story 8

I Am an American

In this chapter, we read the story of Vu, a refugee who left Vietnam at the age of seven on a boat, without his parents, and arrived in the United States at the age of nine, after spending two years as a child refugee in the Philippines. Vu was placed with a foster family who later adopted him. In this story, we read about his journey out of Vietnam and onto American soil. As you read, notice how he writes of his forced migration, his refugee status in the Philippines, and his struggles with second language acquisition in school. Even though he became fluent in spoken English quite rapidly, he struggled with his written proficiency in English for a long time. Pay attention to how he describes his process of acculturation, his socialization into his new American family, and his perception of himself as a successful survivor of the tragic journey. Notice also what he thinks would have happened to him had he stayed in Vietnam.

Vu's Story

In 1987 in Vietnam, my world was centered in the small town of Nha Trang. Life was easy, uncomplicated, and pleasant for me. I was a little boy with few worries. I had no awareness of the turmoil my family suffered at the hands of the Communists when my father fought with the Americans against the Communists during the Vietnam War. With peace also came the Communist rule. Daily life, as well as education, was determined by this government, but I knew no different. We were awakened each day by loudspeakers, which were placed strategically throughout the city and were used to broadcast governmental issues and concerns and even state-approved music. I spent my days in school or skipping school to play on the beach with friends. Education in Vietnam was quite different from what I experienced in the United States. For example, although reading was taught, it was in the context of learning Communist dogma and recitations. Math was also a rote subject. Reading for pleasure was not something that children were exposed to, nor something that adults demonstrated. This early learning shaped my school and adult preferences for reading.

When I was seven years old, one of my sisters took me out of elementary school early one day and brought me home. My parents asked me if I wanted to go to America. This was quite a surprise to me. I had heard stories of America, and it was described to me as the land of extraordinary things, such as wealth, an abundance of goods, and, most of all, opportunities. As a child with limited knowledge of the world, I thought it was a fantasy land. I said yes, knowing nothing about the situation that I was getting into. This little incident changed my life forever.

That same night, my father put me on the back of his motorcycle, and we rode to meet a bus. My father put me on the bus, saying that he would be back to meet me later. I trusted him and proceeded onto the bus. Hours later, the bus arrived at a beach around midnight. I could hear people telling one another to be quiet and not to make sudden moves. Within minutes, we all started to quickly get out of the bus one by one. As my feet met the sandy beach, I did not know where to go or what to do, and all I could see was people running toward the high waves. At this point, I was wandering aimlessly and frantically up and down the beach, not knowing where to go and searching for my father. Eventually a couple of men grabbed hold of my arms and started to carry me toward the water. As we reached the water, I could see a large boat that was a few hundred yards out. I looked around for my father, but he was nowhere to be found in the darkness of night. The men placed me into a basket because I could not swim and pushed me out toward the waiting boat. When we reached the boat, people were swarming in and around the boat, trying to get in, and someone pulled me up. After I was safely on the boat, I searched for a place to keep warm and felt fortunate to find the engine room just below the steering deck, where I stayed for the rest of the night. The next morning when I woke up and saw people walking around on the deck, I looked to the horizon, and land was nowhere in sight. This is when I knew I was on my way to an unknown destination. I felt so lonely and scared, wondering what was going to happen. I became more anxious because I did not have my father to comfort me. I searched everywhere on the boat for my father. From a child's perspective, I believed he must be somewhere on the boat. I tried to find the people who had helped me earlier, but I could not find them either. I looked everywhere on the boat, from the engine room to the steering room to the bow of the ship, but I did not find my father or the people who had helped me. By now, I was hysterical. I did not know anyone, and I had never been alone before.

After two days, I was exhausted from the endless searching for my father. I could hear people whispering that he had probably been captured by the Communists. He had never lied to me before, but finally it became evident to me that my father did not get on the boat. I kept wandering around the boat, taking in what I could. The expressions on most faces began to alleviate my fears. Some people were excited for the opportunity of a lifetime, and some were sad, not knowing what experience awaited them. For seven days and seven nights, there were continuous problems: we encountered tremendous thunderstorms, hunger, quarrels, and sudden deaths. I can remember one storm that hit us so hard that parts of the ship fell off. The refugees were asked to help repair the ship. During another storm, we were sent down to the hold of the ship, where we had to stay for more than two days. Due to the violent shaking and rolling of the ship, people were sick and terrified, crying and praying. On the third day, I vividly remember an old man opening up the door to the deck and the sun shining. All of us were so happy just to be alive. After climbing out of the hold and walking around the boat, I talked to some people and began to gain a better understanding. I had begun to accept the situation and was not quite so hysterical; everything started to come together for me. People explained what we were doing, where we were going, and when we might get there. Hunger was not on my mind during my expedition across the South China Sea. When it was time to eat, we were rationed steamed rice, fried fish, and one cup of fresh water. Most of the time I could not eat, so I gave my food away to others. To some, the meal portions were not enough, so they fought for what they could get to satisfy their thirst and hunger.

One incident that still haunts me is the death of a little baby. I remember this very clearly because I was standing next to the family when they dropped their dead child into the ocean. The entire family stood in a circle silently crying. I thought to myself, if something would ever happen to me, would I be thrown into the ocean and never heard of again? How would my parents know how I died? Who would tell my parents, since no one on this ship knows me? Death was expected on this journey, and it happened daily. However, this was not the way I had experienced death in Vietnam. There were rituals, prayers, and tributes to the deceased. In this instance, death happened, and the person was disposed of.

On the seventh day when land came into sight, we encountered a ship, which turned out to be a pirate ship, and we were told we were going the wrong way. The pirates wanted us to follow them around an island. Our captain started to follow but, fortunately, a fishing boat came along. The fishing boat captain told us not to follow the pirate ship but to follow his boat. If the fishing boat had not come by, we probably would have been killed by the pirates, as had so many before us, I later learned.

The fishing boat led us to land, but we did not know where we were. We later learned we were in the Philippines. Once on land, the native people helped us by giving us food, water, clothes, and a place to stay. We could not understand their native Filipino language, so we could not answer their questions, but eventually we found a bilingual refugee with us who could translate. The next morning, there was a U.S. Navy ship next to ours. I had no idea what this all meant, but the adults appeared overjoyed to be greeted by an American ship. We were taken onboard the ship and were brought to Manila in the Philippines. We stayed in Manila for two nights at a refugee center, and then we were transferred to the primary refugee camp in Palawan, where I remained for two years.

Living in a refugee camp was rigid and different from the home that I knew. After arriving at the camp, I was photographed and interviewed. My refugee status had to be validated. Later, I was placed with a couple who claimed to know my father, but I found out later they did not, so I moved out. I knew of my father's status because the night of the escape my father had given me documents to take along with me. I had kept these documents in case I would need to use them. In this instance, the documentation proved my father's service to the United States. Because I was a child with my father's documentation, many were eager to embrace and care for me, hoping to increase their chances of being granted refugee status or being released from the camp more quickly. People without documentation to qualify them as political refugees often spent many years in Palawan, only to be returned to Vietnam.

Two years in a refugee camp was devastating for me. I missed my parents, my two younger brothers, and my three older sisters. I wondered why I was the chosen one to leave. Was I unloved? Was I bad? I revisited all the naughty things I had done; all the times I was punished; all the times I skipped school to play; all the times I disobeyed my parents, grandparents, or sisters; and all the times my brothers and I fought. I found out later in my adult life that my parents had wanted me to have a better life. In the camp, I did not receive the love and care that I would have received from a normal family, and the majority of the time I was roaming throughout the camp. I was alone, sometimes living in the unaccompanied children's dorm with many other children. I was seven years old when I left Vietnam. Being seven years old without the presence of parents' guidance is disconcerting to a child, but I was fortunate to be placed in the care of a kind family, where I had many friends, until the day I left for America. The new family made sure that I attended school in the camp and brought me to church. School was not my favorite activity; learning English was a goal, but I seemed to learn only to name items, not to speak conversational English. Soon after arriving in America, I found out that the family I lived with in the camp had used me to obtain extra food rations, and they ultimately claimed that they should accompany me to America to care for me, but this ploy ultimately failed them.

In 1989, because of my father's military record, I was able to document my status as a political refugee, and I was accepted as an immigrant through the Unaccompanied Minors Program for resettlement to the United States. Everyone at the camp was so happy and excited for me. It felt like I won the lottery! On May 23, 1989, I arrived in the United States to be greeted by my foster family, the Tylers. I lived with them continuously for 14 years, which is longer than the time I spent with my biological family in Vietnam. Our emotional ties are permanent, and my foster family has become the family I lost.

Throughout my school years, kids asked me if I was adopted, and most of the time I said yes, knowing deep down I wanted the Tylers to be my permanent family. I always used the Tylers' last name, but when I asked my social worker if I could make their name my permanent last name, he told me that I could not be adopted because my family still loved me and wanted to be reunited with me. I did not understand this. I asked my foster family, and they said that social services would not allow adoption because of the Geneva Accord. I did not understand that either. I wanted a family. My foster mother said that if they tried to adopt me, I would be placed in another home. That frightened me. How many families could I lose? How long would I have to wait to be accepted into a family? How many times could I take the chance on loving? I was very happy and secure with my foster family. I had many friends and was doing well in school.

Living in a suburban town provided me with many advantageous educational opportunities and experiences, but no contact with other Vietnamese children. My facility with my native language was quickly diminishing. After six months in the United States, I was fully conversant in my new language. It was becoming difficult to read the letters from my parents in Vietnam. Eventually, my foster parents had to find someone who could translate the letters for me. For about a year, I had a Vietnamese social worker who visited me monthly. He reminded me of my culture and the need to remain in contact with my family and practice my language. I had been placed in an English-speaking home. How was I to practice speaking Vietnamese?

Often I would end up crying because of what he would tell me—how lucky I was, how my family was suffering. I learned that my father had been caught trying to escape and had been put in prison—his second time in a "reeducation" camp. Letters from my mother would tell of her struggles to support my brothers and sisters. When he was caught, the Communists took my family home away from them, and my family had no home. My mother would beg me to send her money. When my foster family learned of this, they wired money to them through Canada, but the requests for money never stopped. At times my parents' advice to me regarding my newly adopted land was contradictory. For example, in one letter I was told to learn English quickly so I could do well, but other letters admonished me to not forget my language, culture, and family. My parents did not speak or write English, so many letters were translated into English prior to being mailed. Many other letters were written in Vietnamese, which I could read only until my second year in the United States. One letter is particularly poignant. It was written, in English, to my foster family from my father in his jail cell where he was held after the escape attempt. He wrote, "My wife has secretly sent your letter into my prison ward, and my roommate help me to translate this letter. . . We are ineffable in words, please accept all our boundless gratitude. I cease my pen with our best wishes to you." Still other letters state that I am now the Tylers' son, and they are grateful for my new family's love and care.

When I was 10 years old, my mother wrote that I should quit school and get a job, so I could send money home like other "good" Vietnamese sons who live in America. Eventually, my social worker had to write to explain how important education was in the United States, that children my age could not work, and that to be able to help them I needed a good education. I was very worried about my dad in the prison because I remembered stories my family had told about his previous imprisonment, which resulted after he stole food for us.

When I entered third grade, I wanted to become as Americanized as possible. Spending time with all my new American friends facilitated assimilation into my new culture. Adjusting to my new culture was not difficult for me because of my easygoing personality; making friends and being accepted was almost effortless for me. I had already decided to acquire the new culture as quickly as possible. I know I did not identify myself as Vietnamese, although I am sure my classmates and teachers saw me as foreign. Nevertheless, I do not ever remember experiencing any prejudice. I was invited to all my friends' parties and dated American girls in high school. Most of my friends were American-born, but I denied that I avoided friendships with other Asian students. When my foster parents asked me about my choice of friends, I explained that there were no other Asian students who played athletics, and I identified with athletes.

The nature of my Vietnamese education differed from a traditional American education. I attended three years of school in Vietnam. School was in session for only half a day, and I frequently skipped school to play with friends, with no consequences. Lessons in Vietnam consisted of memorization and teacher lectures. Students learned by observation, not by experimentation or participation.

The Ministry of Education controlled a national curriculum, which was funded by the government. Students in Vietnam were expected to be orderly, attentive, and quiet; everyone worked on memorizing the same thing at the same time, but not in cooperative groups. The students were fearful of not knowing answers and did not like to be singled out. The teacher was the ultimate authority, but there were no conferences or home–school communication. If the teacher called on the parent, it usually meant that the child had done some terrible wrong. Although I was required to attend school in the Philippines, I did so erratically. I remember that the classes consisted of trying to learn names for things in English.

School in America was something I enjoyed. It was so different from what I remembered in Vietnam and in Palawan. The teachers were nice, laughing and joking with the students. It was clear to me that they liked me. My day-to-day needs did not include my primary language. I did not feel a need to have a cultural connection to my native language. At the beginning of third grade, I was fluent enough to fit in to the expected routines of the class. My foster mother says I adjusted well and had many friends and I appeared to meet classroom expectations. I could read, via decoding, most of the class texts. This was confusing to some of my teachers, who indicated they equated reading with the ability to pronounce the words—which I could do—rather than construct meaning—which I could not do. My elementary school offered a newspaper club after school, and I became a contributing member. I saw myself as being able to participate in all activities offered. I used literacy in many ways, even writing memos to myself, especially when I had done something wrong. When writing, I made errors of syntax, grammar, capitalization, and punctuation, and I still do today.

Although I was a fluent conversationalist fairly soon after arriving in America, my foster mother believed I needed to master the language of the classroom; she raised the issue of programmatic adaptations to accommodate my emerging language. She was met with surprise and was told that I certainly spoke with no accent. There was never any possibility of a language maintenance program in my school district. The only service to second language learners was an English as a second language (ESL) pullout program, which I attended in third, fourth, and fifth grade. After a short time I uncharacteristically complained to my foster mother that I was bored. I told her, "I know 'this is a book,' 'this is a pencil,' and 'this is a chair.'" The program consisted primarily of learning the names for items (something I did routinely all day) and reciting simple conversational sentences with a goal of oral language proficiency. My foster mother was employed in my school district as an administrator, so she intervened with my ESL tutor, and my program was changed to fit my needs. My foster mother's influence on the nature of the support I was receiving resulted in my ESL teacher's work to address specifically the vocabulary that I was expected to use in class, such as spelling words and words from content areas. Because I was a strong visual learner, I was always able to successfully memorize the correct spelling of weekly words. Thus my teachers were confounded when I could not successfully use the words in fill-in-the-blank worksheets.

As academic demands became greater, I appeared to struggle more. By fifth grade, increased classroom emphasis was placed on worksheets to be completed independently. None of the assignments improved my English or added to my fount of knowledge. Teachers were concerned because I worked so hard and yet did not successfully complete all assignments independently. After an evaluation in 1991, I was found to have no special needs; recommendations were to continue with the same support that I had been receiving for two years.

During middle school, I continued to struggle with multiple meanings of words, idioms, and the nuances of the language. In eighth-grade English, almost two full months of classroom instruction were spent in preparation for Word Master, a national competition that tests students' knowledge of words. This preparation involved memorizing lists of words and their definitions. Class time was spent matching words with definitions and figuring out analogies. I could never get more than one or two correct on the weekly test, and my grade was severely affected. What I needed was to be reading good literature, generating ideas and theories, and participating in discussions.

In high school, some English courses offered opportunities to read challenging literature and demanded written responses and essays. At home, I frequently spoke enthusiastically of subjects I was studying. The instruction and assessment that occurred in the classes where I had the most success required active participation, daily writing response to readings, performances and interpretations of readings, and work in cooperative groups. All my grades were B and higher. Again, school was another place where I had to unlearn a cultural lesson. American students would enthusiastically call out answers and actively question the teacher. I was expected to know when I needed help and to ask for it. I was conditioned to not do that. I would never want to make myself known as being unable or unprepared. It took me a long time, with my foster parents' and teachers' help, to assert myself. Nevertheless, my foster mother had to first educate my teachers about my learning needs. Most of my high school courses were at the accelerated level. My teachers stated that I participated in class discussions and was well prepared for class. My homework was always completed on time. They said that I was pleasant and polite and did well in class, but often I performed poorly on exams. Many teachers stated that they were sure I knew much more than the exams exhibited. Teacher comments indicated that my test grades were negatively affecting my report card grade. My success on exams depended on the type of exam administered. Tests that were intended to measure vocabulary competence often consisted of matching items, sentence completions, and identification of antonyms and synonyms. The antonym and synonym items caused me great difficulty. Often the use of multiple-choice or fill-in-the-blank tests is for ease of scoring. The discrepancy between success on authentic measures and failure on standardized tests reveals that I was able to construct my own meaning with the text and to express it effectively, but that I still experienced difficulty when meaning was expected to be boiled down to specific, one-word answers. My scores on standardized tests have never been very high and are not reflective of my true achievement or ability.

I believed that to be successful in America I had to acculturate, forget my previous culture, and become part of the new. I knew the only way to fit in was to be just like all my friends and thus spend less time thinking and talking about my past. I did not want to be associated with Vietnam or have anything to do with it. I wanted to be Americanized. I wanted to forget my Vietnamese language and culture—everything from Vietnam. I used my foster family's last name on everything I wrote and began calling my foster parents "Mom" and "Dad." My social worker scolded me for doing that and insisted on notifying my school about my real legal name, asking that my records reflect that name. I was required to show the social worker school papers and report cards to prove that I was not using my foster parents' last name.

At this time, I knew I was being rebellious against my culture, but I could not figure out why. Maybe because of what my biological parents had put me through—not being there when I needed them, sending me away, I felt, because they did not love me. Eventually, I found out that they did it because they wanted me to have a better life in America.

Accepting the new culture quickly and concealing the old did not concern me, but it worried my foster parents. My foster mom sought me out and dragged me to the cultural events offered by the Unaccompanied Minors Program, but I never wanted to be there. I felt as though I did not fit in; I did not think I was like them. I did not want to listen to Vietnamese music or participate in other Vietnamese cultural celebrations in a nearby city. I did not want to be identified as a refugee, a foster child, a ward of the state, or anything other than an American. As years went by, I began to adapt to my new culture and excel in many things, including sports. My foster family exposed me to skiing, soccer, tennis, swimming, and many other sports, in which I experienced much success and awards. In 1989, I had never seen snow when my foster family took me to a ski mountain where they had a winter home to ski. Within a year, I joined the freestyle ski team, to which my foster brother and sister belonged, and I became a competitor in freestyle skiing, loving skiing, the cold, and the snow. Rushing down mountains, jumping and spinning through the air was a new and wonderful feeling.

I qualified for the freestyle series each year from 1990 to 1997, and ultimately I was invited to compete in the junior nationals in Utah, where I was ranked third in the country in aerials. I was asked to participate in nationals that year. Sports provided me with a way to communicate with my peers. I was so successful, so early, that I gained immediate status and acceptance with the skiing community. During the years I competed, I won numerous meets and enjoyed a national ranking. Self-discovery or introspection showed me that I learned visually, and I achieved my goals easily. Playing sports also placed me in a circle of friends that I would not have had if I had not played sports. Being accepted into this group of athletes ultimately allowed me to forget my own cultural learning, which was in conflict with what I was experiencing. In Vietnam, I was taught not to seek the spotlight or to cause attention to focus on myself. Being considered a star athlete, either in high school sports or in skiing, was exciting yet conflicting. Before coming to America, I remember knowing about an athlete, Michael Jordan, thinking how special and lucky he was. Here I was getting awards. This was very difficult for me; I was not shy, but I did not like to be the center of attention. I did not like going to the podium to receive awards. Ultimately, I conformed to the American culture.

My life has changed dramatically since that dark, frightening night in Vietnam. Had I stayed there, my world would have been quite different. My education would have stopped when I was 12 years old; I would have had no opportunity for a meaningful future. Because I was the oldest son in the family, I would have had the responsibilities that are traditionally demanded of the eldest son. I would have been expected to support my parents and any remaining single siblings for the rest of my life. I would have remained living in my parents' house. They would have expected me to give them financial help and, in addition, to help distant relatives in emergencies. After the death of my father, I would have taken over the role of head of the family. To my understanding, this is because I was the first-born son, and traditionally I would be the caretaker of the family. I remember that the family unit is the most important entity, to which one's first loyalty is owed. Extended family members are accorded the same respect as immediate family members. Parents and all adults demand obedience. Children begin to learn of their responsibility toward their families at a young age. Many generations live together, and the young care for their elders. This was expected of me and culturally accepted in the Vietnamese tradition. I probably would have quit school by the age of 10 years and would have learned to repair bicycles and motorcycles, as my father did. As a little child, I would sit while he worked on repairs and feel that watching him somehow enabled me to be good mechanically. Many times, I have been able to fix something that my foster mother was about to throw away. It is not a skill I learned in America.

American parents are different from Vietnamese parents; they love their children differently. In Vietnam, the children are not the center of the family. A traditional Vietnamese family does not engage children in conversation as equals; children are primarily observers and learn by watching, listening, and imitating. Conformity, obedience, respect, patience, and composure are traits that are valued and expected to be developed. In America, family life revolves around children. In Vietnam, it was expected that parents use physical punishments for wrongdoing. I learned quickly that this is not accepted here. In addition, I had to learn to look adults in the eye when speaking to them. This is contrary to my cultural upbringing. Children in Vietnam show respect by keeping eyes downcast when speaking to an adult. I learned that American parents encourage their children to achieve, in school and in sports, and to set long-term educational and financial goals for themselves. This was unknown to me in Vietnam.

Vietnamese parents never ask for children's opinions or desires. In America, there are so many decisions to be made, such as what to eat, what to wear, where to go, what to play. Children are allowed to voice opinions even when not asked. American children are allowed to set their own bedtime, get monetary allowances, and spend their money as they wish. In Vietnam, I was told what to do and when to do it. If I did not agree or want to obey, I did not voice my objections; I simply did what I wanted and suffered the consequences.

When I came to America, I did not know my birthday; birthdays were not celebrated in Vietnam. The year of birth is important. I know I was born in the Year of the Monkey. Not long after I arrived in America, my mother sent me a birth certificate that differed from the one I left Vietnam with. The new birth certificate indicated I was born in 1978 rather than 1980. Yet I know I was born in 1980 because it was the Year of the Monkey. I later learned that my mother wanted me to appear to be two years older, so I would be allowed to quit school and work more easily. This caused me years of trouble. I had to get waivers in sports to remain eligible. When I got my license at age 18—really age 16—I had to explain, with embarrassment, to my friends and on job, scholarship, and college applications why I was so old on my license. When I was legally adopted, the attorney corrected my birth certificate; however, I am still having repercussions from that. My passport is being held up because the dates on my citizenship certificate and birth certificate do not match. In America, we celebrate birthdays. My ninth birthday occurred three weeks after I arrived in the United

States. I was astonished by the gifts and birthday cake. This was something I never expected and could really learn to like! Years later, in a letter from Vietnam, pictures were included of my family celebrating my sister's birthday. Wow, that surprised me. How could they afford to do that? How did they come to do that? It never happened for me in Vietnam, and I wondered why.

Showing emotion was another new experience for me. Although I would cry when I was hurt in Vietnam, I never remembered displaying sadness or anger or being encouraged to do so. My foster mother had to teach me "grouchy" and that it was "okay" to be out of sorts occasionally and to voice my feelings. I remember one instance when I first arrived at the Tylers' and they took me shopping for new clothes. When my foster mother showed me something that I did not like, my response was "I no like." I came with preconceived notions about how I should dress as an American child but was unsure of how to communicate those desires to them.

My foster family encouraged me to be the most I can be. They pushed me and demanded I stretch myself to achieve, but they never made demands similar to those in my Vietnamese culture. With their encouragement, I participated in all that my school had to offer. At times, it seemed almost impossible to learn a new language and customs and do what my American classmates were doing. There were times when I struggled to do schoolwork because of the language barrier and cultural differences. However, I was able to leave the differences behind and accomplish what needed to be done and move on. Nevertheless, academics, sports, clubs, and social activities have enriched my life. In sports, I played at the varsity level in football, soccer, track, and skiing. These opportunities would not typically happen to foster children. Most foster children leave the system at age 18 years, when the foster parents release them; most are never adopted. I was grateful to my foster family for providing me with a roof over my head, a ski home, a summer ski camp, participation in national competitions, and travel across the United States. I was also accepted to a private college with wonderful scholarships. These are things that I will remember and carry with me for the rest of my life. I became a citizen of the United States in 1997. What opportunities I have been given! I became a citizen of the United States, and all things seem possible.

I have also tried to begin to give back some of the many kindnesses I have received. I volunteered in my town's annual cleanup and at a nursing home. I worked throughout high school with a special education class of severely disabled students. By helping these students, I learned how fortunate I truly am. Things I thought were problems for me were simply difficulties I have been able to overcome with help. Those students will never have the same opportunities as I had because of their disabilities.

I am proud to report that I graduated from a prestigious college and received a well-rounded education. Fifteen years ago, I never dreamed going to college was possible. No one in my Vietnamese family is educated. I have an American family—a mother, a father, a sister, and a brother—who love and believe in me.

A significant event took place on April 18, 2003: my adoption into the Tyler family. I was of legal age, and I was able to choose to be adopted by my former foster family. This is what I had been waiting for since I arrived in America. I now have a forever family with a mother, a father, a brother, a sister, an uncle, and a grandmother, and they all care about me. I know I belong. I can honestly say I have closed a chapter of my early life and have started a new chapter. Furthermore, I am also engaged to marry my girlfriend from high school, who also has a wonderful family who embraced me.

An evaluation of the significance of my experiences necessitates putting on many lenses. Through my child's eyes, I used to only see what I lost—a family, a home, a limited education, Vietnamese culture and my native language, a sense of self, government control, and security. In Vietnam, we were always hungry. Rice and fish were our daily foods, just as they were in the refugee camp. At the dinner table in Vietnam, we were expected to eat in silence and to drink water after the meal. In America, mealtime is a time for conversation, relating the day's events, talking or arguing about events in the news, and planning for fun activities via scheduled play dates or sports events. I learned I could eat and drink as much as I wanted, but I did not like milk. If I were hungry between meals, I could eat then, too. Often there was more food on my plate than I could eat. In Vietnam, there was never food remaining on a plate. I have never been hungry in America, and there are so many new, delicious foods to eat.

Through a young adult's eyes, I see what I have gained—family, a home, security, freedom, education, a culture, and unlimited opportunities. Because I left Vietnam so young, over time my memory has dimmed about many daily experiences and personal interactions with my family. Surely much of which I learned from my culture in my first seven years of life are part of me, but not on a conscious level. The culture I identify with is American. I am an American. I live as an American does. I celebrate occasions as an American does.

On the boat and in the camp, I grieved openly. The picture of me as a new arrival clearly shows a depressed, distraught, young, thin child. Perhaps I rejected my Vietnamese family because anger replaced grief. Perhaps I identified with the family and country that gave me love and security. As I get older, and more mature, I am more comfortable acknowledging my ethnic background. It took me a long time to enjoy going to a Vietnamese restaurant, which I do now, frequently. There is not really a merging of my two worlds. Was I too young to have a strong imprint of my culture? The lessons I learned regarding respect for my elders, authority, and persons of education have served me well, but these are lessons American children are taught also.

I do not consider myself a Vietnamese person but an American. I have also gained a new meaning of life, what my priorities are, and how I can achieve them. I believe that I have lost ties to my Vietnamese heritage, my language, my parents, my responsibilities as the eldest son, and my culture. Today, I try to look at what I have gained more so than what I have lost. What I have gained greatly outweighs, in my mind, what I have left behind. This includes obtaining a wonderful education and graduating from college. I feel I am prepared to adapt and fit into American society.

Content Themes

The major themes of this story are Vu's forced migration and his status as a refugee, the acquisition of English during his school years, and how he views his process of assimilation and Americanization. In addition, he writes about what he considers his gains and losses, how he views his educational and athletic triumphs, and whom he considers his real family.

FORCED MIGRATION AND REFUGEE STATUS

One of the first themes to emerge from Vu's story is that he was forced to leave Vietnam by his family. Vu recalls his traumatic journey at the age of seven years. He continues to describe his state of mind during the journey to the United States as a Vietnamese boat refugee as traumatic. After Vu makes it, miraculously, to the refugee camp in the Philippines, he writes that the two years in the refugee camp were devastating, in part because he wondered if he had been bad or unloved. Although the distinctions between voluntary and involuntary immigration are important, the case of the child forced to migrate and become a refugee needs to be singled out and differentiated from the status and characteristics of the other types of immigrants. Immigrants can choose not to leave their country of origin and have time to plan their migration. Refugees, on the other hand, often have to leave suddenly, sometimes in fear for their lives (Breunlin, Schwartz, & Mac Kune-Karrer, 1997; Grinberg & Grinberg, 2000) due to extreme political or economic hardships. The voluntary immigrant can often return to his or her land, and many immigrants do, but in general refugees cannot, as is the case with Vu. The forced immigration usually closes off the possibilities of an eventual return, at least for the foreseeable future (Daniels, 2002).

Vu explains that some people in the refugee camp resorted to fraudulent activities to make it into the United States. The decline in the arrival of refugees into the United States can probably be attributed, in part, to new efforts to combat fraud. This has slowed the processing of applications but should not be seen as an indication of a drop in need. There are more than 85,000 refugees worldwide who could have been permitted to enter the United States in the last two years to escape hardship and danger but have not entered because of processing issues (Migration Policy Institute, 2004).

After the Vietnam War ended, more refugees began to arrive with no significant amount of money, and many of the so-called boat people were often stripped of what little they did have by pirates or officials in the countries of first asylum (Daniels, 2002), as Vu vividly recounts about his days in the Philippines. Refugees continued to come to the United States in much greater numbers than anticipated throughout the 1990s from the former Yugoslavia, the former Soviet Union, and Vietnam. The Vietnamese do not have a long history of immigration to the United States and are different from all the other major groups of recent immigrants from Asia, in that they tend to be very young, not well educated, and very poor. Many children, such as Vu, were sent alone by their parents in an effort to save at least one child by giving him or her the opportunity to go to the United States. Refugee and asylum policies are very complex and sometimes contradictory because the United States tries to deal with the problem of defining who qualifies as a refugee and who does not, depending on the kind of political regime of the country of origin and whether the refugee is considered an economic or a political one. As Daniels (2002) contends, these complexities seem to be a permanent part of the once simpler matter of emigrating to America.

Children are the ones with the least amount of choice in the decision to emigrate, and Vu's voyage is one of the most dramatic examples of that fact. Refugees crossed the oceans coming from countries devastated by war or political dictatorships. Their parents made a drastic decision that, in their minds, would save their children's lives. In addition, it seems that in Vu's case, at least, the parents also imagined that if Vu's economic prospects were to improve, his parents' economic hardships would diminish as well because as soon as Vu would be old enough to work, he could start sending money back to Vietnam to support the rest of the family. This belief is consistent with that of other families in the poorest countries of the world, who send some of their male offspring to the United States. The forced emigration of children from Vietnam is not an isolated example or a new phenomenon. There are many other countries from which children are forced to emigrate, and, as a practice, it has been going on for centuries (Daniels, 2002).

SECOND LANGUAGE ACQUISITION

The speed and accuracy of the acquisition of a second language varies according to the age, the level of education, and other circumstances of the immigrant. In Vu's case, he was placed with American foster parents who spoke only English, and he did not have any contact with Vietnamese children, which may have accelerated the loss of his native language; he says that after six months in the United States he was fully conversant in his new language. Adolescent immigrant students are generally placed in bilingual education classes of differing quality depending on where the school is located, how it is funded, and the philosophy of the school district. Often immigrant students struggle with second language acquisition. Bilingual education is often used erroneously in a one-size-fits-all approach that does not serve the heterogeneous needs of children with second language acquisition issues. As Vu's story demonstrates, in spite of an oral English proficiency acquired early on in his American school years, he continued to struggle with grammar, writing, and reading, and only a persistent and knowledgeable foster parent was able to help him overcome his literacy concerns. There is evidence that the socioeconomic status of the parents affects immigrants' acquisition of English proficiency (Kuo & Roysircar, 2004). Immigrant parents' academic and occupational past and present history have been demonstrated to influence the second language acquisition process of the school-age child (Nieto, 1999). School personnel who are not well trained may miss the reasons for the differences between oral, written, and reading proficiency in English, may arrive at wrong conclusions, and may suggest interventions that are not well targeted to the immigrant child's needs. Also, schools vary in the degree to which they accept or reject the immigrant child's native culture and language ability, depending on whether the native language is viewed as an asset or a liability (Nieto, 1999). This, in turn, affects the second language acquisition process. Vu's foster (and later adoptive) parents were highly educated and employed all the tools, time, and dedication that upper-middle-class comfort affords to deal with Vu's second language acquisition concerns. This clearly had effects on his successful high school and college performance in later years. Other immigrant children are not so lucky.

ACCULTURATION AND ASSIMILATION PROCESSES

Acculturation and assimilation are complex, nonlinear processes that are further complicated by the different layers, conscious to unconscious; the different levels, from low to high; and the different contexts. How individuals think about themselves may shift depending on where they are—at home or work—or who they are with—their immigrant or their American friends. In terms of his acculturation and assimilation process, Vu clearly wanted to become Americanized, and in his view he succeeded. He remembers that in the third grade he wanted to become as Americanized as possible and that he avoided friendships with other Asian students. As he grew older, he believed he had to forget his previous culture to become part of the new. However, he also states the older he got, the more comfortable he became acknowledging his ethnic background. Another way of looking at Vu's acculturative process is through his depiction of what he had to learn in his new experiences: showing emotions, asserting himself in school, being more talkative during meals, and learning to express which clothes he liked or disliked. Although he acknowledges that his "old self" might be somewhere there unconsciously, he identifies solely with the American culture. This may have been one way for him to cope with his earlier losses when he found himself to be in a strange new world.

SURVIVOR GUILT

Vu's acculturation processes and coping styles can also be understood from the perspective of his traumatic separation and survival. Many immigrants whose experiences are as traumatic as Vu's need to figure out how to deal not only with their separation from their families of origin but also with having survived, psychologically and physically, especially if their parents or siblings did not survive or do as well as the immigrant. Survivor guilt was first identified as affecting survivors of the Holocaust (Vogel, 1999), who were described as exhibiting an intense sense of guilt, which made it difficult for them to be happy knowing that significant members of their immediate families were not. Vu may have "decided" that his biological parents and his siblings are not his "real" family. His stories of forced migration, of his journey from being hungry most of the time during his childhood in Vietnam to having some of the comforts of an upper-middle-class family, and of his encounter with the U.S. school system with its more democratic and less hierarchical treatment of children are all factors that may have contributed to his view of his foster— and later, adoptive—parents as his real parents. Had he not become Americanized, and had he continued to feel and act Vietnamese, how would he have coped with the idea that his parents and siblings were still so poor while he was surviving and thriving in America? It is not unusual for immigrants, particularly those who arrive in the United States very young and who have the opportunity to be exposed to a good educational environment, to do better occupationally, professionally, and financially than the relatives they left behind, which may increase their survivor guilt.

Clinical Applications

It is important for clinicians to assess their clients' status as refugees, their struggles not only with their oral proficiency in English but also with their written proficiency, their experiences in bilingual programs at school, and how they tackle their acculturation and assimilation issues. The interventions include learning the history of the immigrant's country of origin and conducting a psycholinguistic history. Several countertransferential reactions are described.

ASSESSMENT

Forced Migration and Refugee Status

What are the stories of the journey from the country of origin like?

Tell me about the history of your country as it relates to your story of immigration.

How do you think your life has been shaped by your immigration journey?

How did your story affect others who stayed behind?

Who else was affected by or not affected by your immigration journey?

Second Language Acquisition

How easy or difficult was it for you to learn English?

If you were placed in bilingual education programs, what was your experience like with second language acquisition?

Were you encouraged to speak or discouraged from speaking your language of origin?

How do you experience your language of origin in your life today?

Acculturation Processes and Coping Styles

What have you adopted or not adopted of the American way of life?

What have you preserved or not preserved of your background in terms of personality styles, communication styles, values, worldview, and so on?

If you have children, what values of your culture of origin are you interested in them preserving or rejecting?

How do you think of yourself in terms of your cultural identity?

Has the way you think about your cultural identity changed or remained the same over the years?

Survivor Guilt

How did the rest of your family members do in terms of their occupation, health, and social class status as a result of the immigration experience?

Were there differences among them in those areas?

How have you felt in relation to them in those areas?

If there were marked differences between you and the members of your family in terms of health, occupational successes, and social class status, how have you dealt with it?

What meanings have you attributed to those similarities and differences?

TECHNIQUES AND INTERVENTIONS

Acquire Knowledge of History

It is important for the clinician to acquire knowledge about the history of the country of origin, the recent historical factors that may have influenced the cohort of immigrants from that country, and the overall immigration history to the United States from that country. First, it is important for the clinician to acquire some basic knowledge of the history of the country of origin, which includes a general overview of its racial and ethnic diversity or lack of diversity, history of colonialism, class issues, and general educational issues. The majority of countries in the world were colonized by at least one empire at some point in their history. For example, Argentina and Chile were colonized by Spain; Brazil by Portugal; India, Syria, and Israel by Great Britain; North Africa by France; Spain by the Arabs; Korea by Japan; and the United States by Great Britain. This is important because the legacy of colonization explains a good deal of the current racial and ethnic characteristics, idiosyncrasies, sensibilities, political problems, and immigration patterns.

Second, it is important to acquire basic knowledge of recent history, particularly recent economic or political history and weather- or disaster-related history. Were there recent wars, border conflicts, or economic or political circumstances that may have affected the people and encouraged them to emigrate? Were there recent hurricanes, earthquakes, invasions, or revolutionary movements? This is important because immigrants and refugees generally do not immigrate in isolation; they are part of a cohort that tends to immigrate at about the same time, a time related to recent historical, economic, or weather-related events. Knowing the context of the particular immigration pattern helps to understand the client better.

Finally, a general knowledge of the history of emigration from that country is necessary to understand which wave of migration the client joined. One of the most dramatic examples is the history of the Cuban immigration to the United States, in part because of its contrasting nature and effect. The first wave of migration was composed of the professional and managerial elite, fleeing the instauration of the Castro regime. They were received with open arms by the U.S. government and were given immediate permanent resident status. Their experiences of material success after arriving in the United States are well documented. Twenty years later, in contrast, the Mariel Boat Lift exodus of 1980 was composed mainly of poor Cubans, whose levels of education were much lower than those of the first wave of immigrants from Cuba. Many of these new refugees came from jails and institutions for the mentally ill. Some did not acquire permanent resident status for more than a decade and continue to struggle in the lower echelons of society (Daniels, 2002). Some were sent back. In the case of Vu, he belongs to the cohort of Vietnamese immigrants who came to the United States as a result of the end of the Vietnam War.

It is generally accepted that it is better to acquire this information from books, movies, journals, magazine articles, and other media, rather than from the clients. Immigrant clients may believe that counselors who do not know enough about the clients' background will not pay attention to the clinical issues because they are too eager and too curious to gather information from the clients. Once the counselors have the general overview of the main historical facts, the main recent facts, and the immigration cohort, they are better equipped to find out the specific effects on the client.

Psycholinguistic History

Counselors may want to inquire about the particulars of first and second language acquisition to understand clients' past and current struggles and their unique relational and contextual experiences (Perez-Foster, 1996). The age of acquisition of the two languages, the nature of the relationships with people from whom languages were learned, and the environmental context of language acquisition might help a counselor understand the experience of the self of the client when speaking different languages, as well as other important issues that may not otherwise emerge in therapy. When children learn English at an early age, the "forgotten" language is often still there. Clients who at some point were bilingual may want to refer to their early memories, which may include early language memories. People who were bilingual at some point in their lives may have two language codes with which they think about themselves (Perez-Foster, 1996). Some of their earlier interactions with significant people in their lives may linger in affect, modes of expression, and relational characteristics tied in with their early language acquisition. Childhood memories can be uniquely expressed during the therapeutic process because the original language can be seen as a vehicle for reviving the past with a more fully expressed affect (Javier, 1996). This is particularly important for immigrant clients with a traumatic history. Also, the experience with the acquisition of the English language may allow for the emergence of therapeutic themes, such as rejection or acceptance by peers, that may not otherwise emerge. Allowing clients to tell their experiences with the acquisition of each of their languages, and the contextual relationships associated with them, can be helpful in the therapeutic process.

COUNTERTRANSFERENCE

Clients like Vu may elicit in the counselor an excessive curiosity, particularly in the clinician who is not familiar with the culture of the client.

Depending on their ideological position, counselors might be tempted to rush clients into a connection with their cultural background that they may not be ready to make.

Excessive Curiosity About the Client's Background

An intriguing foreign culture may affect the therapeutic process if the counselor loses sight of the therapeutic task (Gorkin, 1996). In the therapeutic intervention section, the need for the provider to gather the information from outside sources was discussed. If the counselor does not do that, he or she will have to rely too much on the client as a source of information. Comas-Diaz and Jacobsen (1991) aptly termed this phenomenon "anthropologist syndrome," during which the clinician may be overly curious about the client's background and spend too much time exploring aspects of the client's culture, at the expense of the client's needs.

Wish to Help Clients Go Back to Their Roots

If a clinician subscribed to the nativist position (i.e., assuming an indigenous or ethnic reaffirmation belief (Falicov, 1998a), he or she would be tempted to challenge Vu to adhere to his Vietnamese culture by returning to his cultural roots after hearing him say, "I am an American." Counselors with this position might be distressed at hearing that Vu is practically disconnected from his real parents, his siblings, and his language and cultural values and might try to convince Vu to embrace his original Vietnamese culture. If the counselor has this ideological point of view, it is necessary to share it with the client and articulate this position as one opinion and not the only possible truth (Falicov, 1998a), or else a client like Vu, who is not interested in an examination of his roots at this time, might drop out of counseling, which the client may have requested for different reasons.

TOOLBOX ACTIVITY—VU			
Resources and Suggested Readings	*Videos*	*Activities*	*Discussion Questions*
Fong, R. (Ed.). (2003). *Culturally competent practice with immigrant and refugee children and families.* New York: Guilford Press. Pipher, M. (2002). *The middle of everywhere: Helping refugees enter the American community.* Orlando, FL: Harcourt. Rasco, L., & Miller, K. (2003). *The mental health of refugees: Ecological approaches to healing and adaptation.* Mahwah, NJ: Lawrence Erlbaum. Suarez-Orozco, C., & Suarez-Orozco, M. (2002). *Children of immigration: The developing child.* Cambridge, MA: Harvard University Press.	*Los Olvidados (The Young and the Damned)* *Europa! Europa!* *Dirty Pretty Things*	Research on the Internet the recent U.S. laws about acceptance and rejection of refugees and the countries where most refugees are coming from. Interview a bilingual individual and ask where he or she speaks the different languages. Ask whether the individual's experience of him or herself is the same or different according to the language the individual is speaking.	Content Themes What other themes do you see emerging in the story that the author did not identify? Assessment Are there any questions you would like to ask Vu? Interventions What other interventions could you propose with Vu? Countertransference What countertransference reactions were emerging in yourself as you read this story? Other Scenarios What would have occurred if Vu had wanted to keep a close relationship with his Vietnamese family? How would Vu's life have been different if he had been raised in several foster homes instead of one? Imagine that Vu is coming to you either several years earlier or several years from now with a presenting problem. Imagine what that presenting problem could be?

Esteban's Story 9

Still Uprooted

Esteban tells the story of his displacement and exile from Cuba at the age of 14 years and his subsequent struggles in orphanages and foster homes in the United States after being separated from his family of origin. We learn about what he lost, the strengths he has used to make sense of his losses, and how he sees himself in the context of his life in the United States. As you read this story, notice how he describes the loss of his family, his social and economic status, and his contexts and language. Pay particular attention to his sophisticated use of written English, which contrasts with how he feels about his accented spoken English. Also, notice how strongly he holds onto his identity as a Cuban and how he longs for a return to the paradisiacal and beloved country of his youth.

Esteban's Story

I was born into an upper-middle-class family of European (French and Spanish) origin in Cuba in 1947, during the years prior to Castro's Communist revolution of 1959. At the time of my birth, and throughout my childhood, my father was an engineer and administrator, who was the director of a large corporation. My mother was an educator and homemaker, who dedicated herself primarily to raising her children and running our household. My sister—who was three years my senior—and I lived in an atmosphere of emotional and financial comfort and stability. In addition, we were the recipients of a sense of psychological security, which was conscientiously bestowed on us by our parents and which simultaneously resulted from our organized style of life.

I experienced my family of origin as a loving, peaceful, nurturing, and well-structured system. My parents enjoyed a long, happy, and stable marriage. They formed a successful team and equally distributed their parenting responsibilities so that both parents provided quality time to my sister and me.

As a result of my parents' socioeconomic position, my earliest identity was formed against the backdrop of Cuba's upper stratum. This was at once a gift and a tragedy, given the devastating, politically imposed, all-encompassing losses that followed Castro's Communist revolution of 1959. The gift was receiving a refined and somewhat privileged reception into human life. The tragedy was that such graciousness did not prepare me for the poverty, emotional devastation, and personal and relational losses I would begin to experience in my early adolescence after the initiation of my forced expatriation.

I, along with more than 14,000 other children, experienced forced expatriation from Cuba in 1962, when I was 14 years old—as an unaccompanied child. My parents sent me into political exile in the United States, through the then-clandestine Operation Peter Pan, which was organized and funded by the Catholic Welfare Bureau and led by Monsignor Bryan O. Walsh. This operation facilitated the largest recorded political exodus of children in the Western Hemisphere. After arriving in the United States, I was sent to a refugee camp for adolescent Cuban boys, which was located south of the Miami area. We lived in Spartan, barracks-type accommodations, which constituted a marked change from the physical comforts and emotional security to which I had been accustomed in Cuba. During the three months I spent in camp, I cried every day under the same pine tree for hours at a time, mourning the loss of part of myself—my family, my comfort, and my existential and phenomenological security.

Subsequently, I received an academic merit scholarship to continue my secondary education in a Catholic high school in Delaware. During the next two years, I resided in a group home for boys, which was administered by a Catholic priest, who was also on the faculty of the high school I attended. Thereafter, I was, once again, relocated to a third destination—an orphanage in Omaha, Nebraska, where I completed my final year of high school in 1967.

I reunited with my parents in Omaha at approximately the time I completed high school. My sister, Anna, was not able to seek political exile because, by the time my parents were able to obtain exit visas in 1967, she had married and had given birth to her first child. Her husband was of military age and would not be allowed to exit Cuba for at least a decade. The reunion with my parents—after five years of separation—was bittersweet. I was angry and disappointed that Castro's government did not allow my sister, with whom I had been quite close, to leave the island. Furthermore, notwithstanding my intense joy at being reunited with my parents in exile, I had to contend with the realization that things would not be the same as they had been in Cuba. For example, my family would never again be complete, and the privileged socioeconomic conditions that my parents had provided for me in Cuba were gone forever. Thus, I found my parents' vulnerability to the harsh conditions of forced expatriation to be quite devastating. It was excruciatingly painful to see that my father—once the powerful and highly respected administrator of a leading international corporation in Cuba—had to accept an insignificant factory position that had nothing to do with his engineering background or administrative expertise to help the family survive financially. My mother, who herself had been a distinguished educator in Cuba, also had no alternative but to accept factory work, which held no relevance to her profession and personal meaning in reference to her life goals. These profound, transcending wounds have left a long-lasting mark on my sense of self and my developing identity.

I perceived my forced expatriation as a highly traumatic phenomenon, which not only represented a series of profound sociopolitical, economic, and cultural losses but also entailed a long separation from my parents at a very sensitive age and a permanent separation from my sister, which culminated in her premature death at the age of 44 years, the result of an "automobile accident" in Cuba in 1988. As such, these critical elements have constituted the loss of my phenomenological framework and original sociocultural context and have come to represent losses of a transcending and irretrievable nature in my life. For example, gone was the psychological security of having an extended family and a support network. Furthermore, our family system was drastically reduced from a comprehensive constellation, which included grandparents and younger-generation aunts, uncles, and cousins, to a nuclear family unit, which was comprised solely by my parents and myself.

My current values are a blend of my mother's and my father's beliefs, life philosophies, and manners of being-in-the-world, and they reflect an unresolved polarity between realistic industriousness and the romantic delusion that one is still a member of the upper class while living in conditions of near poverty, a state which hundreds of thousands of political exiles encountered upon arrival in the United States. My values also constitute the essence of my "received" identity and of the identity I have actively chosen to incorporate into my sense of self, as a conscious, reflective adult. For example, although given my present status as a full-time graduate student, my income is somewhat limited, my values, aspirations, social training, and philosophy of life have nothing to do with this temporary category and continue to correspond to the upper socioeconomic grooming I received as a child. Furthermore, the humanistic values, which I received from both of my parents, I believe, characterize most accurately my consciously chosen manner of being-in-the-world. This is reflected in my chosen profession, as a "wounded healer," in the field of psychology and in my professional dedication—spanning the past 20 years—to providing culturally sensitive services to the most discriminated-against minority populations.

I was brought up as a member of the Caucasian race—both biologically and socioculturally. This has been instrumental in maintaining an intact sense of racial identity in my subsequent experiences as a political exile in a country such as the United States, where ethnicity is often absurdly confounded with race and where even the most explicit and obvious Caucasian individuals of Latin American extraction (mostly of the younger generation) are effectively brainwashed into thinking that they, indeed, are not Caucasian because they were born in a Spanish-speaking country. Such individuals have had to contend with ethnic discrimination, notwithstanding that they indeed are members of the Caucasian race, given the issue that they are not, per se, "classic" representatives of what has been denominated as "culturally White" by a collective of powerful and influential—but highly ignorant and uncultivated—individuals, who have succeeded in establishing the "rules and regulations" for what is, and what is not, "socioculturally White." These individuals have, moreover, established that Whiteness is a "registered trademark" and a monopoly of exclusively one group of Caucasians in the world—namely, the U.S. Anglo-Saxons. In view of these anthropologically absurd antics, which, unfortunately, are widespread, I am quite proud of having arrived in this country as an individual with an already well-developed sense of self, including the dimensions of racial and ethnic identity. I am, furthermore, proud that, notwithstanding the social and academic ignorance of mainstream society, I have remained impervious to the indoctrination of the latter and have not succumbed to the betrayal of my identity as a member of the Caucasian race—for the sake of the so-called ease of not having to swim against the preposterous and absurd current of "mainstream" society's collective and all-encompassing ignorance.

In terms of ethnic or national identity, along with tens of thousands of youngsters, I was deprived of growing up on my own soil and within the emotional security of my own cultural infrastructure. Instead, my cohorts and I have grown up as foreigners in the United States, and, notwithstanding our legal status as permanent residents or American citizens, we shall remain as ontological foreigners for the rest of our lives—our cultural identities split forever between two irreconcilable nations. Along with more than one million other individuals, my family experienced the total confiscation of our businesses, real estate, private property, bank accounts, and other assets by Castro's government. Shortly after the revolution, we were exposed to diverse forms of political oppression, such as the abolishment of the freedoms of speech and press, the abolition of governmental elections, the Marxist-Leninist indoctrination of children at school, the persecution of the clergy, and the eradication of free enterprise. As political dissidents, we were permitted to exit Cuba with only a few personal belongings and very limited funds (i.e., $5 per person).

Experiencing these devastating events during early adolescence, followed by my attempts to consolidate my original national identity with my newly acquired status as a political expatriate living in a foreign country, resulted in profound existential turmoil and a state of cultural uprootedness.

Thus, through the phenomenon of forced expatriation, I, along with hundreds of thousands of exiled Cubans, experienced a resulting, all-encompassing feeling-state of phenomenological uprootedness—that is, a lack of cultural, historical, and national continuity and stability. Many of us who were exiled at an early age may regard ourselves as the lost generation of the late 20th century—a collective of individuals whose lives were developmentally and phenomenologically quartered by the devastating socioeconomic, political, and cultural effects of the Communist revolution and the ensuing chaos of political exile. From a metaphorical perspective, many Cuban expatriates of our generation conceive of ourselves as sociocultural-psychological abortions. This is a state of being that emerges as the result of having lost our original framework to exist (i.e., the conditions of our lives in Cuba, before the Communist revolution), as a consequence of not fitting in, either into what Cuba has become under Communist rule or, ontologically, into the phenomenological sphere of our adopted country of exile, and as a consequence of having had our existential development interrupted.

In my developmental process, this feeling of cultural displacement—of not having roots anywhere—gradually evolved into a perduring, multidimensional sense of existential alienation from postrevolutionary, Communist Cuba and, simultaneously, to some degree, from my country of exile, the United States. It is this inescapable presence of alienation, per se, that comes to form an inextricable part of many Cuban exiles' national identity and existential framework: the nauseating feeling of not belonging anywhere—a perpetual state of being in existential limbo persists even after four decades of political exile. I do not feel completely North American, and I do not feel Cuban in the manner in which Cuba exists geopolitically today. Along with many of my exiled cohorts, I remain inexorably Cuban in my identification with a unique society, with its own phenomenological configuration, which ceased to exist in 1959, following the Communist takeover.

It is important to distinguish here between the experience of an immigrant and that of an expatriate. Cuban expatriates do not practice the mentality or philosophy of immigration, which lends itself to a more adaptive attitude on the part of the individual who, as an immigrant per se, is voluntarily seeking an alternative—and permanent—life in a new country. The early-wave Cuban expatriate who belonged to the island's considerably large upper and middle classes would not have left Cuba seeking a better life in the United States because prior to the revolution there was no socioeconomic need for such action, given the expatriate's level of professional and fiduciary development.

Along with my family and myself, the overwhelming majority of Cuban expatriates believed that our political exile would be short-lived and temporary and that we would return to Cuba after Castro's demise. Forty-four years after our political exile, many Cuban expatriates still consider the possibility of returning to Cuba after the eradication of Communism. For example, many of my peers and I consider it an ethical responsibility as well as a human right and privilege to return to Cuba after Castro's demise and to participate in the long and comprehensive reconstruction process, which will be needed to restore Cuba to the functional first-world nation it was prior to Castro's invasion.

The relevant point is that the majority of Cuban expatriates presently residing in political exile throughout the world would not have left their nation for socioeconomic, migratory reasons. Thus, as a first-wave Cuban expatriate, I consider myself to be in exile solely from Castro's totalitarian government, from the ensuing abolition of the basic human rights that are upheld in a democratic system, and from the preclusion of free enterprise as it is recognized internationally, within a capitalistic infrastructure. As such, I am not in exile from the fatherland, in itself, and I shall continue indefinitely to await Cuba's eventual recovery and restoration to democracy, a key and highly present issue in the execution of my daily existence.

This may be the reason why my struggles with the English language were so severe. English was not spoken at home during my childhood and early adolescence. I had difficulties once I arrived in the United States. The acquisition of English has been a painful process and an instrumental component of my identity construction. I have an idiosyncratic speech pattern that embodies my struggles with losing my original and desirable psychosociocultural framework, the temporality of my forced expatriation, and my resistance to the acquisition of (or the serious attempts to learn) standard English phonemes as a strategy for not being assimilated by the dominant culture, to keep my Cuban identity intact. I know that people still struggle to understand my heavy accent.

Notwithstanding the ravaging experiences connected with my loss of country and forced expatriation, and even after assuming the role of a political exile, my identity was constructed within the values, norms, and structure of an affluent, Cuban-European family. However, even the upper stratum of Cuban society was still considerably influenced by a phallocentric model of psychosocial development and functioned primarily from a patriarchal perspective. Therefore, gender identity formation and sexual orientation issues were clear: heterosexuality was, unquestionably, the only acceptable sexual orientation for both my sister and for me. Gender roles were clearly delineated for men and women, very much in a parallel manner to the upper-class, 1950s society of the United States. In Cuba, as in the United States, a critically differentiating experience in female and male development is generated from the transcultural phenomenon that women are, for the most part, responsible for early child care. Therefore, the development of my masculine traits and my defined male personality took place in relation with and in connection to other individuals to a lesser degree than did my sister's identity formation. As a result, my sister was less individuated than I, and I was more autonomous and self-oriented than she was. For example, through the process of early identification with our mother, my sister developed a sense of self that was continuous with others as well as connected to the world. As a consequence of the fact that women are mostly mothered by women, as a female child, my sister developed within a self-in-relation context of relational capacities and needs, in which significant importance was placed on the mother-daughter connection as an empathic unit of ongoing mutual support and on the values of nurturing and caring for others, kindness and graciousness in human transactions, and self-development within a framework of respecting and supporting the simultaneous progress of others. Conversely, my own gender identity formation was more independent and autonomous and more centered on developing myself as an individual entity versus a being-in-relation-to-others. Decades later, it was the referred independent and autonomous attitude that, in part, contributed to my divorce from my second wife. I now remember that she would often make reference—quite accurately and specifically—to the marked contrast between the manner in which she perceived herself in our relationship (i.e., as a being-in-relationship) and the manner in which she perceived that I behaved in our relationship (i.e., with much less reciprocity and mutuality, focusing more on my personal development versus our development as a team). In retrospect, I realize that this was a valuable lesson to learn.

Furthermore, from a multigenerational perspective, males played a dominant role in both my paternal and maternal ancestors' lives. These phallocentric gender and societal roles were consistently transmitted across the generations to my own family of origin, wherein males enjoyed more personal freedom, individual autonomy, and decision-making power than females and benefited from certain double standards of behavior. For example, at the age of 12 or 13 years, I had more privileges and personal autonomy than my sister, who was then 16 years old. Whereas I received the message that I was *macho, varón, y masculino* and therefore had the upper hand, she received a message of deference to the masculine sex—a message against which she fortunately successfully rebelled.

Again, these previously held values of male dominance ultimately resulted in significant conflicts in my second marriage to a Cuban woman, whose feminist orientation toward gender equality contributed considerably to my progressive rejection of what I now realize is an unfair and quite primitive value system. As a result of many academic discussions with my second former spouse (who presently remains my closest friend and colleague), and of my own consistent reflections on the subject matter, I have adopted a more humanistic and egalitarian worldview and understanding of human relationships, and understand the critical importance of mutuality in all—not just in marital relationships.

In addition, my phallocentric family context affected my first attempt at forming a nuclear family. My daughter, Mabel (from my first marriage), at 10 years old nervously asked me if I wanted or planned to have a son, as if I would not be satisfied with merely having a daughter. By the time Mabel confronted me with this issue, I had divorced my first wife and had remarried, and my value system had evolved to the point that I was able to reassure her that I was ecstatic to have her as an only child and that she would always be my treasured and beautiful offspring.

Another pattern is that all first-born or only sons—including myself—have been consistently and invariably named after their fathers on both sides of the family. Having been given my father's name was at once a great honor and a marked challenge. Given that my father was a highly educated, culturally refined, and sophisticated individual who was gifted in many areas of life, and that he was, simultaneously, a truly accomplished professional in the fields of engineering and technical administration, at times I felt awed by his presence and by the expectation to follow in his footsteps. For example, I was expected to become an engineer and completed 1.5 years of engineering courses.

In addition, because both my sister and I inherited our gender-consistent parental names (i.e., Anna and Esteban), I was resolute not to name my daughter, Mabel, after her mother or anyone else in the family. I voted to choose a name that had no antecedents on either side of the families of origin, thereby presenting Mabel with the opportunity to develop and formulate her own essence as an individual, without preconceived family notions or expectations from prior personas.

Again, although as a Cuban expatriate I am considered to represent an ethnic minority in the United States, I am aware that my simultaneous membership in the Caucasian race has also entitled me to certain privileges that minority groups of color have not been able to receive, including easier upward mobility and the absence of racial discrimination on an almost daily basis, which is part of other minorities' phenomenological experience.

I feel that I have also successfully maintained my identity as a Caucasian individual, despite daily exposure to the absurd stereotyping and social ignorance of mainstream Anglo-American society, which postulates that Anglo-Saxons are the sole ethnicity with rightful claim to authentic membership in the Caucasian race. This latter ability to maintain an intact identity as a member of the Caucasian race despite the endless brainwashing that takes place through all possible mediums of written and verbal communication in the United States at times feels comparable to swimming upstream against a force equitable to that of Niagara Falls and actually surviving; it is, indeed, a significant accomplishment. I feel that as an individual I have attained a certain degree of integrated biculturalism (i.e., the ability to be involved in both my culture of origin and the culture of my host society without having a blended identity), while maintaining an intact sense of identity as a Cuban expatriate. Having had the subjective experience of forced expatriation from my fatherland, Cuba; having had four decades of life in political exile to consciously analyze and reflect on my context as a Cuban national living in the United States, with all the profound levels of loss and reconstruction such a position in life entails; and, finally, having attained an effective level of integration of the two cultures in reference, I feel comfortable with the experience of encountering and understanding the unique processes of cultural transition and acculturation of other individuals in phenomenological transition.

Finally, as a Caucasian, I have developed an effective working knowledge about racial, ethnic, cultural, and religious differences, and, since the time of my residence in Cuba—a time also marked by ethnic and racial diversity—I have actively and consciously worked on developing a nonracist, humanistically oriented, Caucasian identity. As previously stated, I was raised with humanistic, Christian values, which place emphasis on equality and justice for both genders and for individuals of all races, ethnicities, cultures, and socioeconomic backgrounds. Moreover, my parents believed in social justice and equality and ran their household in a democratic and equalitarian manner. Thus, the principles of racial, ethnic, cultural, and gender equality have been of paramount importance in my upbringing and in the development of my sense of identity as a Caucasian of Cuban nationality.

I have successfully become bilingual and bicultural, and I can function quite capably and efficiently in both the mainstream U.S. culture and in my culture of origin, which I consider to be at least as efficient and high-functioning as U.S. mainstream culture. I have been able to incorporate many aspects of U.S. culture without forsaking my own ethnic identity and value system. In addition, I have emerged as a stronger, more sensitive, more insightful human being as a result of this process. However, at a deeper, existential level, it would be absurd to deny that there are still unresolved personal and identity issues, which are the natural consequences of the loss of my cultural framework; of the fact that Cuba has not, as yet, been liberated from Communism; and of the reality that a democratic process has still not been restored to millions of individuals whose human rights continue to be violated by a totalitarian regime.

━ ▪ ━ ▪ ━ ▪ ━ ▪ ━ ▪ ━ ▪ ━ ▪ ━ ▪ ━ ▪ ━ ▪ ━ ▪ ━ ▪ ━

Content Themes

In this story, Esteban tells us about the profound effects his losses have had in his life. He describes the sorrow at his loss of country, family, upper-middle-class comforts, and language, weaving in the themes of acculturation and ethnicity in his relationship with the American cultural milieu.

TRAGIC LOSS

One of the first themes to emerge in the story of Esteban is the issue of loss. Esteban's reaction to his parents' decision to send him to the United States when he was 14 years old still feels raw, and he understands the experience of "psychological uprootedness" as the most traumatic event in his life. He perceives himself as a "sociocultural-psychological abortion." He recalls that during the first three months of residence in the United

States, he "cried every day under the same pine tree." Throughout the story, Esteban talks about losing his economic security, his immediate and extended family, his cultural infrastructure, and his cultural identity.

Esteban describes his losses from the perspective of a child losing the security and comfort of the world that was known to him. The tragedy of the losses is even more evident in him because Esteban came to the United States as an orphan, uprooted from a known and secure world by a decision his own parents made in an effort to offer him a better opportunity in the United States.

LANGUAGE LOSS

The possibility of loss of the language of origin, and the difficulties with the acquisition of the new language, makes it one of the most salient themes for a first-generation immigrant. A second language is best acquired in the first few years of life. Children and early adolescents learn the fastest, and adults the slowest. After age 12 or 14 years, the acquisition of a new language is more difficult (Berger, 2004; Johnson-Powell & Yamamoto, 1997). Complete native speaking and writing command of two or more languages is difficult and quite rare. Generally, individuals with bilingual capabilities have to use translation processes as part of their encoding in the second language, and they need to invest attention in how they say things as well as in what they say, which may make them look detached, vague, anxious, and less real (Marcos, 1976; Marcos & Urcuyo, 1979).

When children and adolescents learn English, they may end up having various degrees of proficiency in English and their language of origin. Some immigrants keep their maternal language intact, whereas others, for reasons other than the age at migration, do not. Esteban has kept his Spanish alive. There seems to be a clear relationship between acculturation and language. The more acculturated the individual, the better the command of English and the more loss of the language of origin; however, that relationship is not necessarily linear (Kuo & Roysircar, 2004; Torres & Rollock, 2004). As is evident in Esteban's writing, his command of written English is highly sophisticated, while at the same time his oral command is not; we know his "idiosyncratic speech pattern" is still intact because people still "struggle to understand" his "heavy accent." An interesting characteristic of Esteban's writing style is the high level of cognitive and intellectual sophistication that makes it look almost cerebral and unemotional. This style can be understood as a coping mechanism he is exhibiting to deal with the traumatic events in his life. It could also be related to his strong accent in English. It is not unusual for an individual who comes from a highly educated family to have well-developed written English proficiency not matched by the level of oral proficiency (Torres & Rollock, 2004). Many educated immigrants possess a good command of the written

English language. The sophistication of written English may also be a way of compensating for concerns about oral proficiency.

An adult immigrant can be affected by the double language loss. Dual encoding in two contexts affects the acquisition and use of both languages. On the one hand, with lack of practice and an inability to encode new material in the native language after migration, the native language gradually becomes obsolete and stale. Immigrants who do not have the opportunity to use words and expressions of their maternal language may end up with holes in the language that come from lack of practice. On the other hand, the acquisition of the second language by an adult lacks the depth and completeness of the language acquisition that takes place during early schooling. The first-generation immigrant ends up characteristically having a hybrid English, mixed with words in the language of origin, and a hybrid language of origin, mixed with English. For example, one of us, Sara, cannot articulate in English information first learned in Spanish in the first 30 years of her life, and it is common for her not to be able to articulate ideas in Spanish encoded in the last 20 years of living, learning, and teaching in the United States. If she is speaking to her mother in Spanish about something she learned originally in English in the United States, she has to use English words and has difficulty saying it in Spanish, whereas if she is speaking to her American friends in English about something encoded as a young child in Argentina, she sometimes sounds inarticulate or unintelligent.

Language can be one of the most profound losses of an immigrant. Because immigrants are so worried about everything that needs to be learned in the process of assimilation into another culture, the loss can be inconspicuous: immigrants might not be aware of the loss until they suddenly realize that they really miss the language. Someone like Esteban may miss speaking in Spanish, reading fiction in Spanish, listening to music in Spanish, and speaking Spanish with friends. Language loss is the equivalent of losing an important relationship.

LANGUAGE, ACCULTURATION, AND ETHNICITY

The relationship between language, acculturation, and ethnicity is complex and multidimensional. The age of migration and the level of education of the immigrant are not the only factors that influence the magnitude of the loss of the native language. There are other factors in play, such as the degree of ambivalence toward the immigration decision, the level of choice in the decision, the experience after entering U.S. cultural contexts, the degree to which the immigrant wishes to acculturate, and many others. This is clear when Esteban talks about his cultural heritage, his accent, and his ethnicity. Esteban talks about his continued struggles with the language, having never lost his accent. As is not uncommon with other Cuban expatriates who had to leave everything behind, he still sees himself as having a Cuban identity that he would have gladly maintained had it not been for tragic political events. There is then a psychological component in Esteban's issues with his second language acquisition that is related to his experience with his involuntary migration and his acculturation process. This has affected both his acquisition of English and how he makes meaning out of his experience of migration. The wife of the professional husband, who reluctantly follows him to the United States from her native country and who would have preferred not to emigrate, might have a harder time learning English and adapting to the new environment than someone in similar circumstances who has her own motivations to emigrate in addition to accompanying her husband in his professional pursuits. This psychological component in language acquisition can be either conscious or unconscious; can affect the immigrant's acquisition of, and relationship with, the second language; and relates to the process of adaptation to a new cultural milieu. Esteban tackles his issues with acculturation with a mixture of nostalgia, rage, and a sense of continued alienation. Esteban says that while growing up in the United States, he felt without root and still considers himself to be in exile. Later in his story, he explains that he has incorporated many aspects of U.S. culture "without forsaking" his own ethnic identity and value system.

In terms of his ethnicity, Esteban considers himself White but explains that he has absurdly been viewed as a minority by the "ignorant" Anglo-American society, feeling at times as if he is "swimming upstream against a force equitable to that of Niagara Falls and actually surviving." Seemingly contradictory identity allegiances, opposing views within himself, and contrasting positions in terms of where he stands in relation to the host culture are not unusual ways of coping with the dislocation and the traumatic nature of Esteban's immigration experience; they are connected to his loss of his original language and his acquisition of the new one and his identity as a Cuban, a White male, and a bicultural American.

IMMIGRATION AND SOCIAL CLASS

Every immigrant's story is in part also a story related to issues of social class. Often immigrants change their social class standing, sometimes quite dramatically. It can go either up or down, rarely staying the same (Breunlin, Schwartz, & Mac Kune-Karrer, 1997; Mirkin, 1998). Sometimes the change in social class status is related to a change in educational status, but not always. Esteban's forced migration carried with it traumatic loss of upper-class comfort.

What one defines as social class markers also varies according to habits and customs of the country of origin. The rise in social class can be as dramatic and challenging as its decline. For the poorest immigrant, the encounter with the American shopping experience, with its array of choices and the availability of credit that allows the illusion of material ownership, can be an overwhelming occurrence. The overwhelming difference between the austerity of the country of origin and the vastness, richness, abundance, and megasizes of the United States is a universally shocking experience for the immigrant.

Immigrant families who are less financially successful in the United States than in their country of origin clearly experience stressors (Mirkin, 1998). For the immigrant from a middle-class or upper-middle-class background in a non-Western society, coming to the United States can mean a dramatic change downward. It is not uncommon for middle-class families in urban areas of Latin America, Africa, or Asia, for example, to have full-time, live-in maids who perform all household duties, a chauffeur, a handyman, delivery people to bring goods to the household, and so on. In hierarchical non-Western societies where labor costs are less expensive, families do not have to be wealthy to have access to inexpensive household help. In the United States, with its more democratic and egalitarian traditions and its high cost of labor, this is not possible except for wealthy families.

In Esteban's case, his parents had to work in menial jobs in the United States after having lived a life that a successful managerial position afforded in the Cuba of the 1950s. It is not unusual for professionals or former managers to find that in the United States they cannot use their training. Esteban's sister died never having been reunited with her parents and her brother in the United States. His way of living in existential limbo and not quite acculturating, his difficulties with the language, and his perception of himself in constant angst may be explained at least in part by his anguish related to the family's loss of social class standing. How can he be happy if his family is not? How can he be happy if his family lost everything they had? With his sister still in Cuba, poor and without the chances to ever improve her social class standing, how can he forget that he is really a Cuban at heart from before the Castro dictatorship? In his view, were he to stop waiting for Castro to be deposed and for the longed-for old social class standing to be restored, he would betray his roots and his own identity as a Cuban.

Clinical Applications

This section includes assessment questions related to the content themes of the story that might be useful to ask with first-generation immigrant clients. The interventions address the technique of language switching, and the countertransference section includes sadness, guilt, denial of the client's culture, and a wish to prove that the clinician is above prejudice.

ASSESSMENT

With first-generation immigrant clients like Esteban, it is important to assess language losses, changes in social class standing, and the clients' views of themselves in terms of their ethnicity and their experiences with the American culture.

Language Loss

Is your writing and oral English proficiency the same or different?

If you have an accent, how do you experience it?

Do you recall experiences about how your accent affects other people?

If you are bilingual, how do you experience yourself when speaking the two different languages?

In what language do you dream, count, curse, talk to yourself, or fantasize?

Shifts in Social Class

What do you think about your current economic and social class standing?

Has the social class or economic status of your family of origin changed?

Has it improved? Worsened?

What are the challenges or benefits related to the change or lack of change in social class?

Ethnicity and Acculturation Views

What are some of your experiences with the American cultural milieu that have affected how you view yourself today?

Does your view of your ethnicity coincide with the way Americans view your ethnicity?

TECHNIQUES AND INTERVENTIONS

Language Switching and Language Mixing

Acculturated individuals with bilingual skills may function effectively in the professional world, for example, but the emotional connections to the early language may appear in surprising contexts. It is not unusual for a bilingual individual to dream, count, curse, or soothe an infant in the language of origin (Perez-Foster, 1996). Language switching is not uncommon, and the experience of self while speaking each language can shift dramatically, depending on the context (Marcos, 1976; Perez-Foster, 1996). Because language is associated with cultural meanings, individuals may perceive themselves as two different persons according to the language that they speak (Marcos & Urcuyo, 1979).

Sometimes bilingual clients may have the need to use the reservoir of emotional connections for early-encoded memories or to express current or old losses. One technique is to allow the clients to express in their language of origin the memory or the feeling state they are trying to convey, even if the counselor does not speak the language of the client (Fuertes, 2004; Perez-Foster, 1996). If the feeling state associated with the memories can be elicited in the language of origin, it might be expressed more fully, more genuinely, and more cathartically, even if the counselors cannot access the meaning of what the client is saying. One possibility is to ask the client to speak first in the language of origin and then ask the client to translate the memories into English. The richness of the memories may emerge more clearly when elicited in the originally encoded language (Javier, 1996). This fosters explorations into how the clients experience themselves in each language (Clauss, 1998).

Allowing clients to mix in words in their language of origin with their communications in English may make them feel freer to express themselves without having to censor the first word that comes to their minds. If clients can use words in their language of origin without fearing a negative reaction from the therapist, their expressions might appear more genuine, less rigid, and more natural.

COUNTERTRANSFERENCE

Clients like Esteban may elicit in their counselors intense sadness for their history of childhood uprooting. In addition, counselors may be confused and ambivalent about Esteban's cultural factors. In some respects, he is not like a stereotypical Hispanic male, and in other respects he may appear to be. He is highly educated and sophisticated. Most of the time, he does not consider himself an American and longs to return to Cuba. He expresses himself aggressively about the "ignorant" Americans who treat him like a "colored" minority. Counselors may feel defensively attacked and may wonder whether to, or how to, tackle the issues of Esteban's identity. Some may wish impatiently for him to give up his allegiance to Cuba, and others may prefer to avoid dealing with the complicated aspects of his identity.

Sadness or Guilt

For clients with immigration stories such as Esteban's, with their histories of early parental loss, refugee status, and struggles at an early age, sadness or guilt about the circumstance of the client's life may not be an unusual reaction (Comas-Diaz & Jacobsen, 1991). If unaware, the counselor could engage in behaviors that may not be helpful. For example, the clinician might feel too much compassion to be helpful, minimizing issues for fear of being labeled ignorant or insensitive. The therapist might be tempted to extend session time, cross boundary lines, encourage dependency, or have an attitude that places responsibility on the clinician and uses an approach of "I am going to be the person who makes all the wrongs go away" (Gorkin, 1996).

Denial of Culture

Because of the complexity of cultural identity issues like those that Esteban presents in his story, counselors may deny the existence of the cultural factors in the clients and treat them with the attitude that all people are more alike than different (Gorkin, 1996). If the counselor is of the same ethnic background as the client, the denial of the cultural issues in the client may be related to thinking that the similarities are so great that there is tacit understanding of what is going on without having to go into cultural issues. If the counselor is of a different ethnic background than that of the client, the identification may come from the supposed sharing of social class or level of education. It is not always easy to engage in conversations about culture, ethnicity, and the painful, sometimes accusatory experiences clients have with these issues. Because dealing with Esteban's cultural factors may appear to be complicated, the counselor may avoid it, creating distance and possibly a cultural myopia (Comas-Diaz & Jacobsen, 1991) that affect the therapeutic process.

Wish to Prove That the Clinician Is Above Prejudice

This is an interesting and often overlooked countertransference reaction that may seep into the therapeutic dyad and, when not acknowledged, may lead to disastrous outcomes (Gorkin, 1996). Often clients and counselors have differing family, political, religious, or sexual values. If a client evokes dislike or feelings of superiority in the counselor, the counselor may secretly feel discomfort for thinking that prejudices are coming to the surface. The concomitant push to bury those feelings and thoughts may stem from the intense need to prove that the counselor is without prejudice. Unacknowledged thoughts and feelings of this kind may result in pushing clients out of the therapeutic process or engaging in passive-aggressive behaviors or other unethical behaviors. These reactions may occur in counselors of the same or of different cultural backgrounds than the clients'.

TOOLBOX ACTIVITY—ESTEBAN			
Resources and Suggested Readings	*Videos*	*Activities*	*Discussion Questions*
Aciman, A. (2000). *Letters of transit: Reflections on exile, identity, language, and loss.* New York: New Press. Dorfman, A. (1999). *Heading south, looking north: A bilingual journey.* New York: Penguin Books. Stavans, I. (2002). *On borrowed words: A memoir on language.* New York: Penguin Books.	*Coming to America* *Moscow on the Hudson* *The Family Perez* *Rabbit-Proof Fence*	Interview recent immigrants and ask them what they like and don't like about living in the United States. Write your reactions in your journal. Write a two-page narrative about the foods, music, and relationships that you are the most nostalgic about or miss the most in your life. Research about recent changes in U.S.-Cuba policy and compare it to the United States' previous policy toward Cuba. What is your opinion about the two?	Content themes What other themes do you see emerging in the story that the author did not identify? Assessment Are there any questions you would like to ask Esteban? Interventions What other interventions could you propose with Esteban? Countertransference What countertransference reactions were emerging in yourself as you read this story? Other Scenarios How would Esteban's life be different had he been able to return to Cuba freely? Would Esteban feel differently about his identity as a Cuban had he been very poor before being forced to move to the United States?

Maria Luz's Story 10

Here We Are Not Free

Maria Luz, a recent immigrant from a small village in Mexico, describes how she arrived in the United States and what she hopes to accomplish. She was interviewed in March 2004, and Sara Schwarzbaum translated the interview from Spanish. When you read her story, notice the ambivalence about her decision to come to the United States, the description of her struggles as an undocumented immigrant who does not speak English, and her longing for her village, where life is different from life in the United States.

Maria Luz's Story

I'm from a small fishing village in Mexico, where I lived with my parents, two brothers, and one sister, until I came to America two years ago. My father does the fishing, and my mother sells the seafood. I used to help my mother sell the seafood in a big city two hours away from our village. We used to take the bus several times a week with our bags full of shrimp, crab, and calamari. Once in the city, we had to move from corner to corner. We couldn't stay in one place because we did not have a permit; we could not afford a city permit to set up a permanent stand. We were always running. That's how we made a living, my mom and me.

We had to support two brothers who went to school, which was in another town, far away from our village, more than an hour away. We had to pay for their transportation, their lunches, their books, their uniforms. I went to primary school. There was no money to send me to secondary school, and, because I was the oldest, I had to start helping my mom. When I started helping my mom sell the seafood, we made some more money, so we were able to send my brothers and sister to high school and a college preparatory school. My sister works in the marina. She went to the preparatory school, so she's doing better already.

We help my mom from here. We send her some money. My parents are still in Mexico. I decided to come here to find out how it was. I had heard a lot about the United States. Back in my village, I used to hear that in the United States, people were free, that life was better, that you could make a lot of money, that jobs paid well. But I didn't know about the obstacles that exist here. First of all, you have to know English; then, you have a have a "good" Social Security number to work here. When I got here, I didn't know anything; I didn't know how complicated it would be.

When we first decided to come to the United States, we arranged for work visas. There are contractors from Louisiana who go to our province to hire people to work for the pine growers, and that's how we got here. They hired us to work for three months in the pine fields. We were supposed to return to our province after the contract expired, but we didn't return to Mexico. We stayed here. If we had returned to Mexico, we would not have been able to come back to the United States. My husband already had a job here in Colorado. After a few months here, I returned to Mexico because I was pregnant with a baby, but I was not well and lost the baby. I stayed in Mexico for about nine months without my husband, and then I came back here, but this time, my husband had to pay someone to help me cross the border.

I walked for 48 hours in the Sonora Desert. There were 20 of us with two "coyotes." I was the only one trying to get to Colorado; all the others wanted to go to California. The coyotes were supposed to help me get to Colorado, but they didn't. They charged my husband $2,000 to get me to Colorado, but they didn't honor that agreement. They took the money and left me in California. I didn't have any money to make it to Colorado. So in California, I had to work in a house preparing meals for workers. I was the only woman. I was there for a month and a half. My husband had to pay again $1,000 to a woman who was to bring me to Colorado. I got here okay, and I started working again. That was two years ago. I worked bussing tables. The restaurant owner paid me $5 an hour. He treated me well. But the waitresses did not. I think they were racists; they used to scream and insult us. I left that job after seven months because I only made $5 an hour, because the waitresses mistreated me, and because I was pregnant. If I hadn't been pregnant, I would have stayed, but it was hard to take all the screaming and the insults. Also, they used to make me clean with harsh cleaning supplies, even though they knew I was pregnant.

The employers pay very little because they know that we don't have papers, that we can't denounce them or accuse them. That's why they pay less than what they are supposed to pay.

I worked without documents. They just gave me the job without asking for any papers. My husband found his job because of his uncle. He does not have any papers either. We bought a Social Security number only to be used in the contract because it's an illegal paper. The employer wants it. My husband's job is good. They used to pay him $6.75 an hour. He's been there for about eight years now. So they pay him $8.75 an hour now. He works 40 hours a week. But the money is not sufficient. We have to be very careful with what we spend. For example, we don't have medical insurance. My daughter was born here. She has public aid because she was born here. I imagined that life here would be beautiful and that we would have more money, that I was going to help my family. It's very different from what I dreamed it was going to be. Here we are not free. In my village, I'm free. I can get out of the house and go wherever I want to go. Here I am trapped between the four walls of my apartment. If we need to go out, we need a car. I don't have a car or friends. I thought we would live better. I wanted to build my house in Mexico. That was my dream when we came: that we were going to be able to work here and make enough money to build the house in Mexico, so we could return there. But it's been almost three years, and it has not happened. I would like to go back because I want to see my parents. I can't leave the United States because, if I leave, I cannot come back in. I would have to come back in as an illegal again and pay a lot of money to return. I would like to stay in the United States because of my daughter. She could be well prepared and learn English, and here there are better opportunities for her. Mexico is a very poor country. To study and go to school you have to have a lot of money, whereas here, we can both work, and she can go to school. At the same time, I would like to go back and see my family. The dream was to come here and work for five years to be able to go back home and build our house. We could not have built a house had we stayed there. We didn't mean to start a family here. We wanted to wait, but I got pregnant by accident, so now I cannot work. But we don't make enough money here. Rent, phone, gas, and electric bills are very expensive. We pay $1,039 in rent. This apartment has two bedrooms, but six people live here, so we can share the rent. We take one bedroom, two other guys take the second, and two of my husband's cousins sleep in the living room. If you have a car, the police stop you because we don't have a driver's license. They are always stopping the cars. One of the guys who lives here does not have a license either. He was detained; they towed his car and took him to the police station. He does not have insurance for his car. He has very bad luck; the police are always detaining him, every month, because he does not have a driver's license. You see, you need a Social Security number to obtain a driver's license, and none of us has a Social Security number.

My daughter gives me strength. We always have problems, with the English, the lack of money, the constant fear of the police, and the troubles at work. She changes our lives. She makes it possible for us to stay here. Now, we prefer to stay here so that we can give our daughter a better education than the one we got. My husband only went to elementary school because he did not want to study; his parents could give him a better education, but he did not want it. The schools in Mexico are public. They don't have high schools in our area. Only big towns have schools. The cost of public education is high because you have to buy the books and the uniforms and pay the admission fees every year. Education is not mandatory in Mexico, so if people don't want to go to school, they don't. Many kids want to go to school, but they can't. The preparatory school does cost a lot of money.

Many people have lots of problems when they come alone, especially women. I came alone. I don't want women to come alone. Something bad happened to me, but with the help of my husband I am getting over it. When it happened, I was not going to tell him. But when I got here, I didn't want him to touch me. Thank God and with the help of the social worker who does the home visits I told him, and he helped me to get over it. When I got pregnant, the social worker also sent me to see a psychologist, who helped me a lot.

The one who raped me was the coyote. The other two ladies who came with me were also raped. They raped us because they knew that we were traveling alone. The other two were traveling alone, too. Nobody else knows about this, not my mother or my brothers and sister; this will stay in my heart forever. These are things that happened to us while traveling. I would have not said this, but I don't want this to happen to other people. It's very difficult. But if you put this in your book, it might be less difficult for other people.

What I like about being here is the city. It's beautiful. I also like the clothes here. Clothes are cheaper here. After one day of work, we can buy clothes. After one day of work, we can buy a week's worth of groceries. The only difference is that here we have to go to a store to buy everything, whereas back in Mexico we grow everything: oranges, plantains, avocados, garlic, potatoes, cabbage, carrots, chilis, onions, and corn. We plant everything, and then we harvest it. Here we have to buy everything.

What I like about the Americans is that they are blond and blue-eyed, so good-looking! They have a lot of opportunities here because they were born here. They live better. I wish I could live like them. They are not all rich. There are rich Americans and poor Americans.

I have a lot of problems with English. People call on the phone, and I don't understand what they are saying. I go to the store and want to buy something, and I don't know how to say it. Sometimes to go to the social service program I have to take a taxi. I have had two problems already with two different taxi drivers who have screamed at me because I don't speak English. I am going to school to learn English, but it's very hard. The teacher only speaks English, and there are a lot of things I don't understand. I am making progress. I can read some. I feel like I am learning. But it is very slow. I walk to school because it's close by. The teacher is very good.

The center also has computer classes. But I can't go because I already pay $4 for two hours of babysitting when I go to the English class; I cannot afford another hour of babysitting to go to the computer class. The center that offers these classes does not have a babysitting service.

I am very proud of myself because the social worker and the nurse told me that I am a good mom, that I take good care of my daughter, and they both told me that they are very proud of me. I always follow their advice. I go to the program classes. Going to those classes distracts me. I only go once a week. No other moms have cars. We have several friends, but I never see them during the week. We cannot visit each other or talk on the phone.

I heard of another person who is having a lot of trouble. The polleros left him in the middle of the desert. I heard that he had to walk 48 hours and drink his urine because he didn't have anything else to drink, until he found a truck driver who had other immigrants, and they picked him up. He is also having a hard time here. His relatives make him pay double what he is supposed to pay: double the rent, double the utilities. They borrow money from him, and they never return it. My husband hears about this at work. He gives him the money, so he does not fight with them. It's his own family. They never return the money that they borrow. He has his wife and children in Mexico, and his mother-in-law is very sick, so he keeps working here to send money back to Mexico and help them.

Occasionally I send money to my parents, $100 here and there. With that they can buy uniforms and pay the enrollment fee that has to be paid twice a year. They also need money for books. The school my brother goes to is a bit more expensive, but it's a better school.

A lot of the people from my village don't come here to the West. They go to a border town, where there are factories that employ Mexicans on the Mexican side. They don't have to be here illegally, and they make good money. It's unusual for a person from my village to be here. Most of the people who are here are from other provinces, not mine.

—— · —— · —— · —— · —— · —— · —— · —— · —— · —— · —— · —— · —— · ——

Content Themes

Maria Luz is here but longs for a small house in Mexico. At the same time, she wants to stay in the United States to provide her daughter with the education she did not have access to in Mexico. She was raped in the process of getting to the United States yet seems proud to be the best mom to her daughter. She has worked through some of the trauma, with the help of the social worker, the counselor, and her husband, and seems to function well, albeit with enormous difficulties, knowing that what keeps her going is the hope that she'll see her family again one day. In this section, we explore her ambivalent feelings about her immigration decision, how her voluntary decision to emigrate turned into a trap, her lack of skills in English, the differences between suburban life in the United States and life in her village, and, finally, the effects of her undocumented status.

AMBIVALENCE

One of the first themes to emerge from reading this and other immigrant stories is the ambivalence about the emigration decision. The desire to leave coexists frequently with the desire to stay (Daniels, 2002; Falicov, 2003; Grinberg & Grinberg, 2000). Maria Luz expresses the temporary nature of her desire to emigrate, so common to a lot of poor immigrants from Mexico and other parts of the world (Johnson-Powell & Yamamoto, 1997). She wants to emigrate only because she thinks she can earn enough money in the United States, but her goal is to return permanently to Mexico, even though she knows that staying in the United States would give her daughter better educational chances. The ambivalent and conflicting decision to emigrate permeates the stories of many people who want to or need to leave and yet wished that they did not have to do so. Whether the immigrant is highly educated or painfully unskilled, an ethnocentric attitude is a common human characteristic: people think that their food, their music, and their streets are the best and rarely want to leave the comfort of familiar sights and sounds (Grinberg & Grinberg, 2000). There has to be something in their country of origin that pushes them to leave (Daniels, 2002). Whether the immigrant comes from such an economically depressed area that leaving is a matter of survival or from an area where physical survival is not at stake, ambivalence is always present.

VOLUNTARY VERSUS INVOLUNTARY MIGRATION

Voluntary migration is frequently understood in opposition to involuntary migration, even though they are far from discrete categories. Voluntary immigration implies a deliberate choice to leave a country of origin to change or improve life, usually for financial, political, or religious reasons. Maria Luz's decision to migrate at first appears to fit in the voluntary immigration category. Because of the limited economic potential in Mexico and the need to help support younger siblings in school, traveling to the United States seemed to be the most logical of choices. In every voluntary immigrant there is an involuntary aspect of the decision to emigrate. If it had been possible for Maria Luz to survive in Mexico, she might not have left. Involuntary immigration is typically associated with forced migration, religious or political persecution, and refugee status. When Maria Luz first migrated, her intention had been to work, support her family, and return to Mexico. But she feels trapped now. The lack of opportunities available to her in Mexico and her current inability to return home, which would force her to be separated from her husband and her child because of her undocumented status, make her an involuntary immigrant.

DOCUMENTED VERSUS UNDOCUMENTED STATUS

The possibilities for employment and inclusion in the mainstream cultural contexts of a society are largely determined by documented or undocumented status. The majority of immigrants to the United States have documented status. They come equipped with student or work visas, or they receive their documented status as part of family reunification programs or their marital status. Documented status can also often be obtained with asylum and refugee status (Daniels, 2002). Other immigrants may be illegal or undocumented. In spite of media depictions and certain public perceptions, undocumented immigrants constitute only a small percentage of the overall American immigrant population. Although accurate calculations are obviously impossible to make, one estimate puts the proportion of undocumented immigrants at about 3 percent of the population of the U.S., with major increases having occurred in the last five years as a result of the increased ability of undocumented immigrants to find employment (Moreno, 2005).

Many hardships stem from immigrants' undocumented status, including low wages, the general inability to go back to the country of origin for family illness or death, and many others, as Maria Luz describes in her story. An immigrant can start out undocumented, as many who cross the borders from Mexico do, or become undocumented after overstaying a tourist visa, a work visa, or a student visa. Once here, the undocumented immigrant typically finds low-wage employment, and the enforcement mechanisms to ensure that employers do not hire them are minimal or isolated. The issue of being undocumented is related to the availability of resources. Without documentation, procurement of a Social Security number or work visa is prohibited. Without the documents, immigrants are unable to receive public aid, a driver's license, better wages, and health insurance, among other benefits. This is clearly reflected in Maria Luz's story. Access to medical care and better working conditions may have prevented her miscarriage.

Other consequences of being undocumented are the additional resources needed for daily living and functioning. Maria Luz and her family are exploited constantly. First, her husband had to pay large amounts of money to have her escorted to this country, which led to her vulnerability to sexual assault. Second, employers are able to pay her less than living wages because the employment situation is illegal. Third, landlords and businesses can charge more for goods and services. Maria Luz addresses these issues in her story.

LANGUAGE ISSUES OF THE FIRST-GENERATION IMMIGRANT

The acquisition of a second language is more difficult for older immigrants of low socioeconomic status. The ability of the first-generation adult immigrant to learn English is more common in people with higher levels of education and more rare in people with less education (Kuo & Roysircar, 2004). For illiterate or quasi-illiterate adult immigrants, the acquisition of a second language is the most difficult (Berger, 2004). Maria Luz came as an adult. Her level of education is low, and not surprisingly, her command of English is poor. Additionally, learning a language takes time. Many first-generation immigrants have to work double shifts. Sometimes, the low wages they earn do not permit them to make ends meet with just one job. If they also are caring for children, the availability of time to learn English is severely limited. In her story, Maria Luz expresses a strong desire coupled with a difficulty to learn English. In general, the desire to learn English in the first-generation immigrant is very strong and rarely is it true that the immigrant refuses to, or is not interested in, learning English, as some wrongly suspect. It is not uncommon for first-generation immigrants with low levels of education to live in the United States for many years and never learn the language, particularly if they don't have time to learn; if they have language brokers, such as spouses, children, or other relatives to help them; if they live in a community where there are a lot of resources in their language of origin, such as Latino barrios, Chinatowns, or Polish villages; or if they come when they are older.

It is clear that Maria Luz is aware that she suffers many barriers due to her lack of English-speaking skills, and she identifies her lack of fluency in English as a great obstacle in her life.

IMMIGRATION AND GEOGRAPHIC ORIGIN

The geographic origin of the immigrant sometimes is more salient than the other themes (Breunlin, Schwartz, & Mac Kune-Karrer, 1997). Immigrants born and raised in rural areas, in close contact with nature, or in small towns where everybody knows everybody else may end up in large urban or suburban areas. Traditionally, immigrants to the United States came to the large urban areas, but they often came from rural areas (Daniels, 2002). In the last several decades, immigrants are settling in suburban areas in numbers that were unprecedented a couple of decades ago. It is unlikely that immigrants will end up in places that are geographically similar to those they came from. Maria Luz expresses this condition when she states, with nostalgia, that in the United States she has to get everything from a store, instead of growing it herself as she did in her village. That shift can have a more dramatic impact on the experience of immigrants and their adaptation than some of the other dimensions.

Clinical Applications

This section discusses clinical applications for working with undocumented and first-generation immigrants. In the assessment sections, it is important to address recent or undocumented immigrants' potential for dropout from services, among other assessment ideas related to the content themes. The interventions section presents the pretherapy orientation technique as a tool to prepare clients for psychotherapy. The countertransference section describes possible clinician reactions, including areas of discomfort.

ASSESSMENT

When working with undocumented or first-generation immigrants, there are a number of issues to consider. First, it is important to assess their familiarity and comfort with participating in therapeutic services. Second, it is important to assess their language issues and preferences and whether they are thinking about staying in the United States or returning to their country of origin. Issues of geographic differences and the influence of these differences on daily living routines and patterns need to be assessed. Finally, documentation status needs to be addressed.

Potential for Dropout From Services

When first-generation immigrants become clients of counseling services, it is important to assess their views of mental health and their ideas about the use of these services very early in the process. Not doing so can result in early dropout from services and an overall impression on the part of the clinician that clients are resistant or unmotivated to receive services.

First-generation immigrant clients, regardless of their level of education or their socioeconomic status, may come from areas of the world where counseling is not viewed as the way to solve individual or family problems (Sue & Sue, 2003). Others come from areas of the world where mental health services are available only for the rich or the upper middle class. When they need mental health services, many immigrants are referred by others to counseling services. This other-referred (Schwarzbaum, 1995) client is different from the typical middle-class client of therapy services, who is self-referred. The self-referred client already has a belief in the helping potential of psychotherapy and knows what to expect from a therapeutic encounter. As a customer (De Shazer, 1988), the client only needs to find a suitable provider to entrust his or her most intimate concerns because he or she has an overall positive view of the process of therapy. In contrast, the typical other-referred client can be a first-generation immigrant, who may have little command of the English language and who may have been referred by a doctor, a school, or another agency for a situation related to a child, substance abuse, domestic violence, or other reasons (Schwarzbaum, 2002). "Others" may think that this prospective client needs counseling services, but the client may not know how therapy works, what is expected of him or her as a client, what therapy entails, how it can help, and whom it can help. Talking to a stranger about matters of the most intimate concern is not always a known—or accepted—practice. The other-referred client places a call to a counseling agency of a mental health center, and the intake worker immediately demands personal information, such as a Social Security number and income information, that the client may not have been ready or willing to share on the first phone encounter with a stranger. The risk of dropout from counseling is higher for first-generation, other-referred immigrant clients than for self-referred, second-generation, or nonimmigrant clients, particularly if they come in contact with agencies that have an ancillary program and not multipurpose service centers that cater to a particular immigrant community (Schwarzbaum, 2004).

High rates of first-session no-show, dropout after intake, and dropout after the first session are common occurrences in mental health centers across the country (Sue & Sue, 2003). These high dropout rates could be prevented, in part, by assessing the potential for dropout very early in the process. Assessing the risk for dropout in the early stages of the therapeutic process is at least as important as assessment of the presenting issues.

Following are questions to assess the beliefs about mental health practices and the risk of dropout of the first-generation immigrant client, followed by questions to assess the issues related to the content themes.

Beliefs About Mental Health Practices

In your country or culture of origin, how do people deal with depression, anxiety, and family problems?

Would anybody you know seek help for these kinds of problems?

What kind of help is available in your community of origin for a person with a concern similar to yours?

Do people in your community ever consult a mental health provider for individual or family problems?

Risk of Dropout From Counseling Services

Do you know anyone who has been helped by talking to a therapist or counselor?

Have you ever been helped by a counselor or therapist?

Do you know what is supposed to happen or not happen in a counseling session?

Do you know what you are supposed to do or not do in a first session of counseling?

In addition to assessing potential for dropout from services, counselors can assess issues related to ambivalence about the immigration decision, language issues, documentation status, and the possible importance of the geographic origin.

Ambivalence About the Immigration Decision

Ambivalence may be related to the presenting problem in overt or covert ways and can affect the client's process of acculturation and assimilation.

How difficult was it to make the decision to emigrate?

Was that difficulty or ease shared with other members of the family?

Originally, did you envision emigrating permanently or on a temporary basis?

Currently, do you wish to return or to stay here?

Are the members of your family in agreement about whether to stay or to return?

Has your answer to that question changed over the years?

To what do you attribute the change or lack of change?

Language Issues

Clinicians need to assess language concerns of clients. Clients with limited English-speaking ability may need to be referred to a provider who speaks their language. If the clients are not bilingual, the language barriers may make it impossible to provide services beyond an initial assessment to an appropriate form of help. There are ways to find out what constitutes a good interpreter, along with recommendations for training of interpreters (Bradford & Munoz, 1993). It may also be important to assess literacy levels in both English and the language of origin. Many clients who appear to speak English because they are able to communicate in a rudimentary way may lead the counselor to think that the clients may indeed speak English, when in reality they may speak only a few words or do not speak it fluently enough to conduct a therapy session in English.

What language do you speak at home?

What language do you use to watch TV, listen to the radio, and talk to family and friends?

What language do your children use to watch TV, listen to the radio, and talk to family and friends?

If you don't speak English well, how do you manage?

Do you have language brokers (i.e., people who translate or interpret for you or help you figure forms out)?

Importance of Geographic Origin

Differences between the geographic regions of origin and the region in the United States where the immigrant settles may need to be assessed. Geographic differences may influence changes in daily living routines and may be contributing factors affecting the degree of ambivalence about the immigration decision and the overall functioning of the client.

Do you come from a place that looks the same or different than the one you are living in today?

How is your current geographic location different than the one you came from?

How is it similar?

How have you and the members of your family experienced the differences or similarities in geographic location?

Did you live in an urban or rural area?

Are you adjusting to being in a rural or urban area?

Has your daily routine been affected by the change in geographical location?

Documentation Status

Social service providers need to assess clients' documentation status. Many undocumented clients may be reluctant to reveal their status for fear of being refused services. In most instances, social service organizations do not have restrictions in providing services to undocumented clients, but clients may not know that. If clients have changed from undocumented to documented status over the years, knowing about their past status may help counselors understand better the hardship and resilience factors of their clients. Many clinical issues may be a result of the clients' undocumented status, ranging from increased stress to poor physical well-being. Lack of access to medical insurance and care, difficulty obtaining a driver's license and car insurance, housing issues, and lack of employment opportunities may affect the functioning of clients, their spouses, and their children and the clients' use of mental health services.

What is the history of your legal status in the United States?

If you started out with undocumented status, how has the documented status changed your life?

If you have undocumented status, how does it affect your life?

Do the members of your family have the same legal status as you, or is it different?

TECHNIQUES AND INTERVENTIONS

Pretherapy Orientation

Lack of motivation and resistance to receiving services are common explanations given about other-referred clients who drop out after the initial appointment at a counseling agency. But this view fails to acknowledge that dropout is an interactional or relational occurrence (Beyebach & Escudero Carranza, 1997; Phillips, Munt, Drury, Stoklosa, & Spink, 1997;

Walitzer, Dermen, & Conners, 1999). Dropout does not need to be viewed as a negative trait the client possesses, but rather as a relational phenomenon that says something about the client–counselor relationship or about the relationship between the client and the organization that offers the help (Lewis & Osborn, 2004; Sue & Sue, 2003). What happens during the initial phone call or during the first hour of contact that prevents so many clients from returning? To what extent is there a fit between the person requesting the services and the clinician or organization offering the help?

The view of the client as unmotivated or resistant to therapy also fails to acknowledge that even though healing as a practice has existed for millennia, the 50-minute hour of psychotherapy is a Western, middle-class, and relatively recent invention (Sue & Sue, 2003). Talking to a stranger about matters of personal or family concern may not be the preferred mode of help-seeking behavior of the immigrant client referred to therapy. Often clients drop out because the organization they come into contact with is not prepared to deal with immigrants and does not make any special adjustments in the way services are delivered (Sue, 1998).

The initial contact (the phone intake, the in-person first interview, and the first session) is what establishes a relationship not only with the counselor but also with the organization where the counselor works and with the idea of therapy as helpful to solve problems. The initial encounter with the organization sets the parameters of what will follow, regardless of the duration of the treatment process. One way to reduce dropout from therapy is the preparation of the client prior to and during the initial encounter with the mental health agency. Pretherapy orientations are tools designed to prepare clients for the process of counseling and can be presented in different formats: as audiotape-recorded scripts or as videotaped orientations available in English and the language of the immigrant (Rosado, 1992; Schwarzbaum, 1995). Written information is also possible, but it has the drawback that it is not helpful for people with limited literacy. The audiotape or the videotape may contain information about what counseling is and is not, how it can help, and the expected behaviors of both clients and therapists. The audiotape or videotape can be supplemented by a conversation during a first appointment to reinforce issues presented in the audiotape or videotape. For example, having this conversation in the first hour may clarify for the client assumptions that he or she may have about the process. It can also help the counselor clarify his or her assumptions about the willingness or the ability of the client to return for more sessions. Making the assumption that the client will indeed return at the end of the first session may be at the heart of many second-session dropouts of the voluntary, other-referred immigrant client. This conversation can also eliminate or minimize other assumptions about what clients know or don't know and about what clients think of the helping process. The importance of this conversation is at least parallel to the need to inquire about the client's presenting problem (Phillips, et al., 1997; Schwarzbaum, 2002).

A well-designed pretherapy orientation program can help decrease dropout rates of immigrant clients, even in cases of clients mandated for therapy, because it offers a collaborative, rather than a paternalistic, approach to counseling the reluctant, other-referred client (Lewis & Osborn, 2004).

COUNTERTRANSFERENCE

There are two primary reactions that may occur from reading Maria Luz's story or from working with first-generation or undocumented immigrants. The first area of concern is documentation status, and the second is language, habits, and customs. First, the media have portrayed undocumented immigrants coming to this country as taking jobs from Americans. Clinicians have to assess their own reactions to undocumented immigrants and immigration policies. Reactions may range from anger over loss of opportunities for Americans to sadness over human rights violations suffered by undocumented immigrants. The second issue is confusion over paperwork for undocumented immigrants. Therapists need to consider billing information and procedures. Therapists may be confused about whether they are legally or ethically responsible for reporting undocumented clients. Parents may be reluctant to participate in treatment with children for fear of deportation. Clinicians who wish for clients to become more acculturated may inadvertently use the documentation status as leverage for finding cultural compromise. For example, therapists may threaten to report child abuse of parents who seem overly strict with their children. Finally, some therapists may romanticize or denigrate the cultural background of the client.

Client's Language, Habits, and Customs

Therapists may have a difficult time with clients' accents in English and may become frustrated at not understanding what clients are saying. Therapists' frustration may also appear if clients do not come to therapy with the information they need to fill out paperwork, such as pay stubs or proof of insurance. If clients are seen in organizations and institutions that are not used to dealing with immigrants, clinicians may expect that immigrant clients will behave in ways that middle-class American clients behave within the "culture" of psychotherapy, and react with annoyance to clients who do not (Whiston, 1996). Someone like Maria Luz may come to a meeting with a therapist accompanied by one or more members of the family if she does not drive or needs help with the paperwork or with English. She may also be less punctual, less task-oriented, and less businesslike. Indirect styles of communication so common in other cultures

(Falicov, 1998b) may annoy the clinician, who is an expert at teaching clients how to communicate directly and assertively.

If clinicians are not used to dealing with immigrant clients, they may appear frustrated, annoyed, and impatient. This may in turn elicit mistrust of the client, which could cause clients to be labeled as unmotivated or resistant to treatment.

Therapist Discomfort and Positive or Negative Stereotypes

Providers of social services may have a tendency to either romanticize or denigrate the culture of the client, depending on their knowledge of—and exposure to—the cultural group, their own worldview and values, or their past experiences with that cultural group (Perez-Foster, 1998). It is important for therapists to examine their own positive or negative stereotypes about the immigrant group because they might be transmitted and projected to the client in direct or indirect ways. When clients come into the therapy room with their marital, parenting, or relationship problems, therapists invariably project onto their clients their hypotheses, interpretations, and solutions based on their own worldview and their own cultural, class, and gender characteristics (Perez-Foster, 1998). Counselors cannot possibly know as much about the clients' culture of origin as their clients do, and this may make some counselors uncomfortable. The ambiguity of not knowing what to do with the concomitant discomfort may make therapists more prone either to romanticizing or denigrating the culture of the client. Therapists need to challenge themselves constantly and tolerate their own discomfort at not always knowing what to do with their immigrant clients. Clinicians need to train themselves to see and hear the larger context of ethnicity, gender, and class (Mirkin, 1998). At the same time, they need to train themselves to tolerate the ambiguity and discomfort of not always knowing what to do. These are necessary, albeit difficult, skills to master if clinicians are to become culturally competent.

TOOLBOX ACTIVITY—MARIA LUZ			
Resources and Suggested Readings	*Videos*	*Activities*	*Discussion Questions*
Bray, I. M. (2006). *How to get a green card* (7th ed.). Berkeley, CA: Nolo Press. Bray, I. M. (2006). *U.S. immigration made easy* (12th ed.). Berkeley, CA: Nolo Press LearningExpress Editors. (2007). *US citizenship* (2nd ed.). New York: LearningExpress, LLC. Weissbrodt, D. (2005). *Immigration law and procedure in a nutshell* (5th ed.). Eagan, MN: West Publishing.	*El Norte* *Lone Star* *Nowhere in Africa* *East-West* *Los Refugiados*	Research the Web site of the Bureau of Citizen and Immigration Services (BCIS) and find the definitions of the following terms: resident alien, nonresident alien, refugee, asylee, immigrant, naturalized citizen, illegal immigrant, and nonimmigrant. On the same Web site, find out the alternatives and requirements for immigrants to reside legally in the United States (e.g., work visas, investor's visas, student visas, tourist visas, family sponsorship programs, visa lottery programs). Research the requirements that foreigners have to fulfill to obtain U.S. citizenship.	Content Themes What other themes do you see emerging in the story that the author did not identify? Assessment Are there any questions you would like to ask Maria Luz? Interventions What other interventions could you propose with Maria Luz? Countertransference What countertransference reactions were emerging in yourself as you read this story? Other Scenarios How would Maria Luz's life be different if she were married to an American?

Teresa's Story 11

I Didn't Want to Go to Church on Sunday

Teresa's story reflects the themes of the second-generation immigrant. Although the immigration story of her parents from Lebanon to the United States is still a powerful organizer of her life and identity, Teresa seems clear on which aspects of the Lebanese culture she is ready to reject. As you read, notice how much the story of her parents' decision to immigrate to the United States and the hard work her mother engaged in influence the way she thinks about her own life. Also, notice the typical second-generation themes of language choice or rejection, and how Teresa has dealt with parental authority and gender issues in her family.

Teresa's Story

Imagine it is November 1980, and you are a 23-year-old Lebanese woman attempting to travel with four small children who are six, four, three, and one and a half years old, without the comfort and support of your family or friends. You're trying to travel from Lebanon to Atlanta; however, you have no means of communication with individuals who do not speak Lebanese. You're also still afraid for your children's safety, and you do not even know if you will be able to make it to your destination.

Furthermore, envision that the first flight you are scheduled to take is 16 hours long, and after you land in Los Angeles you have a connecting flight, which is another four hours, before you land in Atlanta. To make the situation even more complicated, you are moving your family to a country where you do not understand the language or cultural expectations.

While on the plane, as well as at the airport, people attempt to communicate with you. However, the language barriers are too challenging, making it difficult for you to comprehend, so you begin to feel hopeless, questioning if you will ever make it to your destination. Nonetheless, you try to make the best of the situation, and while you are at the airport, you look around for someone who may be of assistance or may have similar ethnic features to translate your travel needs or confusion. (If they look Middle Eastern, they may understand something you're trying to say and help you.)

After several frustrating hours at the airport with four tired and hungry children, you finally observe a couple who may be of assistance to you; you walk up to the couple and ask in Lebanese to be directed to your connecting flight as you wave your tickets at the couple. You realize you are in luck because the couple speaks the same language as you, and to top it all off, they are more than willing to help you out with your frustrating experience. The gentleman assists you with your luggage, and the young lady admires the children as they walk you over to your connecting flight. You can finally breathe because you are on the correct plane, and within hours you will ultimately be reunited with your family members who are already in the United States.

Once you reach your destination, you walk out of the plane and are finally greeted by your son and husband, whom you have not seen in a year and a half, as well as your husband's relatives. You are so overwhelmed you start to cry. You have mixed feelings about landing in Atlanta. You are happy to finally be reunited with your own family; however, you are sad that you left your extended family behind. You still embrace the moment and focus on the future to come.

This scenario was a reality for my mother, my siblings, and me when we traveled from Lebanon to the United States. I do not remember the transition, but my mother and older brother have vivid memories of the experience. They often share their thoughts and feelings regarding the journey, but they both agree that they would not change a thing about it.

My parents' desire to travel to another country and move away from family, friends, and the comforts of familiar cultural surroundings began in 1977. My parents began the immigration process after I was born. It was not finalized until three years later. My parents learned of the American dream from family members who already resided in the United States. My parents dreamed of having a future filled with freedom and independence for the family. So the journey began in 1978, when my father, along with my oldest brother, moved to this country. My mother was pregnant with my younger sister at the time, making travel difficult for her. It was important for my father to immigrate to the United States prior to the rest of the family to establish a home and make some money. The separation was difficult for my mother, but the outcome was eventually worthwhile.

My aunt, who had already lived in the United States for nine years, assisted my family with the immigration proceedings. My parents admired my aunt for leaving Lebanon and coming to this country to experience independence and freedom. My parents dreamed of the transition for years prior to moving. The war in Lebanon became too unbearable to raise a family, so my parents planned the ultimate sacrifice and began their journey to America. (The ultimate sacrifice was leaving my mother's entire family behind to start over in a new country. My father's entire family emigrated to the United States years prior to our family's plan to defect.)

The reason my father and brother moved to the country prior to the rest of the family was to establish a home, employment, and schooling for my siblings and me. My father did not understand the language when he first came to this country. My father counted on my brother and aunt to translate formalities, so he could get a job and enroll my brother in public school.

Our family reunited after a year and a half. Within that time, my father managed to put our living arrangements in order, he enrolled my brother in the neighborhood grammar school, and he managed to find a job in a factory. However, my father still continued to struggle with the American culture and language.

My parents did not have any special skills or education to highlight, because they dropped out of school at an early age. Education was not enforced or emphasized in our culture 25 years ago. Once my mother immigrated to the United States, she immediately began looking for a job of her own. In Lebanon, my mother flourished as the master dressmaker in the family business, which helped her obtain a position in the United States. My mother had friends in this country who assisted her in locating the perfect position. She began working as a dressmaker in a busy theater company. My brother, my sisters, and I hardly ever saw her. She worked from 10 a.m. until 10 p.m. for many years. My siblings and I basically raised ourselves because my father did not contribute to the children's upbringing.

When my mother found a job and established herself, my father injured himself at the factory and eventually quit his job. He realized my mother was able to manage the family as well as the finances on her own, so he did not look for another position. My mother was also receiving monthly government checks to make ends meet, so the lack of income was not that detrimental to the family's budget. Even with the burden of supporting the family, my mother still was able to thrive in this country. She learned the language and taught herself how to read to survive in the American culture. My siblings and I also thrived effortlessly, acculturating to the American worldview. In Lebanon, English is taught to all students, so both my older sisters had an advantage over everyone else in the family. Nonetheless, my brother and I were raised in American surroundings and culture. Because we were so young when we immigrated, our transition was smooth.

As years passed, my siblings and I became more Americanized. We aspired for the same privileges as American children. Yet my father attempted to retain the family's cultural heritage. My siblings and I were forced to go to Armenian school on the weekends, as well as Lebanese church Sunday mornings, and we were required to speak only Armenian at home. Traditionally, within Lebanese and Armenian cultures, the children are taught the language and are expected to speak the native tongue within the household. During family gatherings, my cousins and I would sneak away from the adults and converse in English. When adults were present, we would not dare respond to the adults in any language other than Armenian. My cousins would always respond to their mother by saying "yes, Mother" in Armenian; if they did not, they would be disciplined with the dreadful shoe! (Once you see an Armenian or Lebanese mother take off her shoe, you know it is headed straight for your head, and if she missed the first time, you can guarantee the next time she will make her target!) My mother was not that strict about responding in Armenian. (She's Lebanese and wanted to learn the language.) However, my father would not tolerate or accept us talking in English; he deemed that a lack of respect.

My father was also not accepting of individuals of other ethnic backgrounds. We learned early on that we were expected to marry someone with the same ethnic roots and engage socially with Middle Eastern individuals, but only if he approved of them and their family background. So, needless to say, my siblings and I rarely brought our ethnic friends home. Our social lives revolved solely around schooltime and activities. Traditionally, in Lebanese and Armenian cultures, the head of the household (usually the man) arranges marriages for his daughters. They socialize with local families, looking for eligible husbands. I can recall my father talking to my sisters and me about whether we wanted to meet a nice young man who was available to marry. We basically put my father in his place regarding this situation. I certainly laughed in my father's face, stating I would rather die than have him pick my husband. He was surprisingly not defensive but disappointed that we turned down the offer.

Our childhood was obviously trying. My siblings and I spent most of our time defying our father's strict, domineering rules. We disliked attending Armenian school. We played around during classes, and we eventually expressed our loathing. At first, my father was opposed to us dropping out of school, but with the help of my mother we actually won the battle.

Our second battle to overcome was attending Lebanese church. Our family was more spiritual than religious anyway, so it did not take a lot of effort to win this battle. My siblings and I did not understand Arabic very well, which led to boredom during the church proceedings and constant struggles within the family before church. Because my mother was so understanding, she did not force the issue. She understood that we sought our independence and would choose to go to church on our own if we were not forced to do so, particularly when we understood and observed the spiritual and religious beliefs.

The majority of Lebanese Christian Orthodox followers commonly celebrate and acknowledge the strong spiritual faith passed down from generation to generation. My mother has always been considered a spiritual healer. It was not mandatory for her to attend church masses for her to be enlightened with her gift; the power of prayer and her strong spiritual roots have always guided her. As children, we watched my mother remove the evil eye from people's spirits. It was a very powerful and moving experience. While she was lifting the evil eye, my mother's tears would roll down her face as she yawned. The more she cried and yawned, the stronger the eye was on that individual. My mother always advised us to wear symbols, or charms, on our necklaces, which kept the evil spirits and evil thoughts from others away, so we would not get the evil eye. This sounds a little outrageous, but it is widely known in the Lebanese tradition to own and carry an eye with you at all times. I, on the other hand, do not have an eye currently, but I do have a rosary in my car, which is another religious symbol.

Other traditional celebrations followed by individuals of the Christian Orthodox faith are the elaborate celebrations for Easter, which are celebrated one week after the Americans' Easter. We usually begin the celebration days in advance, making Lebanese cookies, dyeing eggs, and planning the meal for brunch after church. Forty days before Easter, Lebanese Orthodox Christians give up something that they love and cannot live without until Easter. Most people give up meat because Jesus did. The fasting is called Lent.

As years passed, these celebrations were not as elaborate as they had been when we were children. The entire family became too acculturated to the American culture. In 1986 my mother, siblings, and I became citizens; my father did not pass the test. The family still embraced our heritage; however, we were no longer forced to do things. We willingly spoke either English or Armenian at home and attended church. Our social interactions with others from different cultural backgrounds were also accepted. My father did not have so much control in the family anymore. The more my mother became acclimated to the laws and culture of the American worldviews, the more control and power she gained over my father. My mother's role in the family was significant.

The roles within the family dynamic were defined by rules depicted in our nuclear family. The women in my nuclear family were taught to be hard workers and the family breadwinners. My mother received all the respect in the family, even though she did not demand it. My father was viewed as a worthless man who did not contribute to the family system financially or emotionally. He was physically available; however, we could not count on him for anything. My father became the poster father for all Armenian men. I viewed all men of Armenian descent to be deadbeat fathers. This negative image was always reinforced, specifically when I observed my father's friends treating their wives and children similarly to the way I had experienced in my upbringing.

My siblings and I definitely learned some nontraditional male and female roles by observing my parents' behaviors. Through observing my father, we were taught that a woman should serve and pick up after her husband. We were also taught that women were the breadwinners as well as the caretakers. As a result of the constant reminders of a woman's responsibilities, we were taught that the women in the family had to be strong, independent women with an abundance of initiative to succeed.

I'm sure my brother was affected differently. For years he expected my mother, my sisters, and me to take care of him. He also struggled with the image my father implanted in our minds as a useless, incompetent, weak man. He wanted others to know that just because he was my father's son did not mean he was my father. He tried so hard not to be him. My mother continuously talked about the traditional cultural expectations of men and women in our culture to ease all of our minds. She expressed that the situations we observed were not due to cultural traditions but due to her own tolerance. My mother reinforced the notion of shared responsibilities between men and women, even though she did not follow her own advice. She also explained that the traditional norms of men being the breadwinners and women being the sole caretakers no longer existed in Lebanon, especially within Christian religions. (Muslims in Lebanon defiantly abided by the religious and cultural beliefs that men are the superior sex.)

Keeping in mind the false notion of the man as the sole provider and the woman as the caretaker, my siblings and I looked at the gender roles of members in our extended family. We realized that members of both sides of our family are successful in their own ways, regardless of gender. Many individuals in my family own their own businesses. Numerous male and female members of my family have established lucrative businesses without the education typically needed to succeed. Their gender never factored into who was going to run the business or who was going to take care of the children. The idea of joint responsibility was passed down from the older generations and practiced—except in the case of my nuclear family.

Typically, Lebanese and Armenian immigrants come to this country with the intent to start a business. Lebanese families frequently own restaurants, automotive businesses, and liquor stores, whereas Armenians customarily own jewelry stores. It is amazing to me that every member on my mother's and father's sides of the family is living a comfortable life financially, without an education. On the other hand, my nuclear family has struggled for 23 years in this country to get to the comfort level we are at now. It took our family approximately 18 years to completely get out of the welfare system. My mother explains that some years were easier than others. Getting off of welfare was not a problem—staying off was the difficulty.

It is also noteworthy to mention that I am the only member of my nuclear or extended family to ever attend and graduate from college and attend graduate school. Moreover, many older individuals in my family system have not attained a high school diploma. Even more surprising, a common pattern that emerged on the paternal side of my family is that, even though they did not continue their education, several family members own their own businesses. My paternal grandfather owned a restaurant in Lebanon. My two uncles and my aunt also started their own businesses in the United States and Lebanon. Relatives on my mother's side of the family are blue-collar workers. They work for others. However, they are very wealthy.

Another common theme in my family that I deem significant to mention is that out of 14 marriages across generations, only one has ended in divorce. The marriages on my mother's side appear to be more centered on love, equality, and friendship. However, the marriages on my father's side appear to be centered on deceit, connivance, and financial dependence. My paternal relatives have been through many cycles of closeness and distance but have never ended in divorce, with the exception of my cousin Teresa. These marriages have defiantly embraced the true meaning of "till death do us part," regardless of the hardship encountered in the marriage relationships. Being raised in America, there are some aspects of my identity that I can relate to Americans more than Lebanese or Armenians. For example, I can guarantee I would have opted for a divorce if I had been married to my father or several of my uncles. Culture depicts a Lebanese or Armenian woman supporting her husband during moments of weakness, whereas American women quickly get a divorce and seek child support. I have a certain tolerance level for conflict in relationships. However, I do not have the tolerance and patience my ancestors possessed. I could not fathom being married to someone for 35 years (like my parents) and being miserable for the majority of our relationship. I cannot identify with that part of my cultural roots.

Content Themes

Teresa presents the typical second-generation themes of immigrant families. She tells the timeless story of her mother, who, through hard work, sacrifice, and dedication, was able to provide a better future for her children. Teresa also describes her resistance to her father's traditional gender role prescriptions, her achievement at being the first one to attend college in a family of small business owners, and her rejection of some of the prescribed expectations regarding language preservation, religious observance, and decisions about mate selection.

FIRST- VERSUS SECOND-GENERATION IMMIGRANTS

In earlier generations, the ambivalent immigrant did not have access to inexpensive transportation, e-mail, or frequent telephone contact, as many do now. Leaving was tantamount to severing ties with family and friends because once they made the decision it was usually irreversible. This was (and can still be) particularly true in cases of immigrants from faraway countries. The reason Teresa describes her mother's voyage to the United States as the "ultimate sacrifice" is related to this sense of irreversibility in the immigration decision. Teresa's mother must have known that once she left the Middle East, her four Lebanese-born children were going to be raised in the United States, were going to attend American schools, and would speak English. They would become the immigrants of the second generation.

A traditional demographic definition of a first-generation immigrant is that of a person who was not born in the United States, whereas a second-generation immigrant is defined as a person who was born in the United States. Sometimes a second-generation immigrant is defined by where his or her parents were born. However, these categories are not so clear-cut. Someone may have been born in a foreign country and function as a second-generation immigrant (Grinberg & Grinberg, 2000). An immigrant child who comes to the United States at the age of three years might be considered a second-generation immigrant, whereas an individual who comes at the age of 20 years would be considered a first-generation immigrant, even though neither immigrant was born in the United States. What seems to be important is where the person received early schooling, whether English was the primary or the secondary language in the country of origin, and the amount of exposure to American norms, institutions, and peer groups during the formative childhood years, regardless of where the immigrant was born. Teresa would be considered a second-generation immigrant, even though she was born in Lebanon, because she came to the United States at a very young age and, most important, because she received most of her schooling in English and in the United States.

LANGUAGE ISSUES OF THE SECOND GENERATION: LOSS OR REJECTION

Second-generation immigrants vary greatly in the degree to which they preserve their languages of origin. Several psychosocial and acculturation factors exist. The level of conflict within the family, how favorably or unfavorably the language is viewed by the family and the larger community, and the sociocultural pressures to acculturate are among the factors that are influential in determining language preservation. Teresa's mom learned English quickly, did not force Arabic on her children, and acted in ways that encouraged assimilation, for herself and her children, the way earlier immigrants to America did.

Preschool children who are exposed only to their language of origin at home may initially have some difficulty communicating in English to preschool personnel. Some educators still wrongly believe that the reason children may have a delayed literacy in English is that they are exposed to two languages. However, the vast majority of children exposed to two languages during early developmental stages learn both languages equally well (Johnson-Powell & Yamamoto, 1997; Nieto, 1999). Unless the schools offer true bilingual programs, the reality is that immigrant preschool children will most likely use their language of origin at home and use English at school, which often leads to loss of the maternal language because of lack of practice and because children stop the development of literacy skills in their language of origin. When preschool children are placed in English-only settings, they lose not only their first language but also the ability to communicate effectively with their families (Nieto, 1999). Teresa came to the United States when she was one year old and quickly learned English. Even though her father forced her to speak Armenian in the house, she speaks neither Armenian nor Arabic, her mother's language. There is evidence that by the third generation, the language of origin will almost always be lost.

Family members, like Teresa's mother and father, often differ considerably in their English proficiency and in their positive or negative regard to the acquisition of English or to preservation of the language of origin. These differences sometimes become polarized, with language choice symbolizing different sides of the polarized continuum (Falicov, 1998a). The adolescent who refuses to speak the native language can become entangled in loyalty conflicts with parents who do not learn English. Severe generational conflicts may be played out in the family as a result of language issues. In Teresa's recollections, her father forced the children to continue to speak the paternal language, Armenian, which she didn't want to do. It would be difficult to assess whether Teresa fought speaking the native language because her father forced it on her or whether her father attempted to force it because Teresa was fighting it, more interested in becoming "like the others" of her peer group. What seems clear is that Teresa refused to speak Armenian, her father's preferred language, and rejected her father's idea of keeping the traditions of her culture of origin that he wanted her so much to preserve. She seemed to have had a conflicted relationship with him, and it is not surprising, therefore, that she was not making too much of an effort to please her father. Consequently, she does not speak

Armenian. Cohort effects may have already been taking place in Teresa's case. In contrast with Spanish-speaking immigrants, for example, who compose such a large percentage of the American population and who, therefore, might be inclined to continue to use their language, Armenian and Arabic are not as well known or accepted in the United States; therefore, Teresa might not have felt guilty about losing her language of origin.

Some children of the second generation need to act as language brokers (Falicov, 1998a) for their first-generation parents, thus becoming parentified in their roles with their families. When immigrant parents are unable to communicate effectively with their children, they lose the ability to socialize and influence the children, losing the intimacy and closeness that come from passing down values and beliefs (Johnson-Powell & Yamamoto, 1997). This may partly explain the generational conflicts that occur between first- and second-generation immigrants. From this point of view, it is not surprising that Teresa's relationship with her mother seems to have been less conflicted than her relationship with her father, whose command of English was poor.

INTERGENERATIONAL CONFLICTS AND GENDER

Acculturation conflicts may develop for immigrants around shifts in gender and intergenerational roles (Hernandez & McGoldrick, 1999). Relationships between parents and children often become more strained in immigrant families because the old coping support networks may not be there and because the new country may foster less patriarchal and more egalitarian gender and intergenerational roles. These changes do not come without great emotional and psychological costs. Sometimes there exists an inverse relationship between the new and the old gender roles (i.e., the more egalitarian the second-generation immigrant becomes, the more the older generation seems to need to cling to traditional values and gender roles, and the more polarized the generations become). In Teresa's case, the polarization of the gender roles occurred in the context of the intergenerational struggles. Teresa and her father were at opposite ends of the continuum. The more control her father wanted, the more the children rebelled: "My siblings and I spent most of our time defying our father's strict, domineering rules."

Gender role reversals in cultural transitions are not unusual. Because women generally experience more dissatisfaction with narrow gender roles (Breunlin, Schwartz, & Mac Kune-Karrer, 1997), immigrant mothers sometimes are more inclined than fathers to become more Americanized (Comas-Diaz, 1987; Falicov, 1998a; Hernandez & McGoldrick, 1999). Teresa describes how her mother seems to reflect that tendency, how she shifted in her gender identity more than her father did. In the way Teresa tells the story, there was a change in her mother and not in her father.

Teresa's mother was able to find employment, and her father, perhaps due to his disability but most likely because of his gender socialization, continued to expect adherence to the traditional values: "The more my mother became acclimated to the laws and culture of the American worldview, the more control and power she gained over my father." Even though, in the beginning, Teresa was taught that "a woman should serve and pick up after her husband," later she learned that "women in the family had to be strong, independent women with an abundance of initiative to succeed." Not all women in families struggling with cultural transitions make that shift.

Cultural transitions to environments that are more egalitarian and less hierarchical may be very difficult for men who come from cultures with patriarchal family traditions in which women do not work for a living and are not eligible to receive an education and in which adolescents, particularly female adolescents, don't question male parental authority (Breunlin, Schwartz, & Mac Kune-Karrer, 1997). Teresa describes a father who, after making the "ultimate sacrifice" and initially finding housing, employment, and the means to reunite with the rest of his family, eventually and for many reasons lost power and control over his children, who rebelled frequently against him and did not want to adhere to his prescription of the traditional gender roles he had been socialized to support. Losing his ability to work may have forced his wife into more than full-time employment to support the family. In immigrating to America, Teresa's father may have sacrificed more than he bargained for.

Clinical Applications

This section includes assessment of issues that can be of concern for families or individuals of the second generation, a clinical intervention most likely to be useful with conflicts related to the choices of the second generation, and some typical countertransference reactions to these cultural transition issues.

ASSESSMENT

It is important to assess whether clients rejected or lost their language of origin, and the reasons for the rejection or loss. It is also important to assess whether there were parent-adolescent struggles that may have influenced the second-generation immigrants' decisions about choice of mate, lifestyle, or employment. The rejection of the language may have been a reflection of polarized conflicts within the family context, cohort effects, or other reasons.

Language Issues With the Second Generation

Were there expectations related to language preservation in your family?

Did you and your parents agree about issues related to language?

Did you and your siblings or other extended family members agree about issues related to language?

Were there any gains or losses of language?

Intergenerational Conflicts and Gender Roles

Were there conflicts around preservation of traditional gender roles?

How are or were parent-adolescent conflicts handled?

Who was most and least affected by the gender role shifts?

What were the gains and losses related to gender shifts?

TECHNIQUES AND INTERVENTIONS

Untangling Family Conflicts Based on Second-Generation Choices

Counselors vary in how they view the acculturation and assimilation process in their clients. Second-generation immigrant clients often seek help in the midst of the turmoil elicited by the gender role shifts and the intergenerational conflicts that parents and their adolescent or young adult children exhibit. A clinician might see a family, an individual, or a couple in the midst of these conflicts where there are frequent fights about role definitions and open demands for changes in beliefs and actions (Breunlin, Schwartz, & Mac Kune-Karrer, 1997). Counselors might have strong opinions about what they think clients ought to be doing or not doing to solve their problems. For example, had Teresa and her father been in a counseling situation at the time of their cultural transitions, a counselor who thought Teresa should respect her father's hierarchical role in the family would have acted very differently than one who felt the need to encourage Teresa to avoid and discard the traditional, but old-fashioned, gender role expectations her father had for her. Counselors need to be aware of their own ideologies and personal leanings (Falicov, 1998a) and know where they stand in relation to gender and intergenerational conflicts (Breunlin et al., 1997). Are they advocates for acculturation? Do they regard assimilation or preservation of cultural roots as the ultimate goal for immigrant families? The presenting problems related to gender shifts or intergenerational conflicts can be linked to dilemmas of cultural transition by helping clients explore what they are interested in preserving and what they are interested in discarding, rather than the clinician imposing his or her own choices. The clinician can then facilitate clients' choices by acting as a cultural intermediary, helping to build bridges between cultural meanings (Falicov, 1998a), and introducing respectful discussions about the gender constraints that fit the goals of the family (Breunlin, Schwartz, & Mac Kune-Karrer, 1997). Falicov (1998a) and Breunlin, Schwartz, & Mac Kune-Karrer (1997) describe procedures that include drawing attention to differences, contextualizing the differences, reframing problems as dilemmas of coexisting meaning and cultural transitions, and introducing to families the idea that there are many parts to everyone. These interventions help clients highlight the meaning of differences, paying attention to what each member of the family needs from the others. They also help clients understand how those differences in preferences, thoughts, and lifestyle are influenced by socialization and historical and sociocultural patterns. Most important, the interventions help to reduce mutual blaming and polarization by opening the space for personal choice, even if those choices are not correct by the standards of the therapist. Had Teresa and her father been in a therapeutic situation at the time, a therapist might have drawn attention to their differences, might have reframed their struggles as stemming from the cultural transitions, and might have asked them to define what needs each had that were not being addressed. The therapist and the family may have engaged in conversations that might have brought to the forefront each family member's pain, sorrow, losses, and fears. It might also have been useful to explore historical and sociocultural explanations for their generational differences. This in turn might have had the effect of softening their polarized positions. Each family can discover and develop its own manner of living with two cultures, whether through acculturation, alternation, hybridization, or a combination of all these. But dilemmas can be articulated and creative solutions found if therapists show interest, curiosity, and respect for each family member (Falicov, 1998a) instead of taking sides, which increases polarization. People can be helped to increase their options and lift their constraints (Breunlin, Schwartz, & Mac Kune-Karrer, 1997), provided that the family is included in a collaborative way.

COUNTERTRANSFERENCE

Taking Sides

Many immigrant clients seek services because of conflicts between the more acculturated children or young adults and their less acculturated parents. In these cases, members of the same family system seem to be pulled in opposite directions. The request for help may come from the parents, the young adults, or a sibling concerned about the level of distress. For a variety of reasons, many immigrants do not seek help until they are in a time of severe turmoil. A therapist may be pulled in and expected to take sides—and do just that. A common countertransference reaction is that the therapist takes sides with the adolescent against the parents or with the parent against the adolescent (Falicov, 1998a). Taking sides with the client against another member of the family makes some clients feel supported and understood and others feel abandoned, misunderstood, or criticized. Dangerous triangulations occur when clinicians take sides, either overtly or covertly (Nichols & Schwartz, 2001). Taking sides with some members of the family against others violates one of the basic clinical skills, namely, the ability of the therapist to act in a way that will make every member of the family, whether present in the room or not, feel supported by the therapist.

These countertransference reactions stem from differing positions of the counselor about the acculturation and assimilation dilemmas. At one end of the continuum, there are counselors who hold the position that immigrant clients need to become Americanized because gender equality, individuation, and individualism are desirable cultural values. Counselors may openly or covertly despise women who stay with men who exhibit more traditional gender roles and expectations or be openly or secretly critical of parents who hold on to stricter standards to control their rebellious adolescents (Falicov, 1998a). Clinicians with this orientation who had Teresa as a client might have sided with her against her father.

At the other end of the continuum are counselors who assume a position of preservation of ethnic values and heritage (Falicov, 1998a). They may believe that a connection with traditional cultural values, language, and ethnicity is better for the mental health of the client and openly or covertly encourage clients to find their cultural roots, discourage liberation from oppressing values, and promote ethnic pride and resistance to ethnic blending and Americanization. A therapist with this position may have sided with Teresa's father against her. Either of the two extreme positions may constitute a form of cultural imperialism (Falicov, 1998a). The more covert or secret this agenda is, the more damaging its effect on the clients and on the therapeutic situation. Clinicians may have these reactions regardless of the type of counseling they engage in and regardless of how many people attend a session. Counselors can polarize families or couples even if they are conducting individual counseling and may have important influencing effects on the decision-making process about future actions of individual clients.

TOOLBOX ACTIVITY—TERESA			
Resources and Suggested Readings	*Videos*	*Activities*	*Discussion Questions*
Portes, A., & Rumbaud, R. (2001). *Legacies: The story of the immigrant second generation.* Berkeley: University of California Press.	*Avalon* *Coming to America* *Double Happiness*	Use the Internet to find the percentage of Muslim immigrants in the United States. What are some of the names of the countries they come from and the languages they speak? Find information about lesser-known immigrant groups, such as Armenians, Macedonians, and Ethiopians.	Content Themes What other themes do you see emerging in the story that the author did not identify? Assessment Are there any questions you would like to ask Teresa? Interventions What other interventions could you propose with Teresa? Countertransference What countertransference reactions were emerging in yourself as you read this story? Other Scenarios How would Teresa's life be different if she had immigrated as an adolescent instead of as an infant? If Teresa's father hadn't been disabled, how would the life of Teresa's family have been different?

Section IV

Dimensions of Religion and Spirituality

According to recent polls, about 6 out of 10 Americans report that religion is a very important part of their lives, and more than 90 percent report that they believe in God, and believe that religion can answer most of today's problems. Many Americans say they attend religious services at least once a month, and one third of Americans go to services every week or pray regularly even when they do not attend religious services (Religion, n.d.). Religion and spirituality are positively connected to individuals' and families' well-being, sense of belonging, meaning, and purpose (Walsh, 1999b). Additionally, religious resources are among the most utilized when people are dealing with stress, tragedies, illness, death, or poverty (Aponte, 1999), providing resilience, strength, coping, and meaning (Miller, 2003; Walsh, 1999b).

Of those in the surveys, more than 8 in 10 are Christian, including about half who are Protestant and a quarter who are Catholic (Religion, n.d.). Even though most Americans identify as Protestants, other faith communities in the United States include Jews, Hindus, Muslims, Buddhists, Native American spiritual traditions, and many more. This religious diversity assures that clinicians will come into contact with clients of diverse religious backgrounds, no matter where in the country they work.

Spirituality

Spirituality and religion are important components of personality and identity development (Griffith & Griggs, 2001; Standard, Sandhu, & Painter, 2000). Research indicates the importance of spirituality and religion for positive functioning and health and wellness, and the need for therapists to explore the importance of spirituality with their clients (Tolliver, 1997). Spirituality and religion are related, but different, concepts. Spirituality, which includes a notion of transcendence, communal spirit, and a relationship with a higher power, has been used as a source of support and a mechanism for resiliency for many people (Boyd-Franklin, 2004; Johnson, 1995). Spirituality includes a sense of unity or oneness, a connection to people, to nature, and to a higher power. It is connected to a sense of purpose and fulfillment in life. Spirituality is often reflected in the arts, including paintings, music, and body movement (Frame & Williams, 1996; Tolliver, 1997; Walsh, 1999a). There are several identified universal spiritual needs (Fukuyama & Sevig, 1992, 1999). The first spiritual need is to develop a meaningful philosophy of life or a purpose for living (Griffith & Rotter, 1999). The second need is to develop a sense of transcendence, the notion of a greater or common good or of life being more important or greater than individual circumstances. The third need is to develop a deep, trustful relationship with a higher power. The fourth need is to develop meaningful relationships with people and nature, and the fifth need is self-actualization. The development of these needs is often conceptualized as a process or journey (Frame & Williams, 1996). Individuals who are further along in the process of spiritual development are more likely to have a positive outlook on life, a sense of hope and faith, capacity for more intimate relationships and connections, and a sense of optimism. Understanding the spiritual journey may lead to greater self-awareness, consciousness, and a need for service to others (Fukuyama & Sevig, 1999).

Religion

Religion is defined as an organized practice of specific belief systems, traditions, institutional expressions of spirituality and rituals reflective of spiritual beliefs (Dancy & Wynn-Dancy, 1994; Faiver, O'Brien, & Ingersoll, 2000; Frame & Williams, 1996). Religion consists of six components: ritual, doctrine, emotion, knowledge, ethics, and community (Fukuyama & Sevig, 1999). Ritual includes ceremonial behavior and practices, and doctrine includes teachings on the relationship with a higher power. Emotion includes the affective component of spirituality, and knowledge reflects understanding of teachings and principles. Ethics refers to notions of right and wrong, and community refers to psychological, emotional, physical, and social involvement. People with religious faith report higher levels of life satisfaction, personal happiness, social support, and empathy, along with lower levels of depression, blood pressure, and hostility (Griffith & Rotter, 1999). Although religion and spirituality are interconnected, spirituality represents a universal concept, and religion is associated with concrete expressions. Spirituality is personal and subjective, whereas religion tends to be social in nature and is often shared with groups of people or institutions (Standard, et al., 2000). It is important to distinguish between a person's spirituality and their religious faith or upbringing because some people report feeling spiritual while choosing their own way to worship or display it.

The following sections summarize the major characteristics of the most common religious communities found in the United States. First are summarized the three major monotheistic traditions (Christianity, Islam, and Judaism) and then Buddhism and Hinduism, followed by the Native American spiritual traditions.

CHRISTIANITY

The origins of Christianity can be traced back to Jesus of Nazareth, the chosen one (Christ) of God, during the 1st century B.C.E. Jesus was sent as a Messiah, or a savior, and delivered the message of God (Pelikan, 2006). The messages were collected in a sacred text called the Bible, and it served as a record of the major figures in Christianity (Wenner, 2001b). The Bible consists of the Old Testament and the New Testament. The Old Testament is based on the Jewish book of the Torah, and the New Testament chronicles the life of Jesus. Christians believe that Jesus is the savior who was sent by God to take believers to God's kingdom, heaven. According to the New Testament, Jesus performed many miracles in his lifetime, and was arrested for claiming to be the Son of God and crucified (Wenner, 2001b). His crucifixion symbolized to believers that he sacrificed himself for their sins, and salvation comes to those who believe in Him (Wenner, 2001b).

The three major branches of Christianity are Roman Catholicism, Eastern Orthodoxy, and Protestantism (Wenner, 2001b). The Roman Catholic branch formed just after Jesus's death, and the Pope is their spiritual leader. There was a political split in the 4th century due to the division of the Roman Empire into eastern and western regions. This split resulted in the Eastern Orthodox branch being formed, and most Orthodox branches are associated with a particular region: Greece, Rumania, Bulgaria, Russia, the Ukraine, and Armenia (Wenner, 2001b). The last branch to form was the Protestant branch in the 16th and 17th centuries, and this was a split from the Roman Catholicism in an effort to make reforms in the Roman Catholic doctrine and practice (Wenner, 2001b).

Because Christianity originated in the time of the Roman Empire and was accepted by Roman leaders, the ethnicities of many Christians are European in origin. However, due to the proselytizing efforts of Christianity, it has spread through most regions the world. Christianity has an estimated 2.1 billion practitioners. In the U.S., 84.12 percent of the population, or 252 million people, consider themselves Christians (Association of Religious Data Archives, 2006). Christianity is practiced throughout Europe and North, Central, and South America, and Russia. It is widespread across the U.S. in many different forms.

ISLAM

Islam originated in western Arabia and emerged as a religion after Christianity and Judaism in the 7th century C.E. with the Prophet Muhammad ibn Abd Allah (Donner, 1999). Muhammad periodically went on retreats of meditation and reflection, and during such retreats had religious experiences that were revelations from God. These revelations, or messages from Allah, or God, were eventually collected to form the Quran (Koran), which is the sacred scripture of Islam (Donner, 1999). Practitioners of Islam are called Muslims, and they believe in an uncompromising monotheism (Campo, 2006), which includes surrendering to the will of Allah or God.

Muslims believe that this sole God is the ". . . creator, sustainer, and restorer of the world" (Campo, 2006, p. 515). Some other doctrines in the Quran include the belief in an ordered universe in which patterns have been established by God; the view of human pride or arrogance as a cardinal sin; the idea that disobedience to, or disbelief in, God is sinful; a belief in the Last Day, when the world will come to an end and a final judgment will either save or condemn to hell; and a belief that the essence of the human endeavor is a moral struggle (Campo, 2006). In Islam, Muhammad was the last prophet, or divine messenger. Muhammad's messages retold stories of earlier prophets such as Abraham, Moses, David, and Jesus, and although Muhammad's messages were certainly reaffirmations in some respects, they were not well received by his fellow tribespeople, who were adherents to pagan cults of western Arabia (Donner, 1999). Muhammad had to persevere through much opposition and abuse to have his message heard (Donner, 1999).

Upon Muhammad's death, his community of Believers became headed by caliphs, or successors, who lead the Islamic community (Donner, 1999). The way that caliphs were chosen led to three major sects of Islam: Shi'a, Kharijites, and eventually Sunni (Donner, 1999). The Shi'a thought the caliph should become a hereditary lineage, but this did not ensure a spiritually pure leader. This led to the first divide in Islam and the formation of the Kharijites, the seceders (Donner, 1999). The Sunni, or orthodox majority sect of Islam, is the predominant sect today. Sunnis believe in choosing the caliph democratically. The Kharijites have all but disappeared today, and the Shi'a dominate in Iran.

Because Islam does not draw distinctions between religion and the other spheres of life, the Muslim state is, by definition, a religious state. (Campo, 2006). Though Islam had its origins in the Middle East, it is far-reaching today as the world's second-largest religion.

It is estimated that worldwide there are 1.3 billion persons who practice Islam in diverse cultural regions. Islam is spread throughout the world in areas such as Turkey, Central Asia, Africa, India, Mongolia, Russia, Iran, Southeast Asia, and the United Kingdom. In the U.S., 1.55 percent, or 4,650,000 people, identify as Muslim (ARDA, 2006). There are large Muslim populations in Chicago, Detroit, Houston, Los Angeles, New York City, San Francisco, and Washington, D.C. (Muslim Population, 2006).

JUDAISM

Judaism as a religion originated in Israel around 585 B.C.E., among the Hebrew people (Neusner, 2006). Like Christianity and Islam, Judaism is a monotheistic religion that carries the belief that there is only one God. Moses is considered the prophet who delivered the revelations of God to the Jewish people at Mount Sinai. The Torah, or the Five Books of Moses, is considered the sacred text in Judaism and describes the loss and recovery of the Land of Israel, including the sermon given by Moses at Mount Sinai (Neusner, 2006). The Old Testament of the Bible is comprised of the Torah. The Land of Israel was viewed as the land that God had set aside for the Jewish people (Neusner, 2006).

The basic beliefs of Judaism are that there is one God (the Creator), as God's will was revealed to Moses in the form of 10 commandments, and that these commandments were a gift from God so the Jewish people could live their lives according to God's will (Wenner, 2001d). Historically, the Jewish people have been persecuted wherever they lived, outside of Palestine. As Christianity became more widespread as the official religion of the Roman Empire (Neusner, 2006), persecution of the Jewish people increased. Close to six millions Jews were exterminated by the Nazis during World War II. Christians believe that Jesus Christ was the son of God who was sent for the salvation of the people, while the Jewish belief is that Jesus was not the son of God and that the Messiah whom God will send has not yet arrived (Neusner, 2006). The main branches of Judaism are Orthodox, Conservative, Reform, and Reconstructionist. Orthodox Jews are traditionalists who observe Judaism in its purest form, including the dietary and ceremonial laws of Judaism. The Conservative branch places emphasis on the historic and religious aspects of Judaism, and is considered to be less strict than Orthodox Judaism, and less liberal than Reform Judaism. The Reform branch has a more liberal outlook with much less emphasis on doctrine, or religious belief, and has adapted traditional practices to the modern world. Reconstructionist Jews have adapted Jewish ethical teachings to contemporary moral dilemmas and tend to be committed to gender equality.

Judaism is not only a religion, but also an ethnicity. Those who descended from the Hebrew people of the 5th century B.C.E. are considered ethnically Jewish, though they may or may not observe the Jewish religious traditions. For instance, Jesus was ethnically Jewish, but proclaimed to be God's messenger and spread the messages that would become the foundation of Christianity.

Worldwide, there are nearly 15 million Jewish people. In the U.S., there are 5,760,000 Jewish people, roughly 1.92 percent of the population (ARDA, 2006). Today there are large concentrations of Jewish people in Israel, Central and Western Europe, and in the United States, particularly in New York City, Los Angeles, Chicago, Boston, Miami, and Washington, D.C.

BUDDHISM

Buddhism emerged in northern India around 560 B.C.E. It is based on the teachings of Siddhartha Gautama, who became known as Buddha, or "enlightened one" (Wenner, 2001a). The teachings of Buddhism are based on human suffering, or dukkha, and the impermanence of life (Reynolds, 2006). The monastic community of followers, or bhikkhus, whom the Buddha taught was referred to as sangha (Wenner, 2001a).

The beliefs of Buddhism include the concept of no-self, the belief in rebirth (samsara), the doctrine of karma, and attainment of Nirvana (enlightenment) (Reynolds, 2006). For Buddhists, ". . . the aim of religious practice is to be rid of the delusion of the ego, thus freeing oneself from the fetters of the mundane world" (Reynolds, 2006, pp. 148–149). In Buddhism's earliest times, Buddhist monks led a life of wandering, poverty, begging, and sexual abstinence (Reynolds, 2006). This was to cultivate humility, compassion, and selflessness, and to foster freedom from suffering (Reynolds, 2006). Currently, there have been movements to give the Buddhist laity (the nonmonastic community) a larger role, and to relax restrictions on the monastic community, such as allowing Buddhist clergy to marry and have families (Reynolds, 2006).

The two main branches of Buddhism are Mahayana and Theravada (Wenner, 2001a). Mahayana Buddhism is largely practiced in China, Japan, and Vietnam and is based on more than five thousand volumes of holy writings, the oldest writings in Sanskrit. Theravada Buddhism is mainly practiced in Southeast Asia (Sri Lanka, Burma, Thailand, Cambodia, and Laos), and is based on three groups of writings known as Tripitaka, or the "Three Baskets" (Wenner, 2001a). Although Buddhism began in what is now India, it has not remained a strong religion in that region, and Hinduism is the major religion in India today (Reynolds, 2006).

Buddhism maintains about 380,000,000 practitioners worldwide, and about 2,720,000 in the United States (ARDA, 2006). Most Buddhists are concentrated in China, Tibet, Japan, Thailand, Vietnam, and other regions of Southeast Asia. In the United States, Buddhist communities are often found among immigrant groups from Southeast Asia, especially on the West Coast.

HINDUISM

Hinduism originated in northern India, there is no specific founder, and it resulted from the religious practices of Aryan tribes living in India more than 3,000 years ago (Wenner, 2001c). There are sacred texts, the Vedas, which include religious writings and are known collectively as the Book of Knowledge (Hawley, 2006). There are four Vedas: the Samhitas (chants), Brahmanas (sacrificial rituals), Aranyakas (wisdom of the forest), and Upanishads (secret teachings of cosmic correlations) (Hawley, 2006).

Hinduism is based on the caste system, or a ranking system of society, and includes four rankings: Brahmins (priests), Kshatriyas (soldiers), Vaishyas (merchants and farmers), and Harijahns (untouchables, who are extremely poor) (Wenner, 2001c). The Hindus believe in human and animal reincarnation, and it is believed that one's actions in a previous life determine which caste one will belong to in the next life (e.g., if a person behaved well, he or she would be born into a higher caste) (Wenner, 2001c). The caste system was outlawed in 1948 in India, yet it remains influential in the Hindu religion and the complexities of reincarnation. As in Buddhism, there is a peaceful escape from reincarnation, or Nirvana, and the ultimate goal is to transcend reincarnation (Wenner, 2001c).

Hinduism is a complex religion, and a practitioner can be polytheistic, monotheistic, pantheistic, agnostic, or atheistic. Practitioners can choose different paths to reach Nirvana, and these paths include the way of works, the way of knowledge, and the way of devotion (Wenner, 2001c). Hinduism seems to have evolved within its own regional and social context, adapting and incorporating other ideas into its milieu. The beliefs of renunciation of self and the doctrines of reincarnation and liberation seem to be indicative of the Vedic traditions and seem to be rooted in other religions that emerged in northern India (Hawley, 2006).

Hinduism as a world religion has about 870,000,000 practitioners. In the United States, there are about 1.1 million Hindus (Association of Religious Data Archives, 2006). Hinduism is the major religion of India, and is also practiced in Britain and Trinidad. In the U.S., there are temples near Pittsburgh and in Queens, New York City (Hawley, 2006).

NATIVE AMERICAN SPIRITUAL TRADITIONS

Native American spiritual traditions were a part of the precolonial Americas and were as varied as the number of tribal groups that occupied North and South America. Native American spiritual traditions originated 30,000 to 60,000 years ago with the arrival of the first people to the Americas (Doak, 1997) and are now practiced mainly among indigenous peoples of North and South America.

There are no sacred texts or fixed doctrines. These religions are traditions that are embedded in societies of peoples and transmitted orally from generation to generation (Carrasco, 2006). Native American spiritual traditions have developed from ancestral traditions including hunting taboos, animal ceremonialism, beliefs in spirits, and shamanism (Doak, 1997).

Although there are hundreds of different Native American tribes and religions, and it is difficult to generalize without distorting, there are some commonalities. The word "religion" to characterize them is really a misnomer, because they consist of traditions that do not carry the duality of the sacred and the nonsacred of the Western religions. These traditions include rituals and ceremonies that represent the binding together of the living, the departed, the yet-to-be-born, and the human and the natural world. Practices are localized, access to some knowledge is restricted, and participation is more important than belief. There is also the centrality of kinship, and the valuing of generosity and of oral transmission of traditions. Transitions include death and coming-of-age achievements and passages, and joking and clowning are viewed as ceremonial entertainment (Carrasco, 2006). Many tribes had shamans, or those who had a special religious role as thinkers and performers of sacred rituals (Doak, 1997).

Because Native American spiritual traditions have not been organized and recognized religions, they have suffered over the past 500 years as colonization occurred and Christianity was introduced (Carrasco, 2006). Some concerns that continue for traditional Native American spiritual traditions are access to sacred sites, survival of Native American languages, sacred objects being taken illegally and held in museums, misappropriation of traditions by other groups (such as New Agers), and the toll of modern life on traditional values and practices (Carrasco, 2006). Most tribal religions and ceremonies were efforts to achieve a balance with a physical universe inhabited by spiritual entities that were intimately connected to everything else in certain fundamental ways (Deloria, 1993).

The losses of Native American spiritual traditions resulting from the European invasion are massive. Because most of the traditions were maintained orally, whole languages, ceremonies, and narratives were lost. It is difficult to estimate the number of practitioners. Though the number of Native Americans is much higher, the number of people known to be practicing in the Native American Church in the United States is estimated at 250,000 (Doak, 1997). In North as well as in South America, indigenous religious ideas and practices have continued, even in communities that have had a long involvement with Christianity. Christian beliefs and ideas have often been absorbed and reframed to reflect the confluence of Christianity with Native American spiritual traditions. The presence of Native American religious beliefs and ideas within Christian practices is another reason why numbers are difficult to estimate, for many Native Americans converted to Christianity, at least in some respects.

SUMMARY

Most religious faiths have been subject to historical divisions that today are represented by more or less literal adherence to the original texts or stricter or less strict adherence to the teachings of the original prophets. (See Table IV.1.)

The monotheistic religions are known for their ethical tenets and share a belief in the existence of an omnipotent and omniscient God, creator of the world, a recognition of human frailty or weakness that prevent people from making the right choices, an aspiration of human transcendence beyond the self, and a path for salvation or redemption. They also contain fundamental practices that generally include doctrines of faith, the power of prayer, and the establishment of sacred places, sacred days, and sacred foods, as differentiated from those that are nonsacred, or profane.

Buddhism, Hinduism, and the Native American spiritual traditions differ from the monotheistic religions in that the former do not propose the existence of an eternal, personal, omnipotent, omniscient, and all-loving God. In the case of Buddhism, there is a belief in an impersonal and immanent cosmic law; if some of the Buddhist believers turn to the Buddha and worship him, it is because they consider him a savior who brings deliverance, and not as the creator and ruler of the universe. In the case of Hinduism, a vast plurality of gods and goddesses exist as part of the impersonal Brahman, and humans, like all living things, are just manifestations of Brahman. Humans have no individual self, or self-worth. Native American spiritual traditions generally do not distinguish between the natural and the supernatural (Ruvolo, n.d.), while monotheistic traditions are more inclined to emphasize the gulf that separated the pure, spiritual beings in heaven—God, the angels, and saints—from sinful men and women mired in a profane world filled with temptation and evil.

Table IV.1   Overview of Major Religious Faiths

Religion	Major teachings	Scriptures	Tenets	Sects/divisions
Christianity	Focus on person, teaching, and work of Jesus of Nazareth. Jesus is a member of the Trinity.	Christian Bible: Old Testament and New Testament	Seven sacraments based on the doctrine and morals of the church: baptism, confirmation, eucharist (holy communion), reconciliation/ penance, anointing of the sick, marriage, and holy orders. Note: Only Catholics practice all seven sacraments	Catholic, Orthodox, Protestant (Methodist, Lutheran, Calvinist, Anglican, Baptist, Evangelical, Pentecostal), Unitarian
Islam	Belief in unique and absolutely transcendent God. God established a covenant with the children of Adam, and sent prophets.	Quran	Five pillars: witness (Shahadah), worship (Salah), charity (Zakah), fasting (Sawm or Siyam), pilgrimage (Hajj)	Shiite, Sunni, Kharijites
Judaism	Based on belief in one God (Yaweh), covenant with Israel (Jacob)	Bible: Old Testament (Torah, Talmud)	Observation of the "mitzvoth," divine commandments. Regular prayer; Observation of the Shabbat (Sabbath)	Orthodox, Conservative, Reformed, Reconstructionist
Buddhism	Belief in worth and dignity of each living being, respect and compassion for all life. Importance of	Sutras	Four noble truths. Eightfold path: right understanding, right thought, right speech, right conduct, right livelihood, right effort,	

Religion	Major teachings	Scriptures	Tenets	Sects/divisions
	individual finding path to enlightenment and cessation of suffering.		right mindfulness, and right concentration	
Hinduism	One reality behind the universe (Brahman). Reality manifested in gods and goddesses. God takes birth on earth as various incarnations (Avatars). One reality exists in inner soul of man (Atman).	Vedas, Upanishads, Bhagavad Gita	Arati Puja	
Native American	Great Spirits and Evil Sprits. Unity of natural and supernatural.	None	Ceremonies, rituals, communication with invisible world, curing rites	Iroquois, Apache, Dakota/Sioux

Source: The National Conference (1996). Interfaith calendar. Chicago: Author.

Religion and Identity Development

Religious beliefs and practices are an important part of identity development and follow a developmental model in a similar fashion to a spiritual journey (Griffith & Griggs, 2001; Standard, Sandhu, & Painter, 2000). Griffith and Griggs (2001) developed a conceptual framework based on Erikson's and Marcia's identity developmental models. The diffusion religious identity status is characterized by a lack of interest in religion or an externally defined, self-serving form of religion. Individuals may define the relationship with a higher power as an instrumental exchange in which their needs are met. The foreclosure status is defined by conformity or acceptance of religious beliefs to gain acceptance from others. For children, this often includes the tacit acceptance of parental religious beliefs to secure parental approval. Many at this stage may begin to experience a spiritual or religious crisis that highlights the uncritical acceptance or endorsement of beliefs to gain approval. The moratorium status is characterized by an examination period and a critical examination of religious beliefs. This period may also include an exploration of a variety of religious faiths and traditions. The final status, achievement, occurs after the period of questioning and critical examination in moratorium. Here, individuals integrate their religious beliefs into their identity and their spirituality. They become an integral component of life functioning and influence thoughts, actions, and affective experiences. As with other developmental models, individuals can recycle from moratorium to achievement statuses; therefore, it is important for therapists to assess the status level of their clients (Griffith & Griggs, 2001).

RELIGION AND CULTURE

Exploring religious beliefs may lead to understanding culturally specific expressions of spirituality (Fukuyama & Sevig, 1999) and intragroup differences. During developmental or stressful transitions in the life cycle, some people may have a tendency to rely on the continuity and comfort of past traditions and seek connections with their ancestors through prayers, folk medicines, rituals, or magic beliefs. The human tendency to find comfort and stable meanings during times of change by relying on cultural beliefs, known as "ideological ethnicity" (Falicov, 1999, p. 105), can enhance a sense of belonging and continuity. For families experiencing severe trauma, tragedies, losses, or severe poverty, the adherence to cultural religious and spiritual expressions may help them find meaning, solace, resilience, and purpose (Aponte, 1999). For some individuals, spirituality is connected to the concept of animism—the belief that there is a universal life force that exists in all things, both animate and inanimate. The belief in spirits or forces leads to a belief in spiritual causes of mental illness or behavioral problems. Some clients will seek out indigenous healers, such as shamans, curanderos, or faith healers, to find relief for symptoms.

RELIGION AND WELLNESS

Many individuals believe that spirituality is an integral part of the wellness that provides a sense of balance in their lives. There is recognition of the unity of mind, body, and spirit. Many of the wellness models include spirituality along with physical, social, emotional, and mental health. Chandler, Holden, and Kolander (1992) argue, however, that spiritual health needs to be conceptualized as an interactional component of wellness with the other factors. Concentrating on behavioral change in clients without including wellness and spirituality may lead to recidivism of the original symptoms or presenting problems (Chandler, et al., 1992). Research has demonstrated the positive relationship between religiosity and wellness (Miller & Thoresen, 1999; Tolliver, 1997). Health and wellness are concepts that go beyond the mere absence of disease. It is now known that health and wellness are influenced by powerful cultural, social, cognitive, and philosophical factors that include the existence of meaningful relationships and the ability to find meaning and purpose in life (Walsh, 1999a).

REACTIONS TO RELIGIOUS SOCIALIZATION

It is important to understand that there are both positive and negative components to spirituality and religious practices (Faiver, et al., 2000) and that often people can be harmed or wounded by negative experiences. Some religious tenets or rules can be restrictive of behavior or individual expression. Religious beliefs can foster levels of guilt over behaviors and a sense of worthlessness. Guilt can occur from religious teachings and include negative behaviors, excessive guilty thoughts, and affective experiences including depression and anxiety (Faiver, et al., 2000). Individuals struggling with religiously controversial issues, such as homosexuality and abortion, may also feel wounded by religious tenets (Fukuyama & Sevig, 1999). There are also many positive aspects of religions and spiritual beliefs. Religion can mark rites of passages or developmental or transitional periods of life (Fukuyama & Sevig, 1999). Spiritual beliefs can help individuals cope with trauma, grief and loss, or interpersonal difficulties. Spirituality can also help people find self-worth, meaning, and fulfillment in life and increase physical health.

Implications for Professionals

The study of religion has been a neglected subject in the field of psychology in the 20th century. The behavioral sciences have been dominated by a positivist and scientific viewpoint that considered religion to be irrelevant to the study of the human mind (Miller & Thoresen, 2003). In recent times, the scientific study of religion has taken center stage, and there is currently a large body of literature devoted to the investigation of non-observable cognitive and emotional states connected to religious and spiritual experiences (Miller & Thoresen, 2003). This has coincided with a resurgence of the importance of spiritual and religious issues in people who are increasingly seeking the meaning, connectedness, and harmony that they may not have (Walsh, 1999a). Because religion is a fundamental component of many individuals' lives, it is important to consider how religion and spirituality are relevant to clinical practice. Research suggests that many clients wish to include a discussion of spirituality in treatment (Griffith & Rotter, 1999) but surveys find that clinicians may not be accustomed to having conversations with their clients about religion or spirituality because it has generally been a neglected area in psychology (Miller & Thoresen, 2003).

This can be attributed to several reasons. First, training programs do not generally include curricula devoted to religion or spirituality. Second, because they are not familiar with the religious backgrounds of the clients, clinicians' level of comfort may be low and therefore, they avoid the subject of religion altogether. Third, secular clinicians may not believe in the value of discussions related to the religion or spirituality of their clients. It is important for counselors and therapists to assess the religious socialization and religious commitment of their clients. It is also important for clinicians to become comfortable with discussions around religious themes, and find out how clients fulfill their spiritual needs. Finally, it is important to assess whether religion is a source of support or a source of distress for their clients and design interventions according to the outcome of that assessment.

Stories in This Section

There are three stories in this section. Frank's story is that of a minister who learns to follow God more closely. As you read his story, notice the change in his religious identity throughout his lifespan. Bob's story, in contrast, is one of a minister whose changes in religious identity lead him to leave the ministry to serve in other capacities. Katie's story is about how her religious identity changed because she fell in love with someone of a different faith. All three stories highlight how religion and spirituality intersect with self-concept and psychological functioning.

Discussion Questions

Do you agree with the statement that religion and spirituality are key ingredients when working with clients who profess to hold particular religious beliefs?

What are the potential ways that clinicians could convey their discomfort in discussing religion and spirituality in a clinical situation?

What steps could clinicians take to increase their level of comfort?

How does religion help an individual or a family cope with stress, illness, death, or crisis?

What are some specific examples of the relationship between religion and spirituality and well-being?

What are some specific questions that counselors and therapists can pose to assess the religious and spiritual socialization and the religious and spiritual commitment of their clients?

What are some examples of the relationship between religion and culture?

What could be some of the differences between Irish Catholicism and Catholicism in Mexico, for example?

Frank's Story 12

Hearing God's Voice

There are some people whose lives reflect confidence, security, and hope. They seem assured of their futures, even when facing circumstances that are confusing, unclear, or uncertain. When pressed, these individuals often discuss how their spirituality and religious beliefs sustain them, and how they have a personal relationship with a higher power that gives them strength. For them, religion is not just a set of rituals, traditions, or teachings; it is a vital component of who they are. They are what they believe, and their lives reflect this. Fukuyama and Sevig (1992) discuss individuals who are further along on their spiritual journeys. They are optimistic, hopeful, and faithful, and report comfort with the ebbs and flows of life. They report higher levels of intimacy and connection and an appreciation for reverence, aesthetics, and beauty. They also report higher levels of life satisfaction, personal happiness, social support, and empathy, and lower levels of depression, blood pressure, and hostility (Griffith & Rotter, 1999). This first story on religion reflects these principles. Frank is a minister who describes his spiritual and religious development and the intersection of religion with self-concept. Frank reports a close relationship with God and the ability to hear God speaking to him and directing his life. The reader should pay attention to the role of religion in Frank's life and how his relationship influences decisions, values, and expectations. The reader is also invited to pay attention to personal reactions to the religious themes in the story.

Frank's Story

My life is an assimilation of two cultures. I was born and raised in the West Indies in the Caribbean, and now I live in the United States of America. I am

51 years old. I spent 18 formative, foundational, and fantastic years in the Caribbean culture and at present have spent 33 years in the American culture. But there is a thread that binds both cultures, a common nexus that makes my life journey what it is. It has brought purpose and meaning as to why I was so destined. I speak of the church. The church was and is the nucleus of my cultural development, of my values and belief system, and my identity.

The Caribbean culture grounded me in the critical areas of my life: family, work, education, church, friendship, and community. The American culture took the grounding of the Caribbean culture and brought clarity to my cultural identity. I left the Caribbean with a small idea of what I thought I was to be career-wise. But it was the American culture (way of life)—you must get it yourself—that brought me to deepen and define my life's purpose.

The Caribbean culture is laid-back, slow. The American culture is fast-paced, a rat race. In assimilating both cultures, I have learned to live in the middle—a pace that is necessary for my mental state and ability.

My Caribbean background is most interesting. With a British background (we were a colonial state of England), I learned the value of history, country, honor for the queen (our leader), respect for her governmental representative (governor of the Caribbean), and love for one's country. Because of this background, I was able to have a well-rounded education. I acquired a thorough background in English, math, geography, history (mostly British), biology (science), literature, and religious education. These subjects were drilled into me. Throughout my elementary and secondary education, religious education (the study of the Bible) was at the center.

I attended Baptist elementary and secondary schools and had devotionals each morning, which consisted of two hymns, scripture, and prayer. This deepened my appreciation for the great hymns of the church.

My mother plays both the piano and the organ. We grew up with a piano in the house. I can vividly remember gathering around the piano as a family, singing these great hymns. They were so much a part of my life that even after all these years I can still remember all the stanzas of these hymns.

Because my father was (and still is) the pastor of the Alpha Baptist Church, I spent my childhood and youth in Sunday school each Sunday and in vacation Bible school two or three times a year. We attended a special afternoon Sunday school that was held at a neighborhood church. I recall the flannelgraph presentations, the great Bible stories, and the various White teachers. I did not know it then, but I was being deeply grounded in the scriptures, understanding the basic stories and becoming familiar with the major events and persons. One of my favorite Bible characters was and still is Samuel (see 1 Samuel 3:1–10, 19–21). At the Alpha Baptist Church, there were many Sundays when preachers of different ethnicities brought the message. I recall an Indian, a Canadian, and a British preacher; many American White and Black preachers; and preachers from the surrounding Caribbean islands. We grew accustomed to the multicultural flavor from the pulpit. And because my father is a free spirit, we never knew from Sunday to Sunday who would be bringing the message. In fact, when I came to Christ, a White preacher had presented the Gospel message. As I look back over those years, I appreciate very much being exposed to this concept—for the Body of Christ is truly multicultural. There were three childhood experiences that shaped my identity:

1. When we moved to the elementary school to have church, there were very few members at that time. I recall one Sunday morning having severe earaches. I told my father that I was not up to going to church. He granted me permission to stay home. As I lay in bed, something began to happen to me. An overwhelming feeling came over me. I had an irresistible urge to be in church. Before I knew it, I was getting ready. This urge was so great that I walked the 4 miles to church. My father and mother were surprised to see me. I discovered later that it was the Spirit of God that drove me to the church. It was truly an incredible experience.

2. I recall attending an afternoon worship service of the Caribbean Baptist Union, the name of the group of churches with which our church was affiliated. That afternoon, my father was the scheduled preacher. During the sermon, I was standing outside because a great crowd had gathered. As I stood outside, I could hear my father preaching. Suddenly, something gripped me. I was moved to stop what I was doing. Like a camera zooming in to focus on the desired object, my eyes fell on my father. For a few moments, I was mesmerized. I said to myself, "My God, my father is truly preaching!" It was a moment that was indelibly etched on my mind. I can still see myself in that mesmerizing moment.

3. I also recall when we moved to the present location of the Alpha Baptist Church, in the initial building for worship. Here a strange phenomenon occurred. When worship was over, as we prepared to leave the church, I stood behind the pulpit. In the presence of my father, my mother, and a few of my siblings, I said these words, "One day, I will preach from this pulpit." I was barely into my teens when these unforgettable words fell from my lips. I did not know at the time what this experience meant.

These three experiences were all so special, so spirituous and intoxicating that they became foundational in my walk with the Lord.

These snapshots were a prelude to the major purpose that the Lord had in mind for me. In August of 1971, after completing my high school education, I had my conversion experience and my call to preach. I was so taken by the message and convicted by the Spirit of God that before I realized it, I was standing before the church confessing my sins and surrendering my heart and will to the Savior, Jesus the Christ. I was blown away that day. I never before had such an experience. I could not explain what happened, but I was sure of one thing—I would never be the same again.

Many of my friends could not believe what had occurred in my life. They knew my father was a pastor, but my lifestyle was far from that of a Christian. Once they saw how serious and committed I was about my new experience with the Lord, they stopped asking questions. Today, they all call me "Rev."

The church was the nucleus of my cultural experience in the Caribbean and still is the nucleus of my experiences in America. All that has happened to me has its roots in this sacred and hallowed community. It was God's plan all along to make me and use me as a preacher and later as a pastor.

I had no clue about my career when I completed high school. I thought very little about what I would become. I understood much later that the reason for this lack of direction was because my future was already determined for me.

It was God's design to keep me from other areas and interests, so I could be totally committed to what He wanted and had willed for my life. What seemed like a cloudy time, with no sense of direction, was, in reality, a time of preparation and assessing. I recalled that this was a silent time in my life. It was as if I were waiting for something to occur, but was uncertain what it was. Then one day, my father came to me and asked me if I was interested in going to college. At this point, my life was so empty and seemed so boring and monotonous that something needed to happen. Daddy was asking me if I wanted to go to college in Atlanta, Georgia. He was asking me about my future. I knew nothing about Atlanta, Georgia, or, for that matter, college. I did not have a clue. Because preaching was my calling, Daddy was asking me to pursue my studies in this area. He was asking me to matriculate at a particular seminary.

My appreciation for the church I was able to acquire from the passion of my father and the commitment of my mother. I watched them sacrifice their own money, possessions, skills, and time to build the ministry God had called them to perform. Many of their own automobiles were worn out from transporting members and potential members to the church. They labored untiringly. I saw them with my own eyes give money to pay other people's bills and support families who had children in college. They loved the Lord, and it showed in their care for others.

I was not aware of it but their love, attitude, and faith were being transferred into my heart, mind, and spirit. Much of what I do, believe, and practice today came from their great influence on my life. I am truly the son of Everett and Mary Adams. I believe that my pastoral heart and a passion for God's word I received from my daddy, and my musical tendencies and talent, along with a humble spirit, I got from my mother. I can pick up a song or hymn in a heartbeat. I even try to sing on occasion—one of my mother's great gifts. They love people and the church, and I understand why I do. It was instilled in me in my formative years. I did not realize that coming to America meant leaving an established culture and migrating to a new and different culture. This was the first reality check I received. When I arrived in Atlanta, I noticed that there were very many Whites in the airport and on my way to the college. Spending time downtown and in the community, I saw more of them. I was thrown aback by all the Whites. I had grown up in a predominantly Black country. Though many Whites visited as tourists, I usually did not spend much time observing them. My contact with them was very limited. I was accustomed to seeing Blacks in every area of my life—church, school, downtown, hotels, stores, and so on.

I did not realize it at the time, but I was experiencing what is called cultural shock. It was a reality check for me. As I traveled to various locations—grocery stores, gas stations, restaurants, and dry goods stores—I encountered great numbers of Whites. They were everywhere. They seemed to be bombarding me and hemming me in from all sides. I could not get away from them. The limited number of Blacks I encountered, no doubt, magnified and intensified my bewildering experience. Only on the campus and in the church—predominantly Black institutions—was I comfortable and relaxed.

I could not turn to anyone because I wasn't sure what was happening to me. I did not feel any anger or hatred toward them, nor did I feel inferior or even segregated or discriminated against. I was mostly threatened by their presence. There were just so many of them—or too many of them. I had just not been accustomed to this kind of cultural interaction.

My experience of cultural shock in Atlanta was probably magnified by two unforgettable experiences I had as a youth in the Caribbean—one in my early youth, the other in my high school years.

When I was about six years old, we moved from the house that was left to my mother to my grandparents' house (my father's parents; my mother's parents died before she turned six years old, and she was adopted). We were serious about our playtime and outdoor activities. We were adventurous and played all over the area. At the east end of my grandparents' street was a tall wall. It seemed to stretch to the sky, but in reality it was about 12 to 14 feet high and about 3 feet wide. On the top of the wall's surface were broken pieces of glass set in the concrete, and in the middle were steel bars about 3 feet high, also set in the concrete. The steel bars were for the barbed wire that was strung onto it— about six rows of the wire from top to bottom.

As youth, we were nebulous to the danger of this wall. We walked on the wall, seeing who could walk without stepping on the broken glass, while holding on to the wire, avoiding its sharp protruding spikes. At the time, we ignored the potential dangers and were unaware as to why such a wall existed. As we followed the wall, we discovered that it was about 3 miles long, running north to south.

Then we noticed a distinct difference between the houses, roads, trees, and yards on either side. The houses on our side were poor-looking, rundown; the houses on the other side were elaborate, richer-looking. We did not pay much attention to it. We just believed that that was the way it was meant to be. We also noticed that only Whites lived on the other side, while Blacks lived on the poor side.

We then learned that the wall was constructed many years before to separate the natives (Black Caribbeans) from the immigrant Whites from Britain, who had become Caribbeans. It was a shocking discovery—that discrimination and segregation were a reality in our country. That discovery resonated in my spirit. Our lives went on. But today the wall is broken down in strategic places, and the country is independent.

The other experience occurred while I was a student in high school. Among the student body were a few Whites, but they were never treated any differently by most Blacks. One of them told us about a party and invited us to attend. Going to parties was the going thing in that day. When my friends and I arrived, we observed that it was a White party. The friend who ran with us in school responded in a strange manner. He acted like he did not know us and gave us the cold treatment. Our friend felt he was better than us. Needless to say, we did not stay long. We came away from this ordeal confused, angry, disappointed, and sorry for our friend. To say we had mixed emotions is an understatement.

These two experiences were very disturbing, but deep in my spirit I felt that these were the exception rather than the rule. Why do I remember them? I believe because they disturbed and sought to destroy the value and worth I gave to all people. I did not understand it then, but I do now. I had a respect for people, and that respect was not based on their color. It was truly painful and was registered in my memory banks. The reality of what people of color had to deal with was most disturbing.

The early years in America were very challenging. In my college, I lived with African Americans—Blacks from all across the country, and from Africa and the

Caribbean. The Americans treated me very strangely. They asked questions like, "Do you have TV? Do you live in houses? Are there cars in your country? Do you live in huts?" I felt like an alien, and in reality I was—I was in a strange and unfamiliar country.

The proximity of the island to America had a great influence on my formative years—television, movies, food (McDonald's, Kentucky Fried Chicken, and Burger King were among the favorites), and clothes. But these were all disconnected from the American culture because these businesses had to adjust to the Caribbean culture, use Caribbean ingredients, and so on. So I was introduced to the culture, but I discovered that living in the culture was an entirely different experience.

I remember thinking that maybe I had made a mistake by coming to America. The weather was entirely different. My first winter was unforgettable, especially because I did not bring an overcoat. I knew nothing about long johns and had never seen real snow, only snow on TV. I did not know it could get so cold. In the Caribbean, 55 degrees is very cold. I knew nothing about using heat. I was accustomed to driving cars on the left side of the road; driving on the right was a traumatic experience. The food was seasoned and prepared differently. The impact of all of these experiences took its toll as I struggled to adjust, but the difficulty did not interfere with my studies. I was able to keep pace in that area.

The cultural lag did not affect my cognition, but it did affect my daily living. That first semester was the longest time of my life. I was truly relieved when my father sent my plane ticket for me to go home for the semester break. It was a break I really needed. It proved to be the difference for the rest of my college career.

My accent was an ongoing challenge, as people tried to understand me and I tried to understand them. They said I talked too fast, so I had to learn to slow down because, as a preacher, communication was most important. I was fortunate that there were two other Caribbean colleagues on campus, and they were able to buffer my trauma.

I also learned that my secondary education was solid. I spent many nights helping others with their writing, mathematics, English, and Greek, just to name a few. I realized how crucial and valuable a foundational educational background was.

In addition to my cultural adjustments in college, I had many, many fears. As a preacher, I was afraid to stand before people and speak. My fears were so great that I would attend chapel services in college on Mondays, Wednesdays, and Fridays, praying that no one would call on me to preside, to offer prayer, or read the scriptures. I was so relieved when others were chosen. I was very fortunate that no one ever called on me.

I recall on Sundays when I attended the Mt. Mariah Baptist Church in Smyrna, Georgia, that we were invited to dinner after church. Usually my pastor and I would attend these affairs. This was the best meal I received each week as a college student. But because I was afraid of simply being in the pulpit, I developed a nervous stomach. When I ate, I had to dismiss myself from the dinner table and proceed to the bathroom. There all of the delicious meal would find its way back up from my stomach. My fears were deep-seated and many times posed a very difficult problem. I read the scripture in church, but because of my fears, I would stumble over the words. Even familiar scriptures like the 23rd Psalm or the beatitudes became a challenging exercise.

One day, my first pastor in Atlanta became very curious about my inability, ineptness, and clumsy liturgical and clergical functions in the pulpit. He asked me point blank: "Have you been called?" (Being called means that the Lord selected an individual for the preaching ministry. It is not something that the person selects; he is selected.) It was a very penetrating question. I had never really thought about my call until he asked. It was a most propitious moment. Fortunately, I wasted no time in responding. I told him emphatically that I was; I went on to say that I was not sure about other areas of my life, but I was very sure that the Lord had called me into the gospel ministry. This was truly a defining moment in my life. My confidence soared, as the reality of God's hand on my life grew to an all-time high. This, however, did not mean that I was over my turbulence, because my fears continued. My calling was sure, but the daily challenges of that call still lay heavy on me; overcoming my fears would linger for a number of years.

In fact, this question of being called was asked in 1971. It was in the early 1980s, at the First Baptist Church in Frankfort, Kentucky, that I had a recurring dream. This dream terrified me, as well as my wife. I would wake up screaming in a voice that I could never naturally duplicate. The manifestation of a human figure, like the Grim Reaper, would suddenly appear. It would be moving toward me, and once it stood over me I would break out in this terrifying scream. It was a few years later that the Spirit of the Lord came to me and told me the meaning of this dream. He said that this dream was related to my fear of standing before people. Because I came from a small country church in Georgia to a larger congregation in Frankfort, Kentucky, the reality and trauma of my fear intensified. I knew I was fearful standing in the pulpit each Sunday, but I did not connect my fear with my dream. Once I made this discovery, my dream went away. Though I am not fully over my fear, the one thing that always blessed me was that I never stopped going to the pulpit, preaching, praying, speaking, or reading. No one knew that I was struggling with this fear. It did not polarize me or hinder me from standing. It did, on occasion, hinder my effectiveness. But again, no one knew it. The Lord has kept me. This is why Psalm 27:1 was my favorite verse—it reminded me of my fears and how the Lord helped me to deal with them, especially my major fear. Even after 30 years as a pastor and 33 years as a preacher, I still have my moments.

As I developed, it was clear that the church played a major role in my life. I did not know that this was the beginning of a total change. When I met and married my wife of 28 years, Rene, I had already completed two years in the pastoral ministry. Though it was a very small church, the challenge was nonetheless intense. She fit me like a hand in a glove. She was (and is) God's special gift to me. She has brought stability, integrity, and satisfaction to my life and to my ministry. Her role was critical in the 1979 decision to go to First Baptist Church.

The Lord's presence in my life was truly magnified when I came to preach at the First Baptist Church in Frankfort, Kentucky. I was scheduled to preach the second Sunday in August for a friend. Two weeks before I was to meet my obligation, I received a telephone call from one of the deacons in Frankfort. They wanted me to come the same Sunday (second Sunday in August). I told the deacon that I already had an appointment and that they should reschedule me. My wife heard me and called me on the carpet. She told me to call the deacon back and tell him that I would accept the invitation. Then she told me to call my friend and tell him to reschedule me. I did so.

On the second Sunday in August 1979, I came to preach at the First Baptist Church. The side entrance was open, so my wife, my son, and I went in. The entrance led us into the educational section. My wife and son remained behind as I took the time to observe the sanctuary. As I walked into this beautiful sanctuary with its high ceiling, I heard something that would change my life forever. I heard the voice of God. He spoke to me!

Now this was not an audible voice. But God spoke to my mind or in my spirit. He said to me, "You will be the next pastor!" I had never before in my life had such an experience. And when I heard the voice, there was no hesitation on my part. There was no doubt in my mind what I heard. And what I heard, I believed. I was dumbfounded. Then I walked into the vestibule. I noticed on the wall a plaque with all the names of the former pastors. Then it happened again. I heard the voice one more time. It said, "Your name will be next!" It blew me away! Again, I had no doubt. I was very sure that what the voice said to me would come true. Following that experience, the Lord used me to bless His people with His word. The church agreed that I should return. I did so for the next four months. It was on the first Sunday in February 1980 that they called me to be their pastor. It was truly awesome! What God said to me came to pass. I would have missed this important step in my development and ministry if it were not for God's voice and presence in my wife's life. He used her to help me be the preacher and pastor He knew I needed to be. This unique experience in my life was another defining moment. From then on, I heard God speak to me from time to time. My faith and confidence grew to an all-time high. My cultural identity had brought greater awareness and a more authentic and profound faith. I would grow another few inches in my walk with the Lord. Awesome!

That second Sunday experience made quite an impression on me. I was so sure that I would be the next pastor of the church that I went to the church I had been serving with as pastor and resigned the next Sunday. The next day, I called a potential employer. In a few weeks, they hired me as an editor of church literature. This one Sunday experience changed my life totally. I had given up my first pastorate and changed jobs. The church was central in my life's pursuits because the Lord had chosen to use me in this special way.

I worked in a fast-food restaurant before being hired at the publishing board. But though I was the chief cook, I never—I said never—worked on Sundays. And in the restaurant business, Sunday is the biggest day. But again, my cultural identity was my guide and my gauge. It was becoming much clearer to me that it was the very foundation and fruit of my life. There have been a few challenges in my ministry. I recall on the first Sunday in February 1990 I received a small raise from the First Baptist Church and a two-year extension on my position as pastor. I was very upset and decided to leave the church and go to another. In looking back, I see I overreacted. I sent out letters to potential churches and waited for their reply. (In the Baptist Church, candidates for the pastoral office communicate their interest in the pastorate by sending a letter of interest.)

After a few months, I heard from a vacant church in Oklahoma City, Oklahoma. They scheduled for me to preach in May of that same year. My wife and I flew to the city that Saturday and arrived in time for an interview, which I felt went very well. We were given a tour of the facilities. It was a new structure and a very beautiful building. On that Sunday, we attended Sunday school and morning worship. I taught the Sunday school lesson for that Sunday and brought the morning message. It was truly an awesome experience.

When we came away from that experience, my wife and I believed that this was where the Lord was leading us.

In June, we were invited again. This time we drove from Kentucky to Oklahoma. Again, all went well. A few weeks later, a small delegation from the Oklahoma City church came to investigate my ministry in Frankfort, Kentucky. It was a very uncomfortable day because most of the members knew why they had come to worship with us. Somehow we made it through. The church was to call a pastor in a few weeks. I waited and waited and did not hear anything. So I decided to call. I discovered that the business manager of the church (one of the delegates who had come to Frankfort) and the others had given "an evil report" on me. They told the church that they were treated with disrespect and that my family and I were very rude and unkind to them. This, of course, could not be further from the truth. I recall being kind to them, even giving them extra food for their travel back to Oklahoma City.

Then I learned later from one of the members that the business manager had called his own pastor for the job, and I was out of the picture.

As I pondered these events, the Lord came to converse with me. I will never forget what He said to me. He told me that He never gave me permission to go to Oklahoma City. He had nothing to do with it. He said that I took matters into my own hands and went ahead of Him. In fact, He told me that He had nothing to do with the whole experience. Then He went on to say that He should have permitted the church to call me. He told me that He should have allowed me to be the next pastor, so I could fall flat on my face. Then He said to me, "But I saved you from that tragedy. I will grant you my grace. But don't you ever try anything like this again. If you do, you will live to regret it."

I remember thanking Him for being so gracious and kind to me. And I recall saying, "Lord, I will never do anything like this again. If you want me to stay in Frankfort, Kentucky, for the rest of my life, I am prepared to do so. I will go where You want me to go. I will do what You want me to do. Wherever You lead, I will follow."

This was truly a humbling experience. And I learned a very important lesson: my life was not mine; it belonged to the Lord. He was the One who would determine where I would do ministry, and He was the One who would determine when and how I would do that. If this was not enough, when the Murrah Federal Building was bombed in Oklahoma City in 1995, the Lord told me "that He would have fixed it for me to be in that building." I was truly thankful for His grace. And my faith in Him went up another notch.

It was in June of 1991 that the Lord came to speak to me again. I had sent a letter of interest to two churches—one in Anderson, Indiana, the other in Chicago, Illinois. I only did so because a friend kept pestering me to do it. To be rid of him, I sent the letters. I did not expect to get a call. I was only trying to get rid of the constant annoyance about sending these letters. But on the last Sunday in June, my telephone rang. On the other end was the chairman of the board of deacons. He said to me that the church had received my letter, and they needed more information on me and three letters of reference. As I was hanging up the phone, I heard that voice in my ear—it was the voice of the Lord. He told me that I had better get ready, He was sending me to the Peace Baptist

Church in Chicago, Illinois. I was blown away. But I knew it was the Lord because I had heard that voice many times.

My wife and I were scheduled to leave for the Caribbean that Monday. So I hurried to get my information together and was able to secure three letters of reference. It was truly amazing.

I want you to know that from June of 1991 to January of 1992, the Lord kept speaking to me and confirming in my spirit that I was to be the next pastor of the Peace Church. They did call me to be their next pastor. This was an incredible experience. Waiting for this to happen was very easy because almost every week the Lord spoke to me in some special way, confirming His direction for my life. From June to January is seven months, but it was the Lord who helped me stay focused. I learned from Psalm 27:14 that "those who wait on the Lord, He shall strengthen their hearts." This is exactly what the Lord did. He kept me on track with His words of direction.

Needless to say, this was among the most extraordinary experiences of my life. I never dreamt that the Lord would speak to me in this way. And, as I write these words, it has been 12 years since I was called to serve the Peace Church. God has been and is true to His Word. You do know, of course, that my faith in God grew to another level. I could not believe that God would bless such an insignificant and dispensable individual as me. He had favored me. But He has made it very clear that it was not about me—it was all about Him. He blessed me so that I could give Him the glory due unto His name. Awesome!

Two other experiences have occurred since I was called to serve the Peace Baptist Church. One had to do with obeying God and not man. The Lord told me to start a new program. But I could not vote on it. Opposition arose. A group of members met with me and asked me to resign from the church. They said that they would give me a reasonable pay plan and help me move. I told them that I would not.

My future seemed in jeopardy. But nothing became of this meeting because it was unofficial. But I prayed, and the Lord sent me four confirmations that following week: a card, a special cup with an affirming message on it, a telephone call, and a couple who bought me a suit and a pair of shoes. These affirming responses by the Lord were accelerating. The other had to do with prayer. I was invited to offer prayer at the city hall before the city hall members began their regular bimonthly meetings. As I completed my prayer, I closed by saying, "In Jesus's name, I pray. Amen." There was a little commotion about what I said. In the newspaper the next day, it was reported that I had prayed in Jesus's name. It was as though I had done something wrong. I was being made an example of because of my faith.

I came away more determined never to deny my Lord or my faith, if anyone asks. As a resource, I was able to gain strength from God's word and from Neil Anderson's book *The Bondage Breaker*. I was able to turn to my pastor for guidance and direction. With a graduate degree in clinical psychology, and with more than 20 years of pastoral experience, he was able to give some sound and solid counsel. I discovered anew the importance of having a pastor and the importance of professional pastoral counseling. You are aware that my faith grew to another level.

God has helped me in many ways, but let me share one major experience with you. In July of 1996, my youngest brother died from complications with his blood pressure, which led to him contracting pneumonia. In fact, members of the Alpha Baptist Church were visiting our church, and they were preparing to leave for home the next day. I drove home after securing them, and when I drove up to my home, two cars were parked in the driveway. When I walked in, a deacon and the assistant to the pastor were sitting in the living room. When I saw them, I thought my father had passed, but after conversing I learned that it was my 35-year-old brother.

I communicated with my parents, and we grieved together as we remembered my brother and their son. I flew to the Caribbean after being made aware of funeral arrangements. We all gathered the day before to view and inspect the remains of my brother. Those moments we spent in the funeral home felt like a lifetime. We mourned, wept, and grieved as we saw him. The memories abounded as we sat and reminisced.

The next day, the service was to take place at the church. My father assigned me to bring the eulogy. I remember spending the days before in God's word. I recalled when the Lord confirmed the scripture that I was to use for the basis of my message. That scripture was Psalm 27:13–14. It is a very familiar passage. As I prepared my message, I remembered how that scripture began to minister unto me. It gave me so much comfort, strength, and peace. The more its points and principles unfolded, the stronger I became. And when I delivered that message ("God's Prescription for Our Pain"), I was truly strengthened. I couldn't believe it: the word of God has grounded me and lifted me. As I thought about my family, I felt a little bad because I had received so much from God's word. I remembered praying how good it would have been for my family if they had had the opportunity I had. God's word brought me through. I did not break at all during that time. It was not until a few weeks later, as I was sharing with my wife a minor detail about my brother, that the tears began to flow. But even that was a catharsis.

The final experience I will share has to do with my immigration and naturalization status. The decision about this status was again based on my cultural identity. When I got married, I applied for permanent residency in the United States. This immigration status would allow me to live and work in America and maintain my citizenship in the Caribbean.

My wife and I flew to the Caribbean to finalize my status. When we arrived and checked on my status, we discovered that we were missing some very important papers. This meant that my wife had to return to the United States without me. It took about three additional weeks for this status to be granted. It was a very stressful, anxious time, full of tension and trepidation. My wife returned home reluctantly and in tears. But it proved to be an important time for us because it brought us even closer together.

So significant was my desire to be totally involved in the life of my congregation in Chicago that I was moved to become a U.S. citizen. This compulsion grew out of the need to be more involved in the political and social processes. Giving guidance and direction to others without being a citizen became a serious problem for me. I was uncomfortable telling others about participating in our community, when I did not have the proper credentials to do so. In July 1994, I became a citizen of this country. I had assistance with the application process by a very capable and caring citizen, who guided me through the whole procedure. It took me about a year of preparation and actually applying before

I heard from the Immigration and Naturalization Service. I appeared in federal court in downtown Chicago, along with a number of other persons of various citizenship.

My parents came from the Caribbean, and many dignitaries and special friends from the community were present at the awesome celebration that was held that night at the church. I was overwhelmed by their support, and I shouted and thanked the Lord for again favoring me as He had done many times in the past. The following things have made a difference in my life: (1) a strong faith and confidence in God; (2) the power of prayer—God's answers; (3) the importance of associating with others of similar beliefs, who reinforce my commitment; (4) the ability to counsel others, using the presence of God's spirit in my life; (5) the strong support and stability from my lovely wife and precious family. (I am truly blessed. My wife and I are raising eight children, three of our son's children, four adopted children, and a special daughter, who was graciously given to us by two of our grandchildren's mothers.) This blended family has taught me much about love, relationships, honesty, truth, discipline, and the value of a loving and peaceful home. This is interesting because I am from a family of 13 siblings. I am the fifth child and the third son. I guess what I experienced as a youth was so special that I have tried to duplicate it. Like my father and mother, who had no miscarriages and no twins, I am blessed with a special family. I thank God for each of them. Awesome!

Content Themes

Frank's story describes a life that is not only influenced by—but is guided by—religion and a relationship with God. Frank describes an intimate and trusting relationship with God, the third spiritual need (Fukuyama & Sevig, 1992). Most of the adult decisions in Frank's life have been guided by God and serve as a demonstration of Frank's ability and willingness to be led. Frank was socialized into the Baptist faith as a child because his father and other extended family members served as ministers or religious leaders. These experiences, along with his religious training, shaped his cultural and religious identity. It is clear that religion has served as both a source of strength and a resource for Frank. His religion has also helped him to fulfill a calling and to develop a sense of fulfillment in his life and work.

RELATIONSHIP WITH GOD

Most of the major religious faiths include a higher power, a deity that is in charge of human life and nature. The relationship with a higher power can provide strength and comfort, provide answers to life's challenges and dilemmas, and provide a sense of hope and faith. Fukuyama and Sevig (1992) identify this relationship as an important spiritual need and emphasize the nature of trust that exists in the relationship as important. The importance of and influence of God in an individual's life is the first content theme in Frank's story. Frank's relationship with God changed as he grew and developed. As a young child, Frank was socialized into religion by his family through family devotions, church attendance, Sunday school, and vacation Bible school. Frank's relationship with God also has early roots, although he may not have been able to articulate it as a child. Frank was often led by the Spirit to engage in particular activities. Frank describes three early experiences: being led to attend church despite being sick that morning, recognizing and feeling his father preaching during a service, and announcing that he would someday preach from the pulpit. Although he did not fully comprehend these experiences at the time they were occurring, it is clear to him as an adult that he was being led and directed by the Spirit.

Frank continued to grow in his relationship with God as an adolescent and adult. As he was reaching the developmental stages of completing identity and selecting a career, his relationship with God continued to grow and change. It was during high school that he completed his conversion experience and received the call to preach. It is interesting that although he knew he was being saved and receiving the call, he was still not completely sure of the situation. Although he was not certain of the direction, the socialization and training he received allowed him to be confident that his future was secure. As Frank's relationship with God continued to grow during young adulthood, the direction for his life that God gave was revealed more clearly to him. One pivotal moment came when a pastor asked if he was confident that he had been called, and he responded emphatically that he had been called.

Finally, as Frank's relationship became stronger and as his identity became more secure, the direction from God was more direct. He clearly describes his first experience with hearing God's voice, when he was serving as a guest preacher at a church. When he walked into the sanctuary, he heard God tell him he would be the next pastor of the church. This experience was almost replicated when he received his final placement, and God's messages to him were confirmed through other experiences. His ability to listen and heed God's voice demonstrates not only the significance of the relationship but also Frank's willingness to be molded and shaped by it.

SUBMISSION IN RELIGION

The next important theme in Frank's story that is present in many individuals with strong religious faiths is submission. Many clinicians are familiar with the notion of submission or surrender because it is the first step in Alcoholics Anonymous and other self-help groups. The ability to release control, acknowledge weaknesses and limitations, is for many the first step or direction to change. Frank's story is full of experiences related to the development of the ability to be submissive to God and to religious teachings. The most powerful point in the story related to this theme is when Frank overreacted, or reacted from a personal stance, and decided to leave the First Baptist Church. He describes the interview process and his feeling that the Lord had approved his decision to leave the church. However, this move was not directed by God and proved to be a mistake for Frank, but a valuable learning experience about the importance of submitting to God's will. From that point forward, Frank learned to listen more carefully to God's voice and follow God's direction for his life.

There are several benefits to leading a surrendered life or being submitted: a sense of calling, a sense of fulfillment, and confidence in the future. One of the existential needs is a need to develop a sense of purpose or meaning in life (Fukuyama & Sevig, 1999). Many individuals question the purpose of life and their place in the world. Learning to be surrendered or submitted provides that sense of purpose and direction for people. It is clear that when Frank received his calling, his life began to have more purpose and meaning. Being surrendered provides direction for vocational or career choices and allows individuals to experience direction for volunteer and charitable services and for marriage and child rearing. The second benefit to being surrendered is the sense of fulfillment that occurs. The existentialists discuss the process of self-actualization, a sense of personal fulfillment. People who live surrendered lives report not only understanding a purpose in their lives but also a sense of fulfillment for being aligned with their purpose. This is a repeated message in Frank's story—that as he continues to grow with God and understand his purpose his sense of fulfillment and joy continues. The third benefit is the sense of confidence in the future that comes from being surrendered. In Alcoholics Anonymous, Steps 2 and 3 refer to the power of surrendering. (Step 2: Came to believe that a Power greater than ourselves could restore us to sanity. Step 3: Made a decision to turn our will and our lives over to the care of God as we understood Him.) Surrendering control of life to a power that is greater provides a source of confidence. Frank learned to be more confident and was able to wait for God to provide both direction and confirmation in his life.

RELIGION AS A STRENGTH OR RESOURCE

The final theme in Frank's story is the role of religion as a strength and a resource. Religious teachings can help people resolve depressive and anxiety symptoms. Frank experienced social anxiety, particularly a fear of public speaking. He was anxious about reading scriptures and praying in his college years and speaking publicly in the beginning of his preaching ministry. His anxiety was so great that he would often have a nervous stomach. It was after he reaffirmed his ministerial calling that his confidence grew and he was able to begin to overcome his fears. He later had a terrifying recurring nightmare, but through God's interpretation of the dream, he was able to diminish the fear.

Religion can provide comfort during times of loss and grief. Religious teachings on the afterlife and the role of man in relationship to God can be a source of encouragement. When Frank lost a younger brother, his relationship with God and his religious beliefs helped him to handle his grief; they provided strength even as he prepared for and delivered the eulogy. It is interesting that the same scripture served as a resource for dealing with the anxiety of public speaking and with his loss.

Clinical Applications

This section explores the clinical implications of Frank's story for counselors, including assessment of the importance of religion and a relationship with a higher power, techniques and interventions to use in treatment, and countertransference concerns.

ASSESSMENT

Frank's story suggests that clinicians need to assess three important areas in religion and spirituality for clients: the relationship with a higher power, existential concerns, and spirituality as a strength. The following questions are recommended.

Relationship With a Higher Power

Do you have a relationship with God (a higher power)?

Does this relationship serve as a resource, source of support, or comfort?

Do you feel positively connected to God (a higher power)?

Are there times when you have felt abandoned or neglected by God (a higher power)?

Existential Questions

Have you asked yourself these questions: Who am I? What is the meaning of life? What is the purpose of my life?

How do your religious beliefs help you to answer or address these questions?

Do you experience a sense of fulfillment or peace?

What are the conditions that contribute to these feelings?

Religion as Strength

Has your religion served as a source of strength?

Has your spirituality or religious beliefs helped you during times of crisis?

Has your spirituality, religious beliefs, or relationship with God (a higher power) provided comfort for depression or anxiety?

TECHNIQUES AND INTERVENTIONS

When working with people with strong religious faith, it is often important to consult with religious leaders for clinical treatment. Consultation can be valuable to therapists for a number of reasons. First, scripture, religious teachings, and doctrine can serve as resources for the presenting problems of clients. Frank, for example, discussed how several scriptures provided comfort for him. It would be impossible for clinicians to have a good command of the teachings from all religious groups; consulting with a religious leader can provide assistance in this area. Second, most religious institutions and congregations can serve as a resource for financial, physical, and spiritual needs. Congregations can provide money, food, and emergency shelter services, and members of institutions can provide a sense of accountability for individuals who need reinforcement for changes made in clinical treatment. Many churches, mosques, and synagogues provide self-help groups that can reinforce therapy goals. Finally, many individuals consult religious leaders before or in conjunction with their search for clinical services. Consultation will help to provide continuity of services.

Therapists should help clients address their relationship with God. The development of a trusted relatedness with a higher power is a spiritual need (Fukuyama & Sevig, 1992). As with any relationship, clients may experience times of anger or frustration with the higher power. For example, Frank found comfort in his relationship with God after the loss of his brother. One of us, Anita, worked with a client whose son had been tragically killed in an automobile accident. The client entered treatment for her depressive symptoms in relation to the death. When asked about her relationship with God, the client expressed an extreme amount of hostility with God over what she felt was a betrayal of her trust and love for Him. She also felt an extreme amount of guilt over her anger, but felt that her anger was too strong to deny. The client was encouraged to read Bible passages reflecting individuals' anger and frustration and to note God's responses to anger. She was encouraged to discuss her anger with her priest and to join a support group on her loss. If the therapist had not asked directly about her relationship with God, she may not have helped her to completely or appropriately grieve the loss of her son. The loss for her also changed her perceptions of her role as mother and her life's purpose. Again, the discussion of her relationship with God and the meaning of her son's death in relationship to her life helped her to move forward in understanding her purpose.

Clinicians should invite clients to bring scriptures to or share teachings and doctrines during the sessions. Clinicians can respond to the themes present in the teachings and use them to reinforce coping strategies. Clinicians may be confused about how to relate to the discussion of a higher power, from knowing how to address this power to understanding the client's relationship with the power. Griffith and Rotter (1999) discuss constraints in therapy around introducing discussions of God: proscriptive constraints, which prevent discussions of God from occurring; and prescriptive constraints, which limit the level of discussion. Clinicians should help clients to critically examine scriptures. They may also help clients find scriptures on love, forgiveness, marriage, anxiety, courage, faith, patience, and so on.

COUNTERTRANSFERENCE

Stories like Frank's that unfold in clinical offices may provoke a variety of reactions in counselors. Therapists often have strong reactions to religious dialogue presented in treatment, both positive and negative. Some therapists embrace the opportunity to discuss religion and see it as part of a holistic focus of treatment. Other therapists feel overwhelmed by the discussion of religion, particularly if they were not raised with a particular religious faith or practice. As with any other issue, clinicians must very carefully examine their reactions and monitor them, so they do not disrupt the treatment progress or therapeutic relationship. The countertransference issues presented in this story include difficulty integrating spirituality and religion into the treatment, issues involving discussions of God in the conversation, lack of comfort with personal spirituality, lack of knowledge of doctrine or teachings, and concerns that clients are rigidly holding onto beliefs or using religion as a crutch.

Discomfort With Religious Discussions

Historically, psychotherapists have been trained to treat psychology and religion as separate disciplines and have not included religion as part of the therapeutic process. Some counselors may be uncomfortable introducing religion, religious identity, and religious influence into treatment, for a variety of reasons. First, most of the ethical codes for social services professions prohibit professionals from imposing their values. Professionals may fear that introducing spirituality will cause clients undue anxiety or cause clients to fear that the therapist is attempting to proselytize the client (Walsh, 1999a). Therapists should feel comfortable asking clients about their religion and including it in treatment, however. The introduction of the topic does not lead to attempts for either party to indoctrinate others on beliefs, as long as appropriate boundaries are maintained. Therapists also may feel that spirituality and religion have no place in treatment because the primary focus should be on the role of behaviors or cognitions. Many individuals, however, do not have the concept of mind–body duality. Many religious faiths include the notion of body, mind and soul, and spirit. To ignore spirituality would be to ignore a major component of clients' lives (Fukuyama & Sevig, 1999). Wellness models include spirituality as well, and therapists who wish to engage in holistic treatment should include it, despite their concerns about introducing the topic. Therapists should feel encouraged that the field is becoming more accepting of religion in treatment; the latest edition of the *Diagnostic and Statistical Manual* (American Psychiatric Association, 2000) includes a discussion of religious identity (Walsh, 1999a).

Discussions of religion with individuals with strong religious beliefs and convictions may also cause clinicians some discomfort, particularly clinicians who have unanswered questions about their own beliefs or their relationship with God. Therapists may feel inadequately prepared to address clients' concerns and feel as if they do not know doctrine or teachings well enough to be able to aid clients. As with any situation in which the therapist is less knowledgeable than the client, the counselors should allow the clients to lead the discussion and educate the counselor. Counselors should also seek to increase their knowledge of the religious traditions of their clients on their own.

Differences in Religious Beliefs

Finally, therapists may have concerns that clients are rigidly holding onto beliefs or that they are using religion as a crutch. For example, a client facing a terminal disease may choose to deny medical treatment and pray for healing. Therapists may feel that clients are not working actively enough to engage in alternative treatment strategies because clients may insist that their faith and beliefs are enough. Clinicians may experience an ethical dilemma between respecting the client's autonomy and choice to wait for a higher power and intervening by encouraging self-direction for clients. Again, clinicians are encouraged to consult with religious leaders about these issues. There may be times when clients become immobilized with fear and cannot think beyond their beliefs, or times when clients are misinterpreting scripture. Religious leaders may be able to help clients expand their coping skills and strategies.

TOOLBOX ACTIVITY—FRANK		
Resources and Suggested Readings	*Activities*	*Discussion Questions*
Frame, M. W. (2002). *Integrating religion and spirituality into counseling: A comprehensive approach.* New York: Wadsworth. Fukuyama, M. A., & Sevig, T. D. (1999). *Integrating spirituality into multicultural counseling.* Thousand Oaks, CA: Sage Publications. Richards, P. S., & Bergin, A. E. (1997). *A spiritual strategy for counseling and psychotherapy.* Washington, DC: American Psychological Association. Walsh, F. (1999b). *Spiritual resources in family therapy.* New York: Guilford Press.	Research the difference between religion and spirituality. Write an essay examining how Frank's experience would have been different if he had been more spiritual than religious. Make a list of neighborhood or community clergy. Compile a list of resources offered by neighborhood religious services. Interview clergy about their religious teachings and perspectives on counseling.	Content Themes What other themes do you see emerging in the story that the author did not identify? Assessment Are there any questions you would like to ask Frank? Interventions What other interventions could you propose with Frank? Countertransference What countertransference reactions were emerging in yourself as you read this story? Other Scenarios Imagine that Frank is coming to you several years ago or several years from now with a presenting problem. Imagine what that presenting problem could be. How might his religious identity have changed?

Bob's Story 13

The Good Christian Son

I n Bob's story, we read about how he views himself in terms of his cultural identity and the shifts that occurred in his religious life as a result of family relationships, his move from the South to the Northeast, and his rethinking about his role in society and in his family. He also talks about what influenced his first career choice as a minister in an Evangelical Christian church and what accounted for the choice of his second career as a teacher. As you read, pay attention to his shifts in personality traits and in his understanding of his religious affiliation and other shifts in his cultural identity.

Bob's Story

I must admit from the outset that I was somewhat surprised that anyone would even be interested in my story. What I mean by that is, when it comes to culture, I have often thought that my life was somewhat devoid of it. I'm just another White guy with a job, two children, and a wife. I have nothing special to offer in the way of a story, right? Upon further reflection however, I have come to realize that one's cultural heritage is not about being impressive or unique. Rather, each person's history is more significant than he or she could ever imagine—at least to them and those with whom they come in contact. So what follows is a sort of snapshot of my life from a cultural, and especially spiritual, identity standpoint.

I was born in south-central Kentucky in a town that had no hospital. My mother and father had to travel several miles to access the needed medical assistance for my birth. This was not seen as a hardship or even an inconvenience, just how things were. My mother was the daughter of a farmer and a homemaker. She was the youngest of 10 children, 7 daughters and 3 sons. My father was from another town in Kentucky. His father was a professional in the trucking industry, and his mother taught music. My father met my mother while he was a college student in music education. He was also the music director of the small rural Southern Baptist church where my mother was a member.

My mother's ethnic background was Scottish and Welsh. Her maiden name reflects that heritage. My father's ethnic heritage was Dutch and English. I cannot say that these historical roots made any significant contributions to my cultural heritage. Both my parents seemed to prefer the notion that they were "American," and that was all that was necessary to them.

In the region of Kentucky I grew up in, people tended to be either Baptist or "unbelievers." Being an unbeliever meant you did not believe the standard tenets of the Christian faith regarding Jesus, but, most important, being an unbeliever meant you were going to hell. This was not a happy proposition—eternal burning in a lake of fire, gnashing of teeth, and so on.

The Evangelical Christian faith was a significant part of both of my parents' lives from early on. It would prove to be a powerful influence in mine as well. I learned as a child that one's faith was an integral part of decision making. The question of what God's will was in a given situation or relationship was a constant quest: "Does God want my father to take that job?" "Would God be pleased if I were to date this girl?" On and on it went. As a young person, I couldn't help but wonder if God was really all that interested in such minuscule items in light of world hunger, war, and other such global challenges. However, the Bible speaks of God knowing the "number of hairs on your head." In light of that, my older brother and I were taught that God was therefore interested in every detail of our lives. I had friends who literally prayed for good parking places!

Interwoven into this Christian heritage was the fact that I was a White male Southerner. I have extended family members who still refer to the Civil War as "the war of Northern aggression." There was significant pride in being born and raised south of the Mason-Dixon Line. I was taught that those to the north were automatically not to be trusted because of how they had treated us throughout history.

Exposure to persons of color was nearly nonexistent in my upbringing. My family was White. My community was White. My church family was White. In fact, my house was White! Appreciation for cultural diversity was not an intentional part of my upbringing. It came through the back door, so to speak. It came through the arts. I remember growing up in my White neighborhoods and being the only person who knew of Black musicians like Sammy Davis, Jr., Ray Charles, and Nat King Cole. I also knew of Latino musicians, such as Chita Rivera and Tito Fuente. My parents listened to music from different parts of the world, and, as a result, I grew to appreciate sounds that most of my friends did not even know existed. I believe that this exposure made me aware of a world beyond the South. My parents' appreciation for these artists taught me that beauty and talent are to be appreciated, regardless of its origin.

My father eventually left church music and began to teach music in the public schools. My parents listened to music and loved to watch old movies. I was exposed to various art forms at a very early age and began to gain an appreciation for music from around the world. Along with that, my parents had a commitment to treating all people with respect, regardless of skin color. This view was unique compared with the view of many of my friends.

However, there was a merging of my ethnic and regional identity and my spiritual formation that is still difficult for me to distinguish at times. The world around me was seen through so many filters that it became difficult to determine the legitimacy of almost any perspective I adopted. Was I seeing things in a particular way because I was told to? Was I seeing things that way because I wanted to please those around me? These were questions that were nearly impossible for me to answer.

Interestingly, it was evident to me that while my older brother completely embraced his identity as a Southerner, he did not seem to embrace this quest for God's will. He was a person of fierce independence—much to my parents' chagrin. He engaged in all the significant no-no's that we were taught to avoid— smoking, drinking, dancing, card playing, and enjoying the opposite sex. I was not nearly as interested in what I was missing by not doing those things as I was concerned about the pain that my parents were experiencing as they began to conceptualize themselves as failures as parents. My mother and father could not understand why my brother, who is four years my senior, would not respond to their directions or change his behaviors, despite their sometimes harsh punishments. In fact, their hearts were breaking. I knew I could not do the same thing to them.

Thus, I decided to become the ideal Southern Christian son. I did well in school, attended church regularly, was involved in extracurricular activities such as sports and drama club, and held down a part-time job. I graduated as president of my senior class and was motivated to attend the Southern state university my father and grandfather had attended.

During college I began to seriously consider my career options. What did God want me to do with my life? What would please my parents? Later I came to learn that these questions would be almost identical in my conceptualization of them. Ministry seemed like the most obvious choice for a career. God would be happy. My parents would be happy. My brother's deficits would be compensated for. My happiness was not a concern, aside from how well I was meeting the expectations of others. As I look back at this time in my life, I can see where I was being driven by a culture of pleasing God and family, everyone but oneself. This self-deprivation was seen as humble and servantlike.

In point, it became clear to me upon reflection that many of my White Christian peers in the South experienced the same lack of personal agency and integrity. I might have disliked a person or disagreed with him or her, but that person would likely never know it. I was so consumed with being "nice" that how I really felt or what I really thought were altogether lost and unimportant. This inevitably led to forming inauthentic relationships. I did not feel the freedom or have the courage to interact with another honestly if there was a chance that the person might not like me or might not approve of me. Thus, my relationships could not be built honestly. It wasn't until later that I began to realize that it was only when my identity was based on authentic thoughts and feelings that relationships could be meaningful and fulfilling. My mother's death was a significant factor in this shift of character.

It was too risky to not be seen as the good Christian son, so I never thought much about what I wanted. What if what I wanted wasn't Christian or, more important, wasn't perceived as Christian by those to whom I relinquished my locus of control?

I majored in religious studies in college and after graduation went on to seminary, where I received a Master of Divinity. I knew during my studies that the field was not for me, but what could I do? Could I turn my back on God, my family? The time of study, while interesting, became uninteresting to me. I began to feel like I was the wrong person in the wrong place because the priorities of the people around me were not similar to my own. Although I might agree that the issues were important, they were not issues to which I wanted to dedicate my life, personally and professionally. However, because of my continuing fears of what others might think, I completed the degree and worked in congregational ministry for 12 years. I was never happy, but I was always faithful—or so I thought.

The most pivotal moment that served as an important challenge to my culture of pleasing others and Christian fundamentalism came at the untimely death of my mother. She was 60 years old and had suffered a major heart attack. I was serving at a church 90 miles from home in a big city in Kentucky when I was called about her hospitalization. During the drive, I spent substantial time praying and asking God to heal my mother. I was confident that one like me, who had sacrificed so much for God and family, could expect that God would answer my prayers. After all, hadn't I completed a degree that I disliked and been involved in work that I hated for some time now? It was all for Him. He owed me!

My mother was not healed, and her death shook me. It shook my understanding of faith as well as family. I had never realized how matriarchal my family was. My mother led the family, and she often did so through guilt and manipulation. Who would lead us now? Who would dole out affirmation in accordance to our good behavior? Where would our sense of self-esteem come from now?

I became angry. I was angry at God, and I was angry at the church. My ministry at the church began to dissolve, and my wife and I moved to New York City for her to pursue graduate education. I worked for a while in computer and book sales. I was lost.

My name was given to a church in the New York area, and I took the position of minister because I believed I didn't know how to do anything else. Besides, shouldn't that put me back in God's good graces?

Even though the church was made up of White, Christian, transplanted Southerners, things were not what I hoped they would be. The parishioners at this church were people like those with whom I had grown up. They were in the New York area because of career or educational opportunities, but they had not allowed themselves to become integrated into the culturally diverse surroundings that New York offered. They were seeking others like themselves with whom to worship. Within a year of starting at the church, I was unhappy again and found myself looking at classified ads. My wife encouraged me to seek counseling during the time, and I did so. I was forced to ask questions that challenged my understanding of God and how people make decisions. I was forced to answer a question that I had never allowed myself to ask before: "What did I want?" In my cultural understanding of spiritual self, this question had never been an important one. What I wanted was totally unimportant. In fact, it was something to be ignored or changed to please God and family.

I came to learn that what I loved about ministry was service, but what I struggled with was church hierarchy and spiritual oppression. The gifts that I had been given—effective communication and the desire to help others—transitioned well into teaching. I was able to do something meaningful, but I was free within it.

This was new territory for me. I must admit that I still struggle with pleasing others, but I have come to learn that such influences are much more about my own history than with a God who is looking for ways to judge me.

Being a person of faith still serves me. Although the negative aspects motivated significant pain and dissonance, positive aspects of my faith, such as hope, justice, and service to others, have become quite valuable to me. These components of my faith help foster appreciation for what I have and a sense of mission to help those in need. Although this service is no longer motivated by my desire to prove my worth or please others, it is still a vitally important piece of who I am.

Further, my Southern heritage is also valuable. I was raised with very few luxuries and had to work very hard on family farms. The work ethic I was given has challenged me to try to earn the things I receive and not feel entitled to them.

Also, the commitment to family that I was taught, albeit somewhat unhealthy at times, has been tempered through the years with clear boundaries and emotional separation, which enables me to be a more effective husband and father. I have taken my family down home to Kentucky on several occasions and have shown my sons the little house where I was raised in a small town in Kentucky. They have seen the Confederate flags, and I have been able to teach them about the dangers of hatred and prejudice. They have seen my mother's grave, and I have been able to teach them about love and commitment to family.

I believe that I am nowhere near the same person culturally as a resident in New York City that I was as a child in a small town in Kentucky. Yet my skin color, family of origin, and Scottish and Welsh bloodlines remain the same.

Content Themes

There are two important content themes in Bob's story as he describes his religious identity development. The first theme is the socialization to religion that he experienced, not only from his family but also from his community and the region in which he was raised. The second theme is his shift from a fundamentalist Evangelical perspective to his own sense of religion and spirituality.

RELIGIOUS SOCIALIZATION

For Bob, socialization for religion existed in the family and was reinforced through his community and the region where he was born. His family was of an Evangelical Christian faith, and religion was taught to the children as a way of life. Every part of his life was based in or grounded on Biblical teachings and following God. Although Bob felt uncertainty about the importance of God's direction in all parts of his life, he nonetheless followed family socialization and attempted to include God and His will as part of his life. The socialization messages on religion were so strong that

Bob seems to have felt that there was little personal choice. In fact, he was distressed that his older brother seemed not to follow the norms set by the family and engaged in behaviors that upset his parents. To the degree that he took responsibility to spare the suffering of his parents, he became the "good Christian son."

Bob also makes a strong connection among his geographic origin, the rural South, the Evangelical Christian beliefs of his relatives and peers, his work ethic, and his ethnicity. His religious socialization was enforced by his entire ecosystem. For him, it is still difficult to distinguish between his ethnicity, his regional identity, and his religious formation. This is understandable because there is a relationship between geographic origin, ethnic background, and religious affiliation. Bob was raised in the Bible Belt, where religious affiliation, particularly Protestant and Evangelical faiths, is more important than other cultural or personality characteristics. The internalization of this socialization resulted in Bob choosing a career as a minister to please his parents and to become closer to God. What is most interesting is that Bob did not consider himself to have much of a choice in career selection because making choices that were pleasing to his family and God was a lifestyle for him and consistent with the rest of his ecosystem. Even though he knew during his studies that the field of ministry was not for him, he could not turn his back on God and his family.

SHIFT IN RELIGIOUS IDENTITY

The evolving nature of Bob's cultural identity is seen most clearly in the shift in his relationships with God and the church and his change of career from minister to teacher. As Bob traces the beginning of the shifts that occurred in his life, he tells us of the three factors that led to the change: the untimely death of his mother and his subsequent anger at God, his lack of personal fulfillment in working in formal ministry, and his move from the rural South to the urban Northeast. His was a process that culminated in slow but progressive changes in the way he views his religious identity. He talks about shifting from a Christian fundamentalist perspective, which included having a personalized view of his relationship with God and a more literal interpretation of the scriptures to a less fundamentalist view of his relationship with God.

Bob interprets his plunge into Christian fundamentalism and eventually the ministry as a career choice, as having stemmed from the behaviors of his brother, and as a way to please his brokenhearted parents. Although he was unhappy when entering the seminary, he describes how the sense of fulfillment or happiness seemed irrelevant. This changed, however, when his mother became suddenly ill. Because of his level of faith, Bob believed that his prayers for her healing would be answered. He also believed this because he had made sacrifices in his own happiness to serve

God. Bob was confused and overwhelmed by his mother's death and felt disappointed by God. This was an extremely significant occurrence for him and in his words the "most pivotal moment," the one that seemed to initiate his change in religious beliefs. The experience of being lost that Bob described that extended to his career as a minister eventually led to his growing awareness and his acceptance of the lack of fulfillment that he felt in ministry. He moved with his wife and was able to obtain another position in the church. But it was shortly after accepting the new position that he realized that ministry was not for him. His feelings led him to counseling. Such shifts from religious fundamentalism to more liberal views of religious doctrine are not uncommon as individuals begin to question their adherence to the beliefs of the family of origin. After his mother died, Bob may have felt more free to explore the meaning of his religious beliefs and less constrained to continue with the fundamentalist religious beliefs solely to please his parents, which he was previously compelled to do because of his brother's behavior. With hindsight, he now experiences his previous way of life as inauthentic, lacking in personal agency or integrity.

INTERNAL MIGRATION AND RELIGIOUS IDENTITY

Bob's discomfort and dissonance experienced in New York City amid what he describes as the segregated community of Southern Whites transplanted to the Northeast may have influenced his shift just as much as the death of his mother or his own search for authenticity. Internal migrations, such as the one Bob experienced, from the more conservative rural South to the more liberal urban Northeast call for acculturation processes that may be just as relevant as those that take place when people move from one country to another. The sudden exposure to dramatically different cultural milieus within the same country may affect an individual's cultural identity and religious beliefs or practices. It seems fair to wonder to what extent Bob's religious ideas would have shifted had he stayed in the South, in the same community, and around the same peers. At the same time, one wonders if the seeds of change were already present in Bob, and may have made it possible for him to move in the first place, because those who move or emigrate are already open to the idea of dramatically changing their lives (Grinberg & Grinberg, 2000).

Clinical Applications

This section comprises assessment questions related to the theme of shifts in religious beliefs and in career choice.

ASSESSMENT

Conversations about religion are not always easy to conduct, particularly between therapists and clients. There is a well-documented historical relationship between secularism and psychotherapy that persists in the taboo of discussing a person's faith in depth, in the culture in general and in the therapeutic situation in particular. Many therapists, especially if they are unfamiliar with the religious background of the client, may not consider themselves qualified enough to have these conversations. It is important, however, to assess the degree to which a person's religious beliefs, religious affiliations, and religious allegiance may shift according to a person's experience, place of residence, family events, and so on. If someone like Bob were to seek help at the time of the transition, how the therapist handles these issues is of crucial importance for the well-being of the client. It is also important to assess the career choices of individuals and how they arrived at those decisions because many people who are unhappy with their career choices may have a difficult time exploring family connections to their choice or may struggle while figuring out their future if it involves issues of self-determination or authenticity. Many counselors not specifically trained in dealing with the career issues of their clients may fail to address them. Following are some of the relevant questions therapists should ask.

Shifts in Religious Beliefs

Were there any events in your life that may have influenced your religious commitment, fervor, or affiliation?

Has your religious observance, commitment, fervor, or affiliation changed in the course of your life?

Did your parents have the same or different religious affiliations, observance, or commitment?

How has your siblings' level of religious observance, affiliation, or commitment influenced your relationship with them?

Shifts in Career Choice

How did you make your initial career choice? How satisfied are you with your career choice?

Are you aware of familial pressures or traditions that may have influenced your career choice?

If you are switching careers, is it going to be viewed negatively or positively in your family?

TECHNIQUES AND INTERVENTIONS

There were critical events in Bob's life that took him along a different path than the one he was on originally. As Bob describes, his strong religious identity was initially shaped by events in his family, his parents' religious affiliation, the behavior of his sibling, his geographic origin, and his ethnic affiliation as a White, religiously conservative Southerner. At a certain point in his life, he determined that he needed to make a change of course, which took him onto a completely different track. Such dramatic switches can be difficult for the therapist to follow, support, and elicit, particularly if the therapist is of a different religious orientation than that of the client, or if the therapist thinks that he or she has not been trained in dealing with career-related issues. Therapists often treat career, religious, or ethnicity issues as if they were special issues (Giordano & McGoldrick, 1996) rather than basic to understanding personal identity. No matter what stage of the life cycle individuals are going through, helping them sort through important career or religious paths may be one of the most important benefits of therapy for those experiencing dramatic shifts in their life paths. Often, early career decisions and early religious affiliations are closely tied to identifications with family of origin, as in Bob's case. Helping a client tease out these early identifications with family of origin from the personal goals and aspirations may make a difference in clients' lives and help them go from living to please or appease others to a more personally fulfilling career or religious life.

Therapists also need to help clients as they shift and change in their religious identity. Clients often experience loss or trauma that causes a shift in their thinking and religious beliefs. This can create a void that is difficult to fill. Focusing on the spiritual needs of clients (Fukuyama & Sevig, 1999) can be a way to help them begin to sift and tease out religious teachings and beliefs from their socialization experiences.

One useful technique to help clients sort out the different aspects of themselves is called Voice Dialogue and involves identifying parts of the self, naming them, and encouraging dialogues between the self and the part or between the different parts (Zweifel, 2002). Once a part is identified, the self can have a dialogue with the part and ask, "What is your job in my life? What do you want? What do you need? Do you get enough airtime? If you had more airtime, what would you do? What do you know about the other parts?" Eliciting an internal search-and-find mission can lead to integration and more effective decision making (Zweifel, 2002), particularly when it comes to choosing a path that involves lifelong commitments, such as a career or the fulfillment of spiritual needs. The Internal Family Systems Model (Schwartz, 1995) is another model that recognizes the multiple selves of the personality. Allowing the parts to surface is helpful for self-exploration, and that, in turn, can help solve dilemmas.

COUNTERTRANSFERENCE

Clinicians sometimes hold strong opinions about issues that appear to be foreign, strange, or too "other." This can get in the way of sound clinical practice. If the therapist is not able to dissolve the negative countertransference, it might be important to refer the client to someone else. In general terms, it is not possible to conduct meaningful therapeutic work when the counselor is disgusted with, fearful of, or too critical of the choices of their clients.

Negative Reactions to Strict Religious Practices

Clinicians often have strong reactions to individuals raised and socialized with strict evangelical religious traditions. For many, the notion of restricting behaviors, such as dancing, playing cards, wearing makeup, or watching television, seems odd and unusual. However, this is often the case for clients, and clinicians need to be respectful of clients' beliefs. Attempting to teach clients that these beliefs are wrong or too restrictive can be damaging to the therapeutic relationship, particularly if these issues are not related to the presenting problem.

Overreaction to Clients Who Are Excommunicated

The other reaction that counselors often have is to overreact to the hurt that clients feel from their religious background. One of us, Anita, had a client who was excommunicated from her church and family and divorced from her husband because she took her child to the movies, a behavior that was strictly prohibited by the church. When students hear the story, they often become outraged at the church's and the family's response. Although this anger may be a natural reaction to the situation, expressing the anger and encouraging anger in the client may be inappropriate. The client in this case needed to grieve and mourn the loss of her only support system and to reconcile her relationship with God and her religious identity. Although expressing anger was certainly a part of her grieving process, the clinician who focuses too much on this feeling disrupts and hinders the therapeutic process.

Applying Voice Dialogue (Zweifel, 2002) or multiple self-work (Schwartz, 1995) to the countertransference reaction might be a useful way for clinicians to observe the parts of themselves that are rejecting, disgusted by, or angry with the client's decisions, the client's family, or the client's church. Allowing a dialogue between the self of the therapist and the disgusted, rejecting, or angry part of the therapist may bring some interesting information to the surface that may dissolve the disgust or anger of the clinician, increase her or his empathy, and allow for some creative ideas for helping the client move forward.

TOOLBOX ACTIVITY—BOB		
Resources and Suggested Readings	*Activities*	*Discussion Questions*
Burke, M. T., Chauvin, J. C., & Maranti, J. (2003). *Spirituality in counseling and therapy: A developmental and multicultural approach.* New York: Brunner-Routledge. Cloud, H., & Townsend, J. (1995). *12 "Christian" beliefs that can drive you crazy.* Grand Rapids, MI: Zondervan.	Interview someone on important scriptures of their choice, specifically regarding terms such as love, forgiveness, guilt, anger, sin, and redemption. Engage in a discussion about the themes of scriptures and discuss their relationship to spiritual issues. Write an essay on how your own religious beliefs have influenced your career selection. Interview others on the relationship between spirituality and career or volunteer experiences. Write an essay about your familial religious socialization process.	Content Themes What other themes do you see emerging in the stories that the authors did not identify? How important is the theme of Bob's identity as a White Southerner? Assessment Are there any questions you would like to ask? Interventions What other interventions could you propose with Bob? Countertransference What countertransference reactions were emerging in yourself as you read this story? Other Scenarios Imagine that Bob is coming to you several years ago or several years from now with a presenting problem. Imagine what that presenting problem could be. How might his religious identity be different? What if Bob had remained in the ministry? What additional challenges would Bob face had he been gay?

Katie's Story 14

Catholic and Jewish? How Can It Be?

For some individuals, religion is a ritual imposed on them in childhood by their parents, a distant set of memories about church services or school. For others, religion is a practice, a routine that was begun when they were young and is continued through adulthood (Griffith & Griggs, 2001). Yet for others, it is a vibrant, active component of their identity. It shapes who they are and how they function. And the practices and rituals associated with religious beliefs are a way to connect with God, or a higher power; with other believers; and, most important, with themselves. The teachings and doctrines provide a blueprint and guide for living. Work, child rearing, volunteer services, and daily practices are guided by religion. Religion is often conceptualized as a developmental process; connections to religious beliefs change as people grow and mature cognitively and spiritually (Fukuyama & Sevig, 1999; Griffith & Griggs, 2001). Connection to religion also changes as people reach developmental milestones, including graduation, marriage, and child rearing. And religious beliefs change when people face crisis, trauma, or stressors; many people use these times to question spiritual beliefs and their relationship with God.

Katie's story follows this developmental focus. She was raised in the Catholic tradition, and her beliefs and connections changed with her developmental progress. The most important challenges to her religious faith came when she decided to engage in an interfaith marriage and had children. As you read the story, reflect on the intersection of religion, developmental milestones, and life transitions. Also note how current events influenced Katie's development, indirectly influencing her religious beliefs.

Katie's Story

I was born and raised a Catholic, but I did not become one until I married a Jew. I was a Latin-chanting, chapel-veiled, genuflecting, rosary-clicking, Friday-fish-eating Baby Boomer of a Catholic. When I was born in 1954, I was quickly whisked off to the local parish church to be baptized, lest I wind up in limbo if I died a quick death—and which was worse: sudden infant death syndrome (SIDS) or limbo?

My own mother (apparently a secondary player in my spiritual growth) did not attend the ceremony because she was readying for the gathering of relatives. And it would be a large crowd! This Catholic family had grandparents with farm roots, so large families were the norm. The collateral and collective nature of this family beckoned all aunts, uncles, and cousins to mark all major life passages. These gatherings were often colored by which one of my 41 first cousins (on my father's side of the family alone) was wearing the white dress of baptism, or adding the veil, or wearing the grown-up suit for First Communion. The predictable holidays, Holy Days of Obligation, and the Seven Sacraments marked the passage of annual time. These moments brought the certainty and sure knowledge that rote rituals and memorized prayers often provide, especially to the passive viewers so many Catholics had become. We were dictated to by the rigors of the dogmatic Church rules that directed our practices.

Religion was my cultural identity, the sole source of what made me both belong and be distinctive. In my White, upper-middle-class, suburban family, there were only vague hints about any ethnic component to our family: like the Wednesday night sauerkraut-and-sausage dinners or times when my aunts and uncles sang German songs around our piano. I realize now that at that time an Irish Catholic marrying a German Catholic was considered an outmarriage and subject to derogatory terms, such as "shanty Irish." So one ethnic group was expected to take a backseat, and usually this ethnicity belonged to the wife.

Besides, no one had lived on "the old sod" for four generations. I was American, an American Catholic. (Wait! Which was the noun and which the adjective?) I learned the fate of John F. Kennedy when my principal, a nun, came into the class and said, "Our Catholic president has been shot." Yes, I went to Catholic schools, no questions asked. That was what good Catholics did. In my youth, there were only two religions: Catholic and public, each with their own schools. We, of course, knew which one was better because we were told at both church and school that we were The One True Faith. If we Catholics were true, then that meant everyone else's religion was false, right? (They did not call the schools parochial for nothing!)

At school, I dutifully memorized the answers to our Baltimore Catechism, those concise nuggets of theology and dogma that served as the basis of our faith. They are ingrained so deeply into my long-term memory banks through daily repetition and drills that I can today recall the lessons in my first-grade primer almost 45 years later:

Q: Who made the world?

A: God made the world.

Q: Who is God?

A: God is the creator of heaven and earth and of all things.

Q: What is man?

A: Man is made up of body and soul.

Q: How did God make you?

A: God made me in his image and likeness.

Q: Why did God make you?

A: God made me to know Him, to love Him, and to serve Him in this world and in the next.

This made Catholicism seem so easy. Here were all these clear answers—and without the questions ever being asked. Just memorize them and practice. All you need is a good memory. If I did my catechism well, at Confirmation, when the Bishop called on me, I would be able to recite the right response, bringing honor, not shame, to my family.

Weekends were marked by Sunday mass with both Mom and Dad, often after weekly Saturday confession. Mass was one of the few times we were together as a family. Church and services piqued our senses because Catholicism was richly filled with unusual sights, sounds, and smells at that time: incense, chants, the jingle of little bells, holy day pageants, wimpled nuns, collared and cassocked priests. Spectacular, yes—but . . .

It was still Latin mass. Now isn't that something a young child can relate to? We were estranged, marginalized from the adult world as we tried to sit there for the hour listening avidly for God's phone number (*Et cum spiritu tuo* [And with your spirit]). We would try to follow along in the missals (usually a First Communion present, along with a rosary, from a godparent). We could sound out the prayers phonetically, but actually translate them? Make the words meaningful? No. We were present in body but absent in spirit.

The religion of my youth was something that I performed by going through the motions, like a perfect little marionette tied to the long line of family before me. My puppet practices were not hallowed but hollow, wooden. I learned that I was not alone; the whole Catholic Church was chafing under the rigidity of the institution that theologian Martin Marty once termed as "mind-numbing boredom."

I was an adolescent who reached not the Age of Reason but rather the Age of Give-Me-a-Reason-Why-Not. James Fowler, in his seminal work *Stages of Faith* (1981) considers adolescence a watershed moment in faith development, a time when minds and hearts expand their worldviews and either conform to the conventions and standards of the past or break apart the ordered clusters of their values, beliefs, and practices.

I questioned what I had been told was unquestionable; I wondered, though I risked being punished for imagining. If I ever asked those tough "why" questions, the good nuns said, "It's a mystery," which seemed a theological version of the parental "because I told you so." (It really refers to the Greek word *mysterios,* or "drama," but no one told us that.) The problem with Catholic education was that you actually got educated. No longer willing to accept all precepts and practices on blind faith, I wanted to see deeper, and rote rituals and strict rules were blocking me.

The winter of my discontent, fortuitously, coincided with the Church's own. Just as I could hear my inner strains of "Somebody better liven things up around here for me, or I will bail," along came Pope John XXIII, his successor, Pope Paul VI, and the Second Vatican Council, or Vatican II. The *aggiornamento*—the "shaking up" of the Church that Pope John XXIII put into motion—played out before my eyes in high school.

In a short period of time, the sensations of my old Catholicism were changing as if overnight—literally, it seemed. One day, my favorite English teacher was wearing a tight wimple around her face and a long habit, and the next day she had—gulp!—hair! And at mass, they turned the priest around to face the pews. And it was in English! I took communion not placed on my tongue but in my hand, though I had been told in my First Communion preparation that if we ever touched the host our hand would wither. And it didn't! Ha! I was introduced to new titles and words: "People of God," "ecumenism," and "ecumenical." The changes were exciting, odd, hard, scary, and fun. They were more than cosmetic: no longer expected to be passive, I was actually invited to participate in the life of the Church. I was watching. I was relearning and reexamining and beginning to look deeper to find my own place in a new spiritual world.

My aunts and uncles and my father grumbled and complained mightily about the changes, the guitar masses ("Those hootenanny masses," my father said), and, sotto voce, the infallible pope. Ah, yes, they were like Israelites in the desert, grousing at Massah and Meribah about the lack of food, water, and the leadership of that lousy Moses. After all, look what he made them do! Leave slavery! For what? Freedom. But the new way to the Promised Land was messy, hard, and uncomfortable. And they wanted to go back to Egypt! Biblical truth indeed because the first human response to change is usually resistance, and the second is fear or complaining. Change is a struggle, awkward, and stressful. Yet is this crisis a problem, a catastrophe? Or might a radical, new energy to practice be an opportunity for rejuvenation, much needed for spiritual growth?

From 1967 to 1971, I rehearsed these new changes at an all-girl Catholic high school (free from embarrassing myself in front of boys!). My widening vistas saw peers all over America in the throes of massive changes: gender roles, politics, social activism, and so on. I tried on all sorts of nouns and adjectives as well: woman, outspoken, liberated, performer, blond, scholar. I was an eager shopper in an exciting identity mall.

A college education was a given in our family. My father was a first-generation college graduate who came from the poverty of the Depression and quickly worked his way through undergraduate and medical schools, graduating at 21 years of age. When it came my time to choose a college, I made a very bold move—educationally, geographically, psychologically, and spiritually. I chose a non-Catholic university in a major metropolitan area 350 miles from my northern Kentucky family of origin, a university that attracted students from all over the country and the world—Columbia College. I chose theater as a major, a jolting departure from the sciences so valued by my surgeon father and my mother, his nurse, who had reared me. This departure from the family circle was unheard of in my extended family and probably raised some eyebrows at the time. My beloved mentor in high school, who ironically was then a cloistered nun, encouraged me. (She has since left the convent.)

I loved both my college years and the sprawling city of Chicago. Here I stayed, continuing the process of finding myself as a young adult through college and my 20s. I stayed loosely connected to the practices of my Catholicism, still not exactly tied down.

My first job was teaching at a private, all-girl Catholic high school, but I left that after four years to act in the theater instead of simply teaching it. The work hours of theater (and the various day jobs) conflicted with regular Sunday church attendance. I no longer saw myself as Catholic with a capital C but catholic, universal. I was just one fiber in this whole vibrant multicultural tapestry of my adopted city, Chicago.

WAS THIS A "CRISIS" OF FAITH?

In my early 30s, I fell in love, deeply, surprisingly, and irrevocably, with my best friend and could never look at life without him beside me. With him, I never felt more fully in touch with my truest self. What? A transplanted suburban Kentucky, Catholic girl wanting to spend the rest of her life with this urban Chicago, Jewish boy? But there we were. Religious traditions and cultural differences stared us in the face. And we cared deeply enough to care about it. Falling in love reawakened our spirituality, and thus, so naked and tentative, we began exploring our different symbol systems for faith.

Obstacles and changes create disequilibrium. You can either run away, stay stuck in the emotion of uncertainty, or adjust and cope. I was too old, determined, and educated to freeze and too much in love to leave. We encountered the official naysayers in our discovery's way. Indeed, one rabbi railed, "Don't do it. Break up right away! Think of what you are doing to the Jews! Your marriage will fail." Another said, "Technically, you do not exist." Because I was then working at a school renting from a Catholic church, I sought a different tack. "Let's go see one of the priests next door," I suggested. My fiancé was convinced we would be shunned or shamed there, too.

Mentors are, first, angels—surprise strangers marking turning points in lives. We met Father Rick Matthews, the archdiocesan director of young adult ministry in Chicago. We sat down one afternoon at Chicago's Old St. Paul's Church and talked about our hopes.

"Are you in love?" he asked.

"Oh, yes," we replied, beaming.

"Then we are all in the presence of God," he said.

"I suppose it would be easier if I were Catholic, though," my fiancé suggested.

"But being Jewish is who you are," Rick said. "Why should you change that about yourself simply because you are in love with Katie? I think it must be wonderful to be Jewish. In fact, if I weren't Catholic, I'd be Jewish myself."

Then I asked, "What would you suggest about how we should raise our children?"

"What do you do for yourselves?" asked Rick. "You can't expect your kids to do anything except what you as parents are doing with them. That's a sure way to make religion a source of conflict."

"Makes perfect sense," we said, thinking about the pejorative words that had sent us in this priest's direction in the first place.

"Katie goes to church and I go to temple," Daniel said. "Should we take them to temple on Friday night and church on Sunday morning?"

"Absolutely," said Rick.

"Won't they be confused?"

"You can help them understand the differences—and the similarities."

"What should we teach them religiously—Judaism or Catholicism?" I asked.

Rick smiled. "I would teach them both. How can you do otherwise? You two are going to be your children's most important teachers. How can you not?"

Daniel was slightly incredulous. I made mental notes. (Five years later, these seeds took root.)

As our meeting with Father Matthews ended, we asked him if there was a support group that he knew of for couples like us. "There isn't one that I know of," he said, wagging a finger. "But I've been thinking of starting one." (And what that wagging finger foretold!)

THE WEDDING PLANS

Any engaged couple previews the marital adjustment of the first five years in the wedding plans. As an interfaith couple, with additional familial and cultural differences, obstacles seemed compounded. Here is a brief glimpse of our navigations:

The wedding list: His list of 45 friends and relatives for "a small wedding" made me laugh. I had a Catholic family. So 250 relatives and a handful of friends came.

The ceremony: The Baltimore Catechism taught neither wedding etiquette nor canon law. Though I envisioned a beautiful backyard wedding, my church could not allow it outdoors. My Reformed Jewish fiancé did not have the visceral reaction that many Jews feel about entering a church and did not mind being married there. (It was a small hint of how he generously entered all kinds of arenas other Jews might not.)

The celebrants: We wanted a priest and a rabbi, and that put both our mothers in a spin. My mother was convinced she would have to bribe or blackmail the pastor. She knew that in her generation, interfaith couples seeking the Church's blessing were forced to convert and wed in nondescript, private ceremonies, hidden away in the priest's rectory. Not many of us "people in the pews" knew that in 1965, Nostra Aetate had been issued, the Church's official acknowledgment of Judaism as a means of salvation and its hope of rebuilding the special relationship between the two faiths that had been broken apart by painful history. This had paved the way for priests, including our pastor, to happily and publicly perform these interfaith ceremonies between Catholics and Jews.

Indeed, it was finding the rabbi that was the rub because traditional Hallachic (ritually observant) law frowns on marrying outside of Judaism. Fortunately, Cincinnati is home to Hebrew Union College, one of the key

U.S. centers for educating Reform rabbis. We were referred to several studying there and immediately felt comfortable with our first encounter with Rabbi Weiss.

"The Paper": The vestiges of the medieval Catholic Church's fastidiousness about civic record keeping still exist today. The Church bureaucracy keeps great records on births (baptisms), marriages, and deaths. A couple with one non-Catholic is asked to sign a document colloquially called "The Paper" or "The Promise." In the Church of my youth, an interfaith couple was most often a Catholic marrying a Protestant, and I knew that both of them were required to promise to raise the children Catholic, with the subtextual tone of "On pain of death of your immortal soul."

It came to that moment that both Daniel and I dreaded. It was not that we were in disagreement about our children; we were not. We wanted our children to know both religions, but, yes, we would call them Catholic if we had to. Based on the Jewishness of Jesus and the Church's ecumenism, its content allows for more of both. Still . . .

Father John Walsh at Old St. Paul's met with us that day, immediately quelling our queasiness. He explained that Daniel need only acknowledge that I had made this promise. I was promising that in good faith "I would do all within my power" to raise the children Catholic, but sometimes our power might be great and at other times not. The Promise opens up the conversation; it does not close the door. And furthermore, the marriage is more important. Father Walsh—and indeed his entire parish community built around hospitality, acceptance, outreach, and ecumenism—remains another angel in our lives, another person saying, "Come on! Do not be afraid!" There we have found a home.

The ceremony: Even after we secured the two clergymen in Kentucky, it dawned on all four of us that there was no prepared text into which these two men could plug in the names and that the assembled would be able to follow. What resources did we use to thwart another obstacle? We tapped into our basic skills and talents. Daniel is a media writer, and we both were theater majors. We wrote our own ceremony. Because it was unlike anything our family had seen, people in the pews paid alert attention.

AND THE REST OF THE STORY . . . ?

A wedding is one day, but a marriage is daily. Our intercultural differences led us forth in unpredictable ways. For the first time in my adult life, I joined a parish; Old St. Paul's had made both of us—both!—feel welcome and valued for who we are. Daniel's Jewishness is considered quite special there, and never was he asked to change who he was. He also kept his membership at his temple where he grew up but eventually left over the rabbi's stance on interfaith marriage, and we joined two other temples. God is sneaky. Beware the wagging finger! A little less than a year after our 1987 wedding, Father Matthews told us after mass that the interfaith couples' gathering we talked about might be getting off the ground. In June we met for the first time with Father Matthews and the late Father David Monts. This meeting spawned the Catholic-Jewish Couples Group of Chicago, which still exists today. About a year later, Rabbi Albert Sachel joined us. A grassroots support group that we help lead, its membership list has approximately 300 couples in varying stages of relationships. Some people come for one or two meetings; some stay for years. Our monthly meetings address a variety of topics, and we have spun off special interest groups for those planning weddings and birth ceremonies.

Teach your children diligently.

Deuteronomy 6:7

When couples marry, children often follow. In interfaith families, when children come, and the wrestling with early rites of passage is put to rest, the lingering question of "What exactly will we teach the children?" soon arises. There were other families in the group whose children were roughly the same ages as ours. Sending our children to a traditional religious education program alone did not feel quite right, yet could there be such a thing as a Catholic-Jewish Sunday School? If so, what would this look like?

Rick Matthews's advice from years ago to teach them both still resonated. Certainly no established Jewish education program could really teach about Christianity, unless briefly presented as comparative religion. We thought that even suggesting such a course of action would cause rabbis or Jewish educators to shake their heads sadly or even become angry. Indeed, the Union of American Hebrew Congregations (the central organization of Reform Judaism in America) has issued a directive to its religious schools that children who have had religious instruction in other faiths should be discouraged from enrolling in Jewish education programs.

So, as with our wedding ceremony, we rolled up our sleeves and tapped into another talent, education. With seven families, we started our own grassroots religious education program, The Family School, in 1993. Housed at Old St. Paul's, it is a bimonthly, parent-taught cooperative. There we strive for religiocultural competence in two-faith community settings.

I developed a nine-year, K–8 curriculum during the summers, wrote four student texts, and composed a parent curricular overview and guide to teaching the weekly lessons in the curricula. People think I'm nuts, amazed that I would devote all this time for no pay. I knew we were trailblazers, breaking apart and putting together pieces of hidden pathways to the Spirit. I was invigorated, intellectually and spiritually! I did this for three not-so-simple reasons: (1) People told me it couldn't be done, and I wanted to dig in my heels and prove them wrong (a life theme perhaps?); (2) I did not want my own children to learn drivel and junk; and (3) if I were constructing this for my own kids, then why not share my efforts with others now and those to come behind me? As with any good curriculum, I never feel like I am finished, but it is finally in a form that I can share with future Family School families, as well as other groups starting out across the country with similar hopes and dreams just like mine and Daniel's back in 1987.

PRACTICE, PRACTICE, PRACTICE: A PRACTICING CATHOLIC

The expression "I am a 'practicing Catholic' " fascinates me. When I hear it, I want to say right back, "And what the hell does that mean? Aren't we all just practicing?" Usually the phrase is a status report: "I am an active member of this club." Or it is shorthand for expected behaviors: "Yes, I go to church every Sunday, take communion, receive reconciliation at least twice a year (Christmas and Easter obligation, you know), get those ashes on my forehead, fast during Lent on Ash Wednesday and Good Friday, practice only natural birth control," and so on. (That's not fully me.) This expression too often summarizes the external life of the practitioner, not the internal; the extrinsic, not the intrinsic; the level of religiosity, not the depth of spirituality.

The phrase "I am a nonpracticing Catholic" fascinates me, too. Do pieces of your childhood identity ever totally go away? Or is this too just shorthand for the absence of regularity of the rote practices, a hint that you got out of the discipline or habit?

So today I say with a subtle, wry curl at the corner of my lips, "Yes, I am a practicing Catholic," but that means I am still trying to get it right—the untidy discovery part that is active spirituality. I do not practice my faith because I know it all; I practice because I don't know and want to know more. Weekly rituals are no longer rote routines but reminders or catalysts, so repetition and practice are no longer drudgery. The much-maligned Baltimore Catechism of long ago did teach me this (much to my adult surprise): discipline, repetition, imitation, routine, and regularity are learning tools. As with music, dance, and drawing, the basics must be practiced before you can infuse them with your creative spirit to make it become art, transcendent, divine. This reshaping is the start for growing into faith, of being-in-becoming the beloved of the God of love.

If religion is the lens through which we tease out our faith and spirituality and shape our focus of how we see the realities of our world, then today I wear bifocals. Intermarriage woke me up spiritually, or, as the metaphor says in Jesus's baptism stories, "the heavens opened." After 17 years with Daniel, I honestly think of myself as both Catholic and Jewish. It is not that I am Jewish, but that I see my own Catholic practices and stories better, brighter, clearer through the added prism of the rich history, teachings, and traditions of another faith, indeed the very faith that gave mine birth. I like the threads of connection there. This is Catholicism within the light of Judaism. I am comfortable in both worship communities when it is inclusive of diversity, not pejorative.

Indeed, some former Catholics do not practice because of the Church's controversial teachings, theological differences, or the psychic pain because of its myriad scandals, such as clergy abuse of children. I sadly know why some people want to say, "Screw the Catholic Church." Catholic history, past and present, is full of less-than-holy intentions and gestures filled with power and malice, not love and compassion. Yet would I, could I, drop my Caucasian identity because of our repugnant history of slavery and racism? I can't. I have to find ways to reconcile and forgive, without ever forgetting.

Many vocations and roles form parts of my identity, past and present: teacher, actor, waitress, mother, counselor, writer, and wife. I think that what threads these realms—religion, arts, education, and psychology—is this common root: an attempt to take the ordinary human experience and somehow transform it into the extraordinary, whether in body, mind, or spirit. The quality that distinguishes an art, religious practice, or career as disgraceful or grace-filled is the answer to this question: "Am I stuck in an empty, rote, dull space? Or am I vibrantly, dynamically seeking connection?" That indeed makes the ordinary extraordinary. To that I strive in all I do.

My spiritual life is richer because I have been forced to venture into cultural language and stories that were once unfamiliar. Many Catholics gloss over those marvelous Hebrew scriptures. I now enjoy mining these new metaphors for little sparks lighting the way to see kaleidoscopes of "truth." My favorite for life, ethics, and faith is Jacob wrestling with the angel. He wants to reconcile his past mistakes and goes to see his estranged brother. He wrestles all night with "a stranger" and comes out of this close-encounter-of-the-divine-kind wrenched, bruised, and limping but changed, even with a new name: Yakkov, "the liar," becomes Yisrael, "he who wrestled with God and prevailed." Like the old Catholic girl falling in love with a Jew, Jacob's old self gives way to the new future for him and all his children. By marrying Daniel, I have been converted, and for the better. I changed my identity, and my future. That's metanoia!

Renewed, deepened faith practices risk changing the comfort of one's set worldview. But my sense of spirituality is that it is messy, uncomfortable, but then ultimately soothing to the limping self. "Spirit" happens in sneaky, surprising eureka moments. When we encounter anything novel or life-altering, a fevered sense of struggle, anxiety, and strangeness ensues. If you are curious and deeply engaged in breaking apart schemas, mindsets, and rote practices, change will follow. It requires energy to increase knowledge, but only fear can hold you back. (A biblical, angelic motif is, "Do not be afraid.") Humans, not animals, can choose between right and wrong and can push toward transcendence. Do we stay in place, held back by fear, or wrestle with the angel? The higher self may emerge, but the past identity may also linger, pained and limping.

Socrates tells us that an unexamined life is not worth living, and I concur. Any dynamic practitioner of a vocation based on the ethics of care, trust, change, and growth—be it an artist, a musician, an actor, a dancer, a painter, a theologian, a parent, a spouse, a counselor—has to break apart the basic frameworks of the field and reshape it to make it fit his or her own, however kaleidoscopic that framework might become. Otherwise, we risk becoming stagnant, succumbing to our own entropy, and hence dull, dead, lifeless. Dynamic encounters challenge us, and being shaken up makes for personal, professional, or spiritual transformation. First, you have to open all your many eyes (those cultural and spiritual visions) to fully see. Different lenses can take the lead at different moments. Only then will you move beyond life's barriers into the realm of the possible.

Fate and choice have taken me from the closed system of the 1950s South to the horizons of the pluralistic, 21st-century metropolis. My spirit has opened infinite vistas, and I can never be the same. (Love and age have seen to that.) I no longer see my identity as I once did as a child, a teen, a young adult, a middle-aged woman. At this midpoint, I no longer see God in the same way either: God is no longer just a noun but also a verb. I can no longer be cerebral about the human atrocities committed both in the past and today, often done in the name of my God. I hurt because that is not my God.

I chose and vowed to love and honor my beloved, my Daniel. How could I honor him if I were judging the "other" as good or bad? As "us" or "them"? I am a Jacob, wrestling to find out what is valuable and desirable and discarding or restructuring what is dissonant or devalued. I have had to leap, to release, to let it go, to reach out anew. I embraced the "stranger" and made him mine. Together we reconciled our choices to fit our future hopes with fewer barriers for our children to knock down.

Our future, our children! They will forge their own life paths. Oh, yes, I would be hypocritical to bind them too tightly to the family ties of our pasts. It is their journey. Their parents only prepare them with some basics: traditions, values, ethics, curiosity, wonder, and stories. (Oh, never forget the stories! Wrestle those images.) Practice may be rote and dull at times. Give it time. Yet we are really only launching their cultural boats, hoping with all our might that they land happily in body, mind, and spirit on the welcoming shores at a place where "otherness" doesn't divide their futures. To you both: Bon voyage. Peace be with you. Go with God. Go with Good. Shalom.

Content Themes

Katie's story reflects the developmental process of religious beliefs and describes how it changes across time to reflect life transitions and current events. It seems as if Katie's religious beliefs were an important component of her childhood, but strengthened and changed throughout adolescence and high school and certainly when she decided to marry someone of a different faith. Katie's story demonstrates how spirituality and religion permeate all aspects of a person's life and actively influence and affect decision making. There are four important themes. The first theme is the developmental process of religious identity, which corresponds to milestones and life transitions. The second theme is the importance of religion in important decisions, particularly marriage and child rearing. The third theme is the role of socialization in religious identity development. The final theme is the relationship between current events, or the macrosystem and exosystem, and religious identity development.

RELIGIOUS IDENTITY DEVELOPMENT

The development of religious faith and religious identity corresponds to other developmental constructs, such as moral, social, or cognitive development. James Fowler (1981) identified a six-stage model of faith development. In the first stage, intuitive-projective (ages three to seven years), individuals' religious beliefs are based on stories or messages taught by their parents. Because of their cognitive capacities, the stories are primarily fantasy in nature. The second stage, mythical-literal, corresponds to concrete cognitive functioning and includes children's process of separating fantasy stories from reality. The third stage, synthetic-conventional, usually occurring during adolescence, includes a tacit acceptance of values and symbols from the religious faiths and practices. The fourth stage, individual-reflective, is a questioning stage in which people make their beliefs explicit. Individuals question not only their beliefs but also the context in which they developed. The fifth stage, conjunctive, includes a deepening sense of faith and an integration of beliefs. The final stage, universalizing faith, includes integrating ethical principles, including justice and love. It should be noted that, as is the case with most developmental models, individuals may not progress through the stages as outlined.

Katie's spiritual journey seems to follow this path. Her participation in Catholic traditions began in infancy, when she was baptized in the Church. During her school-age years, she attended Catholic schools, and she was indoctrinated with the teachings of the Church through school and religious services. Katie's school-age development seems to reflect Stage 2. For Katie, religion was a rote practice, a part of family functioning, which she took literally and examined in a concrete fashion. Katie reports questioning teachings but being silenced by her teachers. One wonders if she tacitly accepted the teachings at that point, confident in her parents' acceptance of the teachings and doctrine. When Katie entered high school, she began questioning some of the teachings she had previously accepted, partly due to the empowerment she felt from the civil rights movement. She may have entered Fowler's fourth stage during adolescence due to the changes that were occurring within society. Although the primary doctrine of the Church did not change, there was more input from the laity within the service and more participation from parishioners.

When Katie entered college and began to work, as is the case with many, she participated less in religious services, focusing on other developmental tasks. Katie continued to move through the stages as she decided to enter an interfaith marriage. Religious beliefs that had perhaps become routine suddenly took on new meaning as she was faced with the prospect of needing to choose which religious faith to practice. For Katie, love conquers all, and Katie and Daniel examined their faiths within the commitment of the relationship. Although Katie entered the challenges of young adulthood, entering and completing college and establishing a career, her participation in religious activities waned. But certainly the prospect of marriage and the challenge of choosing or defending faith helped Katie to reconnect with spirituality.

There are many issues that may propel individuals into Fowler's fifth stage, conjunctive, in which beliefs are reexamined and integrated. For Katie, it was certainly the decision to marry that caused her to examine her faith and to more fully embrace, accept, and make Daniel's faith a vital part of her life, beginning with the wedding ceremony. Following marriage was childbirth, which led to a new examination of beliefs. For Katie, the prospect of raising children in an interfaith marriage, providing the opportunity to study and embrace both religious traditions, moved her to the sixth stage of development, universalizing faith. People often choose to expose their children to religious teachings, even those who no longer actively practice their faith, to allow their children to choose whether to participate in religion as adults. But because Katie's faith was more developed, she decided not to just expose teachings and practices to her children but to enrich their lives. She was an active participant in their teachings by preparing the curriculum for their studies. Not every person reaches the highest level of spiritual development.

DECISION MAKING

Religious beliefs and teachings often influence people's decision making. Scriptures and teachings, along with religious leaders, are sought for guidance and advice. Religion influences values and determines rules and roles in interpersonal relationships, career decisions, and child-rearing practices. It is clear that Katie was influenced by her religion as she progressed through development. First, Katie's socialization through school reaffirmed values and teachings in the Catholic faith and within her family. For Katie, options for her future were defined by roles prescribed by the Church. When Katie was entering adolescence, the teachings of the Church were beginning to expand, allowing her to have the freedom to explore more options. These changes allowed her to choose to relocate across the country to attend a non-Catholic university, a choice that may not have been available to her before the Church began to change after Vatican II. Katie's next major decision was to choose a career. She chose teaching and theater as a profession and decided to teach at a private, all-girl Catholic high school.

Following developmental trajectories, the next major tasks for Katie were marriage and child rearing, and, as with other aspects of her life, her religious teachings were used as guidance. Although she was taught not to marry someone who was not a practicing Catholic, love had other plans for her, and she fell in love with a Jewish man. Perhaps guided by the changes within the Church and its impact on her identity as an adolescent, she decided to follow her heart. This was not a decision she took lightly, and she and her fiancé decided to seek advice on their marriage. Not only did religion influence her participation in the marriage, but it also dictated the nature of the wedding ceremony, the first challenge to the interfaith relationship. Their commitment to the process led them to developing a support group for interfaith couples. The second challenge came in the attendance of worship services, as the couple decided to worship together in a parish that was accepting of Daniel's belief in Judaism. The final area of decision making in Katie's story is of child rearing, specifically religious teaching and training.

FAMILY SOCIALIZATION

Katie describes the role of the family in the development of her religious identity. Katie was born into a German and Irish Catholic family, and the extended family worshiped together and played a role in her religious development. They were a part of her baptismal ceremony, and the family worshiped and fellowshiped together for all major ceremonies. Katie spent the weekends worshiping with her parents and participating in Saturday confession. The family often dialogued about religious teachings, reflecting and mirroring the teachings from mass and the Catholic school. The extended family, along with her father, for example, expressed discomfort with some of the changes that were happening in the Church, particularly the modernization of the Catholic mass. They also expressed some concern about the interfaith marriage, the wedding ceremony, and the influence on children.

Katie is continuing the family socialization of religious beliefs through her child rearing. She actively developed a curriculum so that her children would receive rich teachings in both Catholicism and Judaism. By ensuring her children's religious education, Katie is working toward securing their futures and aiding them in their spiritual development. Her advice to them, "Practice may be rote and dull at times. Give it time. . . . To you both: Bon voyage. Peace be with you. Go with God. Go with Good. Shalom."

INFLUENCE OF CURRENT EVENTS

Bronfenbrenner's (1977) ecosystem model of development is relevant for understanding religious development. The sociopolitical issues and human rights concerns within the world often influence religious teachings and tenets. When Katie began to question her religious teachings and doctrine, the Church also began to respond to the Zeitgeist and make changes in its policies and the services. Katie experienced high school during the rise of the feminist and civil rights movements, which led to changes in her religious role models. Katie openly embraced the changes that occurred in the services, from having the priest face the congregation to changes in the Eucharist service, but her family was resistant to the changes that were happening. Today there are social justice issues and policy issues that present moral dilemmas for individuals, along with teachings within churches and denominations. Various religious faiths wrestle with issues including abortion rights, civil rights, and same-sex marriages. Individuals, like Katie, look to religious teachings and leaders for guidance. For example, Katie had more freedom to attend colleges and explore careers due to changes within the Church. She was also not as bound to traditional gender role expectations.

Current sociopolitical issues also affected the possibility of mate selection. A generation ago, it would have been more difficult to marry someone of a different religious orientation. Changing attitudes, behaviors, and immigration patterns have literally transformed the past tendency toward homogeneity in mate selection patterns. Intermarriage rates have increased for all ethnic, cultural, and religious groups in the United States (Crohn, 1998). Katie falls into that category by marrying a Jewish man.

Clinical Applications

ASSESSMENT

There are two primary areas of assessment for spirituality and religion as illustrated in this story: religious identity and development and the influence of religion on decision making. First, clinicians should assess the religious socialization practices and teachings of childhood and adolescence. Teachings influence values, decisions, judgments, and relationships, so it is important to assess these early teachings with clients. Because the relationship with religion changes according to developmental stages, it is important to assess how these changes have influenced clients. It is equally important to ask these questions with clients who are no longer practicing a religious faith because often people leave religious institutions because they have been harmed or hurt by particular teachings. The second area of assessment includes the influence of religion on decision making. Clients often seek religious teachings or religious leaders when making choices, and it is important for therapists to understand how these are affecting clients. The following questions are recommended for assessing the importance of religion:

What is your religious background?

Were you raised or socialized in a particular religious faith?

How important is your religious background to you?

How important was religion during your childhood?

How important are religious teachings and practices to you?

Are you currently participating in religious or spiritual practices?

How have your religious beliefs or your connection to religion changed during your development?

How do your religious beliefs influence your decisions?

Do you seek religious leaders for advice in decision making?

How are your religious beliefs related to your presenting problem?

TECHNIQUES AND INTERVENTIONS

Examination of Specific Religious Teachings

Therapists need to help clients examine and explore their specific religious beliefs in treatment. As individuals progress through religious identity development, they begin to question their religious beliefs, separate perceived facts from myths, and understand how their beliefs are related to values and decisions. It is important for therapists to assist clients in their exploration, particularly if their beliefs are related to the presenting problem. It may also be helpful for couples who become overwhelmed by differing religious doctrines to discuss spirituality and spiritual needs. The couple may find more commonality in their sense of purpose in life or transcendence, for example.

Interfaith Relationship Issues

Only since the 1970s have churches and religious faiths sanctioned interfaith marriages; many people have been raised with teachings and practices that prohibited and did not recognize interfaith marriages. Clients who are contemplating these marriages may experience some trepidation because they may feel as if this decision goes against religious teachings and family rules. Therapists can assist clients in two ways. First, clinicians can help clients to outline the important doctrines and teachings from their religions and to find a compromise about worship services, rituals, and traditions. Premarital counseling should help clients explore and face their families' reactions to the marriage. Discussions about how to spend the holidays, particularly the religious holidays, need to be included in the treatment. Counselors can be helpful in assisting clients in the discussion about the actual wedding ceremony as well. Counselors should encourage clients to have realistic discussions about the religious socialization of the children if the couple is planning to have them. Clinicians should suggest to clients that the original conversations in premarital counseling have to be repeated with major life transitions, stressors, or crises. For example, parents may be agreeable about having a civil service ceremony but insist that their grandchildren be socialized in a particular way.

Interfaith couples who are already married or who have children are most likely to seek help when some event in the life cycle disrupts the family's balance (Crohn, 1998). Many couples attempt to deal with their religious differences by trying to forget the past or deny their differences in religious backgrounds or commitments. However, a major life event or trauma may make couples more vulnerable to conflicts around those issues. Many people revert to religious practices and rituals they have been socialized with to deal with the crisis or tragedy, even if, for the sake of being in this interfaith couple, they had denied or rejected their religious practices in the past. Helping couples clarify their needs, differences, worries, and anxieties about the religious differences is important. It is also important for the therapist to help interfaith couples create their own religious rituals, routines, and traditions.

COUNTERTRANSFERENCE

Two areas of countertransference are raised in this story: moral dilemmas and confusion around interfaith relationships.

Moral Dilemmas

Katie's story and her religious identity show the influence of current affairs, sociopolitical issues, and the cultural ideology on functioning. Religion influences our decisions and behaviors. When religious teachings and practices change, people are left confused over what to believe or how to behave. Likewise, individuals may experience a lack of change in religious teachings and think that their religious training and beliefs are not relevant to today and leave their religion. Counselors will experience these same feelings and be confused about how to assist their clients. For example, a person with an unplanned pregnancy may be confused about whether to terminate the pregnancy, which would go against their religious training. Therapists are advised to be aware of their own positions and be careful not to impose them on their clients. A Rogerian approach that focuses on active listening may be useful in helping people with moral dilemmas (Rogers, 1980). The narrative approach that focuses on helping people understand the meaning they are constructing may also be beneficial in this area (Freedman & Combs, 1995).

Confusion About Interfaith Differences

Clinicians may become overwhelmed by working with clients who were socialized in two different religious traditions. Therapists who share a similar religious tradition and strong religious beliefs with one member of the couple may find it difficult to understand how and why the couple is interested in an interfaith relationship. Therapists with no religious training may underestimate the significance of the relationship and the troubles the clients will face. Clients need assistance in sorting out and prioritizing religious beliefs and family reactions. Clinicians may want to consult with religious leaders to assist in the process of helping the couple achieve a balanced view of their differences (Falicov, 1995).

TOOLBOX ACTIVITY—KATIE		
Resources and Suggested Readings	*Activities*	*Discussion Questions*
Cowan, P., & Cowan, R. (1989). *Mixed blessings: Overcoming the stumbling blocks in an interfaith marriage.* New York: Penguin. Hawxhurst, J. C. (1998). *The interfaith family guidebook: Practical advice for Jewish and Christian partners.* Boston, KY: Dovetail. Mogel, W. (2001). *The blessing of a skinned knee: Using Jewish teachings to raise self reliant children.* New York: Penguin. Rosenbaum, M. H., & Rosenbaum, S. (1998). *Celebrating our differences: Living two faiths in one marriage.* New York: Ragged Edge Press. Yob, I. (1998). *Keys to interfaith parenting.* Hauppauge, NY: Barron's Educational Series.	Research a religious faith that differs from yours. Imagine marrying a person from that faith. Write an essay on the challenges you would have to face. Develop a list of essential religious teachings that you would want to share with your children.	Content themes What other themes do you see emerging in the story that the author did not identify? Assessment Are there any questions you would like to ask? Interventions What other interventions could you propose with Katie? Countertransference What countertransference reactions were emerging in yourself as you read this story? Other Scenarios Imagine that Katie married another Catholic. How would this marriage have shaped her religious identity? Imagine that Katie married someone of the Islamic faith. What challenges would they have?

Section V

Dimensions of Social Class

Social class is one of the more confusing and less visible dimensions when it comes to understanding the diversity of individuals and families. The challenge comes from defining the concept of social class and understanding the nature of existing cultural myths, due mainly to the dominant American discourse, which generally does not acknowledge class inequalities (Kliman & Madsen, 2005) and perpetuates the myth of the United States as a classless society (Langston, 2000). This is a powerful myth in American social and political life that affects the way people think about themselves. It stems, in part, from the historical differences between a stratified British society at the time of independence—in which climbing from the social class of one's origin to another, higher one, was virtually impossible—and the emerging democracy of the New World, which allowed a certain segment (White males) to go from the "mailroom to the boardroom," regardless of birth origins. This myth contains within it the idea that hard work, motivation, ambition, and intelligence alone are responsible for people's success, and conceals the reality by giving the working class and the poor false hopes (Langston, 2000). The social mobility that characterized America in the 20th century was not available to all members of society, and the possibilities for continued social mobility have been declining steadily in the past two decades (APA Task Force on Socioeconomic Status, 2007).

Dominant discourses tend not only to deny the existence of class differences and inequalities but also attribute those inequalities to personal characteristics, as if poverty or wealth were the result of lower or higher levels of motivation or lower or higher capabilities. While it is true that within groups, certain people are more capable or more motivated than others, most social class inequalities are the result of favorable or unfavorable conditions in which a person grows up (Kliman & Madsen, 2005; Prilleltensky & Prilleltensky, 2006).

The difficulties of defining social class, compounded by the dominant discourses that portray America as a classless society, make it one of the least examined issues in the clinical situation and an almost invisible variable in the training of counselors and psychologists. Though training programs vary in the degree to which they offer coursework in working with the poor, the disadvantaged, or the marginalized members of society, they often overemphasize poverty over other social classes. They also may not focus on the relationship between poverty and other dimensions (i.e., the relationships among poverty, ethnicity, and gender), disregard the relationships between social classes, and might not examine the effect of any social class on individual functioning. These theories of intersectionality are significantly influencing how social class is conceptualized (APA Task Force on Socioeconomic Status, 2007).

It is as important for clinicians to understand, assess, examine, and have conversations about social class as it is to examine other variables, because social class, socioeconomic status, and the relationship among social classes influence behaviors, lifestyle, values, expectations, and overall functioning. Social class also affects life expectancy, the sequences of the life cycle, access to resources, risks for illnesses, opportunities to fulfill personal or collective needs, relationships with friends, choices of mates, and a myriad of other human dimensions. Understanding social class is also important because it is a primary factor in intragroup differences. For example, within the same social class, people differ according to their geographic origin, and within the same ethnic group there may be substantial differences according to social class. In some situations, differences in social class may be more salient than differences in ethnicity.

Socioeconomic status is the term used to denote salary and income levels for individuals. Social class, a more inclusive term, includes wealth, salary and wages, real estate, educational levels, and assets (Kliman, 1998). Social class has sociopolitical connotations and carries with it sociological and psychological implications (Boyd-Franklin, 2003) because it is tied to issues of race and ethnicity. For example, poverty is associated with ethnic minorities, and middle-class values are connected to the White or dominant experience. The standards associated with social class are different according to racial and ethnic groups, so what constitutes a poor class in one setting may be a middle-class community according to that particular group (Boyd-Franklin, 2003). Additionally, there are numerous subjective representations of social class that may include people's relationship with social capital, human capital, or cultural capital. There can be a multiplicity of middle-class cultures, each with different values, motivations, and expectations (Liu, Soleck, Hopps, Dunston, & Pickett, 2004). Because most Americans define themselves as middle-class, the term has little descriptive value (Kliman & Madsen, 2005). Typically, income, education, and occupation are used to place people in a hierarchical framework. Five sociological social class categories can be identified: the underclass, the working poor, salaried workers, managerial/professional workers, and the nonruling capitalist class (Kliman, 1998).

The underclass includes individuals who are near or below the poverty level. Assumptions about the underclass include lower levels of education (high school diplomas or less), illiteracy, and laziness. Members of the underclass are also assumed to be less psychologically sophisticated than members of other classes, and to not have the capacity for insight or long-term psychotherapy. Members of the underclass are also assumed to engage in criminal activity or illicit behaviors, including gang involvement, drug dealing, prostitution, robbery, and burglary.

In fact, criminal activity in the underclass is often glamorized in the media, including a focus in news reports and in movies such as *Boyz n the Hood, Colors,* and *Striptease.*

The working poor include individuals whose employment involves manual labor or menial tasks. Assumptions about the working poor include that they have limited education, most likely a high school diploma or GED. They are seen as hard workers but still not psychologically sophisticated. They are not considered cultured or refined. Many live in poverty and have no health care or other benefits.

The salaried workers class is reflective of the middle-class images in this country. Members of the salaried workers class often are employed in positions that require high school diplomas or college experience. With the decline of real wages, higher health and housing costs, the disappearance of manufacturing jobs, and the realities of corporate downsizing, many salaried workers face insecurities that did not exist a generation ago for members of the middle class. Members of the middle class are seen as more psychologically sophisticated than members of lower classes.

The professional/managerial class is equivalent to the economic upper middle class, although from the sociological model they may have lower income levels than the salaried workers class. They are assumed to have college experience, most likely to have completed a college degree and graduate studies. Members of this class tend to delay coupling or having children, and once their children reach young adulthood, they might have more trouble becoming independent than in previous generations. Many members of this class depend on members of the working poor for help with their children, the elderly, or the disabled while they are at work. They are more likely to participate in fine arts and culture, enjoying the educational experiences of museums, plays, and concerts. Members of this social class are assumed to be psychologically sophisticated, capable of insight, and good candidates for psychotherapy.

The nonruling capitalist class is equivalent to the upper class and is considered to own most of the total wealth of the country. Although they are often assumed to come from "old money," their educational levels vary. They are the only social class without economic insecurity, although their members are not without worries and pressures, including maintaining the family legacy, social obligations, and in many cases, the lack of emotional connections of its members. They are assumed to be the most cultured and refined, attending the symphony and opera, and to have high levels of psychological sophistication.

This previous stratified view of social class, while helpful to take into consideration, is limited because strict hierarchical ideas of social class are insufficient to understand how people perceive themselves or are perceived by others (Liu, et al., 2004), and it is important to understand each social class as it relates to the others. For example, for some people, how their income level compares with that of others may be more important than their actual income. Also, there is a relationship between wealth, power, and privilege, and between poverty, marginalization, and oppression. In general, the wealthier the individual or the group, the more power they exert and the more privileges they are afforded.

One of the most important values related to social class is its relationship to education and work. Education is seen as providing access to opportunities and resources. The importance of education and the belief that education can aid in career development vary according to social class status, with members of the upper class often placing more importance and value on education. Although a higher educational level can lead to career development and higher salaries, some individuals in the lower classes may feel that the pursuit of higher education will not bring benefits, or they may doubt their ability to afford continuing education. Therefore, it is important to explore the differences in career aspirations and career expectations. Career aspirations refer to the dreams or ideals that individuals hold regarding career choice and occupational status. Most of us begin dreaming about careers at an early age, with our hopes of becoming doctors, police officers, or nurses. Career expectations refer to the beliefs that individuals hold about the likelihood of attaining a particular position, including the likelihood of attaining a particular educational level. Career aspirations and expectations may differ drastically. For example, a child of a recent immigrant may dream of practicing medicine in this country but not expect to attend medical school due to the economic need to work to bring additional family members to the country. An African American student may aspire to become a lawyer but not expect to achieve this goal due to a lack of role models in the community or a financial inability to attend college.

Finally, social class is related to values of spending and access to resources. Total wealth includes salary and income, assets, real estate, stocks and mutual funds, and professional level (Kliman, 1998). Social class standing allows individuals access to resources, including credit lines, loans, and temporary assistance during financial crises. Members of the working class often do not meet the requirements for public benefits or social service benefits (Breunlin, Schwartz, & Mac Kune-Karrer, 1997), and they may not be able to afford loans for additional resources. In addition to educational opportunities, social class status also provides access to health care services. The cost of medical care has to be considered in understanding an individual's functioning. Individuals without health insurance can incur significant amounts of debt if sickness occurs. It is important to assess clients' access to resources because it often influences priorities for individuals and the assumptions held about members of particular classes. If a family is coping with providing meals, it is unrealistic to expect the family to be interested in focusing on self-esteem or actualization.

When providing therapy for members of those in poverty or in the working class, different types of interventions that focus on providing resources or coordinating services may be warranted. Spending habits and priorities regarding savings plans also are influenced by social class. Members of the middle class may face issues regarding consumerism and the accumulation of debt (Breunlin, Schwartz, & Mac Kune-Karrer, 1997). Therapists should remember that counseling services might contribute to the debt or financial difficulties that clients sometimes face.

Social Class and Social Justice

Clinicians are probably most familiar and comfortable working with clients who come from middle- or upper-class backgrounds (Roland, 1996) and most of their training reflects that bias. Counselors and psychologists are generally trained to work individually with clients who are interested in self-awareness and self-improvement and take responsibility for their own change.

Psychotherapy can be understood, then, as a middle-class, Western invention (Robinson, 2005; Roland, 1996; Sue & Sue, 2003), even though, in the United States, a large percentage of consumers of counseling services are poor. Social service providers, practitioners in the mental health field, counselors, and other professionals have a witting or unwitting role as either social reproducers or social reformers, as either promoters of change or as proponents of the preservation of the status quo (Prilleltensky, 1994). From that point of view, psychology, social work, and counseling are not, nor have they ever been, professions devoid of political implications (Toporek & Williams, 2006; Vera & Speight, 2003) because psychological theories and practices are always affected by the social and cultural context from which they derive.

In spite of the fact that the issues of social justice have recently begun to take center stage in the multicultural literature, many training programs do not offer coursework in social justice, simply because most accrediting bodies do not require it either (Talleyrand, Chung, & Bemak, 2006). Counseling and psychology programs do not emphasize preparing students to actively engage in systemic change processes (Vera & Speight, 2003), and the great majority of students learn social justice skills on the job (Talleryrand, Chung, & Bemak, 2006). Though social work programs often offer an exception, it is not clear how often the course offerings promote a social justice perspective. It is imperative that students develop the knowledge and the skills necessary to engage in social justice work when they engage in clinical work with the poor. Obviously, work for social justice involves more that just working with the poor. But poverty is such a big risk factor (and has such broad effects) that it is included in this section.

As an example of the necessity of social justice interventions when working with the poor, let us examine the education achievement gap in the United States. The education achievement gap between African American children and their White counterparts, or between middle-class and poor children (the two measures tend to overlap) is very high (Tough, 2006). It has now become clear that one of the reasons for this gap is related to the different cognitive and emotional skills that middle-class children develop in their homes compared to the skills that poor children develop in theirs. For example, a study shows that middle-class children are exposed to many more encouraging verbalizations on the part of their caretakers than poor children (Hart & Risley, 1995). The exposure to large vocabularies affects the vocabulary development of the children. By the time they reach first grade, middle-class children have a much larger vocabulary than poor children do. The size of the vocabulary is, in turn, positively related to IQ, which in turn affects scholastic achievement, and therefore work-related opportunities, and so on. But the achievement gap between rich and poor children is only partially explained by the vocabulary gap. Another part of the explanation resides in what is known as the "education apartheid" (Street, 2005), which perpetuates inequality based on race, ethnicity, and social class. First, the best teachers tend to go where they get paid better, to suburban schools where the majority of students are White. Second, spending per student is lower in states that have more poor children. Third, school districts are funded primarily by property taxes in most states, hence, the lower the property taxes in a school district, the lower the funding for education.

Ethnic minorities are highly represented in the poor communities. The median annual income of African Americans and Latino families in the U.S. is much lower than the median annual income of White families (APA Task Force on Socioeconomic Status, 2007). When counselors and psychologists work with poor families, they are often working with mostly ethnic minorities, particularly women and children, who are disproportionably represented in lower socioeconomic strata. If they intervene only at the level of the individual child or family, they are most likely engaging in social control tactics, in blaming-the-victim approaches, and in the perpetuation of the status quo (Peirson, 2005). Instead, work for social justice could include both formal and informal interventions. One form of social justice work involves advocacy and includes empowerment; raising the class, racial, ethnic, and gender consciousness of the clients; promoting the active participation of families in assessing their own needs; and providing families with access to social networks (Prilleltensky & Prilleltensky, 2006). But advocacy is only one form of social justice work. Many forms of social activism can be implemented at the community level, including doing policy work, lobbying, coalition building, and other forms of social and political action aimed at working toward promoting a more equitable educational system. From the social justice perspective, it is clear that efforts devoted to making changes at the individual or family level only will not be sufficient to decrease the achievement gap.

Implications for Professionals

First, it is important for clinicians to understand the relationships among their clients' ethnicity, gender, and social class standing in society. Second, professionals need to understand the relationship between client's social class and the compression or expansion of the life cycle events associated with social class standing. Third, clinicians need to be aware of the existence of a middle-class bias in counseling and psychotherapy that may affect how they view their clients, their clients' worldviews, and their clients' choices. Fourth, it is important for clinicians to assess, discuss, and take into account any drastic or sudden changes in social class standing in their clients' history, the effect of clients' social class on their worldview, as well as their clients' perception of their social class. Finally, clinicians need to be interested in assessing their clients' strengths, resilience factors, and coping styles.

Stories in This Section

This section includes two stories. The first describes Carla's struggles to overcome the multigenerational effects of poverty. Note the legacy and influence of teenage pregnancy and the lack of education on social class. The second story of Anthony discusses the influence of a change in socioeconomic status on self-concept and identity development.

Anthony's mother moved to the working class after her divorce, and as a result Anthony struggled with alienation and isolation for much of his childhood and adolescence. The reader is encouraged to think about how to work with people of various social classes.

Discussion Questions

1. How does the myth of America as a classless society impact the provision of social services? Do you agree with the statement that social class needs to be made a more visible dimension in the helping professions?

2. How do you understand social justice, and what are the steps that individual providers can take to ensure that their practice reflects a social justice orientation? What are some of the political implications of the provision of counseling and psychological services for the poor?

3. In what ways can a middle-class bias be reflected in the provision of counseling services?

4. Have you ever had the experience of making an assumption regarding the social class (high or low) of a person, only to be proven wrong upon further fact gathering? What are the possible clinical implications of such an a priori reaction?

5. What are the possible consequences of drastic and/or sudden changes in the socioeconomic status of an individual or a family? Does a drastic or sudden change in status necessarily result in a change in social class identity?

Carla's Story 15

One More Mile

S ome of the most difficult commercials to watch on television portray starving children, with sad faces and protruding stomachs. The narrator pleads for pennies a day, so children can be rescued from poverty and hunger. They are always shown in distant, underdeveloped, Third World countries, far from the comforts of America. The commercials convince us that poverty is an issue for other countries. And yet census data indicate that 12.1 percent of individuals and families live in poverty within the United States. It is hard to imagine, but children here often struggle to find meals, and if they were shown on a television commercial, these U.S. children might closely resemble the children from Third World countries.

Socioeconomic status influences values and functioning. For those in poverty, decisions are made in view of available resources and satisfaction of current needs. Social class standing, with the accompanying sociological implications, includes assumptions about characteristics of people. Those in the lower or working class may struggle to find employment and educational opportunities. This leads them to decisions that often go against the dominant middle-class standards and values and at times may be illegal. What often occurs is a cycle of poverty or lower-class standing, connected to feelings of confusion, depression, helplessness, and hopelessness. Carla's story is one of overcoming the cycle of poverty. She represents clients who are struggling to meet basic physical survival needs, to the neglect of other psychological needs. As you read, notice the connections between middle-class standards and issues of race and oppression. Also notice the generational patterns of social class status and the role of education in relieving poverty.

Carla's Story

I'm a 48-year-old, brown-skinned woman; maybe I even have a few hidden freckles. I'm a little-past-middle-age Black woman who decided to return to school after being out for what seems like an eternity. I never understood about being Black because my skin color is brown, or at least it is one of the colors you see in a box of crayons. I was born and raised in Dallas, Texas. It took me a long time to be able to identify myself as a Black, African American, or Negro. I accepted Jesus as my savior and Lord about 15 years ago. Well, actually, I know that Jesus has always been a part of my life, ever since I was a little girl. I have overcome a lot of obstacles in my life. I know the Lord was present in my life, and this is the only reason I made it this far; as the old women from my culture used to say, "on a prayer and a wing," meaning praying and soaring on the celestial throne of God.

I refused even at an early age to let my color dictate to me. By this, I mean when I was growing up it was like a crime to be Black, even if you knew you were Black. "One more mile" is what I call this autobiography because of all the obstacles of being Black, poor, and raised in a single-parent home, though this life still came with benefits. The only thing I felt that the White people could not take from me was my color. Eventually, my mother explained it was not the color, and if you're really going to make a White person dislike you, get an education. I was seven years old. What did I know about color or education? I just knew I was treated differently because of the color of my skin.

I knew there was a difference by the time I turned seven in the second grade. The White children dressed better, and they even had better lunches. White children seemed to have better homes, and every necessity any human could want, including me. This had me asking myself questions about my Black identity and how come I could not give this evil, bad color back. How come I could not trade me in for a White version that got respect, that did not go hungry, that did not want for a pretty dress? I heard people talking about the new bleaching cream that had just come out. I thought maybe if my mother bought some, I could use it and turn White. It should have been a requirement not an obligation for children, no matter what nationality, to not be deprived of the essentials of life, such as food. All my girlfriends, the ones who were White, always spoke about their mothers and fathers. My Black girlfriends would speak of their mothers and their fathers visiting. Most of the time, it would be them visiting their father and stepmother. The average Black family when I grew up only knew that the so-called American dream pertained to a White family—a mother, a father, and their children. But the American dream to some Black families was mother and maybe a stepfather. I know I had some Black girlfriends who actually told me that their mother told them Mr. Welfare was their father, meaning the public aid assistant for needy families was their father.

These are the words that played in my head that my mother would tell us: "When you leave this house, you become actors and actresses. No matter what's going on around you, it's not about you, and keep your head up and a smile on your face. Always keep people on the outside, never let them on the inside." See, my mother believed that if people knew that calling you names and treating you badly bothered you, then they knew how to push you emotionally. But if you ignored them and let them call you names, they could not get control over you mentally or physically because you refused to play into their hands.

The challenges of school coming up in the 1960s and 1970s were true for most Black children. You had to work harder because the books were a year behind and the teacher was not adapted to teaching Black children with their "incorrect" language—no proper pronunciations of language, only the language learned in the home. So, if your mother had a Southern accent, you would also have that same accent. Trying hard to talk like the White man or White woman or White kids was like having a full-time job. The only time I was able to sound White was when I was repeating some disturbing things some White child had said to me.

Being the second-eldest of seven children was hard. We lived in a kitchenette apartment. My mother and father were separated at this point. I did not know or understand what this meant at the time. With no resources, this was all my mother could afford. When I asked my mother about my father, she said he was in the army. I noticed that all of my friends' fathers were always at home and not in the army. I would tell my mother that my friends' fathers were at home; she would state that my friends' fathers were White—like I knew what that meant. All I knew was Maggie had a father, and my father was in the army because we were Black and poor, and if he had been White, he would not be in the army. At six years of age, what did I know?

When my mother and father were together, all they did was fight. My mother was an alcoholic, and my father was abusive. After they separated, her only relief was more alcohol. No money, no help, we weren't eligible for assistance from public aid until my mother proved that she was not getting assistance from my father, who was of course in the army. She never missed sending my siblings and me to church services in the morning because they served breakfast, and sometimes that was a meal we did not have at home. In that day and time, you did not tell what went on in the home; you just endured, no matter what happened in your life.

I would go to my White friends' houses because they always had food. Later on, I found out that my mother was barely 13 when she married my father, and my father was 18—a shotgun wedding. My mother was pregnant, and back at that time, you married the man, no ifs, ands, or buts. After my mother and father went their separate ways, times became unreal. But, as I said earlier, one more mile—I could go on; because of God this was possible. Sometimes my mother would play like we had an expensive steak, and it would only be peanut butter and jelly for breakfast, lunch, and dinner. We received public assistance because my father was not in our home and my mother had no other way to support us. Literally, trying to raise seven children alone took a toll on her, and she started escaping in a bottle of liquor. She was a strong Black woman. Married at 13, she did not have a childhood. She had to be a wife. Culturally, being a Black child meant that you became grown at an early age. Being a Black woman meant that you were considered the strong, I-can-take-anything woman, the man's backbone, the mother and father. You did not have rules and regulations pertaining to raising your children and being the missing father; you made it up as you went along. The way my mother handled my father not being there was to become the substitute, and her seven children ended up a substitute for her.

When I turned 10 years old, some glimmer of light came into my life—my mother went on the wagon. My mother was getting public assistance and had found a part-time job in the hospital. We moved to a larger apartment, one with three bedrooms. With six siblings, that was like living in a mansion compared to the kitchenette, which was one room less than living in a small studio apartment. Even though I have experienced many dilemmas in my past that included different types of rejection, I know my mother did the best she could under the circumstances—a Black woman with no education, no husband, and seven children to raise by herself. We always had dinner at 4 p.m., no later than 5 p.m., and took our baths and were in bed by 6 p.m. At seven years of age, I knew how to iron, wash, and cook. When I turned nine, I realized from some inner feeling and from other children in the community where we lived that my mother was very young and Black. She had her first child when she was 13 years old and was married. The child died in her arms. She had a nervous breakdown and received no help to deal with her grief and the death of her child. She was a child, a Black child in the 1950s, with no coping mechanism to help her endure depression and grief over her lost child. African Americans did not believe in going to psychologists. When I was much older, it was told to me that you did not want the community in which you live to think that you were crazy. My grandfather was a preacher, so he tried to console her when my grandmother would let her go to her father's house. When it became overbearing, they sent her back to her husband's family since he was the one who caused the problem.

My grandmother used to tell me that she could tell the Lord her problems. Why pay the White man money to talk to them when they would only have the White man's answer for a Black problem? My grandmother was from the South, where she picked cotton; sometimes I would ask her about picking cotton. She would laugh and say, "I did not pick cotton; I used to be the lady of night." My grandmother had problems going to a regular medical doctor. She had all types of remedies, such as goose grease if you had the mumps or a swollen gland. We used Father John cough syrup and cod liver oil for most if not all sicknesses. There were all types of remedies that the Black woman used to keep from going to the White doctor for a Black illness. Just like my grandmother at one time did not understand the logic of going to the White man's doctor.

My mother, at 14 and pregnant again, was devastated for a young girl—not just a mother and wife but a young girl. My mother was an only child, so she had no brothers or sisters she could talk to. The lack of love in my mother's life had my mother seeking love; this would be a cycle my family would go through. My mother did not embrace us and say "I love you" because she did not know how. This is how my mother ended up with my father; she dressed up and pretended to be something she was not. I did not know that I had a grandmother until I was 13. I had never seen this woman; I had only heard about her. My mother did not know how to be mother at 13 and 14.

My mother's drinking problem was getting worse. Children and Family Services came out. I remember someone called on my mother, but when the family services came out, we denied the charges because we were taught that what happened in the house stayed in the house. We knew my mother was sick. I remember at one time we did not have any lights. I was about 13. We told all our friends who came over that we were religious, and we used candles because we were not allowed to use lights for a week. But this was when my mother was supposed to get her public aid check and get the lights back on. This was a very rundown apartment we lived in that needed a lot of work, but it was all my mother could afford to pay for with seven children. I was 14 and a freshman in high school. My sister and I would have to walk because my mother did not have car fare for us to get to school. Thank God that we were on public aid; at least we were able to eat free lunch at the school. One more mile I would have to overcome. I thought I found the solution to my mother's drinking problem. My mother loved to drink vodka, and she would leave the bottle in the refrigerator. So I told my sisters if we drank half of the vodka and put water in the bottle, she would not be as drunk. This proved to be disastrous because my sisters and I were just as drunk as our mother.

Without the proper help, such as psychologists or psychiatrists, my mother went into her own world. Just when I thought that things couldn't get any worse, my mother started disappearing for three to four days, and we would not even have food to eat. I had three younger siblings who did not have friends' houses where they could go visit and stay for dinner. This became the responsibility of me and my two other siblings, to provide the necessary food for the younger siblings.

At 14, I had to do something. I met this young man who worked in a store right across the street from my house. He was 18, and he liked me a lot. I couldn't say I liked him the same, but I did not know what having a relationship or love was all about. My mother was not stable; she did not know love or how to express it. I was able to secure food because he liked me. We started dating; I told him I was going on 17 years of age, that vicious cycle I talked about earlier. One more mile—there is nothing free in life. I had to decide whether to have a sexual encounter with this guy to keep feeding my siblings and myself. Especially since I lied and told him I was 17. Families had unity but no help. Your family stuck together no matter what. At 15, I found out I was pregnant. At gym one day, I got really sick and went to the nurse, and she did a pregnancy test. The school informed me that when I began showing, I would have to quit until I had the baby or they were going to drop me out of school because the school was not insured for this type of problem. I lost a lot of friends because their mothers would not let them be friends with me because they would become pregnant. Even I did not realize that it was not contagious.

My mother was laid off her job, but she was still receiving public aid. I signed up to go to Dante Skill Center to secure a clerical certificate, while I was waiting for my child to be born. I was under the NYC-II Program (Neighborhood Youth & Counseling Program) for Black people whose parents were not working or were getting assistance from the government and whose children were not going back to high school. After my daughter was born, I did go back to high school and the Dante Skill Center in the evening. This was against the law, but I needed the money, which was $154, to help support my siblings and my daughter. It wasn't much, and the government paid the rent.

One of my mother's drunken friends had put the gas on illegally, and Human Services paid for our lights because I had a new baby. One day I came home from school, but before I got there I just knew something was wrong. First, I passed by this lounge my mother loved to go to. They told me that my mother and daughter had been in there earlier, and they had collected about $20 from people in the lounge who said my daughter was really cute. When I finally got to my house, my mother was passed out on the floor and my baby was crawling around eating off the floor. I picked up my baby, and I cried and wished for a normal family like the White family I saw on television. I made up my mind that I had to move.

I took my money and rented a room owned by my girlfriend's mother, Ms. Shells. It was a men's rooming house that housed men. My baby's father would come and spend the night, so I would not be scared, but he had also become very abusive. When my baby's father went to jail, this was the best thing I figured could happen, so I could move. I went to the public aid office to get assistance, but they told me that as long as I was underage, my mother still had to get the check for my children and me. I had two children by the time I turned 18.

While at the public aid office, I ran into a girl I went to high school with. I was standing waiting for the bus with my new baby and my eldest little girl, who was two years old. I began to cry, but I did not have anywhere to go, and I was really worried about my children. Social Services only helped adults. I knew now how my mother must have felt, all alone and no one to go to. I really needed psychological help, but I did not know what that meant at the time. I just heard people say this. I was depressed and felt there was no hope, but I still had a strong sense of spirituality that God was enough in spite of what I was going through. The girl told me to come home with her and talk to her mother and maybe we could work out something so I would not be on the streets. I told her mother all the money I received was $154 from training school and that I had two more months and then I would be graduating from there.

A new home is what I received, and some special friends. I slept on the floor of my girlfriend's bedroom with my two-year-old child and my three-month-old baby. Once I put the children to sleep, I would go to these two lounges across the street from each other to get milk and diaper money from the men at the lounge. This is how I would do it. Once a week, I would go sit at the bar; the men would give me money for cigarettes and to play the jukebox and buy myself a drink. I would order a soda and pocket the rest of the money and tell them I was going to the washroom. Then I'd leave. I was able to do this until I started getting checks from school. My baby wasn't on formula like other babies because I could not afford to buy it. I did not even have a medical card to take her to the doctor. The medical card was the poor people's insurance. My baby survived as well as myself on what I could muster up.

I only knew Black antidotes—alcohol, drugs, and men, anything that would give us what we considered a little peace in the White man's world. My friend's mother agreed to keep the children while I attended business college downtown. This was a government program for poor people who want to get a trade and a stipend for car fare. The school had 6 spaces out of 100 for poor families to go to school to learn a trade. They had a special scholarship, so you had to show that you were really poor and could not even afford to come to school. I put in an application and was accepted because I had a high school diploma. About 90 percent of the students at this school were White. One of the significant life events that happened to me while in this school was, besides my teacher being White, I became one of her prized students to use in class to the other White students as "the poor Black student who was able to come to school on scholarship"; she would tell them, "If she can make it, you people should make it that much more."

The teacher used to tell me that I was Black; she must have figured I did not know that. Then she would say that I would never learn how to type because my hands were like a dwarf's—too short to reach the keyboard. The reality of the situation is that culturally I was not White, but I was not an idiot, either. The teacher always used the three Black students as her escape to try to make the White students succeed.

I was used to the dilemma of racism and some White people speaking as if we learned by example, by looking and not by using our brains. I used my teacher to inspire me to complete the program, and everything she said I could not accomplish I did better than accomplish. I graduated from the program with honors, and I graduated out of the 12-month program typing 73 words a minute. Education was always a big part of me; my mother stressed the importance of it. This is when I met the man who would become my husband. I was seeking love when I did not know what love was. I got married because I got tired of trying to support myself and get by on my own. I signed up at YMCA College, majoring in court reporting and music. These dreams were put on hold temporarily. At 18 and with two children, I married but did not know the man or his family.

I was married 23 years. In all the years I was married, this was past a challenge. The marriage was not made in heaven. I had encountered a family who believed in selling drugs and gang-banging. I finally got tired, two more children later. I moved to the opposite side of town than my husband with my four children, no job, nothing to support my family. I had quit my state job to move and have food for my children and to get away from my husband. So I started sending out résumés and putting in job applications. One more mile—I had to have closure. Sure, life had thrown me more lemons, but I was always able to make lemonade, and after my divorce from this man, I decided to better myself by going back to college. I had been doing temporary work for several years and decided something had to happen for the better. At this point, I needed to seek psychological help, social services, and anything or anybody who could explain why it may have been destiny that I would still be going through hell, just because it never came easy being a Black person. Presently, I'm working as a secretary. I completed a double degree in criminal justice in a college that has a returning adult program. Eventually, I want to work in juvenile probation or a juvenile correctional center or perhaps even one day open up a facility that would help young pregnant girls survive the system.

One more mile of culturally challenging things—I kept seeking to better myself and become something I saw all my life. You are not disabled because you are Black, White, or green. You disable yourself because you give up and allow yourself to believe that education is only for White people. This story has just lightly touched the events that I dare not share with anyone except my God and children because they have always been a part of my big picture. I know if it had not been for the grace of God and His mercy, I would have not lived to tell my story.

Content Themes

Carla's story teaches us about the influence of social class and socioeconomic status on functioning, values, and behaviors. It is clear from the story that Carla's family lived in a generational cycle of poverty, with accompanying feelings of helplessness and depression. Because both Carla and her mother had children as teenagers, the available sources of public aid and other resources for them were limited, exacerbating the issues of poverty and leading to questionable solutions. Carla's story also highlights the importance of education as a means of changing or shifting in socioeconomic status. Finally, the intersection of social class with dominant standards, race, and oppression are highlighted in the story.

THE IMPACT OF POVERTY

Carla's mother was poor, and although it is not mentioned in the story, Carla's grandparents may have been working class or poor as well. Carla's mother had her first child as a teenager and was unable to support her family once the relationship with the child's father dissolved. To receive public aid, she had to prove that she was not receiving financial assistance from her husband. Although she was eventually awarded aid, by the time she had seven children, the aid did not provide enough support to be able to sustain the children. Carla's mother ended up abusing alcohol as a way to overcome the depression and helplessness she felt from her circumstances. It seems as if she felt she had no way out of poverty, probably because she did not receive financial or emotional support from her family of origin and did not receive enough government support to feed her children.

The influence of poverty is apparent throughout the story. The first effect was the hopelessness and negative emotions that were felt by the family members. It appears that Carla's mother attempted to make the most of situations—for example, helping the children to feel as if their meals were more luxurious than they were. The level of poverty in the family often kept them from having minimal survival needs met. However, having children at a young age with little support seemed to eventually take a toll on her. She began to drink more and to leave her children unattended and without supervision. When individuals need to receive services but are denied for a variety of reasons, feelings of depression occur. The inability to see a way out of poverty, combined with real physical needs, extends the depression to a sense of hopelessness and helplessness. One can only imagine the pain that Carla's mother experienced not being able to provide for her children's basic needs and in seeing them hungry and comparing themselves negatively to others. The injustice of the situation without the voice to be heard can lead to increased helplessness. There is also a sense of shame that comes from being in poverty. The second effect of poverty is that it often forces children to behave as if they are older than their biological age. Older siblings often have to be responsible for the care and support of the younger children; they often need to drop out of school to work part-time jobs to feed siblings. It is clear that Carla felt this responsibility for her younger siblings. Older siblings often serve as intercessors at school for parents who may be unable to attend conferences. This creates role ambiguity and confusion for siblings who are forced to take on responsibilities before they are ready (Kliman & Madsen, 2005). In gang- and drug-infested neighborhoods, children often work selling drugs to make up for the lack of funding provided by public aid.

This of course is the third effect of poverty: the choice to engage in risky or illegal behaviors to meet basic survival needs. Boyd-Franklin (2003) discusses the necessity of street survival skills that is often a part of the culture of poverty. Although selling drugs may not be the best long-term solution, for many it provides more immediate and substantial cash than working a minimum-wage job or receiving part-time wages. Fortunately, Carla's family was able to receive some assistance from public aid, churches, the school, and friends, so none of the children had to turn to drugs to provide money for the family. Carla, however, did engage in questionable behaviors to provide for her younger siblings. Carla had to find ways to obtain money for food and was placed in the vulnerable position of needing to exchange sexual favors for money. This behavior continued even after she began to have her own children. Even when making more healthy choices, the consequences may be negative. Carla married as a way to gain financial support but ended up in an abusive relationship.

The final effect of poverty is the intergenerational transmission of poverty. In poor families, the family life cycle between generations may be compressed (Kliman & Madsen, 1999). Young mothers, with or without partners, may be raising children at a much younger age than their middle-class counterparts. By the age when a middle-class mother has her first child, it is not unusual for a poor mother to have grandchildren. This pattern gets repeated from one generation to the next. Although Carla attempted to provide money for the family, she became pregnant, propelling her into poverty. She had to quit high school because she was pregnant, which prevented her from finding suitable employment. The end results for Carla were the similar feelings of helplessness, hopelessness, and depression that her mother experienced. Carla was fortunate that another family took her and her children in until she completed school and could begin working. Many individuals remain in a cycle of poverty (Boyd-Franklin, 2003). Parents are unable to care for their children, who begin to make decisions that keep them in the lower socioeconomic status. There are generations of families, for example, who remain in public housing because they cannot develop enough resources to move. Carla does not discuss her children, but it is possible that they are also receiving public assistance and maintaining the intergenerational cycle of poverty.

LACK OF ACCESS TO RESOURCES

One of the major consequences of living in poverty or the working class is the lack of resources available to individuals and families. Although the U.S. government offers subsidy programs, they often do not provide enough to fully support families. Many of the welfare-to-work programs in states, introduced by the 1996 Personal Responsibility and Work Opportunity Reconciliation Act, offer limited assistance to families, for example, five years of funding to engage in training and job placement. When the five-year period is over, people are removed from welfare rolls and have to become financially independent. Individuals who are unable to receive employment that pays a living wage often have mental disorders that prevent them from maintaining full-time employment. Those not able to work due to child care concerns are left without public assistance. Members of the working class often make too much money to receive assistance but lack sufficient income to provide for their families. The effect of poverty tends to be even more severe on women and children of color (Boyd-Franklin, 2003; Robinson, 2005). The percentage of minorities in poverty is disproportionately higher than that for White people (Boyd- Franklin, 2003; Kliman & Madsen, 1999). Individuals in impoverished rural areas may have less access to resources (Sayger & Heid, 1990; Weigel & Baker, 2002).

Although Carla's family received public assistance, it was not adequate to take care of the seven siblings. Her mother had to rely on support from other social service organizations. Carla also spent time with friends and ate at their homes. Carla was also able to participate in the free lunch program at school, and that sometimes served as her only meal. Carla faced barriers of her own after she had her first child. She reports that, at the time, social services and public aid were provided only to individuals over the age of 18 years. The lack of access to resources led Carla and her family to cheat the system—for example, they had utilities turned on illegally, and Carla enrolled in a program illegally to earn an education to find employment. Many individuals often remain single but live together, receiving benefits illegally. Other individuals lie about their age to receive services.

Oppression and poverty increase vulnerability to chronic stressors (Boyd-Franklin, 2003). This is related to increases in drug and alcohol abuse and chronic health problems. And the lack of resources extends to medical and therapeutic services. Carla did not have enough money to provide appropriate nutrition for her daughter. Fortunately for Carla, her baby did not require medical attention because she could not have afforded quality medical care for her. Women of color often have the least amount of access to medical and psychological services (Robinson, 2005). Many individuals remain in poverty if they require extensive medical care and build up debt from medical bills. In fact, individuals often become poor due to medical problems that are not covered by insurance. Individuals in poverty often do not receive psychological services, either. Because their primary focus is on food, clothing, and shelter, despite feelings of depression or anxiety, therapy is not seen as an option. If individuals are able to enter treatment, they are more likely to attend sporadically due to difficulty with transportation or work schedules (Boyd-Franklin, 2003). They may also feel that it is not necessary to participate in insight-oriented work and rather want the therapist to serve more as a case manager, or to advocate for them with social services organizations. The lack of availability of therapeutic services can be detrimental for individuals and families in poverty, who experience chronic stress and trauma and exposure to violence, gang activity, crime, drugs, and alcohol (Boyd-Franklin, 2003).

IMPORTANCE OF EDUCATION

Carla's story highlights the importance of education as a means out of poverty. Her mother became pregnant for the first time and married at the age of 13 years, preventing her from completing high school. The lack of a high school education probably contributed to her being unable to find suitable employment to care for her children. Carla repeated this cycle, becoming a teenage mother, which forced her from high school. Carla's mother stressed the importance of education, so Carla continued to pursue vocational training, even using illegal means to continue. Education proved to be a way out of lower socioeconomic status for her. She eventually completed her college degree, despite experiences of racism along her educational path. Many do not have that opportunity or the heroic personal characteristics or perseverance to sustain the path despite chronic exposure to racism.

LINK TO RACE/DOMINANT VALUES

The exposure to middle-class norms and values has an influence on individuals of all class levels, particularly due to the prevalence of television viewing. Aponte (1995) discusses the "new poor," who are bombarded with images of wealth, greed, and consumerism via television, leading to a sense of injustice, helplessness, and sometimes rage. For Carla, these images were not viewed via television but in vivo through her attendance at predominantly White schools. As a child, Carla combined the notions of race and class, with wealth and comfort associated with being White and poverty with being Black. Early on, Carla felt a sense of injustice about the lack of equity in resources. In addition to class associations, Carla connected family structure with race, believing that only Whites had intact nuclear families, whereas Black families were predominantly single-parent households. Many African Americans view economic situations, educational opportunities, and employment through the lens of race (Boyd-Franklin, 2003).

Clinical Applications

ASSESSMENT

Clinicians must assess the influence of both social class and socioeconomic status on clients for a number of reasons. Social class determines the level of access to resources. Participating in therapeutic services is in many ways a luxury and can become a financial burden to clients who do not have insurance to cover payment. Clients in lower social classes suffering from psychological disorders with a neurological or biological basis may not be able to afford to maintain medication. They may also have some unaddressed medical concerns that are contributing to their presenting problems. Socioeconomic status is also linked to basic and psychological needs of individuals. Clients may have more pressing concerns than behavioral change, such as providing food and shelter. It is also important to assess clients' strengths, coping, and resiliency factors. The following are recommended as questions to assess social class:

What is your current income, wage, or salary level?

Are you making enough money to meet basic needs?

Are you receiving financial assistance? Does this assistance allow you to meet basic needs?

What is your educational level? Are you receiving a living wage?

Do you have access to appropriate medical care?

Do you have a budget?

Are you able to maintain your budget?

Are you in debt?

How do you cope with the struggles?

What makes you strong?

TECHNIQUES AND INTERVENTIONS

Social class standing should influence treatment goals and interventions. Many clients in poverty are referred through third parties, such as court or legal systems or schools. Although it is important to address the treatment concerns of the referral source, therapists may also need to serve as case managers with other social service agencies and as advocates for clients. Aponte (1995) calls for therapeutic services that address the ecosystem of the client, noting the importance of interventions at the individual, family, and community levels. He outlines three general goals for treatment of the poor. First, the poor need to feel control over their lives, particularly ownership of therapy. This need serves to counterbalance the sense of helplessness that often develops due to the lack of available resources and the inability to meet basic needs. The second goal for treatment is to help clients to develop a sense of purpose or meaning in life. Children who live in housing projects in urban areas often are pessimistic about even reaching 18 years of age due to violence in the neighborhood. This pessimism contributes to a sense of meaninglessness. The lack of gainful employment or the ability to contribute to society may also add a sense of the futility of life. Clients need to move beyond basic survival needs to address other psychological needs, including a sense of meaning and fulfillment. The third goal of treatment is to focus on changing the community in which clients live and function. Again, therapists need to be willing to expand beyond providing individual counseling.

Therapists need to remember that the client's therapy goals may be focused more on present-oriented or basic needs. Clients at the poverty level may enter treatment for depression or anxiety, but the inability to meet basic needs or the lack of available resources often exacerbates psychological symptoms. Clients at this social class may appear infrequently in treatment. They may call clinicians to be seen on an emergency basis, which generally involves an immediate family crisis, a situation with work, or a medical need. Clinicians may deem insight-oriented or long-term therapy as useful, but clients may identify other uses for the therapist, including assistance through crises. Behavioral approaches and brief therapeutic approaches may be most helpful for clients.

Special care needs to be taken to establish a working alliance with clients of economically disadvantaged backgrounds. Initiating a clinical encounter with an assessment of strengths and coping and resilience factors may be most beneficial to the establishment of the therapeutic alliance (Kilpatrick & Holland, 2002). If clients are engaging in illegal activity, they may not feel comfortable disclosing information in treatment. For example, a single mother may be living in public housing with her children's father but may be unwilling to acknowledge her partner for fear of losing benefits if the government discovers her living arrangement. Clinicians have to consult with the ethical codes from their professions and state laws regarding reporting criminal activity. In all cases, it is important to provide informed consent for reportable offenses as part of establishing the therapeutic relationship. Therapists working with clients in rural areas need to address dual relationships in treatment, particularly because therapists are advocating for them and seeking resources (Sayger & Heid, 1990; Weigel & Baker, 2002).

Family Therapy

Family therapy, particularly structural therapy or ecostructural therapy (Aponte, 1995), is also recommended for individuals who are economically poor (Minuchin, Colapinto, & Minuchin, 1998). Families often lose structure as children, especially older siblings, take on more adult and parental responsibilities. Children may also be called on to serve as parents to their own parents, who are incapacitated due to depression, anxiety, or substance abuse. It is also not unusual for multiple generations to be living together and for parents to be treated as siblings of their children. Family therapy can help to restore structure to families, empowering parents.

Home therapy or home visits are recommended for treatment (Aponte, 1995). Home visits may help the clinicians meet with the families or clients on a weekly basis. The visits also provide the therapist with an opportunity to see the clients' living space and community and to meet important family members. Visiting the home also provides the clinician with the opportunity to provide more informal psychotherapy groups as a benefit to the community.

Community Interventions

Clients also need to be empowered through community interventions. Therapists may need to help clients coordinate services through various agencies and may need to serve as advocates for clients. Boyd-Franklin (2003) recommends developing an ecomap, a diagram of the agencies and services that clients receive. The diagrams help to coordinate services and serve as tools to help clients empower themselves.

Parent Education

A common experience of poor families is to be referred for services by the state's children and family services agency, schools, and community counseling centers. Typically, parent education programs consist of a teacher with a curriculum telling parents how to be better parents. This involves several underlying assumptions: that the parents are bad parents, that the teacher knows how to parent the children of these parents better than the parents themselves, that the parents are going to absorb a curriculum they had no input in designing, and that after the teacher teaches the curriculum, the parents are going to have an "aha!" moment and become better parents of their children after they gain insight into their mistakes. When parents do not demonstrate that they have learned the correct way of parenting the children, they are labeled unmotivated, resistant, or abusive. In the United States, "protecting" the family often means controlling the family (Iglehart & Becerra, 1995). Despite the worthy goal of protecting the children from abusive and neglectful parents, institutionalized violence in the form of curriculum-based parent education is exerted on the family in disrespectful and damaging ways (Minuchin, et al., 1998).

Traditional parent education curricula are generally not designed with regard to the social class status of the parents and are delivered by providers who are not involved in the community, with little input from the parents. Culturally sensitive parent education can start by involving the targeted parents in a needs assessment of the community. Abuse and neglect do not take place in a vacuum but are part of a community that needs help with affordable housing, employment, health care, and other issues. Even parents who are mandated to take parenting classes can be encouraged to become collaboratively involved in the identification of their needs and the implementation of the needed changes as the stages of change, the motivational interviewing, and the solution-focused models demonstrate (De Shazer, 1988; Miller & Rollnick, 1991; Prochaska, Norcross, & Di Clemente, 1995). When parents identify parent education as one of their needs, they are much more likely to benefit from it. For meaningful change to occur, counselors should not be thinking for their clients and should not be their "surrogate frontal lobe" (Hoyt, 2001, p. 113). A facilitated discussion could take place in a school, for example, with a facilitator who poses questions to the group. These discussions can take place during parent university days and parent-teacher conference nights, in day care centers, or in community youth programs, and they may be more successful than curriculum-based parent education programs.

The following are some questions that a parent educator could use to springboard discussions. The questions are intended to elicit answers from the parents themselves, and not from the facilitator.

What are the best ways to motivate a child?

What works when it comes to getting kids to do what the parent wants?

What works to modify a child's behavior? What does not work?

How do you get a child to stop or start doing something?

What did your parents do when you were a child that worked?

What did your parents do when you were growing up that didn't work?

What did you learn about how to raise your children from the ways your parents raised you?

When you know what works, can you implement it? How so?

What hinders your implementation of what works?

What are the characteristics of a good mother or father? What are the characteristics of an ineffective mother or father?

Is there anything you do or don't do that makes you feel like a good mother or father?

Is there anything you do or don't do that makes you feel like you are not a good mother or father?

Do you know what happens to you that makes you behave in one way and not another way with your children?

Make a list of what works for you. Now make a list of what does not work. When do you do things from one list, and when do you do things from the other list? What do you notice about the two lists?

When parents are given an opportunity to talk about the best way to change a child's behavior, they often say that patience works and screaming does not. When asked for the best way to raise a child's self-esteem, parents often say that praise, love, and attention are better than punishment and neglect. In other words, parents may already know what works and what does not.

COUNTERTRANSFERENCE

There are many areas in which therapists may have strong personal reactions. Working with people of differing social classes may invoke strong feelings, value differences, and ethical dilemmas. Clinicians should carefully monitor their reactions, especially when working with people in lower social class levels.

Feelings of Helplessness

The first typical reaction of clinicians is to overidentify with feelings of helplessness and hopelessness (Comas-Diaz & Jacobsen, 1991). It can be frustrating to hear stories of deprivation and hunger, especially when children are involved. Clinicians who feel overly sympathetic may offer solutions that clients have already tried or solutions that are not viable, inadvertently enhancing the frustration of the clients. They may feel guilty for their own middle- or upper-class status (Robinson, 2005). Therapists may also be tempted to cross therapeutic boundaries and take care of clients by offering money or transportation services. Clinicians may also be tempted to provide housing for children in poverty. Therapists may also engage in the parallel process of helplessness and hopelessness, leading them to provide false hope to clients or to make clients feel stuck in treatment. The frustration may lead therapists to blame the clients for their circumstances.

Feelings of Anger

The second reaction is to feel angry with the clients, particularly if clients seem to have values different from those of the middle-class clinicians (Gorkin, 1996). A common complaint in supervision is that clients have inappropriate spending habits or values around money. Therapists may also be angry with clients who are wearing expensive clothing, shoes, or jewelry. Many clients, however, buy designer clothing at thrift stores or secondhand stores or receive donated clothing from companies or social services organizations. Many clients spend money on nice clothing because they feel that it is important to look presentable and decent: "We may be poor but we don't have to look poor" is the philosophy that is often presented by individuals in poverty. Maintaining appearances can be a way to maintain a sense of self-worth and dignity. It is important to remember that clients have free will and autonomy and can choose to spend money as they see fit. If therapists feel that the value differences hinder the therapeutic relationship, they should discuss their concerns with the clients. Clinicians may also feel angry with clients who engage in illegal activities to provide for themselves and families. Therapists may be able to see the shortsightedness of illegal solutions but have difficulty with helping clients find more suitable solutions. Therapists may also face an ethical dilemma when hearing about illegal activity regarding their duty to report the activity to the police. Clinicians need to check with state regulation boards.

Standard English

Clinicians may have difficulty with clients from lower social class backgrounds who do not speak standard English proficiently (Robinson, 2005; Sue & Sue, 2003). Similar to working with immigrant clients, therapists may struggle with understanding slang terms. Clinicians may also assume that clients who do not speak standard English are illiterate or unintelligent or have difficulties learning.

TOOLBOX ACTIVITY—CARLA			
Resources and Suggested Readings	*Web Sites*	*Activities*	*Discussion Questions*
Kotlowitz, A. (1992). *There are no children here: The story of two boys growing up in the other America.* New York: Anchor. Minuchin, P., Colapinto, J., & Minuchin, S. (1998). *Working with families of the poor.* New York: Guilford Press.	www.hud.gov www.doleta.gov/wtw/	You are a single parent planning to attend the local community college this year with the goal of transferring to a four-year college in two years. You are currently receiving Food Stamps and a housing subsidy and have a part-time salary of $9,000. Two courses cost $600. Plan a monthly budget including costs for housing, utilities, food, child care, transportation, entertainment, and miscellaneous expenses. Research the application process for public housing and public welfare programs in your state. Research the application process for unemployment.	Content Themes What other themes do you see emerging in the story that the author did not identify? Assessment Are there any questions you would like to ask Carla? Interventions What other interventions could you propose with Carla? Countertransference What countertransference reactions were emerging in yourself as you read this story? Other Scenarios Imagine that Carla is coming to you several years ago or several years from now with a presenting problem. What might that presenting problem be?

Anthony's Story 16

From Radical to Bohemian to Suit Me

Our social class status distinguishes us from other people, yet it is sometimes so invisible that, although differences between us are recognized, we do not attribute them to class. The differences in class and socioeconomic status begin in childhood. For example, there are certain brands of blue jeans or sneakers that children just "must have" because everyone is wearing them. Other differences can be seen at lunch in the cafeteria, through distinctions between the meals purchased through free lunch programs to homemade meals of peanut butter sandwiches or left-over veal. It is clear that some people are poor: they seem to be unkempt, may smell, and have to eat free lunches. And it is equally clear that some are rich: they drive their own cars to high school. These are the visible differences that are superficial, and although they are at times linked to popularity or attractiveness, social class issues are not generally labeled as such. But it is important to recognize that social class is also linked to values, standards, and norms for behaviors, less visible characteristics.

Individuals are socialized within a particular social class structure. Although social class is fluid, the values associated with it are developed through childhood socialization (Robinson, 2005). Social class is linked to values, including the importance of education, vocation, and achievement. Class is related to interpersonal relationships, influencing the activities people share. Relationships with authority figures, whether they are treated with respect or disdain, are often determined through social class socialization. Socialization begun in childhood is reinforced in high school, as adolescents begin to make decisions on vocational aspirations and college attendance. Decisions are often based on parental income level, the perception of opportunities, role models within the community, and family expectations. When people are faced with the challenges of adulthood, issues of social class and accompanying values come to the surface.

However, the values of social class may emerge at earlier times in individuals' lives, particularly if change occurs in socioeconomic class levels. The predominant media image is that of a positive change in class standing. Television is filled with shows on which individuals can go from rags to riches. The American dream of being able to own a home and have a family is something that many aspire to. In fact, one of the stereotypes of immigrants is that they come to the United States for economic gain, to be a part of the American dream. Rarely does one think of social class change in the opposite direction: of losing income. But many Americans are laid off, fired, or downsized from their positions. Parents divorce, causing women and children to sometimes move to poverty level. This change in class standing can influence self-concept and identity development. Anthony's story is one of changes within social class. The reader should note the effect that change in social class status has not only on his self-concept and identity, but also on his social activities and interpersonal relationships.

Anthony's Story

An old Italian jibe states, "How do you get an Italian to keep quiet? Easy. Tie his hands behind his back." The truth fundamental to the joke is that Italians are, by and large, an expressive bunch who routinely gesture in their storytelling.

While growing up, I confess, my family expressed their private joys, public triumphs, and collective pain in storytelling. To them, no subject was considered either too taboo or too sacrosanct. Political correctness, a virtue embraced by the larger culture, was largely absent from my family. Decorum was judged by the level of audience interest. Through their frequent retelling, the stories grew in revision and refinement.

At an early age, I was taught that plain-spoken pilgrims and their pursuit of religious freedom shaped America. By inference, they built a dominant culture and extended its benefits to the world. My family, on the surface, appears to embody this story. With historical veracity, I can trace my lineage back to the founding of the nation as a registered son of the Mayflower. This fact, coupled with my Anglo-Saxon-sounding surname, suggests that I am ethnically White. Granted, I realize that by tracing my lineage back to Plymouth Rock, I admit English heritage, but an uncomfortable fact emerges: I can claim only one immediate ancestor in 16 as Anglo-Saxon. That ancestor, my grandfather, is not strictly English himself. He is a mix of English and Black Irish. My name aside, I strain to understand what it means to be White.

As family lore and history books explain, the Black Irish were the survivors of the unsuccessful Spanish naval invasion of England. As fate would have it, they washed up on Irish beaches and married the local girls. In 1930, my grandfather married a Sicilian woman after his arrival from Tennessee. She, an Italian immigrant, had ancestors who emigrated from France in the 1800s. It appears that not all of Napoleon's soldiers returned home after the war.

The lineage on my mother's side is equally as convoluted. My maternal grandfather, a southern Italian, married a Scottish-Hungarian woman. As a result, both my father and my mother grew up in bicultural households with prevailing Italian cultural norms. As a result, I trace my identity back to Italian, Hungarian, Scottish, Irish, English, and French ancestors—Italian American, for short.

The social patterns embedded in an Italian heritage are obvious from the media images. My family is loud, emotionally extravagant, and profligate in storytelling. Communication was, and is, next to impossible without operatic gestures and crescendoing falsettos. To paraphrase Shakespeare in literature and my family in life, "All is but a stage."

Indeed, not only is life a stage but a loud one at that. My family routinely performed at dinnertime. Dinner was both an open forum and, simultaneously, an audition. Moreover, if someone's story became boring and uninteresting, it was then expected, if not required, that another family member save dinner from destruction and take up the reins of conversation. Outside the family, we dichotomized relationships into the tidy categories of family and everyone else. Notwithstanding, different measures of conduct applied. In times of stress, the family turned to itself for strength and excluded the demands of the dominant culture. Usually, this was accomplished through sarcasm and aloof observation. Stock phrases would be taken out of our cultural vault and deployed against any of the dominant culture's claims on our time, our money, or our allegiance.

Not surprisingly and tragically, we became firmly convinced of our own cultural integrity. In retrospect, after making the necessary concessions to the family's fear of change, I have since come to view their traits in terms of strength and resilience, rather than simple fear and ignorance. A few short years into my life and my parents' marriage, they divorced. As a result of their divorce, my family's finances plummeted. A sharp thud later, I awoke to form a fuzzy picture of my financial standing vis-à-vis the other seven-year-olds in the area.

Not long after, as I sat on my front stoop in my Sedgefield jeans with the knees blown wide apart, I collected my thoughts. I quickly reasoned that the new erratic dinner schedule was not due to spontaneity, novelty, and stoicism, nor was it a passionate commitment to child-centered learning. It was a consequence of the divorce. Scarce meals accompanied my mother's erratic work schedule. I plummeted in all the relevant measures of physical fitness: height, weight, and resistance to illness. Other consequences soon followed. Baseball, a pastime in the neighborhood, required strict attention to detail: uniforms, snug caps, well-oiled gloves, and a litany of bats, wooden and aluminum. Moreover, it required a basic understanding of the concept of strike zone, catching technique, and swinging basics. Shell-shocked from my father's rapid exit, I found all this talk overwhelming and alienating. As a result, I shied away from organized sports.

Not long after her divorce, my mother returned to her childhood home with me and my brother in tow. We toddled along, only later becoming aware that our postcard-perfect smiles opened closed doors. My grandfather insisted that he provide a second phone line in his home. Magnanimously and publicly, he trumpeted this as a grand gesture to provide for his children. The sleek burgundy phone with its 10 feet of unspooled line sat on a faux-mahogany table. Later, he used this gift, this phone, to whisper his illicit passion into his mistress's ear. I would often sit in the jagged, dry silence trying to swallow my revulsion.

Implicitly, I understood the exchange: shelter for silence. My grandmother, however, played by another set of rules. Stammering over herself in convoluted emotional somersaults, she lashed out, and my grandfather remained complicit in his silence. Quickly, I became the convenient alibi for his indiscretions and an unwilling accomplice in his attempts to shelter time, money, and emotional availability from his wife, my grandmother. Her legendary rants pierced my already fragile psyche. Before long, and fully realizing the consequences of the Faustian exchange, I simply tuned out. Amid the emotional abuse, willful manipulation, and emasculating atmosphere, I realized the road to happiness would be a bumpy one. To survive, I stripped down my expectations to a bare minimum and deeply buried my emotional needs. I understood that if I could survive until college, I could unpack my troubled identity.

Growing up in such an environment, I attempted to lessen the stigma of poverty by controlling my environment. Initially, I enforced this by not placing myself in any potentially embarrassing situations where my deprivations would be exposed. Often, when confronted with a happy two-parent family with a bright economic future, I ridiculed them. Importantly, it must be noted that rarely were these thoughts verbalized. Eventually, I turned the ridicule inward on myself. Often this cycle culminated in a racing heart rate, a constriction of my vision, and a near blackout.

To cope with what I saw as a debilitating condition, I recast the entire experience into my family's far-left political language. My earliest childhood recollections include a moment where my mother cooed over me: "Who is my little radical?" Prompted, I responded that indeed I was her little radical. With Pink Floyd's "Dark Side of the Moon" wafting in the background, I was strongly encouraged to never work for the corporations because they were evil incarnate.

My mother's idealism, countercultural spin, and politics led her in the early 1970s to entertain some unconventional notions of mainstream culture. In short, a radical group recruited my mother to bomb an abortion clinic. After deliberation, she refused, but only after considering the repercussions on her two infant sons. Her beliefs framed the radical-left character of the family's politics. Later, I trained myself to crucify any hope of economic betterment, and I purged myself of friendships and experiences that could conceivably testify to other alternatives. Surprisingly, I found that poverty was quite resistant and had a life of its own, replete with its self-sustaining mores, norms, and values. By the time I entered college, I began to question my conclusions. As a student in the early 1980s, I unflinchingly sized up the local high school. Consequently, I understood that my future lay elsewhere. Seeking to escape a substandard education, I, along with a handful of resolute ragtag urban city dwellers, clambered onto the bus. We peered out at the passing urban landscape as our bus bent its way to the north transit terminal considered by all Westsiders to be the equivalent of the Brandenburg Gate. There, I exchanged the frayed city green for the crisp suburban blue. After running the gauntlet across the city's edge, I longingly gazed on suburban West Park's ample lawns and sturdy stone homes. I traveled a snug suburban mile to Carnegie College Prep, an academy for the well-heeled. Again, I was the kid with the Anglo last name but misplaced Italian heritage. Even more to the point, as a city dweller, I was regarded as disadvantaged and potentially violent. As a result of having a confused heritage, a questionable pedigree, and a checkered financial legacy, I soon became marginalized and encountered difficulty in assimilating.

Inside the classroom, I adjusted to the academic demands. However, outside the classroom, I strained to find common ground with my classmates because their conversations revolved around experiences beyond my reach. I could not identify with the gated communities, the downtown business internships, and the jaunts to Europe. I felt I needed stories and experiences of my own to counter the wide net cast by Carnegie College Prep. Confused, I tried to put an affirming spin on my shame. Inwardly, I agreed with the stereotypes to create a "violent identity" for myself. I concluded that I would always remain a second-class citizen, a poster child for the downtrodden—in short, a pity project. I hardened my childhood flirtations with alcohol, drugs, and gangs into a more active participation. Working in the city at a local banquet hall opened the door to the purchase, barter, and, often, the outright theft of hard liquor. Jack Daniel's, marijuana, and hash became my drugs of choice, and my friends who passed through the criminal system gave me instant clout in the rarified air of Carnegie College Prep.

In a Conradesque way, I became the anti-wonder-boy of the community. I dealt them alternative stories, beautifully tragic, to counter my own sense of inadequacy. I tried to project myself as an embodiment of their upper-class fears. After years of this borderline self-destructive behavior, I gladly parted with this ill-fitting identity and embraced Christianity. I traded my alcoholic tales and drug-induced visions for a new story of redemption and healing. At last, I felt I had a road map to reconstruct my fractured sense of self. Although I successfully eliminated most of the destructive symptoms of my pain, the root confusion still remained. During the nonthreatening environment of college, I attempted to clarify my struggle. I attempted to patch my identity together with spiritual and aesthetic glue. Comical in retrospect, I endeavored to solve my questions by transcending them.

Clove cigarettes, Echo and his Bunnymen, and late-night Marxism—Bohemia beckoned, and I felt the allure irresistible. In defining myself as an artist, I felt I could leave all the inconvenient talk of heritage, ethnicity, and duty behind and replace it with the lively topics of beauty, inspiration, and class warfare. After my best imitation of Jasper Johns, and an unsuccessful storming of a government building to protest late-night Nicaraguan romps by the Contras, I grew tired of being so countercultural. I concluded that being a Bohemian was a definite dead-ender. Against my better radical judgment, I fancied that there may be something to the tired talk of heritage, ethnicity, and duty. But before beginning a systematic exploration of my roots, I took a 10-year detour through second-generation Asian America.

After college, my childhood imps of despair and fatalism feverishly gnawed on my relationships. I lived with a robust fear of the "spontaneous meal" or the "unplanned movie." I feared if my social encounters drifted into unexpected expenses, I would meet three equally unsettling choices: (1) invent an indecorous excuse; (2) accept someone's charity; or (3) commit myself to an expense I could ill afford. As a result, any sustained effort at intimacy became difficult. A cycle of shame and anxiety danced in my head. I reasoned if I chose friendship over finances, the unexpected would create feelings of worthlessness, a loss of control, and a sense of being less than masculine. After surveying these thoughts, I often returned to the cycle of anxiety and blackouts. So I chose to limit my relationships. With good reason, I equated my singleness with my financial situation.

With an eye on the inevitable emotional hangover, I routinely stayed in on weekends. I reached out to the Christian community, and they thankfully responded. I firmly believe that my God has an incredible sense of humor. He took me, an angry and broken Italian American, and placed me into the tightly woven community of second-generation Korean American Christians. This Asian faith community provided the reliable and predictable behavior I needed to heal my identity, while I deconstructed my Anglo-Italian, liberal, artistic upbringing. In time, and only after receiving much support, wisdom, and healing, I began to test the limits of my adopted culture. Soon, a majority of my social life centered on the Korean community. I became a youth pastor to a Korean church, roomed with a second-generation Korean American, and socialized almost exclusively within the Korean American community. Thankfully, I healed my identity in a community dedicated to the pursuit of truth and harmony. These two ideals balanced the excesses of my heritage. Later, when I became confident of my identity, I found it necessary to separate my ethnic identity from my growing spirituality. That necessitated a break from the Korean American community. Struggling against post-college poverty, I perceived that my socioeconomic position sharply contrasted with my aspiration to be White. I persistently wrestled with my sense of belonging. My pigmentation allowed me to pass for White in the dominant culture, whereas my mannerisms frequently aroused suspicion. Often, I was asked to tone down because I caused distraction. It was explained to me that "most people do not act like that." This variance created in me a desire to further define myself according to my family's radical political legacy. I entertained two questions: "How could I, a second-generation radical, push the envelope beyond the limits set by my former hippie parents?" and, second, and not as crucial to my identity but imperative to my immediate survival: "How can I eat regularly?" Thankfully, I found an acceptable balance of these two competing needs. I betrayed my family's mores, values, and trust. I snapped a conservative navy blazer into place and laced up for success. I decided that I needed to work for the corporations.

Working as an agent, I received a regular paycheck, which alleviated my immediate financial crisis. More important, my job served as a convenient wedge between me and my near-hysterical mother. It allowed me the necessary psychological space to complete my identity formation. Inwardly, I delighted in the shrewdness of my seemingly mundane career choice; I valued it as the pièce de résistance of my post-college identity development. However, in the long run, I could not separate this job from my emergent identity. Eventually, I found the job ill suited for both my temperament and my sense of belonging. Suffice to say, I could not reconcile the White, affluent business world with my ethnic and class understanding. In retrospect, I should have been tipped off by the constant lunchtime dry heaves.

I left the corporate world after a two-year stint and went headlong into teaching. Initially, I resisted the idea because it reflected my father's failings, himself a public school teacher. After, taking inventory of my gifts, talents, and temperament, I realized that the road to healing ran straight through my father's profession.

My six-year journey to teaching was difficult and offered little immediate relief. In my pursuit of my dream, I culled eight meals from my weekly budget, compromised on air quality with my apartment's toxic mold, and studied late into the night amid the sounds of the bustling city rats scurrying under the floorboards.

Undeterred, I courted my present situation with a ripening sense of purpose. I taught for six years as a substitute teacher while pursuing my teaching certificate. While back in school, I separated from both the radical notions of my childhood and the Asian culture that supported my healing. I found peace and a growing sense of my identity.

I left the Asian community to deepen my spirituality. Ironically, as I left, I reconciled with my father and found a faith community that fit both of us. It was there that I met my wife, an Asian American. My wife and I continue to explore our shared bicultural and biracial experience. Importantly, our cultural differences are undergirded by a common faith. The most noticeable differences in our marriage revolve around time management, conflict style, and in-laws. Our conflict with time might humorously be relegated to the time differential between Los Angeles and Seoul. Small underlying conflicts have occasionally spilled into larger cultural messes. My Italian heritage gives full vent to emotional expression. As a result, most of the cultural cues of tone, facial expression, and nonverbal language are readily understood. In the same vein, Korean culture relies on a subsequent series of cultural cues, protracted periods of silence, and nonverbal protocol to express meaning.

To illustrate, my wife and I temporarily shared living space with a couple while our home was being built. While seated on a couch rapt by CNN's coverage of the Second Gulf War, I observed our Korean American friend express, albeit nonverbally, a sense of displeasure. Moreover, as I readily understood her mild displeasure, I intuited it had nothing to do with the war or my viewing of it.

After a quick internal check of possible offenses, I concluded none existed. As a result, I continued watching the broadcast. Later, this friend exploded into unmitigated rage. On the surface, she explained that she was angry that I neglected to bring in the newspaper. It soon became evident that her rage was directed at my reluctance to probe for a more complete understanding of her distress and my unwillingness to respond to her discomfort with a kind act of service. The Korean word "nunchi" expresses this dynamic. From my predominately Italian American understanding, nunchi is tantamount to being held an emotional hostage. My inner Tony Soprano mumbled, "If she's got a problem with me, then she needs to tell me." My cultural paradigm informed me of three things: People need to take responsibility for their own discomfort, responsibility involves expression, and if people choose not to verbally communicate their anger or frustration, then the problem resides with them. In contrast, the Korean concept of nunchi places great emphasis on the nonverbal and demands a response by the recipient. Additionally, the act of verbalizing is viewed as somehow diminishing the value of the exchange. I have since translated nunchi into the more readily understood concepts of being empathic, thoughtful, and proactive. Still, the cultural assumptions of the role verbal expression plays in relationships present ongoing challenges. Returning to the nature of in-laws, I have, of late, more fully embraced my mother-in-law. Our relationship has gone through a series of awkward steps but has culminated into full acceptance with the birth of her grandson. Initially we were on a first-name basis, which reflects the American value of informality. Now, often I refer to her as Chung-mo-nim, the Korean term of respect given by a son-in-law. Occasionally, I refer to her as Nana, my son's version of "Grandmother."

Building on this belief, I have come to understand that my ethnic identity and sociocultural history, along with the indwelling of the Holy Spirit, define me. The answer to my own identity struggle is a complex one. Recently, I have rejoiced in the fact that I can lay claim to a bicultural identity. My identity remains primarily rooted in my faith but is open to new experiences. The intensity and raw emotionality of my Italian heritage are being refined in my marriage to a Korean American. Emotional expressiveness is giving way to thoughtful restraint. Storytelling is ceding ground to acts of service.

Content Themes

Anthony's story is rich with images around social class and socioeconomic status and their influence on self-concept and identity. There are two central themes in the story: the influence of changes in social class and the influence of dominant middle-class values.

CHANGES IN SOCIOECONOMIC STATUS AND SOCIAL CLASS

The first major content theme is the change in social class status that Anthony experienced and the influence of this change on his self-concept and identity. When his parents divorced, it is likely that he dropped from middle-class to working-class status. His mother moved to her parents' home because she may not have been able to afford her own place and perhaps because she wanted to receive child care for her children. It is not uncommon for individuals, particularly women, to move into a household with their parents or extended family members immediately following a divorce to save on housing costs, reduce child care expenses, and receive emotional support. If individuals do not have family for financial support, the change in social standing most likely would be from the middle class to poverty level. Anthony's mother was fortunate to be able to relocate with her parents. Nonetheless, there must have been a drastic change in status because Anthony reports consequences to his physical status.

The changes had effects on Anthony's development and social activities. The initial effect was on his peer relationships in the neighborhood, which seemed to result from changes in family structure and social class. When the children in the neighborhood talked about baseball, Anthony became overwhelmed and began to withdraw. When in high school, Anthony experienced a similar disconnection from his peers. He was not able to associate through the middle- and upper-class activities and discussions.

Anthony felt the other students assumed that, because he was from the city, he was "disadvantaged and potentially violent." He began to construct his identity based on the stereotypes projected onto him and his inability to connect with his peers. Unfortunately, Anthony chose to participate in illicit activities to define himself.

Anthony's transition is similar to the character portrayed by Judd Nelson in the movie *The Breakfast Club*. His peers were all more financially stable and seemed to come from intact nuclear families. To hide his shame and embarrassment, he took on the role of the delinquent. His real personality, of being sensitive, empathic, and caring, was revealed as he spent time with the other characters. Many adolescents who feel alienated and disconnected from the mainstream may choose this path to define themselves; the tough-guy stance serves as protection against rejection and hurt. Had Anthony continued with his behaviors, he may have ended up dropping out of high school or possibly imprisoned. Fortunately, his desire to be able to feed himself helped him to find career direction and to pursue college. Anthony also found solace in the Christian community.

The sense of social isolation continued after college and after he entered the workforce. Anthony decided to reenter school to pursue his teaching career, which left him on a tight budget. He became fearful of being invited out for spontaneous outings because he could not afford meals, movies, or activities outside of his budget. Anthony chose to isolate himself from peers and to remain single due to the shame of his social class position. Unfortunately for Anthony, the pressure to fit within the dominant culture continued through young adulthood, college, and employment. It also continued to influence interpersonal relationships.

DOMINANT CLASS STANDARDS

Anthony begins his story discussing his mixed ethnic heritage and his claim to the Italian American culture. His family sounds as if they were loud and boisterous, shared many heated discussions, and enjoyed each other's company. Of course, even in the introduction, Anthony discusses his relationship with the dominant culture and his feeling of separation from it. Although racially he identifies with being White, it is clear that, for Anthony, his cultural identity is more rooted in his Italian American heritage than in his Whiteness. However, examining his relationship to social class and interpersonal relationships, it is clear that his socialization was influenced by dominant White, middle-class values, which he eventually internalized, even though he fought them earlier.

White middle-class values include the importance of individualism; independence; autonomy, achievement, and competition; the Protestant work ethic; a future time orientation; status and power; and ownership of goods and property (Robinson, 2005; Sue & Sue, 2003). Although some of

Anthony's values may have differed from mainstream values due to ethnic variations, it is also likely that they differed due to social class status. Anthony was able to attend a high school noted for academics and to pursue college, so it is clear that he endorsed the mainstream values of achievement and autonomy. He reported that his college experience was "nonthreatening." When choosing a career, however, the socialization that Anthony experienced influenced his choice, which differed from mainstream values. He reports that his mother was a "hippie" who taught him that valuing money was inappropriate. The notion of status and power and ownership of property, goods, and assets may not have been important or a priority for the family. However, his quest to stay aligned with his family's values contradicted his need to eat and support himself, so he attempted to acculturate to the dominant mainstream values and began to work for a corporation. Working in this environment was unsettling for Anthony, however, and seemed to make him physically sick. The differences in values may have been too overwhelming for him.

Making the choice to leave corporate America and to pursue a teaching career returned Anthony to his working-class status. He followed the Protestant work ethic by attending school to earn his teaching degree, so he meets the dominant standards in some regards. However, few would take the option of leaving a well-paying job to move to a place where rats could be seen or heard, making his choice different from the choice other White middle-class men would have made. One wonders if this option would have been available to him if he were married and had children.

Clinical Applications

This section addresses assessment concerns, techniques and interventions, and countertransference issues.

ASSESSMENT

Social class influences values, standards, and norms for behavior, along with interpersonal relationships. Therapists need to assess clients to determine how they have been socialized regarding class. Therapists also need to assess changes within generations, as well as within individual lifetimes, regarding socioeconomic status. Clinicians may also want to assess how social class influences interpersonal relationships and their clients' internalized classism. Internalized classism can manifest itself in "anger, frustration, feelings of failure, anxiety or depression related to not being able to meet the demands of his or her economic culture" (Liu, Soleck, Hopps, Dunston, & Pickett, 2004, p. 109).

The following assessment questions are recommended:

What is your current social class level?

Has there been a change in your social class?

Have you recently received a promotion or raise at work?

Have you been downsized, laid off, or fired?

Has there been a change in your family's social class?

What messages did your parents or other family members give you regarding finances or economics?

Were you encouraged to save money or plan for the future?

What messages did you receive regarding education, achievement, or career aspirations?

How were your relationships influenced by your socioeconomic status?

To assess internalized classism, the following questions are recommended:

How do you view your own social class in relation to your friends, neighbors, or relatives?

Has that view change over time or did it remain the same?

How comfortable or uncomfortable are you with members of a different social class?

How do you feel about disclosing your social class status to other people?

How do you understand the reasons for your economic successes or your failures?

TECHNIQUES AND INTERVENTIONS

Anthony's story teaches about the influence of social class on self-concept and interpersonal relationships. Clinicians need to be sensitive to changes in social class and how the changes influence functioning. A number of techniques are recommended for treatment.

Dominant Values

First, clinicians need to address social class norms and standards and help clients who feel as if they differ from the norms. Middle-class values predominate in the media, along with the drive for consumerism, and influence self-concept and self-esteem. Clinicians should help clients understand how their socialization experience, values, and self-concept are related to social class. Exploring childhood experiences around social class might be a useful way of helping clients elicit values related to class. Focusing on clothing, toys, games, and accessories may be a useful way for clinicians to begin. Children are socialized early about the importance of material goods; in preschool, friendship changes based on who has the best new toy. By school age, children use ownership of goods as a way to assess worth and to measure self-esteem. These messages may be supported by parents, who often go into debt to buy extravagant gifts for children during holiday seasons and birthdays; even birthday parties are becoming expensive affairs, with goody bags and treats for children who attend. The macrosystem and general cultural ideology of consumerism reinforce these values. Helping clients explore the relationship between their self-concept and their class-related values may elicit an awareness previously not present of how they go about selecting their mates, their careers, and other lifestyle options and how these choices are intimately related to their socialization and to their social class. For example, clients often consider themselves "less than" in terms of their social class standing and their background and may wrongly assume that they do not have access to certain professions or future mates, solely based on a self-deprecating view of themselves and on their social class. A woman with a professional degree who was raised in a working-class environment may feel that she is not a suitable partner for a professional man raised in the upper middle class, although their current social class is the same. Others may consider themselves "more than" and avoid making a professional or occupational choice because they may consider themselves above it. For example, executives who are downsized may refuse to accept employment below a certain salary level or a particular job title.

Many dual-career families may feel like failures because they cannot obtain the same status that previous generations could obtain living on one income (Kliman, 1998). As disparities in income grow and media images continue to depict upper-middle-class comfort that few people can afford, therapeutic conversations about historical phenomena and class disparities may help normalize this issue and decrease shame for these couples and families. Having clarifying conversations with clients can be revealing and life changing.

Clients should also be encouraged to discuss educational and career goals and their relationship to social class. The Protestant work ethic is part of mainstream culture, along with the notion of the importance of achievement, accomplishment, and status. Again, children are socialized with these messages and, therefore, may be encouraged to prepare for standardized tests and to begin to think of a vocation at an early age. Clinicians should discuss individuals' career expectations and aspirations, especially when working with adolescents, because these aspirations and expectations may differ based on social class. For example, a teenager growing up in an urban inner city may aspire to become a physician. However, due to expectations about the cost of college and medical school, the lack of role models within the community, and the lack of access to information regarding available scholarships, the adolescent may decide that pursuing college is an impossible dream. Clients of all ages should be assisted in finding resources to pursue career aspirations and vocational goals.

Budgets

Many live with high levels of debt; it is easier to buy items on credit today than at any other point in history, an effect of the interaction of the macrosystem ideology of consumerism and the chronosystem in which consumer spending is seen as the answer for economic recessions and slowdowns. Although it may feel outside the arena of treatment, therapists should explore financial wellness with clients. Teaching clients how to balance a checkbook and avoid credit card debt can be an important tool for fiscal responsibility. Clients should also be encouraged to develop reasonable and manageable budgets for living expenses. Living in debt, with the fear of being pursued by creditors, can create undue stress and pressure for individuals. As we saw in Anthony's story, it can also lead to a sense of social isolation. Clinicians should refer clients to reputable nonprofit credit counseling agencies. Therapists must be cautioned that the cost of therapeutic services can exacerbate the financial stress clients face. Even if clients make a small copayment, the cost of therapy should be carefully considered and included in budgets. Therapists are encouraged to follow suggestions present in many of the ethical codes and consider providing pro bono services; this may be a preferred option, along with a reduced fee, for clients who are in need of treatment services but are experiencing financial stress.

COUNTERTRANSFERENCE

It is tempting for counselors to avoid or ignore issues of social class in the counseling relationship when counselors perceive themselves as being of the same social class as their clients. However, it is important for counselors not to assume that their clients share similar worldviews and expectations, even if they are perceived to belong to the same social class. Hearing stories such as Anthony's can elicit emotional reactions in clinicians, including sadness and sympathy for his social class differences and confusion about his financial choices. The importance of mainstream middle-class values and their influence on counseling also need to be addressed. Anthony experienced social isolation throughout school based on his perception of alienation from his peers. Clinicians who have experienced a similar sense of isolation based on social class may over-identify with clients such as Anthony. This hinders therapists' ability to display genuine empathy for clients. Therapists who were socialized and raised in the middle and upper classes may associate clients such as Anthony with delinquent or criminal behaviors. Stereotyping clients also hinders the development of the therapeutic relationship.

Differences in Values

Therapists may feel confused about Anthony's decision to struggle financially by leaving a job in a corporation to pursue a teaching degree. Becoming wealthier seems to be a part of the mainstream values because status, power, and financial gain are valued. Individuals with education who choose to live in poverty are viewed as deviant. "Being poor in American society and staying poor is not valued. Being poor and then becoming rich is often admired; the values of hard work, pulling oneself up by one's bootstraps, change, and perseverance are showcased" (Robinson, 2005, p. 178). Special care may have to be taken to work with clients whose value systems differ from mainstream middle-class norms. Therapists need to determine what is "normal" according to their social class socialization and how that perception of normal influences their perceptions of clients.

Finally, clinicians should remember that counseling occurs within a particular context and follows mainstream values (Sue & Sue, 2003). In addition to valuing independence and autonomy in individuals, counseling reinforces the notions of hard work, perseverance, and self-control. This includes the concept that change is the responsibility of clients and emphasizes an internal locus of control. Clients whose cultural values are different from mainstream values may expect different approaches to treatment.

Classism

Counselors have to address their own reactions to social class and classism. Social class is related to classism, which is defined as prejudice directed toward someone of a different social class. Downward classism is the typical classist idea, involving prejudice and discrimination against people perceived to be in a lower social class. But individuals can also express upward, lateral, and internalized classism (Liu, et al., 2004), paralleling issues with racism. Counselors need to assess their own level of internalized classism and examine whether downward, lateral, or upward classism is present in interactions with their clients.

TOOLBOX ACTIVITY—ANTHONY		
Resources and Suggested Readings	*Activities*	*Discussion Questions*
Ehrenreich, B. (2002). *Nickel and dimed: On (not) getting by in America*. New York: Owl Books. Shipler, D. K. (2004). *The working poor: Invisible in America*. New York: Knopf.	Conduct a values auction. Determine which values are most important to you and how they are related to social class (see Pedersen & Hernandez, 1996). Write an essay about the social class values you hold and their influence on your professional work as a provider of social services.	Content Themes What other themes do you see emerging in the story that the author did not identify? Assessment Are there any questions you would like to ask Anthony? Interventions What other interventions could you propose with Anthony? Countertransference What countertransference reactions were emerging in yourself as you read this story? Other Scenarios Imagine that Anthony decided to remain in his corporate position for fear of being poor. How would you help him deal with his stress?

Section VI

Dimensions of Sexual Orientation

Sexual orientation is the romantic, sexual, or emotional attraction to another person. It is important to distinguish sexual orientation from other concepts with which it is often confused. Sexual orientation is different from biological sex, which refers to the physical sexual characteristics with which people are born. Sexual orientation is also different from gender identity, which is the psychological sense of being male or female. Finally, sexual orientation needs to be distinguished from the term gender, which can be defined as the socially constructed adherence to cultural norms for feminine and masculine behavior, thoughts, and feelings (Answers to your Questions, n.d.).

Sexual orientation cannot be viewed as a dichotomous variable since it exists along a continuum that ranges from exclusive homosexuality to exclusive heterosexuality and includes various forms of bisexuality (Answers to your Questions, n.d.; Elze, 2006; McClellan, 2006). The traditional polarization of sexual orientation into two discrete categories, homosexuality and heterosexuality, leaves out bisexuality and other sexual orientations (Division 44, 2000). An understanding of the differences among gender identity, gender expression, and sexual orientation is important. Sexual orientation refers to one's sexual attraction to men, women, or both, whereas gender identity refers to one's sense of oneself as male, female, or transgender, and gender expression is the behavioral expression of either the gender identity or the sexual orientation (Answers to your Questions, n.d.).

This section is divided into two subsections. The first subsection, Heterosexuality, Homosexuality, and Bisexual Gender Orientations, focuses on gay, lesbian, and bisexual orientations and contains an introduction to these topics followed by the story of Karen, a woman who found out, after having been married for several years, that she was attracted to another woman. We read about her journey toward self-knowledge, self- expression, and self-acceptance. The second subsection, titled Transgender and Intersex Sexuality, focuses on transgender and intersex issues and contains an introduction to these topics, followed by a story written by the mother of a transgendered child, in which we read about the transformation of Ryan into Rachel. Each story has its own Content Themes and Clinical Applications sections, and each includes its own Toolbox Activity.

Heterosexuality, Homosexuality, and Bisexual Gender Orientations

Homosexuality can be defined as the orientation of people who "identify inwardly as male or female in accordance with their genitals, and whose primary erotic attraction is to their own sex" (Johnson, 2004, p. 79). People with a heterosexual orientation are commonly referred to as straights, and people with a homosexual orientation are sometimes referred to as gay (both men and women) or as lesbian (women only). Bisexual individuals can experience sexual attraction to both their own and the opposite sex, regardless of their behavior (McClellan, 2006).

The best estimate of individuals who are gay or lesbian in the U.S. was made by Alfred Kinsey in his study of sexuality in the 1940s and 1950s. Kinsey's data suggest that 10 percent of the U.S. population was homosexual (Miller, 1995). More recent data suggest that anywhere between 2 percent and 10 percent of the population is gay or lesbian (Smith & Gates, 2001). It is difficult to estimate the number of people who identify as gay, lesbian, or bisexual, because there is a fear of discrimination or victimization by identifying as other than heterosexual (Smith & Gates, 2001). The "Don't ask, don't tell" policy in the United States military, which advocates for hiding one's sexual orientation in order to serve in the military (Gates, 2004) mirrors the written or unwritten policies in work, family, and social environments where people do not feel free to reveal their sexual orientation.

HISTORICAL DATA

Same-sex intimacies have been documented in all historical periods. Same-sex eroticism was considered acceptable and expected at some historical times and places and condemned in others (Tully, 2000). By the end of the Middle Ages, homoerotic activity was equated with sodomy, which was considered a sin (Tully, 2000). As homosexuality began to be understood as a biological expression in the 19th century, public attitudes looked to science to explain and eventually condemn homosexuality (Moses, 1982). Although same-sex behavior has always existed, sexual orientation is a relatively new concept, and the idea of homosexuality as a category is only about 100 years old (GLBT Fact Sheets, n.d.; Roseneil, 2002; Tully, 2000). Homosexuality was often referred to as the practice of the "invert," the "third sex," and the "intermediate sex" until 1869 (Miller, 1995). These terms reflect an evolution in 19th-century thought from a "moral and religious attitude toward same-sex relations to a scientific one" (Miller, 1995, p. 13). Homosexuality went from being considered a sin to a medical and scientific category (Miller, 1995) viewed as deviant, pathological, and criminal (Moses, 1982). The term "homosexual" was first used in 1869 by a German campaigner for decriminalization of sexual relations between men (Miller, 1995). The creation of this term, however, did not mean acceptance.

Homosexuality as a category meant a medical condition in need of a cure. Freud contributed to this view by theorizing that homosexuality was caused by arrested development at an early developmental stage that prevented the young man or woman from reaching the developmental goal of heterosexuality (Miller, 1995). Freud did contend, however, that everyone is innately bisexual, and rejected the idea that it was possible to transform homosexuals into heterosexuals, which was an unusually tolerant position for his time. He considered that sexual orientation was *both* constitutional *and* at the same time acquired during the early developmental years. He believed sexual orientation to be well established before adolescence and that attempting to change it was neither a feasible nor a desirable goal of therapy. Freud was convinced that it was as difficult to change the sexual orientation of gays or lesbians as it was to change the sexual orientation of heterosexuals. He was also sure of the bisexual disposition in all people, regardless of their sexual orientation (Gay, 1989; Miller, 1995). Freud's view of arrested development, however, contributed to the belief that homosexuality is, therefore, learned and can be cured. The medical-oriented approach resulted in viewing gayness in terms of mental illness with a slant toward rehabilitation (Moses, 1982). Treatments that were often forced upon patients included induced seizures, nausea-inducing drugs, electroshock, covert sensitization, having gay men masturbate while viewing pictures of a nude woman, lobotomies, castration, and implantation of "normal" testes (Hunter & Hickerson, 2003). The members of the early American psychiatric establishment maintained that homosexuality could be corrected with treatment until 1973, when the American Psychiatric Association altered its position by declaring that homosexuality is not a mental disorder. The classification of homosexuality as a mental disorder was not changed until the 1987 revised edition of the DSM-III (Hunter & Hickerson, 2003).

Currently, conversion therapies or reparative therapies are practiced and encouraged (Spitzer, 2003), even though they have been rejected as unscientific by the American Psychological Association (DeLeon, 1998), the American Psychiatric Association, the American Psychiatric Association Commission (2000), the American Counseling Association (Whitman, Glosoff, Kocet, & Tarvydas, 2006), and the National Association of Social Workers (Hunter & Hickerson, 2003). Not only are conversion therapies scientifically unproven, but serious ethical questions arise when using a form of therapy that may be harmful to clients. The American Psychiatric Association board noted that conversion therapy can cause depression, anxiety, and self-harming behavior and voted in 1998 to renounce any therapy with the goal of converting gay and lesbian individuals (Hunter & Hickerson, 2003).

"Gay" is a term generally used to describe men who are attracted to, or sexually involved with, someone of the same sex. It came into use within the subculture in the 1920s, and became used by the general public in the U.S. after Pearl Harbor (Miller, 1995). Lesbian is a term used to describe women who are attracted to, or sexually involved with, someone of the same sex. In the Victorian era, lesbianism was known as "romantic friendship," and in the 1950s as "the love that dare not speak its name." The term "lesbian" came into popular use in the early 20th century (Faderman, 1991, p. 139). Bisexual experimentation gained popularity in the 1920s as the Victorian era faded, a new rebellious culture emerged, people took notice of Freud's assertion of all human beings' bisexual nature, and World War I created a culture of separate sexes (Faderman, 1991). Sociological research in the 1930s and 1940s led to the view of gays and lesbians as social deviants, which pointed to environmental causes for the deviance (Moses, 1982).

The rise in social activism movements spawned by the civil rights movement is a recent development. The gay liberation movement was born at the time of the Stonewall Rebellion of 1969 in Greenwich Village, which was an important historical marker of the gay civil rights movement (Miller, 1995). After years of police raids on gay bars and harassment by the police, the patrons of the Stonewall Inn fought back during a police raid on June, 28, 1969 that spurred a three-night riot between the police and the crowd at the Stonewall Inn. While homosexuality, bisexuality, and transgender issues are "coming out of the closet" (Blumenfeld, 2000, p. 261), so is the backlash against this trend. Hate crimes against lesbians, gays, bisexuals, and transgenders are on the rise (PFLAG, n.d.).

CURRENT VIEWS ON GENDER SOCIALIZATION AND SEXUAL ORIENTATION

The relationship between sexuality, sexual orientation, and gender is a complex one involving multiple cultural, biological, social, cultural, and genetic aspects (Birke, 2002). Current scholarship regarding gender social-ization generally reveals a description of a permanent interaction between biological and cultural/constructivist perspectives (Mitchell & Black, 1995). Gender socialization is understood as a complex psychological and social construction, not as a simple extension of either anatomically based reproductive capacities or brain physiology. In terms of gender socializa-tion, this means that people are not only born as male or female, but "learn to be women and men" (Lorber, 2000, p. 204) in reciprocal interactions between anatomy, social expectations of male and female behavior, and other complex, gender-based socialization experiences, such as gender role expectations and gender role responsibilities (Moses, 1982). Genes, hor-mones, and biology contribute as much as social practices to the construc-tion of gender socialization. It is now understood that, as with anything else that is human, gender identity cannot be thought of as devoid of the influence of culture.

With respect to sexual orientation, there is controversy in the medical and social science literature regarding the importance of determining its causes. The controversy surrounding the origins of sexual orientation has strong political, religious, and social implications. Research on the origin of sexual orientation shows contradictory and inconclusive data. Scientists do not know what "causes" homosexuality, any more than they know what "causes" heterosexuality. The complex interactions among genes, sex hor-mones, prenatal, and environmental determinants has not been eluci-dated. The idea that early exposure to homosexual experiences or that exposure to early homoerotic abuse leads to later homosexual develop-ment is generally not supported in the scholarly literature (Butke, 2002; Johnson, 2004), though childhood sexual abuse can accelerate or retard identification of a gay sexual orientation (Arey, 2002). There is some evi-dence that suggests that biological or genetic markers and brain structural differences for sexual orientation may exist (Birke, 2002; Johnson, 2004). In addition to genetic and other biological factors, it is suspected that a multitude of environmental and psychosocial factors may have a profound influence on the sexual differentiation of the brain, and later, on the devel-opment of children and adolescents (Birke, 2002). There is also some indi-cation that the biological and environmental mechanisms underlying homosexuality may be different for males and females and for people with a bisexual orientation (Esterberg, 2002).

Regarding the need to understand the origins of homosexuality, impor-tant questions arise. If homosexuality were not a stigmatized behavior, would there be an interest in finding out the reasons for its origin? Why is there not a similar push to find out the reasons for heterosexuality? If het-erosexuality was not viewed as the norm, from which homosexuality devi-ates, would the question: "What makes people gay?" have any meaning at all? There is a lot at stake in the answers to these questions. Some supporters of gay rights contend that finding the genetic markers of homosexuality would end the controversy and advance the gay rights cause by reducing discrimination and putting an end to the idea that homosexuality can be contagious (Birke, 2002). Other scholars contend that, on the contrary, focusing on the causes and origins of homosexuality is itself a homophobic activity that merely reinforces the prejudices. From that point of view, "What makes people gay?" is not an important or even a relevant question (Blades, 1994).

To frame the issue of homosexuality as one that oscillates between biological determinism and social constructionism only is to attempt to simplify the complexity of the issues. Some examples of that complexity follow. First, there may be numerous forms of homosexuality and heterosexuality. Some authors contend that homosexuality is fixed and cannot be changed or consciously chosen (Answers to your questions, n.d.; Butke, 2002). Other authors argue that sexual orientation is fluid and that people can fall anywhere along a continuum (Roseneil, 2002), and that "there is not a homosexuality, but homosexualities" (Nardi, 2002, p. 46). Second, sexual behavior cannot be the only dimension considered; fantasy, sexual attraction and desire, love, self-identification, and culturally sanctioned expectations and behaviors also need to be taken into consideration. Third, there is diversity within sexual orientations and there can be different typologies of gays, lesbians, or bisexuals. For example, in "Latin bisexuality" found in some Latin American societies, men may engage in overt same-sex behavior, and as long as men play the active or "insertive" role, they are not considered homosexual (Esterberg, 2002, p. 219).

For most people, sexual orientation emerges in early adolescence without any prior sexual experiences. It appears that men, on average, know that they are gay earlier than women (Arey, 2002). Many men and women generally report knowing they were gay from very early on, but some women awaken to their lesbian sexual orientation later in life. It is unclear whether a post-adolescent awakening is even possible, whether it is a result of the denial and repression of earlier homosexual feelings or tendencies, or whether it is a reflection of differences between men's and women's origins of homosexuality (Esterberg, 2002).

The lack of full consensus surrounding many of the issues about sexual orientation is a reflection of the lack of available knowledge, but is also a reflection of the profound social, cultural, and political implications of each position.

Clinical Considerations

When counseling gay, lesbian, or bisexual (GLB) clients or their families, it is important for clinicians to take into account several considerations.

HOMOPHOBIA

As a sexual minority, GLBs are at high risk of stigmatization, discrimination, marginalization, and violence (Tully, 2000; Swan, 1997). Blatant discrimination has existed under authoritative pretexts, and excluded many from military service, employment, and housing. Sometimes GLBs suffer at the hands of their own parents, siblings, and other close relatives. As with members of other oppressed groups, there has been historical hostility and stigmatization of those who have not identified as heterosexual, considered to be the norm with which homosexual and bisexual orientations are compared. The persecution and oppression are often based on religious grounds, but also on scientific ones. As with other oppressive experiences, homophobia can become internalized, exerting its influence from within by instilling shame, self-hatred, and self-deprecating behaviors, influencing self-acceptance and the expression of same-sex sexual feelings. When counseling GLB clients, it is important to assess homophobic experiences and the presence of internalized homophobia.

ETHNICITY AND SEXUAL ORIENTATION

The importance of the intersection between gay or lesbian identity and ethnic minority status cannot be overlooked. Latinos and Latinas, African Americans, or Muslim gay, lesbian, or bisexual people are considered minorities within minorities and experience multiple layers of oppression (Harper, Jernwall, & Zea, 2004; Meyer, 1995; Parks, Hughes, & Matthews, 2004). There is data supporting the fact that much of the violence, discrimination, and marginalization against ethnic minority gay men and lesbians is perpetrated at the hands of their own families (Azimi, 2006; Hunter & Hickerson, 2003; Tully, 2000). Because of cultural values, fear of shaming their families, and negative views of homosexuality, many gays and lesbians may hide their same-sex behaviors, and lead double lives (Hunter & Hickerson, 2003).

In ethnic groups with conservative religious or family values, the issues around coming out are more complicated. There is some indication that minority youth identity formation may be delayed (Rosario, Schrimshaw, Hunter, & Brown, 2004). The representations of homophobia and internalized homophobia have their own characteristics that are embedded in the cultural characteristics of a particular individual (Sanchez, Liu, & Vilain, 2006). Gays or lesbians who belong to an ethnic minority may be less likely to come out to peers, family members, or in the workplace, leading a more isolated or ostracized life (Morales, 2006). For a Latino gay man, for example, who wants to stay connected with his family, but has internalized the message of the injunction that machismo means "do not be like a woman," hiding his sexual orientation from his family members may be more adaptive than coming out for fear of being rejected. Latino and Latina gays or lesbians may defer coming out indefinitely for fear of hurting their families or to avoid disapproval (Hunter & Hickerson, 2003; Morales, 2006).

In many Muslim countries, homosexuality is against the law and criminalized. Gay Muslims often engage in marriages of convenience or marry lesbians. This is not unusual, considering that homosexual men are often beaten, tortured, and forced to become informants of other homosexual men (Azimi, 2006). Also, because the rights of the family are considered to be above the rights of individuals, many Muslims would not consider depriving their families of honor and pride or risk engulfing them in public shame (Azimi, 2006).

Gay men of color are often subject to racism within the gay community and may find it more difficult to find social support (Ryan & Gruskin, 2006). This added component may further compound the need among men of color to hide their sexual orientation.

SUICIDE AND SUBSTANCE ABUSE

It appears that gays, lesbians, and bisexuals are more at risk of suicide and substance abuse than the general population. A study that included 5,000 homosexual men and women revealed that 40 percent of adult gay males and 39 percent of adult lesbians had either attempted or seriously contemplated suicide (Jay & Young, as cited in McFarland, 1998). Another study reported that gay and lesbian adolescents were two to three times more likely to attempt suicide and may account for as many as 30 percent of completed youth suicides each year (Gibson, as cited in MacFarland, 1998). Higher rates of suicidality may be due to fear of parental rejection, lack of coping skills, exposure to homophobia, and internalized homophobia.

The GLB community is also at higher risk of substance abuse. In a study by Cochran, Ackerman, Mays, & Ross (2004), consistent patterns of elevated drug use by gay men and lesbians were found to exist. Gay men and lesbians have a higher prevalence of abuse and problems associated with illicit drugs (Cochran, Ackerman, Mays, & Ross, 2004). The most commonly used substance was marijuana, although daily use of marijuana and cocaine was found to occur more among homosexual men than heterosexual men (Cochran, et al., 2004). Substance use also provides unique counseling concerns because of the increased chance for engaging in high-risk sex while using (Hirshfield, Remien, Humberstone, Walavalkar, & Chiasson, 2004). Hirshfield, et al., (2004) also reported that human immunodeficiency virus (HIV) transmission among homosexual men had increased 17 percent since 1999. The use of drugs to enhance sexual experiences, such as ecstasy, crystal meth, and poppers, has been associated with high-risk behaviors during sexual experiences, such as engaging in unprotected sex (Hirshfield, et al., 2004). Cheng (2003) states that "(al)though lesbians and gay men have a higher rate of substance abuse compared to that of the general population, only 1% of the clients of substance abuse programs identify themselves as being gay or lesbian."

Homophobia is part of the reason that many in the GLB community do not seek mental health counseling or substance abuse counseling. Substance use may be a way to combat tension created by external homophobia and to lessen one's own negative feelings toward the self (Cheng, 2003). It is important to assess suicidal ideation and substance abuse in the GLB client population.

HIV

The HIV epidemic continues to devastate countless gay men and their families, friends, and partners. The HIV epidemic surged through the gay community in the 1980s, and out of 8,797 persons infected by 1985, 70 percent were gay and bisexual men (Miller, 1995), and as many as 50 to 60 percent of sexually active gay men tested positive for HIV. The risk factors for transmission of HIV were found to be contact with body fluids, blood, or blood products, and the sharing of hypodermic needles (Miller, 1995). Currently, men who have sex with men still have the highest rates of HIV infection in the U.S. (Ryan & Gruskin, 2006). The Centers for Disease Control and Prevention reported that more than half of the HIV infections among young men in 2000 were due to same-sex contact (Ryan & Gruskin, 2006). Young adults seem to be a very high-risk group, accounting for four in five cases of sexually transmitted diseases (STDs) (Ryan & Gruskin, 2006). Ryan & Gruskin (2006) discuss another high-risk group: men with same-sex partners who identify as heterosexual, particularly men of color. The Centers for Disease Control and Prevention indicated in 2000 that of 8,000 men of color, up to 24 percent of African American men and 15 percent of Latino men had same-sex partners, identified as heterosexual, and often did not disclose same-sex behaviors to their female partners (Ryan & Gruskin, 2006). When GLBs lead double lives, they are putting themselves and their partners at risk (Dube, Savin-Williams, & Diamond, 2001; Ryan & Gruskin, 2006).

Due to the risk of HIV infections, it is important to assess disclosures regarding sexual orientation and the losses of a GLB in a clinical situation. Many people have lost friends, partners, and relatives. It is also important, therefore, to assess depression stemming from losses, and anxiety about the HIV diagnosis.

GAY AND LESBIAN YOUTH

Adolescent gays and lesbians are at higher risk of suicide, substance use, abuse, and homelessness than their heterosexual peers (Hunter & Hickerson, 2003). Factors such as disrupted peer relationships, family conflict around disclosure of sexual orientation, struggles with GLB sexual identity, feelings of isolation, being a target for discrimination, harassment, violence due to sexual orientation, and having anxiety about sexual health are all stressors that could contribute to a GLB youth's risks. One study found that gay and lesbian adolescents accounted for up to 30 percent of completed youth suicides per year, and were two to three times more likely to attempt suicide than their heterosexual peers (McFarland, 1998; Hunter & Hickerson, 2003).

Reasons for homelessness include being expelled from the home by parents and running away from home (Hunter & Hickerson, 2003). Studies in Los Angeles and Seattle estimate that between 25 and 40 percent of runaway and homeless youth are gay (Hunter & Hickerson, 2003). Hunter & Hickerson (2003) cite studies that indicate the additional risks of being homeless for these youth such as: "... they are likely to be overtaken by assaults and sexual exploitation, drug usage, prostitution, pregnancy, criminal activity, or HIV" (p. 325). A study by Rotheram-Borus and colleagues found that GLB youth subjects, compared to subjects in national surveys, had lifetime prevalence rates of substance use that were 50 percent higher for alcohol, three times higher for marijuana, and eight times higher for cocaine or crack (as cited in Hunter & Hickerson, 2003). Compound the homelessness of GLB youth and substance use, and the findings are even more devastating. In a study by Shifrin & Solis of 72 homeless gay youth and 3 homeless lesbian youth, 100 percent were addicted to crack or cocaine. Hunter & Hickerson (2003) state: "(c)hemicals numb anxiety and depression and act as antidotes to the pain of exclusion, ridicule, and rejection" (p. 326).

A major drawback of citing these statistics is that the information focuses on the negative aspects of GLB youth, giving the impression that homosexuality invariably leads to unhappiness, suffering, distress, and psychopathology, and not giving a full account of the characteristics of this population (Miceli, 2002). Many GLB youth are politically active, fighting stigma and homophobia, and organizing grassroots movements in schools and other institutions. This activity has the effect of educating GLB youth and results in resilient and strong young men and women. The current viewpoint is that although there are certain risk factors for GLB youth, overall most are able to manage their lives well (Hunter & Hickerson, 2003). Rotheram-Borus & Langabeer (2001) suggest that a shift toward positive attitudes about GLB individuals in mainstream culture may be helpful in alleviating societal pressures in GLB youth. This in turn can empower these individuals as they work through their coming-out issues as they may feel more supported by others in society. Designing programs that help to lessen or remove the stigma of GLB identities could be an important factor in supporting GLB youth (Rotheram-Borus & Langabeer, 2001). Identifying risk factors and addressing these in support groups for GLB youth could be another way to allow for positive identification and acceptance for GLB youth (Hunter & Hickerson, 2003).

HUMAN RIGHTS ISSUES

Another issue of importance when working with gay and lesbian clients is the issue of human rights and legal rights. Gay men and lesbians face discrimination in various arenas, including employment, housing, the military, immigration, student organizations, child custody, and personal relationships (Hunter & Hickerson, 2003); many states still have sodomy laws that restrict consensual sex acts between adults (Hunter & Hickerson, 2003). Knowing about federal, state, and local laws that may restrict gay and lesbian clients is important when helping GLB clients. Counselors must also be prepared to advocate for their clients and their clients' rights from a human rights perspective.

GLB CLIENT/CLINICIAN MATCH

Research on GLB client/counselor match is contradictory and inconclusive. Many GLB clients prefer a counselor of the same sexual orientation. Kaufman & Carlozzi (1997) found that the importance of having a counselor with the same sexual orientation as well as the same gender was more prominent for lesbians than for gay men or bisexuals. The importance of the sexual orientation of the counselor may depend on the presenting issues for counseling. For issues regarding sex-related problems, it may be more important to have a match than for issues such as work-related problems (Kaufman & Carlozzi, 1997). McDermott, Tyndall, & Lichtenberg (1989) found that 49 percent of their sample indicated a preference for a counselor of the same sexual orientation, yet 39 percent reported that sexual orientation of the counselor made no difference.

When working with GLB clients, counselors need to be aware of the process of coming out and the never-ending process of disclosure (Hunter & Hickerson, 2003; Morrow, 2006a). Indication of a good match for GLB clients is a counselor who can provide a safe and nonjudgmental place for GLB clients to work through their feelings; openness and complete confidentiality on the part of the counselor; and the counselor's awareness of community services and resources specific to the GLB community (Hunter & Hickerson, 2003). Sensitivity to the unique concerns of GLB individuals and knowledge of GLB relationships and family issues is also instrumental for a good client/clinician match.

GAY AND LESBIAN COUPLES AND FAMILIES

Gay and lesbian couples and families have unique needs and concerns. Lesbians and gay men are engaged in long-term relationships, having babies, and creating families, redefining commitments and what families can be. Since the 1970s, there has been a substantial increase in the number of children raised by gay and lesbian parents (Bowe, 2006). With few models to draw upon, these couples and families often need the services of clinicians to help them navigate the complicated legal, social, and emotional issues they face in a society that bans or shuns gay marriage and may discriminate against the children of gay couples. Often in the case of gay or lesbian parents who previously had children in a heterosexual marriage, it can be difficult to secure custody or even visitation rights, especially in the case of gay men (Hunter & Hickerson, 2003). The strain and discrimination experienced by gay and lesbian parents, as well as the loss of family and contact with their children, would be important to explore with these clients.

One aspect of heterosexism is the denial by mental health professionals of the unique needs and concerns of GLB individuals, and the insistence of approaching GLB clients with a heterosexist bias (Hunter & Hickerson, 2003), as if there were no differences. When looking at gay and lesbian relationships, counselors will need to examine their own beliefs about gender roles, for example (Moses, 1982). While some GLB couples may be comfortable conforming to gender-typed behaviors and play opposite gender roles, others may differ from traditional heterosexual expectations (Moses, 1982; Morrow, 2006). A counselor who looks at a gay relationship from a heterosexist viewpoint may feel that a couple should fit into opposite gender roles, and frustrate clients who do not view themselves in a specific gender role within the relationship. Hunter & Hickerson (2003) point out that gay and lesbian couples receive little or no validation for their relationships or their families due to heterosexist notions and disapproval of same-gender relationships. Another heterosexist assumption is that both parents are legal guardians of their child. Many times in gay and lesbian relationships, only one parent is the legal guardian, and the other parent may have no legal rights (Hunter & Hickerson, 2003). Gay and lesbian parents often have less support from their communities than do heterosexual couples (Hunter & Hickerson, 2003). This can lead these families to feel isolated, physically and emotionally.

Overall, research has shown that children of gay and lesbian parents experience no significant distinctions or disadvantages when compared to children with heterosexual parents. A study of lesbian and gay stepfamilies found that there were: " . . . unique strengths and flexibility in discovering creative ways to be families that nourish and support all members" (Lynch as cited in Hunter & Hickerson, 2003, p. 180). Patterson's study of 37 children with lesbian mothers indicated that these children were normal in their social competencies and self-concepts, and their sex and gender role behaviors were considered to be typical when compared to normative samples (as cited in Hunter & Hickerson, 2003). In another study by Tasker & Golombok that followed children of lesbian mothers for 25 years, there were no significant differences in mental health difficulties experienced by these individuals as compared to children of heterosexual mothers (as cited in Hunter & Hickerson, 2003). As stated by McKinney (2006), "Children from gay and lesbian families tend to be more tolerant of others, less judgmental, and more open to new experiences than children reared in heterosexual families" (p. 208).

SOCIAL SUPPORT

Counselors can help locate sources of social support for parents of GLB children. Organizations such as Parents, Families, and Friends of Lesbians and Gays (PFLAG) can provide parents opportunities for networking with other parents and gaining a greater understanding of and comfort with their GLB children (Hunter & Hickerson, 2003). Other organizations, such as the Human Rights Campaign (HRC), provide resources for parents, families, and GLB individuals (Morrow, 2006). Connecting parents with these resources and forms of social support can help to lessen feelings of isolation that they may experience. Other referrals for parents could be anger management groups and groups that help develop techniques for resolving disputes and stilted communication (Hunter & Hickerson, 2003). It may also be helpful to approach the child's coming out as GLB as a loss for the parent, and therefore using stages of grief as a model for working through the parent's emotional responses (Hunter & Hickerson, 2003). Availability and use of social support for GLB clients and their families is correlated with better mental health.

RESILIENCY FACTORS

Obviously, not all GLB individuals suffer from depression, anxiety, suicidal ideation, or other mental health issues. With all the oppression, heterosexism, and homophobia that GLB clients face, what helps them to lead happy and productive lives? Perhaps one of the biggest signs of resiliency in the GLB community was the birth of the gay liberation movement in 1969. The GLB community fought back against continual police oppression, and this resulted in a series of riots known as the Stonewall Rebellion, which symbolized the growing voice of the gay community; they would no longer live in secrecy and silence (Tully, 2000). The lambda sign (a symbol used by the gay community) means "dignity in the face of oppression" (Tully, 2000, p. 31). The gay community continued the work of liberation by lobbying to have homosexuality removed from the *Diagnostic and Statistic Manual of Mental Disorders,* and finally achieved this by the 1987 printing of the DSM-III-TR (Hunter & Hickerson, 2003).

Currently, GLB individuals and couples are lobbying for marriage rights and the rights to adopt children. Many are having children and starting their own families. Antidiscrimination laws for the workplace, housing, and education are being passed as a result of the GLB community's efforts for their basic human rights (Hunter & Hickerson, 2003). Community centers in urban areas have been established, as well as mental health centers and medical centers. The GLB community has put forth enormous efforts in the face of the oppression that its members have endured, and through the formation of advocacy groups, social support groups, and social service centers, they persevere and thrive (Hunter & Hickerson, 2003).

Implications for Professionals

Clinicians might work with GLB clients directly or with their siblings, parents, spouses, or children and should be aware of the preceding clinical issues. Professionals need to be comfortable making assessments, asking appropriate questions, and providing help in finding support. Counselors need to be aware of state regulations and ethical guidelines regarding exceptions to confidentiality around issues of HIV and acquired immunodeficiency syndrome (AIDS) disclosures to third parties, and that there are multiple pathways toward the successful synthesis of an individual's sexual identity.

This subsection includes the story of Karen.

Discussion Questions

1. What are the differences between sexual orientation and gender socialization?

2. What are the differences between gender socialization, gender identity, and gender expression?

3. In your view, how important is it to understand the origins of sexual orientation?

4. In your view, how important is it to have a GLB client/GLB clinician match? Are your reasons the same or different than arguing for an ethnic client/counselor match?

5. What steps could you take to increase your level of comfort to work with GLB clients?

Karen's Story 17

Midlife Growing Pains

Karen writes about her 14-year marriage to Steve, the discovery of her attraction to another woman, and the steps she took after that discovery. She tells us about her subsequent relationships, her unfortunate encounters with violence and homophobia, and how she dealt with her family of origin and the work-related issues of her coming out. As you read, notice the fluctuations in her identity awareness.

Karen's Story

At the age of 35, I began another growth spurt. This change crossed many dimensions including physical, cognitive, emotional, social, familial, occupational, and sexual. After 14 years of marriage to Steve, my high school sweetheart, I found myself being attracted to a woman. This attraction was causing me to question my integrity as a woman, a friend, and a married wife. Never before had I felt such incredible exciting stirrings inside, nor such torment. Whether or not to act on these feelings and desires became a weight that I carried with me in all settings. What would this do to my marriage and more importantly my friendship with Steve? What would happen at work, since Gwen, the woman I was attracted to, was a coworker at the school where I was a librarian? What would my friends say? What about family? Is this a choice or is this something that has been building inside of me, remaining dormant until I was ready to face it? Is this love or just lust? Is it the person you love regardless of their gender? Is this adultery if it is with the same sex? Why is God doing this to me? And finally, am I going crazy?

I shared some of my questions separately with Steve and my best friend, Meg. To my amazement, both of them were not surprised that I had this attraction. They had always suspected or at least acknowledged the possibility that I might have lesbian tendencies. This was an incredible surprise to me that they had thought this but had never talked with me about it. I cannot remember ever entertaining the thought but I always found myself open to differences in people, welcoming diversity, enjoying the study of relationships and social interactions in psychology, feminism, humanism, and the role of faith and the values of independence, responsibility, caring, and resiliency. I had strayed from the religious teachings of my Southern Baptist upbringing many years before and preferred a more secular view of faith. This allowed me to attend churches that were welcoming to people from all walks of life and to not pass judgment on others. However, this did not keep me from judging myself.

The conversations Steve and I were to have over the next couple of months became more and more difficult. The stirrings grew. An overwhelming curiosity and desire to explore collided with my devotion to him, my life on the farm, and my fear of what might come. As I moved into the spare room and came home later and later, so that I could spend time just being with her, I could see the toll that this was taking on him. This tender man had supported me emotionally and economically while I worked on my master's degree in library science. He surprised me with weekend getaways to the beach. He held me even when I was writhing in tears over what I was going to do with these feelings. How could I end a marriage that so many of our friends idealized? And that I idealized? The guilt and pressure mounted, but then so did the stirrings.

As I spent time with Gwen during the work week, I began to have an awakening deep inside. Almost as if discovering a part of me that had been waiting for the door to open for the light to come in. I drove away from her on our meetings yearning for both solitude to think it all out and planning for when we could meet next. I began to feel alive in a way I had never felt possible. In my past, I was prone to bouts of melancholy and perhaps a cynical if not pessimistic view of life. This experience was leaving me soaring to heights and depths I never new possible. I was recognizing beauty all around me, feeling fortunate and blessed, tapping into physical energy to function on less than 3 hours of sleep, eating ravishingly or not eating at all and crying in rages of self hate and blame. The full gambit of life revealed.

Whoever said the coming-out process is a spiritual one was correct. Learning who you are as a sexual human being after decades of never having to think about it at all makes you question your whole purpose of life. As I began to redefine myself, my old support systems began to change. I couldn't talk about what was happening to me but to a couple of close friends. As the strain of my actions began to take a toll on my relationship with Steve, resentment, bitterness, and anger began to be the undercurrent of our talks. I moved away from my home on the 85-acre farm within six months to a one-bedroom condo in town. I began a Dr. Doolittle sort of push me–pull me routine with Gwen.

I sought help from conversations with God and a therapist, began taking medicine for sleep, and walked on eggshells around my family and at work. I was not prepared to talk with my parents and siblings and struggled with how to explain why I had moved out.

My family was very supportive of my decisions and never pried. For this I am extremely thankful as I don't know how I would have handled their questions about "why." Being the youngest of four children and sometimes forgotten, more formally educated and the one everyone considered "different" gave me some freedom from the inquisition that others might have in their families. I felt supported by them because "blood takes care of blood" but I did not feel close enough to them to share this part of my life even though all of my immediate family lived in the same town. I'm sure they talked among themselves and wondered why the perfect marriage was failing, but few questions were asked. My parents checked on me routinely and always offered to help if I needed them.

While living in the condo, I spent a good deal of time at Gwen's house. She lived in a very rural setting, which gave me comfort since leaving the woods, river, and meadow of the farm. One drizzly afternoon, we took her dog for a walk down the dirt road past her house. While walking back home we passed a car that had stopped at a bridge over the small river that was full from the rain. Soon after passing the car, it pulled up ahead of us and stopped. We walked on by thinking it unusual but unaware that the man, a stranger in the car, had intentions of harming us. He got out of the car with a baseball bat and struck Gwen in the leg, then came after me. He hit me in the knee as I shoved my umbrella in his face. I yelled for Gwen to run, and we both took off with him following us. Gwen fell down, and I turned to defend both of us. I began talking to him in as calm a voice as I could muster, told her to run and then I began running backwards still telling him that he needed to go home to his family and leave us alone. He finally turned back to his car and we got to her house and locked the door. Physically, Gwen was okay, but I had ligament damage to my knee. Later that night, my father drove both of us to a convenience store where the police had apprehended the attacker and I gave a positive ID. In court, we learned of several previous charges for this man including several for assault on a female. He received more jail time for his assault on us. As we were leaving the courtroom, members of his family called out words of profanity to us intermixed with words like "dyke," "lesbian," and "fags." Was this to be my first experience of sexual orientation discrimination? Even my landlord said to me that there is a lot of hate out there for lesbians when he learned of the crime, but I had never spoken to him about my sexual orientation. Did this mean that I now was attaining the appearance of a lesbian? Was I being outed by just my looks and my presence with Gwen? What was going to happen at work? Could I get fired?

At work I found support not condemnation from the faculty and administration. When I returned to work on crutches, people showed genuine concern for my health and never asked too many questions. My school library colleague was wonderful. She introduced me to feminism and goddess-based faith through tarot cards and readings that I had never encountered before. She opened her home to Gwen and me and began to share more of her personal life with me to help me understand that everyone has questions they are searching answers for. Her husband shared in this support and became a consistent ally. She even spoke individually with a student who was passing a note around about Gwen and I being lesbians. She was an incredible safety net and her understanding allowed me to begin to develop my own understanding of what was happening.

The depth of darkness I found myself slipping into from time to time after leaving the farm was directly related to the fact that I had planned my whole future around my infallible belief that Steve and I would be together as friends, if not husband and wife, forever. When he began dating again, I realized that he could be happy with someone else but that perhaps I couldn't if it meant losing contact with him forever. The woman he was now living with became intensely jealous, and contact with him was stressed and awkward. I wanted to come home, but he was in a different place now, and I had to accept the change.

About three months after the assault incident, Gwen and I moved in together in a small rental house in the country. Anytime you share living space, there are changes and compromises to be made. Here is a journal entry during that first few months together.

June 4—I went for a walk this afternoon looking for nothing but then something. I went up the start of a logging road cut through the woods with poison ivy and all. Then I got on another red clay road to the top of the mountain. At the top I looked around some to check out where I could go next time I wanted to hike. The logging road looked like a big gash that had begun to heal some but had many scars running through it becoming smooth yet jagged in places. I asked the trees if they talked. The response was a cry—not a new cry but a mourning sorrowful one. The woods were still in recovery from the damage done by the road work. The gash and scars were still very sensitive and healing slowly. Yet, the trees had learned that life continued, things were constant as before. The wind still blew, the birds came, and leaves were new and green. It was as though a metaphor existed for me on the ridge. The scars were the changes in my life, the loss of the relationship with Steve, the cuts in my heart. Still very sensitive but healing, recognizing that some things are the same: friends, family, interests, laughter and play. This brings me to wondering why I am reluctant to make a greater commitment to Gwen. I keep trying to hold on to the image of the relationship with Steve as perfect and it is the relationship with Gwen that has created the wound that I now carry as a scar. Yet standing on that ridge with the trees looking at the road, I realize it is the relationship with Steve, the silence, the anger with him and with myself that has created the wound. I keep wanting to blame Gwen for the scar but it's not her. She is one of the constants that helps the woods [me] gain the energy and strength to heal and look beyond the road.

Why can't I let this happen? Maybe it's like the road. My scar is still quite sensitive and changing in its look every day. Maybe once I can go beyond the focus of the scar I can really heal and breathe easy again.

While we were living together, Gwen quit her job to go back to school to become a physical therapist. To the public, family, and some friends we were housemates saving money for other adventures. To our close friends, we were a couple. It was not possible to show public forms of affection as I still worked in the school setting and it just didn't feel safe even in a town as progressive as the one we lived in.

It was on a trip to Atlanta to visit some of Gwen's gay friends that we were able to be more open. It was also on this trip that I learned how to not look gay. We went out to a local restaurant that is frequented by gay men, lesbians, and bisexuals. I began to take notice of the women's hair and clothing. Many of these women did not fit the stereotype. They did not have short hair, rather they had long flowing, permed, curled, bunned, or braided hair. They wore dress suits, makeup, jewelry, skirts, and feminine blouses and carried pocketbooks. I laughed out loud when I realized that I could not tell who was gay and who wasn't. From this experience, I coined the notion that you can tell a lesbian by her haircut, and whether or not she wears a black belt with a silver buckle and carries a pocketbook. I became very conscious of how I dressed, keeping long hair, wearing brown belts, and carrying a pocketbook. I even had people whom I outed myself to say, "No you're not, you don't look or act like one."

The relationship with Gwen lasted for seven years. When I look back on the experience with her, I can sometime feel remorse for the losses I and others endured for me to follow what felt natural. The journal writing during this time of forming a new identity allowed me a chance to express what was heartfelt and sometimes unthinkable to say out loud. The breakup with Gwen left me swirling into a period of self-doubt, condemnation, resentment, and ultimately depression. I allowed myself to become physically sick, dehydrated with rapid weight loss, intense anxiety, and stagnation in my growth. I sought the comfort of friends, my family, therapist (a new one), a church support group, a women's support group, and antidepressants. My whole world was reeling with confusion about direction, questioning of my ability to survive the emotional pain of the loss. Here I had chosen to be in a relationship with a woman that led to the loss of my home, friends, my sense of identity, changes in my approach to work, social settings, and family gatherings, and the dreams of the future I had shaped while married, and now that relationship was over. My whole outlook on life had changed. How could this have happened?

I turned to reading as much as I could on Buddhist beliefs about attachment and letting go, forgiveness, and how to be alone. I didn't like being alone, yet I knew this was what I needed to do to learn how to survive. I reached out to others who were incredibly patient with me. I joined a social organization for lesbians so to meet others and have new lesbian friends to hike and go to the movies with. I sought out lesbian retreats. And yes, I was looking for a companion to fill the void left by Gwen.

At this point I was and am still today not totally convinced that I am a lesbian. My experience with Gwen allowed me to open up to parts of myself that needed to come to the surface if I was to continue to grow as a human being. I find the definition of bisexuality more fitting for me, but then that brings up another set of concerns. No one really wants to hear that you are bisexual because that means you are a frustrated lesbian or you can't make up your mind.

After Gwen I dated some women, entertained the idea of dating a male friend of a friend, flirted a little with people of both genders, and finally decided to enter a doctoral program. I had always talked about wanting to work at the collegiate level even when I was married and just finishing my undergraduate degree. This was the dream of the future I had kept in my head since I was 18 years old. Now at 42, I began to save as much money as possible to make the commitment to a doctoral program without the help of a partner. I found a person who became a friend to share my house with and take care of my pets while I was in school during the week. And in two years, I was through with my coursework and ready to reenter the real world again. It was in November of the second semester I went to a movie with Savannah, a woman whom I had worked for during the summer months. I had stopped looking for "the one" by this time, especially since my studies dominated my time and thoughts. Much to my surprise when I dropped her off after the movie, she asked "Was this a date?" I didn't even know she was interested in women, let alone me. We will be celebrating our third year together this winter as I continue to increase my awareness of my sexual identity. I don't believe sexual orientation is a continuum for me. I think it is much more fluid and especially for women who discover these aspects of themselves later in life. I read a book titled *From Wedded Wife to Lesbian Life* edited by Deborah Abbott and Ellen Farmer and was able to see myself in many of the stories. I have learned that women (and men) at midlife can have growing pains, and we must listen to them in order to know how to heal.

I completed my dissertation on the training of school administrators on issues of sexual orientation and today, I am an assistant principal, and I teach part time at the university about research, multicultural education, and the education of children and adolescents. I rely on my 15 years of experience working in schools to provide examples and scenarios for class discussion. I have also given myself the gift of being out with my students at the university. I realize that I am taking a risk by doing this, but at this time in my life I really don't like hiding who I am. Yet, you will most likely not see me holding my partner's hand in public. Being aware of my surroundings and of the prejudice that exists in many people's views allows me to keep a balance that sometimes is frustrating but very real.

All of my siblings now know of my orientation. My father is deceased and my mother is supportive without asking questions. My longtime friend Meg, who is now the mother of two boys, has told me to feel comfortable showing affection with my partner in front of them. It is so freeing to know that they and others are welcoming of people who are not heterosexual, and that my orientation is seen as only part of who I am. Yesterday I put up grape jelly from my own grapes and tomorrow I will make squash casserole to share with friends who just had a baby. Who knows what next week might bring?

Content Themes

In this story, Karen tells us of her journey of coming out both to herself and to those around her. She shares her difficulty in coming out to her family. Karen also addresses the confusion that she experienced coming to terms with her bisexuality and reveals to us that the process has not completely ended for her. We sense her confusion with labels and her desire to "love whom she loves" regardless of their gender. The final theme that we learn from her story is her shame and internal judgment about who she is becoming.

COMING OUT

The disclosure of sexual orientation, also known as of "coming out of the closet," needs to be understood as a process rather than an event (Morrow, 2006). Coming out is a twin process that involves several areas. First there is coming out to the self, or thinking of oneself as gay or lesbian, and second there is coming out to others, in which one identifies as gay or lesbian to other people (Moses, 1982; Morrow, 2006). The coming-out process can be understood as related to the individual's level of identity development. There are several models of sexual identity formation (Cass, 1979; Coleman, 1981; Fassinger & Miller, 1996; Fox, 1995; Grace, 1992) that conceptualize the development of sexual identity as consisting of stages. When working with GLB adolescents and adults, it is important to understand at what level of identity development they place themselves (Ryan & Futterman, 2001). Cass's sexual identity formation (SIF) model proposes six stages of coming out: (1) Identity confusion; (2) identity comparison; (3) identity tolerance; (4) identity acceptance; (5) identity pride; and (6) identity synthesis (as cited in Hunter & Hickerson, 2003).

The focus on identity development models, however, while important to foster self-acceptance in a hostile environment, can be also limiting and simplistic (Miceli, 2002). Ryan and Futterman (2001) present coming out as a process that involves: " . . . recogniz[ing] the impact of stigma, . . . unfold[ing] over a period of time, . . . increasing acceptance of a 'homosexual' identity, and . . . disclosure to nongay persons" (p. 3). The process of coming out and the realization of society's negative reactions is often managed by GLB individuals without support and modeling from parents or other family members (Ryan & Futterman, 2001). This lack of support can lead to feelings of isolation, more feelings of stress, and a greater chance of being victimized by others. It is also imperative that GLB clients be allowed to identify and define themselves, and that the counselor does not do the labeling for them (Savin-Williams, 2005). Though labels can be liberating, they can also be considered reductionist and unable to capture the full extent of sexuality. "Identity terms box [gay and lesbians] in . . . and oversimplify a complex aspect of the self" (Savin-Williams, 2005, p. 18). It is important to help clients understand that there are multiple trajectories and that there exist several different ways of synthesizing and develop their sexual identity (Yarhouse, Tan, & Pawlowski, 2005).

Coming out can lead to negative repercussions including loss of job, family, and friends (Ryan & Futterman, 2001). As this story suggests, coming out can also lead to victimization and violence, which increases the fear of disclosing one's sexual orientation (Ryan & Futterman, 2001). Hunter & Hickerson (2003) discuss working with clients to identify the possible repercussions of disclosing sexual identity in order to realistically assess what the client will be able to handle. Morrow (2006) addresses the possibility of rejection from the family and the subsequent loss of one's parents when coming out. Clients may want to carefully consider each context in their lives to decide when, where, how, and to whom disclosure is appropriate (Hunter & Hickerson, 2003). Hunter & Hickerson (2003) also suggest that "Clients . . . make disclosures when they are feeling positive about themselves rather than when they are feeling vulnerable. They should feel prepared instead of making impulsive or reactive disclosures"

(p. 252). Counselors may utilize techniques such as visualization or role plays in order to help clients rehearse coming out to others (Hunter & Hickerson, 2003).

The coming-out process for ethnic minority individuals may present additional challenges and an understanding of their cultures (Hunter & Hickerson, 2003). Morrow (2006) discusses the cultural implications of coming out for African American GLB people, such as strong religious ties that value heterosexuality, emphasis on traditional gender roles, valuing procreation, and devaluation of same-sex relationships. Some considerations when working with Asian American GLB persons would be fear of rejection by families, lack of understanding from parents, fear of bringing shame onto the family, and stigma associated with utilizing mental health services (Hunter & Hickerson, 2003; Morrow, 2006). In Latino cultures, there is often a strong tie to Catholicism, an emphasis on traditional gender roles, and procreation-based values (Hunter & Hickerson, 2003; Morrow, 2006). When working with Native American clients, Hunter & Hickerson (2003) suggest assessing the level of acculturation and cultural values, and helping clients to find a "culturally relevant way to come out" (p. 258).

The other aspect of the coming-out process involves its effect on the parents, children, and peers of GLB youth and adults. Gays and lesbians and their parents are often not prepared to handle the effect of the coming-out process on the extended family because of the cultural milieu that is discriminatory and stigmatizing. The disclosure of a GLB orientation could be distressing to the parents, siblings, and other relatives. Family members' reactions can also be conceived as a process not unlike that of the grieving process and can include alternate states and varying degrees of denial, rejection, acceptance, tolerance, embarrassment, shame, guilt, and loss. The reactions of the parents of gay and lesbian offspring may depend on their age, their ethnicity, and their religious background. Also, their experiences in dealing with past crises, their degree of acceptance of differences, past exposure to gay people, and the availability of support and information (Herdt & Koff, 2000) may impact the nature of their reaction. Some parents go through a grieving process that may include wondering what they did "wrong" to cause the homosexuality of their children, embarrassment, or a feeling of loss of the illusion of having a "normal" child. Other parents' love and devotion to their children help them to find strength and a new way of looking at the world, overcoming a system that stigmatizes and tyrannizes their children. Clinicians will need to be aware that parents will move through these patterns at different rates, to allow them time, and to stay "with" them as they move through the phases toward acceptance (Hunter & Hickerson, 2003). Hunter & Hickerson (2003) suggest helping parents with these emotional responses, encouraging them not to trivialize their children, respecting the courage their GLB children had in coming out to them, and dispelling them of their misconceptions, stereotypes, and negative attitudes of GLB persons. Some questions that parents may have when discovering their child's GLB identity may be as follows: (1) How did it happen? (2) Is it permanent? (3) What kind of future is there for my child? and (4) What about disclosures outside of the family? (Hunter & Hickerson, 2003).

In her story, Karen describes going through the process of coming out as an adult while she is in a heterosexual marriage. Though most people come out to themselves generally at a younger age, Karen's is not an uncommon experience. Karen felt that her marriage was "everything," yet she found herself attracted to another woman. This realization started a process of self-evaluation and self-questioning. Karen's terms for her coming out to herself were "an awakening" and "stirrings inside." She talks about "discovering a part of herself" that she had not previously known.

Karen's coming out to others proved just as difficult, as it often is. She describes her difficulties talking to the members of her family. For many GLBs, coming out to friends, coworkers, the community, and people at the store, on the street, and in all other public areas of a person's life is a continual struggle, in part because others have the assumption that an individual is straight. It is not surprising that Karen would experience difficulty in coming out to others and find it overwhelming to do so. In Karen's coming-out process, she experiences a lot of discomfort in Cass's identity confusion stage. When in this stage, she feels very confused about her sexual orientation, her desires, her needs, and her self-concept (Hunter & Hickerson, 2003). She also goes back and forth in her feelings, sometimes thinking of her husband and her marriage, and sometimes thinking of Gwen and their relationship. Although the feelings that she has in this stage are expected, when working with clients in this stage counselors would need to understand the enormity of the confusion and the flip-flop nature of the client's feelings. As people move through all the different aspects of the coming-out process, they may move backward and forward, as Karen does, hesitating and affirming at different times in a fluctuating, nonlinear manner. The fact that Karen is not totally comfortable holding hands in public may be a reflection of her continued struggle that may be due to the geographical area where she resides, in which case it would constitute a self-protective measure, or may be due to her internalized homophobia, or both.

BISEXUALITY

Like Karen, many lesbians tend to have their first same-gender relationships later than gay men do (Tully, 2000). Women may be conditioned by society to have relationships with men, and often marry in their twenties. For lesbians whose sexual orientation may be unfolding at the same period in their lives, this can create confusion for those women who may have internal feelings of same-gender attraction, but are conditioned by society to marry men (Burgess, 1997). Because of the expectation to have children, many of these women may have already had children with the man whom they have married when they begin to come to terms with the feelings that they have toward other women (Burgess, 1997), as happened to Karen.

Kinsey suggested in the late 1950s that bisexuality was much more widespread than previously thought, and he argued that exclusive heterosexuality and exclusive homosexuality were the two poles of a continuum and that most people could be placed somewhere in the middle (Esterberg, 2002). Bisexuality is also diverse, and a case could be made for a typology of bisexuality. But attempts at defining the types and categories of bisexuality encourage labeling and stereotyping. Karen expresses that she is not comfortable labeling herself as lesbian, and although she identifies as bisexual at the time, she is not comfortable with society's view of that label either. The way that an individual feels or acts sexually may change over time, just as it did in Karen's story. Because Karen and others may see their sexuality as fluid, not as a continuum, trying to identify themselves with a label at any given moment may prove a difficult task (Feinberg, 1996). Rosario, Schrimshaw, Hunter, & Braun (2006) suggest that sexual identity development is a process of finding congruence among sexual orientation, sexual behavior, and sexual identity. Rosario and colleagues (2006) state: ". . . (i)dentity formation consists of becoming aware of one's unfolding sexual orientation, beginning to question whether one may be GLB, and exploring that emerging GLB identity . . ." (p. 47). Because GLB individuals are usually not raised in a community of others who are like them where they would learn about that identity, as the sexual identity development process takes hold, these individuals often seek out gay-related social activities and sexual experiences (Rosario, et al., 2006).

The complexity involved in a bisexual orientation presents its unique struggles. The bisexually oriented individual cannot look to heterosexual society or homosexual society for support of that identity (McClellan, 2006). The prevalent dichotomous view of sexual orientation is a factor that presents confusion for those who may identify as bisexual (Hunter & Hickerson, 2003; McClellan, 2006). Hunter & Hickerson (2003) go further to state: "Because of the stereotypes and myths associated with bisexual persons, they may have trouble attaining social validation from heterosexual and gay and lesbian persons" (p. 248).

Recent scholarly literature based on lesbians and bisexual women suggests that sexual identities are far more changeable in the course of the life cycle than originally thought and that identity development does not necessarily occur only in one direction (i.e., from straight to gay or lesbian) (Esterberg, 2002). What is important is to allow individuals to define how they think of themselves, as Karen is doing. It appears that, in terms of sexual history or behavior, "it is the meaning they make of their experiences that leads some women to think of themselves as bisexual and others as lesbian" (Esterberg, 2002, p. 220). Karen seems to have resolved the fact that she has been attracted to others both heterosexually and homosexually, and accepts this piece of herself. She has realized that she is not completely heterosexual and has accepted this part of herself, yet she still struggles with what her identity truly is. She frames the self-evaluation of her identity as fluid and changing, yet in her own words, she became very conscious of how she dressed and presented herself because she did not want to appear lesbian. She mentions that she is "not totally convinced" that she is lesbian, feels that the definition of bisexuality is more fitting, and states that her "sexual identity awareness keeps forming," and she also says that she would most likely not hold her partner's hand in public. Karen is out to her family and friends, has extensively researched issues of sexual orientation, and expresses that she does not want to hide who she is. Karen recognizes that her sexual orientation is one piece of who she is, and continues to work on developing awareness of that piece of herself.

SHAME AND INTERNAL JUDGMENT

Karen talks about judging herself. As Kaufman & Raphael (1996) state, "embedded in these judgments are distinct, though sometimes hidden, expressions of shame" (p. 6). Shame is deeply rooted in ourselves and is formed from the judgments of others and then internalized; it preys on self-esteem, affecting identity and sexual intimacy (Kaufman & Raphael, 1996).

Some factors that may perpetuate feelings of shame in Karen are society's stigmatization of homosexuality, and the relative acceptance of homophobia. The historical condemnation of homosexuality provides a framework of judgment, criticism, and inferiority that, once internalized, produces shame (Kaufman & Raphael, 1996). This shame causes some to hide in fear, which Karen expresses at different points in her story. Heterosexism is another factor that may contribute to judgment, as it "... functions to shame anyone who is different and ... [often] silence[s] lesbians and gay men in many situations where their heterosexuality is assumed" (Kaufman & Raphael, 1996, p. 95). Another significant factor that contributes to shame is the feeling of powerlessness that gay men and lesbians experience due to their sexual preference (Tully, 2000). The attack on Karen and her partner by the male stranger may have reinforced judgment, shame, and feelings of powerlessness.

Clinical Applications

This section explores the clinical implications of Karen's story for counselors, including assessment of sexual identity and level of comfort with being out, techniques and interventions of use, and countertransference issues.

ASSESSMENT

Assessment of Identity

When working with clients who are exploring acknowledging their sexual orientation to themselves and others, it will be important to assess how they choose to identify, what they are struggling with, and how they feel about themselves and their families. What to ask depends on the age of the clients, their level of self-acceptance or rejection, their fears or their shame, and the nature of their families and other social support systems. Some individuals will be comfortable discussing these issues with a counselor sooner than others, some are comfortable in certain circles (i.e., among the GLB community), and some are not comfortable at all for a long time. These differences need to be respected, and the client should not be pressured to move in a direction where they are not ready to go, according to their level in the gay and lesbian identity development models.

It is important to assess sexual attraction, behavior, and fantasies as well as sexual and emotional attractions.

Following are some questions that counselors can ask clients who are presenting with issues dealing with their sexual orientation. Before asking these questions, it is important to find out whether clients are comfortable discussing issues regarding sexual thoughts, feelings, or behavior with the clinician.

Who do you mostly socialize with?

Which sex or sexes are you attracted to?

Which sex or sexes are in your fantasies, daydreams, and dreams?

With which sex or sexes do you engage in sexual relations?

How are you dealing with what is happening to you (from self-acceptance to shame)?

How do you label or identity yourself (lesbian, gay, bisexual, or other)?

How comfortable or uncomfortable are you discussing issues regarding what is going on with your parents, siblings, friends, and colleagues?

What messages have you received from society about your sexual identity?

How, if at all, is your sexual orientation related to your presenting problem?

TECHNIQUES AND INTERVENTIONS

Helping Clients With Their Coming-Out Process

One of the most important functions that counselors, psychologists, and social workers can engage in is helping GLB clients with their coming-out process. This involves several areas. First, it is important to help clients assess whether or not coming out, and to whom, is a wise decision. For example, for teenagers who live in religiously conservative environments and are financially dependent on their families, coming out may put them in a high risk of homelessness. For people who live in remote rural areas, or in city neighborhoods that may not be safe, it might be more protective not to come out. Second, it is important to educate clients that coming out to oneself may involve getting over self-loathing, disgust, or denial. Not all GLBs will express these negative emotions, but for those who do, it is important to help clients understand that this is a normal aspect of the coming out to oneself, and that these feelings can be overcome. This is a particularly important topic because self-loathing, inner conflicts, denial, and disgust of one's own characteristics can lead to self-destructive behaviors. To deal with self-loathing and lack of self-respect, strategies may need to be implemented that include educating clients about the myths associated with sexual orientation, helping clients learn coping strategies to deal with homophobia, encouraging clients to conduct research on the realities of gay and lesbian life, and seeking out role models and gay-friendly people. Clinicians can encourage clients to seek support with online bulletin boards or community groups to develop a family of friends, find out information about HIV and AIDS, and become acquainted with the faces of internalized homophobia. Finally, clinicians can help clients with the process of coming out to others. Clients need to know that the coming-out process involves steps such as: planning, timing, anticipating the reactions of others, dealing with frustrating experiences, and weathering bad responses. They also need to know that disclosure to the closest family members is often the most difficult task (Bass & Kaufman, 1996; Signorile, 1995).

Feelings of Shame and Internal Judgment

When working with gay and lesbian clients, there may be feelings of shame that result from internalized homophobia or internalized judgments. Directing clients to identify and understand these feelings may help the client to lessen the feelings of shame. Kaufman & Raphael (1996) suggest working with the client to develop self-esteem, find self-nurturing activities, participate in self-forgiveness, re-own previously disowned parts of the self, and develop a positive identification of oneself as gay or lesbian in order to dissolve feelings of shame. Working to create a self-affirming identity, a whole and integrated self, and self-value can help clients to transcend their feelings of shame and empower them (Tully, 2000). Kaufman & Raphael (1996) suggest refocusing attention as a tool for releasing shame, whereby an individual refocuses his inward attention, such as inner scrutiny and self-consciousness, into attention outside of himself. This could be accomplished by encouraging clients to focus on external things when they are experiencing internal judgment. Another technique suggested by Kaufman & Raphael (1996) is changing scripts, or modifying self-shaming scripts into self-affirming scripts. Additionally, encouraging clients to get in touch with gay community resources, gay subcultures, and to form families of choice, results in the reduction of shame (Tully, 2000).

COUNTERTRANSFERENCE

Counselors need to cultivate awareness of their reactions to GLB clients and their expectations for gender role behavior, their homophobia, their heterosexism, and their acceptance or rejection of their clients' choices. Clinicians' countertransference reactions may vary depending on whether clinicians are GLB or not.

GLB Clinicians

Clinicians who are GLB may identify too much with the experiences of their clients and fail to be helpful (Hunter & Hickerson, 2003). As in other clinical situations, the dangers of identifying too much with their client may prevent clinicians from listening to the uniqueness of their client's story and fail to recognize the differences (Hunter & Hickerson, 2003). Thinking that they know "what is best" for them, GLB clinicians may push clients in a direction they are not ready to go, or may fail to push clients who might need some encouragement, affirmation, or assertiveness. A GLB clinician of color working with another sexual minority of color might minimize clients' other problems, or be at risk of engaging in dual relationships (Lowe & Mascher, 2001). It is important for clinicians to provide education, recommend interventions, and make suggestions to clients without projecting their own experiences or agendas onto their clients.

Clinicians who are not GLB

Excessive Curiosity or Guilt: Clinicians who are not GLB, on the other hand, may have excessive curiosity about the clients' sexual behavior and other issues of which the clinician may not be sufficiently aware. It is important for the clinician to learn from sources other than the client some basic information, so that session time can be spent on client-specific issues. Insecure therapists may feel uncomfortable, guilty, or inadequate dealing with sexual minority clients and may act out or lack boundaries (Lowe & Mascher, 2001).

Wish to Change or Rejection: Some counselors may accept working with GLB clients as long as they do not have to deal with relationship issues, because they feel an intense rejection of the clients' sexuality. If a counselor feels the need to change a client or reacts with much distress, then referral should be considered (Moses, 1982; Morrow & Tyson, 2006). Clinicians who do not support gay and lesbian human rights need to refrain from working with GLB clients because it may be unethical to work with a population that the therapist does not support (Twist, Murphy, Green, & Palmanteer, 2006). However, the issue of referral based on ethical principles of competence or differences in values is complex and has important ethical and legal ramifications. Counselors who would be comfortable helping a GLB individual client but refuse to counsel clients on relationship issues on the grounds that homosexual relationships go against their religious beliefs might be violating important ethical principles. Recent court decisions (Herman & Richter Herlihy, 2006) indicate that using religious beliefs to justify refusing services based on sexual orientation violates the principle of beneficence, the first—and possibly the main— obligation of a clinician (American Counseling Association, 2005).

TOOLBOX ACTIVITY—KAREN			
Resources and Suggested Readings	*Videos*	*Activities*	*Discussion Questions*
Abbott, D., & Farmer, E. (Eds.). (1995). *From wedded wife to lesbian life: Stories of transformation.* Freedom, CA: The Crossing Press.	*Claire of the Moon* *If These Walls Could Talk 2* *De Colores: Lesbian and Gay Latinos: Stories of Strength, Family, and Love.*	Compile a list of the resources available for GLB youth in your community. Interview clergy who perform commitment ceremonies and those who do not. Write a paper about the differences. Include how this information could help you as a counselor.	Content Themes What other themes do you see emerging in the story that the authors did not identify? Assessment Are there any questions you would like to ask Karen? Interventions What other interventions could you propose with Karen?
Bass, E., & Kaufman, K. (1996). *Free your mind: The book for gay, lesbian, and bisexual youth and their allies.* New York: HarperCollins.			
Burgess, C. A. (1997). The impact of lesbian/gay sensitive policies on the behavior and health of lesbians in the workplace. In W. K. Swan (Ed.), *Gay/lesbian/bisexual/ transgender public policy issues.* New York: The Harrington Park Press.			Countertransference What countertransference reactions were emerging in yourself as you read this story? Other Scenarios How would Karen's life be different if she had children? As a counselor, how could you help her?
Jennings, K. (1994). *One teacher in 10: Gay and lesbian educators tell their stories.* Los Angeles: Alyson Books.			Imagine that Karen came to you after her initial struggles with the attraction to another woman. What could you have said to her upon finding out that she is a teacher in an elementary school? A high school?
Nava, M., & Dawidoff, R. (1995). *Created equal: Why gay rights matter to America.* New York: St. Martin's Press.			
Sinclair, A. (1995). *Coffee will make you Black.* New York: Harper Paperbacks.			

Transgender and Intersex Sexuality 18

Heterosexuality and homosexuality need to be differentiated from the concept of transgender sexuality and intersex conditions. Transgender is an umbrella term used to describe people whose gender identity (i.e., their sense of themselves as male or female), or gender expression (i.e., their behavior), differs from that usually associated with the sex with which they were born) (APA Task Force on Gender Identity/transgender, n.d.; Hunter & Hickerson, 2003; Martin & Yonkin, 2006). Intersex is a term that describes people who are born with atypical genitalia that may include both male and female external (genitalia) or internal (reproductive) attributes. Intersex individuals were formerly referred to as hermaphrodites, but the term has been rejected to depathologize and destigmatize the conditions (Martin & Yonkin, 2006).

Historically, gender variant experiences seem to have existed in all cultures. Particularly in the context of the performing arts and sports, cross-dressing has been (and still is) an accepted form of transgender expression. Gender variance and sexual orientation are, generally, not related concepts. Transgender and intersex individuals can be straight or gay and can vary across several dimensions, including their biological sex, their psychological identity, their social presentation, and their legal sex (Lombardi & Davis, 2006). There are several types of transgender individuals, including cross-dressers and transsexuals, also known as gender variant. (Martin & Yonkin, 2006). The majority of gender variances are expressed in cross-dressing. The majority of cross-dressers are heterosexual males (Martin & Yonkin, 2006).

A few transgender individuals live either part or their lives or most of their lives as transsexuals. Male-to-female (MTF) or female-to-male (FTM) transsexuals, for example, experience intense dissatisfaction with their birth sex or with the gender role associated with that and often seek sex reassignment with surgical procedures. According to the APA Task

Force on Gender Identity/transgender (n.d.), "Transsexuals who are attracted to women prior to transition continue to be attracted to women after transition, and transsexuals who are attracted to men prior to transition continue to be attracted to men after transition" (p. 1). For example, a male who is attracted to females will be attracted to females, after transitioning to female, and may regard herself as a lesbian.

According to Feinberg (1996), transgender can be used to describe a person who reassigns the sex that he or she was labeled with at birth. Feinberg asserts, "transgender people traverse, bridge, or blur the boundary of the gender expression they were assigned at birth" (p. x). Feinberg (1996) goes on to explain how this differs from transsexual because, "transsexual men and women traverse the boundary of the sex they were assigned at birth" (p. x). For some, there is a surgical gender reassignment, for some it is dressing and living as the opposite gender, and for some it is blurring the feminine and masculine sides and living as "bigender" (Feinberg, 1996). Estimates of the number of people who are transgender are difficult to make. Transsexuals who are biologically male are about 1 in 10,000 and biologically female are about 1 in 30,000 (APA Task Force on Gender Identity/transgender, n.d.). It is estimated that as many as 2 to 3 percent of biological males engage in cross-dressing, at least occasionally (APA Task Force on Gender Identity/transgender, n.d.). Research conducted on the brains of transsexuals has indicated that the brains of male-to-female transsexuals are similar to those of straight females, and that female-to-male transsexuals' brains are similar to those of straight males (Johnson, 2004). Biological factors seem to be most responsible for the development of genetic maleness or femaleness. Five components comprise the biological makeup of sex determination: somatotype (chromosomes), hormones, internal genitalia, external genitalia, and gonads (Moses, 1982). Each of these aspects is subject to variation, so one's gender can be distinctly male or female, or fall on a continuum of male and female qualities (Moses, 1982). When the external appearance and the other biological factors (hormones, internal genitalia, and so on) are incongruent, it can lead someone who is socialized to be one gender to "feel" that he or she is really the opposite gender, or bigendered (male and female).

Intersex individuals are those who are born with genitalia of both sexes involving atypical features in the external genitals, internal reproductive organs, sex chromosomes, or sex-related hormones (Martin & Yonkin, 2006). Often infants who are born with ambiguous genitals (without a penis or without a vagina) are surgically and hormonally assigned a gender to give them a male or female identity (APA Task Force on Gender Identity/intersex, n.d.). Other reasons for surgical and hormonal treatments include preserving fertility, bowel and bladder function, or genital function. Intersex conditions are not always apparent at birth, though, and some intersex conditions are not discovered until puberty, when decisions about surgical or hormonal treatment are made. Sometimes, decisions about surgical corrections at birth are made without the parents' consent, and often the child is never told that he or she was born intersex (Martin & Yonkin, 2006). It is estimated that 1 in every 1,500 babies is born with ambiguous genitals that cannot be easily classified as male or female (APA Task Force on Gender Identity/intersex, n.d.).

The Division 44 of the American Psychological Association did not include transgender or intersex individuals in their 2000 guidelines for psychotherapy with lesbian, gay, and bisexual clients (Division 44, 2000), and as of the current edition of the DSM (DSM-IV-TR), there is a classification for Gender Identity Disorder, which is explained as, " . . . a strong and persistent cross-gender identification, which is the desire to be, or the insistence that one is, of the other sex" (American Psychiatric Association, 2000, p. 576). This diagnosis is highly controversial (Martin & Yonkin, 2006; Lombardi & Davis, 2006). The argument that the diagnosis is essential to ensure access to care, particularly for those seeking medical, surgical, or hormonal procedures (APA Task Force on Gender Identity/intersex, n.d.) is not supported by several authors (Lombardi & Davis, 2006; Martin & Yonkin, 2006). Advocacy groups are working toward reforming the DSM IV classification of Gender Identity Disorder on the basis that it pathologizes gender diversity (GID Reform, n.d.).

Recently, there has been movement toward the recognition that the push toward the selection of one gender or another is not absolutely necessary for people to live productive lives, and that the pressure to attain a specific gender appearance need not be followed in order to function adequately (Lombardi & Davis, 2006). Individuals holding these views challenge the existing Western binary and categorical sex-gender system, increasingly identifying as bigender, gender blender, or gender-free. In some cases, they realize that they can live as transgendered without surgical or hormonal alternations (Hunter & Hickerson, 2003).

Implications for Professionals

Providing support and information is the first task of the counselor working with transgender or intersex individuals. Helping to find the right medical care, educating the family, advocating for the individuals and their families, and securing supportive environments can be facilitated by providing a nonjudgmental and safe place to discuss these issues. In addition, the clinical considerations described in Section VI ("Heterosexuality, Homosexuality, and Bisexual Gender Orientation") are also applicable, including homophobia, human immunodeficiency virus (HIV), suicidality, substance abuse, resiliency factors, and others.

Discussion Questions

1. Do you agree that the concept of homosexuality needs to be differentiated from the concept of transgender sexuality?

2. Discuss the differences between gender variance and sexual orientation.

3. Discuss how you could help transgender individuals reconcile their social presentation with their legal sex.

4. What are your views of the diagnosis of gender identity disorder?

5. In a continuum from total comfort to total discomfort related to discussing issues related to transgender sexuality, where would you place yourself? If your level is low, what steps could you take to increase your level of comfort with the issues presented in this section?

Rachel's Story   **19**

Nurturing the Spirit

This is a mother's account of raising a transgendered child. Rachel's mother is the author of this story. She writes about the first few years of Rachel's life, when she was known as Ryan. This is the story of how Ryan became Rachel.

Rachel's Story

Rachel is a beautiful, well-adjusted, happy and healthy, nine-year-old little girl. She likes to do all the things little girls at this age like to do. Sleepovers and ice cream sundaes are by far her favorite things in life. But her life to this point has not been easy. Rachel was born with a boy's body. This is our story . . .

In 1996, I gave birth to twins, a boy and a girl, Ryan and Alissa. They were the most beautiful babies I had ever seen. I had struggled to have children; these two were the result of 11 in vitro fertilizations in five years, with five miscarriages along the way. This was, by far, the happiest day of my life.

I was not the type of mom who learned everything from books; I thought that the best parenting would come from within and I wanted to tap into my maternal instincts. I had no expectations for my children's lives; I just wanted to raise happy, secure, productive adults.

It was apparent from the beginning that these two kids were completely different. Alissa was active and alert and always needing to know what was going on; she slept in short intervals. Ryan was very quiet and serious, he enjoyed cuddling and sleeping, and he hated to be held by different people. My mom and I would joke, "Typical boy."

By two and a half, both children were active and speaking. Ryan would always correct us when we said things like "Good boy," or "Boys do it like this." He would say, "But I'm a girl." He would get upset when he wore blue while his sister was dressed in pink. He was not interested in typical boys' toys, nor did he like us to describe him as "handsome"; he insisted on "pretty" or "beautiful."

We attributed all these behaviors and confusions to having a twin sister who hit her milestones earlier. She was the first to crawl, the first to walk, the first to speak, and the first to potty train. Ryan was always competitive, even early on, so we thought that Ryan just wanted to be like Alissa.

One night I was bathing the kids; they weren't three yet. After the kids played and washed up, I took them from the tub and wrapped them in towels. I left the bathroom for a moment to get something (I can't remember what) and when I returned, Ryan was trying to remove his penis with an unopened nail clipper. Shocked, I said, "Hey buddy, what are you doing?" He replied, very innocently, "I have to cut this off, it doesn't go there." I told him that it would hurt and took the clippers. We continued with the rest of the nightly activities; I went on as best I could.

As time went on, Ryan's need to express like a girl became more and more apparent. He loved nail polish and lipstick. He liked to play dress-up for hours, to the point where girls' clothes became his daily attire. He gave us a hard time when it was time to go somewhere. He got upset when his sister would be able to wear a dress and he couldn't. He stopped attending his own birthday parties and refused to open gifts. Even Christmas was disappointing; he needed to be coaxed through each present, constantly eyeing his sister's booty.

Ryan's mood was more and more depressed and he was only four years old. I kept hoping that this was just confusion or a phase, but it wasn't ending, it was getting worse. At home during the day, he was happy in his dress-up things or wearing some of his sister's old clothes. He played with other little girls in the neighborhood, and it was really apparent to the other moms that Ryan was very feminine in both his actions and his activities.

Ryan and Alissa started kindergarten at age five. I went in and met Ryan's teacher and told her that he preferred to play as a girl and that was okay with his father and me. I asked her to tell me if there were any problems or if kids started picking on him and she promised that she would. She supported a child's right to be happy, even if it meant not behaving as defined by our society's roles for gender.

Kindergarten was uneventful. Ryan's grades were average, and his friends were girls in his class. Mornings were brutal, however; he never wanted to go to school, and he never wanted to get dressed. It was a constant struggle. Just before first grade began, one hot August night, I was putting him to bed and we were saying our prayers. When he ended, he looked at me and said "I'm so mad at God. Every night after I say my prayers, I close my eyes and ask God to make me into a girl, and every morning when I wake up I'm still a boy. God made a mistake, mommy, and He won't fix it, no matter how hard I wish."

My heart broke. I said, "I know, honey. I know you want to be a girl. And when I was your age I wanted to be a boy. But when I grew up I was glad I was a girl." And he asked "What if I grow up and I still don't want to be a boy, what then?" I replied, "Then I'll help you find a doctor that can change your body into a girl's." His face lit up like it was Christmas. "You mean like when I'm 25?" I said "Yes, when you're 25." He slept that night with a smile on his face.

When first grade started, I explained his needs to the teacher and again asked that she watch for bullying. This teacher, too, was supportive and understanding. Each day was again met with a struggle, and matters got worse. At school, Ryan began to have panic attacks; he had emotional breakdowns daily. He was unable to do his work; he could not concentrate or pay attention.

He would say things to me like "You don't know what its like to be me," or "Mom, I wish I was dead." We had long talks about his need to be a girl, but he would not discuss these issues with anyone else. My heart was breaking. I could not find a doctor who understood what he was going through. Doctors didn't want to get involved with a child so young, for fear of lawsuits in the future. Ryan was only happy when he was able to express as a girl, so I found myself becoming more and more lenient with this behavior. His father, on the other hand, was doing his best to "mold his son" into a boy. This caused added tension in a house that was already in turmoil.

It was an agony. I was often accused of "encouraging" Ryan's feminine behavior, but I couldn't have stopped it if I tried. To me, it didn't seem right to force a child to like things he didn't like, or dress in a way that made him uncomfortable, or play in a way that wasn't fun, just to please everyone else. My gut told me something was wrong, and the solution was uncomfortable for everyone except me and my child.

I remember making the analogy of having a child who was trapped in a wheelchair. If this were the case, and I could do something to allow this child to run and play like all other kids for a few hours a day, wouldn't I be lax as a mother if I didn't allow this miracle to occur? To me, Ryan had a little girl trapped inside, and letting her out made him happy, and seeing him happy made me happy, no matter what it took.

I always believed that each child is born with a spirit, a reason to be. It was my greatest responsibility as a parent to nurture that spirit and help him become who he was meant to be, not who I wanted him to be. But how do you, as a mom, allow your child to express behaviors that are appalling to society? My dilemma was clear, and so was my mission. I needed to create an environment where Ryan could be happy and others could accept him. But how?

By six years old, Ryan was suicidal. We had to lock the windows upstairs because he threatened, on a regular basis, to jump out and end his life. I spent my days crying to anyone who would listen, insurance people, care providers, doctors, secretaries, receptionists, teachers, family members, and friends . . . the list goes on.

In March of that year, we found a pediatric doctor who specialized in child behavioral and gender issues. She explained that Ryan has Gender Identity Disorder; he is transgendered. Putting it into laymen's terms, she told us that while not much is known about this condition, it is believed to be caused when the child's brain develops like that of the opposite gender, in this case female. This development takes place in utero; a signal from the fetus, depending on the biologic gender, tells the mother's body to produce estrogen or to masculinize that estrogen into a form of testosterone. The hormones produced then wash the brain, causing a part of the hypothalamus to develop differently in men than in women. The XX and XY chromosomes control fetal body development only.

It is believed that something in the hormonal wash goes wrong, or the signal from the fetus is misinterpreted, and the brain develops resembling that of the opposite sex as opposed to that of the biologic sex. That is why Ryan felt like a girl inside, because, chances are, that his brain was developed as such.

The good news was there was a diagnosis. The bad news was that the only "cure" for such a condition was to allow an individual to express as the identified gender. She was not aware of any cases where a child this young was allowed to express openly in this manner. She explained the Harry Benjamin Standards of Care for Transgendered Adults, and said that if we chose to allow our child to follow these standards, she would support us, but it was going to be a tough road for all.

Slowly, Ryan began his transition. It started at home and in the neighborhood. He was allowed to freely wear whatever clothing he liked; I began purchasing him his own wardrobe of "girl's clothes." I also spoke to anyone who would listen, explaining the best I could, what this condition was and how it affected him. People were understanding, and for the most part, accepting; but I always got the feeling they walked away saying, "Wow, she's got a handful, glad that's not my kid." But I was glad that Ryan wasn't theirs, too.

Ryan started second grade as Reggi; his initials are REG (and Reggi was the girl character in his favorite cartoon). Because of his anxiety during first grade and his inability to learn or retain, he began second grade testing at a mid-year kindergarten level. I explained his recent diagnosis to the teachers and administrators; all were accepting and understanding and willing to do whatever it took to help him out.

The first few months seemed to be confusing for everyone but Reggi. His hair was growing a little longer; his clothing was all purchased in girl's departments, but "unisex" would be the word I would use to describe his attire. Reggi was happy: happy to go to school, happy to be learning, participating in all the lessons for the first time in his life.

All the teachers noticed his change, but so did the other students. While I could go to the staff and explain what was occurring, no one could discuss the subject with the other students without parental permission. So the kids asked questions like: "Hey, is your kid a boy or a girl?" and I would reply: "It doesn't matter to me as long as Reggi is happy." Funnier yet, no one knew what pronouns to use, so everyone avoided them. I would joke with the teachers that we all spoke like Elmo on *Sesame Street*.

Reggi settled into second grade and had an incredible year. For the first time, he was invited to a birthday party. He came home and said, "Mom, I got invited to Julia's birthday party for next Saturday. All the girls in the class were invited! Can I go? Please?" Of course my child was attending.

In March of Reggi's seventh year, I found an incredible Internet support group, www.transfamily.org, that provided a method of communication among parents of transgendered children. Most of the parents on the list were moms of children in their 20s and 30s, but several of the moms had children as young as Reggi. Within 48 hours of finding this site, I found more information than I could have imagined about children suffering in bodies that don't match their identified gender.

After discussing this new information with the rest of the family, I went to the school and told Reggi's teacher that we were ready to start using female pronouns. This was, by far, the hardest part of our transition, using "she" and "her" instead of "he" and "him," but the teachers seemed get the hang of it right away; the other children caught on quickly as well. At home it was a little rougher, but each time we made a mistake and used a male pronoun, we corrected ourselves and moved on with our discussion.

We watched our child's spirit come to life. It was like witnessing the metamorphosis a caterpillar makes to become a beautiful butterfly. As her outward appearance started to resemble who "she" felt like inside, her academics and social skills improved as well. Soon she was reading and spelling with little or no effort, and that year, she completed second-grade testing on a fourth-grade level.

Reggi began to excel in all areas. She was being invited to friends' homes for playtime and sleepovers, and her grades became all As and Bs. But the children who couldn't understand what had happened, and who couldn't forget that Ryan was in their kindergarten and first-grade classes, started to become abusive. They would reserve their comments to times when an adult wasn't present, like on the playground or on the bus. They called her "gay-boy" or "the girl with a dick"; they tried to trip her or entice her into a physical confrontation. But Reggi, loving who she was allowed to be, didn't respond; she seemed to just want it to go away. In fact, the only reason I found out what was happening was that Alissa, Reggi's twin, was usually present but had been sworn to secrecy by Reggi.

One day Alissa got off the bus crying. "Mom, I can't take it anymore," she cried. The kids on the bus had a yearbook from the previous year and they were harassing Reggi, pointing out pictures from first grade captioned "Ryan" and saying things like "See, you're a boy that likes to wear skirts, you little fag," or "No matter what you call yourself, you'll always be Ryan Grant, Ryan Grant" (tantalizing her with her birth name like it was a bad word). Even the bus driver pointed out the name on the bus pass was "Ryan," so "he" had to be a boy.

Reggi's response was slight of emotion. She just said "Mom, I don't care what those kids say. They are jerks and I wouldn't play with them even if they were nice to me." I knew inside she had to hurt, but I realized why she could not tell anyone; to repeat what was happening just caused the event to go on—and she just wanted it all to go away.

The school, once again, handled it great. They brought the children into the counselor's office in small groups and discussed what was happening and tried to explain what Reggi was dealing with. They allowed the children to ask questions and discuss their behavior in the security of other children and without repercussion. To this day, out of some 600 students that experienced Reggi's transition, only one or two bullies continue, very subtly and infrequently, and the school takes a "no-tolerance" approach toward the behavior.

In August of 2005, Ryan's name was legally changed to Rachel Elizabeth; Reggi would still work as a nickname. This was done so that all school records could be changed, and class lists would be distributed with a girl's name as opposed to a boy's. In this way, Rachel would not be singled out by substitutes or bus drivers; nor would explanations be necessary in many settings.

As Rachel approaches puberty, a whole new set of issues arise, which we can only prepare ourselves for. Our plan is to wait until we notice signs of secondary sex changes, such as body hair or voice change. We then will probably use hormone blockers to prevent these changes. If all is on track (if she still expresses as a female and desires to live as one) we will begin hormone replacement therapy (HRT) and allow her body to develop with feminine characteristics. Surgery, at this point, will be her decision when she is of legal age to decide.

But this is just our plan. If puberty changes her internal feelings, then Rachel will be able to grow into a man. This has to be Rachel's choice, with our guidance and support. She has already begun seeing a therapist, who will keep her in touch with her internal feelings, alerting us to any confusions that may arise.

The one thing I learned through this journey is never to make a plan that can't be changed. So many "life rules" I took for granted have been questioned over and over, and now I live with a truly open mind and heart. There are so many basic facts, like the sun will rise in the morning and will set at night, and what goes up must come down, that I didn't question when I gave birth to a girl, that she would grow to be a woman or when I gave birth to a boy he would grow to be a man.

But now I look at life a little differently. I ask myself: "What if . . . ?" What if I throw something up into the air and it doesn't return—would that necessarily be a bad thing? Or what if the sun forgot to rise; if my life continued in some way, would that be all bad?

My child has taught me more in nine years than I learned in the entire 37 years before she was born. She has taught me the true meaning of tolerance, perseverance, and patience. She has taught me to take nothing for granted and not to be scared of the "what-ifs" in life. These are life's challenges and adventures, which, when celebrated rather than feared, make our life experience whole.

Content Themes

This is a story that describes the beginning of the difficult transition from Ryan to Rachel and the mother's journey to help her struggling child. Ryan genuinely felt that he was a girl and that "God made a mistake." This story illustrates the issues related to the discovery of transgender characteristics, the effects of the discovery on the family, the school, and the child, and finally the transition from Ryan to Rachel. The final piece of the mother's story gives us a sense of the harassment that Rachel has begun to experience from a society that does not understand gender identity incongruities.

TRAPPED IN WRONG BODY/GENDER IDENTITY

The biological development of gender has several components, and inconsistencies within these components can cause conflict between a person's internal feelings of gender and his or her external gender appearance. Recent research points to prenatal influences during the third trimester, when sex hormones affect the brain organization of the developing fetus. This research indicates that it is possible to be born with the biological makeup of one gender, and the brain organization of the opposite gender (Looy & Bouma, 2005). The mother in the story talks about this research and the possibility that Ryan was born with the brain organization of a female. As soon as Ryan becomes verbal, he expresses that he feels that he is a girl and insists that he is a girl. The disparity between Ryan's mind and body create confusion, depression, and suicidal ideation within him. Van Huekelem presents a case that is similar to Ryan's, in which a young girl named Halle felt that she was really a boy, and by age six became depressed and suicidal (as cited in Looy & Bouma, 2005). Ryan's struggle is something that most people take for granted; most people experience a certain harmony between their biological sex and their psychological experience of gender (Looy & Bouma, 2005).

TRANSITION

Ryan's mother talks about the term Gender Identity Disorder (GID). Ryan was diagnosed with GID at six years old, which meant that his gender identity varied from his biological sex (Mallon & DeCrescenzo, 2006). Although categorizing GID as a mental disorder is debatable (at one time homosexuality was categorized as a mental disorder), currently if an individual wants to explore gender reassignment, there must be a diagnosis of GID (Lev, 2004). There are certain standards of care that are addressed in the process of transitioning—the Harry Benjamin International Gender Dysphoria Association (HBIGDA) has set up therapeutic guidelines and standards of care for transgendered clients (Lev, 2004). As Ryan was allowed to express as Rachel, his mother and doctor proceeded under the Harry Benjamin Standards of Care. The transition for a child would be similar to that for an adult, whereby the child would begin to express as the identified gender.

Another transition in this story occurs with Ryan/Rachel's mother. The mother indicates that her husband was having a more difficult time with Ryan's insistence that he was a girl, and tried to "mold" Ryan into a boy. Cooper (1998) suggests that family members go through a transition as well, which often involves confusion, anger, disappointment, guilt, and grief. Cooper (1998) states: ". . . families may find it difficult to adjust to the use of new pronouns, or the use of a new name for a family member" (p. 124). Support for family members as well as for the transgendered individual is essential, especially during periods of transition.

HARASSMENT

In the mother's story, we learn of the harassment Rachel experienced from her peers as she transitioned into her preferred gender identity. This harassment was not only from peers, but also from adults, including a school bus driver. This type of harassment is quite overt and obvious. Social stigmatization and the pathologization of transgendered individuals are more covert ways in which youth may experience harassment

(Mallon & DeCrescenzo, 2006). Other forms of harassment include with-holding of support by friends or family, parents' refusal to allow preferred gender expression, and discrimination because of transgender issues (Mallon & DeCrescenzo, 2006).

Fortunately, Rachel's mother is supportive of her preferred gender iden-tity and is seeking out support for both of them. Her mother has found a doctor who is willing to work with them according to the Harry Benjamin Standards of Care. As Rachel emerges from her insulated world among her family, she may experience more harassment, such as social stigmatization. Again, Rachel's mother has helped by having her name legally changed to avoid the stigmatization of Rachel by teachers, bus drivers, and other adults who may have not have previously known Rachel.

Clinical Applications

This section explores the clinical implications of the mother's story for counselors, including assessment of expression of gender identity, useful techniques and interventions, and countertransference issues.

ASSESSMENT

Cross-Gender Expression and Transgender Identity

Cross-gender behavior need not be confused with transgender identity or intersex conditions, and early expression of GID does not mean that an individual will continue to want to be the other gender (Mallon & DeCrescenzo, 2006). Not every child who experiences a discrepancy between assigned gender and biological sex will continue to experience this discrepancy as an adult (Hunter & Hickerson, 2003). Assessment is critical because many children are mislabeled with GID due to any type of cross-gender behavior, even when these children are not dissatisfied with their gender identity (Mallon & DeCrescenzo, 2006).

The following questions may make it possible to differentiate cross-gender behavior from transgender identity in a child or adolescent:

Does the child repeatedly states a desire to be, or insists that he or she is the other sex?

Does the child state a persistent discomfort with, or aversion to, the characteristics of his or her own sex, such as disgust with his own penis for a boy or rejecting urinating in a sitting position for a girl?

Does the child appear to be constantly distressed in social situations or in the school setting because of the above mentioned aversion, desires, or disgust?

Does the child's overall functioning appear to be impaired because of desires of being the other sex?

TECHNIQUES AND INTERVENTIONS

The following paragraphs describe strategies found in the literature that may be helpful once it is determined that the child, adolescent, or adult is transgender or has an intersex condition.

Expression and Acceptance of Gender Identity

As in the story presented by Ryan/Rachel's mother, the process of discovering one's gender identity can be extremely difficult when the individual feels that his or her gender identity does not match his or her biological gender. Other psychological issues such as depression and suicidal ideation may arise, and clinicians need to be aware of and treat associated conditions that result (Mallon, 1999). Generating and facilitating love, acceptance, and compassion from the individual's family and from the clinician herself can help to keep communication open and create a safe environment for children experiencing gender discrepancies (Mallon, 1999; Martin & Yonkin, 2006).

Counselors will need to develop understanding and patience, and provide support for these clients and their families throughout the process, whether clients choose to transition or not. Helping families to understand gender identity expression, to grieve the loss of the expected gender identity, and to build a new relationship with the transgendered individual will be paramount in assisting the families through transitions (Cooper, 1998). Support and education are essential for the child and the family as well as the community of which the child is a part.

The transition from biological gender to identified gender involves not only the transgender client, but also the people surrounding the transgender individual (Lev, 2006). Educating family members about the nature of transgender sexuality and the process of transitioning is an important factor in helping to create support for the transgender client (Lev, 2006). Clinicians will need to be prepared to address family feelings of anger, guilt, denial, sadness, rejection, and grief (Mallon & DeCrescenzo, 2006). Finding support for the family will be essential to healing the family system around these issues.

Transitioning and Working Through Harassment

As Rachel's mother mentioned in her story, the Harry Benjamin Standards of Care can be used to navigate the transition process. Because gender-variant individuals may have a sense of isolation due to societal oppression, validating and exploring feelings that result from social stigmatization can be a part of the counseling process (Lev, 2006).

As in the case of Rachel, counselors may need to prepare transgender children by helping them to develop strategies for dealing with bullying, name-calling, and other forms of harassment (Mallon, 1999). Mallon (1999) suggests that every aspect of the gender-variant client's culture should be addressed, including race, religion, and experiences. Mallon (1999) states that, "Transgendered children of color and their families face compounded stressors resulting from transgenderphobia and racism and may need additional emotional and social support, as well as legal redress of discrimination" (p. 62). Awareness of the possibility of violence within and outside the family toward the gender-variant individual is something that counselors need to keep in mind and watch out for (Mallon, 1999).

Belief in Client Competency

A pitfall that counselors may encounter is being overconcerned with their client's gendered appearance and behavior (Lombardi & Davis, 2006). Counselors need to let their clients decide how they want to express their gender and to what extent. Some clients may be comfortable with a more androgynous appearance, and Lombardi & Davis (2006) suggest that counselors be comfortable with trusting the competency of their clients. Because hormone replacement therapy (HRT) is a part of transitioning, counselors may find themselves in the "gatekeeper" role (Martin & Yonkin, 2006). Counselors might need to provide letters to medical providers for HRT and for gender reassignment surgery, and Martin & Yonkin (2006) suggest that this can place a counselor in a conflict of roles—that of mental health provider and unilateral decision maker for the client. Counselors need to be cognizant of ways to include their transgender clients in the decision-making process and to allow these clients to express their competency. Also, as noted, not all transgender people want the binary experience of sex and gender and may choose not to use tools to feminize or masculinize their appearance (Martin & Yonkin, 2006), and clinicians are encouraged to empower their clients and their families to find adequate care.

COUNTERTRANSFERENCE

As with counselor reactions to gays and lesbians, counselors need to be aware of their own levels of transphobia. Due to GID being classified as a mental disorder in the DSM-IV-TR, professionals may feel justified in pathologizing individuals who are transgendered (Lombardi & Davis, 2006). Another concern for counseling professionals working with transgender clients is falling into the role of "gatekeeper" and viewing these clients as incompetent in making decisions for transitioning. Sexism, classism, racism, and heterosexism can also hinder the relationships (Lombardi & Davis, 2006).

Pathologizing Transgender Clients/Transphobia

The mere presence of GID as a diagnostic category in the DSM-IV-TR gives counselors power over the lives of transgender individuals (Hunter & Hickerson, 2003). A concern that is raised about this pathologization of transgender individuals is its use in institutionalizing children and adolescents with GID (Hunter & Hickerson, 2003). Because of its diagnosability as a mental illness, counselors need to be aware of their interpretation of GID and their potential view of their clients as "mentally ill." Transgender behavior and identity have not been shown to directly impair a person's life. Of those people who seek mental health services, transgender individuals are no more likely to have impairment than those who are not (Hunter & Hickerson, 2003). Counselors working with these clients will need to be careful in their assessments, look beyond gender-stereotyped roles, and look at environmental stressors that could contribute to problems presented by transgender clients.

TOOLBOX ACTIVITY—RACHEL			
Resources and Suggested Readings	*Videos*	*Activities*	*Discussion Questions*
Feinberg, L. (1996). *Transgender warriors: Making history.* Boston: Beacon Press. Lev, A. I. (2004). *Transgender emergence: Therapeutic guidelines for working with gender-variant people and their families.* New York: The Haworth Clinical Practice Press. Mallon, G. P. (Ed.). (1999). *Social services with transgendered youth.* New York: Harrington Park Press. Morrow, D. F., & Messinger, L. (Eds.), (2006). *Sexual orientation and gender expression in social work practice.* New York: Columbia University Press.	*Normal* *TransAmerica*	Interview male-to-female and female-to-male transsexuals and ask them about their experiences with counseling professionals. Write a paper about what were the most helpful and least helpful counseling interventions. If you don't have access to transsexual individuals, research the topic of most and least helpful interventions for transsexuals and write a paper about them.	Content Themes What other themes do you see emerging in the story that the authors did not identify? Assessment Are there any questions you would like to ask Rachel or Rachel's mom? Interventions What other interventions could you propose with Rachel or Rachel's mom? Countertransference What countertransference reactions were emerging in yourself as you read this story? Other Scenarios Imagine that Ryan's mom comes to you when he is 20 years old and talks to you with some trepidation regarding his impending sex change operation. How could you help Ryan's mom as he transitions to Rachel?

Appendix

Author Guidelines

You are invited to write a cultural autobiography, a story of your life, your identity, and your experiences. The story should tell who you are, how you see yourself, and how you arrived at your perceptions. There is no set format for the story; it should be as creative or reflective of your life as you would like. The following questions are general guidelines to assist in writing the chapter. You do not need to answer each question, nor are they intended to be included in any particular order.

How do you identify yourself?

What factor do you most identify with as your cultural identity? Why? What significant events in your life have contributed to your cultural identity? What meaning does it provide for your life?

What is your most distinguishing cultural factor? Does it differ from the most important? If so, how? Why?

Has your cultural identity served as a detriment, challenge, problem, difficulty, or deterrent in your life? Has your cultural identity felt like a burden? If so, how?

What childhood messages did you receive about your cultural identity or background?

How has your cultural identity served as a source of strength in your life?

Have you used your identity as a coping skill or problem-solving tool? If so, when and how?

Does the factor that you identify most strongly with differ from the cultural factor with which others identify you? How has that affected your identity development? Are there significant life events associated with this factor?

Have you encountered any difficulties with your cultural identity? If so, what kind? How have you coped with them? What resources have you needed to cope with them? How have the difficulties contributed to your identity?

What strengths do you associate with your cultural identity? What are the areas of pride associated with them?

Multicultural Genogram

The genogram is a useful tool for assessing families and determining multigenerational patterns, significant life events, rituals, roles, and the nature of relationships between family members. The genogram often provides direction for treatment. The multicultural genogram provides all the information listed previously, but includes an assessment of worldview that often affects behaviors of members. Worldview can be defined as an individual's perception of his or her relationship with the world. Specific questions on cultural factors can be included in the genogram to enrich the process.

ETHNICITY

1. What is the ethnicity of each family member?
2. What roles does ethnicity determine for different members?
3. What roles are assigned due to ethnicity?
4. What are similar characteristics across various ethnic groups?
5. What are differences between ethnic groups?
6. How is conflict handled according to ethnic groups?
7. How do family members handle conflicts across ethnicity?
8. What are specific rules for marriage and child rearing according to ethnicity?

IMMIGRATION/ACCULTURATION

1. What is the family's history of immigration?
2. When did individual members migrate to America, and why?
3. Are there plans to return to the country of origin?
4. What difficulties did the family face during immigration?
5. Has each member acculturated to the majority culture?
6. Is there conflict between members who retain culture of origin and members who have acculturated?

GENDER

1. What is the role of gender for each member as defined by the ethnicity/culture of origin?

2. What behaviors, characteristics, beliefs, and values are defined by gender?

3. How are gender roles divided in the family? In the family of origin?

4. How is conflict between gender roles handled?

5. How do beliefs about gender roles influence child-rearing beliefs?

SOCIOECONOMIC STATUS (SES)

1. What role or meaning does SES have for members?

2. Does class differ across generations?

3. What resources are available to members due to SES?

4. Has there been a change in current SES?

SPIRITUALITY

1. What is the family's religious history?

2. What characteristics, values, and beliefs are influenced by religion?

3. If members differ according to religion, what are the similarities in values and beliefs?

4. What are the differences in values and beliefs according to religion?

5. How are conflicts due to different religious values resolved?

OTHER AREAS OF CONCERN

Majority or minority status

Sexual orientation

Regional background

Physical disabilities

Adapted from Thomas, A. J. (1998). Understanding worldview and culture in family systems: Use of the multicultural genogram. In *The Family Journal: Counseling and Therapy for Couples and Families, 6,* 24–32. Reprinted with permission.

References

Aciman, A. (2000). *Letters of transit: Reflections on exile, identity, language, and loss.* New York: New Press.

Adams, M. (2000a). Antisemitism. In M. Adams, W. Blumenfeld, R. Castaneda, H. Hackman, M. Peters, & X. Zuniga (Eds.), *Readings for diversity and social justice* (pp. 133–137). New York: Routledge.

Adams, M. (2000b). Classism. In M. Adams, W. Blumenfeld, R. Castaneda, H. Hackman, M. Peters, & X. Zuniga (Eds.), *Readings for diversity and social justice* (pp. 379–381). New York: Routledge.

Adams, M. (2000c). Readings for diversity and social justice: A general introduction. In M. Adams, W. Blumenfeld, R. Castaneda, H. Hackman, M. Peters, & X. Zuniga (Eds.), *Readings for diversity and social justice* (pp. 1–4). New York: Routledge.

Almeida, R., Woods, R., Messineo, T., & Font, R. (1998). The cultural context model: An overview. In M. McGoldrick (Ed.), *Re-visioning family therapy: Race, culture and gender in clinical practice* (pp. 414–429). New York: Guilford Press.

Alvarez, J. (1992). *How the Garcia girls lost their accent.* New York: Plume Books.

American Anthropological Association. (1998). *American Anthropological Association statement on "race."* Retrieved August 4, 2007, from http://www.aaanet.org/stmts/racepp.htm

American Counseling Association. (2005). *American Counseling Association Code of Ethics.* Alexandria, VA: Author.

American Psychiatric Association. (2000). *Diagnostic and statistical manual of mental disorders* (4th ed.). Washington, DC: Author.

American Psychiatric Association. (2000). *Diagnostic and statistical manual of mental disorders* (4th ed. – TR). Washington, DC: Author.

American Psychiatric Association Commission on Psychotherapy by Psychiatrists (COPP). (2000). Position statement on therapies focused on attempts to change sexual orientation (Reparative or conversion therapies) [Electronic Version]. *American Journal of Psychiatry, 157,* 1719–1721.

American Psychological Association. (2002). *APA guidelines on multicultural education, training, research, practice, and organizational change for psychologists.* Retrieved May 28, 2007, from http://www.apa.org/divisions/div45/resources.htm#guidelines

American Psychological Association. (2005, August). *Resolution on anti-Semitic and anti-Jewish prejudice.* Retrieved November 14, 2006, from http://www.apa.org/pi/antisemitic_jewish_prejudice.pdf

Anderson, S. K., & Middleton, V. A. (2004). *Explorations in privilege, oppression, and diversity.* Belmont, CA: Wadsworth.

Annual ADL Audit. (2006, April 5). *Anti-Semitic incidents decline in 2005 but levels still of concern in U.S.* [Antisemitism USA press release]. Retrieved April 5, 2006, from http://www.adl.org/PresRele/ASUS_12/audit_2005.htm

Answers to your questions about sexual orientation and homosexuality. (n.d.). Washington, DC: APA Office of Public and Member Communications. Retrieved November 21, 2006, from http://www.apa.org/topics/orientation.html

Anti-Defamation League. (n.d.). *Antisemitism.* Retrieved December 8, 2006, from http://www.adl.org/main_Anti_Semitism_Domestic/default.htm

APA Task Force on Gender Identity, Gender Variance, and Intersex Conditions. (n.d.). *Answers to your questions about transgender individuals and gender identity.* Washington, DC: APA Office of Public and Member Communications. Retrieved November 21, 2006, from http://www.apa.org/topics/transgender.html

APA Task Force on Gender Identity, Gender Variance, and Intersex Conditions. (n.d.). *Answers to your questions about individuals with intersex conditions.* Washington, DC: APA Office of Public and Member Communications. Retrieved November 21, 2006, from http://www.apa.org/topics/intersx.html

APA Task Force on Socioeconomic Status. (2007). *Report of the APA task force on socioeconomic status.* American Psychological Association. Retrieved August 22, 2007, from http://www.apa.org/pi/ses/homepage.html

Aponte, H. (1995). *Bread and spirit: Therapy with the new poor.* New York: W. W. Norton.

Aponte, H. J. (1999). The stress of poverty and the comfort of spirituality. In F. Walsh (Ed.), *Spiritual resources in family therapy* (pp. 76–89). New York: Guilford Press.

Appiah, K. A. (2006, January 1). The case for contamination. *The New York Times Magazine, 155,* (53446), 30–52.

Arey, D. (2002). Gay males and sexual child abuse. In L. Aronson Fontes (Ed.), *Sexual abuse in nine North American cultures: Treatment and prevention* (pp. 200–235). Thousand Oaks, CA: Sage Publications.

Armstrong, K. (2001). *The battle for God: A history of fundamentalism.* New York: Ballantine.

Arredondo, P., & Perez, P. (2003). Expanding multicultural competence through social justice leadership. *The Counseling Psychologist, 31*(3), 282–289.

Arredondo, P., Toporek, R., Brown, S. P., Jones, J., Locke, D. C., Sanchez, J., & Stadler, H. (1996). Operationalization of the multicultural counseling competencies. *Journal of Multicultural Counseling and Development, 24,* 42–78.

Ashemberg Straussner, S. L. (2001). Jewish substance abusers: Existing but invisible. In S. L. Ashemberg Straussner (Ed.), *Ethnocultural factors in substance abuse treatment* (pp. 291–317). New York: Guilford Press.

Association of Religious Data Archives. (2006). Retrieved September 21, 2006, from http://www.thearda.com/internationalData/countries/Country_234_2.asp

Atkinson, D. (2003). *Counseling American minorities: A cross-cultural perspective* (6th ed.). New York: McGraw-Hill.

Atkinson, R. (1998). *The life story interview.* Thousand Oaks, CA: Sage Publications.

Atkinson, D. R., Morten, G., & Sue, D. W. (1998). *Counseling American minorities* (5th ed). Boston: McGraw-Hill.

Azimi, N. (2006, December 3). Prisoners of sex. *The New York Times Magazine,* p. 63.

Balls Organista, P., Organista, K. C., & Kurasaki, K. (2003). The relationship between acculturation and ethnic minority mental health. In K. M. Chun, P. Balls Organista, & G. Marin, (Eds.), *Acculturation: Advances in theory, measurement, and applied research* (pp. 139–161). Washington, DC: American Psychological Association.

Bartee, J. (2007). Personal communication. April 2007.

Bass, E., & Kaufman, K. (1996). *Free your mind: The book for gay, lesbian, and bisexual youth and their allies.* New York: HarperCollins.

Beauvais, E., Chavez, E. L., Oetting, E. R., Deffenbacher, J. L., & Cornell, G. R. (1996). Drug use, violence, and victimization among White American, Mexican American, and American Indian dropouts, students with academic problems and students in good academic standing. *Journal of Counseling Psychology, 43,* 292–299.

Ben-Sasson, H. (1985). *History of the Jewish people.* Cambridge, MA: Harvard University Press.

Berger, K. S. (2004). *The developing person through the lifespan* (6th ed.). New York: Worth.

Bernal, G., Trimble, J. E., Burlew, A. K. & Leong, F. T. L. (2003). Introduction. In G. Bernal, J. E. Trimble, A. K. Burlew, & F. T. L. Leong (Eds.), *Handbook of racial and ethnic minority psychology* (pp. 1–12). Thousand Oaks, CA: Sage Publications.

Bernal, G., Trimble, J. E., Burlew, A. K. & Leong, F. T. L. (2003). *Handbook of racial and ethnic minority psychology.* Thousand Oaks, CA: Sage Publications.

Berry, J. W. (2003). Conceptual approaches to acculturation. In K. M. Chun, P. Balls Organista, & G. Marin (Eds.), *Acculturation: Advances in theory, measurement, and applied research* (pp. 17–37). Washington, DC: American Psychological Association.

Berry, J., Phinney, J., Sam, D., & Vedder, P. (2006). *Immigrant youth in cultural transition: Acculturation, identity, and adaptation across national contexts.* New Jersey: Lawrence Erlbaum.

Beth-Shalom, U., & Horenczyk, G. (2003). Acculturation orientation: A facet theory perspective on the bidimensional model. *Journal of Cross Cultural Psychology, 34*(2), 176–188.

Bettelheim, B. (1980). *Surviving and other essays.* New York: Vintage.

Beyebach, M., & Escudero Carranza, V. (1997). Therapeutic interactions and dropout: Measuring relational communication in solution-focused therapy. *Journal of Family Therapy, 19,* 173–212.

Birke, L. (2002). Unusual fingers: Scientific studies of sexual orientation. In D. Richardson & S. Seidman (Eds.), *Handbook of lesbian and gay studies* (pp. 55–71). Thousand Oaks, CA: Sage Publications.

Birman, D. (1994). Acculturation and human diversity in a multicultural society. In E. J. Trickett, R. J. Watts, & D. Birman (Eds.), *Human diversity: Perspectives on people in context* (pp. 261–284). San Francisco: Jossey-Bass.

Blades, E. (1994). The causes of homosexuality are irrelevant. In M. E. Williams (Ed.), *Opposing viewpoints: Homosexuality* (pp. 47–51). San Diego, CA: Greenhaven.

Blumenfeld, W. (2006). Christian privilege and the promotion of "secular" and not so "secular" mainline Christianity in public schooling and in the larger society. *Equity and Excellence in Education, 39,* 195–210.

Blumenfeld, W. J. (2000). Heterosexism. In M. Adams, W. Blumenfeld, R. Castaneda, H. Hackman, M. Peters, & X. Zuniga (Eds.), *Readings for diversity and social justice* (pp. 261–266). New York: Routledge.

Blumenfeld, W. J. & Raymond, D. (2000). Prejudice and discrimination. In M. Adams, W. Blumenfeld, R. Castaneda, H. Hackman, M. Peters, & X. Zuniga (Eds.), *Readings for diversity and social justice* (pp. 21–30). New York: Routledge.

Bowe, J. (2006, November 19). Gay donor or gay dad? *The New York Times Magazine*, p. 66.

Boyd-Franklin, N. (2003). Race, class, and poverty. In F. Walsh (Ed.), *Normal family processes* (pp. 260–279). New York: Guilford Press.

Boyd-Franklin, N. (2004). *Black families in therapy: Understanding the African American experience* (2nd ed.). New York: Guilford Press.

Boykin, A. W, & Toms, F. D. (1985). Black child socialization: A conceptual framework. In H. P. McAdoo & J. L. McAdoo (Eds.), *Black children: Social, educational, and parental environments* (pp. 33–52). Newbury Park, CA: Sage Publications.

Bradford, D. T., & Munoz, A. (1993). Translation in bilingual psychotherapy. *Professional Psychology: Research and Practice, 24*(1), 52–61.

Bray, I. M. (2006). *How to get a green card* (7th ed.). Berkeley, CA: Nolo Press.

Bray, I. M. (2006). *U.S. immigration made easy* (12th ed.). Berkeley, CA: Nolo Press.

Breunlin, D. C., Schwartz, R. C., & Mac Kune-Karrer, B. (1997). *Metaframeworks: Transcending the models of family therapy.* San Francisco: Jossey-Bass.

Bronfenbrenner, U. (1977). Toward an experimental ecology of human development. *American Psychologist, 32,* 513–531.

Burgess, C. A. (1997). The impact of lesbian/gay sensitive policies on the behavior and health of lesbians in the workplace. In W. K. Swan (Ed.), *Gay/lesbian/bisexual/transgender public policy issues* (pp. 35–48). New York: The Harrington Park Press.

Burke, M. T., Chauvin, J. C., & Maranti, J. (2003). *Spirituality in counseling and therapy: A developmental and multicultural approach.* New York: Brunner-Routledge.

Butke, M. (2002). Lesbians and sexual child abuse. In L. Aronson Fontes (Ed.), *Sexual abuse in nine North American cultures: Treatment and prevention* (pp. 236–258). Thousand Oaks, CA: Sage Publications.

Campo, J. (2006). Islam. In W. Doniger (Ed.), *Britannica encyclopedia of world religions* (pp. 515–563). Chicago: Encyclopaedia Britannica.

Carrasco, D. (2006). Native American religions. In W. Doniger (Ed.), *Britannica encyclopedia of world religions* (pp. 515–692). Chicago: Encyclopaedia Britannica.

Casas, J. M., Ponterotto, J. G., & Gutierrez, J. M. (1986). An ethical indictment of counseling research and training: The cross-cultural perspective. *Journal of Counseling & Development, 64,* 347–349.

Cass, V. C. (1979). Homosexual identity formation: A theoretical model. *Journal of Homosexuality, 4,* 219–235.

Cassidy, C., O'Connor, R. C., Howe, C., & Warden, D. (2004). Perceived discrimination and psychological distress: The role of personal and ethnic self-esteem. *Journal of Counseling Psychology, 51*(3), 329–339.

Castaneda, R., & Peters, M. (2000). Ableism. In M. Adams, W. Blumenfeld, R. Castaneda, H. Hackman, M. Peters, & X. Zuniga (Eds.), *Readings for diversity and social justice* (pp. 319–323). New York: Routledge.

Chandler, C. K., Holden, J. M., & Kolander, C. A. (1992). Counseling for spiritual wellness: Theory and practice. *Journal of Counseling & Development, 71,* 168–175.

Cheng, Z. (2003). Issues and standards in counseling lesbians and gay men with substance abuse concerns. *Journal of Mental Health Counseling, 25*(4), 323–336.

Chun, K. M., Balls Organista, P., & Marin, G. (Eds.). (2003). *Acculturation: Advances in theory, measurement, and applied research.* Washington, DC: American Psychological Association.

Cisneros, S. (1991). *The house on Mango Street.* New York: Vintage Books.

Clark, C. S. (1997). The new immigrants: Do they threaten the American identity? *Congressional Quarterly, 7*(3), 49–72.

Clark, R., Anderson, N. B., Clark, V. R., & Williams, D. R. (1999). Racism as a stressor for African Americans: A biopsychosocial model. *American Psychologist, 54,* 805–816.

Clauss, C. S. (1998). Language: The unspoken variable in psychotherapy practice. *Psychotherapy, 35*(2), 188–196.

Cloud, H., & Townsend, J. (1995). *12 "Christian" beliefs that can drive you crazy.* Grand Rapids, MI: Zondervan.

Cochran, S. D., Ackerman, D., Mays, V. M., & Ross, M. W. (2004). Prevalence of non-medical drug use and dependence among homosexually active men and women in the US population. *Society for the Study of Addiction, 99,* 989–998.

Cokely, K. O. (2002). Testing Cross's revised racial identity model: An examination of the relationship between racial identity and internalized racialism. *Journal of Counseling Psychology, 49,* 476–483.

Cole, M. (2006). The eclipse of the non-European: Historical and current manifestations of racialization in the US. *Ethnic and Racial Studies, 29*(1), 173–185.

Coleman, E. (1981). Developmental stages of the coming out process. *Journal of Homosexuality, 7*(2–3), 31–43.

Comas-Diaz, L. (1987). Feminist therapy with mainland Puerto Rican women. *Psychology of Women Quarterly, 11,* 461–474.

Comas-Diaz, L., & Jacobsen, F. M. (1991). Ethnocultural transference and countertransference in the therapeutic dyad. *American Journal of Orthopsychiatry, 61,* 392–402.

Constantine, M. G. (2007). Racial microaggressions against African American clients in cross-racial counseling relationships. *Journal of Counseling Psychology, 54*(1), 1–16.

Constantine, M. G., & Sue, D. W. (2007). Perceptions of racial microaggressions among black supervisees in cross-racial dyads. *Journal of Counseling Psychology, 54*(2), 142–153.

Cooper, K. (1998). Social work practice with transgendered youth and their families. In G. P. Mallon (Ed.), *Social services for transgendered youth* (pp. 111–131). New York: Haworth Press.

Cowan, P., & Cowan, R. (1989). *Mixed blessings: Overcoming the stumbling blocks in an interfaith marriage.* New York: Penguin.

Crohn, J. (1998). Intercultural couples. In M. McGoldrick (Ed.), *Re-visioning family therapy: Race culture and gender in clinical practice* (pp. 295–308). New York: Guilford Press.

Cross, W. E. (1995). The psychology of nigrescence: Revising the Cross model. In J. G. Ponterotto, J. M. Casas, L. A. Suzuki, & C. M. Alexander (Eds.), *Handbook of multicultural counseling* (pp. 93–122). Thousand Oaks, CA: Sage Publications.

Dancy, J. J., & Wynn-Dancy, M. L. (1994). Faith of our fathers (mothers) living still: Spirituality as a force for the transmission of family values within the Black community. *Activities, Adaptation, and Aging, 19,* 87–105.

D'Andrea, M., & Daniels, J. (2001). Expanding our thinking about white racism: Facing the challenge of multicultural counseling in the 21st century. In J. G. Ponterotto, J. M. Casas, L. A. Suzuki, & C. M. Alexander (Eds.), *Handbook of multicultural counseling* (pp. 289–310). Thousand Oaks, CA: Sage Publications.

D'Andrea, M., Daniels, J., Arredondo, P., Ivey, M. B., Ivey, A. E., Locke, D. C., O'Bryant, B., Parham, T. A., & Sue, D. W. (2001). Fostering organizational changes to realize the revolutionary potential of the multicultural movement: An updated case study. In J. G. Ponterotto, J. M. Casas, L. A. Suzuki, & C. M. Alexander (Eds.), *Handbook of multicultural counseling* (pp. 222–253). Thousand Oaks, CA: Sage Publications.

Daniels, R. (1997). *Not like us: Immigrants and minorities in America, 1890–1924.* Chicago: Ivan Dee.

Daniels, R. (2002). *Coming to America: A history of immigration and ethnicity in American life* (2nd ed.). New York: HarperCollins.

DeLeon, P. H. (1998). Proceedings of the American Psychological Association, Incorporated, for the legislative year 1997: Minutes of the Annual Meeting of the Council of Representatives, August 14 and 17, Chicago, Illinois; and June, August and December 1997 meetings of the Board of Directors [Electronic Version]. *American Psychologist, 53,* 882–939.

Deloria, V. (1993). *Teaching about Native American religions.* Retrieved October 3, 2006, from http://puffin.creighton.edu/lakota/teaching.html

De Shazer, S. (1988). *Investigating solutions in brief therapy.* New York: W. W. Norton.

Dinnerstein, L. (2000). The Christian heritage. In M. Adams, W. Blumenfeld, R. Castaneda, H. Hackman, M. Peters, & X. Zuniga (Eds.), *Readings for diversity and social justice* (pp. 144–150). New York: Routledge.

Division 44/Committee on Lesbian, Gay, and Bisexual Concerns joint task force on guidelines for psychotherapy with lesbian, gay, and bisexual clients. (2000). Guidelines for psychotherapy with lesbian, gay and bisexual clients. *American Psychologist, 55*(12), 1440–1451.

Doak, M. (1997). *Religious movements.* Retrieved October 3, 2006, from http://religiousmovements.lib.virginia.edu/nrms/naspirit.html

Dolan-Del Vecchio, K. (1998). Dismantling White male privilege within family therapy. In M. McGoldrick (Ed.), *Re-visioning family therapy: Race, culture, and gender in clinical practice* (pp. 159–175). New York: Guilford Press.

Doniger, W. (Ed.). (2006). *Britannica encyclopedia of world religions.* Chicago: Encyclopaedia Britannica.

Donner, F. (1999). Muhammad and the caliphate. In J. L. Esposito (Ed.), *The Oxford history of Islam* (pp. 1–62). New York: Oxford University Press.

Dorfman, A. (1999). *Heading south, looking north: A bilingual journey.* New York: Penguin Books.

Dube, E. M., Savin-Williams, R. C., & Diamond, L. M. (2001). Intimacy development, gender, and ethnicity among sexual-minority youths. In A. R. D'Augelli & C. J. Patterson (Eds.), *Lesbian, gay, and bisexual identities and youth* (pp. 129–154). New York: Oxford University Press.

Duncan, B., Miller, S., & Sparks, J. (2004). *The heroic client: A revolutionary way to improve effectiveness through client-directed, outcome-informed therapy.* San Francisco: Jossey-Bass.

Ehrenreich, B. (2002). *Nickel and dimed: On (not) getting by in America.* New York: Owl Books.

Elliott, A. (2005, May 12). Study by Muslim group says bias crime up 50% in 2004. *The New York Times,* p. B5.

Ellis-Hill, C. S., & Horn, S. (2000). Change in identity and self-concept: A new theoretical approach to recovery following a stroke. *Clinical Rehabilitation, 14,* 279–287.

Elon, A. (2002). *The pity of it all: A portrait of the German-Jewish epoch 1743–1933.* New York: Picador.

Elze, D. E. (2006). Oppression, prejudice, and discrimination. In D. F. Morrow & L. Messinger (Eds.), *Sexual orientation and gender expression in social work practice* (pp. 43–78). New York: Columbia University Press.

Epston, M. (1993). Internalized other questioning with couples: The New Zealand version. In S. Gilligan & R. Price (Eds.), *Therapeutic conversations* (pp. 183–189). New York: W. W. Norton.

Erikson, E. (1968). *Identity, youth, and crisis.* New York: W. W. Norton.

Esterberg, K. G. (2002). The bisexual menace: Or, will the real bisexual please stand up? In D. Richardson & S. Seidman (Eds.), *Handbook of lesbian and gay studies* (pp. 215–227). Thousand Oaks, CA: Sage Publications.

Everall, R. D., Altrows, K. J., & Paulson, B. L. (2006). Creating a future: A study of resilience in suicidal female adolescents. *Journal of Counseling and Development, 84,* 461–470.

Faderman, L. (1991). *Odd girls and twilight lovers: A history of lesbian life in twentieth-century America.* New York: Columbia University Press.

Faiver, C. M., O'Brien, E. M., & Ingersoll, E. R. (2000). Religion, guilt, and mental health. *Journal of Counseling & Development, 78,* 155–161.

Falicov, C. J. (1995). Cross-cultural marriages. In N. S. Jacobson & A. S. Gurman (Eds.), *Clinical handbook of couple therapy* (2nd ed., pp. 231–246). New York: Guilford Press.

Falicov, C. J. (1998a). *Latino families in therapy: A guide to multicultural practice.* New York: Guilford Press.

Falicov, C. J. (1998b). The cultural meaning of family triangles. In M. McGoldrick (Ed.), *Re-visioning family therapy: Race, culture, and gender in clinical practice* (pp. 37–49). New York: Guilford Press.

Falicov, C. J. (1999). Religion and spiritual folk traditions in immigrant families: Therapeutic resources with Latinos. In F. Walsh (Ed.), *Spiritual resources in family therapy* (pp. 104–120). New York: Guilford Press.

Falicov, C. J. (2003). Immigrant family processes. In F. Walsh (Ed.), *Normal family process* (3rd ed., pp. 260–279). New York: Guilford Press.

Faludi, S. (1992). *Backlash: The undeclared war against American women.* New York: Anchor.

Fassinger, R. E., & Miller, B. A. (1996). Validation of an inclusive model of sexual minority identity formation on a sample of gay men. *Journal of Homosexuality, 32,* 53–78.

Feagin, J. R., & Feagin, C. (2002). *Racial and ethnic relations.* Englewood Cliffs, NJ: Prentice Hall.

Feagin, J., & Sikes, M. P. (1995). *Living with racism: The Black middle-class experience.* Boston: Beacon Press.

Feinberg, L. (1996). *Transgender warriors: Making history.* Boston: Beacon Press.

Fong, R. (Ed.). (2003). *Culturally competent practice with immigrant and refugee children and families.* New York: Guilford Press.

Fordham, S. (1988). Racelessness as a factor in Black students' school success: Pragmatic strategy or Pyrrhic victory? *Harvard Educational Review, 58,* 54–84.

Fouad, N. A., Gerstein, L. H. & Toporek, R. L. (2006). Social justice and counseling psychology in context. In R. L. Toporek, L. H. Gerstein, N. A. Fouad, G. Roysircar, & T. Israel (Eds.), *Handbook for social justice in counseling psychology: Leadership, vision, and action* (pp. 1–16). Thousand Oaks, CA: Sage Publications.

Fowler, J. E. (1981). *Stages of faith.* New York: Harper & Row.

Fox, D. R. (2003). Awareness is good, but action is better. *The Counseling Psychologist, 31*(3), 299–304.

Fox, R. C. (1995) Bisexual identities. In A. R. D'Augelli & C. J. Patterson (Eds.), *Lesbian, gay, and bisexual identities over the lifespan: Psychological perspectives* (pp. 48–86). New York and Oxford: Oxford University Press.

Frame, M. W. (2002). *Integrating religion and spirituality into counseling: A comprehensive approach.* New York: Wadsworth.

Frame, M. W., & Williams, C. B. (1996). Counseling African Americans: Integrating spirituality in therapy. *Counseling and Values, 41,* 16–28.

Freedman, J., & Combs, G. (1995). *Narrative therapy: The social construction of preferred realities.* New York: W. W. Norton.

Freire, P. (1970/2001). *Pedagogy of the oppressed.* New York: Continuum.

Freire, P. (1999). *Pedagogy of hope.* New York: Continuum.

Fuertes, J. N. (2004). Supervision in bilingual counseling: Service delivery, training, and research considerations. *Journal of Multicultural Counseling and Development, 32*(2), 84–94.

Fuertes, J. N., & Gretchen, D. (2001). Emerging theories of multicultural counseling. In J. G. Ponterotto, J. M. Casas, L. A. Suzuki, & C. M. Alexander (Eds.), *Handbook of multicultural counseling* (pp. 509–541). Thousand Oaks, CA: Sage Publications.

Fukuyama, M. (1990). Multicultural and spiritual issues in counseling. Workshop presented at the American Association for Counseling and Development Annual Conference, Cincinnati, OH.

Fukuyama, M. A., & Sevig, T. D. (1992, November). Integrating spirituality and multicultural awareness. Workshop presented at Loyola University Chicago.

Fukuyama, M. A., & Sevig, T. D. (1999). *Integrating spirituality into multicultural counseling.* Thousand Oaks, CA: Sage Publications.

Garcia-Prieto, N. (1996). Puerto Rican families. In M. McGoldrick (Ed.), *Re-visioning family therapy: Race culture and gender in clinical practice* (pp. 183–199). New York: Guilford Press.

Garrett, J. T., & Garrett, M. W. (1994). The path of good medicine: Understanding and counseling Native American Indians. *Journal of Multicultural Counseling and Development, 22,* 134–144.

Gates, G. (2004). *Gay men and lesbians in the U.S. military.* Retrieved October 17, 2006, from http://www.urban.org/publications/411069.html

Gay, P. (Ed.). (1989). *The Freud reader.* New York: W. W. Norton.

Gergen, K. (1991). *The saturated self: Dilemmas of identity in contemporary life.* New York: Basic Books.

GID Reform (n.d.). Retrieved November 28, 2006, from http://www.gidreform.org/

Gilbert, M. (2000). The Holocaust maps. In M. Adams, W. Blumenfeld, R. Castaneda, H. Hackman, M. Peters, & X. Zuniga (Eds.), *Readings for diversity and social justice* (pp. 151–162). New York: Routledge.

Gimenez, M. (2005). Capitalism and the oppression of women: Marx revisited. *Science and society, 69*(1), 11–32.

Giordano, J., & McGoldrick, M. (1996). European families: An overview. In M. McGoldrick, J. Giordano, & J. K. Pierce (Eds.), *Ethnicity and family therapy* (2nd ed., pp. 427–441). New York: Guilford Press.

GLBT Fact Sheets (n.d.). Retrieved November 21, 2006, from http://www.aglp.org/pages/cfactsheets.html

Gonzalez, G. M. (1997). The emergence of Chicanos in the twenty-first century: Implications for counseling, research and policy. *Journal of Multicultural Counseling and Development, 25,* 94–106.

Gorkin, M. (1996). Countertransference in cross-cultural psychotherapy. In R. Perez Foster, M. Moskowitz, & R. Javier (Eds.), *Reaching across boundaries of culture and class: Widening the scope of psychotherapy* (pp. 160–173). Northvale, NJ: Jason Aronson.

Grace, J. (1992). Affirming gay and lesbian adulthood. In N. J. Woodman (Ed.), *Lesbian and gay lifestyles: A guide for counseling and education* (pp. 33–47). New York: Irvington.

Green, R. J. (1998). Race and the field of family therapy. In M. McGoldrick (Ed.), *Re-visioning family therapy: Race, culture, and gender in clinical practice* (pp. 93–110). New York: Guilford Press.

Greene, B., White, J. C., & Whitten, L. (2000). Hair texture, length, and style as a metaphor in the African American mother-daughter relationship: Considerations in psychodynamic psychotherapy. In L. C. Jackson & B. Greene (Eds.), *Psychotherapy with African American women: Innovations in psychodynamic perspectives* (pp. 166–193). New York: Guilford Press.

Greene, B. L. (1992). Racial socialization as a tool in psychotherapy with African American children. In L. A. Vargas & J. D. Koss-Chioino (Eds.), *Working with culture: Psychotherapeutic interventions with ethnic minority children and adolescents* (pp. 63–81). San Francisco: Jossey-Bass.

Grieco, E. M., & Cassidy, C. R. (2001, March). Overview of race and Hispanic origin: Census 2000 brief. Retrieved August 8, 2007, from http://eric.ed.gov/ERICDocs/data/ericdocs2sql/content_storage_01/0000019b/80/17/10/06.pdf

Griffith, B. A., & Griggs, J. C. (2001). Religious identity status as a model to understand, assess, and interact with client spirituality. *Counseling and Values, 46,* 14–24.

Griffith, B. A., & Rotter, J. (1999). Families and spirituality: Therapists as facilitators. *The Family Journal: Counseling and Therapy for Couples and Families, 7,* 161–164.

Grinberg, L., & Grinberg, R. (2000). *Psychoanalytic perspectives on migration and exile.* New Haven, CT: Yale University Press.

Gushue, G. V. (1993). Cultural-identity development and family assessment: An interaction model. *Counseling Psychologist, 21,* 487–513.

Gutierrez, D. (1995). *Walls and mirrors: Mexican Americans, Mexican immigrants, and the politics of ethnicity.* Berkeley: University of California Press.

Hackman, H. W. (2000). Sexism. In M. Adams, W. Blumenfeld, R. Castaneda, H. Hackman, M. Peters, & X. Zuniga (Eds.), *Readings for diversity and social justice* (pp. 199–203). New York: Routledge.

Hanna, F., Talley, B., & Guindon, M. (2000). The power of perception: Toward a model of cultural oppression and liberation. *Journal of Counseling & Development, 78,* 430–441.

Haraucourt, E. (n.d.). Seul, "Rondel de l'adieu" (S. Schwarzbaum, Trans.). Retrieved February 27, 2005, from http://perso.wanadoo.fr/college.claudel.chevigny/poesie/poeme4.htm

Hardiman, R. (1982). White identity development: A process oriented model for describing the racial consciousness of White Americans. *Dissertation Abstracts International, 43,* 104A. (University Microfilms No. 82-10330).

Harper, G. W., Jernwall, N., & Zea, M. C. (2004). Giving voice to emerging science and theory for lesbian, gay, and bisexual people of color. *Cultural Diversity and Ethnic Minority Psychology, 10*(3), 187–199.

Harrell, S. P. (2000). A multidimensional conceptualization of racism-related stress: Implications for the well-being of people of color. *American Journal of Orthopsychiatry, 70,* 42–57.

Hart, B. & Risley, T. R. (1995). *Meaningful differences in the everyday experience of young American children.* Baltimore: Brookes.

Hawley, J. S. (2006). Hinduism. In W. Doniger (Ed.), *Britannica encyclopedia of world religions* (pp. 177–199). Chicago: Encyclopaedia Britannica.

Hawxhurst, J. C. (1998). *The interfaith family guidebook: Practical advice for Jewish and Christian partners.* Boston, KY: Dovetail.

Hays, D., Chang, D., & Dean, J. K. (2004). White counselors' conceptualization of privilege and oppression: Implications for counselor training. *Counselor Education and Supervision, 43,* 242–257.

Hays, P. (2001). *Addressing cultural complexities in practice.* Washington, DC: American Psychological Association.

Helms, J. E. (1995). An update of Helms's White and people of color racial identity models. In J. G. Ponterotto, J. M. Casas, L. A. Suzuki, & C. M. Alexander (Eds.), *Handbook of multicultural counseling* (pp. 181–198). Thousand Oaks, CA: Sage Publications.

Herdt, G., & Koff, B. (2000). *Something to tell you: The road families travel when a child is gay.* New York: Columbia University Press.

Herman, M. A., & Richter Herlihy, B. (2006). Legal and ethical implications of refusing to counsel homosexual clients. *Journal of Counseling & Development, 84,* 414–418.

Hernandez, M., & McGoldrick, M. (1999). Migration and the family life cycle. In B. Carter & M. McGoldrick (Eds.), *The expanded family life cycle: Individual, family and social perspectives* (3rd ed., pp. 169–184). Boston: Allyn & Bacon.

Herring, R. D. (1999). *Counseling with Native American Indians and Alaskan Natives.* Thousand Oaks, CA: Sage Publications.

Hines, P. M., Garcia-Preto, N., McGoldrick, M., Almeida, R., & Weltman, S. (1992). Intergenerational relationships across cultures. *Families in Society, 73,* 323–338.

Hirshfield, S., Remien, R. H., Humberstone, M., Walavalkar, I., & Chiasson, M. A. (2004). Substance use and high-risk sex among men who have sex with men: A national online study in the USA. *AIDS Care, 16*(8), 1036–1047.

Hopson, D. P., & Hopson, D. S. (1992). *Different and wonderful: Raising Black children in a race-conscious society.* New York: Fireside.

Hoyt, M. (2001). Cognitive-behavioral treatment of posttraumatic stress disorder from a narrative constructivist perspective: A conversation with Donald Meichenbaum. In M. Hoyt (Ed.), *Interview with brief therapy experts* (pp. 97–120). Philadelphia: Brunner-Routledge.

Hunter, S., & Hickerson, J. C. (2003). *Affirmative practice: Understanding and working with lesbian, gay, bisexual, and transgender persons.* Washington, DC: NASW Press.

Ibrahim, F. A. (1991). Contribution of cultural worldview to generic counseling and development. *Journal of Counseling & Development, 70,* 13–19.

Iglehart, A. P., & Becerra, R. M. (1995). *Social services and the ethnic community.* Prospect Heights, IL: Waveland.

Imber-Black, E., Roberts, J., & Whiting, R. A. (Eds.). (1988). *Rituals in families and family therapy.* New York: W. W. Norton.

Ingoldsby, B. (1995). Poverty and patriarchy in Latin America. In B. Ingoldsby & A. Smith (Eds.), *Families in multicultural perspective* (pp. 335–351). New York: Guilford Press.

Isom, D. (2002). *Me, I got many parts: An exploration of racialized gender with African American youth.* Unpublished dissertation.

Jackson, J. S., Brown, T. N., Williams, D. R., Torres, M., Sellers, S. L., & Brown, K. (1996). Racism and the physical and mental health status of African Americans: A thirteen-year national panel study. *Ethnicity and Disease, 6,* 132–147.

Javier, R. A. (1996). In search of repressed memories in bilingual individuals. In R. Perez-Foster, M. Moskowitz, & R. A. Javier (Eds.), *Reaching across boundaries of culture and class: Widening the scope of psychotherapy* (pp. 225–242). Northvale, NJ: Jason Aronson.

Johnson, O. S. (2004). *The sexual spectrum: Explaining human diversity.* Vancouver: Raincoast Books.

Johnson, A. C. (1995). Resiliency mechanisms in culturally diverse families. *The Family Journal: Counseling and Therapy for Couples and Families, 3,* 316–324.

Johnson-Powell, G., & Yamamoto, J. (Eds.). (1997). *Transcultural child development: Psychological assessment and treatment.* New York: Wiley.

Kagan, C., & Burton, M. (2005). Marginalization. In G. Nelson & I. Prilleltensky (Eds.), *Community psychology: In pursuit of liberation and well-being* (pp. 293–308). New York: Palgrave.

Kandel, B., & Halebian, C. (1997). *Growing up biracial: Trevor's story.* New York: Lerner.

Katz, J. (2000). Pornography and men's consciousness. In M. Adams, W. Blumenfeld, R. Castaneda, H. Hackman, M. Peters, & X. Zuniga (Eds.), *Readings for diversity and social justice* (pp. 247–249). New York: Routledge.

Katz, J. H. (1985). The sociopolitical nature of counseling. *The Counseling Psychologist, 13,* 615–624.

Katz, K. (2002). *The colors of us.* New York: Henry Holt.

Kaufman, G., & Raphael, L. (1996). *Coming out of shame.* New York: Doubleday.

Kaufman, J. S., & Carlozzi, A. F. (1997). Factors influencing therapist selections among gays, lesbians and bisexuals. *Counseling Psychology, 10*(3), 287–297.

Kennedy, J. F. (1964). *A nation of immigrants.* New York: Harper & Row.

Kerwin, C., & Ponterotto, J. G. (1995). Biracial identity development: Theory and research. In J. G. Ponterotto, J. M. Casas, L. A. Suzuki, & C. M. Alexander (Eds.), *Handbook of multicultural counseling* (pp. 199–217). Thousand Oaks, CA: Sage Publications.

Kilpatrick, A. C., & Holland, T. P. (2002). *Working with families: An integrative model according to the level of need.* Boston: Allyn & Bacon.

Kim, J. (1981). The process of Asian American identity development: A study of Japanese-American women's perceptions of their struggle to achieve personal identities as Americans of Asian ancestry. *Dissertations Abstracts International, 42,* 155 1A. (University Microfilms No. 81-18080).

Kirkpatrick, D. D. (2005, February 11). House passes tightening of laws on immigration. *The New York Times,* p. A13.

Kliman, J. (1998). Social class as a relationship: Implications for family therapy. In M. McGoldrick (Ed.), *Re-visioning family therapy: Race, culture, and gender in clinical practice* (pp. 50–61). New York: Guilford Press.

Kliman, J., & Madsen, W. (1999). Social class and the family life cycle. In B. Carter & M. McGoldrick (Eds.), *The expanded family life cycle: Individual, family and social perspectives* (pp. 88–106). Boston: Allyn & Bacon.

Kliman, J., & Madsen, W. (2005). Social class and the family life cycle. In B. Carter & M. McGoldrick (Eds). *The expanded family life cycle: Individual, family and social perspectives* (3rd ed., pp. 88–105). New York: Pearson.

Klonoff, E. A., Landrine, H., & Ullman, J. B. (1999). Racial discrimination and psychiatric symptoms among Blacks. *Cultural Diversity and Ethnic Minority Psychology, 5,* 329–339.

Kotkin, J. (2006, October 17). 400,000,000: American demographics examined. *The Wall Street Journal.*

Kotlowitz, A. (1992). *There are no children here: The story of two boys growing up in the other America.* New York: Anchor.

Krieger, N. (1996). Racial and gender discrimination: Risk factors for high blood pressure. *Social Science and Medicine, 30,* 1273–1281.

Kuo, B. C. H., & Roysircar, G. (2004). Predictors of acculturation for Chinese adolescents in Canada: Age of arrival, length of stay, social class, and English reading ability. *Journal of Multicultural Counseling and Development, 32*(3), 143–154.

LaFromboise, T., Coleman, H. L. K., & Gerton, J. (1993). Psychological impact of biculturalism: Evidence and theory. *Psychological Bulletin, 114,* 395–412.

Landrine, H., & Klonoff, E. A. (1996). The schedule of racist events: A measure of racial discrimination and a study of its negative physical and mental health consequences. *Journal of Black Psychology, 22,* 144–168.

Langston, D. (2000). Tired of playing Monopoly? In M. Adams, W. Blumenfeld, R. Castaneda, H. Hackman, M. Peters, & X. Zuniga (Eds.), *Readings for diversity and social justice* (pp. 397–401). New York: Routledge.

LearningExpress Editors. (2007). *US citizenship* (2nd ed.). New York: LearningExpress, LLC.

Leonhardt, D. (2006). Scant progress in closing gap in women's pay. *The New York Times, 156,* (53803), pp. 1–18.

Lev, A. I. (2004). *Transgender emergence: Therapeutic guidelines for working with gender-variant people and their families.* New York: The Haworth Clinical Practice Press.

Lewis, T. F., & Osborn, C. (2004). Solution-focused counseling and motivational interviewing: A consideration of confluence. *Journal of Counseling & Development, 82*(1), 38–48.

Lipsitz Bem, S. (2000). The conundrum of difference. In M. Adams, W. Blumenfeld, R. Castaneda, H. Hackman, M. Peters, & X. Zuniga (Eds.), *Readings for diversity and social justice* (pp. 35–36). New York: Routledge.

Liu, W. M., Soleck, G., Hopps, J., Dunston, K., & Pickett, T., Jr. (2004). A new framework to understand social class in counseling: The social class worldview model and modern classism theory. *Journal of Multicultural Counseling and Development, 32*(2), 95–122.

Liu, W. M. (2002). The social class related experiences of men: Integrating theory and practice. *Professional Psychology: Research and Practice, 33*(4), 355–359.

Lombardi, E., & Davis, S. M. (2006). Transgender health issues. In D. F. Morrow & L. Messinger (Eds.), *Sexual orientation and gender expression in social work practice* (pp. 344–363). New York: Columbia University Press.

Looy, H. & Bouma III, H. (2005). The nature of gender: Gender identity in persons who are intersexed or transgendered. *Journal of Psychology and Theology, 53*(3), 166–178.

Lorber, J. (2000). "Night to his day": The social construction of gender. In M. Adams, W. Blumenfeld, R. Castaneda, H. Hackman, M. Peters, & X. Zuniga (Eds.), *Readings for diversity and social justice* (pp. 203–213). New York: Routledge.

Lorber, J. (2005). *Gender inequality: Feminist theories and politics.* Los Angeles: Roxbury.

Lowe, S., & Mascher, J. (2001). The role of sexual orientation in multicultural counseling. In J. G. Ponterotto, J. M. Casas, L. A. Suzuki, & C. M. Alexander (Eds.), *Handbook of Multicultural Counseling* (pp. 755–778). Thousand Oaks, CA: Sage Publications.

Lum, D. (2006). *Culturally competent practice: A framework for understanding diverse groups and justice issues.* Belmont, CA: Wadsworth.

Lum, D., & and Lu, Y. E. (1997). Developing cultural competency within a culturally sensitive environment. Paper presented at the Council on Social Work Education annual program meeting, Chicago, Illinois.

Luthar, S. S., & Cicchetti, D. (2000). The construct of resilience: Implications for interventions and social policies. *Development and psychopathology, 12,* 857–885.

Luthar, S. S. (2006). Resilience in development: A synthesis of research across five decades. In D. Cicchetti & D. J. Cohen (Eds.), *Developmental psychopathology: Risk, disorder, and adaptation,* Volume 3 (2nd ed.). New York: Wiley.

Macedo, D. (2001). In P. Freire (Ed.), *Pedagogy of the oppressed* (pp. 11–27). New York: Continuum.

Mallon, G. P. (Ed.). (1999). *Social services with transgendered youth.* New York: Harrington Park Press.

Mallon, G. P., & DeCrescenzo, T. (2006). Transgender children and youth: A child welfare perspective. *Child Welfare, 85*(2) 215–241.

Marcia, J. (1994). The empirical study of ego identity. In H. Bosma, T. Graafsma, H. Grotevant, & D. de Levita (Eds.), *Identity and development: An interdisciplinary approach* (pp. 67–80). Thousand Oaks, CA: Sage Publications.

Marcia, J. E. (1966). Development and validation of ego identity status. *Journal of Personality and Social Psychology, 3*, 551–558.

Marcos, L. R. (1976). Bilinguals in psychotherapy: Language as an emotional barrier. *American Journal of Psychotherapy, 30*, 552–560.

Marcos, L. R., & Urcuyo, L. (1979). Dynamic psychotherapy with the bilingual patient. *American Journal of Psychotherapy, 33*(3), 332–338.

Marin, G., Balls Organista, P., & Chun, K. (2003). Acculturation research: Current issues and findings. In G. Bernal, J. E. Trimble, A. K. Burlew & F. T. L. Leong (Eds.), *Handbook of racial and ethnic minority psychology* (pp. 206–219). Thousand Oaks, CA: Sage Publications.

Martin, J. I., & Yonkin, D. R. (2006). Transgender identity. In D. F. Morrow & L. Messinger (Eds.), *Sexual orientation and gender expression in social work practice* (pp. 106–128). New York: Columbia University Press.

McBride, J. (1997). *The color of water: A Black man's tribute to his white mother.* New York: Riverhead Books.

McCarthy, J., & Holliday, E. I. (2004). Help-seeking and counseling within a traditional male gender role: An examination from a multicultural perspective. *Journal of Counseling & Development, 82*(1), 25–30.

McClellan, J. (2006). Bisexual relationships and families. In D. F. Morrow & L. Messinger (Eds.), *Sexual orientation and gender expression in social work practice* (pp. 243–262). New York: Columbia University Press.

McDermott, D., Tyndall, L., & Lichtenberg, J. W. (1989). Factors related to counselor preference among gays and lesbians. *Journal of Counseling & Development, 68*(1), 31–35.

McFarland, W. P. (1998). Gay, lesbian, and bisexual student suicide. *Professional School Counseling, 1*(3), 26–29.

McGill, D. W., & Pierce, J. K. (1996). American families with English ancestors from the colonial era: Anglo Americans. In M. McGoldrick, J. Giordano, & J. K. Pierce (Eds.), *Ethnicity and family therapy* (pp. 451–466). New York: Guilford Press.

McGoldrick, M. (2003). Culture: A challenge to concepts of normality. In F. Walsh (Ed.), *Normal family process* (3rd ed., pp. 235–259). New York: Guilford Press.

McGoldrick, M., & Giordano, J. (1996). Overview: Ethnicity and family therapy. In M. McGoldrick, J. Giordano, & J. K. Pierce (Eds.), *Ethnicity and family therapy* (pp. 1–27). New York: Guilford Press.

McGoldrick, M., Giordano, J., & Pierce, J. K. (1996). *Ethnicity and family therapy.* New York: Guilford Press.

McGoldrick, M., & Preto, N. G. (1984). Ethnic intermarriage: Implications for therapy. *Family Process, 23*, 347–364.

McIntosh, P. (1998). White privilege: Unpacking the invisible knapsack. In M. McGoldrick (Ed.), *Re-visioning family therapy: Race, culture, and gender in clinical practice* (pp. 147–152). New York: Guilford Press.

McKinley, J. C. (2005, January 6). A Mexican manual for illegal immigrants upsets some in U.S. *The New York Times,* p. A5.

McKinney, R.E. (2006). Gay male relationships and families. In D. F. Morrow & L. Messinger (Eds.), *Sexual orientation and gender expression in social work practice* (pp. 196–215). New York: Columbia University Press.

Mead, J. C. (2004, June 20). Ticket to nowhere. *The New York Times,* p. L1.

Merriam-Webster. (1998). *Deluxe dictionary: Tenth collegiate edition.* Pleasantville, NY: Reader's Digest.

Merriam-Webster Online Dictionary. (n.d.). Retrieved October 10, 2006, from http://www.m-w.com/dictionary

Meyer, I. (1995). Minority stress and mental health in gay men. *Journal of Health and Social Behavior, 36*(1), 38–56.

Meyer, I. H. (2003). Prejudice, social stress, and mental health in lesbian, gay, and bisexual populations: Conceptual issues and research evidence. *Psychological Bulletin, 129*(5), 674–697.

Mezzich, J. E., Ruiz, P., & Muñoz, R. A. (1999). Mental health care for Hispanic Americans: A current perspective. *Cultural Diversity and Ethnic Minority Psychology, 5*(2), 91–102.

Miceli, M. S. (2002). Gay, lesbian, and bisexual youth. In D. Richardson & S. Seidman (Eds.), *Handbook of lesbian and gay studies* (pp. 200–214). Thousand Oaks, CA: Sage Publications.

Migration Information Source. (2006). Retrieved May 22, 2007, from http://www.migrationinformation.org/Feature/display.cfm?ID=585

Migration Policy Institute. (2004). *Coming to America: Two years after September 11, 2001.* Retrieved January 24, 2005, from http://www.migrationpolicy.org/pubs/Immigration_Since_9–11.pdf

Miller, G. (2003). *Incorporating spirituality in counseling and psychotherapy.* Hoboken, NJ: Wiley.

Miller, N. (1995). *Out of the past: Gay and lesbian history from 1869 to the present.* New York: Vintage Books.

Miller, W. R., & Rollnick, S. (1991). *Motivational interviewing: Preparing people to change addictive behaviors.* New York: Guilford Press.

Miller, W. R., & Thoresen, C. E. (1999). Spirituality and health. In W. R. Miller (Ed.), *Integrating spirituality into treatment: Resources for practitioners* (pp. 3–18). Washington, DC: American Psychological Association.

Mills, N., (Ed.). (1994). *Arguing immigration.* New York: Touchstone.

Minuchin, P., Colapinto, J., & Minuchin, S. (1998). *Working with families of the poor.* New York: Guilford Press.

Mio, J. S. (2003). On teaching multiculturalism. In G. Bernal, J. E. Trimble, A. K. Burlew, & F. T. L. Leong (Eds.), *Handbook of racial and ethnic minority psychology* (pp. 119–146). Thousand Oaks, CA: Sage Publications.

Mirkin, M. P. (1998). The impact of multiple contexts on recent immigrant families. In M. McGoldrick (Ed.), *Re-visioning family therapy: Race, culture, and gender in clinical practice* (pp. 370–384). New York: Guilford Press.

Mitchell, S. A., & Black, M. J. (1995). *Freud and beyond: A history of modern psychoanalytic thought.* New York: Basic Books.

Mogel, W. (2001). *The blessing of a skinned knee: Using Jewish teachings to raise self-reliant children.* New York: Penguin.

Morales, E. (2006). *Counseling Latino gays and lesbians: Identity formation and psychosocial issues.* Paper presented at the 2006 National Latino/a Psychologists Association Conference, October 13, Milwaukee, WI.

Morales, E. E. & Trotman, F. K. (2004). *Promoting academic resilience in multicultural America: Factors affecting student success.* New York: Lang.

Moreno, S. (2005). Flow of illegal immigrants to U.S. unabated. *Washington Post.* Retrieved May 22, 2007, from http://www.washingtonpost.com/wp-dyn/articles/A55202-2005Mar21.html

Morrison, T. (1970/2000). *The bluest eye.* New York: Plume.

Morrow, D. F., & Tyson, B. (2006). Religion and spirituality. In D. F. Morrow & L. Messinger (Eds.), *Sexual orientation and gender expression in social work practice* (pp. 384–404). New York: Columbia University Press.

Morrow, D. F. (2006a). Coming out as gay, lesbian, bisexual, and transgender. In D. F. Morrow & L. Messinger (Eds.), *Sexual orientation and gender expression in social work practice* (pp. 129–149). New York: Columbia University Press.

Morrow, D. F. (2006b). Sexual orientation and gender identity expression. In D. F. Morrow & L. Messinger (Eds.), *Sexual orientation and gender expression in social work practice* (pp. 3–17). New York: Columbia University Press.

Morrow, D. F. (2006c). Gay, lesbian, bisexual, and transgender adolescents. In D. F. Morrow & L. Messinger (Eds.), *Sexual orientation and gender expression in social work practice* (pp. 177–195). New York: Columbia University Press.

Morrow, S. L., Hawxhurst, D. M., Montes de Vegas, A.Y., Abousleman, T. M., & Castaneda, C. L. (2006). Toward a radical feminist multicultural therapy: Renewing a commitment to activism. In R. L. Toporek, L. H. Gerstein, N. A. Fouad, G. Roysircar, & T. Israel (Eds.), *Handbook for social justice in counseling psychology: Leadership, vision, and action* (pp. 231–247). Thousand Oaks, CA: Sage Publications.

Morrow, S. L., & Hawxhurst, D. M. (1998). Feminist therapy: Integrating political analysis in counseling and psychotherapy. *Women and Therapy, 21*(2), 37–50.

Moses, A. E. (1982). *Counseling lesbian women and gay men.* St. Louis: The C. V. Mosby Company.

Muslim Population. (2006). Retrieved September 27, 2006 from http://www.theislamproject.org/education/United_States.html

Myer, I. (2003). Prejudice, social stress, and mental health in lesbian, gay and bisexual populations: Conceptual issues and research evidence. *Psychological Bulletin, 129*(5), 674–697.

Nakazawa, D. J. (2004). *Does anybody else look like me? A parent's guide to raising multiracial children.* New York: DaCapo.

Nardi, P. M. (2002). The mainstreaming of lesbian and gay studies? In D. Richardson & S. Seidman (Eds.), *Handbook of lesbian and gay studies* (pp. 45–54). Thousand Oaks, CA: Sage Publications.

The National Conference. (1996). *Interfaith calendar.* Chicago: Author.

Nava, G. (Director). (1983). *El norte* [The North] [Videotape]. (Available from Filmco A/S, 9718 Glenoaks Blvd., #A, Sun Valley, CA 91352).

Nelson, G., & Prilleltensky, I. (Eds.). (2005). *Community psychology: In pursuit of liberation and well-being.* New York: Palgrave.

Neusner, J. (2006). Judaism. In W. Doniger (Ed.), *Britannica encyclopedia of world religions* (pp. 412–491). Chicago: Encyclopaedia Britannica.

Neville, H. A, Worthington, R. L., & Spanierman, L. B. (2001). Race, power, and multicultural counseling psychology: Understanding white privilege and color-blind racial attitudes. In J. G. Ponterotto, J. M. Casas, L. A. Suzuki, & C. M. Alexander (Eds.), *Handbook of multicultural counseling* (pp. 257–288). Thousand Oaks, CA: Sage Publications.

Nichols, M. P., & Schwartz, R. (2001). *Family therapy: Concepts and methods* (5th ed.). Boston: Allyn & Bacon.

Nieto, S. (1999). *The light in their eyes: Creating multicultural learning communities.* New York: Teachers College Press.

Nieves, E. (1999, July 30). California calls off effort to carry out immigration measure. *The New York Times*, p. A1.

O'Hearn, C. C. (1998). *Half and half: Writers on growing up biracial and bicultural.* New York: Pantheon.

Parham, T. A. (2001). Afterword: Beyond intolerance: Bridging the gap between imposition and acceptance. In J. G. Ponterotto, J. M. Casas, L. A. Suzuki, & C. M. Alexander (Eds.), *Handbook of multicultural counseling* (pp. 871–881). Thousand Oaks, CA: Sage Publications.

Parks, C. A., Hughes, T. L., & Matthews, A. K. (2004). Race, ethnicity and sexual orientation: Intersecting identities. *Cultural Diversity and Ethnic Minority Psychology, 10*(3), 241–254.

Parks, C. A., & Humphreys, N. A. (2006). Lesbian relationships and families. In D. F. Morrow & L. Messinger (Eds.), *Sexual orientation and gender expression in social work practice* (pp. 216–242). New York: Columbia University Press.

Pedersen, P. B. (1991). Multiculturalism as a generic approach to counseling. *Journal of Counseling & Development, 70,* 6–12.

Pedersen, P., & Hernandez, D. (1996). *Decisional dialogues in a cultural context: Structured exercises.* Thousand Oaks, CA: Sage Publications.

Peirson, L. (2005). Disadvantaged children and families. In G. Nelson & I. Prilleltensky (Eds.), *Community psychology: In pursuit of liberation and well-being* (pp. 448–467). New York: Palgrave.

Pelikan, J. (2006). Christianity. In W. Doniger (Ed.), *Britannica encyclopedia of world religions.* Chicago: Encyclopaedia Britannica.

Perez-Foster, R. (1996). Assessing the psychodynamic function of language in the bilingual patient. In R. Perez-Foster, M. Moskowitz, & R. Javier (Eds.), *Reaching across boundaries of culture and class: Widening the scope of psychotherapy* (pp. 243–264). Northvale, NJ: Jason Aronson.

Perez-Foster, R. (1998). The clinician's cultural countertransference: The psychodynamics of culturally competent practice. *Clinical Social Work Journal, 26*(3), 253–269.

PFLAG. (n.d.). Retrieved August 27, 2007, from http://www.pflag.org/Hate_Crimes.hatecrimes.0.html

Phillips, R., Munt, G., Drury, J., Stoklosa, M., & Spink, J. (1997). Dropouts in family therapy. *The Australian and New Zealand Journal of Family Therapy, 18*(2), 115–118.

Phinney, J. S. (1996). When we talk about American ethnic groups, what do we mean? *American Psychologist, 51,* 918–927.

Phinney, J. S. (2003). Ethnic identity and acculturation. In K. M. Chun, P. Balls Organista, & G. Marin (Eds.), *Acculturation: Advances in theory, measurement, and applied research.* (pp. 63–81). Washington, DC: American Psychological Association.

Phinney, J. S., Madden, T., & Santos, L. J. (1998). Psychological variables as predictors of perceived ethnic discrimination among minority and immigrant adolescents. *Journal of Applied Social Psychology, 28,* 937–953.

Pipher, M. (2002). *The middle of everywhere: Helping refugees enter the American community.* Orlando, FL: Harcourt.

Pinderhughes, E. (1989). *Understanding race, ethnicity, and power: The key to efficacy in clinical practice.* New York: Free Press.

Ponterotto, J. G., Casas, J. M., Suzuki, L. A., & Alexander, C. M. (Eds.). (2001). *Handbook of multicultural counseling.* Thousand Oaks, CA: Sage Publications.

Ponterotto, J. G., Jackson, M. A., & Nutini, C. D. (2001). Reflections on the life stories of pioneers in multicultural counseling. In J. G. Ponterotto, J. M. Casas, L. A. Suzuki, & C. M. Alexander (Eds.), *Handbook of Multicultural Counseling* (pp. 138–161). Thousand Oaks, CA: Sage Publications.

Ponterotto, J. G., Utsey, S. O., & Pedersen, P. B. (2006). *Preventing prejudice: A guide for counselors, educators, and parents* (2nd ed.). Thousand Oaks, CA: Sage Publications.

Pope-Davis, D. B., Liu, W. M., Toporek, R. L., & Brittan-Powell, C. S. (2001). What's missing from multicultural competency research: Review, introspection, and recommendations. *Cultural Diversity and Ethnic Minority Psychology, 7*(2), 121–138.

Portes, A., & Rumbaud, R. (2001). *Legacies: The story of the immigrant second generation.* Berkeley: University of California Press.

Potts, R. G. & Watts, R. J. (2003). Conceptualizations and models: The meaning of difference in racial and ethnic minority psychology. In G. Bernal, J. E. Trimble, A. K. Burlew, & F. T. L. Leong (Eds.), *Handbook of racial and ethnic minority psychology* (pp. 65–75). Thousand Oaks, CA: Sage Publications.

Prilleltensky, I. (1994). *The morals and politics of psychology: Psychological discourse and the status quo.* Albany, NY: State University of New York.

Prilleltensky, I., & Prilleltensky, O. (2003). Synergies for wellness and liberation in counseling psychology. *The Counseling Psychologist, 31*(3), 273–281.

Prilleltensky, I., & Prilleltensky, O. (2006). *Promoting well-being: Linking personal, organizational, and community change.* New Jersey: Wiley.

Prochaska, J. O., Norcross, J. C., & Di Clemente, C. C. (1995). *Changing for good.* New York: Morrow.

Quintana, S. M. (1998). Children's developmental understanding of ethnicity and race. *Applied and Preventive Psychology, 7,* 27–45.

Quintana, S. M., Castaneda-English, P., & Ybarra, V. C. (1999). Role of perspective-taking abilities and ethnic socialization in development of adolescent ethnic identity. *Journal of Research on Adolescence, 9,* 161–184.

Rahman, O., & Rollock, D. (2004). Acculturation, competence, and mental health among South Asian students in the United States. *Journal of Multicultural Counseling and Development, 32,* 130–142.

Rasco, L., & Miller, K. (2003). *The mental health of refugees: Ecological approaches to healing and adaptation.* Mahwah, NJ: Lawrence Erlbaum.

Remafedi, G., Farrow, J. A., & Deisher, R. W. (1991). Risk factors for attempted suicide in gay and bisexual youth. *Pediatrics, 87*(6), 869–875.

Religion. (n.d.). Retreived from http://www.gallup.com/poll/1690/Religion.aspx

Report: Undocumented immigrant population surges (2005). *USA Today.* Retrieved May 22, 2007, from http://www.usatoday.com/news/washington/2005-03-21-undocumented-immigrants_x.htm

Reynolds, F. (2006). Buddhism. In W. Doniger (Ed.), *Britannica encyclopedia of world religions* (pp. 172–264). Chicago: Encyclopaedia Britannica.

Richards, P. S., & Bergin, A. E. (1997). *A spiritual strategy for counseling and psychotherapy.* Washington, DC: American Psychological Association.

Rivers, I., & D'Augelli, A. R. (2001). The victimization of lesbian, gay, and bisexual youths. In A. R. D'Augelli & C. J. Patterson (Eds.), *Lesbian, gay, and bisexual identities and youth: Psychological perspectives* (pp. 199–223). New York: Oxford University Press.

Roberts, S. (2006, August 30). Census figures show scant improvement in city poverty rate. *The New York Times,* pp. B1–B4.

Roberts, S. (2007, August 9). Minorities now form a majority in one third of most populous counties. *The New York Times,* p. A5.

Robinson, T. L. (2005). *The convergence of race, ethnicity, and gender: Multiple identities in counseling.* Upper Saddle River, NJ: Prentice Hall.

Rockquemore, K. A., & Brunsma, D. L. (2001). *Beyond Black: Biracial identity in America.* Thousand Oaks, CA: Sage Publications.

Rockquemore, K. A., & Laszloffy, T. A. (2003). Multiple realities: A relational narrative approach in therapy with Black-White mixed-race clients. *Family Relations, 52,* 119–128.

Rodriguez, R. (2002). *Brown: The last discovery of America.* New York: Viking.

Rogers, C. R. (1980). *A way of being.* Boston: Houghton Mifflin.

Roland, A. (1996). How universal is the psychoanalytic self? In R. Perez-Foster, M. Moskowitz, & R. Javier (Eds.), *Reaching across boundaries of culture and class: Widening the scope of psychotherapy* (pp. 71–90). Northvale, NJ: Jason Aronson.

Rosado, R. J. (1992). *The effects of pretreatment orientations on the utilization of treatment by Spanish speaking Hispanics, bilingual Hispanics and non-Hispanics in treatment at a child guidance center.* Ann Arbor, MI: University Microfilms International.

Rosario, M., Schrimshaw, E. W., & Hunter, J. (2004). Ethnic/racial differences in the coming-out process of lesbian, gay and bisexual youths: A comparison of sexual identity development over time. *Cultural Diversity and Ethnic Minority Psychology, 10*(3), 215–228.

Rosario, M., Schrimshaw, E. W., Hunter, J., & Braun, L. (2006). Sexual identity development among lesbian, gay, and bisexual youths: Consistency and change over time. *Journal of Sex Research, 43*(1), 46–58.

Rosen, E. (1995). Mourning in different cultures: Jewish families. In F. Walsh & M. McGoldrick (Eds.), *Living beyond loss: Death in the family* (pp. 194–200). New York: W. W. Norton.

Rosen, E., & Weltman, S. (1996). Jewish families: An overview. In M. McGoldrick (Ed.), *Ethnicity and family therapy* (pp. 611–630). New York: Guilford Press.

Rosenbaum, M. H., & Rosenbaum, S. (1998). *Celebrating our differences: Living two faiths in one marriage.* New York: Ragged Edge Press.

Roseneil, S. (2002). The heterosexual/homosexual binary: Past, present and future. In D. Richardson & S. Seidman (Eds.), *Handbook of lesbian and gay studies* (pp. 55–71). Thousand Oaks, CA: Sage Publications.

Rossman, L. (1997). Sexual orientation issues impact K–12 education. In W. Swan (Ed.), *Gay/lesbian/bisexual/transgender public policy issues* (pp. 63–74). New York: The Harrington Park Press.

Ross, M. W., & Rosser, B. R. S. (1996). Measurement and correlates of internalized homophobia: A factor analytic study. *Journal of Clinical Psychology, 52*(1), 15–21.

Rotheram-Borus, M. J., & Langabeer, K. A. (2001). Developmental trajectories of gay, lesbian, and bisexual youths. In A. R. D'Augelli & C. J. Patterson (Eds.), *Lesbian, gay, and bisexual identities and youth: Psychological perspectives* (pp. 97–128). New York: Oxford University Press.

Rowe, W., Bennett, S., & Atkinson, D. R. (1994). White racial identity models: A critique and alternative proposal. *The Counseling Psychologist, 22,* 120–146.

Ruiz, A. S. (1990). Ethnic identity: Crisis and resolution. *Journal of Multicultural Counseling and Development, 18,* 29–40.

Ruvolo, D. (n.d.). *A summary of Native American religions.* Retrieved November 30, 2006, from http://are.as.wvu.edu/ruvolo.htm

Ryan, C., & Futterman, D. (2001). Lesbian and gay adolescents: Identity development. *The Prevention Researcher, 8*(1), 1, 3–5.

Ryan, C., & Gruskin, E. (2006). Health concerns for lesbians, gay men, and bisexuals. In D. F. Morrow & L. Messinger (Eds.), *Sexual orientation and gender expression in social work practice* (pp. 343–359). New York: Columbia University Press.

Ryan, C. (2001). Counseling lesbian, gay, and bisexual youths. In A. R. D'Augelli & C. J. Patterson (Eds.), *Lesbian, gay, and bisexual identities and youth: Psychological perspectives* (pp. 224–250). New York: Oxford University Press.

Saba, G. W., Karrer, B. M., & Hardy, K. V. (Eds.). (1989). *Minorities and family therapy.* New York: Haworth.

Sanchez, F. J., Liu, W. M., & Vilain, E. (2006). *Gender role conflict and negative self-identity among Gay Latino men.* Poster presented at the 2006 National Latino/a Psychologists Association Conference, October 12–14, Milwaukee, WI.

Savin-Williams, R.C. (2005). The new gay teen: Shunning labels. *Gay & Lesbian Review Worldwide, 12*(6), 16–19.

Sayger, T. V., & Heid, K. O. (1990). Counseling the impoverished rural client: Issues for family therapists. *Psychotherapy Patient, 7,* 161–168.

Schlesinger, A. M., Jr. (1998). *The disuniting of America* (revised ed.). New York: W. W. Norton and Company.

Schwartz, R. (1995). *Internal family systems therapy.* New York: Guilford Press.

Schwarzbaum, S. (1995). The effect of a combined pretherapy orientation on Hispanic clients' utilization of counseling services. *Dissertation Abstracts International, 57*(01B), 0710. UMI Number 9614897. Ann Arbor, MI: University Microfilms International.

Schwarzbaum, S. (2002). Dropout from counseling services by low-income Latinos/as: Historical and current explanations. *Illinois Counseling Association Journal, 149,* 25–37.

Schwarzbaum, S. (2004). Low-income Latinos and dropout: Strategies to prevent dropout. *Journal of Multicultural Counseling and Development, 32,* 296–306.

Schwarzbaum, S., Consoli, A., & Zalaquett, C. (2006). *Interventions that facilitate access to services of low income, first generation, immigrant Latino/a clients in therapy and prevent dropout.* Presentation at the National Latino/a Psychological Association Conference, October 13, Milwaukee, WI.

Scott, J. (2005). Life at the top in America isn't just better, it's longer. *The New York Times, 154,* (53216), A1–A18.

Section by section summary of the Sensenbrenner Bill. (2005). *Siskind's Immigration Bulletin.* Retrieved May 24, 2007, from http://www.visalaw.com/05dec2/3dec 205.html

Seligman, M. (2006). *Learned optimism: How you can change your mind and your life.* New York: Vintage Books.

Sellers, R. M., Smith, M. A., Shelton, J. N., Rowley, S. A. J., & Chavous, T. M. (1998). Multidimensional model of racial identity: A reconceptualization of African American racial identity. *Personality and Social Psychology Review, 2,* 18–39.

Selman, R. L. (1971). Taking another's perspective: Role-taking development in early childhood. *Child Development, 42,* 1721–1734.

Shipler, D. K. (2004). *The working poor: Invisible in America.* New York: Knopf.

Signorile, M. (1995). *Outing yourself: How to come out as lesbian or gay to your family, friends, and coworkers.* New York: Random House.

Smith, D. M., & Gates, G. (2001). *Gay and lesbian families in the United States.* Retrieved October 17, 2006, from http://www.urban.org/publications/1000491.html

Sonn, C. C., & Fisher, A. T. (2005). Immigration and adaptation: Confronting the challenges of cultural diversity. In G. Nelson & I. Prilleltensky (Eds.), *Community psychology: In pursuit of liberation and well-being* (pp. 405–425). New York: Palgrave.

Speight, S. L., Myers, L. J., Cox, C. I., & Highlen, P. S. (1991). A redefinition of multicultural counseling. *Journal of Counseling & Development, 70,* 29–36.

Spitzer, R. L. (2003). Can some gay men and lesbians change their sexual orientation? 200 participants reporting a change from homosexual to heterosexual orientation. *Archives of Sexual Behavior, 32*(5), 403–417.

Standard, R. P., Sandhu, D. S., & Painter, L. C. (2000). Assessment of spirituality in counseling. *Journal of Counseling & Development, 78,* 204–210.

Standards for Cultural Competence in Social Work Practice. Retrieved May 28, 2007, from http://www.socialworkers.org/sections/credentials/cultural_comp.asp

Stavans, I. (2002). *On borrowed words: A memoir on language.* New York: Penguin Books.

Steele, S. (2006). *White guilt.* New York: HarperCollins.

Steinberg, S. (2001). *The ethnic myth: Race, ethnicity, and class in America* (3rd ed.). Boston: Beacon Press.

Steinem, G. (2000). Revving up for the next twenty-five years. In M. Adams, W. Blumenfeld, R. Castaneda, H. Hackman, M. Peters, & X. Zuniga (Eds.), *Readings for diversity and social justice* (pp. 256–260). New York: Routledge.

Stevenson, H. C., Cameron, R., Herrero-Taylor, T., & Davis, G. Y. (2002). Development of the Teenager Experience of Racial Socialization scale: Correlates of race related socialization frequency from the perspective of Black youth. *Journal of Black Psychology, 28,* 84–106.

Street, P. (2005). *Segregated schools: Educational apartheid in post-civil rights America.* New York: Routledge.

Study of immigrants links lighter skin and higher income. (2007, January 28). *The New York Times,* National Report, p. 19.

Suarez-Orozco, C., & Suarez-Orozco, M. (2002). *Children of immigration: The developing child.* Cambridge, MA: Harvard University Press.

Sue, D. W., & Sue, D. (2003). *Counseling the culturally diverse.* New York: Wiley.

Sue, D. W., Ivey, A. E., & Pedersen, P. B. (1996). *A theory of multicultural counseling and therapy.* Belmont, CA: Thomson Brooks/Cole.

Sue, D. W., Arredondo, P., & McDavis, R. J. (1992). Multicultural counseling competencies and standards: A call to the profession. *Journal of Counseling & Development, 70*, 477–486.

Sue, S. (1998). In search of cultural competence in psychotherapy and counseling. *American Psychologist, 53*, 440–448.

Swan, W. (1997). Workplaces, schools, partnerships, and justice: An intersection that causes confrontation. In W. Swan (Ed.), *Gay/lesbian/bisexual/transgender public policy issues* (pp. 15–21). New York: The Harrington Park Press.

Swarns, R. L. (2007, March 11). Against odds, Iraqi refugees reach U.S. *The New York Times*, p. A20.

Takaki, R. (1993). *A different mirror: A history of multicultural America.* Boston: Little, Brown & Company.

Talleyrand, R. M., Chung, R. C. Y., & Bemak, F. (2006). Incorporating social justice in counselor training programs. In R. L. Toporek, L. H. Gerstein, N. A. Fouad, G. Roysircar, & T. Israel (Eds.), *Handbook for social justice in counseling psychology: Leadership, vision, and action* (pp. 44–58). Thousand Oaks, CA: Sage Publications.

Tatum, B. (2002). *Why are all the Black kids sitting together in the cafeteria?* New York: Basic Books.

Tavernise, S., & Worth, R. F. (2007, January 2). As Iraqis flee, few are gaining sanctuary in U.S. *The New York Times*, p. A1.

Thernstrom, S. (1980). *Harvard encyclopedia of American ethnic groups.* Boston: Belknap Press.

Thomas, A. J. (1998). Understanding worldview and culture in family systems: Use of the multicultural genogram. *The Family Journal: Counseling and Therapy for Couples and Families, 6*, 24–32.

Thomas, A. J., & Speight, S. L. (1999). Racial identity and racial socialization attitudes of African-American parents. *Journal of Black Psychology, 22*, 152–170.

Thompson, G., & Ochoa, S. (2004, June 13). By a back door to the U.S.: A migrant's grim sea voyage. *The New York Times*, p. A1.

Thompson, V. L. S. (1996). Perceived experiences of racism as stressful life events. *Community Mental Health Journal, 32*, 223–233.

Todorov, T. (1984). *The conquest of America: The question of the other.* New York: Harper & Row.

Tolliver, W. F. (1997). Invoking the spirit: A model for incorporating the spiritual dimension of human functioning into social work practice. *Smith College Studies in Social Work, 67*, 477–486.

Tomm, K. (1988). Interventive interviewing: Part III. Intending to ask lineal, circular, strategic and reflexive questions. *Family Process, 27*, 1–16.

Tomm, K. (1989). Externalizing the problems and internalizing the personal agency. *Journal of Strategic and Systemic Therapies, 8*, 54–59.

Toporek, R. L., & McNally, C. J. (2006). Social justice training in counseling psychology: Needs and innovations. In R. L. Toporek, L. H. Gerstein, N. A. Fouad, G. Roysircar, & T. Israel (Eds.), *Handbook for social justice in counseling psychology: Leadership, vision, and action* (pp. 37–43). Thousand Oaks, CA: Sage Publications.

Toporek, R. L., & Williams, R. A. (2006). Ethics and professional issues related to the practice of social justice in counseling psychology. In R. L. Toporek, L. H. Gerstein, N. A. Fouad, G. Roysircar, & T. Israel (Eds.), *Handbook for social justice in counseling psychology: Leadership, vision, and action* (pp. 17–34). Thousand Oaks, CA: Sage Publications.

Torres, L., & Rollock, D. (2004). Acculturative distress among Hispanics: The role of acculturation, coping, and intercultural competence. *Journal of Multicultural Counseling and Development, 32,* 155–167.

Tough, P. (2006, November 26). What it takes to make a student. *The New York Times Magazine,* pp. 44–77.

Trickett, E. J., Watts, R. J., & Birman, D. (1994). Toward an overarchieving framework for diversity. In E. J. Trickett, R. J. Watts, & D. Birman (Eds.), *Human diversity: Perspectives on people in context* (pp. 7–26). San Francisco: Jossey-Bass.

Trimble, J. E. (2003). Introduction: Social change and acculturation. In K. M. Chun, P. Balls Organista, & G. Marin (Eds.), *Acculturation: Advances in theory, measurement, and applied research* (pp. 3–13). Washington, DC: American Psychological Association.

Trimble, J. E., Helms, J. E., & Root, M. P. P. (2003). Social and psychological perspectives on ethnic and racial identity. In G. Bernal, J. E. Trimble, A. K. Burlew, & F. T. L. Leong (Eds.), *Handbook of racial and ethnic minority psychology* (pp. 239–275). Thousand Oaks, CA: Sage Publications.

Tully, C. T. (2000). *Lesbians, gays, & the empowerment perspective.* New York: Columbia University Press.

Turner, J. & Simmons, A. (2006). Transnational resilience and resistance: Key concepts for working with refugees. In AFTA Monograph series: *Immigrant families and immigration: Therapeutic work, 2*(1), 6–22.

Twist, M., Murphy, M., Green, M. S., & Palmanteer, D. (2006). Therapists' support of gay and lesbian human rights. *Guidance & Counseling, 21*(2), 107–113.

Undocumented immigrants: Facts and figures. (2004). Retrieved May 22, 2007, from http://www.urban.org/publications/1000587.html

Ungar, M. (2004). *Nurturing hidden resilience in troubled youth.* Toronto: University of Toronto.

U.S. Bureau of Labor Statistics. (September, 2006). [Report 995, pp. 1–40.] Retrieved November 15, 2006, from http://www.bls.gov/cps/cpswom2005.pdf

U.S. Bureau of the Census. (2000). Retrieved November 1, 2004, from http://www.census.gov/main.www.cen2000.html

U.S. Bureau of the Census. (2005). Retrieved August 17, 2005, from http://www.census.gov/prod/2001pubs/c2kbr01-4.pdf

Utsey, S. O., Gernat, C. A., & Bolden, M. A. (2003). Teaching racial identity development and racism awareness: Training in professional psychology programs. In G. Bernal, J. E. Trimble, A. K. Burlew, & F. T. L. Leong (Eds.), *Handbook of racial and ethnic minority psychology* (pp. 147–166). Thousand Oaks, CA: Sage Publications.

Utsey, S. O., Ponterotto, J. G., Reynolds, A. L., & Cancelli, A. A. (2000). Racial discrimination, coping, life satisfaction, and self-esteem among African Americans. *Journal of Counseling and Development, 78,* 72–81.

van der Kolk, B. A., MacFarlane, A. C., & Weisaeth, L. (1995). *Traumatic stress: The effects of overwhelming experience on mind, body and society.* New York: Guilford Press.

Vazquez-Nuttall, E., Romero-Garcia, I., & De Leon, B. (1987). Sex roles and perceptions of femininity and masculinity of Hispanic women: A review of the literature. *Psychology of Women Quarterly, 11,* 409–425.

Vera, E. M., & Speight, S. L. (2003). Multicultural competence, social justice, and counseling psychology: Expanding our roles. *The Counseling Psychologist, 31*(3), 253–272.

Vogel, R. (1999). A control mastery approach to short-term couple therapy. In J. M. Donovan (Ed.), *Short-term couple therapy* (pp. 63–100). New York: Guilford Press.

Wald, M. L. (2004, December 9). U.S. to specify documents needed for driver's licenses. *The New York Times,* p. A36.

Waldegrave, C. (1998). The challenges of culture to psychology and postmodern thinking. In M. McGoldrick (Ed.), *Re-visioning family therapy: Race, culture, and gender in clinical practice* (pp. 404–413). New York: Guilford Press.

Walitzer, K. S., Dermen, K. H., & Conners, G. J. (1999). Strategies for preparing clients for treatment: A review. *Behavior Modification, 23*(1), 129–151.

Walsh, F. (1999a). Religion and spirituality: Wellsprings for healing and resilience. In F. Walsh (Ed.), *Spiritual resources in family therapy* (pp. 3–27). New York: Guilford Press.

Walsh, F. (1999b). *Spiritual resources in family therapy.* New York: Guilford Press.

Walsh, F. (1998). *Strengthening family resilience.* New York: Guilford Press.

Walters, M., Carter, B., Papp, P., & Silverstein, O. (1991). *The invisible web: Gender patterns in family relationships.* New York: Guilford Press.

Washburn, J. J., Manley, T. & Holiwski, F. (2003). Teaching on racism: Tools for consultant training. *Journal of Educational and Psychological Consultations, 14*(3 & 4), 387–399.

Waters, M. (1990). *Ethnic options: Choosing ethnic identities in America.* Berkeley: University of California Press.

Watts, R. J., & Abdul-Adil, J. K. (1997). Promoting critical consciousness in young, African-American men. *Journal of Prevention and Intervention in the Community, 16,* 63–86.

Weigel, D. J., & Baker, B. G. (2002). Unique issues in rural couple and family counseling. *The Family Journal: Counseling and Therapy for Couples and Families, 10,* 61–69.

Weiner-Davis, M. (1993). *Divorce busting: A step-by-step approach to making your marriage loving again.* New York: Simon & Schuster.

Weissbrodt, D. (2005). *Immigration law and procedure in a nutshell* (5th ed.). Eagan, MN: West Publishing.

Wenner, S. (2001a). *Buddhism.* Retrieved March 7, 2006, from http://www.mnsu .edu/emuseum/cultural/religion/buddhism/buddhism.html

Wenner, S. (2001b). *Christianity.* Retrieved March 7, 2006, from http://www.mnsu.edu/ emuseum/cultural/religion/christianity/christianity.html

Wenner, S. (2001c). *Hinduism.* Retrieved March 7, 2006, from http://www.mnsu .edu/emuseum/cultural/religion/hinduism/hinduism.html

Wenner, S. (2001d). *Judaism.* Retrieved March 7, 2006, from http://www.mnsu .edu/emuseum/cultural/religion/judaism/judaism.html

Werner, E. E., & Smith, R. S. (2001). *Journeys from childhood to midlife: Risk, resilience, and recovery.* Ithaca, NY: Cornell University Press.

Whiston, G. (1996). Working-class issues. In R. Perez Foster, M. Moskowitz, & R. Javier (Eds.), *Reaching across boundaries of culture and class: Widening the scope of psychotherapy* (pp. 143–158). Northvale, NJ: Jason Aronson.

White, G. (2005). Ableism. In G. Nelson & I. Prilleltensky (Eds.), *Community psychology: In pursuit of liberation and well-being* (pp. 405–425). New York: Palgrave MacMillan.

Whitman, J. S., Glosoff, H. L., Kocet, M. M., & Tarvydas, V. (2006). Exploring ethical issues related to conversion or reparative therapy [electronic version]. *Counseling Today, 49*(1), 14–15.

Wright, M. A. (1999). *I'm chocolate, you're vanilla: Raising healthy Black and biracial children in a race-conscious world.* San Francisco: Jossey-Bass.

Wyman, D. S. (2000). The setting: Europe and America. In M. Adams, W. Blumenfeld, R. Castaneda, H. Hackman, M. Peters, & X. Zuniga (Eds.), *Readings for diversity and social justice* (pp. 163–169). New York: Routledge.

Yarhouse, M. A., Tan, E. S. N., & Pawlowski, L. M. (2005). Sexual identity development and synthesis among LGB-identified and LGB dis-identified persons. *Journal of Psychology and Theology, 33*(1), 3–16.

Yob, I. (1998). *Keys to interfaith parenting.* Hauppauge, NY: Barron's Educational Series.

Young, I. M. (1990). *Justice and the politics of difference.* Princeton, NJ: Princeton University Press.

Ziegler, P., & Hiller, T. (2001). *Recreating partnership: A solution-oriented, collaborative approach to couples therapy.* New York: W. W. Norton.

Zutlevics, T. L. (2002). Toward a theory of oppression. *Ratio, 15*(1), 80–102.

Zweifel, J. (2002). *Will the real me please stand up?* Naperville, IL: Nell Thurber Press.

Index

Ableism, 22–23
Acculturation, 157–160
  assessment and, 178
  language and, 192–193
  process of, 176
  See also Immigration
Activity, 5
African Americans
  characteristics of, 64–66
  forced immigration of, 151–152
  internalized oppression and, 21
  racial/ethnic identity models
    and, 58–62
  racism and, 28–29
  sexual orientation and, 343–344
  social class and, 299–301
  See also Butch's story; Carla's story;
    Frank's story; Julie's story
Ambivalence, 111, 154, 157, 203
Anger toward clients, 319
Anthony's story
  clinical applications, 330–334
  content themes, 328–330
  narrative, 322–328
Anti-immigrant sentiment, 30–31.
    See also Ethnocentrism; Nativism;
  Xenophobia
Anti-Semitism, 23–24
Asians, 69–70
Assessment
  acculturation processes, 178
  ethnicity and, 125–126, 142–143
  forced migration and, 177–178
  homosexuality and, 362
  immigration and, 142–143
  language loss and, 195
  multiracial individuals and, 106
  oppression and, 39
  race and, 83–84
  racism and, 142–143
  religion and, 259–260, 272, 291

  resilience and, 40
  second-generation immigrants
    and, 224–225
  second-language acquisition and, 178
  social class and, 142–143, 314, 330–331
  socioeconomic shifts and, 195
  survivor guilt and, 178
  transgender and intersex conditions
    and, 378–379
  undocumented immigrants and, 206–210
Assimilation, 176
Attachment, 35
Authentic self, 82–85
Author guidelines, 383–384
Autonomy, 15

Behavioral approaches, 5
Betsie's story
  clinical applications, 125–130
  content themes, 121–124
  narrative, 111–120
Bilingualism, 195–196
Bisexuality, 340, 342, 359–361. *See also*
    Homosexuality
Bob's story
  clinical applications, 271–274
  content themes, 269–271
  narrative, 265–269
Buddhism, 234–235
Budgets, 333
Butch's story
  clinical applications, 105–109
  content themes, 101–105
  narrative, 92–101

Camouflage, cultural, 126
Capitalist class, nonruling, 298
Carla's story
  clinical applications, 314–319
  content themes, 310–314
  narrative, 304–309

Christianity, 231–232
Circular questions, 127
Class, social
    assessment and, 142–143, 330–331
    changes in, 328–329
    differences in, 334
    dimensions of, 295–299
    immigration and, 193–194
    implications for professionals, 301
    shifts in, 195
    social justice and, 299–301
    See also Anthony's story;
        Carla's story; Maribel's story
Classism, 24–25, 334
Cognitive appraisal, 36
Colonialism, 179
Coming out, 356–359, 362–363
Community interventions, 316
Community psychology, 7
Competence, cultural, 3–4, 9–11
Consciousness, 9
Coping strategies, 36
Countertransference
    economically disadvantaged clients
        and, 318–319
    ethnicity and, 127–130
    homosexuality and, 364–365
    moral dilemmas and, 293
    multiracial individuals and, 107
    power imbalances and, 146–147
    race and, 86–88
    religion and, 261–262, 274
    sadness and, 197
    second-generation immigrants and,
        226–227
    social class and, 333–334
    transgender and intersex conditions
        and, 380–381
    undocumented immigrants and, 212–213
    unfamiliar cultures and, 180–181
Course, multicultural counseling, xiv
Critical consciousness, 84–85
Cultural deficiency model, 6
Curiosity, 180–181, 364
Current events, 290–291

Decision making, 289
Deficiency, models of, 5–6
Denial of culture, 197
Development, 45–48
Dilemmas, moral, 293
Disability, 22–23
Diversity
    defined, 8
    inequality and, 15

Dominant class standards,
    329–330, 331–333
Dropout, 210–212
Dyad, client–counselor
    race and, 87–88
    sexual orientation and, 347

Ecosystem framework, 102, 290
Esteban's story
    clinical applications, 194–198
    content themes, 190–194
    narrative, 183–190
Ethnicity
    African Americans and, 64–66
    Asians and, 69–70
    assessment and, 125–126, 142–143
    concept of, 53–54
    countertransference and, 127–130
    family values and, 122–123
    implications for professionals, 70
    intergroup differences and, 57, 63
    intragroup differences and, 54–56
    language and, 140
    Latin Americans and, 67–69
    models of, 58–62
    Native Americans and, 66–67
    overview, 52–53
    pressure to conform and, 123–124
    pride in, 121–122
    religion and, 124
    sexual orientation and, 343–344
    White Europeans and, 63–64
    See also Betsie's story; Maribel's story
Ethnocentrism, 26
Exploitation, 17

Families
    connectedness of, 37
    gay and lesbian, 348–349
    socialization within, 103, 107, 290
    therapy for, 316
Family values, 122–123
Fourth force, multicultural theory as, 5–8
Frank's story
    clinical applications, 259–262
    content themes, 256–259
    narrative, 245–256

Gay and lesbian clients. See Homosexuality
Gender, 37. See also Sexism
Gender Identity Disorder (GID). See
    Transgender and Intersex Conditions
Gender role shifts, 141–143, 223–224
Genetic deficiency model, 5–6
Genograms, 384–385

Geographic origin, 206
GLB clients. *See* Homosexuality
God, relationship with, 256–257
*Guidelines on Multicultural Education,
    Training, Research, Practice, and
    Organizational Change for
    Psychologists* (American
    Psychological Association), 10
Guilt
    on clinician's part, 197
    religion and, 241
    survivor, 176–177

Helplessness, feelings of, 318–319
Help-seeking behavior, 36–37
Heritage, racial, 85
Heterosexuality, 337–338
Hinduism, 235–236
Hispanics, 67–69
History, acquiring knowledge of, 179–180
History of psychotherapy, 4–5
HIV, 345
Homophobia, 26–27, 343
Homosexuality
    clinical applications, 342–350
    current views, 340–342
    defined, 338
    historical data, 338–340
    implications for professionals, 350
    See also Karen's story
Humanistic approaches, 5
Human nature, 5
Human rights issues, 347
Hybrid identities, 140–141, 143
Hypothesis-making, 146

Identity
    developmental models and, 45–47
    models of, 58–62
    religious, 239–241, 270–271, 287–289
    sociohistorical context and, 124–125
    See also Self
Identity development
    importance of context, 102–103
    multicultural theory and, 9
Illegal activities, 315–316
Illegal immigrants, 204–205. *See also*
    Maria Luz's story
Immigration
    assessment and, 142–143
    current controversies, 154–156
    first- vs. second-generation
        immigrants, 221
    forced, 151–152, 174–175
    geographic origin and, 205–206

historical dimensions, 149–154
    implications for professionals, 160–161
    language issues, 205–206
    reasons for, 157–160
    social class and, 193–194
    voluntary vs. involuntary, 204
    See also Esteban's story; Maria Luz's
        story; Maribel's story; Teresa's
        story; Vu's story; Xenophobia
Imperialism, cultural, 18
Individuals, characteristics of, 3
Institutional oppression, 20–21
Interfaith marriages, 292–293. *See also*
    Katie's story
Intergenerational conflicts, 223–224
Intergroup differences
    African Americans and, 64–66
    Asians and, 69–70
    ethnicity and, 57, 63
    Latin Americans and, 67–69
    Native Americans and, 66–67
    White Europeans and, 63–64
Internalized oppression, 21–22
Internalized-other
    interviewing, 126–127
Internal migration, 271
Interpersonal oppression, 20
Intersex clients. *See* Transgender and
    Intersex Conditions
Intragroup differences
    ethnicity and, 54–56
    multiracial individuals and, 104
Islam, 232–233

Judaism, 23–24, 233–234. *See also*
    Anti-Semitism
Julie's story
    clinical applications, 83–88
    content themes, 79–83
    narrative, 74–79
Justice, social
    multicultural competence and, 12
    multicultural competency training
        and, 7
    oppression and, 11–12
    social class and, 300–301

Karen's story
    clinical applications, 361–365
    content themes, 356–361
    narrative, 351–356
Katie's story
    clinical applications, 291–293
    content themes, 287–291
    narrative, 278–287

Language
  acculturation and, 192–193
  clinical use of language of origin,
    195–196
  ethnicity and, 140
  first-generation immigrants and,
    205–206
  loss of, 191–192, 195
  second-generation immigrants and,
    221–223
  second language acquisition,
    175–176, 180
  use of standard English, 319
Latin Americans, 67–69
Latinos
  ethnicity and, 52
  ethnocentrism and, 26
  internalized oppression and, 21
  racism and, 28
  racial/ethnic identity models and, 58–62
  sexual orientation and, 343–344
  See also Latin Americans
Leaders, religious, 260
Lesbians. See Homosexuality
Loss, 190–191

Marginalization, 17
Maria Luz's story
  clinical applications, 206–213
  content themes, 203
  narrative, 199–203
Maribel's story
  clinical applications, 142–147
  content themes, 139–142
  narrative, 134–138
Metatheory, multicultural theory as, 8
Modalities, multiple, 9
Moral dilemmas, 293
Multicultural theory
  course in, xiv
  as fourth force, 5–8
  propositions of, 8–9
Multiple identities
  in history of multicultural theory, 7
  as proposition of multicultural theory, 9
Multiracial individuals
  countertransference and, 107
  myths about, 106–108
  See also Butch's story

Native Americans
  characteristics of, 66–67
  spiritual traditions of, 236–237
Nativism, 180–181

Nature, relationship with, 5
Nonruling capitalist class, 298
Nurturance, 35

Oppression
  assessment of, 39
  clinicians and, 40–43
  defined, 14–15
  institutional, 20–21
  internalized, 21–22
  models of, 16–19
  multicultural competence and, 11–12
  overview, 13–14
  personal and interpersonal, 19–20
  privilege and, 15–16
  types of, 22–31
  See also Resilience
Outside perspective questions, 127

Parent education, 316–317
Personal oppression, 19–20
Poverty, 310–312. See also Carla's story
Powerlessness, 17
Prejudice, 197–198
Pretherapy orientation, 210–212
Pride, ethnic, 121–122
Privilege, 15–16
Problem-solving focus, 36
Professional/managerial class, 297
Protective factors, 35–37
Psychodynamic approaches, 5
Psycholinguistic history, 180

Race
  assessment and, 83–84
  as concept, 51–52
  identity development and, 80
  See also Butch's story; Ethnicity;
    Julie's story
Rachel's story
  clinical applications, 378–381
  content themes, 376–378
  narrative, 371–376
Racism
  assessment and, 142–143
  as type of oppression, 28–29
  Julie's story and, 81–82
  See also Butch's story; Julie's story;
    Maribel's story
Reflexive questions, 127
Refugees, 174–175. See also Esteban's
    story; Vu's story
Relationship questions, 127
Relationships, social, 5

Religion
    clinical applications, 259–262
    defined, 230–231
    ethnicity and, 124
    identity development and, 239–241
    implications for professionals, 241–242
    overview of major faiths, 231–239
    resilience and, 37
    strength as, 258–259
    submission in, 257–258
    See also Bob's story; Frank's story;
        Katie's story
Reportable offenses, 315–316
Resilience
    assessment of, 40
    associated factors, 34–37
    autonomy and, 18
    clinical work and, 38–39
    defined, 33–34
    family connectedness and, 37
    gender differences, 37
    homosexuality and, 349–350
    overview, 32–33
    spirituality and, 37
Resources, lack of access to, 312–313
Role reversal questions, 127

Salaried workers, 297
Second-generation immigrants
    family conflicts and, 225–226
    vs. first-generation immigrants, 221
    See also Maribel's story; Teresa's story
Second-language acquisition, 175–176,
        180, 205–206
Self
    contextual dimensions of, 48–49
    development of, 47–48
Self-definition, 82–83
Self-determination, 15
Self-esteem, 35–36
Self-hatred, 108–109
Self-image, 105
Self-regulation, 36
Sexism, 29–30
Sexual orientation, 337–338
    current views on, 340
    ethnicity and, 343
    HIV and, 345
    homophobia and, 26, 343
    implications for professionals, 350
    resilience and, 345
    See also Bisexuality; Heterosexuality;
        Homophobia; Homosexuality;
        Karen's story; Rachel's story

Shame, 361, 363–364
Silence, culture of, 19
Social class. See Class, social
Social competence, 36
Socialization
    family, 290
    racial, 85–86
    religious, 241, 269–270
Social support, 349
Sociohistorical context, 124–125
Spirituality
    defined, 230
    resilience and, 37
Standard English, 319
Standards for Cultural Competence in
        Social Work Practice (National
        Association of Social Workers), 11
Substance abuse, 344–345
Suicide, 344–345
Support, 35
Survivor guilt, 176–177, 178

Taking sides, 226–227
Teresa's story
    clinical applications, 224–227
    content themes, 220–224
    narrative, 215–220
Third-party referrals, 315
Time perspective, 5
Toolbox activities
    Anthony's story, 335
    Betsie's story, 131
    Bob's story, 275
    Butch's story, 109
    Carla's story, 320
    Esteban's story, 198
    Frank's story, 263
    Julie's story, 89
    Karen's story, 366
    Katie's story, 294
    Maria Luz's story, 214
    Rachel's story, 382
    Teresa's story, 228
    Vu's story, 182
Training
    about oppression, 41–42
    multicultural competency, 7
Transgender and intersex conditions
    implications for professionals, 369
    overview, 367–369
    See also Gender Identity Disorder;
        Rachel's story
Underclass, 297
Undocumented status, 204–205, 210

Values
    of dominant class, 329–330, 331–333
    race and, 313–314
Violence, 18–19
Voice Dialogue, 273
Vu's story
    clinical applications, 177–181
    content themes, 173–177
    narrative, 163–173

Wellness, 240–241
White Europeans, 63–64
Working poor, 297
Worldview, 4–5

Xenophobia, 30–31

Youth, gay and lesbian,
    346–347

About the Authors

Sara E. Schwarzbaum, Ed.D., LCPC, is a family therapist with a specialization in working with Latinos. She earned her master's degree in clinical psychology from Universidad de Belgrano in Buenos Aires, Argentina. She received her doctoral degree in counseling with an emphasis in family therapy from Northern Illinois University. She is currently a professor in the Department of Counselor Education and a coordinator of the Master's in Couple and Family Counseling Program at Northeastern Illinois University in Chicago, where she teaches internship seminars, family therapy, and multicultural counseling courses. Formerly, she coordinated the Latino Family Counseling Program of Lake County, Illinois, where she provided services for Latino families and trained bilingual clinicians. She is also a family therapist in private practice in Lincolnshire, Illinois, and a consultant, trainer, and presenter at state and national conferences, mental health centers, hospitals, community agencies, and universities, where she frequently conducts workshops on clinical issues with Latino clients, the multicultural competency of clinicians, psychotherapy with immigrant families, and ethnocultural countertransference, as well as other topics. She is the coauthor, with Anita Thomas, of *Culture and Identity: Life Stories for Counselors and Therapists.*

Anita Jones Thomas, Ph.D., is a counseling psychologist with specializations in multicultural counseling and family therapy. She earned her bachelor's degree in human development and social policy from Northwestern University, and her master's degree in community counseling and her doctorate in counseling psychology from Loyola University Chicago. She is assistant professor at Loyola University Chicago, where she teaches courses in multicultural counseling, family therapy, and school counseling. Her research interests include racial identity, racial socialization, and parenting issues for African Americans. She also conducts training seminars and workshops on multicultural issues for state and national professional organizations in counseling and psychology, hospitals, and corporations and has served as a consultant for human services organizations. She has served as governor for the Illinois Counseling Association, as president of the Illinois Association for Couples and Family Counseling, and as corresponding secretary for the Chicago chapter of the Association of Black Psychologists. She is the coauthor, with Sara Schwarzbaum, of *Culture and Identity: Life Stories for Counselors and Therapists* (Sage Publications, 2006).